ADAMS

JOB INTERVIEW ALMANAC

Second Edition

ADAMS MEDIA
Avon, Massachusetts

CREDITS

Project Editor: Richard Wallace

Composition: Electronic Publishing Services, Inc., Tennessee

Published by Adams Media, an F+W Publications Company

57 Littlefield Street

Avon, MA 02322

www.adamsmedia.com

ISBN: 1-59337-292-2

Printed in Canada.

A B C D E F G H I J

Library of Congress Cataloguing-in-Publication Data

The Adams job interview almanac / [the editors of Adams Media].-- 2nd ed.
    p. cm.
ISBN 1-59337-292-2
1. Employment interviewing / editors of Adams Media. 2. Job hunting. I. Title: Job interview almanac. II. Adams Media.

HF5549.5.I6A3 2005
650.14'4--dc22

2004030284

CONTENTS

PART III
AFTER THE JOB INTERVIEW

6. Clinching the Deal. 118
How to follow up on first interviews and handle later interviews with finesse.

7. The Art of Negotiation 123
Salary, benefits, and other important factors to consider. Expert negotiating techniques to help you get what you want.

PART IV
SAMPLE JOB INTERVIEWS

15. Health and Medicine

16. Legal and Protective Services

17. Marketing and Sales

18. Science

19. Service

ACKNOWLEDGMENTS

Thanks to the following people whose generous time and expertise made this book possible:

Virginia Alonzo, Javier Amador-Peña, Linda Armstrong, Linda Arslanian, Jennifer Barr, Elise Bauman, Susan Beale, Edward Beaudoin, Julianne Bennett, Jeff Benson, Bill Brands, Russell Brothers, Rob Bunnell, Michael J. Carriero, Christopher Ciaschini, Nicole Coady, Marisa Cohen, Andrew J. Conn, Susan Crawford, Catherine Crowder, Elizabeth Clarke, Bob Davis, Dental Fill-Ins, Laura DiBenedetti, John J. Diggins, Richard Dreier, James B. Earley, Lisa Edenton, Katy Edmonson, Jeff Eisnaugle, Anny Ellis, Glen Fassinger, Joanne Franco, Jill Gabbe, Jan Gentry, Clifton Gerring, Dov Goldman, Al Golub, Jeffrey M. Graeber, Jim Grobman, Ron Grover, Steve Grune, Bob Hale, Pete Harper, Gary Hayden, Margot T. Healy, Catherine A. Hegan, Catherine Holsen, Denise Humphrey, Beryl Israel, Wayne Jackson, Michelle Johnson, Chuck Kelly, Keith Kleinsmith, J. Patrick Knuff, Linda Kosarin, Jennifer Kove, Rowena R. Krum, Heather Kuty, David E. Lambert, Jr., Ann C. Lee, Howard Levinson, Pam Liflander, Mark A. Linnus, Andrew Lobo, Michael G. McArdle, Mark McAuley, John McCauley, Nancy McGovern, Terence McGovern, Jim Mellarkey, Bruce Menin, Arnold Most, Jennifer Most, Karen M. Nichols, Elizabeth O'Brien, Carrie Oliver, Richard Oliver, Susan Oliver, Guy Pacitti, Stefan Pagacik, Thomas V. Patton, Pam Perry, Joe Petrie, Jeff Phillips, Rosalie Prosser, Jan Quiram, Rodney Ramsey, Gigi Ranno, Andy Richardson, Gary P. Richardson, Alan Ritchie, Kent Rodgers, Bob Rogers, Thomas J. Rusin, David Ryback, Jeremy M. Sherber, Donna Shervanian, Aryana Soebagjo, Judy Spinella, John Stagliano, Joseph Steur, Deborah Story, Allan Tatel, Bob Teague, Jill Todd, Nancy True, Catherine Tuttle, K.A. Vlahos, Mark Waldstein, David Williams, Ron Wilson, Frank Winslow, David S. Wolff, Bill York, Diane V. Yurkewicz, Reeve Zimmerman, Michael Zitomer, and Frank J. Zych, Jr.

HOW TO USE THIS BOOK

The *Adams Job Interview Almanac* is the most comprehensive guide to job interviewing available. It is the only book of its kind that features complete job interviews from hiring managers in all fields and industries. Are you a seasoned marketing manager? If so, you'll find twenty interview questions with examples of effective responses, and hints on how to increase your odds of getting job offers, in Chapter 17. Or are you a recent college graduate trying to break into public relations? Turn to Chapter 11 to learn what questions you might encounter in a job interview and how you can distinguish yourself from the competition. In fact, we've included more than 100 job interviews for positions in:

Accounting and Finance
Administration
Art and Design
Communications
Computers and Engineering
Education
Executive and Management
Health and Medicine
Legal and Protective Services
Marketing and Sales
Science
Service
Social and Human Services
Technical

No matter what career you're interested in, you're guaranteed to find it within these pages!

Additionally, we'll show you how to land job interviews, find and research potential employers, and develop your own themes for the interview. We've included valuable advice for handling stress interviews, strategies for second and third interviews, and information on how to negotiate job offers to get what you want. As if that isn't enough, you'll also find industry-specific advice for entry-level job seekers, career changers, experienced professionals, and people re-entering the workforce.

Answering a battery of interview questions can feel something like running a gauntlet. A little preparation, though, and the help of this book can help see you through, safe and sound. The interview questions and answers included here should give you a sense of how questions should be handled. They shouldn't be used as the basis of "canned" or scripted answers. Adapt these responses to your own circumstances, and remember that the way you respond can be just as important as what you actually say.

Keep in mind as you're reading that behind every interview question is a hiring manager's concern. And even though you may not encounter precisely the same questions that are included here, the concerns of the hiring manager remain the same. Your job is to define each concern and then alleviate it with a well-thought-out response. This book is designed to help you do just that.

So keep reading, and remember—you're on your way to a fabulous career!

Part I

Before the Job Interview

CHAPTER 1
GETTING YOUR FOOT IN THE DOOR

Beginning Your Job Search

As is the case with anything that requires consistent effort and self-discipline, getting started on your job search is the toughest part. Think about it. It's just like exercise. Whether you work out in a gym, in your basement, or anywhere else, the hardest part is usually getting yourself off the couch and into your sweats. But once you've started, and you're focused on your regular routine, it all becomes much easier.

So where exactly does one begin? At the beginning. Not by writing a new draft of your resume, not by calling XYZ Corporation down the street because a friend of a friend says they're hiring. Before you even *think* about wading through the help-wanteds or buying new stationery, focus on two big questions:

What do you want?
What do you have to offer?

Let's look at the first question. What do you want? One of the biggest mistakes job seekers make is to start looking for a job before they're really ready—even before they have a well-defined goal. Setting goals is critical in all areas of your life, but it's especially important when it comes to obtaining a job. You need to define your objectives clearly.

Defining your job objectives is also known as career planning (or life planning, for those who wish to emphasize the importance of combining the two). Career planning has become a field of study in and of itself. If you're thinking of choosing or switching careers, remember two things. First, choose a career in which you'll enjoy most of the day-to-day tasks. This sounds obvious, but most of us have at one point or another been attracted by a glamour industry or a prestigious-sounding job without asking ourselves: Would I really like doing the job day in and day out?

Second, remember that you're not just choosing a career—you're also making a choice about the life you want to lead. Time and time again career counselors report that one of the most common problems job seekers run into is that they don't consider whether or not they're suited for a particular position or career. For example, some people attracted to management consulting by good salaries, early responsibility, and high-level corporate exposure find that they can't stand the long hours, heavy travel, and constant pressure to produce. So be sure to ask yourself not only how you might adapt to the day-to-day duties and working environment that a specific job carries with it, but also how you might adjust to the long-term demands of that career and that industry.

One formalized way to focus on your interests is to take a standardized interest-inventory test. These are multiple-choice tests designed to help you figure out your likes and dislikes and determine which jobs are best for you. To give you an idea of the types of questions you might find on an interest-inventory test, we've included ten questions that you should consider. Look at each of these questions. Do they describe your job- and career-related interests? If so, leave a check mark.

I enjoy:

- Working with things most of the time
- Working with people most of the time
- Working in an office or business environment
- Doing scientific and technical studies
- Doing routine or repetitive activities
- Doing abstract and creative activities
- Working with people in a helping role
- Working with machines most of the time
- Working for prestige and the admiration of others
- Seeing concrete results of my work almost immediately

Although it's been said that you are what you do, think about turning this phrase around: you do what you are. Your personality, likes, dislikes, values, and goals should determine where you work and what you do, not the other way around. Look at The Big Picture. Take a moment to see beyond whether you want to work "in an office" or "outdoors" and consider trying the exercise that's been asked of many creative-writing students. Write your epitaph. It doesn't have to be a one-line composition. Write for as long as you want. But answer this question: "What do you want to be remembered for?"

These exercises, of course, are just a beginning. Think of as many questions of your own as you can. Ask a friend or family member who knows you well to help you come up with some. Even if you believe you have a clear idea about where your interests lie, even if you're not entering the job market for the first time, try these exercises. Remember: you're not just looking for a paycheck. Use this time to figure out what's important to you.

Once you've thought about what interests you and what's really important to you, the next step is to think about the second big issue: what you have to offer to employers. Again, broadly speaking, what are your skills? Don't answer by guessing your typing speed; for now, think more broadly than that.

Which of the following describe your skills?

- The ability to understand and use words well
- The ability to do arithmetic quickly and accurately
- The ability to think geometrically
- The ability to see details
- The ability to make precise movements quickly
- The ability to coordinate your hand and foot movements with things you see
- The ability to work well as part of a team
- The ability to work well independently
- The ability to take a position and then defend it

If you've answered these questions, you're almost ready to start your search in earnest. Now's the time to use what you've learned about yourself to decide on the industry, job, and part of the country that appeal to you. One reason to do this is that it makes your job search easier; if you try to pursue too many different avenues, you'll only frustrate yourself. Having a well-developed plan based on objectives you've taken time to think about is easier on you—and will make you a stronger candidate, as well. Remember: employers like job candidates who have real interests and a clear direction. They know that if you're interested in a particular industry, company, or job, you're more likely to enjoy the position, do a good job, and stay with the company. Recruiters don't like to hear that you aren't at all discriminating—that you'll take whatever job they have available.

Developing Your Strategy

Assuming that you've established your career objectives, the next step of the job search is to develop a strategy. If you don't take the time to lay out a plan, you may find yourself going around in circles after several weeks of randomly searching for jobs that always seem just beyond your reach. The first step is to decide on the best method for contacting employers, so you should be familiar with the most common techniques and their advantages and disadvantages. Among the most popular resources and methods are the following:

1. Direct contact
2. Networking
3. Help-wanted ads
4. Employment services
5. Alumni-placement offices
6. Professional associations
7. Online databases

I. Direct Contact

Direct contact (also called "cold contact") means making a professional, personal approach to a select group of companies. Done well, it can be an excellent method for most job seekers, leading to many interviews and, possibly, job offers.

As a general rule, you should always *try* to contact a department head or president of any company you're considering working for. This will probably be easier to do at smaller companies, where the president of the company him- or herself may be directly involved in the hiring process. However, when you contact larger companies, you'll find yourself more often bumped back to the personnel office. If this happens to you, try to contact a key decision maker within personnel.

The first step you should take is to send out your resume with a personalized cover letter. The letter should be addressed to a specific person; if you're not sure whom to send it to, call the company and ask, making sure you get the correct spelling of the contact's name. You should further personalize each letter by including a reference to something you know about that particular company (presumably through your research). This can make all the difference between getting an interview and getting passed over.

One important benefit of contacting employers directly is that you have the chance to do the necessary research to determine whether you'd like to work for that company and exactly how your skills would fit in there. However, that doesn't mean you should bury every firm within 100 miles with mail and phone calls. Mass mailings rarely work in the job hunt. This also applies to those letters that are personalized—but dehumanized—on an automatic typewriter or word-processing program. Don't waste your time or money on such a project; you'll fool no one but yourself.

The Sixty-Second Pitch

Approximately one week after you've sent your resume to a key decision maker, you should follow up with a phone call. Don't simply ask if your resume has been received—this can be frustrating to employers who are inundated with hundreds of resumes. A better approach is to state that you've sent your resume and explain, in sixty seconds or less, why you think you're the best candidate for the position. Your "sixty-second pitch" should be a clear and concise summary of yourself, including three important elements:

- What kind of work you do (or want to do)
- What your strongest skills and accomplishments are
- What kind of position you're seeking

If you're invited to an interview after you've pitched yourself to the hiring manager, great! If not, don't let it end there! Ask if there are any particular qualifications that he or she is looking for in a candidate. Is there anything else you can do or any additional information that you can send (writing samples, clippings, or portfolio) to help the hiring manager make a decision? Even if the person says no, that your resume is sufficient, he or she may be impressed by your interest and enthusiasm.

If you haven't already done so, specifically ask the employer if he or she would have a few minutes to meet with you. If that doesn't work, ask if that person knows anyone who might be interested in speaking to someone with your qualifications. If you're unable to arrange an interview or to get a referral, ask the employer if he or she would mind if you called back in a month or so. The goal is to get a positive response from the phone call—whether it's an interview or simply a scrap of job-hunting advice. Don't give up too easily, but be professional and courteous at all times.

2. Networking

Another excellent method of finding work is through networking, a strategy that focuses primarily on developing a network of "insider" contacts. Networking is the most effective of all job-hunting tools. In fact, experts indicate that as many as 86 percent of all jobs are found through networking. Many people think that only highly connected executives use networking; however, it can work for anyone—even people with few or no contacts in the business world.

If you feel hesitant about networking, you're not alone. Many job seekers mistakenly think that networking is somehow degrading or manipulative. They suspect that networking really means pestering strangers for a job and begging for scraps of help and sympathy. They opt not to use this important tool and end up needlessly limiting their opportunities.

The problem is that these people don't understand what networking really is. Networking means letting people you know—personally and professionally—that you're looking for a job. You simply ask them to keep you in mind if they hear of any appropriate openings or know anyone who might need someone with your skills.

At first you might not think you have many contacts at your disposal—but if you think carefully, you'll realize you do. Let's say there are fifteen people you can initially contact. Each of these fifteen contacts may introduce you to three more people, giving you a total of forty-five additional contacts. Then each of these people may introduce you to three additional people, which brings you 135 additional contacts. And that's a lot of people!

Of course, developing your network of contacts doesn't usually work as smoothly as the theory suggests, because some people won't be able to introduce you to anyone. The further you stray from your initial contact base, the weaker your references may be. So it's important to begin building your contact base with as many people you know personally as you can. Dig into your personal address book and your holiday greeting-card list and locate old classmates from school. If you know a lawyer, accountant, banker, doctor, stockbroker, or insurance agent, give each of them a call. These people will help you develop a very broad contact base due to the nature of their jobs.

Your network can be a rich source of both hidden and publicized opportunities. From your network of contacts you can often glean referrals to professionals in your field of interest, or get an "insider's view" of a company's growth prospects. Ask people in your network about any potential openings they anticipate over the next few months. Are any groups growing at a particularly fast rate? Are there any areas where a company could use someone like you or where the hiring managers have had difficulty attracting the kind of skills you offer?

As always with any leads, follow up directly, as well as with the person who gave you the lead. Try to secure a meeting to discuss how your qualifications might be a potential benefit to an organization. If a networking contact has been particularly helpful to you, by all means send a thank-you note. Not only is this courteous, it keeps your contacts current.

3. Help-Wanted Ads

Contrary to popular belief, newspaper classified ads are not a good source of opportunities for job hunters. Few people find jobs this way, although many spend a tremendous amount of time and effort poring over newspaper after newspaper.

According to career-development consultant Charles Logue, fewer than 3 percent of all job openings are advertised in classified ads. Worse, so many applicants respond to these ads that the competition is extremely fierce. Even if your qualifications are good, your chances of getting an interview are not.

One moderate-sized employer told us about an experience advertising in the help-wanted section of a major Sunday newspaper: "It was a disaster. We had more than 500 responses from this relatively small ad in just one week. We have only two phone lines in this office, and one was totally knocked out. We'll never advertise for professional help again."

If you insist on following up on help-wanted ads, then research a firm before you reply to an ad. Doing research might help to separate you from everyone else responding to that ad. That said, you should be sure to focus only a small portion of your job-search efforts in this direction.

Blind Ads

"Blind ads" are newspaper advertisements that don't identify the employer. Job seekers are usually instructed to send their resumes to a post-office-box number. Although they may seem suspicious, blind ads can be a source of legitimate job opportunities. A firm may choose to run a blind advertisement because it may not wish to be deluged with telephone calls, or it may be trying to replace an employee who hasn't been terminated yet.

You should be aware, though, that blind ads are sometimes used for deceitful purposes, such as selling employment-marketing services or harassing unsuspecting callers. The best advice is to trust your instincts and don't allow yourself to be put in a situation that makes you feel uncomfortable.

4. Employment Services

Employment services fall into four basic categories: executive-search firms, employment agencies, counseling services, and executive-marketing or -outplacement firms. There are also important distinctions among the organizations listed within each basic category.

Executive-Search Firms

Have you ever heard the term "headhunter" used in relation to a job search? What's really being talked about are executive search firms. If you're considering using one, here's a summary of what they are, what they do, and whom they're for. Essentially, there are two types: those that operate on retainer for their client companies, and those that operate on a contingency basis, meaning that they receive payment only when a successful search is concluded.

It's important to know that these firms aren't for everybody. Executive-search firms handle only experienced executives, focus only on positions in the higher salary ranges, and generally don't specialize in any particular industry. They're always hired and paid by the employer, and they're just as likely to contact and recruit candidates who aren't even looking as those who are currently in the job market. Search firms are interested only in executives with successful, proven track records in jobs that directly apply to their clients' needs. For this reason they often file the names of tens of thousands of possible candidates for placement.

After receiving an assignment a search firm will go through its own records and through other sources, then limit its search to a few hundred names, depending on the position being filled. Then, after studying the backgrounds of these candidates and discussing them with sources in the industry, the firm narrows its choices to a few dozen candidates. Finally, the firm will present the strongest candidates to its client. If you're an experienced executive, you may want to send your resume to one or more executive search firms, but don't bother to follow up with a phone call—and don't expect an interview unless your background happens to match the firm's current needs.

These organizations aren't licensed, so if you decide to go with an executive-search firm, make sure it has a solid reputation. You can find names of search firms by contacting the following:

Association of Executive Search Consultants (AESC)
230 Park Avenue, Suite 1549
New York, NY 10169
(212) 949-9556
www.aesc.com

American Management Association (AMA)
Management Services Department
1601 Broadway
New York, NY 10019
(212) 586-8100
www.amanet.org

As with help-wanted ads, you shouldn't let an executive-search firm become a critical element in your job-search campaign—no matter how encouraging it may sound. Continue to seek out your own opportunities actively and keep all of your options open.

Employment Agencies

Much more common than headhunters are general employment agencies. These can be divided into private agencies and state-government agencies. State agencies place a much wider range of people, including many hard-to-place, low-skill workers, although they do place others as well and shouldn't necessarily be ruled out as a valuable resource. More often, though, job seekers looking for professional positions will have better luck with private employment agencies.

In some states private employment agencies can charge job seekers a fee, but the employer pays the vast majority of these agencies. Typically, employment agencies charge the employer a fee based on a percentage of the new employee's first-year salary.

A word of caution: Unfortunately, a few less-than-ethical employment agencies have done a great deal to tarnish the reputation of the entire industry. Some firms, especially those specializing in lower-end placement—for secretarial and office help, for example—are notorious for running ads for openings that don't exist, and for pitching fictional candidates to employers. Because placement fees can run in the $1,500 to $2,000 range, even for a secretarial position, some agencies feel pressure to push a job seeker to take a position they know the person won't enjoy. Another danger sign: If your agency tries to have you stop by the office both before and after job interviews, odds are they're actually trying to monopolize your time. Naturally, once you've signed on, they don't want you to go to another agency (or, for that matter, find work on your own).

If you're unsure about a particular agency, keep in mind that employment agencies must be licensed by the state in which they operate. Some states can give you the number of business complaints that have been lodged against an agency. The vast majority of employment agencies place great importance on their reputation. Companies that engage in shady business practices generally aren't around long before they're exposed, and tend to get forced out of business. To play it safe, though, review the following list before choosing an agency:

- Find out when the company was founded. If it's been around awhile, chances are you're dealing with a reputable, established company.
- Consider choosing an agency that specializes in your profession. In general, these agencies are more likely to be reputable because they operate in only one industry—and bad word of mouth can travel quickly. Employers in certain high-demand fields rely heavily on specialized employment services to find good candidates. These fields include banking, finance, advertising, data processing, health care, insurance, publishing, retailing, sales, and a variety of technical industries. Like executive-search firms, specialized employment agencies aren't particularly interested in people with little or no experience in the industry, or in those thinking about switching careers. But because these agencies fill fewer senior-level positions than do executive-search firms, a specialized employment agency will probably be interested in trying to place you if you're a professional with, say, five to ten years of relevant experience in the industry.
- Find out if the agency belongs to a national or regional professional organization. The industry's most notable national organization is the National Association of Personnel Consultants (NAPC). Thousands of agencies across the country belong to this group; members are required to follow the prescribed business practices of the organization, known as the Standards of Ethical Practice, and the NAPC Code of Ethics.

If you decide to register with an agency, your best bet is to find one that's recommended by a friend or associate. Barring that, you can find names of agencies in the yellow pages or by contacting the following:

National Association of Personnel Services
10905 Fort Washington Road, Suite 400
Fort Washington, Maryland 20744
(301) 203-6700
www.recruitinglife.com

After you've selected a few agencies (three to five is best), send them your resume and cover letter. Make a follow-up phone call and try to schedule an interview. Be prepared to take a number of tests (vocational, psychological, and other) on the day of your interview.

Above all, don't expect too much. Only a small percentage of all professional, managerial, and executive jobs are listed with these agencies, so they're not a terrific source of opportunities. Use them as an addition to your job-search campaign, but focus your efforts on other, more promising methods.

Career-Counseling Services and Executive-Marketing Firms

Counseling services are even more diverse than employment agencies. Many nonprofit organizations—colleges, universities, and private associations—offer free or very inexpensive counseling services. For-profit counseling services, on the other hand, can charge a broad range of fees, depending on their services. Services include individual career counseling, internship programs, specialized workshops in areas such as resume and interview preparation, and aptitude and interest testing. You can find them listed in your local phone book, or write to:

National Board for Certified Counselors
3D Terrace Way
Greensboro, NC 27403
(336) 547-0607
www.nbcc.org

Executive-marketing firms, or outplacement firms, are sometimes confused with career counselors. The distinctions are important, though: a career counselor will teach you how to conduct your own job search; an executive-marketing firm will conduct a search for you. (Executive-marketing firms can also be confused with executive-search firms. For the most part, executive-search firms work for client companies, not for the job seekers whose resumes they keep on file.) If you're considering an outplacement company, check it out carefully. Some of these firms charge upwards of $3,000 and do little more than circulate your resume. Many will promise you the moon and stars but won't guarantee results. Best bet: check with the local Better Business Bureau and ask for information on the firm.

5. Alumni-Placement Offices

These services are now part of many universities and colleges. They function basically as a clearinghouse for interested companies attempting to match job-seeking alumni to their needs. Although most are not well supported, either financially or with staff, they shouldn't be overlooked as a source. If your school doesn't offer placement services, try to take advantage of the membership listings many alumni associations make available, as they can serve as a valuable source for contacts.

6. Professional Associations

Many of these organizations have established placement services for members' use. Companies, either via the association's mailings or through society meetings, put your resume in a referral system for review. Employers use some of these services quite extensively. Contact these associations directly to inquire if they offer any employment services.

Even if a particular association doesn't offer placement services, it's still a valuable resource. Many professional associations have annual meetings or hold conferences and seminars, which are great opportunities for making contacts and keeping abreast of industry trends. For a comprehensive nationwide directory of professional associations, check your library for the *Encyclopedia of Associations* published by Gale Research.

7. Online Databases

Below, you will find a directory of helpful online databases. Some allow you to conduct free searches, while others require users to buy a subscription. The list is broken down into two parts—the first being those sites that are specifically geared to job seekers, and the second being information services that may also be helpful in your research on a particular company or industry.

Career-Related Online Databases

CareerBuilder
Offers company listings, classifieds, and more.
(866) 438-1485
www.careerbuilder.com

Federal Career Opportunities
Lists federal jobs across the U.S. from GS5 to SES levels. The online system is updated daily, and job information may also be accessed through a newsletter updated every two weeks.
(703) 281-0200
www.usajobs.com

HotJobs
An online career network providing job listings and career advice.
www.hotjobs.com

Monster.com
An online career network providing job listings and career advice.
(800) MONSTER
www.monster.com

For Company and Industry Research

The Bureau of Labor Statistics
www.bls.gov

Dun's Electronic Business Directory
www.dnb.com

Dow Jones Factiva
www.factiva.com

Gale Research Group
Publishes a broad range of databases including Gale Digital Archives and
Gale Reference Library.
www.galegroup.com

Hoover's Online
(800) 486-8666
www.hoovers.com

LexisNexis
www.lexisnexis.com

Standard & Poor's Online Services
www.standardandpoors.com

Managing Your Most Important Resource: Time

Job searches aren't something most people do regularly, and so it may be
hard to estimate how long each step will take. Nonetheless, it's important to
have a plan so that you can see the progress you're making.

When outlining your job-search schedule, you should have a realistic
time frame in mind. If you'll be job searching full-time, your search will probably take at least two months. If you can devote yourself only part-time, it
will probably take at least four months.

You probably know a few people who seem to spend their whole lives
searching for a better job in their spare time. Don't be one of them. Even if
you can search only part-time, give the effort your whole-hearted attention.
If you've got a job and don't feel like devoting a lot of energy to finding a new

one right now, then wait. Focus on enjoying your present position, do your best, and store energy for when you're really ready to begin your job search.

If you're currently unemployed, remember that job hunting is tough work physically and emotionally. It's also intellectually demanding work that requires you to be at your best. So don't tire yourself out by working on your job campaign around the clock. At the same time, you must be sure to discipline yourself. The most logical way to manage your time while looking for a job is to keep regular working hours.

If you're still employed, job searching will be especially tough; don't work yourself to the point where you show up for interviews looking exhausted, or where your current job begins to suffer. On the other hand, don't be tempted to quit the job you already have! Employers prefer hiring applicants who are already working somewhere. The long hours are worth it. If you're searching for a job while you have one, you're in a position of real strength.

If you're searching full-time and have decided to use several different contact methods, divide each week, allotting time for each method. For instance, you might devote Mondays to answering newspaper ads, because most of them appear in Sunday papers. You might devote Tuesday and Wednesday mornings to developing your contacts and calling a few employment services. You could spend the rest of the week contacting companies directly. This is just one plan that may or may not work for you.

By trying several methods at once, you'll make your job search more interesting, and you'll be better able to evaluate the potential of each method, altering your schedule accordingly. Take care, however, not to judge the success of a method simply by the number of interviews you obtain. Positions advertised in the newspaper, for instance, are likely to generate many more interviews per opening than are unadvertised positions. But there are far more of the latter.

If you're searching part-time and decide to try several different contact methods, we recommend that you try them sequentially. You simply won't have enough time to put a meaningful amount of effort into more than one method at once. So estimate the length of your job search, then allocate so many weeks or months for each contact method you'll use.

If you're expected to be in your office during the day, then you have an additional problem to deal with. How can you work interviews into business hours? And if you work in an open office, how can you even call to schedule interviews? You should make every effort to keep up both performance and appearance on your present job, so maximize your use of the lunch hour, early mornings, and late afternoons for calling. If you keep trying, you may be surprised how easy it is to reach a particular executive after office hours. Often you can catch people as early as 8 A.M. and as late as 6 P.M. Jot down a plan each night on how you'll be using every minute of your precious lunch break.

Your inability to interview at any time other than lunch just might work to your advantage. Set up as many interviews as possible for your lunch hour and schedule them to take place at a mutually convenient restaurant. This will go a long way toward creating a relaxed rapport with the interviewer. (Who isn't happy when eating?) But be sure the interviews don't stray too far from the issue at hand.

Lunchtime interviews are much easier to obtain if you have substantial career experience. People with less experience often find no alternative to taking time off work. If you have to take time off, take time off, but try to do so as discreetly as possible. You might want to take the whole day off to avoid being too obvious about your job search, scheduling two to three interviews on the same day—but no more. It's very difficult to maintain an optimum level of energy for more than three interviews in one day. Explain to the interviewer why you might have to juggle your interview schedule—he or she should be impressed with the consideration you're showing your current employer by minimizing your days off, and will probably appreciate the fact that another prospective employer is interested in you.

If you're searching for a job—especially part-time—you must get out there and do the necessary tasks to the best of your ability and get them over with. Don't let your job search drag on endlessly. Finally, remember that all schedules are meant to be broken. The purpose of a job-search schedule is not to rush you to your goal but to help you map out the road ahead, and then to evaluate periodically how you're progressing.

So You've Been Fired or Laid Off

If you've been fired or laid off, bear in mind that you're not the first and won't be the last to go through this traumatic experience. In today's changing economy thousands of professionals lose their jobs every year. Remember, losing your job is not a reflection of your worth as a person; it's usually a reflection of either your company's staffing needs or your employer's perception of your performance. If you weren't performing up to par or if you weren't enjoying your work, then you'll almost certainly be better off making a new start.

Don't begin your job search with a flurry of unplanned activity. A thorough search could take months, so your first priority is to negotiate a reasonable severance package and determine what benefits, such as health insurance, you're still legally entitled to. Also, register for unemployment compensation immediately. Don't be surprised to find other professionals collecting unemployment as well—it's for everyone who's lost a job.

The next step is to develop a strategy and form a plan. Now is not the time for major changes in your life. If possible, remain in the same career and the same geographic location, at least until you've been working again for a while. On the other hand, if the only industry for which you're trained is leaving town or is severely depressed in your area, then you should give prompt consideration to moving or switching careers.

Avoid mentioning that you were fired while arranging your interviews—but be prepared for the question "Why were you fired?" during an interview. If you were laid off as a result of downsizing, briefly explain, and be sure to emphasize that your job loss wasn't due to performance. If you were in fact fired, be honest, but try to put the best possible spin on the situation while letting the interviewer know that you've learned from your mistakes. If you're confident one of your past managers will give you a good reference, tell the interviewer to contact that person. Don't speak negatively of your past employer, and try not to sound particularly worried that you're temporarily unemployed.

Finally, don't spend too much time reflecting on why you were let go or how you might have avoided it. Think positively, look to the future, and be sure to follow a careful plan during your job search.

The College Student: How to Conduct Your First Job Search

Although you'll be able to apply many of the basics covered earlier in this chapter to your job search, there are some situations unique to the college student's job search.

Perhaps the biggest problem college students face is lack of experience. Many schools have internship programs designed to give students exposure to the field of their choice, as well as the opportunity to make valuable contacts. Check out your school's career-services department to see what internships are available. If your school doesn't have a formal internship program, or if there are no available internships that appeal to you, try contacting local businesses and offering your services—often businesses will be more than willing to have an extra pair of hands (especially if those hands are unpaid!) for a day or two each week. Either way, try to begin building experience as early as possible in your college career.

What do you do if, for whatever reason, you aren't able to get experience directly related to your desired career? First, decide if there's anything about your previous jobs that you can highlight. Did your duties include supervising or training other employees? Did you reorganize the accounting system, or come up with a new way to boost productivity? Accomplishments like these demonstrate leadership, responsibility, and innovation—qualities that most companies look for in employees. And don't forget volunteer activities and school clubs, which can also showcase these traits.

Companies will often send recruiters to interview on-site at various colleges. This gives students a chance to obtain interviews with companies that might not have interviewed them otherwise, particularly if the recruiter schedules "open" interviews, in which the only screening process is signing up. Of course, since many more applicants gain interviews this way, many more people are rejected. The on-campus interview is generally a screening interview, to determine if it's worth the company's time to invite you for a second interview. So do everything possible to make yourself stand out from the crowd.

The first step, of course, is to check out any and all information your school's career center may have on the company. If the information seems out-of-date, call the company's headquarters and ask to be sent the latest annual report, or any other printed information.

Many companies will host an informational meeting for interviewees, often on the evening before interviews are scheduled to take place. Do not miss this meeting. The recruiter will almost certainly ask if you attended. Make an effort to stay after the meeting and talk with the company's representatives. Not only does this give you an opportunity to obtain more information about both the company and the position, it also makes you stand out in the recruiter's mind. If there's a particular company that you have your heart set on, but you're not able to get an interview with the recruiter, attend the information session anyway. You may be able to convince the recruiter to squeeze you into the schedule. (Or you may discover that the company really isn't suited for you, after all.)

Try to check out the interview site beforehand. Some colleges may conduct "mock" interviews that take place in one of the standard interview rooms. Or you may be able to convince a career counselor (or even a custodian) to let you sneak a peek during off-hours. Either way, having an idea of the room's setup will help you prepare mentally.

Be sure to be at least fifteen minutes early for the interview. The recruiter may be running ahead of schedule and might like to take you early. But don't be surprised if previous interviews have run over, resulting in your thirty-minute slot being reduced to twenty minutes (or less). Don't complain; just use whatever time you have as efficiently as possible to showcase the reasons you're the ideal candidate.

Last Words
A parting word of advice. Again and again during your job search you'll be rejected. You'll be rejected when you apply for interviews; you'll be rejected after interviews. For every job offer you receive, you will probably have been rejected numerous times. Don't let rejections slow you down. Keep reminding yourself that the sooner you get started on your job search—and get those rejections flowing in—the closer you'll be to obtaining the job you want.

CHAPTER 2
PREPARING FOR THE INTERVIEW

Too many job seekers jump right into a full-scale job search without much advance preparation other than putting together a resume. A serious mistake! Although your resume may get you job interviews, to win job offers, you must prepare yourself further. It's vitally important to distinguish yourself in some positive way from other candidates vying for the same position. One way of accomplishing this is by developing several themes that you continually refer to throughout the job interview. This enables you to emphasize your strongest points and ensures that you'll leave a strong, positive impression in the recruiter's mind.

Developing Your Personal Themes for the Job Interview
There are twelve types of information recruiters seek in a typical job interview. Knowing what these points are, and being able to discuss readily how each point relates to you, will make you better prepared and more in control of the interviewing process. Think of your twelve themes as sales messages. Each is designed to showcase your best skills and qualifications. Together, they make up a twelve-point strategy that will enable you to sell your qualifications in virtually any interview situation.

Read through the following twelve topics. Develop a personalized approach to each and practice talking about it. Think of specific examples in your background that correspond to each topic. You can't possibly be prepared for every situation, but once you've developed your twelve key messages, you'll be able to apply them to almost any interview question you face.

Next, turn to Chapter 4 to review common interview questions relating to each of the twelve themes. Try to answer each question aloud, incorporating the themes you've developed. Then evaluate your progress. You may discover that you need more practice in order to become comfortable discussing the topics in a clear and concise manner. Nothing that you say for the first time will come out the way you like. Practice aloud delivering your twelve key messages until the words come easily in an organized yet comfortable, conversational way.

1. Passion for the Business
Ask yourself, "Why am I interested in working in this field in this industry?" Do you feel a passion for the business? If so, why? Give specific examples of the things that excite you. These could be anything from enjoying the challenge of meeting increasingly higher sales goals, to a sense of satisfaction

derived from developing a product from the creation stage to final production. Offer personal experience where possible.

2. Motivation and Purpose

Interviewers will want to know why you want to work for their particular company. Ask yourself, "Why do I want this interview?" Don't simply repeat your resume and employment history. What's the most compelling case you can make to prove your interest? Have you used the company's products or talked to its customers or competitors? (Refer to the section that follows, Researching Potential Employers, to learn how you can locate this kind of information about companies you're interested in.)

3. Skills and Experience

Consider your key skills and how you'll use them in this job. Avoid clichés and generalities; instead, offer specific evidence. Think about your weaknesses and how you can minimize and balance them with your strengths. Try to describe yourself as objectively as possible. Avoid sounding arrogant or defensive.

4. Diligence and Professionalism

Describe your professional character, including thoroughness, diligence, and accountability. Give proof that you persevere to see important projects through, and that you achieve desired results. Demonstrate how you gather resources, how you predict obstacles, and how you manage stress.

5. Creativity and Leadership

Offer proof of your effectiveness, including creativity, initiative, resourcefulness, and leadership. What examples can you provide for each? Focus on how you overcome problems, how you take advantage of opportunities that might otherwise be overlooked, and how you rally the support of others to accomplish goals.

6. Compatibility with the Job

Discuss your specific qualifications for the job. How well do they fit the requirements of the position? Your answer should describe both positive and negative aspects of recent jobs, without dwelling on the negatives. Conclude by focusing on what you're seeking in your next job. Keep in mind that your response should match closely the position you're applying for.

7. Personality and Cultural Compatibility

Consider your personality on the job. How do you fit in with other types of personalities? What types of people would enjoy working with you for hours at a time? How would the company's customers or clients react to you? Your goal is to develop responses that make the interviewer feel confident there won't be any surprises after hire about your personality on the job.

8. Management Style and Interpersonal Skills

Talk about the management style and the interpersonal skills you use with peer groups and leaders. Focus on how you work rather than on what type of work you do well. What kind of boss, colleague, and employee will you be? Give personal or popular examples of leaders you believe are effective. Why are those people able to accomplish so much?

9. Problem-Solving Ability

Offer proof, with examples, of your problem-solving ability. How have you resolved difficult issues in the past? Are you practical in how you apply technical skills? Are you realistic? Focus on real issues, on logical value-added solutions, on practical outcomes of your work, and on realistic measures of judging these outcomes.

10. Accomplishments

Think about your initiative and accomplishments. Offer examples in which you've delivered more than what was expected. Don't give long descriptions of situations; instead, focus your answer on the action you took and the positive results you obtained. If you were hired, what situations would you handle especially well? What can you contribute to the organization?

11. Career Aspirations

Tailor your aspirations to the realities of this particular job and its career path. Avoid listing job titles or offering unrealistic performance deadlines. Instead, reiterate the skills and strengths you want to develop further. Do you want cross-functional experience, a larger budget, or more supervisory responsibility? Why would you be effective with that additional experience?

12. Personal Interests and Hobbies

Do you have a balanced lifestyle? Is your personality reflected in the type of job you choose as well as in the outside activities you pursue? Are your personal and career interests compatible? The interviewer will also be interested in your community involvement. How commendably would you reflect the company's image?

After you feel comfortable with your twelve sales messages, develop them in a brief summary. This is a useful tool that you can use effectively at the end of the interview, when the interviewer says something like "Is there anything else you'd like to tell me?" Never let an interview end without summarizing your twelve key messages.

Researching Potential Employers

There are two good reasons why you should set aside some time early in your job search to research companies in your field of interest. First, it's a great way to locate potential employers. Second, it's an effective way to learn more about particular companies you're considering working for.

Researching potential employers can be time-consuming, but it's well worth the effort. To use your time effectively, however, you should divide your research into two distinct phases. The first phase should involve gathering only basic information about many different companies, including:

- Company name, address, phone and fax numbers
- Names and job titles of key contacts
- Whether the company is privately or publicly held
- Products and/or services
- Year of incorporation
- Number of employees

The second phase of research begins as you start to schedule job interviews. This involves gathering more detailed information about each company you're interviewing with. Your goal is to be able to walk into an interview knowing the organization inside and out. You need to know the company's products, types of customers, subsidiaries, parent company, principal locations, rank in the industry, sales and profit trends, type of ownership, size, current plans, principal competitors and their relative performance, and much more. Incorporating this knowledge into your discussions is certain to impress the toughest of interviewers and will distinguish you from the competition. The more time you spend on this phase, the better prepared you'll be. Even if you feel extremely pressed for time, you should set aside at least twelve hours for pre-interview research.

Where to Look

To find the information you need, you'll have to dig into every resource you can find. Libraries are a fantastic source of both publicized and hidden job opportunities. Most have a vast array of resources, including major newspapers like the *New York Times* and the *Wall Street Journal* and trade journals like *Advertising Age* and *Publishers Weekly*. To identify publications in your field of interest, consult the *Encyclopedia of Business Information Sources* or *Predicasts F&S Index*.

There are a number of other resources you can use to find listings of companies, most of which can also be found at your local library. Ask the reference librarian to help you locate the many directories that list basic information about companies in your field of interest. Be sure not to overlook these great tools:

Million Dollar Database from Dun and Bradstreet is a good place to begin your research. It lists approximately 1,600,000 companies that are both publicly and privately held and is updated annually.

Standard & Poor's Register of Corporations provides valuable biographical information on thousands of company officials. The *Register* is comprised of three volumes: Volume 1 provides information on both public and private corporations, Volume 2 contains biographical information on corporate executives and directors, and Volume 3 contains indices.

Corporate Technology Directory (CorpTech Technology Company Information) focuses on the products of approximately 50,000 companies. This is a great resource for job seekers interested in high-tech industries, including computers, biotechnology, environmental engineering, chemical and pharmaceutical, and transportation.

The National JobBank (Adams Media) lists key contacts at more than 20,000 small and large companies. It includes information on common positions filled and educational backgrounds desired, and is updated annually.

Directory of Human Resources Executives (Hunt–Scanlon) names human-resource executives and provides information on number of employees and area of specialization of 10,000 public and private companies.

Directory of Corporate Affiliations (LexisNexis) is one of the few places where you can find information on a company's divisions and subsidiaries. Through its print, CD, and database products, DCA provides access to information on more than 170,000 companies.

Also, don't overlook the countless industry-specific directories that are available, such as *Dunn's Directory of Service Companies*, *Martindale-Hubbell Law Directory*, and *Standard Directory of Advertisers*. These are a terrific place to find potential employers and often include information on professional associations and industry trends.

Many of these resources can also be found on CD-ROM at your library. These "books on disk" are easy to use and can save you a lot of time. They are often attached to printers, so you can print the information you need. Usually, libraries will provide free access to CD-ROM databases.

Your local library is not the only place to look for valuable company information. Why not go straight to the source? Call the investor-relations departments of companies you're interested in and request their annual report. (This approach will generally work only with larger companies.) Call the sales office or PR office of the parent company to get a copy of any literature distributed to consumers, including product literature, recent press releases, or even annual reports (for public companies). If the company is public, call a stockbroker and ask for additional information to supplement what's already in your file. If the firm has a human-resources department, ask for a recruitment package or any other information available to job seekers. If you're interested in a smaller company that doesn't have a human-resources department or publish annual reports, don't panic! Most companies have brochures or catalogs of their products or services that they'll send to you upon request. If possible, speak to someone at the firm before the interview. If you can't do this, speak to someone at a competing firm. The more time you spend, the better.

Use all of your research to develop educated, informed opinions. You'll be better prepared to exchange ideas, create interesting conversation, and make a positive impression on the interviewer. Refer to Part 4 of this book for specific examples of how you can use this information to impress hiring managers and win job offers.

The Informational Interview

Particularly if you're an entry-level job seeker or a career changer, you should consider conducting at least one informational interview. An informational interview is simply a meeting that you arrange to talk to someone in a field, industry, or company that interests you. With the help of this kind of interview you can prepare for a real job interview in several ways, including:

- Examining your compatibility with the company by comparing the realities of the field (skills required, working conditions, schedules, and common traits of people you meet) to your own personal interest
- Finding out how people in a particular business, industry, or job view their roles and the growth opportunities in their businesses
- Conducting primary research on companies and industries
- Gaining insight into the kinds of topics your potential interviewers will be concerned about and the methods for interviewing
- Getting feedback on your relative strengths and weaknesses as a potential job candidate
- Becoming comfortable talking to people in the industry and learning the industry jargon
- Building your network, which can lead to further valuable information and opportunities

To set up an informational appointment, request a meeting with someone who has at least several years' experience working in your field of interest. Your goal is to learn how that person got into the business, what he or she likes about it, and what kind of advice someone with experience might pass on to someone who's interested in entering the field.

Tell your contact right away that you'd like to learn more about the industry or company, and that you'll be the one asking all the questions. Most people won't feel threatened (especially if you assure them you're not asking them for a job) and will usually be inclined to help you.

If you tell a contact that all you want is advice, though, make sure you mean it. Never approach an informational interview as though it were a job interview—just stick to gathering information and leads and see what happens. Also, unless specifically requested to do so, sending your resume to someone you'd like to meet for an informational interview will probably give the wrong impression.

Conducting Informational Interviews

Now that you've scheduled an informational interview, make sure you're prepared to take the lead. After all, you're the one doing the interviewing—not vice versa. Prepare a list of ten to twenty questions, such as:

- How did you get started in this business?
- What experience helped you to be prepared and qualified for this job? (How did you get to this point in your career?)
- What do you believe is the ideal education and background?
- What are your primary responsibilities in your current job?
- What do you like most about your job, your company, and your industry?
- What do you dislike most about them?
- What's been your greatest challenge?
- If you could work with anybody in this field, whom would you want to work with?
- Five years out, what are your career goals?
- What are typical career path options from here?
- If you could change something about your career path, what would you change?
- What are the most valuable skills to have in this field?
- What specific experiences helped you build these skills?
- What opportunities do you see in this business?
- Why did you want this job?
- What would you say are the current career opportunities for someone with my qualifications in the industry?
- If you were in the job market tomorrow, how would you get started? What would you do?
- What are the basic requirements for an entry-level position in the industry?
- What do you consider a must-read list in your field?
- Where do you see the industry heading in the near future?
- Is there a trade association that might aid me in my job search?
- What things impress you when you interview candidates for positions in this field?
- What would be turn offs when you interview candidates?
- What critical questions should I expect to be asked in a job interview?

- What advice would you give to someone looking for a job in the industry?
- Is there anything else I should know about the industry?
- Do you know of anyone who might be looking for someone with my qualifications?
- Is there anything you think I should've brought up (but didn't) that should be a consideration? (What have I missed in this line of questioning?)

Always end by thanking the person and promising to follow up on any important leads he or she has provided, and to let the person know how things turn out. You should also send a thank-you note within one or two days of the informational interview.

Follow up periodically with everyone in your network—even after you get a job. Once you develop a network, it's important not to lose those contacts. You want to translate your informational network into a support network and maintain it throughout your career.

Preparing for Telephone Interviews

Telephone-screening interviews are becoming more commonplace because companies want to reduce their hiring costs by avoiding travel at screening stages in interviews. Using phone interviews, recruiters can quickly weed out most candidates and decide on the best candidates to pursue—that is, to invite for a face-to-face interview.

Here's why planning for a telephone interview is so important: unlike a planned first interview, for which you have done all the preparation already discussed, a telephone interview can come at any time and from any company. Also, once you begin to network, a phone interview may result when all you expected was possible leads. Sometimes recruiters will call to schedule an interview at a later time, but more often they'll call hoping to catch you in and interview you on the spot.

Here are some general tips for handling a phone interview:

- If you feel unprepared or uncomfortable with your phone skills, practice with a friend. Role-play and ask your friend to question you over the phone. Also, you can make good use of your answering machine, here; call when you're away from home and leave yourself a message emphasizing one of your themes. When you get home, listen to how you sound; listen to your voice pattern (enthusiasm, highs/lows, pauses, and so on). Also listen to the content—was your message clear and direct? Keep practicing until you're comfortable with the results.
- Always be prepared, with your twelve themes ready to go. The basic guidelines of a screening interview apply here as well.

- Keep a copy of your resume by the phone along with a list of key words representing the themes you think are relevant to the industry or job category you're pursuing.
- You can't count on clues from an interviewer's body language, eye contact, or other such signs. You'll have to pay close attention, instead, to their voice pattern, and you must use your own voice—simple, direct, enthusiastic responses—to keep the conversation interesting and easy to follow.
- Listen very carefully and maintain your highest level of concentration. Have a phone set up where you can sit more or less as you'd sit for an interview. Keep a pen and some paper near the phone along with your resume and notes. Take very careful notes about what you're asked and what seemed most critical to the recruiter. (This information will help you follow up later with a letter.)
- Avoid long pauses; provide quick summaries of your key themes or points with clear examples of how you've made positive contributions where you've been and how you could contribute to this company.
- Make sure you get the name (spelled correctly), number, and address of the person who called.
- Reaffirm your interest—if you're interested after this first round. Find out what happens next and what you can do to make yourself competitive. Follow up with a thank-you note, just as you would for a screening interview. Your goal is to get face-to-face in the next round.

Collecting References

At some point before you start interviewing, you'll need to prepare a list of three to five references. Unless you're new to the workforce, at least two of these should be professional references from previous employers or close business associates. Other potential sources of references include teachers, professors, volunteer committee heads, and friends who are well respected in business circles. Don't list family members as references.

Be sure to ask people for their permission before you cite them as references. If they agree, be sure you have their job title, the name of the company where they work, and their work address and phone number. Then prepare a neat, typed list of your reference contacts with your name at the top of the page. You should make several copies and have them on hand during your job interviews. Don't make the mistake of listing your references on your resume, as this is commonly considered inappropriate and unprofessional.

Don't forget to send each of your references a thank-you note when your job search is over. Proper etiquette aside, this practice will help keep your contacts current. You never know when you might need their help again sometime down the road.

Preparing Questions for the Interviewer

Toward the end of a typical job interview the interviewer will usually ask if you have any questions. You should be prepared with one or two, or the employer may think you're not really interested in the company. Use this time to ask questions that subtly demonstrate your knowledge of the firm and the industry, and that underscore your interest in a long-term career with that company. At the same time, don't allow this opportunity to become an interrogation. Two or three thoughtful questions are usually sufficient.

What questions should you ask? Here are some examples:

Q: **"What position or positions does this job typically lead to?"**

Q: **"Assuming I was hired and performed well for a number of years, what additional opportunities might this job lead to?"**

These questions imply that you're an achievement-oriented individual looking for a company in which you can build a long-term career.

Q: **"I've noticed in the trade press that your firm has a terrific reputation in marketing. What are the major insights into the marketing process that I might gain from this position?"**

Q: **"I understand that your company is the market leader in industrial drill bits in North America. I'm curious to know how much of the product line is sold overseas—and whether there are many career opportunities in marketing abroad."**

These questions imply that you're very interested in a long-term career in the industry and that you might lean toward pursuing a career with this firm because of its solid reputation. Your well-timed and appropriate questions are sure to impress even the toughest interviewer.

Q: **"What skills are considered most useful for success in the job I'm applying for?"**

This question implies that you really care about your success at your first job, and provides important information you can use to your advantage in the future.

Q: **"I'd really like to work for your firm. I think it's a great company and I'm confident I could do this job well. What's the next step of the selection process?"**

More than a question, this is a powerful statement that will quickly set you apart from other job hunters. However, you should make such a statement only if you mean it. If you're offered the position but then say you need two weeks to think it over, you'll lose your credibility. However, even after responding in this manner, it's reasonable to ask for one or two days to give an offer some thought.

Be sure to save your questions about salary, benefits, and related issues for later, after you receive an offer. You'll still be free to negotiate—or to decline the position—at that point. Also, avoid asking questions that will be difficult or awkward for the recruiter to answer. For example, this is not an appropriate time to ask, "Does your company use recycled paper for all its advertising brochures?"

Part II

During the Job Interview

CHAPTER 3
SETTING THE RIGHT TONE

You're on your way to a job interview.

By now, you've probably spent a great deal of time preparing. However, you must not let your practice and preparation become a disadvantage. Once the interview begins, you must focus on interacting effectively with the interviewer—as opposed to trying to recall precisely the responses you practiced earlier. If you've prepared adequately for the interview, your conduct and responses should effortlessly convey to the interviewer the image you want to project.

It's important for you to know that the interviewer's decision about whether or not you'll be invited back for an additional interview will probably be influenced by your attitude and personality as much as by your qualifications. So although preparation is important, your performance during an interview can make an even greater difference. Generally, you should try to stress the following qualities in your choice of words, your tone of voice, and your body language:

- Capability
- Confidence
- Dependability
- Easygoing manner
- Enthusiasm
- Flexibility
- Resourcefulness
- Strong work ethic

A word of caution: Don't concentrate too much on trying to project the perfect image. Just try to relax, visualize yourself as smooth and confident, and you'll almost certainly do well.

Dressing for Success

How important is proper dress for a job interview? Although the final selection of a job candidate will rarely be determined by dress, first-round candidates are often eliminated because they've dressed inappropriately. This is not to say you should invest in a new wardrobe; just be sure that you're able to put together an adequate interview outfit. A good rule of thumb is to dress for a position just above the one you're applying for.

For a business interview, men should wear a clean, conservative, two-piece suit, a white shirt, and a silk tie. Good dress shoes, such as lace-up wing tips, are your best bet for shoes. This is the basic corporate wardrobe; however, in some industries, a quality jacket, pants, shirt, and tie are fine. But if you're not sure what dress is appropriate at a certain firm, play it safe and opt for a two-piece suit. A man should always wear a jacket and tie to an interview—even if everyone else in the office is in shirtsleeves. Dressing this way shows that you're taking the interview seriously and treating the company with respect.

For women, a professional-looking dress or suit with low-heeled shoes makes the best impression. In more conservative industries, like law or banking, a suit's probably your best choice. However, some hiring managers in "creative" industries, like advertising or publishing, look for a more informal, stylish look that reflects the applicant's individuality. Use your best judgment and wear whatever is both professional and comfortable for you. However, be sure to avoid excess jewelry or makeup.

Impeccable personal grooming is even more important than finding the "perfect" outfit. Be sure that your clothes are clean, pressed, and well fitting, and that your shoes are polished. Hair should be neat and businesslike, and your nails should be clean and trimmed. Both men and women are advised to skip the cologne or perfume—you never know if the person interviewing you will be violently allergic to the cologne you're wearing.

Timing Is Everything

Although it may seem hard to believe, many job seekers arrive late for interviews. This is easy enough to do—you might simply take a little unplanned extra time to prepare for your interview, or underestimate how long it will take to get to the interview location. Don't let yourself make this fatal mistake!

Allow plenty of time to get ready for, and to travel to, your job interview. You shouldn't arrive at the interviewer's office more than ten minutes in advance. However, if you're driving across town, allowing yourself an extra ten minutes probably isn't enough. Try to get to the location at least thirty minutes early; you can then spend twenty minutes in a nearby coffee shop or take a walk around the building. Interviews are important enough to build in a little extra time. Here's another tip: if you've never been to the interview location, visit it the day before so you know exactly how to get there, how to access the building, and where to park.

Sometimes the interviewer will be running behind schedule. Don't be upset: be sympathetic. Interviewers are often pressured to see a lot of candidates and to fill a demanding position quickly. So be sure to come to your interview with good reading material to keep yourself occupied and relaxed.

What to Have on Hand

A briefcase or leather-bound folder, if you have one, will help complete the professional, polished look you want to achieve. Women should avoid carrying a purse if they plan on carrying a briefcase—it may detract from a professional image. And don't forget to wear a watch!

Before leaving for the interview be sure that you have good directions and the phone numbers and names of the people you'll be meeting with. You should also bring the following items with you to the interview:

- Several unfolded copies of your resume and cover letter
- A notepad and pen (for taking notes during the interview)
- A list of professional references
- Examples of your work, such as writing samples or clippings (taking care that these don't breach the confidentiality of previous employers)

Body Language

The first minutes of the interview are the most important. A recruiter begins sizing up your potential the instant you walk into the room. If you make a bad impression from the start, you may be ruled out immediately, and the interviewer may pay little attention to your performance during the rest of the interview. An excellent initial impression, on the other hand, will put a favorable glow on everything else you say during the rest of the interview—and could well encourage the recruiter to ask less demanding questions.

How can you ensure that you make a terrific first impression? The easiest answer is to be sure you're dressed well. When the recruiter meets you, he or she will notice your clothes and grooming first. Nothing other than impeccable grooming is acceptable. Your attire must be professional and squeaky clean.

Your body language will also speak volumes, even before you and the interviewer exchange a word. Any recruiter will unconsciously pick up on and react to the subtle signals of body language. Here are some important things to think about:

- Do you smile when you meet?
- Do you make just enough eye contact without staring at the recruiter?
- Do you walk into the office with a self-assured and confident stride?
- Do you shake hands firmly?
- Are your briefcase, notepad, and coat in your left hand, or do you have to juggle them around in order to shake hands?
- Do your eyes travel naturally to and from the recruiter's face as you begin to talk?
- Do you remember the recruiter's name and pronounce it with confidence?
- Do you make small talk easily, or do you act formal and reserved, as though under attack?

It's human nature to judge people by that first impression, so make sure yours is a good one. But most of all, try to be yourself.

Overcoming Nervousness

As if formulating solid answers to interview questions isn't tough enough, you'll also have to overcome a quite natural, inevitable nervousness. Most employers won't think less of a job candidate for a bit of nervous behavior—but they will pay close attention to how you hold up under pressure. Displaying excessive nervousness can easily eliminate you from further consideration.

One good way to overcome pre-interview jitters is to exercise positive thinking. If you're feeling nervous about an upcoming interview, imagine in detail what the experience will be like: think of what you'll say, the questions you'll be asked, and how you'll answer them. Picture yourself responding calmly, effectively, and in a controlled manner. This type of mental rehearsing won't guarantee success, but it should help you feel more optimistic and self-confident, which will undoubtedly enhance your final presentation.

Above all, you should practice interviewing as much as you can. You'll become more confident and your answers will become more polished with each interview you have.

Navigating the Dynamics of Interview Conversation

All your preparation should be evident when the conversation gets going. Make sure your tone remains conversational; don't let the interview turn into an interrogation. Start by thanking the interviewer for the opportunity to talk with him or her and explain up front why you're interested in the position. Be ready to answer and to ask questions, including occasionally asking the interviewer for his or her own perspective on a subject.

After small talk the interviewer may well begin by telling you about the company, the division, the department, or perhaps the position. Because of your detailed research, information about the company should be already familiar to you. The interviewer will probably like nothing better than to avoid this regurgitation of company history, so if you can do so tactfully, indicate that you're very familiar with the firm. If the interviewer seems determined to provide you with background information despite your hints, then listen attentively. If you can manage to initiate a brief, appropriate discussion of the company or industry at this point, that's great. It will help you to build rapport, underscore your interest, and increase your impact.

Soon the interviewer will begin to ask you questions. This period of the interview may be structured or unstructured, or somewhere in between. In a structured interview the interviewer asks a prescribed set of questions, seeking relatively brief answers. In the unstructured interview the interviewer asks more open-ended questions to prod you into giving longer responses and revealing as much as possible about yourself, your background, and your aspirations. Some interviewers will mix both styles, typically beginning with more objective questions and asking more open-ended questions as the interview progresses.

Try to determine as quickly as possible which direction the interviewer is going, and respond to the questions accordingly. As you answer the questions, watch for signals from the employer as to whether your responses are too short or too long. For example, if the employer is nodding or looking away, wrap up your answer as quickly as possible. Following the style the interviewer establishes will make the interview easier and more comfortable and will help you make a more favorable impression.

Once you begin to feel more confident about interviewing, you may wish to think strategically about each interview. One effective tactic is to adjust your speed of speech to match that of the interviewer's. People tend to talk at the speed at which they like to be spoken to. If you can adjust your speech rate to that of the recruiter without sounding unnatural, the recruiter will probably feel more comfortable (after all, interviewing others isn't much fun, either) and have a more favorable impression of you.

Another strategy is to adapt your answers to match the type of company for which you're interviewing. For example, if you're interviewing for a job at a large product-marketing company that emphasizes group decision making and spends much of its energy focused on battles for market share with its competitors, you might want to talk about how much you enjoy team sports—especially being part of a team and competing to win.

Concentrate on the themes you've developed in Chapter 2 and be alert for opportunities to mention them. If applicable, draw parallels between your experience and the demands of the position as described by the interviewer. Talk about your past experience, emphasizing results and achievements and not merely recounting activities. If you listen carefully (listening is a very important part of the interviewing process), the interviewer might very well give you an idea of the skills needed for the position. Don't exaggerate. Be on the level about your abilities.

Try not to be negative about anything during the interview—especially about any past employer or previous job. Be cheerful. Everyone likes to work with someone who seems to be happy.

Don't let a tough question throw you off base. If you don't know the answer to a question, say so simply—don't apologize. Just smile. Nobody can answer every question—particularly some of the questions that are asked in job interviews.

Try not to cover too much ground during the first interview. This interview, in which many candidates are screened out, is often the toughest. If you're interviewing for a very competitive position, you'll have to make an impression that will last. Focus on a few of your greatest strengths that are relevant to the position. Develop these points carefully, state them again in different words, and then try to summarize them briefly at the end of the interview.

Above all else, keep the conversation flowing. Don't talk too much or too little; watch the recruiter for signals. A job interview is a conversation between two people who are hoping to discover they have a common interest. Move around if you have to so that you don't appear stiff, but be careful not to fidget. Try to appear relaxed, enthusiastic, and determined—all at the same time!

Turning the Tables

Often the interviewer will pause toward the end and ask if you have any questions. Particularly in a structured interview, this might be the one chance to communicate your knowledge of, and interest in, the firm. Have a list prepared of specific questions that are of real interest to you. Let your questions subtly show your research and your knowledge of the firm's activities. It's wise to memorize an extensive list of questions, as several of them may be answered during the interview.

When asking the interviewer your questions, follow these guidelines:

- Don't let this opportunity turn into an interrogation. Don't bring your list of questions to the interview.
- Ask questions that you're fairly certain the interviewer can answer. (Remember how you feel when you can't answer a question during an interview.)
- If you're unable to determine the salary range beforehand, don't ask about it during the first interview. You can always ask about it later.
- Don't ask about fringe benefits until you've been offered a position. (Then be sure to get all the details.) You should be able to determine the company's policy on benefits relatively easily before the interview.
- If it looks as though your skills and background don't match the position your interviewer was hoping to fill, ask if there's another division or subsidiary that perhaps could profit from your talents.

A Final Note

Interviewing is like almost everything else—the more you do it, the better you become. Don't expect to give a perfect performance—especially in your first few interviews. Even experienced professionals who haven't interviewed in a while are bound to be rusty.

And if you have a terrible interview, don't let it shake your confidence! Remember that everyone has a bad interview experience sooner or later. Learn from it, work on your performance, and keep looking for other opportunities.

CHAPTER 4
WHAT YOU CAN EXPECT

The First Interview

As mentioned earlier, the first interview is often a screening interview conducted by a human-resource-department representative or an employment interviewer. The types of questions are general in nature—rarely specific to the technical aspects of the job. This is why it's important that you've developed themes related to the most relevant aspects of your own experiences and achievements. (See Chapter 2 for more information on this strategy.)

The primary purpose of the first interview is to determine qualities like motivation, industry or functional skills, work ethic, communication skills, and critical-thinking skills. You should communicate genuine interest in the job, the industry, and the city or region of the country if relocation is part of the package. You need to demonstrate compatibility with the company culture and show that you can sell that compatibility in subsequent interviews if the recruiter moves you to the next round in the process. Recruiters are always concerned about weeding out any candidate who might embarrass them in a second interview; they must believe that they really got to know you and that you won't present any surprises in subsequent interviews. After all, their reputation and judgment are on the line if they recommend you for a second interview.

Practicing Your Answers

You can never be sure exactly what you'll be asked at a job interview, but certain questions are more likely to be asked than others, and you should be prepared for them. By developing solid answers to possible questions, you'll be in a better position to answer questions that you haven't anticipated.

Try to structure your responses in a way that conveys that you're someone the employer would want to hire. In other words, project yourself as someone who's likely to stay with the company for a number of years, who's achievement oriented, who'll fit in well with the other employees, who's likable. Of course, you should also try to present yourself as someone who's capable of performing extremely well in the position.

You should avoid giving generic answers like "I'm a people person" or "I've excellent written and oral communication skills." Your response should always be specific (with supporting examples), and it should relate specifically to the job, the industry, or other personal factors to help your answer (and you!) stand out. Particularly in screening interviews, where generic questions are often asked, recruiters are looking to eliminate the average respondent.

You can't afford a predictable, nondescript response. You must turn a common question into a memorable answer.

Go through the practice interview questions we've included here. (The questions are organized according to the twelve themes outlined in Chapter 2.) At first you may wish to read the sample responses and the accompanying discussion. Later, as you begin to feel more comfortable with the questions, try answering them without any help, as you would during a real interview. How did you do?

1. Passion for the Business

Q: Why do you want to work in this industry?

A: *I've always wanted to work in an industry that makes tools. One of my hobbies is home-improvement projects, so I've collected a number of saws manufactured by your company. I could be an accountant anywhere, but I'd rather work for a company whose products I trust.*

Tell a story about how you first became interested in this type of work. Point out any similarities between the job you're interviewing for and your current or most recent job. Provide proof that you aren't simply "shopping" in this interview. Make your passion for your work a theme that you allude to continually throughout the interview.

Q: Why would you be particularly good at this business?

A: *I was a pastry chef, so I understand dessert products well and can help you with new product development. Recent preservatives have come a long way toward eliminating texture difference in pastry dough. This means we can investigate many more products than before.*

Show how you keep up due to natural inquisitiveness, reading, and so on. Do you have sufficient natural interest to go that extra step and channel appropriate energy into your work? Give a specific answer.

Q: How do you stay current?

A: *I pore over the* Wall Street Journal, *the* Times, Institutional Investor, *and several mutual fund newsletters. And I've a number of friends who are analysts.*

Demonstrate natural interest in the industry or career field by describing publications or trade associations that are compatible with your goal.

Q: Why do you think this industry would sustain your interest over the long haul?

A: *The technology in the industry is changing so rapidly that I see lots of room for job enhancement regardless of promotions. I'm particularly interested in the many applications for multimedia as a training tool.*

What expectations or projections do you have for the business that would enable you to grow without necessarily advancing? What excites you about the business? What proof can you offer that your interest has already come from a deep curiosity—perhaps going back at least a few years—rather than a current whim you'll outgrow?

Q: Where do you want to be in five years?

A: *I'd like to have the opportunity to work in a plant as well as at the home office. I also hope to develop my management skills, perhaps by managing a small staff.*

Don't give specific time frames or job titles. Talk about what you enjoy, skills that are natural to you, realistic problems or opportunities you'd expect in your chosen field or industry, and what you hope to learn from those experiences. You shouldn't discuss your goals in a field or industry unrelated to the job you're applying for. This may sound obvious, but too many job candidates make this mistake, unwittingly demonstrating a real lack of interest in their current field or industry. Needless to say, such a gaffe will immediately eliminate you from further consideration.

Q: Describe your ideal career.

A: *I'd like to stay in a field related to training no matter what happens. I was too interested in business to work at a university, but I believe that teaching is somehow in my blood. I've been good at sales because I took the time to educate my clients. Now I look forward to training the new hires.*

Talk about what you enjoy, skills that are natural to you, realistic problems or opportunities you'd expect in this particular job or industry, and what you hope to learn from those experiences. Avoid mentioning specific time frames or job titles.

Q: If you had unlimited time and financial resources, how would you spend them?

A: *I'd love to be able to take several executive seminars on financial management that aren't geared toward financial experts. I'd also love to be able to shut down my department long enough to send everyone through an Outward Bound-type program. Finally, I'd probably travel and look at foreign competitors, and enjoy the food along the way. What would you do?*

Although it's tempting to discuss things you'd do for fun, stick to job- or industry-related pursuits, or to skill-building efforts that could transfer to the job you're applying for. For example, if you're applying for a teaching job, you might also be interested in volunteering for an adult literacy program; this demonstrates a passion for your field—a belief in the importance of education—even without pay as an incentive.

2. Motivation and Purpose

Q: Tell me about yourself.

A: *I'm the kind of person who thrives in an environment where I have to coordinate lots of people and lots of different agendas and schedules. That skill is what I believe has earned me success in brand management. It's also the reason I couldn't imagine having a job in which I followed a routine or had only one or two responsibilities.*

This question invites you to describe your motivation. Don't repeat your resume or employment history. Interpret one or two items to explain why you're talking to this company. What's the most compelling item you can describe to prove your interest? This is probably the most commonly asked interview question, and it's usually one of the first questions asked. Be sure to have a sixty-second pitch ready for the interviewer. (See Chapter 1 for information on how to develop your sixty-second pitch.)

Q: Tell me something about yourself that I didn't know from reading your resume.

A: *You wouldn't know that I've managed my own small portfolio since I was six, but I believe that it's important for you to understand my interest in investment sales. I've averaged a 2 percent return over the past eight years.*

Don't just repeat what's on your resume. Think of a talent or skill that didn't quite fit into your employment history, but that's unique and reveals something intriguing about your personality or past experience.

Q: Tell me what you know about this company.

A: *I served as an intern to a restaurant analyst last summer, so I followed all the steak-house chains closely. What you've done especially well is focus on a limited menu with great consistency among locations; the business traveler trusts your product anywhere in the United States. I'm particularly interested in your real-estate finance group and expansion plans.*

Describe your first encounter or a recent encounter with the company or its products and services. What would be particularly motivating to you about working there as opposed to working the same type of job in a different company? The recruiter will look for evidence of genuine interest and more than just surface research on the company. Reciting the annual report isn't likely to impress most recruiters, but feedback from customers and employees will.

Q: What have you learned about our company from customers, employees, or others?

A: *I actually called several of the key accounts mentioned in your brochure. Two of the customers I spoke with explained why they continued to buy from you year after year. Your distribution operation is phenomenal. Are there any service improvements you think could still be made?*

Describe how your interest has grown from personal dealings with company representatives. Think creatively in preparing for job interviews. For example, prior to your job interview, speak with retailers or workers at other distribution points about the company's product line. What can they tell you? Give one or two examples of what you've learned to explain why you're interested in this company. What's the most compelling example you can describe to prove your interest?

Q: Why do you want to work here?

A: *I lost a bid several years ago to your company. I realized then that products in the computer industry are becoming increasingly similar. They're so similar now, and retail prices are so competitive, that service is the best way for a company to distinguish itself from the competition. This company has the best service record of all its competitors, and I believe it will dominate the business in the long run.*

Your preparation and research should become apparent here. Give one or two reasons why you're interested in the company, and what in particular piqued your interest. What's the most compelling thing you can describe about your personal experience with the company, its products, or its employees? Possible answers include the company's reputation, the job description itself, or a desire to get involved with the industry.

Q: What particular aspect of the company interests you most?

A: *I'm most interested in your Latin American developments. My father was an army officer, so we lived for three years in Latin America. I know you've just entered joint ventures with two processing companies there. What are your plans for the next few years?*

This is another opportunity for you to showcase your special knowledge of the company. If you did the proper research, as described in Chapter 2, you should have no problem answering this question with ease.

Q: **What's your favorite product made by our company?**

A: *I've used Softer Than Ever shampoo for years. In fact, my initial contact with the company was the brand manager for Softer Than Ever. She encouraged me to apply for an HR position here.*

Describe personal use—why do you use the company's products? What do you think are new market opportunities for that product?

Q: **What do you think of our newest product and ads?**

A: *It seems that your new ads are trying to show that breakfast time is family time, with a certain wholesomeness. Are you doing this to balance against the recent bad press about high-fat foods, without attacking the issue directly?*

You should be familiar enough with the company's new products and advertising campaigns to make informed, intelligent comments about them. Offer specific suggestions and positive comments.

Q: **Tell me what you think our distinctive advantage is within the industry.**

A: *With your low-cost-producer status and headquarters operation in a low-cost area of the country, you seem in a better position to be able to spend aggressively on R&D, even in a down year, compared to your closest rival.*

Describe things you believe the company does very well, particularly compared to its competition. Explain how the financial strength of the company is important.

Q: **Where do you think we're the most vulnerable as a business?**

A: *Your cash position and strong product presence make you an attractive target for a takeover. That's my only major concern. I've already worked for one organization that merged with another, but I also know I can weather the storm.*

Describe things you believe the company does not do well compared to its competition. Explain how the company's financial strength is important. If you've a passion for the business, the future of the job is probably always on your mind.

Q: **What would you do differently if you ran the company?**

A: *I might investigate whether to sell off the light-manufacturing businesses and start an aggressive supplier-relations program.*

In a constructive way demonstrate that you have enough knowledge about the business to answer this question convincingly. One way to gain such knowledge is by talking to a sufficient number of company insiders, which is why this question can quickly weed out the "shoppers" from more serious job candidates. You can also turn the question around—ask for the recruiter's ideas, too. You might learn something valuable.

Q: **What other firms are you interviewing with, and for what positions?**

A: *Actually, I've definitely decided to pursue a career as a restaurant manager, so I'm applying only for restaurant management training programs. I've recently had interviews with several other large national fast-food chains, such as Super Burger and Clackey's Chicken.*

Often the candidate will try to impress the employer by naming some large firms in unrelated industries with completely different types of jobs. This is a big mistake! What employers want to hear is that you're interviewing for similar jobs in the same industry at similar firms (such as their competitors). This illustrates that you're committed to finding a job in your field of interest and are likely to be a low-risk hire.

Q: **Describe our competition as you see it.**

A: *Most of your competitors have tried to do too many things. As a result, most have had difficulty expanding and maintaining consistent quality.*

Give evidence that you've researched the company and industry carefully and acquired more than superficial knowledge. Point out positive and/or negative aspects of the company's competitors. Discuss how the company's initiatives are better suited to your personal interests.

Q: **What would you do if one of our competitors offered you a position?**

A: *I'd say no. I'm not interested in other players in this industry. I want to work for Nike because I won a number of races wearing the Nike brand. Because of my positive experience with Nike, I know I'd be convincing selling your product to retailers.*

The interviewer is trying to determine whether the candidate is truly interested in the industry and company, or whether he or she has chosen the company randomly. Contrast your perceptions of the company with its competitors, and talk about the company's products or services that you've encountered. In the long run, which players do you believe are most viable and why? This is also a good place to ask the interviewer for his or her opinion.

Q: **Why are you ready to leave your current job?**

A: *My interest lies in returning to the banking industry. I can work in human-resources management in many environments, but I believe that my experience as a lender prepares me exceptionally well for recruiting new lenders into the training program.*

Give two or three reasons why you're ready to leave your current job. Focus on limitations in growth, or lack of challenge, in your current job. Make sure you point out why you believe the position you're interviewing for would provide the challenge and additional responsibilities that you desire.

Q: What do you want out of your next job?

A: *I'm really interested in taking over a territory where we aren't very well positioned. My sales successes to date have been in areas where we already had a decent market share. I also want a very aggressive commission structure if I'm able to turn around a problem territory.*

This question is similar to "Why are you ready to leave your current job?" Give one or two examples from your current work experience that explain why you're interviewing for the position. Focus on your desire for greater challenge. For example, "I've gone as far as I can go in my current job unless someone vacates a position." Make sure you point out why you believe the job at hand provides the additional responsibilities you're seeking.

Q: What's your dream job?

A: *My dream job would include all of the responsibilities and duties in this position you're trying to fill. I also thrive in a fast-changing environment where there's business growth. Your plans call for expanding internationally during the next year, and this would satisfy one of my ultimate goals of being involved in an international corporation.*

This is your ideal chance to sell your aptitudes that fit the job description. Show an interest in finding new ways these skills can be put to use in a new job with additional responsibilities. Tie in the industry, size of the company, or other factors where appropriate.

Q: What motivates you to do this kind of work?

A: *I've been fortunate in my own schooling; I had wonderful teachers. I want to be that same kind of teacher—who not only encourages kids to learn but also sets an example that inspires others to want to teach. In the long run, that's our best chance of turning around the quality of education in this state.*

The interviewer will want to know about your belief in the products or services of the company. Use personal experience to demonstrate your interests and strengths. In an interview for your ideal job, you'd be highly motivated to get paid for working at something you liked. The interviewer will want to know if your natural interests are compatible with this particular job.

Q: What are your salary goals or expectations?

A: *Based on your job description, which mentions that you prefer someone with a master's degree in engineering, I hope you consider the fact that my skills meet your highest standards. Therefore, I'd expect a salary at the high end of your pay range for the position classification. Can you give me some indication of your range?*

Recruiters want to weed out people whose financial goals are unrealistic. This question is a direct hit—it forces a response about a touchy subject. If you mention a salary that's too low, you may seem uninformed; too high, and you may outprice yourself or ruin your ability to bargain. It's best to turn the question back on the recruiter. Ask what the salary range is for the position; then ask the recruiter to consider how your qualifications rate compared to the "average" requirements for the position.

Q: What new skills or ideas do you bring to the job that other candidates aren't likely to offer?

A: *Because I've worked with the oldest player in this industry, I can help you avoid some of the mistakes we made in our established markets. I think that retaining your core customer base is more important than securing new accounts right now.*

This question addresses the candidate's motivation for adding "true value" (beyond what's expected) to the job. Have you thought about the job carefully, considering current limitations or weaknesses in the current department and your unique abilities? If you're running neck and neck with another candidate, your ability here to prove "I offer what you need and then some" could land you the job.

Q: What interests you most about this job?

A: *I'd love the opportunity to work with John Doe, whom I watched build the financial-services practice under bank deregulation. I think our utilities clients will go through a lot of the same problems that banks faced in the eighties. John's insights will be sound, and John and I have worked well together on several projects.*

Point out the new experiences you look forward to in the job as well as reasons you believe you're uniquely suited to the position. Point out similarities to some of your past jobs in which you enjoyed success.

Q: What would you like to accomplish that you weren't able to accomplish in your last position?

A: *I was hampered by a small budget that limited our marketing efforts to print ads and other traditional resources. I'd like to explore interactive media, because the eight-to-twenty-five-year-old category responds to computer-based media.*

This question should be answered in the same way you'd answer "Why are you ready to leave your current job?" Remain positive—discuss things you enjoy and have an aptitude for, but avoid dwelling on the limitations of your last job.

Q: We have a number of applicants interviewing for this position. Why should we take a closer look at you?

A: *I'm probably one of the few CPAs you'll find who's worked in two Hispanic countries. With all the production that you're outsourcing to Mexico, I may be able to provide some assistance with your inventory planning.*

This is similar to the question "Why should I hire you?" What's the most compelling item you can describe to prove your qualifications and interest? Is there something extra you offer besides the basic job qualifications? Be specific in your answer. Whatever answer you prepare, try using it when you wrap up the interview, if you haven't yet been asked this question.

Q: Prove to me that your interest is sincere.

A: *I actually tried to get an internship here last summer, when I was a senior in college, but the manager whom I was going to work with was transferred to another office, and the internship fell through. Since that time, I've closely followed developments in the industry and at this company through trade journals and by speaking with my contacts in the field.*

Your answer here can combine elements from your prepared responses to the questions "Why should I hire you?" "What have you learned about our company?" and "What interests you most about this job?" You must go beyond a superficial comment and truly demonstrate a passion for some aspect of the work.

Q: How have your career motivations changed over the past few years?

A: *When I started in sales, I didn't realize how much I'd miss it if I left. Now I want to stay close to the field organization, even though I'm looking at marketing jobs. Your firm attracts me because the account-team concept would keep me in tune with customer needs.*

Describe what you've learned from your past jobs, especially where your skills and natural instincts have become apparent. Your current motivation should relate strongly to the job you're interviewing for.

Q: Why should I hire you?

A: *My uncle had a company that was a small-scale manufacturer in the industry, and although he later sold the business, I worked there for five summers doing all sorts of odd jobs. For that reason I believe I know this business from the ground up, and you can be assured that I know what I'd be getting into as a plant manager here.*

Don't repeat your resume or employment history. Offer one or two examples to explain why you're talking to this particular company. What's the most compelling example you can give to prove your interest? This question often remains unasked, but it's always in the back of a recruiter's mind. Even if this question isn't asked, you should find an opportunity to use your prepared response sometime during the interview, perhaps in your closing remarks.

3. Skills and Experience

Q: What are your key skills?

A: *After working six years as a senior systems analyst, I've developed a number of key skills, including business modeling, process re-engineering, software-package evaluation, and excellent programming skills in UNIX and C environments. I was very pleased to discover that these are the skills you're seeking. Do you want to hear about specific examples of my work?*

Talk about your key skills and how you'll use them in this job. Avoid clichés or generalities. Offer specific evidence, drawing parallels from your current or previous job to the job you're interviewing for.

Q: What sets you apart from the crowd?

A: *Once I'm committed to a job or a project, I tackle it with tremendous intensity. I want to learn everything I can, and my goal is to achieve results beyond the expectations of my supervisor. I guess you might say I'm very competitive and like to excel at everything I do.*

Your answer should communicate self-confidence, but avoid sounding arrogant. Talk about observations other people have made about your work, talents, or successes.

Q: What are your strengths?

A: *My strengths are interpersonal skills, and I can usually win people over to my point of view. Also, I have good judgment about people and an intuitive sense of their talents and their ability to contribute to a given problem. These skills seem to me directly related to the job. I notice that you require three* years' work experience for this job. Although my resume shows that I've only two years' experience, it doesn't show that I took two evening college courses related to my field and have been active in one of the professional societies. I also try to gain knowledge by reading the industry's trade journals. I'm certain that my combined knowledge and skill level is the equivalent of that of other people who actually do have three years' work experience. I'm also currently enrolled in a time-management course; I can already see the effects of this course at work on my present job.

Describe two or three skills you have that are most relevant to the job. Avoid clichés or generalities; offer specific evidence. Describe new ways these skills could be put to use in the new position. If you have to talk about weaknesses, be honest without shooting yourself in the foot—avoid pointing out a weakness that might be a major obstacle to landing the job. For example, it might be wise to mention that you barely have the required work experience for the job; the interviewer has surely noticed this much, and then you can explain how you're qualified for the job nonetheless.

Q: What are your weaknesses?

A: *One of my weaknesses is that I tend to take on a little too much responsibility, then feel that I have to carry it myself. I need to be more willing to talk to my supervisors or coworkers, ask for their advice and suggestions, and even seek their help from time to time.*

Be honest, but discuss how you'd balance your weaknesses with appropriate strengths. Avoid sounding defensive, perhaps by explaining why you haven't yet had an opportunity to develop a particular skill, even though you're interested in acquiring that skill. Don't assume that by avoiding this discussion the interviewer won't notice any deficiencies you may have. You're better off bringing up this topic yourself; you can then address and defend your position and change the recruiter's mind.

Q: How is your experience relevant to this job?

A: *In my current job I've recently completed three re-engineering projects. I gathered all the necessary market data, developed a benchmarking program, and put together a team to do the evaluation and analysis. As a result I'm ready to tackle the major re-engineering project that you've listed as the priority of this job during the first year. In my past job I was the liaison between the project engineering group and the instrumentation group in the testing of a new turbo engine. This experience will also help me tackle this job, which involves a close and careful working relationship between your technical group and your field-testing group.*

Draw parallels from your current or previous job to the requirements of this job. A similarity that seems obvious to you may not be so obvious to the recruiter. Ask questions about the job, if necessary, to get the interviewer to accept your rationale.

Q: What skills do you think are most critical to this job?

A: *The ability to evaluate all of the regulatory and competitive requirements for your new product are critical. I've had considerable experience in this area as a strategic-marketing and regulatory-policy analyst in my most recent job, and also in my first job.*

Describe the immediate relevance of your past experience. Draw parallels from your current or previous job to the requirements of this job.

Q: What skills would you like to develop in this job?

A: *I'd like to develop my negotiating skills. I've had considerable experience interpreting and implementing large contracts, but I've been limited in negotiating the actual conditions, costs, and standards for a major contract. I believe this job will offer me the opportunity to be a member of a negotiating team and thereby to begin acquiring the skills necessary to lead the team.*

Describe several aptitudes you haven't been able to develop fully in your current job. For example, your opportunity to manage the department might have been hindered because your supervisor plans to stay in his or her job at least five more years.

Q: If you had to stay in your current job, what would you spend more time on? Why?

A: *If I stay in my current job, I'd like to gain more experience in labor negotiating. In particular, I'd like to help negotiate labor contracts, resolve grievances at the step-4 level, and prepare grievances for arbitration. My background in all other areas of human resources is strong, and I believe labor-relations experience will round out my skills so that I can have the opportunity to move up as a department head or a vice president in the future.*

What interests you most about your job? Describe the responsibilities that give you the most satisfaction. In addition, show a real interest in upgrading the job, staying on the leading edge, and so on.

Q: How could you enrich your current job?

A: *When I was a research assistant for the cable and wireless company back in ninety-nine, at a time when we were experiencing rapid growth, our pricing analyst abruptly resigned for a better job. During the search to fill his position,*

I volunteered to help out with one of the major government projects. I worked considerable overtime, studied on my own, and helped bring the project to conclusion. I was commended for my effort and was told I'd be in line for the next opening in the pricing group.

Show an ability to add value continually to your job. What new opportunities exist that could challenge your skills and intellect? The interviewer will want to feel confident that you won't get bored or disenchanted with your work.

Q: **How do you explain your job successes?**

A: *I never assume our customers are satisfied with our product, so I do my best to follow up with every customer. This feedback has provided valuable insight into the quality and characteristics of our products. The customer, as well, always appreciates this follow-up, especially when something hasn't gone right and you still have the opportunity to correct it on a timely basis. In addition, I'm able to pass on information to our design and production units to help improve both process and product.*

Be candid without sounding arrogant. Mention observations other people have made about your work strengths or talents. This question is similar to the question "What sets you apart from the crowd?"

Q: **Tell me about a project in which you were disappointed with your performance.**

A: *In my last job as an operations analyst for a manufacturing company, I had to analyze all the supplier bids and present recommendations to the vice president of logistics. Because the supplier bids weren't in a uniform format, my analysis often consisted of comparing dissimilar items. This caused some confusion in my final report, and by the time I reworked it and presented it to the vice president, we'd lost the critical time we needed to improve our approval process for these bids. In hindsight I should have taken a simpler approach to the problem and not tried to make it as complex or all-inclusive, so that I could have good recommendations in a timely manner.*

Describe roadblocks and what you did to try to get around them. How did your skills come into play? In hindsight, what could you have done differently? What lessons have you learned?

Q: **What aspects of your work are most often criticized?**

A: *I remember in my first job as a marketing assistant, I spent endless hours analyzing a particular problem. I came up with a revised marketing plan that was extremely well received. Unfortunately, when I had to present it to top management, I didn't give the necessary time and attention to the actual presentation— overheads and slides—and the proposal was turned down because I didn't* *make clear the savings that would result. I spent the next two weeks working on my presentation, and on my second try I was much more persuasive and convinced management that, indeed, this was the way to go. They approved it, and my recommendations were carried out to everyone's satisfaction.*

Focus your answer here on some weakness in a job you held early in your career. What did you or your supervisor do about it? Demonstrate improvement over the years.

Q: Compared to others with a similar background in your field, how would you rate yourself?

A: *I've been consistently ranked in the top 10 percent nationally for all salespeople in my field. I sell advertising space for a national news publication. My clients are primarily large ad agencies that represent corporate America. I've always enjoyed the challenge of selling to advertising-agency executives because they always set high standards and really know our product well. This brings out the very best in my competitive nature, and I'm consistently at the top, both within my publishing company and within the industry.*

Be honest and self-confident without sounding arrogant. Give clear, convincing reasons for your answer. If you've been in the top 10 percent in sales nationally, this is a good time to bring it up!

Q: Does the frequent travel required for this work fit into your lifestyle?

A: *The frequent travel necessary for this position would not be a problem. My wife also travels on business on occasion, and we are both familiar with the necessities of traveling for a position.*

Offer what you're comfortable divulging about your family situation if it helps prove your flexibility. By all means, don't be dishonest with yourself or the recruiter.

Q: Why have you changed jobs so frequently?

A: *My frequent job changes over the last five years have resulted primarily from the rapid change in my profession. As you know, my jobs have been based on government contracts, and over the last several years the congressional appropriations have been up and down, causing some contracts to be canceled, while other companies get unexpected, huge contracts. Although this volatility creates good opportunities to move on, it also creates a lot of uncertainty in the industry. Since your business is based mostly on consumer products and not on government products, I welcome an opportunity in which the business cycle is more stable and predictable.*

Expect questions about what may seem like possible deficiencies in your background, and give candid answers. Try to demonstrate convincingly, for instance, why you moved on for personal growth, a larger budget, or other career-enhancing experiences. Tell the interviewer why you're interested in his or her company for the long haul.

Q: **Have you ever been fired or asked to resign?**

A: *During one of my summer internships while in college, I was working for a software consulting company. Midway through the summer a new president was appointed because of some financial difficulties, and he requested the resignation of my entire group. I was the most junior member of the project, and I was swept out with the others, even though my work had never been criticized.*

This is also a difficult question—but, again, be honest. If you aren't, and the recruiter contacts your references, he or she may have grounds for dismissal, or for revoking an offer.

4. Diligence and Professionalism

Q: **Tell me about your most difficult work or personal experience.**

A: *My coworker went through rehab for six months after a wreck, and I picked up a lot of additional work to help him out. I know, too, that he would've done the same for me. It's important for me to have that kind of trust among my work group.*

Demonstrate effectively how you manage stress and remain professional by describing a specific situation, but be careful not to divulge information that's too personal. For example, if you've just been treated for cancer, you may want to keep that to yourself, so the recruiter doesn't fear a recurrence that could affect your work.

Q: **Give an example of how you saw a project through, despite obstacles.**

A: *I actually rotated off an account but kept my hand in it as an adviser, because the client had threatened to pull the account if he wasn't dealing with me. Over three months I was able to make the client more comfortable with my replacement while I slowly decreased my presence.*

Demonstrate how you gather resources and foresee and manage obstacles. Focus your answer on the solution and execution, not on the obstacles themselves.

Q: Share an example of your determination.

A: *I led an effort to change our production system over to dedicated lines. The biggest problem was convincing the factory workers that this strategy made sense, even though they'd have to learn to do their jobs differently. I assured them that within a few months their jobs would be easier, and we'd save about four man-hours per employee per week. I convinced management to increase the profit-sharing account using half of those savings, which also helped get the employees on my side.*

Describe a time you persevered to accomplish a goal. A personal goal (for example, one that reflects an interest in developing a new skill) would be appropriate here. Demonstrate how you gather resources, predict obstacles, and manage stress.

Q: Share an example of your diligence or perseverance.

A: *About halfway through our last system installation the client changed her requirements. Our partner agreed that, at the new costs the client would incur, we could still meet the original completion date. It took about seventy to eighty hours a week for us to get the job done, but we did it, knowing that it would be over within three months.*

Describe your professional character, including thoroughness, diligence, and accountability. Demonstrate how you gather resources, use time-management techniques, or go the extra mile. Use a specific example.

Q: Describe a time when you tackled a tough or unpopular assignment.

A: *I had to determine which budgets would be cut within my division to yield an overall 5 percent cost reduction. I tried to remain objective and keep the personalities of department heads out of the decision. Ultimately, I ended up getting each department head to commit to a .25 percent reduction through frugal travel-expense planning, which was an enormous part of our sales division's costs. We accomplished most of the savings by combining trips and by securing two-week-advance airline reservations whenever possible.*

Describe a time you were willing, or even volunteered, to solve a problem that had remained unresolved after earlier attempts. Or describe something you accomplished that was important to the company's long-term interests, even if short-term implications were less than favorable. Your answer might involve a problem employee or a process-improvement plan, for example.

Q: Would your current boss describe you as the kind of employee who goes the extra mile?

A: *Absolutely. In fact, on my annual evaluations she writes that I'm the most dependable and flexible person on her staff. I think this is mostly because of my ability to juggle and prioritize. Would you like an example?*

Be ready to offer proof that you persevere to see important projects through, and to achieve important results. Share an example that demonstrates your dependability or willingness to tackle a tough project. If you describe "long hours of work," make sure you demonstrate that the hours were productive, and not the result of poor time management.

Q: **Tell me about a time you didn't perform to your capabilities.**

A: *The first time I had to give a presentation to our board, I failed to anticipate some of their questions. I was unprepared for anything other than what I wanted to report. Now my director and I brainstorm all the what-ifs in advance.*

This question forces the candidate to describe a negative situation. Do so in the context of an early career mistake based on inexperience, then demonstrate the better judgment you now have as a result of that learning experience.

Q: **How have you handled criticism of your work?**

A: *The first time I had a complaint from a client, I had difficulty keeping the complaint separate from my personal service of the account. The client was upset about the downtime on ATM machines. I learned that showing empathy usually calms the situation; I also learned that no client is going to be happy with everything, even if the overall experience is positive.*

Describe your accountability and professional attitude. Offer a specific project or work habit that caused you a problem until you faced up to it and overcame it. How have you minimized a weakness? You could also describe a time you responded objectively and professionally to an attack on your work.

Q: **Employees tend to be either concept oriented or task oriented. How do you describe yourself?**

A: *It's important for me to have clear direction on each project. That's why I'm good in support roles, with managers who have very specific ideas. I'm thorough at carrying out the tasks.*

With this question the interviewer looks for a match between the candidate's preferred level of detail and the level of detail required by the job. Problems might arise if the job requires delegation but the candidate enjoys working independently. When you've completed projects in the past, have you performed within the scope of the task assigned?

Q: **What would your colleagues tell me about your attention to detail?**

A: *My coworkers always count on me to help them think through what might have been overlooked, so they'd probably tell you I think through processes from A to Z.*

Here the interviewer is interested in the candidate's dependability and follow-through. Are you responsible? Have you contributed productively to a team effort without getting caught up in unnecessary detail? Do you use your time efficiently? If you do, mention specific praise given by one of your peers.

Q: **How do you manage stress in your daily work?**

A: *I try to get out for lunch at least once during the week to clear my head. I also have a personal rule that stops me from reacting to any problem until I feel calm about it. I think, then act—but I've learned to do that over time.*

It might be helpful here to describe a stressful project you've worked on and the specific actions you took to organize each step and see the project through. How do you keep yourself calm and professional under pressure?

Q: **How do you regroup when things haven't gone as planned?**

A: *I start by trying to imagine the worst possible outcome; then I back up and identify precautions I can take to avoid that scenario. In this way I usually end up with a result close to the original goal. The training example I described earlier is proof of that skill.*

Describe a time when some obstacle forced you to change your original plan, but you were still able to achieve the desired result. Did you rally the support of others to make this happen? With hindsight, how might you have better predicted the obstacle?

Q: **How have you prioritized or juggled your workload in your current job?**

A: *I juggle by working only on my two major accounts early in the day. That way, if interruptions occur, my most critical customers are taken care of.*

Demonstrate how you gather resources, how you predict obstacles, and how you manage stress. Describe personal habits that allow you to move ahead on priorities and avoid micromanaging or putting out fires. In what ways have you become better at managing time over the years?

Q: **Describe a professional skill you've developed in your most recent job.**

A: *I'm most proud of my new skills in applying database technology—for example, in our mailing services. What used to take us days of manual sorting now takes five minutes through a quick-search feature.*

Describe a skill you've improved in order to manage your work more efficiently. Typical examples might include learning a new software application, taking a professional seminar, or taking adult-education classes.

Q: When have your skills in diplomacy been put to the test?

A: *A customer came in once and demanded money back for an evening dress that had apparently been worn. She claimed it was a different color after dry cleaning and that the cleaner said the fabric was faulty. I quickly told her we'd happily return her money, even though I didn't think she was being honest. I decided it was more important to keep other customers from hearing her and maybe doubting our high-quality merchandise.*

Describe a problem situation with a client or a work associate that you resolved by remaining objective. How did you show empathy and build rapport?

Q: How do you manage your work week and make realistic deadlines?

A: *I always reserve two hours of dead time every day to handle any unanticipated problems that may occur. I used to plan for eight or nine hours of project time, but now I find that I'm able to manage my own projects, as well as whatever my boss and staff need from me.*

To answer this question effectively, describe in detail how you establish priorities, set deadlines, and determine schedules.

Q: Tell me about a time you had to extend a deadline.

A: *Two weeks into a job, it was clear that our client expected us to add more features as we went along. I renegotiated with the client, outlined his goals, and showed him a price structure similar to a menu, from which he could choose more features at a higher cost and in a longer time frame. He opted for something in the middle that he understood would cause a three-week adjustment to the schedule.*

Describe your accountability and willingness to adjust a deadline in order to satisfy the overall goals of a project. Had you not adjusted the deadline, what goal would have been compromised?

Q: What personal skill or work habit have you struggled to improve?

A: *I had to learn to say no. I used to be helpful to the point that other staff abused my goodwill. Now I offer to help by countering with something I'd like help on in return. On balance I believe the trade-off is more equitable, and cooperation in our office has improved over time.*

This question is similar to "Describe a professional skill you've developed in your most recent job." However, here you probably want to discuss an improvement from the earliest days of your career, or from your relatively distant past. Make sure you convince the interviewer that this particular work habit is no longer an obstacle.

5. Creativity and Leadership

Q: **What's the most creative or innovative project you've worked on?**

A: *During my summer job at Cellular One, I noticed that the sales inquiries were distributed haphazardly to all the marketing assistants in the office. I decided to set up a system grouping inquiries according to region or according to company size. This approach enabled the entire marketing team to come up with better and more creative solutions to our sales problems.*

Provide examples of your initiative and resourcefulness. Discuss how your leadership skills have helped you accomplish your goals. Give a specific example that shows a creative, new, or unusual approach to reaching your goals.

Q: **Describe a time when you've creatively overcome an obstacle.**

A: *My publishing company could never get an appointment with a major Fortune 500 company. After several sales representatives gave up in frustration, I volunteered to take a crack at the account. Instead of contacting the vice president of advertising, I decided to target the VP's administrative assistant. I scheduled an appointment with the assistant and gave him my sales pitch. I really made an impression, because the assistant convinced the vice president that she should schedule an appointment with me. In fact, she penciled me in on her calendar on the spot. I had the appointment, and we got the order two weeks later.*

In answer to this question, it's often helpful to focus on how you overcome problems by rallying the support of your coworkers. How have you approached a problem differently from how others might have addressed the same problem? Emphasize your creative solution and its positive results.

Q: **Why do you think that some companies with good products fail?**

A: *Employees who are involved in the design and/or manufacture of a product must totally understand and believe in the product and use it on a regular basis. Only in this way can they continually modify and improve it to the* *customer's satisfaction. Any product must be constantly fine-tuned to meet the changing needs and demands of the consumer. Only by getting the employees involved with the product and excited about it can this improvement occur.*

This is a question about the candidate's vision as a leader. If you're asked this question, you'll do well to discuss a specific example of a product or idea that failed because of poor enthusiasm from employees or other consumers. Without being overly critical, you should discuss what you would have done differently.

Q: How resourceful are you?

A: *At one time, for all of our new product launches, our chief engineer would release a press statement about its virtues. But when I was given responsibility for a new launch, I decided to get three of our largest customers to videotape an endorsement for use in our marketing campaign. The result was a far higher level of credibility, and we exceeded our six-month sales quota. We now use personal endorsements routinely when we launch our products.*

This is a question about the candidate's creativity and initiative. Provide an example of how you've changed your plan or direction and achieved the same, or a better, result. You might want to focus on how you obtained crucial information, or how you changed your personal style to get someone to cooperate.

Q: Give me proof of your persuasiveness.

A: *During my summer internship I was assigned the task of conducting a benchmarking study for all the communication expenditures for a major utility. I had to get the consensus of employees in several different departments. Unfortunately, they resented the fact that I was just a summer intern, and they refused to cooperate. I had to schedule individual meetings with every employee and persuade each one that what I was doing would be ultimately beneficial to his or her own department and to the company. After a frustrating month I finally got everyone's cooperation, the project went flawlessly, and in the end I received a bonus for my efforts.*

This is a question about leadership, but try not to use an example in which you were the designated leader. If possible, describe a time when you didn't really have authority but instead used your powers of persuasion to get people on your side. Describe your goal and the outcome of your efforts. Why did people trust or believe you?

Q: What would your last supervisor say about your initiative?

A: *In any job I hold I can usually find inefficiencies in a process, and I always try to take some initiative to come up with a solution for improvement. My last* *supervisor was a little surprised and flustered the first few months when I was constantly coming to him with my ideas for improvements. He finally accepted the fact that I had some good ideas and encouraged me to write up in a proposal every month my one best idea, so that he could get me the resources to tackle the solution on a formal basis. My first big project had to do with improving the inventory control in one of our manufacturing shops. Because the records for inventory receivable were inconsistent, I set up an entirely new inventory-order system and used that data to trace the history of the inventory—for example, when it was used, how it was used, and my recommendations for necessary replacement. I reduced the total value of the inventory we had to carry the first year by 23 percent. As a result, my supervisor would always use me as an example of someone who's constantly taking the initiative.*

Describe a project you volunteered to work on to solve an existing problem or to avoid a potential problem. How did you approach your supervisor with the idea initially? Focus on the creativity of the idea, your approach, and the result you obtained.

Q: Describe an improvement you personally initiated.

A: *I improved the inventory-management system for all laboratory supplies and equipment in a department of medicine at the university where I previously worked. The system was one that had been handed down year after year, and no one had ever bothered to question its efficiency. I decided we needed a whole new system, and I took it upon myself to design and implement one. This required several extra hours of work after my routine duties were completed, but I felt good about making this additional contribution to our department.*

Give proof of your effectiveness, dedication to the job, and ability to "think outside of the box."

Q: Describe a time in your work experience when the existing process didn't work, and what you did about it.

A: *The order-entry system at the telecommunications company where I worked was a mess. Orders weren't being processed properly, or in a timely manner. I did a work-flow analysis to identify the bottlenecks, and then I convinced my boss that we needed to spend $100,000 on a totally new system. He reluctantly agreed, but with the caveat that "This had better save us money." After one year the project had paid for the investment twofold.*

The interviewer wants to know what initiatives this candidate took to change a faulty process in a creative way. Show that you can approach a problem creatively and manage a situation that isn't working. Did you achieve the result you needed?

Q: **Describe a time you had to alter your leadership style.**

A: *I'm normally a strong leader who has good vision and enjoys delegating, but I expect my orders to be carried out promptly. When I was assigned a project to increase our product exports and was given a committee of nine people to work with, I immediately assumed I had the best plan and began my normal routine of delegating. I quickly realized, though, that this group of employees, with international backgrounds, wasn't responding well. In fact, they asked to have input into my plan. I agreed to spend half a day talking with them, and then I realized that they, too, had good ideas. The only way to move ahead on the project was to encourage the entire group to offer solutions to our export problem. I think these people would agree that I'm flexible and willing to modify my leadership style when the need arises.*

Your answer to this question should emphasize your ability to make different kinds of people feel comfortable, so that a reasonable working relationship results. Be specific. What initiatives did you take to improve a less than ideal situation? What would the other people involved say about you now?

Q: **Tell me about a good process that you made even better.**

A: *Recently, when I started a new job at a manufacturing company, the processes in place were very efficient and effective. However, soon after beginning the job, I was told I'd have to reduce the budget by 20 percent. The only way to do this while maintaining the current workload was to make the processes even more efficient. I called my team together and issued a challenge that we had to take these already good processes and make them even better in order to meet the corporate objective. We exceeded even our own expectations and showed that any process can be improved, with critical evaluation and creative thinking.*

The interviewer wants specific examples of how the candidate has added value, even when an existing situation was already good. In response to a question like this, prove you're creative enough to bring a new level of quality to the job. Can you demonstrate the value you've added in every past job?

Q: **Tell me about a time you persuaded others to adopt your idea.**

A: *Our customer retention at the biotech company where I worked was poor. I thought we could understand and improve this situation by conducting a thorough customer-attitude survey. My boss thought this would be a waste of time, but I finally persuaded him that we could uncover some of the core reasons why retention had been getting progressively worse. I showed him how our competitors had been using customer surveys to their advantage. He agreed, and the surveys were used to make a number of changes in how we dealt with customers. For example, the survey revealed that customers were frustrated at not being able to quickly get through to the order-entry department—that the* *phone would often ring five or six times before someone would answer it. As one of the new supervisors, I started grabbing the phone on the first ring and helping to process the order. My initiative was noticed, and a few other supervisors started pitching in and doing the same thing, and before long everyone was involved in answering the phone when we had an overload of incoming calls. This not only improved the efficiency of our order-entry process, but caused all of the workers to take note that the supervisors truly were involved and interested in the department. Their efficiency also began to improve.*

Emphasize here your ability to rally support and to make people comfortable with your ideas. Be specific. This question is common in interviews for sales positions.

Q: How would a former colleague or subordinate describe your leadership style?

A: *My colleagues would probably say that my leadership style is the strong, silent type. I don't make a big deal about being in charge or making decisions. I try to involve everyone around me in the decision-making process and in carrying out a plan of action. My colleagues truly believe that I bring a lot of positive energy to our group and that I help motivate others.*

The interviewer is trying to determine what the candidate's references or colleagues will say if they're called. Be objective and realistic without embellishing or being overly modest. Describe candidly your leadership style, giving specific examples that reflect your personal approach. Would former colleagues describe your contributions as generally positive for the department?

Q: Do you believe that your job appraisals have adequately portrayed your leadership abilities?

A: *Although I had limited opportunity to demonstrate my leadership abilities in my previous job, I'm certain my appraisals would mention that I'm extremely thorough and dependable with my assignments. I take the time to make sure that all those around me clearly understand what our objectives are. This quality has enabled me to gain the confidence and respect of my coworkers and has been mentioned by my supervisor during performance appraisals.*

This question is especially important if an outcome in your past work experience wasn't positive despite your efforts, or if you haven't had an opportunity to play a real leadership role.

Q: Tell me about one of your projects that failed.

A: *I've always had a tendency to be a workaholic, and have the attitude that I can tackle anything successfully. During the hurricane of 1992 my insurance* company was inundated with claims. I immediately thought I could handle all the claims in my area and jumped in with both feet to work twelve-hour days. I quickly realized that there was no way I could complete all the claims on time, and I had to start delegating responsibility for claims to my investigators. This experience showed me that no matter how efficient and competent you are, there are times when you can't achieve everything you'd like to, and it's essential to delegate or to ask for help.

Show that you have the ability to be humble and to learn from your mistakes. In hindsight, what would you have done differently? How has your leadership style changed because of the experience?

Q: **Describe the situations in which you're most comfortable as a leader.**

A: *One of my talents is to take complex issues or problems and break them down into their simplest parts. I'm also good at teaching other people. As a result, whenever I'm faced with a complex problem, other people tend to let me find a solution and instruct them on how to proceed. As a result, I've found that I'm an effective leader in this kind of situation. I'm not a particularly effective leader, though, in a highly charged political environment. My preference is to deal with facts and data. When there are other issues like political or emotional factors to consider, I often prefer that someone else take the lead, and I simply resolve to be a good team player. In all other situations I normally surface as a leader.*

Describe situations in which you've had experience as a creative leader and people have trusted you. Why do people tend to follow your lead in these situations? This is more an issue of earned authority than of outright authority. Conversely, if you're asked to describe situations in which you're a better contributor than leader, you can define types of problems that you're less comfortable working on, or situations in which you feel you're too opinionated or biased to lead without controlling the group unfairly. Then end by describing instances when you've played the leader well.

Q: **Describe your comfort level working with people of higher rank and people of lower rank.**

A: *The person that delivers our mail twice a day has become a good friend. I've invited him to my house to meet my family, and we'll often go to baseball games together on the weekends. I can also relate well to my general manager. We both have common interests, which include sailing, and elk hunting in the winter.*

Be specific here. Tell the interviewer how you've developed a style that's worked with a variety of people.

6. Job Compatibility

Q: **What were the most rewarding aspects of your most recent job?**

A: *My favorite aspect of being a recruiter is the feeling of accomplishment you get when you know you've made a good match. I always make periodic checks on the recent recruits and their managers. Positive progress reports keep me motivated.*

The interviewer is interested in how well suited the candidate is to the job. What do you do particularly well and want to do more of in your next position? Conclude by focusing on the new experiences you're seeking in your career. Your response should correspond closely to the position you're applying for.

Q: **What things have frustrated you in your previous jobs?**

A: *What was most difficult about my last job was the physical layout—our R&D facility was three states away, so, as a technical-product manager, I found it difficult to develop rapport with my design team. Your facility seems well geared for good communication, since you're all right here in Atlanta.*

Here again the interviewer is seeking to determine if job and candidate are compatible. Your answer should describe both negative and positive aspects of recent jobs, without dwelling on the negatives. Conclude by focusing on the positives you seek in your next job.

Q: **What are the limitations of your current job?**

A: *My job now is limited because the industry's simply not in a growth mode. Actually, that's why I became skilled in defensive marketing—retaining customers through customer-satisfaction programs that enhance our reputation and give us an edge over the competition.*

Briefly explain one or two reasons why your current position doesn't allow for the growth you desire. Think about the question "Why are you ready to leave your current job?" Above all, remain positive, focusing on what you do well and want to emphasize in your work.

Q: **What do you want to achieve in your next job?**

A: *I hope to be able to move into finance in a manufacturing group, since I started at the home office. I think that's important to my overall understanding of the company's core business.*

Your answer should describe your ideal job. Focus on what you seek in your next job, taking care that your response closely matches the position you're applying for. Wherever you're unsure, ask questions of the interviewer—for example, "In this job would there be an opportunity to ..."

Q: Describe your ideal job.

A: *My ideal job would combine a sales territory that I managed and additional responsibility for sales training, so I could use my teaching background.*

This question is similar to the previous one. Whatever response you prepare, make sure that it closely matches the position you're applying for.

Q: What interests you most about this job?

A: *I was excited to watch your successful acquisitions in South America. Because of my exchange-program experience there, I believe I could help in your Latin American marketing effort.*

Describe your qualifications for the job and how well the job fits your natural skills and abilities. Give evidence that you've performed well in similar work. What proof can you offer that you'll excel in this job?

Q: What interests you least about this job?

A: *One of the things I hope not to do is prospect extensively by meeting one on one with small-account representatives. I found in my last sales territory that I gave superior service to my major accounts by focusing my on-site time with them. I was able to grow my key account business 20 percent.*

You might want to ask the interviewer, "What did the last person in the job find difficult about the position?" Whatever the answer, respond appropriately, then describe what interests you most about the job.

Q: What aspects of this job do you feel most confident about?

A: *I believe that I can engage an audience really effectively. When I get up in front of a room to present a new idea, I can usually get people on my side rather quickly.*

Sell what you do best, and try to match it to the tasks you know are part of the job. Ask the interviewer if your skills might have been helpful in some recent project. Try to convince the interviewer that what you have to offer is truly in demand at the company, in this job, in the industry.

Q: What concerns you most about performing this job?

A: *My clinical experience gives me confidence that I can perform the job. Other than the fact that I've not formally managed an outpatient clinic, I'm worried about whether the support staff is readily available to answer the phones. To* *get the results you want with your hot line, staff will have to be available at all times to answer questions about our services.*

You may want to turn the question around; ask the interviewer if he or she has any concerns about your qualifications. Then address those concerns and affirm your confidence that your skills are the right ones and your interests are compatible with the position. Offer proof that will dispel any doubts the interviewer may have.

Q: **What skills do you offer that are most relevant to this job?**

A: *My engineering background gives me a logical problem-solving ability that I know will be useful in assessing client needs. That background will also help your consulting firm sell business to manufacturers who themselves employ many engineers.*

Your answer should be similar to your prepared response to the question "What interests you most about this job?" Use examples to back up the most relevant information from your resume.

Q: **Considering your own resume, what are your weaknesses in relation to this job?**

A: *What are you most concerned about? If you're worried about my sincerity in working for a nonprofit organization, I hope that my discussion about my family's philanthropic efforts has made you more comfortable with my motives.*

The best approach here is to turn the question around and get the interviewer to disclose what he or she believes are your weaknesses. Then use the opportunity to change the interviewer's mind. As always, give specific examples of your suitability for the position.

Q: **How did the realities differ from your expectations in your last job?**

A: *The hardest thing to foresee was how other departments within the company would view my market-research department's work. Unfortunately, I found that many groups prefer to go outside for specialized research services, and that's really the reason I decided to contact your firm.*

The interviewer is trying to determine if, in the past, the candidate was realistic about judging his or her suitability for a job. If, for the most part, you've been a pretty good judge of such things, you've probably screened yourself carefully for this job. The recruiter also wants to ensure that any past disenchantment won't be repeated in this job.

Q: **How would you enrich your current (or most recent) job?**

A: *If I decide to stay with my current job, I'm going to volunteer to be on the communications task force, which is trying to get all of our offices linked to the Internet and other resources.*

Without dwelling on the negatives, describe how you've improved the quality of your job so that you've continued to develop your skills and enjoy your work. Don't give the interviewer the impression that, if dissatisfied, you're unable to work on a solution or a plan for improvement. Conclude by focusing on the qualities you seek in your next job. Your response should correspond closely to the description of the position you're applying for.

Q: Would you be able to travel or to work extended hours as necessary to perform the job?

A: *If I have forty-eight hours' notice, I can arrange to be available in the evening. As it is, I usually work until at least 6 P.M., because I get a lot done after the business office closes at 5, and I travel about once a month for my current job.*

Your response should be consistent with the demands of the position you're currently applying for, reflecting a realistic understanding of the work and time required. Inquire about seasonality of work, if you're unsure, and show a willingness to spend extended hours periodically.

Q: Why is this a particularly good job for someone with your qualifications?

A: *Based on what you've told me about the last person who excelled in this job, I'm confident that I've the same skills in spreadsheet analysis and statistics. I'd also work well with your audit team, because I come from that kind of environment and know what a client can do to make the consulting relationship more productive.*

The best answer here will describe positive experiences and results of recent jobs that were comparable to this one.

Q: What's your most productive or ideal work setting?

A: *I like having at least one hour of uninterrupted time in the early morning to plan my day. I usually start around 7 A.M. Otherwise, I enjoy an office with open doors, constant feedback, and lots of energy and activity. It helps me work more productively when I sense how busy everyone else is, too.*

The interviewer wants to know the impact that the candidate's working environment has on his or her job performance. How well would you fit the position, physical layout of the department, and attitudes of the particular work group? Emphasize your ability to work in a variety of settings, and how you've managed to be productive in less than ideal work environments.

Q: Tell me about two or three aspects of your last job that you'd never want to repeat.

A: *I'm glad that I have experience in credit collections, but it isn't something I want to do again. That background has enabled me to make better risk assessments, though.*

In a constructive way, describe two or three things you've done that you didn't personally enjoy or that didn't play upon your strengths. Then describe your strengths and their relevance to the job you're applying for.

Q: Do you prefer continuity in structure or frequent change in your daily work?

A: *I enjoy change and challenge, which is why I frequently ask for the tough assignments. The last two projects we discussed were ones that I asked for. I don't allow myself to get bored.*

Your answer should be consistent with the job description. Describe environments that have allowed you to remain interested and learn new things without getting bored.

7. Personality and Cultural Compatibility

Q: What would your friends tell me about you?

A: *My friends would tell you that I move faster than most people, eat more than most people, work later than most people, and still manage to spend time with friends despite my schedule. I believe in doing lots of things with gusto.*

Talk about parts of your personality that will naturally be revealed on the job.

Q: Tell me about your relationship with your previous bosses.

A: *My bosses would tell you that I've often acted as a sounding board for them. With all three of my bosses, we've mentored each other, although the obvious balance of wisdom and expertise was theirs. I was always helpful to them in their decisions about customer problems.*

The interviewer is interested in whether the candidate and the supervisor for the position will work well together. As you describe each previous boss, the interviewer will most likely be making mental comparisons to the supervisor. The interviewer must feel confident that he or she has uncovered any surprises about your working relationships, and that you won't end up clashing with your new boss. Try to be honest without being negative. Emphasize the type of boss you work well with.

Q: Describe your working relationship with your colleagues.

A: *They'd probably tell you that nothing ever shocks me or sets me back too much, and that I'm really an asset as an adviser when they suffer a roadblock, as in the case we discussed about the contractor. I'm constant and dependable.*

What types of people do you enjoy working with? How would the company's customers or clients react to you? From your answer the interviewer must feel confident that any surprises about your work personality have been uncovered. Give examples of how you pitched in, how you know to ask for help when you need it, and your concern for the group's accomplishments.

Q: Describe your personality beneath the professional image.

A: *I laugh a lot at my own shortcomings. I see irony in most things and I'm outspoken, but I bring a sense of humor to any office. I think it provides a nice balance of warmth in a work setting.*

This is similar to the question "What would your friends tell me about you?" Concentrate on how your personality reflects your job skills or interests.

Q: What environments allow you to be especially effective?

A: *Although I can work effectively in most environments, I prefer environments where people are their own bosses, within reason. I like to have a goal but be able to draw my own map to get there. To accomplish goals, I rely on asking questions and finding people receptive, so cooperation and access are important to me in a work group.*

Emphasize your flexibility and your ability to work in many different types of environments. Your answer should not consist of a "laundry list" of requirements (private office, few interruptions, and so on) or the interviewer may conclude that you will be difficult to satisfy.

Q: Describe an environment that is ineffective for you.

A: *I don't do terribly well when someone has an exact idea of how one of my goals should be accomplished. That doesn't allow me any latitude to make adjustments to suit my own style. I do well when I can draw my own map.*

This is the negative side of "What environments allow you to be especially effective?" Focus on environments you prefer or that increase your effectiveness.

Q: What situations excite and motivate you?

A: *I really enjoy working on any re-engineering project where a true improvement results—for example, the JIT project in which we saved more than $10,000 per month in inventory costs.*

The interviewer wants a clearer perspective as to what kind of work inspires you. There is no one right answer to this question, but your answer should be at least somewhat compatible with the position you're applying for. For example, you should not say that highly creative work motivates you if you're applying for a position that involves somewhat monotonous, repetitive work, such as data entry or assembly line work.

Q: Tell me about a situation that frustrated you at work.

A: *I was frustrated when one of my clients, who had insisted on a high-growth stock, called in a panic because the stock price dropped more than twenty points in one day. I had a hard time convincing him to ride it out rather than cut his losses. This happened despite my attempts up front to explain the short-term volatility of that stock.*

Describe how you've remained diplomatic, objective, or professional in a difficult situation. The interviewer will want to know if you're likely to run into similar frustrating experiences at his or her company, and that you can handle such stumbling blocks with ease.

Q: How would your last employer describe your work habits and ethics?

A: *Let me put it this way: I received an MVP award from my division for the extra efforts I put into one of our customer relationships. The customer had threatened to pull the account, so I stepped in and debugged the system, even though it required me to work through a holiday weekend.*

Do you think your current or last employer would hire you again? Are you reliable, thorough, dependable? Give examples of your reliability, dedication, and corporate loyalty.

Q: Did your customers or clients enjoy working with you?

A: *My client base changed very little, except that billings increased, so I think that's evidence the clients were satisfied enough to stay with me for more than three years. That's particularly unusual in the ad-agency business, too. They simply knew they could count on me to treat their business as if it were my own.*

How would the company's customers or clients react to you? Can you give specific feedback from a client? How many of your clients were repeat customers? Why do you believe you kept their business?

Q: How will you complement this department?

A: *I enjoy an environment in which people bounce ideas off each other and have the flexibility to ask for help when they need it. I'm usually a great troubleshooter* *for PC problems in my office, and I'm often going to ask for help proofreading important memos. I believe in give-and-take.*

Describe how your personality and/or skills would help round out the department. What types of people enjoy working with you for hours at a time? How would the company's customers or clients react? Assure the interviewer that there will be no surprises about your work personality.

Q: Tell me about a problem you've had getting along with a work associate.

A: *We brought in a new associate who was very bossy—to the point where he continually offended one of our most easygoing interns. I actually pulled him aside and told him that I found it more productive to ask people for help than to give orders. Unfortunately, it didn't work, but we were more careful when we hired new staff after that.*

Your example might describe a work associate whose standards of excellence were perhaps less stringent than yours, and there was a clear difference in quality of work. Avoid discussing a mere personality clash; focus instead on a difference in work ethic or something with which the interviewer is likely to empathize.

Q: Whom did you choose as your references, and why?

A: *I selected a former boss, a peer, and a customer as references, to demonstrate that I'm a pretty well-rounded person and get along with all the important work associates in my life.*

The interviewer is looking for a logical mix of people without any obvious omissions. For example, a former salesperson would do well to include a former salesperson as a reference. Describe what you'd expect each of your references to say. Include a diverse group—senior to junior, an associate from work, an old professor from college.

Q: Can we call all of your references?

A: *I'd prefer that you call my current boss only after you've made me a firm offer of employment and I've had a chance to tell her myself that I'm changing jobs. Then, of course, I understand your need to verify that my application was accurate.*

This is a question designed to protect you. If your current employer doesn't know you're looking for a new job (as is most often the case), you can request that the interviewer contact your current employer only after you've accepted a position and given your notice to your current employer.

Q: Tell me what you learned from a recent book.

A: *I enjoy reading biographies, especially of people who lived in a different era. I recently read Churchill's biography, which taught me a lot about the value of leadership and good PR under times of stress.*

The interviewer wants to know if the candidate has interests in common with others at the company. Do you use your spare time as a productive, yet relaxing, way to learn new things? What are you naturally inquisitive about?

Q: **Tell me about a work group you really enjoyed.**

A: *My group in our new-product-launch department really meshed. When one of us was approaching the final day before a launch, we all rolled up our sleeves and helped put press packets together or whatever else was the last item to be shipped to the sales force. Although it was an administrative task, it had to be done, and it was a good time for us all to speculate on the success of the product and any major concerns.*

This question is a combination of "Describe your working relationship with your colleagues," and "Did your customers or clients enjoy working with you?" Demonstrate your ability to work well with others and to establish solid, ongoing working relationships.

Q: **What would your last boss want to change about your work habits?**

A: *He'd want me to be a morning person rather than a night owl. I like to stay late; he loves to be at work by 7 A.M. The business day is so busy that we usually talk during lunch when we need to discuss something without interruptions.*

Describe a weakness that you and your boss have worked on and improved. It's also reasonable to point out differences of preference (for example, I'm a morning person, she likes to work late) that don't indicate a problem of work-ethic or motivation differences. Talk about your personality on the job. The interviewer will want to know how you'll fit in with your future boss and coworkers. What types of people would enjoy working with you? How would the company's customers or clients react to you?

Q: **Describe a time when you had to assist a coworker.**

A: *I once helped an associate understand survey methodology in order to write a report. He had never taken a research course and didn't know how to structure questions.*

Demonstrate a willingness to pitch in. Discuss a time when your objective advice or special expertise produced a positive outcome for a coworker and for the department.

Q: **Are you most productive working alone or in a group?**

A: *I need some private time for planning, but otherwise I like the activity and noise of people around me and the ability to share ideas. I think most writers need reinforcement, because we all get writer's block occasionally.*

The interviewer is looking for someone who can work in an environment without the environment disrupting the candidate's preferred way of getting work done. Be honest but communicate that you're a flexible and reasonably adaptable employee.

Q: **Tell me about a situation in which it was difficult to remain objective.**

A: *I'd researched a new online source for our library, and my manager decided to pull funding at the last minute. It was frustrating for me because I'd gotten excited about the product, liked the vendor, and had even told some people to count on having the resource. But I understand the need to revise budgets, and the matter was out of my control at the time.*

The obvious example here is a time when you've worked long hours on a project only to have the project canceled. Or perhaps you found that the project was less strategically sound than you'd hoped. Were you able to readjust your thinking and do what was best in the long run?

8. Management Style and Interpersonal Skills

Q: **Tell me about an effective manager, supervisor, or other person in a leading role you've known.**

A: *The best professor I ever had always reviewed the most important points from our last class before he moved on to new material. He also watched our faces carefully and repeated information whenever he saw a blank stare. Sometimes he would just ask for feedback by saying, "What are you having difficulty with?" He never assumed too much or made us feel dumb for not grasping a concept quickly.*

Talk about a supervisor's management style and interpersonal skills. Focus on the positive—how the person worked rather than what type of work he or she did. How was the person able to accomplish so much and get your support?

Q: **Tell me about your least favorite manager or supervisor.**

A: *I worked with a manager once who was inaccessible. If you walked into his office to ask a question, you got the sense that you were bothering him, so we just learned to get help from each other instead.*

Turn this question around to talk about your own management style and the type of boss, employee, and peer you'll be. What negative example has taught you what's important? Focus on what you learned from one negative experience; however, if you're going to talk about a former boss, be tactful and avoid heated criticism.

Q: What type of management style do you think is effective?

A: *I've always learned well from people who act as coaches rather than experts. When someone comes to me with a problem, I try to act as if I'm reasoning through the problem with the person, learning as I go. I never just give an answer. I want employees to develop confidence in creating answers for themselves.*

This is similar to the question "Tell me about an effective manager or supervisor you've known." Give a personal or popular example of a leader you believe is effective. Why is this person able to accomplish so much? Talk about your management style and interpersonal skills with peer groups and leaders, and describe how you've incorporated habits from leaders you admire.

Q: Describe your personal management style.

A: *I repeat what someone has told me, but I reorganize the information in a way that helps them see the problem or answer themselves. Sometimes I just ask questions until they see a clear solution. I learned this from watching a friend who's a successful trial lawyer.*

Talk about your management style and interpersonal skills with peer groups and leaders, and describe how you've incorporated a habit from a leader you admire.

Q: What type of people do you work with most effectively?

A: *I tend to work well with people who are confident and straightforward. It's more difficult for me to be around timid people, because I move quickly and am decisive.*

Focus on the positive here. What type of boss, employee, and colleague would you be? Keep in mind that the interviewer wants to find out how well you would fit in with the other personalities in the company—not how well the other personalities in the company would suit you.

Q: What are some of the things your supervisor did that you disliked?

A: *The only thing I really don't like is to get feedback in front of others. I want to hear good or bad feedback in private, so that I have time to think and react* to the issue without other distractions. I believe that's the fair way to improve learning or to change future behavior.

Try to describe a positive learning experience from a difficult situation, avoiding personal criticism of an ex-boss or manager, if possible.

Q: **How do you organize and plan for major projects?**

A: *I love to brainstorm a best, worst, and most likely scenario. Then I set a time-table that's realistic. What I usually find is that some combination of my best and worst cases evolves; I can adjust my schedule easily as these things unfold because I've already visualized what could happen and how I'd react.*

Give the interviewer a good idea of your general approach to mastering complex tasks. You may wish to include here how you decide on time frames, set deadlines, determine priorities, delegate tasks, and decide what to do for yourself.

Q: **Describe a time when you've worked under intense pressure.**

A: *I had to complete an end-of-quarter report once while I was on the road for two consecutive weeks. The amount of telephoning back and forth was incredible, because I couldn't bring my office files with me. Luckily I had a great secretary and a logical filing system, so we located everything we needed.*

A good idea when answering a question like this is to concentrate on your time-management skills. Give a specific example, with enough detail to communicate both the intensity of the situation and the ease with which you handled it.

Q: **How do you deal with tension between you and your boss?**

A: *The only tension I've ever felt was one time when we both got too busy to keep each other informed. My boss overcommitted me with a short deadline, not knowing that I was bogged down by another client problem. I believe firmly in the importance of staff meetings so that we can respect the demands on each other's time.*

The safest ground here is to describe an example of a miscommunication early in your relationship with your boss and how you resolved it. The interviewer will want to know how you avoided a recurrence of the problem.

Q: **How do you manage your time on a typical day?**

A: *I've always given priority to work with established clients, because they offer a better risk/return value. The last thing I do is general correspondence, especially internal correspondence, which I take care of at the end of the day or week.*

Here the interviewer wants evidence that the candidate can juggle priorities as necessary based on the work team, departmental adjustments, and nature of the tasks. He or she will also want to be sure that you don't give priority to "fun" work and avoid dull, necessary routines that are important in the long run.

Q: **Describe a time when you acted on someone's suggestion.**

A: *I changed my open office hours because several of my employees found it difficult to visit me except in the early mornings.*

Be specific here in demonstrating your flexibility and your interpersonal skills. Do people feel comfortable offering you suggestions? Do they believe you'll listen fairly and objectively? When you do take their advice, do you give credit where credit is due? Reassure the interviewer that your approach to management is reasonable and fair, and that you respect other people's good ideas.

Q: **Tell me about a time when you had to defend an idea to your boss.**

A: *Once I had to convince my boss to change PR firms. I really believed that our interests on the West Coast weren't being met by our Chicago-based firm. I was able to convince him after showing him the demographic shift in our customer base.*

This is the flip side of "Describe a time when you acted on someone's suggestion." Can you give advice constructively and get someone to understand "your side"? Give a specific example.

Q: **What aspect of your management style would you like to change?**

A: *I've been working on holding back the urge to tell people the answers when they ask for advice. I think it's more important to teach people how to solve their own problems. I've gotten better at coaching and presenting questions and feedback without telling people what to do.*

Talk about one aspect of your management style that you're working to improve. Tell the interviewer the steps you're taking and give evidence that you're making progress.

Q: **Have you ever felt defensive around your boss or peers?**

A: *I had to explain once why I thought a black-and-white brochure was more suitable for the content of an insurance-product brochure. No one in my office liked the idea initially, because we were all used to color brochures, and everybody felt that black and white looked cheap. Eventually I convinced them* *that a more subtle approach would work better to present information about a difficult topic—death benefits.*

Pick a specific example of a time when you had to defend an idea. Avoid any discussion of personality clashes, feelings of resentment, or heated exchanges. How did you get others to see your view of things? What was the outcome? Be sure to end on a positive note.

Q: **Tell me about a learning experience that affected your management style.**

A: *Early in my job at the bank, I wrote a letter to an EVP but failed to copy the two AVPs who worked for him. One of them was impacted by the content of the memo and concluded that I'd circumvented him on purpose. I've really been careful about chain of command ever since.*

Use a variation of your answer to the question "Tell me about your least-favorite manager or supervisor," in which you describe an experience, either positive or negative, that taught you a lesson about effective management. Or describe the tactics of a manager who got you to perform more than you thought was possible. How did he or she motivate you?

Q: **Have you patterned your management style after someone in particular?**

A: *I've emulated my first boss in many ways. I keep a file for each member of my staff on my desk. They can throw notes, ideas, work they want me to review, or anything else in there, and I do the same with material I have for them. It's an extra form of communication whenever one of us gets an idea. Then, when we sit down to talk, the issues we need to cover are in one place, at our fingertips.*

Your answer should describe someone you've known personally—a boss who motivated you in a positive way to achieve beyond your own goals. Be specific about how he or she accomplished this.

Q: **Describe a leader you admire.**

A: *I've always admired the president of my company. He's visible, he doesn't want a special parking place or table in the cafeteria, and he gives you the feeling that he's just another member of the team.*

Give personal or popular examples of leaders you believe are effective. Why do you believe those people are able to accomplish so much? What tricks have you learned from the leaders you admire?

Q: **What personal characteristics add to your effectiveness?**

A: *I always stay in touch with my network. If I see an article that might be of interest to someone I know, I clip it and send it to that person. Then, when I need help and make a phone call to that person, the phone call gets returned promptly.*

Talk about what makes your personal style unique and effective. For example, how are you able to get cooperation from others? What specific skills and traits help you get results, and why?

9. Problem-Solving Ability

Q: **How have your technical skills been an asset?**

A: *Although I never planned on a career as a writer or publisher, much of my job in marketing has depended on good writing and creative layout skills. My part-time college job with a newspaper taught me a lot about desktop publishing, how to position something on a page effectively, and how to write short sentences with maximum impact. In all of my marketing jobs I've been able to explain my goals clearly to graphic designers, which has helped me avoid costly design revisions.*

Describe how you've used technical skills to solve a problem. Tell a specific story. Demonstrate how these same skills have been useful in other situations or in most of the jobs you've held. If you're hired, what situations will you handle particularly well?

Q: **Describe a situation in which you've applied technical skills to solve a problem.**

A: *One of our components kept arriving at distribution points with stress cracks. My materials-science background helped me to diagnose the problem as one of storage temperature during shipping. Although our equipment was safely stored at both end points, it had been sitting in un-air-conditioned cargo space for up to thirty hours before reaching its destination. We're now using a different shipping company, and we've improved our labeling on large shipments to reflect the user's warning about temperature extremes.*

Quickly define the problem for the interviewer, then focus on how your skills enabled you to tackle it. What actions did you take, and what was the outcome?

Q: **How do your technical skills, combined with other skills, add to your effectiveness on the job?**

A: *My strong economics background, along with my computer-sales experience, provide a balanced set of skills to perform financial research on the computer* *industry. Most of my contacts and hobbies are also related to high-tech, so I offer a natural curiosity that helps me stay abreast of changes in the industry.*

This question gives you a chance to sell the package deal—why is the unique combination of your skills effective? Give one or two specific examples of projects you're frequently asked to handle.

Q: **Describe how you've used a problem-solving process.**

A: *We once had several customers who'd arranged numerous free hotel stays around the country using our 100 percent satisfaction guarantee. I suggested leading a PC task force to set up a warning system that flags any guest name corresponding to a previous reported complaint or free service. Now when a guest checks in and we type in a name, we know immediately that the person has had an unpleasant experience at one of our hotels. We proactively approach the guest, acknowledge we're aware of the problem, and offer our commitment to do everything possible to provide them with impeccable service. This practice warns the potentially fraudulent guest; at the same time, it warns our staff to be especially careful with any guest who's giving our hotel a second chance. Our satisfaction rate has improved, and fraudulent cases have decreased.*

Describe for the interviewer, step by step, how a problem-solving process you initiated came to a successful conclusion. What measures or benchmarks did you use to control or manage the process? What were the results?

Q: **How do you usually go about solving a problem?**

A: *When I need to solve a problem, I generally start by writing down as many ideas as I can think of about possible causes. Next I look for relationships among causes so I can group together symptoms of bigger problems. Usually, after I study these groups of problems, the real cause becomes readily apparent.*

The interviewer will want to hear the logic you use to solve problems as well as the outcomes you're able to achieve. Are you decisive? How do you narrow the options and make decisions? What do people say about your reasoning skills? What examples would they cite of your effective decision making?

Q: **How do you measure the success of your work?**

A: *I measure reactions of customers. When my customers call me with a referral, I know they're happy. And I have to say that repeat business to me is more satisfying than winning a new account. People have a tendency to try a new company because of that company's reputation or product, but they come back because of the relationship they've learned to trust.*

What results or evidence do you need to evaluate the success of your work? What type of feedback or reward system is important to you? The reviewer will want to establish that these needs can be satisfied in the job.

Q: **How practical or pragmatic are you?**

A: *I can usually pick up on an underlying problem, even if it's not too obvious. I recall an investment banker who visited our real-estate-finance class and asked us what might cause the Tokyo investment community a problem attracting local investment dollars. A number of finance M.B.A.s in the class started trying to think of some complicated set of reasons. I decided it would have to do with getting out of a bad market quickly, and that a nonliquid investment would create problems. I said investors would be unsettled if the primary investment is local real estate and inflation has caused the paper value to exaggerate the real street value. As it ended up, that was the answer he wanted.*

Give the interviewer an example of some practical or sensible approach you've used to solve a problem. When was a simple solution the best solution? Had others overlooked the obvious? In this example, you'll want to show off your commonsense skills rather than your "academic" skills.

Q: **How do you balance your reliance on facts with your reliance on intuition?**

A: *Facts are important but often neglect point-in-time influences, especially with market research. One survey that I was uncomfortable with involved pricing data that was collected just after a major presidential election. The timing caused me to doubt that consumers would really spend as much as the survey indicated they would for new cars. So we ended up holding on to the last quarter's pricing structure. We sold more cars while, as interest rates climbed, some of our competitors had expensive inventory carryover.*

Describe a specific time when your intuition helped you solve a problem that might have been handled badly if you'd followed the facts or standard procedure. Demonstrate an ability to "think outside of the box."

Q: **What was your greatest problem in your last job?**

A: *I had to get longtime employees with few or no computer skills to embrace a new e-mail system. I started by explaining the need for less paper in everyone's job. Then I decided to create a temporary e-mail account with one daily riddle on the system; everyone who responded correctly got their name put in a weekly drawing. Each week for one month a person from the drawing got a dinner for four at a nice local restaurant. This approach went over well as a device to get people to use the system.*

The interviewer wants to hear about a problem area the candidate improved in his or her last job. If you're asked this question, don't complain without showing solutions. Demonstrate an ability to offer solutions, not merely to point out problems.

Q: **Tell me about a problem that you failed to anticipate.**

A: *My boss asked me to solve an ongoing scheduling problem. I failed to realize that the person who had lived with the problem would see me as an antagonist. By the time I realized it, I'd already done some of the groundwork. If I'd started by asking for the person's opinion, I would have been able to get him on my side early on.*

This question forces you to be humble but gives you an opportunity to relate an incident from which you learned an important lesson. What warning signs should you have seen? How has your judgment improved as a result of this experience?

Q: **Have you ever resolved a long-standing problem?**

A: *We used to batch our guests' personal faxes—sometimes as many as ten outgoing fax requests per hour—to put less strain on our administrative staff. We had guests who weren't happy about that. I arranged a lease deal on an outgoing fax machine for guest self-serve access. This freed up more time for staff, and they were able to maintain control of incoming faxes, protecting incoming information until they could locate the appropriate guest in person.*

Tell the interviewer about a problem you championed within a work setting or other organization. How did you overcome or circumvent the obstacles? What were the results? What motivated you to tackle the problem to begin with?

Q: **Describe a time you found it necessary to make an unpopular decision.**

A: *I had to start a policy of no food in work areas, including private offices, because the production workers were unhappy with the inequity. For safety reasons workers couldn't have food anywhere near expensive equipment. Now it's forgotten, but at the time a number of supervisors were angry at me. I thought the matter was important and that the solution was consistent with other new policies, like doing away with assigned parking spaces for high-level employees. So far we've been progressive enough to keep unions out of our company.*

Sometimes an important long-term result is achieved only with short-term sacrifices. This question measures the candidate's ability to make important value judgments with long-term results. Be sure to give a specific example if you're asked a question like this.

Q: Tell me about the most difficult problem you've ever dealt with.

A: *I was promoted to manage a new department. A coworker in that group resented me from the beginning. I soon learned that her best friend had been turned down for the position. I actually confronted her about it; I explained that I had once put a friendship to the test because I'd worked too closely with someone and we found that we spent our leisure time talking about work. A few weeks after our talk she admitted that she'd never thought about the potential results of working too closely with a personal friend. Our working relationship was fine after that.*

Discuss the problem here briefly, then focus on what actions you took and what results you obtained. Be candid—why was this problem personally hard for you? How did you remain objective and professional?

Q: Describe a time when a problem wasn't resolved to your satisfaction.

A: *I thought once that we'd let a customer down by not responding quickly enough to resolve a problem; our production capacity wasn't sufficient to deliver the customer's complete order during the holiday season. That customer ended up asking for a discount, and I thought we should have offered the discount first, without waiting to be asked. The sense of goodwill would have been stronger.*

This question focuses on the candidate's standards of quality. Describe a situation in which you foresaw long-term complications from a problem that was poorly handled. Did you do anything to try to resolve the issue?

Q: Tell me about a time when there was no rule or precedent to help you attack a problem.

A: *I was the first employee in a newly created position. I spent the first week developing an understanding of the history that had led to creation of the position. Only then did a method for setting priorities on the job become clear.*

Can you operate without structure? Describe your problem-solving process, especially the steps you took and measures you established in a particularly trying situation. Demonstrate confidence and the willingness to take on new challenges.

Q: Describe a time when you failed to resolve a conflict.

A: *I wasn't able to keep a good employee who'd been in our manufacturing facility for ten years. His position across our division was rewritten to require computer skills. I offered to send him to night classes, but he refused the help. I had no option other than to replace him. In retrospect, if I'd been encouraging him and other employees to acquire new training periodically, he might not* have been overwhelmed when his position was reworked. Now I'm vigilant about encouraging my group to attend seminars and courses to enhance their job skills and to avoid becoming outdated.

If you're asked a question like this, you may be wise to choose a conflict that wasn't yours to solve. If you must discuss a personal conflict, focus on the positive steps you'd take if you could do it again. In what ways are you smarter now?

Q: When do you have difficulty making choices?

A: I'm not particularly good at interpreting survey data. I've really worked to get to know our research staff and librarians. I rely on them and am careful to thank them formally in front of my vice president. We're definitely a team, and I'm careful not to take credit for our industry reports, which we publish for the Pacific Region of our firm.

Be honest. What situations are difficult for you to resolve? What people, or other resources, do you gather in these instances to help you make decisions?

Q: Describe an opportunity in which you felt the risks far outweighed the rewards.

A: At one point we had an opportunity to purchase conveyor equipment at thirty cents on the dollar from a company that had dissolved. Although we anticipated an overhaul of our distribution facility five years down the road, I felt it was too far into the future to spend money only to have idle capacity for a five-year period. If market conditions had shown more promise for new sales in the initial two-year period, I would have gone ahead with it.

The interviewer wants to see that the candidate has an interest in taking reasonable risks without inclining toward foolishness. Demonstrate with an example your logic for deciding against some plan. How was the outcome preferable to what might have happened?

10. Accomplishments

Q: Tell me about a major accomplishment.

A: I'm really proud of the business I obtained with XYZ Wholesale Club. I believe that these types of companies will continue to thrive in the next few years.

Offer proof of your accomplishments using real examples. Don't give long descriptions of situations. Focus your answer on the actions you took and the positive results you obtained. The interviewer will want to know what you can contribute to the company.

Q: Talk about a contribution you've made to a team.

A: *I helped my last team put together more cohesive presentations for a client. I think our practice and preparation made a statement about how committed we would be to the details of the system installation. In the end, we landed the account.*

Tell the interviewer about your initiative within a team. Offer proof, using specific examples, that you delivered more than the team expected and that the team would compliment your contributions to the group's efforts. What special role did you play?

Q: Talk about a special contribution you've made to an employer.

A: *In my last job I ran the United Way campaign for three consecutive years. I believe it's an important cause, and I know it's difficult for the company to find volunteers, so I stepped in.*

Let the interviewer know that you deliver more than your employer expects. If you were hired, what situations would you handle especially well? What unique contributions can you make to the organization? How would you go the extra mile?

Q: Tell me about an organization outside of work that's benefited from your participation.

A: *I've been involved in Junior Achievement. I was an economics undergrad, and I liked seeing the high-school kids get excited about what they read in the paper and about how economics affects their lives.*

Discuss in some detail your initiative with something you volunteered for— such as working for a charitable organization. In other words, what things are important motivators for you? Could your employer benefit from these interests in some way? What kind of corporate citizen are you?

Q: Give me an example of a time you delivered more than was expected.

A: *In my last job my boss asked me to take over all the uncollected accounts. I was able to recover 20 percent more than his goal. I convinced people that I was willing to work out an affordable schedule based on their needs, and I did this by asking about their problems. Once they vented, they would usually listen to me.*

Give an example of a time when you truly excelled at a given task. Chances are you're likely to repeat similar results in your new position. In other words, give the interviewer an indication of the situations you might handle especially well if you were hired.

Q: **What accomplishment is your greatest source of pride?**

A: *I'm proud of how we turned a profit at our hospital in the first year under private management. Now that goal's been accomplished, and I'm ready to do the same for another hospital; that's why consulting within the industry appeals to me so much.*

Your answer will hint at the kinds of projects you'd like to do in the future. Focus on goals related specifically to the job you're applying for. The interviewer will want to know how your past initiative and accomplishments can translate to success for his or her company.

Q: **If I hired you today, what would you accomplish first?**

A: *I could help you increase your business within the OEM market. As an OEM contractor for four years, I understand how to structure deals that will be profitable.*

Give the interviewer clear, tangible evidence that the company will benefit immediately upon hiring you. Focus your answer on the action you would take, and make sure your goals are realistic. Can you demonstrate specific knowledge about the company and industry and how it relates to the role of your department and job?

Q: **What accomplishment was the most difficult for you to achieve?**

A: *I found it intimidating to work with the marketing-research staff when I started my job, mostly because I hadn't done well in statistics or market research during college. What I decided to do was enroll in an executive seminar on market research, which really boosted my confidence. Now I don't feel at a disadvantage when I meet with the research group, and I know what questions to ask to get information that's meaningful to me.*

Describe something you've accomplished despite obstacles, lack of training, or inadequate experience. This question allows you to talk about overcoming a weakness.

Q: **Tell me about a time you saved money for an employer or an organization.**

A: *I was able to eliminate a middleman we'd worked with for years in getting our employee magazine printed. We planned the issues, collected research, wrote the articles, did most of the editing, and then handed the information to him, which he took to a designer and printer. After I managed this process twice, I decided to do the coordinating work myself. The additional time it cost me was eight hours, but we saved a 10 percent markup, and even better, the issues now get completed faster and with greater accuracy.*

Be specific and quantify your results when answering your question, but don't give long descriptions of situations. Offer proof using a clear, convincing example.

Q: What's your greatest achievement to date?

A: *I'm proud of the fact that I graduated on time with a solid GPA while I played varsity basketball for four years. A lot of the women on my team either took a reduced course load or let their grades suffer. I believe the reason I got through it all was sheer determination; I never even let myself visualize anything but finishing on time and with good grades. So I firmly believe, as a professional counselor, in the importance of a positive outlook.*

Be sure that the achievement you describe here is relevant to the job you're interviewing for. Also, be careful that your answer doesn't sound as if the best is behind you. Mention something great that you've achieved, but clearly communicate your belief that the best is yet to come.

Q: Tell me about a person or group you had to work with to achieve something important.

A: *My law-school class really worked hard to improve the image of our school with employers. We put together our own promotional book, which we sent to law firms and alumni; the book presented a mock courtroom case in which other law schools filed a class-action suit arguing that the quality of the student body and teaching at our school had caused an erosion of interest in other law programs; they proved to the court that both teaching and student statistics clearly had led to positive placements for our graduates, which in turn killed the chances for students from other programs. The format of our brochure was so unusual that it got the attention of the major press, which served our purpose nicely.*

Give an example that demonstrates your use of teamwork to produce a better result than you could have achieved by yourself. Acknowledge your contributions and those of your team members.

Q: Tell me about something you accomplished that required discipline.

A: *I had to work two jobs to put myself through graduate school. I interned at the newspaper while I studied journalism during the week. Then on weekends I sold real estate. Juggling those three schedules was a challenge, but I did it because it was important to me to graduate without school loans.*

This is your opportunity to discuss a skill you worked to develop, or a time when the quantity of your work required solid time-management skills. How did you remain focused?

Q: **What situations do your colleagues rely on you to handle?**

A: *People often rely on me to handle client confrontations. I'm known as a person who never loses my temper in front of customers.*

This question provides a good opportunity for the candidate to showcase his or her dependability, strength of character, and professionalism. The interviewer will be impressed if you can also demonstrate that you work well with others and clearly enjoy your colleagues' respect.

Q: **Tell me about a need you fulfilled within a group or a committee.**

A: *I worked on the committee to review our company's policy on sick leave. One of our employees was abusing the system in order to gain vacation time. I served as the objective member of the group, having used virtually no sick leave in five years of employment. I ended up presenting an idea that the company's now considering, which is to allow up to one week of sick time to be voluntarily allocated to extra family-leave time.*

Tell the interviewer about your initiative in group projects. In teams, what roles do you usually play?

Q: **Tell me how you've supported and helped attain a corporate goal.**

A: *I helped meet our goal of value to stockholders by holding a fire sale of goods to clean out our warehouse. The public was invited, with a preview for customers, suppliers, vendors, and stockholders. Attendees bought new but visually imperfect electronics components at 70 percent reductions. We cleared $20,000 from sales of equipment we'd written off.*

Here the interviewer asks for evidence that the candidate completes projects with the corporation's goals in mind. What other groups, departments, or customers benefited from a similar effort on your part? Give specific examples, not generalizations. Focus on how you've enriched your job by expanding the benefits of your action beyond your own group or department.

Q: **Tell me about a quantifiable outcome of one of your efforts.**

A: *I reorganized inventory planning and was able to automate the inventory-reorder function, which used to be a forty-hour process and now takes only three hours.*

Describe a specific accomplishment, the outcome of which produced a clear benefit. Offer proof, using real examples, that you deliver more than what's expected. Did you exceed your expected outcome? How?

Q: **Describe an ongoing problem you were able to overcome.**

A: *We had three groups with different homegrown schedules, even though each group relied on the other's work and timing. I got us all connected via a computer network and held a training session to brainstorm our communications plan. We now talk regularly via e-mail and a network scheduler, and we all have the information we need.*

This question is similar to "Tell me about a time you tackled an unpopular assignment." Focus on how you achieved good results through the use of a creative technique or through greater diligence than others had previously devoted to the project.

Q: Tell me about a project you completed ahead of schedule.

A: *I was in charge of a new product rollout. In general we completed each phase without a major setback—which was partially luck—but I also systematically called two days ahead of every deadline to check the status with all groups involved. I believe that made the difference. The launch took place two weeks ahead of plan—a significant period of time in our industry, where shelf life for products is generally less than one year.*

Focus here on how you set goals and schedules, measured results, and championed the outcome of a project. This question is aimed at your diligence in accomplishing tasks and, assuming the project required group effort, at your leadership skills.

11. Career Aspirations

Q: Where do you want to be in five years?

A: *In five years I'd like to have progressed to the point where I have bottom-line budget responsibility, and I'm also in charge of a production unit where I have labor-relations, quality-control, design, and manufacturing responsibilities. I believe this job will allow me the opportunity to meet my personal goals in the next five years.*

Avoid the temptation to suggest job titles; this makes you seem unbending and unrealistic, since you don't know or control the system of promotion. Likewise, you don't know how long it might have taken your interviewer to reach certain levels, and you wouldn't want to insult. Describe new experiences or responsibilities you'd like to add that build on the job you're applying for.

Q: What are your long-term career plans?

A: *My long-term career goals are to become known as an industry expert and to have earned a respectable management position with responsibility for a major piece of the business. I'd like to think I'll have experience in many parts of the business over time.*

It's reasonable to see ahead about five years but probably no more, given the changing nature of businesses. Especially in high-tech fields, which change dramatically in a short time, it's impossible to project accurately how you might fit into a specific job. Therefore, focus on types of experiences (not job titles) you hope to gain over time.

Q: **Since this will be your first job, how do you know you'll like the career path?**

A: *Although it's true that I've never worked a job in your industry, I've talked to many friends and alums at my school who've been successful in your company. I always ask them the question, What's the most frustrating thing about your job, and What's the most rewarding thing about your job? From the information I've gained, I'm confident that I'll be able to adapt quickly to your culture and will find the next few years rewarding, based on my goals and values.*

This can be a difficult question to answer convincingly, unless you've done a little bit of preparation. Discuss, for example, an internship or a conversation that's allowed you to assess the culture of the organization, or to preview the work involved. Describe other people in the profession who have been mentors or who have taught you about the field. Also, point out why you're interested, how you learned more about the industry, and how you stay current with industry trends.

Q: **Why is this job right for you at this time in your career?**

A: *This job would build on my extensive technical background both as a navy communications officer and in the two software companies where I've worked. I believe I'm now ready to assume broader responsibilities as a project manager. I've demonstrated my ability to handle the responsibility for both a diverse team of programmers and engineers and for major capital budgets.*

Describe the experiences you want to pursue that build on your current skills and interests. Be as specific as you can, based on what you know about the current or future direction of the position and the department. Demonstrate why this position fits with your personal career goals. How can you create job growth for yourself?

Q: **What are your aspirations beyond this job?**

A: *Beyond this job as a marketing assistant, I see myself moving up through marketing analysis into brand management and eventually running a category. I'm aware that there are several skills I need to develop in the interval, and I believe with your continuing-education program and my own motivation for self-improvement, I'll have those skills when the opportunities arise for greater responsibility. That's why I'm determined to learn from the ground up, starting as a marketing assistant.*

Again, don't fall into the trap of specifying job titles. Stick to a natural progression you see as plausible. How should this job grow for the good of the organization? Then turn your attention once again to the job at hand. If you seem too interested in what lies beyond this job, the interviewer will fear that you won't stick around for long.

Q: **What new challenges would you enjoy?**

A: *I've worked in the hospitality industry for over eight years and have progressively worked in larger, more prestigious hotels. I've learned the food-and-beverage side of the business and the hotel-management side, and now I believe I'm ready to be a convention- or conference-sales manager.*

Describe the natural next step in your skill development based on what you've learned and enjoyed in your last job. What do you feel ready to tackle next? Be as specific as you can, considering what you know about the current or future direction of the position and department.

Q: **If you could start all over again, what direction would your career take?**

A: *I've always enjoyed consumer sales as I've moved up in my career. Looking back, I wish I'd gotten a bit more experience in market research earlier in my career, because it's important to understand the types of quantitative models and technical-research techniques that are now important for a regional sales manager to know.*

The interviewer will want to see if your career path (including this job interview) is less than ideal for you. Be careful to show that your heart lies in this field, but offer some insights so that someone else following in your footsteps might quicken the learning curve, time frame, and so on.

Q: **What achievements have eluded you?**

A: *I've achieved considerable success at the finance department of my company, a large corporation. I've worked in two different plants as the director of finance. I've worked in capital budgets at the corporate office and in the business-planning area. Unfortunately, I've never had the opportunity to work in the treasury department. Based on my graduate finance education and my several years' finance experience, I'm now convinced that I'm ready to handle this responsibility and that it'll be the next step in my learning curve toward a top finance-executive position.*

Describe a responsibility you'd like but haven't yet earned. What do you feel ready to tackle next? Explain why you haven't yet had the opportunity to assume such a responsibility, but take care not to sound passive. Describe some continuing efforts to reach your goals. Ask yourself, Would your current employer agree that you're ready?

Q: How long do you think you'd continue to grow in this job?

A: *My own personal measure of growth in a job is acquiring new skills, new knowledge, and new insights into the industry. As long as I can measure this type of growth, I consider myself successful. I'm a believer in stretching a job by reaching out to learn more about other areas that are peripheral to the job I'm in.*

This is a variation on the question "Where do you want to be in five years?" Be as specific as you can, considering what you know about the position. Don't mention a job title you'd want next, or the interviewer will wonder if you're already preoccupied with moving on.

Q: What career path interests you within the company?

A: *I'd like to work toward becoming a senior project manager within your commercial real-estate firm. My background includes working in several areas within commercial real estate, including architectural design, working with governmental departments and agencies, working with banks in the finance area, and, finally, working in sales and leasing. I'd like to pull all this background together in the next few years and eventually have project-management responsibility.*

Demonstrate your knowledge of the typical career path, if you're familiar with it. If not, turn this answer into a question: "What's the typical career path for someone with my skills?" Focus principally on businesses or divisions of the company that interest you, as well as skills and challenges you hope to master in the next few years.

Q: I see you've been out of work for a while. What difficulties have you had in finding a suitable job that fits your interests?

A: *It's true that I've been out of my field for the last four years, but I've had a number of tempting offers to jump back in. However, I felt that it was important to stay home with my new baby and also continue a part-time family business that I ran out of our home while my husband completed law school. Now that that's behind us, I'm ready to return to my career in the entertainment industry.*

What the interviewer really wants to know is why someone else hasn't hired this candidate. Why isn't she in greater demand? Is she being too unrealistic, or is she pursuing positions randomly? Is there something in her past that others have discovered? Tell the interviewer the positive things your references or former work associates will say about your skills, and make sure your references are strong.

Q: **Compare this job to others you're pursuing.**

A: *I've narrowed my job search to only those large securities firms within the finance industry. The basic skills necessary with all of these firms are similar: strong quantitative and analytical abilities, the ability to make decisions quickly, and good interpersonal skills to react to a customer's needs.*

Some consistency or thread of commonality among your other prospects is important here. Your choices must reflect your career aspirations. What common skills are clearly needed in all the jobs you're pursuing?

Q: **Have you progressed in your career as you expected?**

A: *My six years with a major gas company have included solid experience in price analysis, capital budgets, and financial planning. I now believe I'm ready to take on departmental responsibility for the entire finance function within a finance company.*

Review the positive learning experiences from your past jobs and the next steps you're ready to take as a result, but also be realistic in admitting the areas where you need more experience. Honesty is important here without demonstrating either pessimism or unrealistic expectations.

Q: **Tell me about your salary expectations.**

A: *I've become a little frustrated in the past year because the downturn in our industry has caused limited promotional opportunities. Based upon salary information published by our national association, the market price for someone with my experience and educational background is in the broad range of $30,000 to $40,000 per year. Although I'm not certain how your salaries compare to the national norms, my feeling is that my value would certainly be in the upper half of this national range. I hope you'll share with me some of your salary ranges relative to the national norms.*

A well-prepared candidate can effectively turn this question around. Ask first for the company's salary range, then answer in general terms based on your qualifications in relation to the job requirements.

Q: **What do you reasonably expect to earn within five years?**

A: *My expectation for the next five years is that my contributions will be recognized and appropriately rewarded. I realize that salary levels are based on a number of factors, including the company's profitability and the general business cycle that affects our industry, but I expect to take on greater responsibility each year and to be appropriately compensated for my efforts and contributions.*

Again, turn this question around and ask what's typical for the career path. Then consider, based on your skills and performance, the areas you'll excel in. Leave it to the interviewer to determine the appropriate "time frames" for promotions. Don't speculate, or you'll risk sounding arrogant, unrealistic, or the opposite—too reserved or too tentative.

Q: **Why did you stay in your last job so long?**

A: *I was in my last job for over seven years. During this time I completed an advanced technical degree at night school and also had two six-month assignments during which I was loaned out to different departments. As a result, I acquired some additional skills that normally aren't associated with the job I've held. Therefore, I feel I've made good progress and I'm ready to accept the next challenge.*

The interviewer wants to know about the candidate's interest in personal improvement, tackling new assignments, and so on. A seven-year stay in one job might indicate someone who's a bit too comfortable with the status quo. Demonstrate how you've developed your job responsibilities in meaningful new ways.

Q: **Have you ever taken a position that didn't fit into your long-term plan?**

A: *Back in the late eighties, when Wall Street was booming, I was lured away with a high-paying offer in a firm that was trading commodities on the Asian market. Even though I had success in the job, I quickly realized that the work wasn't fulfilling or challenging enough to keep me happy. So, after two years, I jumped back into the corporate world as a controller for one of the metal plants of my corporation. I've since moved up in the finance area, and my long-term plans include staying in this industry and assuming greater responsibility in the area of financial planning and control.*

The interviewer is trying to determine here how wisely the candidate can pick jobs to match his or her interests and aspirations. If you've been side-tracked by some job, you'll probably have to convince the recruiter that you're on the right track pursuing this position.

12. Personal Interests and Hobbies

Q: **Other than work, tell me about an activity you've remained interested in over several years.**

A: *I've been involved in Cancer Society fundraising ever since my grandmother died from the disease. In the back of my mind I guess I'm hoping that the research can lead to findings in time to save the life of someone else in my family.*

The interviewer is looking here for a history of commitment over time, and consistency of interests. Do you sustain your hobbies over a period of time, or do you have a different hobby every year? Are your interests compatible with the job you're applying for? Would they be of value in any way to the company?

Q: What do you do in your spare time?

A: *I really enjoy getting outside—I often go camping and hiking. I've learned a lot about different fabrics that are good for various weather conditions. That's why I'm so interested in your textile operations.*

The interviewer wants evidence that you're well-rounded, not just one-dimensional. He or she is also looking for shared interests or common ground. You should always, in some way, relate your answer to the job description.

Q: Do you have a balanced lifestyle?

A: *I make an effort to get out of the office at a reasonable hour twice a week. I go home and walk my dog. That's one of the most relaxing things I do, but it often helps me think of solutions for problems at work, even though I'm not consciously trying to solve those problems.*

Do you have an outlet, a way to get a break from work, so that you show up each day refreshed and ready to perform at your highest level? Describe something specific that allows you to relax. Are your personal and career interests compatible in terms of their logic or thought processes?

Q: What outside activities complement your work interests?

A: *I've always enjoyed tennis. In many ways it's a game of strategy and pacing. When something isn't working in the first set, you have to change your strategy for the second set. You also have to pace your energy in case you go to a third set, and constantly watch and read your opponent's reactions. I'm a gutsy tennis player—I go for the big points sometimes—but I'm careful with timing. That's the way I am at work too.*

The interviewer is interested to see if the candidate's personality is reflected in both work and outside activities. Your answer to this question will shed light on your personality and thus possibly on your compatibility with the job.

Q: Tell me about a time you were in a recreational setting and got an idea that helped in your work.

A: *I was on vacation in Mexico and saw a woman with a homemade seesaw she was using to lift her laundry basket when she needed something out of it. It gave me an idea for a new type of scaffolding, which I designed when I got* *back to work. Now our brick masons have a rotating bench that keeps their materials at waist level, which reduces back fatigue.*

The interviewer will want to know if you have the ability to synthesize information and apply what you see to your profession. Show that your work is something you're naturally inquisitive about, rather than something you have to do. Are you able to "think outside of the box" to come up with fresh ideas? Be sure to give specific examples.

Q: How is your personality reflected in the kinds of activities you enjoy?

A: *I love to cook and entertain. That's the salesman coming out in me. I love sharing experiences with people, and I'm very outgoing. I don't particularly enjoy being alone. I always feel as if I should be "doing something."*

Describe how your natural skills and values are reflected in various things you do, from work to leisure. What are your comfortable patterns of operating? For example, a detailed, precise hobby reflects something different from a risk-oriented, aggressive sport.

Q: What kinds of leisure activities help you perform your work better?

A: *I enjoy sitting outside during lunch and talking with students. It gives me a chance to get fresh air, but it also helps the students get comfortable with me, so they're more likely to seek my help when they need it.*

The recruiter will want to know that you have an outlet to relax. Just about any hobby or leisure activity will help you perform more efficiently at work, but if you can tie the activity directly to job performance, so much the better.

Q: What do you do to relax?

A: *I have a great family. Weekends are like a vacation for me. When I'm at work, I focus on work, but when I'm home on weekends, work really is far from my mind. One of the smartest things I did was to move twenty miles outside of town; even the drive home is relaxing.*

An admission that work is far from your mind when you're relaxing is not necessarily a bad thing. This candidate attractively reveals additional information about his or her character and, at the same time, lets the interviewer know that there is plenty of psychic energy stored for the work day.

Q: If you found yourself getting burned out, what would you do to revitalize your energy?

A: *I don't allow myself to get involved in a routine to the point that I get burned out. I've always been the type of person who asks for new assignments so that I stay motivated and interested.*

Are you disciplined enough to avoid burnout? When you're not being productive, do you recognize it? What do you do to cope with stress?

Q: Our company believes that employees should give time back to the community. How do you feel about it?

A: *I believe that, too. In my last job as manager I told each of my employees that they could spend one Friday afternoon a month at a charity of their choice on company time as long as they weren't all gone on the same Friday. Ironically, productivity didn't decrease at all; they got more done in the morning—and I guess Friday afternoons weren't that productive to begin with. I've spent my afternoons with an adult reading program.*

Describe a time you gave something to a community or organization as a volunteer. Do you go above and beyond what's expected of you? Do you use your skills productively? Are you unselfish—a team player? Demonstrate how your personal interests make you productive even when you aren't being paid. What incentives other than a paycheck inspire you?

Q: What community projects that can use your professional skills are particularly interesting to you?

A: *As a marketing person, I've offered free advice to our local high school for its fund-raisers, as well as to a local real-estate office whose success could help my rural community's real-estate values.*

This interviewer wants to know if the candidate will be a good corporate citizen. The question also gives the interviewer a sense of the job seeker's values. Try to focus your answer on productive applications of your work-related skills. Don't get sidetracked describing a cause that doesn't demonstrate job-related skills. Avoid discussing any charity or organization that may be considered controversial.

Q: If you had unlimited leisure time, how would you spend that time?

A: *I don't think I could ever be happy with lots of spare time. I'd probably travel, learn another language, and spend more time with my two charities. I'd also take more courses in accounting.*

In answering this question, demonstrate that you'd use your time to increase your skills, or to give something back to the community or a good cause. When possible, choose an activity that's career- or job-oriented; for example, if you're in marketing, say you'd get involved with Junior Achievement and teach young people about careers in business. Your answer should reflect your energy and capacity for work, as well as your natural curiosity. Don't say something like "I don't know; I'd just like to relax."

Q: **Describe how a sport or hobby taught you a lesson in teamwork or discipline.**

A: *My football coach from high school taught me always to watch out for the other guy. If you do, he'll cover you when you need him to. I've applied that principle in all my work groups, especially on the trading floor.*

Tell about a time you had to use teamwork to get a desired result. Tell a specific story, then explain how the same skill or lesson has been used in your work.

Q: **When you aren't at work, do you prefer to stick to a schedule, or do you prefer to be spontaneous? Why?**

A: *My workday is very structured, because I'm generally in four or five meetings a day. On the weekends, I like to have a plan, but not necessarily a set schedule. That in itself is a relaxing change of pace for me, but I feel I'd be wasting time with no plan at all.*

Be careful that, whichever answer you choose, it's consistent with the job you're interviewing for. For example, since accounting is a profession that requires discipline and precision, your answer should reflect your natural inclination toward agendas, schedules, and precision. However, for a sales job you'd probably want to show that you're prepared to "wing it." This question is essentially about your personality but is also about your compatibility with the job.

Q: **Tell me about an interest that you outgrew.**

A: *Early on, I wanted to be a research physician. Then I spent time in a chemistry lab and realized I wasn't looking forward to the next two years of lab work. That's why I've chosen marketing for medical equipment instead. It combines my respect for the medical profession with a job that's more suited to my personality.*

Describe a former interest or hobby that you no longer pursue, making sure that the interest isn't related in some way to the job you're interviewing for. Talk about why you outgrew the interest and how it's not compatible with your current interests. Be sure to discuss how your current interests are related to your career.

Q: Describe a recent book or movie that you really identified with.

A: *I loved one part of an otherwise depressing movie, One Flew over the Cuckoo's Nest. In one scene the nurse refuses to turn on the TV for the World Series, so Jack Nicholson looks at the blank screen and starts narrating as though the game were actually on. The other patients gather around him and follow the game. I thought that scene was an example of the power of visualization in making things happen.*

Demonstrate that you can assimilate knowledge from a wide variety of sources, including books and movies. Tell the interviewer about a specific book or movie that taught you something. Discuss how and where you've applied that knowledge.

CHAPTER 5
ZINGERS!

One of the biggest fears that job candidates harbor about interviews is the unanticipated question for which they have no answer. To make matters worse, some recruiters may ask a question knowing full well that you can't possibly answer it. These types of questions are known as "stress questions" and are designed for their shock effect. Sometimes recruiters ask stress questions not because they enjoy seeing you squirm in your seat, but because they want to judge how well you might react to pressure or tension on the job.

If you encounter a stress question, your best bet is to stay calm, diplomatic, and positive in your response. Don't get defensive or allow your confidence to be shaken, and try to answer the question to the best of your ability. If you simply can't answer the question, think about it for a few seconds. Then, with a confident smile and without apology, simply say, "I can't answer that question."

Following are fifty of the most challenging questions you'll ever face. If you're able to answer these questions, you'll be prepared to handle just about anything the recruiter comes up with.

Q: Tell me about yourself.

A: *I'm a production assistant with a B.A. in communications and three years of solid broadcasting and public-relations experience. I have extensive experience developing and researching topics, preinterviewing guests, and producing on-location videotapings. I have a tremendous amount of energy and love to be challenged. I'm constantly trying to take on additional responsibilities and learn new things. I've been watching your station for some time now, and I've been impressed with your innovative approach and your fast growth. I'd like to be a part of that winning team.*

This is a perfect opportunity to "sell" your qualifications to the interviewer. Using the sixty-second pitch you developed in Chapter 1 as a guideline, briefly describe your experience, skills, accomplishments, goals, and personal qualities. Explain your interest in the company you're interviewing with, and how you plan on making a contribution there. If you're a recent college graduate, be sure to discuss your educational qualifications as well, emphasizing the specific classes you took that are relevant to the position.

Q: What is your biggest weakness?

A: *I admit to being a bit of a perfectionist. I take a great deal of pride in my work and am committed to producing the highest-quality work I can. Sometimes if I'm not careful, though, I can go a bit overboard. I've learned that it's not always possible or even practical to try to perfect your work—sometimes you have to decide what's important and ignore the rest in order to be productive. It's a question of trade-offs. I also pay a lot of attention to pacing my work, so that I don't get too caught up in perfecting every last detail.*

This is a great example of what's known as a negative question. Negative questions are a favorite among interviewers, because they're effective for uncovering problems or weaknesses. The key to answering negative questions is to give them a positive spin. For this particular question your best bet is to admit to a weakness that isn't catastrophic, inconsistent, or currently disruptive to your chosen professional field, and to emphasize how you've overcome or minimized the problem. Whatever you do, don't answer this question with a cop-out like "I can't think of any," or even worse, "I don't really have any major weaknesses." This kind of response is likely to eliminate you from contention.

Q: Tell me about a project in which you were disappointed with your personal performance.

A: *In my last job for a manufacturing company I had to analyze all of the supplier bids and present recommendations to the vice president of logistics. Because the supplier bids weren't in a uniform format, my analysis often consisted of comparing dissimilar items. This caused some confusion in my final report, and by the time I'd reworked it and presented it to the vice president, we'd lost the critical time we needed to improve our approval process for these bids. In hindsight I should have taken a simpler approach to the problem and not tried to make it so complex or all inclusive. Ever since, I've paid more attention to making recommendations in a timely manner.*

Describe roadblocks and what you've done to try to get around them. How have your skills come into play? In hindsight, what could you have done differently? What lessons have you learned?

Q: Tell me about your most difficult work or personal experience.

A: *One time my coworker went through rehab for six months after a wreck, and I picked up a lot of additional work to help him out. I know he would've done the same for me, and it's important for me to have that kind of trust among the members of my work group.*

The interviewer will want to know how you hold up under pressure. Describe a situation, either personal or professional, that involved a great deal of conflict and challenge and placed you under an unusual amount of stress. What, specifically, were the problems, and what did you do to resolve them?

Q: **What was your greatest challenge in your last job?**

A: *I had to get longtime employees with few or no computer skills to embrace a new e-mail system. I started by explaining the need for less paper in everyone's job. Then I decided to create a temporary e-mail account with one daily riddle on the system; everyone who responded correctly got his or her name put in a weekly drawing. Each week for one month a person from the drawing won a dinner for four at a nice local restaurant. This idea worked well as a device to get people to use the system.*

Describe a problem area that you improved in your last job, emphasizing the solution you devised. If you're relatively inexperienced and can't boast of solving a tremendously difficult or involved problem, like saving the company from a hostile takeover, that's okay. Simply describe a relatively minor problem you've solved creatively, as this candidate does.

Q: **Tell me about the most difficult problem you've dealt with.**

A: *That would be the time I was promoted to manage a new department. A coworker in the department resented me from the beginning. I soon learned that her best friend had been turned down for the position. I actually confronted her about it; I explained that I had once put a relationship of my own to the test working too closely with a friend—we found that we spent all our leisure time talking about work. A few weeks after our talk she admitted that she'd never thought about the potential results of working too closely with a friend. Our working relationship was fine after that.*

Discuss the problem briefly, then focus on what actions you took and the results you obtained. Be revealing: Why was this problem personally hard for you? How did you remain objective and professional?

Q: **Describe a time when you failed to resolve a conflict.**

A: *I wasn't able to keep a good employee once who'd been in our manufacturing facility for ten years. His job description was rewritten to require computer skills. I offered to send him to night classes, but he refused the help. I had no option but to replace him. In retrospect, if I'd encouraged him and other employees to acquire new training periodically, he might not have been overwhelmed by the time his position was reworked. Now I'm vigilant about encouraging my group to attend seminars and courses to enhance their job skills and to avoid becoming outdated.*

The ideal solution here is to discuss a conflict that wasn't yours to solve in the first place. If you must discuss a personal conflict, focus on the positive steps you'd take if you could go back and do it over again. What have you learned as a result of this experience?

Q: How have you handled criticism of your work?

A: *The first time I had a complaint from a client, I found it difficult to keep the complaint separate from my professional service of the account. The client was upset about the downtime on ATM machines. I learned that showing empathy usually calms an unpleasant situation; I also learned that no client is going to be happy with everything, even if that client's overall experience is positive.*

The interviewer is looking for an indication of the candidate's accountability and professional character. Describe a specific project or work habit that caused you a problem until you faced up to it and overcame it. Alternatively, you might describe a time you responded objectively and professionally to particularly harsh or unreasonable criticism of your work.

Q: Give an example of how you've handled rejection.

A: *I remember in my first job as a marketing assistant, I spent endless hours analyzing a particular problem. I came up with a revised marketing plan that was extremely well received. Unfortunately when I had to present it to top management I didn't put in the necessary time and attention to the actual presentation—overheads and slides—and the result was that it was turned down because I did not make it clear the savings that would result from this new marketing plan. I spent the next two weeks working on my presentation and at my second try I was extremely persuasive and convinced top management that indeed, this was the way to go. They approved it and my recommendations were carried out to everyone's satisfaction.*

Ideally, you should cite an example from an early stage in your career. Explain why you met with rejection and describe how you managed to overcome it. Demonstrate your improvement in that area over the years.

Q: What might your current boss want to change about your work habits?

A: *I'm a morning person and she's a night owl. I like to come into the office at least an hour early, usually by seven, to get a jump start on my work. My boss likes to come in after nine and work late into the evening. So I think if she could change one thing about me, she'd probably make me into a night owl, too, so that I'd be available during many of the same hours she likes to work.*

The interviewer will want to know how you'll fit in with your future boss and coworkers, and will also want to feel confident that he or she has uncovered any surprises about your corporate style. One good way to answer this question is to point out minor differences of preference. Alternatively, you might describe a weakness that you and your boss have worked on and improved.

Q: **Tell me about two or three aspects of your last job you'd never want to repeat.**

A: *I'm glad that I have experience in credit collections because it's enabled me to make better risk assessments. I really didn't enjoy the work, though, and it isn't something I want to do again.*

In a constructive way describe two or three things you've done that you didn't especially enjoy or that didn't play upon your strengths. Then describe your strengths and their relevance to the job you're applying for.

Q: **Tell me about a time when your employer wasn't happy with your job performance.**

A: *That would be during my first week on the job as a paralegal. I gave her two letters that had typos in them. Frankly, I'd simply been a little sloppy—but that's the only example that comes to mind. Ms. Heilman did tell me regularly that she was very happy with my work.*

Again, be sure to discuss a relatively minor incident here. Also, show a willingness to accept responsibility for the problem—don't blame others or make excuses. Simply describe what happened and how you successfully resolved the situation.

Q: **Have you ever been passed up for a promotion that you felt you deserved?**

A: *A couple of times in my early career I thought that I was unfairly passed up for a promotion. However, in retrospect I now realize that in all likelihood I wasn't ready to perform in those jobs—and, in fact, the additional training experience I gained remaining where I was proved invaluable in the last few years, as I've made significant progress moving up the corporate ladder. I've also learned to appreciate that being ready for a promotion doesn't necessarily mean it'll happen. There are many external factors that influence the nature and timing of promotions, aside from a person's performance and capabilities.*

The interviewer wants to gauge the candidate's self-confidence, as well as his or her objectivity about personal or professional limitations. Give evidence here that you have enough patience to learn what's important before you get bored or frustrated. After you've mastered your own job, would you stay motivated long enough to be productive?

Q: Have you ever been fired?

A: *During one of my summer internships while in college, I worked for a software consulting company. Midway through the summer a new president was appointed because of some financial difficulties, and he requested the resignation of my entire group. I was swept out with everyone else, even though my work performance had never been criticized.*

If you've never been fired, of course, this is a simple question to answer. But if you have been fired, you'll need to be prepared to discuss the situation in detail and possibly answer a series of very specific follow-up questions. If the termination was a result of a situation beyond your control, such as corporate downsizing, most interviewers will be very understanding. But if you were fired due to poor performance or some other problem, you'll need to admit your fault and convince the interviewer that you've corrected the problem. Although this may be a difficult question to answer, you should be completely honest. If you aren't, and the recruiter finds out as much from your references, you may be subject to immediate dismissal, or your job offer may be revoked.

Q: Why have you changed jobs so frequently?

A: *My frequent job changes over the last five years have been due to the rapid changes in my profession. My jobs have been based on government contracts, and over the last several years congressional appropriations have been up and down, causing some companies' contracts to be canceled, while other companies land huge, unexpected contracts. This volatility creates some good opportunities, but it also creates a lot of uncertainty. Because your business is based mostly on consumer products, and not on government products, I welcome the opportunity to work in an environment where the business cycle is more stable and predictable.*

Be candid here. Personal growth, a larger budget, or other career-enhancing experiences are all valid reasons for moving on. Convince the interviewer that you're interested in his or her company for the long haul.

Q: Why did you stay in your last job so long?

A: *I was in my last job over seven years. During that time I completed an advanced technical degree at an evening university and also had two six-month assignments in which I was loaned out to different departments. As a result, I acquired some additional skills that normally aren't associated with that particular job. Therefore, I think I've made good progress and am ready to accept the next challenge.*

The interviewer may be curious about your interest in personal improvement, tackling new assignments, and so on. He or she may also be concerned about whether you have a tendency to get too comfortable with the status quo. Demonstrate how you've developed job responsibilities in meaningful new ways.

Q: **Tell me about a problem you've had getting along with a work associate.**

A: *I'm pretty easygoing and tend to get along with most people. But I remember one time when we brought in a new associate who was very bossy—to the point where he offended one of our interns with his attitude. I actually pulled him aside and told him that I found it more productive to ask people for help than to give orders. Unfortunately, my advice didn't seem to help much, but we were more careful when we hired new staff after that.*

Avoid discussing a personality clash; focus instead on a difference in work ethic between you and an associate, or something else with which the interviewer is likely to empathize. For example, you might describe someone whose standards of excellence were perhaps less stringent than yours.

Q: **Tell me about your least-favorite manager or professor.**

A: *Well, I've been pretty fortunate as far as managers go, and I didn't have any problems with my professors. In my first job out of college I worked with a manager who was pretty inaccessible. If you walked into his office to ask a question, you got the sense that you were bothering him, so we just learned to get help from each other instead. I wouldn't say he was my least-favorite manager, because he was a good manager in a lot of ways, but I would have preferred that he'd made himself more available to us and given us more direction.*

Answering this question will be a little bit like walking across a loaded minefield, so beware! Keep in mind that the interviewer doesn't want to learn about your former supervisors; he or she does want to learn about the way you speak about them. Though the interviewer may bait you to make a negative statement about your former employer, doing so can create a host of problems. Even if your claim is completely true and entirely justified, the recruiter may conclude either that you don't get along well with people or that you shift blame to others. The best way around this dilemma is to choose an example that's not too negative, touch upon it briefly, then focus the rest of your answer on what you learned from the experience.

Q: **Who's the toughest employer you've ever had, and why?**

A: *That would be Ms. Henson at Franklin Associates. She'd push people to their limits when things got busy, and she was a stickler for detail. But she was always fair, and she rewarded good, hard work. I'd call her a tough boss, but a good boss.*

Again, you should avoid making negative statements about your previous employers, at all costs. Turn the question around with a positive, upbeat response, as this candidate does.

Q: **Have you ever had to work with a manager who was unfair to you, or who was just plain hard to get along with?**

A: *Actually, I've never run into that. Of course, my current boss has to work under time constraints—just like everyone else—and she sometimes has to phrase things succinctly if our department is going to meet its goals. But I've never considered that unfair or hard to handle. It's just part of the job. My supervisors and I have always gotten along quite well.*

Never, under any circumstances, criticize a current or former employer, no matter how many times the interviewer gives you the opportunity to do so. What the interviewer is trying to find out here is not whether the candidate has worked for difficult people, but if he or she is willing to bad-mouth them.

Q: **What are some of the things your supervisor has done that you disliked?**

A: *The only thing I really don't like is to get feedback in front of others. I want to hear good or bad feedback in private, so that I have time to think and react to the issue without other distractions. I believe that's the fair way to improve learning or to change future behavior.*

Again, avoid being overly negative when talking about your ex-boss or manager. Discuss a relatively minor example or one with which the interviewer is likely to empathize. Put a positive spin on your answer by describing what you learned from this difficult situation.

Q: **How do you handle tension with your boss?**

A: *The only tension I've ever felt was once when we both got too busy to keep each other informed. My boss overcommitted me with a short deadline, not knowing that I was bogged down with another client problem. I believe firmly in the importance of staff meetings so that coworkers can respect the demands on each other's time.*

The safest ground here is to describe an example of a miscommunication in your early relationship with a boss and how you resolved it. The interviewer will want to know how you avoided a recurrence of the problem.

Q: **What are your salary requirements?**

A: *I'd expect a salary that's comparable to the going rate for someone in my field with my skills and expertise. Salary, however, isn't my only consideration. I'm most interested in this opportunity because I think it represents a good match between what you're looking for and my qualifications. What kind of figure do you have in mind?*

Recruiters want to weed out people whose financial goals are unrealistic. This question is a direct hit—it forces a response about a touchy subject. If you mention a salary that's too low, you may seem uninformed or desperate; too high, and you may eliminate yourself from further consideration. It's best to turn the question back on the recruiter. Ask the salary range for the position; then ask the recruiter to consider how your qualifications compare to the average requirements for the position.

Q: What is your current salary?

A: *I currently earn an annual salary of $35,000 with full benefits.*

By all means, if you're asked about your salary history, don't embellish. More and more companies are starting to verify applicants' pay history, some even demanding to see W-2 forms from job seekers. If you get the job, a falsehood discovered even years later may be grounds for immediate dismissal. Don't leave yourself open to this kind of trouble.

Q: Would you be willing to relocate to another city?

A: *I'd prefer to be based here, but it's certainly a possibility I'd be willing to consider.*

You may, even in some first interviews, be asked questions that seem to elicit a tremendous commitment on your behalf, such as this one. Although such questions may be unfair during an initial job interview, you may well conclude that you have nothing to gain and everything to lose with a negative response. If you're asked such a question unexpectedly during an initial job interview, simply say something like "That's certainly a possibility" or "I'm willing to consider that." Later, if you receive an offer, you can find out the specific work conditions and then decide if you wish to accept the position. Remember, at the job-offer stage you have the most negotiating power, and the employer may be willing to accommodate your needs. If that isn't the case, you might wish to explain that upon reflection, you've decided you can't (for instance) relocate, but you'd like to be considered for other positions that might open up in the future.

Q: Does the frequent travel required for this work fit into your lifestyle?

A: *The frequent travel in this consulting position is no problem for me or my family. I was recently married, but my wife is an airline flight attendant, so neither of us follows the typical nine-to-five routine.*

If you're comfortable divulging information about your family situation, now is the time to do so. The interviewer is concerned here that the candidate may not be able to travel as much as the job requires. Emphasize your flexibility, or explain why travel wouldn't be a problem, in order to alleviate these concerns.

Q: **Would you be able to work extended hours as necessary to perform the job?**

A: *I'm accustomed to working long hours during the week. I usually work until at least six-thirty, because I get a lot done after the business office closes at five. I can make arrangements to be available on weekends, if necessary, though I do prefer to have at least twenty-four hours' notice.*

Your response should match closely the position you're applying for and should reflect a realistic understanding of the work and time required. Ask about seasonality of work, if you're unsure, and show a willingness to work occasional extended hours.

Q: **Sell me this stapler.**

A: *This is a professional-quality stapler, designed to be functional as well as attractive. It will help you reduce clutter on your desk by enabling you to fasten pages together. And since papers relating to the same subject will now be attached, you'll be more efficient and will save time searching for papers. Finally, its sleek shape and black color are coordinated to match the rest of your office furniture.*

With this kind of question the interviewer will want to determine how quickly you think on your feet, as well as your ability to communicate effectively and succinctly. Be prepared to give a thirty-second speech on the benefits and advantages of virtually any common office object, from a paper clip to a telephone, particularly if you're interviewing for a sales position.

Q: **Why should I hire you?**

A: *I offer over fifteen years of expertise in management, including electronic assembly for a major computer manufacturer, and injection-molding operations for a prominent plastics company. Because I have the ability to adjust and learn new skills quickly, I've often been called upon to start new operations. I'm confident on the basis of my skills and experience that I can help improve production by leading a team effort directed at achieving your company's goals.*

You'll usually encounter this question toward the end of a job interview; how you answer it can make or break your candidacy. Instead of reiterating your resume, emphasize only a few of your strongest qualifications and relate them to the position in question. Even if you're not asked this question, you should be sure to wrap up the interview by saying something like, "I'd like to emphasize my interest in the position. Particularly after speaking with you today, I feel stronger than ever that I'm the right candidate for the job. I offer over ..."

Q: **Prove to me that your interest is sincere.**

A: *I know that a lot of people want to get into television because of the money or because they just want to be on camera. But to me communicating well is an art and the television industry is the ultimate test of how well one communicates. Working in television isn't like working for a newspaper, where if a reader misses a fact, he or she can just go back and reread it. A television news story can go by in a flash, and the challenge is to make sure the audience understands it, learns from it, and, in a broader sense, can use the information to better their lives or their situations. It's the way television can evoke action that's always made me want to be a part of the industry. I'm particularly interested in this station because I like your focus on the community. Though the on-air products have a great nineties look, it's to your credit that the station seems to remain focused on the tradition of local news and what matters to its audience. The special reports that emphasize town politics, that go on location each week to a different town for a live shot, that explain the big issues facing a community, make the viewer feel that the station is a part of the community. In my opinion this is a great way to maintain a loyal audience.*

Being unprepared to answer this question can eliminate you from further consideration. On the other hand, if you're able to demonstrate a strong interest in the company and in the position, you'll have an advantage over the competition.

Q: **What would you do if I told you that I thought you were giving a very poor interview today?**

A: *Well, the first thing I'd do is ask you if there was any specific part of the interview that you thought I might have mishandled. After that I'd think back and try to remember if there had been any faulty communication on my part. Then I'd try to review possible problems I had understanding your questions, and I'd ask for clarification if I needed it. Finally, if we had time, I'd try to respond more fully and appropriately to the problem areas you identified for me.*

Interviewers like to ask stress questions like these to see how well you hold up under pressure. Your best bet is to stay calm, relaxed, and don't allow your confidence to be shaken.

Q: **You have seven minutes to convince me why you're the best candidate for this position. Go.**

Instead of following a traditional question-and-answer format for a job interview, some recruiters have been known to ask no more than this one question. Only the most prepared candidates will survive this type of interview. If you run into this question, your best bet is to discuss the various sales themes you developed in Chapter 2, emphasizing throughout one or two of your strongest qualifications for the position.

Q: **How would you respond to a defaulted form Z-65 counterderivative renewal request if your manager ordered you to do so, and if the policy under which the executive board resolves such issues were currently under review?**

Sometimes recruiters ask seemingly impossible questions, just to see how you'll respond. It's not so much that they want to see you squirm in your seat as that they want to judge how you might respond to pressure or tension on the job. No matter how you may feel at the time, being subjected to a ridiculous question like this one is probably a very good sign. If you're asked a tough question that you simply can't answer, think about it for a few seconds. Then, with a confident smile and without apology, simply say something like "I don't know, but if you hire me, I'll sure find out for you."

Special Situations
Interviewing can be even more stressful when you find yourself in what we call a "special situation." Perhaps you lack paid job experience, have been out of the workplace to raise children, are concerned about possible discrimination because of age or disability, or are trying to enter a field in which you have no practical experience. Not to worry! The key to improving your chances in an interview is to emphasize your strengths. Focus on your marketable skills (whether they were acquired in the workplace or elsewhere), and highlight impressive achievements, relevant education and training, and/or related interests. And, of course, you should take care to downplay or eliminate any information that may be construed as a weakness.

For example, if you are a "displaced homemaker" (a homemaker entering the job market for the first time), you can highlight the special skills you've acquired over the years while downplaying your lack of paid job experience.

Questions for Students and Recent Graduates
Whether you're graduating from high school or college, those of you with little or no work history face the same dilemma: it's tough to get a job without experience, and it seems impossible to gain experience without getting hired. But, as you'll see, there are ways to get around this problem by emphasizing your strengths and educational achievements.

Q: **Why weren't your grades better?**

A: *School was a wonderful experience for me. I really enjoyed learning new ideas, I studied consistently, and I was attentive in class. But I never believed in cramming before the night of an exam just to get a higher grade or staying up all night to finish a term paper. I really believe I learned just as much as many students who went for the grades.*

It's likely that if you've made it to the interview stage, you fulfill the basic criteria for the position, including the education requirements. The recruiter is probably trying to judge here how well the candidate handles adversity. It's important not to get defensive or to place blame. Instead, try to put a positive spin on the question—for example, by concentrating on what you learned and the extra effort you put in, rather than on the grades you received.

Q: **Why did you decide to major in history?**

A: *It was a difficult choice because I was also attracted to government, international relations, and economics. But the study of history allowed me to combine all three, especially by focusing on economic history. What's more, I found several of the professors in the department to be exceptionally knowledgeable and stimulating.*

Show that you have solid, logical reasons for choosing your major. If you can't defend your choice of major, the interviewer will wonder how much thought you've put into choosing a career. You should also be sure that your reasons for choosing your major are compatible with your career choice. For instance, don't say you were an English major because you love literature and writing if you're applying for a position as a banker.

Q: **Was there a course that you found particularly challenging?**

A: *Initially I was completely overwhelmed by the introductory chemistry course that I took last year. No matter how hard I studied, I seemed to be getting nowhere. I failed the first three quizzes. So I tried a new approach. Instead of just studying by myself, I asked a friend who's a chemistry major to help me with my studies. I also began seeking help from the professor after class. And I found that more time spent in the lab was critical. I ended up with a B-plus in the course and thought I achieved a solid understanding of the material. More than that, I learned that tackling a new field of study sometimes requires a new approach, not just hard work, and that the help of others can be crucial!*

The interviewer will want to see how well you respond to difficult situations. Demonstrate that you won't fold in the face of difficulty, and that you're willing to put in the extra effort to meet a challenge.

Q: **Why didn't you participate more in extracurricular activities?**

A: *I wanted to give as much effort as possible to my studies. I came from a high school in a very small town, where I received a lot of A's, but this didn't prepare me very well for college. So I studied very hard. I have, however, found time to explore the city and make new friends, and I do socialize informally on weekends.*

The interviewer may be worried that if you don't have many outside interests, you may eventually suffer from burnout. Employers like candidates who are well-rounded and have interests outside of work. If you didn't participate in formal extracurricular activities in college, you still may want to talk about some of your interests, such as reading or exercising, that you participated in on a more informal level. For instance, you may have a passion for running even if you weren't on the college track team.

Questions for Career Changers

For those of you who've devoted your careers exclusively to one profession or industry, work experience really isn't an issue. You have lots of experience—but none of it relates to your current job objective. No problem! Instead of emphasizing your job history, you'll just have to emphasize the skills you've acquired that apply to the job you're seeking. For example, let's say your career has been in real estate and, in your spare time, you like to run in marathons. Recently you heard about an opening in the sales-and-marketing department at an athletic-shoe manufacturer. What you need to do is emphasize the skills you have that the employer is looking for. Not only do you have strong sales experience, you're familiar with the needs of the company's market, and that's a powerful combination!

Q: **Why do you want to leave your current position?**

A: *I've learned quite a bit about the plastics industry in my current position and am very glad to have had the opportunities I've had at Fiske, Inc. However, I've found that my interests really lie in research and development, which Fiske has recently decided to phase out over the next two years. And that's why I'm so interested in this organization, because, as I understand, Randy Corporation places a great deal of emphasis on R&D, and is also a highly respected leader in the industry.*

The interviewer's foremost concern with career changers will always be why they want to switch careers. Show the interviewer that your decision has been based on careful consideration. Explain why you decided upon this particular position, as well as how the position will allow you to further your natural skills and interests.

Q: **Why would you want to leave an established career at an employment agency for an essentially entry-level position in marketing?**

A: *I've enjoyed my work at the agency and have gained many valuable skills from it. At the same time, however, I feel as if I've stopped growing. I'm no longer challenged by my work. I've thought about this for a long time, and I'm confident that it's time for a change. As for my interest in marketing, last year my teenage children and some of the other neighborhood kids decided to design and sell T-shirts to benefit a local family who'd lost their home to a fire. I pitched in by designing and distributing posters, placing advertisements in local newspapers, and selling shirts outside grocery stores and shopping malls. At first I really didn't give the project a lot of thought, but when I saw the fruits of my labor, I began to get very excited about it. I learned that you can have a great product and a great cause, but if nobody knows about it, you're dead in the water. I finally felt as if I was making a difference—and I was good at it, too. Since then I've taken two introductory marketing courses and am planning to enroll in a part-time degree program this fall. Furthermore, I'll be able to use many of the skills and abilities I've gained at the employment agency in the marketing field. After all, working for an employment agency is marketing—marketing the agency to corporate clients and job seekers, and marketing job seekers to corporate clients.*

The interviewer is trying to determine two things: the candidate's motivation for choosing a new career, and the likelihood that the candidate will be comfortable in a position where he or she will probably have less power and responsibility than in previous jobs. To dispel the interviewer's fears, discuss your reasons for switching careers, and be sure to show that you have a solid understanding of the position and the industry in general. Many candidates expect to start their new careers in a job comparable to the one they held previously. But the truth is that most career changers must start in lower—if not entry-level—positions in their new company to gain basic experience and knowledge of the field.

Questions for Candidates Re-entering the Job Market

There's no doubt about it, if you've been out of the workforce for a while, you're facing some troubling issues. You may be feeling anxious, wondering if you've still got what it takes to make it out there. The key element for you is to make sure all of your skills are up-to-date. If they aren't, you should consider retraining, which might mean learning a new computer program or taking a class at the local college. If your skills are current, not to worry. What you'll need to emphasize is your previous job experience and skills, ways you've kept up-to-date during your leave (reading trade journals, doing freelance work, attending seminars), and the skills you've learned at home that can be transferred to the workplace.

Q: Your resume doesn't list any job experience in the past few years. Why not?

A: *I took five years off to raise my son, Jason, who's now in kindergarten. It was a difficult decision for me, but at the time I decided I wouldn't be able to commit myself 100 percent to my career with such tremendous responsibilities at home. And I didn't think it would be fair to my employer to give any less than my complete and total commitment. I believe it was the right decision for me at the time, but now I feel refreshed and ready to devote myself full-time to my career.*

Whatever the reason for your hiatus, be honest. Discuss the decisions behind your absence, whether they were to stay home and raise a family or to recuperate from a debilitating injury. Tell the interviewer why you're now ready to return to work. Most important, emphasize your eagerness to resume your career.

Q: I see you've been out of work for a while. What difficulties have you had in finding a job that's compatible with your interests?

A: *It's true that I've been out of my field for the last four years, but I've had a number of tempting offers to jump back in. However, I thought it was important to stay home with my new baby and also continue a part-time family business, which I ran out of our home while my husband was completing law school. Now that that's behind us, I'm ready to return to my career in the entertainment industry.*

The real question behind the interviewer's curiosity here is why someone else hasn't taken this candidate off the market. Why isn't the candidate in greater demand? Is he or she being too unrealistic, or perhaps going after random positions? Is there something in the job seeker's past that others have discovered? You'll need to alleviate such concerns by frankly discussing your situation. Be sure to emphasize how you've remained involved in your career during your sabbatical, as well as your eagerness to rejoin the workforce.

Q: Your resume indicates that you've been working for the past two years as a part-time clerk at Reliable Insurance Brokers. How will this experience help you in your banking career?

A: *Reliable was in the process of computerizing its files, and I was hired primarily to check the computerized files for accuracy vis-à-vis the manual files. I recorded premium payments, prepared bank deposits, and sorted payables. Not only did this work help me keep my accounting skills current, I also learned valuable computer skills that will certainly help me become even more efficient and productive in my next position in banking.*

The interviewer may be concerned here that the candidate is simply applying for any available job, rather than for a specific position in a specific field. Explain how your experience relates to the position you're applying for, and discuss any skills you've gained that are transferable to the position and company.

Illegal Interview Questions

Illegal interview questions probe into your private life or personal background. Federal law forbids employers from discriminating against any person on the basis of sex, age, race, national origin, or religion. For instance, an interviewer may not ask you about your age or your date of birth. However, she or he may ask you if you're over eighteen years of age.

If you're asked an illegal question at a job interview, keep in mind that many employers simply don't know what's legal and illegal. One strategy is to try to discover the concerns behind the question and then address them. For instance, if the employer asks you about your plans to have children, he or she may be concerned that you won't be able to fulfill the travel requirements of the position. Sexist? You bet. But it's to your advantage to try to alleviate those concerns.

Try to get to the heart of the issue behind the question by saying something like "I'm not quite sure I understand what you're getting at. Would you please explain to me how this issue is relevant to the position?" Once the interviewer's real concerns are on the table, you can allay those concerns by saying something like "I'm very interested in developing my career. Travel is definitely not a problem for me—in fact, I enjoy it tremendously. Now, let me direct your attention to my experience and expertise in . . ."

Alternatively, you may choose to answer the question or to gracefully point out that the question is illegal and decline to respond. Avoid reacting in a hostile fashion—remember that you can always decide later to decline a job offer.

Any of the following responses are acceptable ways to handle these tricky situations without blowing your chances for a job offer. Choose the response that's most comfortable for you.

Q: **What religion do you practice?**

> *Answer 1: I make it a point not to mix my personal beliefs with my work, if that's what you mean. I assure you that I value my career too much for that.*

> *Answer 2: I'm not quite sure I understand what you're getting at. Would you please explain to me how this issue is relevant to the position?*

> *Answer 3: That question makes me uncomfortable. I'd really rather not answer it.*

Q: How old are you?

Answer 1: *I'm in my fifties and have over thirty years of experience in this industry. My area of expertise is in ...*

Answer 2: *I'm too young to retire, but I'm old enough to know better than to answer a question like that.*

Answer 3: *I'm not quite sure I understand what you're getting at. Would you please explain to me how this issue is relevant to the position?*

Answer 4: *That question makes me uncomfortable. I'd really rather not answer it.*

Q: Are you married?

Answer 1: *No.*

Answer 2: *Yes, I am. But I keep my family life separate from my work life so that I can put all my effort into my job. I'm flexible when it comes to travel and late hours, as my references can confirm.*

Answer 3: *I'm not quite sure I understand what you're getting at. Would you please explain to me how this issue is relevant to the position?*

Answer 4: *That question makes me uncomfortable. I'd really rather not answer it.*

Q: Do you have children?

Answer 1: *No.*

Answer 2: *Yes, I do. But I keep my family life separate from my work life so that I can put all my effort into my job. I'm flexible when it comes to travel and late hours, as my references can confirm.*

Answer 3: *I'm not quite sure I understand what you're getting at. Would you please explain to me how this issue is relevant to the position?*

Answer 4: *That question makes me uncomfortable. I'd really rather not answer it.*

Q: Do you plan to have children?

Answer 1: *No.*

Answer 2: *It's certainly a consideration, but if I do, it won't be for some time. I want to do the best job I can for this company and have no plans to leave just as I begin to make meaningful contributions.*

Answer 3: *I can't answer that right now. But if I ever do decide to have children, I wouldn't let it detract from my work. Becoming a parent is important, but my career is certainly very important to me, too. I plan on putting all of my efforts into this job and this company.*

Answer 4: *I'm not quite sure I understand what you're getting at. Would you please explain to me how this issue is relevant to the position?*

Answer 5: *That question makes me uncomfortable. I'd really rather not answer it.*

Part III

After the Job Interview

CHAPTER 6
CLINCHING THE DEAL

You've made it through the toughest part—but now what? First, breathe a sigh of relief! Then, as soon as you've left the interview site, write down your thoughts about the interview while they're still fresh in your mind. Ask yourself these key questions:

- What does the position entail?
- What do you like and dislike about the position and the company?
- Did you make any mistakes or have trouble answering any of the questions?
- Did you feel you were well prepared?
- If not, what could you do to improve your performance in the future?

Carefully consider all of these questions; if you find that your performance was lacking, work to improve it.

Be sure to record the name and title of the person you interviewed with, as well as the names and titles of anyone else you may have met. Ideally, you'll have collected their business cards. Don't forget to write down what the next agreed-upon step will be. Will the recruiter contact you? How soon?

Writing Your Follow-Up Letter

It's fair to say that follow-up letters won't necessarily help you secure the job, but not sending one will most certainly hurt your chances. You should write a follow-up letter immediately after each interview you have, ideally within twenty-four hours. The letter should be brief (no more than a page) and personalized. In your letter you should be sure to:

- Express your appreciation for the opportunity to interview with the recruiter.
- Express your continued enthusiasm about the position and the company.
- Recap your strengths, being careful to relate them to the requirements of the job and the company.
- Request to meet again.

The following is an example of a good follow-up letter:

SAMPLE FOLLOW-UP LETTER

178 N. Green Street
Chicago, IL 60657
(312) 555-5555
(312) 555-5050

October 2, 2005

Pat Cummings
Personnel Manager
Any Corporation
1140 State Street
Chicago, IL 60601

Dear Ms. Cummings:

It was a pleasure meeting with you yesterday regarding the research-assistant position. I enjoyed learning more about the opportunity and about Any Corporation.

The position is exciting and seems to encompass a diversity of responsibilities. I believe that with my experience and skills, I'm qualified to make a valuable contribution to your organization.

Should you require additional information, please don't hesitate to contact me at either telephone number listed above or at (312) 444-4444. I look forward to hearing from you.

Sincerely,

Chris Smith

Allow the interviewer five to ten business days to contact you after receiving your letter. If you still haven't heard anything after that time, you should follow up with a phone call. Express your continued interest in the firm and the position, and inquire as to whether or not a decision has been made or when you'll be notified.

In the meantime it's important to keep your candidacy fresh in the interviewer's mind. Send work that intrigued the interviewer (for example, brochures or writing samples). If the conversation during the interview provided any possibilities for follow-up, such as reading an article or book, drop a note to the interviewer mentioning how much you learned from the piece. Or if you discovered during the interview that you share common interests with the interviewer, such as sailing or rock climbing, consider sending the person a great article you just found on the topic. Not only will this ensure that you don't get "lost in the shuffle," but it will help you establish a sense of camaraderie with the interviewer. Though this technique won't guarantee you the position, it certainly can't hurt if it gets the interviewer in your corner!

Taking the Next Step

Don't be discouraged if you don't receive an immediate response from an employer—most companies interview many applicants before making a final decision. Take advantage of this time to contact other firms, and to schedule more interviews, so that if a rejection does come, you have other options open. Continuing to job-hunt and to interview will have been a good idea even if you end up receiving the job offer. Ultimately, you may have a number of opportunities to choose from, and you'll be in a better position to negotiate terms.

If you place too much importance on a single interview, not only are you bound to be unduly disappointed if the offer doesn't come through, you'll be wasting valuable time and energy. So keep plugging away!

Handling Rejection

Rejection is inevitable, and it's bound to happen to you just as it happens to all other job hunters. The key is to be prepared for it and not to take it personally.

One way you can turn rejection around is by contacting each person who sends you a rejection letter. Thank your contact for considering you for the position and request that he or she keep you in mind for future openings. If you feel comfortable, you may want to ask the person for suggestions to help you improve your chances of getting a job in that industry or for the names of people who might be looking for someone with your skills. You may want to say something like "What would you do in my situation? Whom would you call?"

Two cautions are in order: First, don't ask employers to tell you why they didn't hire you. Not only will this place a recruiter in a very awkward position, you'll probably get a very negative reaction. Second, keep in mind that if you contact employers solely for impartial feedback, not everyone will be willing to talk to you.

A well-written thank-you note, mailed within one or two days of receiving notice of rejection, makes a positive statement. When Danny P. was turned down for a position as a publicity director, he quickly wrote his interviewer a letter that expressed his disappointment at not being offered the job, but also his thanks for the company's consideration of his qualifications. The interviewer was so impressed by Danny's initiative, she provided him several contact names to assist in his continued search.

In your letter emphasize an ongoing interest in being considered for future openings. Also, be very careful to use an upbeat tone. Although you may be disappointed, you don't want to put the employer on the defensive or imply that you don't respect his or her decision. Above all, don't give up! Stay positive and motivated, and learn from the process. Success could be right around the corner!

Strategies for Later Interviews

When filling professional career positions, few companies will make a job offer after only one interview. Usually, the purpose of the first interview is to narrow the field of applicants to a small number of very promising candidates. During the first meeting, then, the ideal strategy is to stand out from a large field of competitors in a positive way. The best way to do this is to emphasize subtly one or two of your key strengths as much as possible throughout the interview.

During later interviews the competition for the position will drop off, and employers will tend to look not for strengths, but for weaknesses. At this point you should focus on presenting yourself as a well-balanced choice for the position. Listen carefully to the interviewer's questions so you can determine his or her underlying concerns and try to dispel them. On the other hand, if later interviews are primarily with people who are in a position to veto your hiring, but not to push it forward, you should focus primarily on building rapport as opposed to reiterating and developing your key strengths.

Another way in which second interviews differ from first interviews is that the questions become much more specific and technical. The company must now test the depth of your knowledge of the field, including how well you're able to apply your education and past work experience to the job at hand. At this stage the interviewer isn't a recruiter; you may have one or more interviewers, each of whom has a job related to the one you're applying for. Typically these interviewers will represent your potential boss, professional peer group, or executives who oversee the work group.

The second round of interviews can last one to two days, during which you might meet with as few as several people or as many as fifteen or more over the course of the visit. These interviews typically last longer than initial interviews. For many executive positions you may also have meetings around breakfast, lunch, or dinner. In all cases, remember—you're still in an interview. You may be having a dinner conversation about a recent topic of concern to the industry as a whole—be ready with opinions, and be equally ready to listen and to ask good questions. You may be asked to demonstrate how you'd go about performing some aspect of the job; be ready in case you're presented with a tough problem and asked to tackle it as though you'd already started your first day on the job. Use what you said in the screening interview as an outline (It's gotten you this far!) but be prepared to build on this outline in meaningful ways with more developed details, examples, and ideas.

Usually you can count on attending at least two interviews for most professional positions, or three for high-level positions, though some firms, such as some professional partnerships, are famous for conducting a minimum of six interviews for all professional positions. Though you should be more relaxed as you return for subsequent interviews, the pressure will still be on. The more prepared you are, the better.

CHAPTER 7
THE ART OF NEGOTIATION

In today's tough economy one of the most nerve-racking steps on the trail to a new job is near the end of the path: deciding whether or not to accept an offer. On the one hand, if you've been in the job market for some time, your instinct may scream, "I'll take it, I'll take it," before the last syllables of the offer are out of the recruiter's mouth. On the other, you may also be worrying that the salary won't even cover the cost of all those stamps you've used to send out resumes and cover letters over the past few months.

Faced with these conflicting emotions, many job seekers can make unnecessary, costly mistakes during this final, vitally important stage. Far too many people sell themselves short without even exploring their options. Others have wildly unrealistic expectations of the level of compensation they should expect. Still others get so wrapped up in money questions they forget to consider any other issues—a big mistake.

Important Factors to Consider
If you're going to consider a job offer seriously, be confident that this is a job you really want. If you're just graduating, is the job in the field you'd like to pursue? Are you willing to live and work in the area in question? Would you enjoy the work schedule? The way of life?

Whether or not a job will help your career progress is ultimately a much more important question than what your starting salary will be. In some organizations you may be given a lot of responsibility right away but then find your upward progress blocked. Make sure you know if there are opportunities for advancement. Ask about performance reviews: how often are they conducted?

Other information you should have in order to make a sound decision includes:

- Start date
- Job title and associated responsibilities
- Salary, overtime, and compensation
- Bonus structure
- Tuition reimbursement
- Vacation and parental-leave policy
- Life-, medical-, and dental-insurance coverage
- Pension plan
- Travel requirements

Ideally, these issues will have been covered during the course of the interview process or at the time the job offer is made. But if you're unsure of any of this information, don't assume that the specifics will be to your satisfaction. Contact the personnel representative or recruiter and confirm all-important details.

Work Environment

Another important factor to consider is the kind of environment you'll be working in. Is the company's atmosphere comfortable, challenging, and exciting? Consider specifics, including office or workstation setting, privacy, proximity to other staff, amount of space, noise level, and lighting. How much interaction occurs between coworkers? Some organizations strongly encourage teamwork and dialogue among staff, whereas others prefer to emphasize individual accomplishment. Which approach works better for you? Remember: if you don't like the work environment before you accept the job, you probably won't like it as an employee.

Salary and Benefits

Money may seem like the biggest criterion in accepting a job, but it can often cloud the decision-making process. Don't accept a job that you're not enthusiastic about simply because the starting salary is a few thousand dollars higher than what you're currently making. It's probably more important to find a job that lets you do something you enjoy. Ask yourself whether the position presents a career path with upward movement and long-range income potential.

Benefits can make a big difference in your compensation package, so don't overlook them! Perhaps the most important benefit to consider is health insurance. With health-insurance costs skyrocketing, you should be sure to find out if the company covers these costs in full. If the company, like many others, pays only a percentage of these costs, make certain that you can afford to pay the difference out of your own pocket.

And what about life, dental, and disability insurance? Does the company have a bonus structure or profit-sharing plan? These things can contribute significantly to your salary. Is there a pension plan? How many vacation days or sick days will you get? You should consider all of these factors carefully.

If you plan to continue your education, it's important to find out if the organization will pay for your tuition and if the employer will give you time to attend classes. Some organizations offer tuition incentives but require so much overtime that it's very difficult to take advantage of the benefit.

Do Your Homework

Supplement the information that the organization provides by searching journals and newspapers for articles about the company and, if possible, by talking to current employees. Try to get objective comments—not, for instance, information from someone who was recently fired by the company. Alumni of your college or university who hold similar positions or are employed by the same organization may be an excellent source of information.

Negotiating the Offer

The prospect of negotiating salary and benefits strikes fear into the hearts of many job seekers young and old. But handling the inevitable money questions doesn't have to be difficult. And the more you think about them in advance, the easier they'll be for you to answer. Let's go through the process step by step.

First, the basics. Never try to negotiate salary or benefits until after you've gotten an offer. Try it, and you'll look as if you care more about money than about putting your skills to work for the company. Your goals at an interview are simple: (1) prove to the recruiter that you're well-suited to the job as you understand it, and (2) make sure that you feel comfortable with the prospect of performing the job and working in the environment the company offers.

If you've been offered a position, congratulations! The hard part is over. If you feel uncomfortable about negotiating for a salary, relax. The tables are now turned in your favor. Think about it—you've already gotten what you want. Until you say yes to the offer, the burden is on the recruiter. He or she has put a lot of time and effort into finding the right candidate and has decided that you are that person. If you say no, the recruiter will have wasted a lot of energy and may have to go back to square one to find another candidate.

So don't worry about the recruiter's withdrawing his or her handshake and showing you the door if you dare to ask if the company's offer is flexible. The worst case might be that the employer tells you your salary is set by company policy and there's really no room to negotiate. But the recruiter may just as likely tell you he or she can't give you an immediate answer and will have to get back to you.

The most important thing to remember about salary negotiations is that most salaries are negotiable. That doesn't mean that you name a figure and the employer either matches it or doesn't. It means that you're ready to listen to what the recruiter has to offer, and give it consideration. To succeed in negotiation, both parties have to reach an agreement with which both are happy. If you somehow succeed at winning yourself a bigger paycheck but antagonize your future boss in doing so, trouble lies ahead. If, on the other hand, you set realistic expectations and realize that you may not get everything you want, you'll probably do just fine.

Just how do you know how much you should expect? The answer is the same as in every other step of your job search: do your homework. Contact your professional association or read the trade journals for your industry. Call employment agencies to find out salaries of jobs listed with them; read the newspaper help-wanted ads. Alumni of your college or university in similar positions (or employed by the same organization) may also be an excellent source of information. Doing this research will give you an idea of the general salary level you can realistically expect.

Setting realistic expectations is especially important for the entry-level job seeker or recent graduate. If you don't have a lot of professional experience, you don't leave the recruiter with much hard evidence on which to base a decision. Instead, you're asking him or her to take a leap of faith based on potential that you've demonstrated in classes, internships, volunteer work, or extracurricular activities. Without a track record of professional experience, your arsenal is missing a powerful weapon. This is why the marketplace often determines entry-level salaries. That leaves you very little leverage with which to negotiate. Even so, that doesn't mean you can't give it a try.

On the other hand, if you have some experience under your belt and are looking for a midlevel or executive-level position, your negotiating power might be much greater. For a lucky (or unlucky) few at the top of the heap, salary and benefit negotiations can be as complex and painstakingly slow as a bill passing through Congress. If you're like most people, you're not in that group. Whatever your level of experience, your task is to try to figure out just how high the employer is likely to go.

If, after listening politely to the specifics of the offer, you're left hoping for a higher salary, greater health coverage, or something else, it's okay to say so (calmly). Find out if the offer is firm. If it seems there may be some room to negotiate, make sure you have a specific figure in mind, because if the recruiter does have the freedom to barter, he or she will probably ask you point-blank to supply a figure that would satisfy you.

When you're asked that question, rule number one is as follows: don't tip your hand by giving the interviewer a concrete number for which you're willing to settle. You don't want to take yourself out of the running by naming a figure that's absurdly optimistic, and you certainly don't want to risk naming a figure that's lower than what the employer is ready to offer. Instead of naming your price, say something like, "Based on my experience and skills, and the demands of the position, I'd expect to earn an appropriate figure. Can you give me some idea what kind of range you have in mind?"

If you're pressed about salary requirements during an interview and you feel you must name a figure, give a salary range instead of your most recent salary. And don't forget to add in the value of your insurance, pension, or any other benefits you had, says Rebecca Jesperson Anthony and Gerald Roe, career specialists at the University of Iowa.

Naming a salary range gives you a chance to hook on to a figure that's also in the range the company has in mind. In fact, many companies base their offers on sliding salary scales. Therefore, if you name a range of, say, $25,000 to $30,000, it just may be that the company was considering a range of $22,000 to $28,000. In this case, you'll be more likely to receive an offer in the middle to upper end of your range. Of course, your experience and qualifications also play a part here. If you're just starting out and have little experience, the recruiter may be more likely to stick toward the lower end of the scale.

A few words about projecting the right attitude when discussing money— try not to reveal what you're thinking. Even if the salary offer seems barely above poverty level, it wouldn't be wise to inform the recruiter of that fact. Similarly, if the offer is much higher than you expected, doing cartwheels around the room probably wouldn't be appropriate, either.

In all seriousness, though your appearance and demeanor are important throughout your career, they are especially important at the interview and offer stage. If you want to be a professional, start right away by acting like one.

Some final notes. The point of your job search isn't salary negotiation; it's finding a job that you'll be happy with, that you'll grow with, and that will allow you to be yourself. If your starting salary isn't the one you dreamed about, but the job presents the right opportunity, think about the possibility of commanding a higher salary once you've had a chance to make yourself invaluable to the organization.

On the other hand, if the salary or benefits fall far short of your realistic expectations, despite all your efforts to negotiate, nothing says you have to take the job. Don't make the mistake of accepting a position with which you're fundamentally unhappy. Trust your instincts—if you're dissatisfied with the employer before your start date, don't bet that the situation will improve after you start.

Part IV

Sample Job Interviews

CHAPTER 8

ACCOUNTING AND FINANCE

Accounts Payable Clerk

Q: **What are your qualifications for this position?**

A: *I have three years' experience as an accounts payable clerk, processing accounts payable in a high-volume environment, as well as working knowledge of data processing.*

Most accounts payable positions require at least one year of experience. You should also be familiar with the latest accounting software.

Q: **Tell me about an average working day. In detail, describe your responsibilities and how you post invoices to the accounting system.**

A: *I start by opening and sorting the prior day's mail. I match the incoming vendor invoices with the purchase orders and packing slips. I then verify the pricing against the purchase order for propriety, test the extensions, and test for invoice accuracy. Then, choosing the correct general-ledger account, I post the transactions to the accounting system. In addition, I'm responsible for weekly computerized check runs, all manual check disbursements, and I summarize all journal entries and post them to the general ledger.*

The interviewer is trying to determine the level of your experience and actual understanding of the functions you presently perform. Be specific, and list your duties. Give examples when possible.

Q: **How would you handle the following situation: unusual bills are received, and though a purchase order is referenced, the money due exceeds the amount authorized?**

First-time Job Seekers: Any kind of bookkeeping, data entry, or general office experience will be of great value. Offer a firm handshake and make direct eye contact. Don't be shy about mentioning specific achievements and successes.

A: *I'd ask the person who originated the purchase order to explain the cost overage and why the invoice should be paid as submitted. I'd then request an authorization from the appropriate manager to exceed the amount authorized. I would also advise the vendor of the discrepancy and explain that invoices in excess of the purchase-order amounts must be approved in writing before any additional work is done or quantities are billed.*

This is a common situation with a fairly straightforward and universal solution. The questioner is probing the candidate's problem-solving skills, but more important, his or her ability to interact with coworkers and valued customers.

Q: What do you like most and least about doing this kind of work?

A: *It's a steady and consistent job, and I've always enjoyed working with numbers. I like making things balance and tie out both on a daily basis and at the end of the month. The pressure at month's end can be draining, but the satisfaction of contributing to the department is well worth the added work.*

The interviewer is probing the candidate's personality and compatibility with the job. Is the candidate being straightforward or trying to give the "expected" answers? In most smaller companies this position is not the first step to the corner office. It's a job filled by people who like numbers, can handle some pressure, and work well toward "team" goals. Because of this you'll want to portray yourself as a positive person who'll fit in with the rest of the staff.

Q: How long would it take you to post an average daily batch?

A: *I usually post the bills once or twice a week. Sometimes it takes days to prepare a batch by verifying POs, checking with the receiving department and getting approvals for cost overrides. But I can usually post a week's worth of payables in a day.*

The interviewer wants to determine the candidate's work pace and see if his or her experience is compatible with the position available.

Q: What do you think are the most important aspects of this job?

A: *Attention to detail is clearly the most important part of any job in accounting. Meeting deadlines and schedules is important, as well as being able to interact effectively with others in the company.*

Career Changers: Stress past achievements and freely discuss your desire to move into the accounting field. Give an example of your ability to learn new things. If your career has been banking, you may find it difficult to make this switch, as people with banking experience typically require more retraining.

This question merits some careful thought and discussion. The employer is trying to determine the nature of the candidate's work ethic, and the effort that he or she willingly expends to get the job done accurately and effectively. It's extremely important that an applicant have the type of personality that will fit in at the company.

Q: **Describe in detail the process you're familiar with when preparing and running a batch of checks.**

A: *After accessing the accounts payable report module of the accounting system and selecting the open-invoice report, I prepare a list of all invoices currently due. My supervisor selects the vendors that will be paid on this check run and returns the list to me. I then key the items to be paid into the accounts payable system and verify the totals per the batch run against my manual total. If the two match, I print the checks, match them up with the corresponding invoices and POs, and present them for signature.*

This question gets to the basic "mechanics" of an accounting position: what do you do and how do you do it? The successful applicant will demonstrate a working knowledge of all the basics, attention to detail, and a fundamental understanding of the process.

Q: **What type of computerized systems are you familiar with?**

A: *I'm familiar with PCs and local-area network systems, as well as IBM minis like the '36 or the AS/400. I've worked with RealWorld, Solomon, Macola, Great Plains, and MAS90.*

The interviewer is trying to determine the complexity of the accounting packages with which the candidate has experience. Since most modern systems are essentially quite similar, the interviewer is mainly trying to ensure that there won't be a lengthy training period for a new employee. If you're not familiar with the system that the employer uses, emphasize your enthusiasm and your ability to learn new programs quickly.

Q: **Have you ever worked with any of the major spreadsheet programs? If so, describe how and why it was used.**

Experienced Professionals: You've obviously done this work before. Be straightforward and confident—try to put all your experience on the table with being overly aggressive. Stress your experience with major customer accounts and the high volume of work you're able to handle. Your extensive customer contact will also be very attractive to employers.

A: *I'm proficient in Excel. I've used it extensively to help with bank reconciliation, and to prepare the daily cash sheet, listing both cash receipts and disbursements, which is then submitted to senior management to help them make their operating decisions.*

The interviewer will try to determine all the skills that you might bring to the company. Have you used spreadsheets to assist in routine daily work? Have you developed something that led to a major increase in productivity?

Q: Do you prefer to work alone or in a group?

A: *Half of my job requires that I interact with vendors and fellow employees. The rest of the time I spend working on individual projects. I really don't have a preference, as long as this job provides a challenge and the chance to vary my working situation.*

The interviewer is interested here in the personality of the applicant. The "department team" needs someone with a balanced approach. The stereotypical green-eyed grouch sitting in the corner balancing the books won't work in today's fast-paced business world; however, the water cooler "hang about" won't fill the bill either.

Q: Why do you want to leave your present position?

A: *I'm looking for a chance to assume more responsibility and to increase my earning potential. My present employer is experiencing a downsizing. As I was the last person hired in the department, I'll most likely be the first to go.*

Since this is basically a clerical position, if you're an experienced A/P person, you should say that you're looking for more money or a positive change of scenery. This is also the type of question that will help the interviewer get a feel for your personality. Will you criticize your employer? If so, this will reflect poorly on your candidacy. You should always try to be straightforward and diplomatic in your job interviews.

Candidates Re-entering the Workforce: Emphasize your desire to work. Stress your ability to work with numbers, and don't be bashful about discussing prior jobs. Make sure you're up-to-date on the latest accounting software.

Accounts Receivable/
Cash Receipts Clerk

Q: **What are your qualifications for this position?**

A: *I have three years' experience in an accounts-receivable position at a manufacturing company. We have approximately 1,000 customers and receive about 100 checks a day. I also have an extensive working knowledge of the data-processing function, as I do order entry and post cash at my present position.*

Most accounts-receivable positions require at least one year of experience. You should also be familiar with the latest accounting software.

Q: **Tell me about an average working day. In detail, describe your responsibilities and how you post transactions into the accounting system.**

A: *I start by opening and sorting the day's mail. I then match the checks received against the customers' open-invoice file, verify the accuracy, note any variances, and post it to the computerized A/R system. This is done by preparing a batch, approximately twenty-five checks at a time, calculating a manual total, then doing the data entry into the system, running the edits, and verifying the total of the batch entered against the one I calculated. Once the two agree, I update the system. I am also responsible for making the bank deposits. Generally, these are done two to three times per week. I prepare all the month-end customer statements, run the month-end aged trial balance A/R agings, and perform the sales analyses.*

The interviewer is trying to determine the candidate's level of experience and understanding of the functions he or she presently performs. Be specific, and list your duties. Give examples where possible.

First-time Job Seekers: Any kind of bookkeeping, data entry, or general office experience will be of great value. Offer a firm handshake and make direct eye contact. Don't be shy about mentioning specific achievements and successes.

Q: **Have you ever performed the order-entry function, billing function, or customer-service function?**

A: *Yes. In fact, my first job out of high school was an order-entry position. After twelve months I was promoted to customer service. I believe that this experience helps me do a better job in accounts receivable, since I'm able to see the whole picture. When problems arise, I'm usually able to solve them promptly on my own.*

The interviewer is looking for a broader knowledge of the process derived from the candidate's familiarity with data entry, products, and/or pricing. Discuss in detail any experience you may have in these areas, and emphasize your adaptability and problem-solving skills.

Q: **How would you handle the following situation: an important, regular customer overpays an open invoice.**

A: *I'd first check to see if the customer had more than one customer-account number. If not, I'd check with the collections or sales departments to find out if the customer was prepaying for an order. If not, I'd call the customer about the overpayment, or duplicate payment, advising that we would apply it to the account, to be used against other open invoices. If crediting the account was not acceptable, I'd offer to refund the overpayment if it was a large amount.*

This is a common situation with a fairly straightforward and universal solution. The questioner is probing the candidate's problem-solving skills, but more importantly, his or her ability to interact with valued customers.

Q: **What do you like most and least about doing this kind of work?**

A: *I have always enjoyed working with numbers. I like making things balance as well as dealing with customers in order to effect problem resolution. I'm very detail oriented and like to stay busy. The pressure at month's end can be draining, but the satisfaction of contributing to the department is well worth the added work. The thing I like least is photocopying all the checks. In fact, I recently suggested to my supervisor that we set up a lock box at our bank. This would eliminate having to make copies, but more important, would speed up the collection of money.*

Career Changers: Stress past achievements and freely discuss your desire to move into the accounting field. Give an example of your ability to learn new things. If your career has been banking, you may find it difficult to make this switch, as people with banking experience typically require more retraining.

The interviewer is probing the candidate's personality and compatibility with the job. Is the candidate being straightforward or trying to give the "expected" answers? These jobs are filled by people who like numbers, can handle some pressure, and work well toward "team" goals. Because of this, you'll want to portray yourself as a positive person who'll fit in with the rest of the staff.

Q: How long would it take you to post an average daily batch?

A: *As I mentioned earlier, we receive about 100 checks a day. From the time the envelopes are opened, researched for account numbers, invoice, or credit number to actual posting, about six hours. It probably takes another half hour to an hour to photocopy all the checks and prepare the bank deposit for delivery to the bank.*

The interviewer wants to determine the candidate's work pace to see if his or her experience is compatible with the position.

Q: What do you think are the most important aspects of this job?

A: *Attention to detail is clearly the most important part of any job in accounting. Meeting deadlines and schedules is important as well.*

This question merits some careful thought and discussion. The employer is trying to determine the nature of the candidate's work ethic. Do you have the type of personality that will fit in with the company?

Q: What type of computerized systems are you familiar with?

A: *I'm familiar with PCs and local-area network systems, as well as IBM minis like the '36 or the AS/400. I've worked with RealWorld, Solomon, Macola, Great Plains, and MAS90.*

The interviewer is trying to determine the candidate's experience with specific accounting packages. Since most modern systems are essentially quite similar, the interviewer is mainly trying to ensure there won't be a lengthy training period for a new employee. If you're not familiar with the system the employer uses, emphasize your enthusiasm and ability to learn new programs quickly.

Experienced Professionals: You've obviously done this work before. Be straightforward and confident—try to put all your experience on the table with being overly aggressive. Stress your experience with major customer accounts and the high volume of work you're able to handle. Your extensive customer contact will also be very attractive to employers.

Q: **What are you ideally looking for in this company and job?**

A: *I'm looking for a steady job with a solid company. I want to become part of a team and to enjoy working with people in the accounting department and other departments in the company.*

Employers want to fill these positions with serious people who are likely to remain for an extended period. In small to midsized companies the accounts-receivable position is a crucial one that requires a unique type of personality and set of skills.

Candidates Re-entering the Workforce: Emphasize your desire to work. Stress your ability to work with numbers, and don't be bashful about discussing prior jobs.

Actuarial Analyst

Q: **Describe your knowledge and level of expertise as it relates to computer systems and software.**

A: *I'm PC literate and fluent in many of the popular programming languages. I develop spreadsheets using Excel. I'm also capable of manipulating data and can do routine customizing of software.*

The interviewer is trying to assess what software the candidate uses and for what purposes. In addition to naming specific applications, you should discuss your level of expertise or comfort with those applications.

Q: **Describe your knowledge of, or expertise with, the valuation process and, specifically, the role you play in such projects.**

A: *I do the data collection, benefits calculations, and statements. I also run complete valuations, with the exception of preparing reports. Typically, my work is reviewed or checked by a supervisor.*

This question allows the interviewer to gauge how thorough the candidate's knowledge is of the valuation process, and how active he or she is in pension consulting. Be prepared to discuss such matters in detail.

Q: **What other kinds of actuarial projects do you participate in?**

A: *Although valuations are my main responsibility, I participate in other projects involving plan terminations and nondiscrimination testing. I'm also developing expert knowledge in FASB accounting regulations.*

The interviewer is trying to evaluate the breadth of the candidate's actuarial exposure and his or her knowledge beyond core valuations. This response demonstrates that the candidate is developing beyond a narrow actuarial focus.

First-time Job Seekers: The best advice for you is to prepare, prepare, prepare. You must have knowledge of the company you're interviewing with, what it does, and what areas interest you. Don't make the interviewer struggle to define your employment objectives. If you can't articulate why you're interviewing with a particular company, you're not prepared to take the interview.

Q: **Do you participate in other specialized projects? If so, describe them.**

A: *Yes. I have experience with asset/liability modeling, some union negotiations, and early-retirement windows. In addition, I've sat in on a few plan-design discussions with senior actuaries.*

This answer demonstrates the breadth of the candidate's experience beyond routine actuarial issues. The comment about plan design is good because it demonstrates rudimentary exposure to more strategic-oriented issues.

Q: **Describe your exam progress to date and your intentions regarding enrollment and fellowship designations.**

A: *I've completed ninety credits, having failed two sittings so far. My passing scores have ranged between six and eight. I plan to attain ASA within the next two years and will pursue enrollment. I'm currently undecided about FSA.*

The interviewer will want to gauge your rate of progress and success rate in passing (that is, your ability to work and pass exams). This response indicates ambition and goal orientation in terms of timing for ASA. It also illustrates the candidate's honesty with respect to uncertainty about FSA. Such information is important to know—particularly if the position or career path requires minimum credentials.

Q: **Generally, how do you acquire your professional knowledge, beyond the academic experience of exam sitting?**

A: *Most of my training is on the job, through participation on project teams. I work in a team environment that uses a full-circle feedback process. I also love to read any professional material I can get my hands on.*

This answer demonstrates the candidate's ability to work with others and to develop in a relatively unstructured environment. Similarly, you'll want to convey a "team orientation," a natural thirst for knowledge, and a desire for self-improvement.

Career Changers: Make sure you have basic knowledge of the company you're interviewing with, what it does, and what areas interest you. Equally important, you must think through what your existing knowledge and skills sets are and how they can be "transferred" to the new job. Thoroughly research a new industry by reading, conducting informational interviews, and so on.

Q: **What kinds of skills and knowledge do you hope to acquire if you join us?**

A: *I want to learn FAS106 accounting and develop expertise in plan-design issues. If possible, I'd like to broaden my exposure to include group and managed-care projects.*

You should demonstrate a breadth of interest. This is important if the firm's culture promotes generalist- over specialist-type development.

Q: **Have you participated in any marketing-related activities? In general, how do you feel about marketing and business-development responsibilities?**

A: *Yes, I've participated in marketing-related activities, but so far it's been purely of a support nature. I participate on proposal teams, and on occasion I attend new-business presentations as an observer.*

This answer demonstrates the candidate's progress in building employer confidence. He or she is a relatively inexperienced individual who's been exposed to such sophisticated activities as marketing and client interactions.

Q: **Describe to me what client service means to you and how you promote this activity on the job.**

A: *To me, client service means listening to, and understanding, the client. It also means delivering what the client needs on time and making sure the work is right. I do this by trying to meet all my deadlines. I also try to anticipate my clients' needs and to give more than is requested.*

The interviewer isn't looking for a canned response here but is trying to elicit a more realistic answer that demonstrates an understanding of the importance of client servicing, and of the candidate's role in helping an employer achieve this goal. This answer, particularly in its emphasis on anticipating a client's interest, is excellent and demonstrates initiative.

Q: **Describe your level of responsibility in your current job.**

Experienced Professional: Although it's important to demonstrate what you know and can do, it's equally important to articulate goals toward furthering your professional development. Spend sometime assessing your strengths, weaknesses, goals, and ambitions. Do a hard, honest, thorough "balance sheet" analysis of your life's experiences and come to the interview with a purpose in mind.

A: *I have accountability for managing to completion that portion of a project assigned to me. On occasion a junior analyst supports me and I check that person's work. I've also assumed an informal responsibility for training new staff about our valuation system.*

This response demonstrates the candidate's growing responsibility and what, specifically, he or she is entrusted to do. Training is excellent exposure, and if you have some, definitely comment on it. It demonstrates not only your mastery of the work but your ability to impart knowledge to others.

Q: Describe the kind of environment you function best in. What kinds of cultural qualities motivate you?

A: *I like a cooperative environment, where teamwork is encouraged, and one that's flexible enough to permit me latitude in directing my own career development. I also want an environment that supports risk taking, which means having a reasonable tolerance for mistakes—provided, of course, that a mistake is the product of experimentation and not negligence.*

All candidates are faced with two key questions when evaluating a job. First, is it the kind of work they can enjoy and grow with? More important, however, is there a cultural fit or "marriage"? "Cultural fit" is the "soil" that promotes or retards growth, and this question helps the interviewer evaluate the efficacy of hiring a particular candidate.

Q: What are you passionate about?

A: *That's an interesting question. I guess I'd have to say that I'm passionate about racquetball. I learned the sport about five years ago, and I've been playing ever since. Though it's sometimes difficult to fit it into my busy schedule, I try to play at least three times a week. I find it's not only a lot of fun, it helps me let off a little steam.*

This response, aimed at discovering the candidate's interests, provides the interviewer with some deeper insight into the candidate's dedication to a cause

Candidates Re-entering the Workforce: Have confidence in your worth! Don't apologize or act defensively about a career hiatus. Employers today are more likely to understand an individual's decision to leave the workforce for a time. Explain how you've remained productive while you were away by taking courses, keeping up on professional developments, maintaining professional contacts, developing a skill or knowledge you didn't have when you left the workforce. It doesn't matter precisely how you've been productive as long as you've done something that will be perceived as having professional value.

or principle. There is, of course, no right answer. However, you shouldn't say something like, "I'm not really sure. I mean, I like golf and theater, but I've never thought of these as passions. I don't know what I'm passionate about," which demonstrates that the individual is either not in touch with him- or herself or simply doesn't get excited about anything, which may translate into lackluster performance on the job.

Q: **What motivates you to excel at what you do?**

A: *Obviously, I must have an interest in what I'm doing. With this as a given, I excel in problem-solving situations that require a lot of creativity. I get real satisfaction out of knowing my involvement in something has made a difference.*

The interviewer wants to evaluate whether the candidate and the job are suited to one another. Your answer should touch upon personal qualities that mesh well with the position you're seeking. For example, if you were applying for a repetitive job, such as a drill-press operator or an assembly-line worker, this wouldn't be a good answer.

Q: **Why do you want this job?**

A: *I want to work for a company that has, as a core capability, pension-plan design. This is the profession I'm dedicating myself to. Your company is a leader and offers one of the most state-of-the-art environments in the business. It's clear to me that I can learn and grow here and reach a potential not possible at my current company.*

This is a question that you must be prepared to answer. First, it cuts to the chase about why you're sitting in front of the interviewer and forces a direct response to a question your potential employer must answer—that is, "Why should I hire this person?" Second, it permits the interviewer to evaluate your ability to "sell yourself." Spend some time before the interview thinking about this question—your answer could make or break your candidacy.

Banking Officer

Q: **Why are you interested in banking?**

A: *I'm interested in banking because the role of bankers is expanding and is much more exciting than it used to be. Bankers are responsible for a lot more than just bringing in loans; they are now relationship managers. Their role is to ensure that their customers can come to them for just about any financing need, and they line up the specialists within the bank for whatever service is needed.*

This answer demonstrates that the candidate is well tuned in to recent changes in the banking industry, now that banks, under deregulation, are allowed to provide a wide array of services formerly restricted to investment firms. Because local banks can now provide a full range of services, the role of relationship manager has evolved. Banking professionals often rotate among the specialty departments (e.g., trust services, international, real estate) and among banking-officer positions, where they are primarily in charge of client management. This question may not always be asked, but it's always foremost in an interviewer's mind. Here the candidate demonstrates that he or she is knowledgeable about how banking has changed and how officers are adopting a more finance-generalist approach. With one answer the candidate has effectively addressed several potential questions.

Q: **And why are you interested in our bank specifically?**

A: *I like your association with a larger national bank, despite the fact that you operate under a regional name here. One of your AVPs I spoke with explained that two transactions she managed recently were actually booked at the parent bank, which has been number one in loan syndications for years and is well-known for agented deals and the high-yield market. The advantage of that relationship for clients is one-stop shopping. If the parent bank is better set up for a certain type of transaction, you can move the business up there. It seems to me that most banks are more segmented; they don't share business back and forth the way you do.*

Banks have different specialties as well as affiliations with other banks. This answer is strong for two reasons: it establishes the candidate's genuine interest by indicating that he or she has taken time to talk to insiders; and it establishes the reason this candidate is interested in this specific bank—because of its strength in syndications. The candidate's answer thus demonstrates to the interviewer that a job offer will likely be matched by a job acceptance, even if the candidate has several other options.

Q: **Tell me about your early career development in banking.**

A: *I'd talked to several alumni from my college who'd gone through typical management-associate or officer-development programs at banks. These people generally had strong accounting skills, as I do. Following their advice, I decided to concentrate my studies in accounting, then do rotations in various departments and learn banking from the ground up. What appealed to me about this approach was that while I waited to decide on a specialization, I was using both my finance and my accounting skills. I actually found several departments of interest to me, and I went into trust services initially. I'm looking at your bank now because I want the best bank in my specialization, which is capital markets.*

Rotational training experience among departments is critical, because it indicates that the candidate has knowledge of the full range of banking-service possibilities. As relationship managers, banking officers often have to cross-sell a bank's many services. Most people who climb up the banking-system ladder have participated in a rotational training program to begin their banking careers. The major banks all have some form of a rotational training program, which can last from several months to a year or more. During this time candidates learn about different banking departments and services and attend classes. (Note: Robert Morris Associates of Philadelphia publishes a banking diagnostic exam about fundamentals of corporate banking, which is used in many banks' training classes. Some typical topics covered in the exam are included in this interview.)

Q: **Describe your ideal banking job.**

A: *I'd like to be a participation/syndication manager with a key role in portfolio management for large corporate issues (around $1 billion to $5 billion) and*

First-time Job Seekers: Training programs are ideal, because banks that sponsors rotational training programs don't generally demand prior experience and usually aren't willing to pay much for it, as new recruiters won't be productive to the organization until they're out of the training program. Rotations also provide a good way for a new hire to preview several departments. You gain a great education about how various departments coordinate efforts, and you get to choose a specialty after you've gotten the insider's perspective. Generally banks target new college graduates and some M.B.A's for these programs; people coming in with M.B.A.s or fulltime experience are often put into an accelerated form of the training program.

Selection criteria for bank-training programs generally include a bachelor's degree in a business discipline with a minimum of six hours of college credit in accounting; sales aptitude, or even better, some sales experience; and a genuine interest in banking.

secondary market trading. I've worked large commercial deals in the past and would be happy to discuss that experience with you. Ultimately, I'd like to specialize within an industry category, such as energy or retail.

The important goal in answering this type of question is to be specific; that means matching your interests to a bank where those interests are a known strength. (We assume the bank in this interview is indeed known for corporate lending to energy and retail clients.)

Q: **Why are you so interested in loan syndications?**

A: *Syndication is lucrative to the large commercial banks because of up-front fees, and is therefore growing. Not only does that mean good opportunity for me to be challenged, but it also makes sense for the bank. You can take on an uncomfortable percentage of debt to gain up-front fees—let's say, by helping a fast-growing national corporation issue a large amount in bank debt—and then turn around and sell those issues easily on a secondary market. This creates a very liquid market for these issues to smaller banks.*

This answer hits home because it shows the candidate's interest in the bank's bottom line (that is, it keeps the recruiter's interests up front). The candidate uses a good example of a growing company, which would need the debt financing for expansion; the example of potential benefits to a large company is good indication of the candidate's sales ability.

Q: **What key skills would make you successful in syndication work?**

A: *I have strong recollection of quantitative information, which is important, because you often have to recall quickly where you bought and sold something. Then sales and negotiation skills are critical, because once you've secured a large issue of stock, you want to sell it on the secondary market quickly, and your relationship with the smaller banks is critical.*

This is a skill-assessment question. Although this recruiter is kind enough to remind the candidate to relate skills specifically to the job, you may be asked a more generic question, so the burden is on you to relate your skills as directly as possible to the position you're applying for. This answer is good because each skill is presented in the context of how it's used and why it's important.

Q: **If the consumer price index is off this month, how does that impact our bank?**

A: *The CPI influences consumer confidence, so if you're holding a lot in, let's say, a retail portfolio, that's not good.*

This type of question examines specific skills and problem-solving ability relevant to banking and finance. The candidate is tested on comprehension of cause and effect. The answer, though short, is effective because it's confident and relates to a specific example (retail).

Q: **Suppose your portfolio under management consisted of automotive corporate bonds, retail department store corporate bonds, and options on a major retailer's stock. How would you balance the risk in that?**

A: *I'd add to it something countercyclical to retail consumer confidence. I might look for an investment in hard goods or heavy manufacturing that's not tied to retail buying cycles.*

Here the candidate is tested on decision-making skills and demonstrates an understanding of the economic weighting of a diversification strategy in a well-run investment portfolio. The recruiter might be interested to hear about some particularly creative or unusual investment choice, so a follow-up question might be "If you were managing this portfolio, tell me two or three specific companies you might invest in to diversify." Be ready with a few of your favorite choices.

Q: **If you were looking at how a company financed a large equipment purchase, where would you find that information?**

A: *I'd consult the company's statement of cash flows to examine capital expenditures.*

Here the recruiter assesses the candidate's skills, particularly accounting skills. Banking officers must have strong knowledge of accounting statements when looking for insight into a particular company's financial strength. Only then can they make good risk assessments, determining which companies the bank wants to do business with.

Q: **If you're an account officer and are presented with a problem loan, what would you want to do?**

A: *I might increase the pricing to reflect the increased risk. Or I might review loan and collateral documentation to see what other options were available.*

Career Changers: The instance of seasoned professionals entering banking for the first time is very limited, as the training programs are the general career track for most banking professionals. Exceptions include such great trust administration, where a CPA or an attorney might be hired because of estate-planning experience.

This question addresses the candidate's judgment and effectiveness with bank customers. You wouldn't want to demand payment immediately or agree orally to accept late payment. It's in the bank's best interests to work out such problems and continue to earn interest on money lent to the borrower, not to call in the loan.

Q: Lender-liability claims might arise in what type of situation?

A: *You might have a discretionary line of credit—demand line—where the bank decides not to lend the money. The decision may be made for a number of reasons: perhaps there's been considerable overuse of the line with no paydown period anytime during the year. Or perhaps there are late interest payments, or the borrower is consistently not meeting collateral requirements of receivable balances.*

Because this question tests the candidate's knowledge of specific banking conditions, it would be addressed only to a more seasoned candidate in banking. The answer is effective because it demonstrates that the candidate knows how to protect the bank's interests.

Q: Suppose you were holding a large portfolio of interest-sensitive investments, like financing/leasing companies, and the domestic balance of trade looked unfavorable for the upcoming months. What would you want to do?

A: *I wouldn't sell the interest-sensitive investments because, by then, the price would already be affected by the trade projection. With prices rising the companies you're holding will eventually increase their loan rates. At the same time the government will lower its rates, so the leasing companies will benefit from the larger spreads. I'd counterbalance the portfolio in the interim; I'd pick up some higher-end, longer-term securities.*

This is an excellent problem-solving question for a banking officer interview, as the candidate is tested specifically on cause and effect. Again, this type of question is likely to be asked of a more seasoned person with banking experience, or a candidate with an advanced degree, such as an M.B.A.

Q: So many deals in the corporate finance group take a long time to develop. Describe a time when persistence over the long run got you the desired result.

A: *I worked in sales of expensive industrial equipment. Usually I had to help my customers arrange financing, sometimes including long-term lease arrangements. Often, after convincing them to buy, I had to do the financing legwork, but once financing was arranged, the company still might not buy right away. However, most companies appreciated my diligence, and I'd stay in touch* *regardless. Many times I'd earn business one or two years later, even when the financing terms weren't as favorable as before, because I'd earned the customer's trust.*

Corporate finance products like leveraged lease transactions take a long time. Banks are looking for candidates who understand this. This answer demonstrates that the candidate has the right attitude and experience in arranging financing, even though his or her past job was considered a "sales" job.

Q: **What are appropriate actions to take after you've made a proposal to a potential banking customer? How would you follow up?**

A: *I'd follow up within a week and see if the customer needed further information. I wouldn't rush someone more quickly than that, because in the case of choosing a corporate lender, the client has a big decision to make and shouldn't feel rushed. During the phone call I'd try to determine whether I'd really gotten to the decision maker.*

This question addresses the candidate's determination as well as personal skills and judgment. In the conservative field of banking, especially corporate banking, you should demonstrate that you can be patient. When dealing with a consumer loan, however, you might choose to follow up faster, as the loan amount will be lower and less risky and the time frame needed for the consumer's decision shorter.

Q: **Tell me how your prior banking experience could help you here.**

A: *I've done corporate lending, so I have considerable knowledge of what's involved and how to be successful. I've worked extensively in trust services. I've always been active in my community in various organizations, and I've developed a strong network that's helped me establish new banking contacts. As I've progressed, I've often brought in business with people I've met through my association with Big Brothers and the Special Olympics.*

This answer demonstrates that the candidate has transferable skills—prior lending experience, trust experience, and networking skills. The candidate's network of contacts will tend to benefit whichever bank he or she works for—another strong selling point.

Experienced Professionals: Your best bet is to try to find a position that allows for immediate contributions to the bank's performance with no training required. Most training programs are geared toward young professionals just starting out, and the company's pay range for trainees is fairly tight.

Q: **What have you found most difficult in your role as a banking officer?**

A: *I'd say developing my cold-calling skills was hard. Quite honestly, I'm much more secure in my accounting and analytical skills than in my cold-calling skills, so I've always worked hard to try to network to get more comfortable meeting people for the first time. My networking skills in general have gotten much better, and I do have a strong business network, especially in my home state, where your bank has been expanding.*

The candidate effectively demonstrates humility here by admitting that cold calling hasn't been his or her forte—a tactic that will probably save the candidate from later being asked a question about a weakness. This rather negative information is presented in a positive way that shows the job seeker did something to improve his or her comfort level with cold calling. Indicating that one's contacts are strong in an area where the bank is trying to attract new business is also a smart approach.

Q: **Suppose you had to cold-call for the bank. What might you do?**

A: *I've actually learned from several mentors how they've developed their own cold-calling skills. One thing I've learned is that you don't accomplish much by sticking to vague, safe conversation. You have to ask tough questions, like the prospect's opinion of the bank. Does that person think we're a top choice, or do we fail even to make his or her short list? When you ask these kinds of questions, you get good, competitive information, and you know what you're up against trying to turn it into new business.*

The most important thing is simply to have a plan. This answer is memorable, well articulated, and strongly establishes the candidate's opinion. Although the opinion may be debatable, it's much preferable to the candidate's sitting on the fence. The strength of this statement leaves the recruiter confident that this person will get results.

Q: **As banks move toward relationship management, what does that mean to you?**

A: *We're the corporate finance group, in a sense; we're responsible for helping a client with any financing need, not just with loans. That means we have to know the various specialists within our bank and be able to call quickly upon them to cross-sell our bank's services. That's where my knowledge from rotational training in four different banking areas—private banking, treasury management, international, and bank consolidations—will help me be effective.*

This is a question of job computability, where the recruiter seeks to determine if the candidate's business philosophy is consistent with the bank's. (There's no right or wrong answer here; the candidate simply gives an opinion, hoping that it's shared by the bank's management.) As national banks continue to provide one-stop shopping or full financial-management services, they'll definitely want to hire candidates with knowledge of all the bank's services. This candidate does a good job of showing a well-rounded knowledge of different banking services.

Q: **Tell me how your accounting skills have come into play in banking.**

A: *They help because I'm always doing financial modeling—for example, a client may be considering an acquisition. Or I may need to look carefully at pension issues or balance-sheet items with a client.*

This question indicates that the recruiter is intrigued by the candidate's accounting skills or believes they're important. The candidate simply needs to demonstrate their relevance. The answer here is direct and projects confidence.

Q: **In your relationship-manager role, how have you cultivated your client base?**

A: *I've used a prospecting list of companies that are in my territory, that have a strong growth record, and that might be good targets for full-service investment banking. I'm not trying to compete with a local bank for operating-loan business.*

This question demands that you have a starting point. How do you think? How do you organize yourself? The candidate's answer is effective, because it shows the choices or trade-offs the candidate must make to focus his or her energy carefully.

Candidates Re-entering the Workforce: Training programs can be a great way to re-enter the job market, because they're designed on the assumption that you're just beginning, as if you're a first-time job seeker. However, you won't be paid at a significantly higher rate than a fresh college graduate. Chances are you can graduate quickly from the training program because of well-developed networking skills, general management skills, and prior experience. Make sure you demonstrate interest and knowledge of the ways banking has changed since you were last in the workforce.

Candidates with prior banking experience can usually get rehired into their specialty. Banks have been very progressive about helping people into job-sharing and part-time professional positions, performing their prior jobs at reduced hours per week. For example, an investment-sales representative for the bank may have to re-establish a book of contacts but can assume the same job with a smaller group of clients.

Q: **How do you compare to your peers as a banking officer?**

A: *I brought in about $350,000 in revenue last year. Most of our officers brought in between $250,000 to $300,000.*

The recruiter is looking for hard results, and the candidate delivers. At the entry level an officer might be expected to bring in about $140,000 or more in transaction revenue; then the expectation increases. This candidate shows that his or her performance exceeded the average or expected revenue. The answer could be improved with some insight into the candidate's thoughts about why he or she was able to outperform the bank's expectation.

Credit Analyst

Q: Describe your credit-analysis experience.

A: *I've been doing commercial credit analysis at a large bank for two years, learning about various loan structures and industries.*

The interviewer wants to determine where the candidate's experience lies, for example, in commercial-, residential-, or consumer-loan areas. If you're a first-time job seeker, you could cite an internship or related college work instead of actual job experience. For example, you could say something like, "In my financial-management courses we routinely calculated and analyzed performance-and-condition ratios to determine the health of a company. This can be directly related to credit-analysis work in banking." Competitive pressures have instilled in bankers the need to cut costs. This in turn has meant the elimination of many in-house training programs. Therefore, it's important for you to convince the interviewer that you can be productive with little additional training.

Q: What do you see as the role of the credit department in a lending operation?

A: *The lender's primary responsibility is to bring in new loan business. The credit department must take an objective look at the prospective borrower—to make sure that the borrower is creditworthy and that the proposed loan conforms to bank policy. The key is to be able to act as a "watchdog" while maintaining a good working relationship with lenders.*

The credit analyst must have the maturity and confidence to deal with lenders who have higher-level positions in the bank, and who have production goals to meet. You must demonstrate that you can maintain your objectivity and stand up to pressure from lenders without forgetting the need to work as a team.

Q: How big are the loans you have typically dealt with?

A: *I've worked on loans mainly in the $500,000 to $1 million range, but I believe that the same skills used to analyze credits in this range can be applied to loans both larger and smaller.*

The interviewer wants to determine if the candidate's experience matches the credit size usually processed by the credit department. It's important to stress how your experience can be applied to any size loan.

Q: **What types of borrowers have you analyzed?**

A: *I've worked on manufacturers, distributors, and service companies. Each requires similar skills, but each also requires thinking about how the business flows, who the suppliers are, and who the customers are. I've also looked at real-estate developers and builders.*

Familiarity with the interviewing bank's customer base is a plus. If you don't have that kind of information, do some research. This could be as simple as asking for a copy of any annual report, calling the lending area with a few questions, and/or conducting an informational interview.

Q: **What types of loans were involved in your analyses?**

A: *Businesses need various types of loans for various purposes. I've looked at commercial real-estate loans for both construction and permanent financing, lines of credit, and term loans.*

Each type of loan involves different issues. Experience with those types of loans made by the interviewing bank would, of course, be helpful. Before your interview make a point of finding out what types of loans the bank makes.

Q: **How would you approach a commercial mortgage loan?**

A: *Commercial mortgage loans require knowledge of the building, the owner, and the tenants. Building information includes age, condition, structure, current and proposed use, and location. Much of this information can be obtained from an appraisal or from bank personnel with knowledge of the area. The marketability of the neighborhood must also be considered. The bank obviously doesn't want to rule out a property based on location, but location is a factor. A residential property in an industrial neighborhood could have a lower value*

First-time Job Seekers: The adage "Knowledge is Power" certainly applies here. Know as much as possible about the industry, the bank, and the job opening before your job interview. Informational interviews are great sources of information and guidance—start by calling the bank and asking to speak to an analyst. Most people are flattered to be asked for advice—just be aware of the time pressure people may be under. Read the Wall Street Journal and the business pages of your local and regional newspapers so that you become familiar with industry lingo and can "talk the talk."

College placement offices can also be terrific sources of information. Many will help you with resume preparation, training suggestions, job leads, and referrals sources. Contact the American Banking Association, your state's banking association, and Robert Morris Association (which as local, state, and national chapters) for more information about the banking industry.

than the same building in a residential neighborhood. A building that's suited only for a single use may have less value than one that could house many types of operations. The financial stability of the owner, of course, is an indication of how promptly the loan payments will be made. If the owner is not the tenant, the leases and the tenants should be evaluated as well—that's where the cash will come from to make those payments.

Commercial real-estate loans can be complicated. Knowledge of the issues involved will show that you can be productive in this new position without additional training, which can be costly and time-consuming.

Q: **Describe the important factors to consider in a construction loan request.**

A: *Key issues in considering a construction-loan request include whether the project is under contract or is speculative, the background of the builder or developer, the type of construction, and the market. If the project is under contract, a key issue is whether or not the builder has the financial backing to complete the project. What is his or her experience in this type of building? Does the ultimate user have the financial ability to complete the project? If the project is speculative, how many similar projects are in process in the area? What is the developer's experience in that area? Will funds be disbursed only for a completed work? How will this be monitored?*

Ideally, before your job interview you'll have done research into the types of loans the bank makes. If the bank you're interviewing with does construction loans, it may be important for you to be familiar with them. If you aren't, emphasize your ability to pick up new information quickly and your enthusiasm to learn new skills.

Q: **What would you consider when analyzing a business-loan request?**

A: *I'd start with the business itself by looking at what the company does. Is there a market for that company's products or services? The experience of management and the length of time the company has been in business are very important. The company's profitability and financial condition are obviously*

Career Changers: Networking helps a lot. Get the word out that you're interested in pursuing a career in banking. Leads can come from unlikely places. Even though you may not know anyone in banking, some of your friends, relatives, and business contacts are certain to. And their friends and associates may know still more people. Check with the American banking association, and the Robert Morris association (which has local, state, and national chapters) for more networking contacts.

also very important. I'd evaluate the trends in the operation and that of its industry. Also, the type and amount of loan should be in line with bank policy and should make sense.

This is a basic-quiz question. Although the credit manager may be able to train you regarding a specific loan type or business structure, you must have an understanding of what the common issues are when analyzing a potential borrower. Reassure the interviewer that you have a solid understanding of these issues.

Q: How would you handle a line of credit?

A: *A line of credit provides a company with short-term working capital—generally to support solid assets like receivables or inventory. The first thing to consider is the reason for the loan. The bank would want to finance growth in the assets, not in obsolete inventory or in collection accounts. The amount should be in line with the normal level of such assets. The frequency with which they turn over each year is key for two reasons: first, you want to make sure that you're financing growth and not stale assets, and second, the source of repayment for a line of credit is the conversion of inventory into receivables and then into cash.*

It's important for you to show the interviewer that you have some basic knowledge of common loan requests, thus indicating that you'll become a contributing asset to the department fairly quickly.

Q: How would a term-loan analysis differ from that of a line of credit?

Experienced Professionals: If you have a job interview, it's probably safe to assume that you have all the qualifications necessary for the position. Your best bet is to try to distinguish yourself from the other qualified candidates vying for the position. A great way to do this is by researching before your job interview. Familiarize yourself with bank's customer base by asking for a copy of its annual report or by calling the lending area with a few questions. You should also make sure that you're familiar with the different type of loans the bank makes. Stress this "insider" knowledge in you interview and emphasize your interest in the position. Bring a sample presentation with you, with all identifying information omitted, to illustrate the quality and breadth of your work experience.

It's common for credit analysts to move into credit management or lending after a few years of solid experience. If this is your goal, you should be prepared to explain why you want to make the transition and how your previous experience and skills have prepared you for the position you're applying for.

A: *A term loan is usually used to finance the purchase of equipment or other fixed assets. The term of the loan should not exceed the useful life of the asset purchased. Since repayment for this type of loan comes from profits, it's important to make sure that the company is earning enough to meet payment requirements.*

Being familiar with the differences between various loan types is important. A review of a finance textbook, or informational interviews with experienced analysts, could provide the information you need to impress an interviewer.

Q: Can you provide a sample presentation?

A: *Yes. I've brought sample analyses I've done in the past. Of course, for the sake of confidentiality, the name of the borrower and all other identifying information has been omitted.*

Analyses form the basis of the credit decision. They're read by both internal decision makers and external auditors/examiners and must present the pertinent facts and conclusions in a clear, concise fashion. If you lack related experience, or just don't have a sample analysis, an excerpt from a research paper or other writing samples could serve the same purpose.

Q: What software have you used?

A: *I am quite familiar with Excel, Windows, and Microsoft Word. I've used various statement spreading programs such as STAN from Baker Hill.*

The important ideas to get across here are a basic familiarity with how general- and special-purpose software works and the flexibility to pick up quickly the particular systems used by the bank.

Q: Have you done industry surveys? Describe why and how.

A: *To understand how a company is doing, you need to compare it with its industry. This could be as simple as looking up a D & B rating. If I'm unfamiliar with the industry and a significant loan amount is involved, I may have to check other industry sources. This is similar to doing a research paper.*

Candidates Re-entering the Workforce: Make sure your resume includes information about how you've kept busy during your hiatus, for example, by doing volunteer work or taking a class. In your interview relate how this experience can help you on the job. You should also be up-to-date on the latest software used in the industry. If you have no experience with the particular systems used by the bank, emphasize your basic familiarity in general- and special-purpose software and your ability to learn new systems quickly.

The interviewer wants to know how resourceful the candidate can be. Give an example of a time when you needed a greater understanding of something, and explain how you obtained the information you needed.

Q: How do you deal with multiple priorities?

A: *Many times the bank sets the priorities in its policy. Loans that require committee approval, for example, take precedence when a committee meeting is approaching. Generally, I look at the larger, riskier credit first.*

The ability to prioritize is very important. Management will have final say on how priorities are set, but you must evidence the ability to juggle several tasks at once.

Q: Do you see your future in credit or in lending?

A: *I like looking at a variety of different types of deals, something a credit department position would allow. Furthermore, my strongest skills are in technical areas rather than in sales, so I'm primarily interested in a career in credit management.*

The credit-analyst position can be a starting point for a career in credit or in lending. The interviewer wants to know where the applicant's future interests lie. It's common for a credit analyst to move eventually into lending; as long as you make it clear that you're willing to stay for at least a couple of years, an interest in lending shouldn't pose a problem.

Financial Analyst
(Consumer and Personal Care Products)

Q: **Do you have an M.B.A.?**

A: *Yes, I do. I graduated last May with an M.B.A. from New York University. I took two to three classes at night for the past three years.*

The recruiter will probably ask you this question before you're asked anything else. If you don't have an M.B.A., you should probably not be in the interview. This candidate's answer is particularly good because it demonstrates the amazing dedication and determination that he or she has.

Q: **What are your qualifications?**

A: *I have a BS in finance as well as an M.B.A. I also have three years' work experience in finance with a Fortune 500 company. I have two years' additional financial experience in another major company as well.*

The most important thing that the recruiter will be looking for is the proper experience and background. Generally, he or she will be looking for an M.B.A., but if you have other academic qualifications that would serve you well in this position, talk about them. This response reflects the proper education and experience of a financial analyst.

Q: **What class have you taken that has helped you the most in the business place?**

A: *One class that I took in business school that was not required as part of my finance concentration was Cost Accounting, which probably helped me more than anything else in my first job.*

The recruiter, of course, will be looking for a person well suited to the job. This means someone who has the necessary educational background, and who will be willing to spend the greater portion of his or her career with the company. The recruiter will want to know if you're qualified for the job from an academic standpoint.

Q: **If you were a finance or accounting person new to the job at a manufacturing plant, and you wanted to know how your costs compared, whether good or bad, what would you do? Where would you start?**

A: *I would compare benchmarking among divisions and manufacturing sites within the company. I would also benchmark outside the company with any industry data available for that type of manufacturing process.*

Once the recruiter has determined that you have the right bank of knowledge and the right personality for the company, he or she will then try to see how quickly you'll be able to jump in. Brush up before the interview and be able to respond comparably to similar questions.

Q: What software-presentation packages do you use?

A: *I'm equally comfortable on a Macintosh and a PC. Although I'm very familiar with Microsoft Excel, Microsoft Word, and Microsoft PowerPoint.*

This candidate shows a high level of computer proficiency and is familiar with the main software-presentation packages. If you don't know how to use some or all of these programs, take a seminar before the interview.

Q: What do you think being a financial analyst really means?

A: *It means putting the numbers together and seeing if they work. If they don't, the financial analyst must uncover the problem, and find out why things aren't working.*

This is a model answer: crisp, clear, and to the point. The candidate precisely understands what this job title means and has succinctly described it.

Q: What are the best tracking methods?

A: *It absolutely depends on the situation and what the problem points to. When I did some tracking for accounts payable, I looked at inputs, approvals, and deletions. I compared the number removed from the outstanding.*

This is a good, sound answer. This candidate proves that he or she knows the ropes. Be prepared with actual samples of reports that you've written.

Q: How good are your writing abilities?

First-time Job Seekers: The most important thing that recruiters will be looking for us the proper experience and background. Generally, they'll be looking for an M.B.A., but if you have other academic qualifications that would serve you well in the position, be sure to talk about them. Employers also look for eagerness, determination, and confidence in entry-level hires, but you don't want to come across as cocky. As one hiring manager put it, you should be "reachable, teachable, and updatable."

A: *I really concentrated on further developing my writing skills while I got my M.B.A. I took an entrepreneurial class in which the chief assignment was developing, writing, and continually rewriting a very involved business plan.*

This is an excellent answer. Have a business plan or something similar ready to show the recruiter. Leave your business plan with the recruiter after the interview. The recruiter will be looking for a candidate with writing ability, because as a financial analyst, you'll be expected to write a lot of memos.

Q: How good a communicator are you?

A: *While getting my M.B.A., I think I further honed an existing set of solid communication skills. For example, before I started business school, I could do a presentation to a group just fine, but I didn't feel all that comfortable. I was a bit nervous, and I couldn't relax and enjoy myself. By the end of business school I had given so many group presentations that it didn't, and still doesn't, faze me.*

This answer is quite commendable. The candidate has avoided the biggest mistake—answering the question affirmatively without giving proof or an example of why it is so. The recruiter is looking for someone with exceptional verbal skills, because you have to be able to communicate what you analyze.

Q: Tell me about something you analyzed.

A: *I incorporated many accounts payable records into one account. To do this, I looked at what was outstanding in each account. From the consolidated report that I prepared as a result, the financial officers were able to determine some significant benchmarking.*

Expect vague questions such as this during your interview for a financial-analyst position. The candidate has answered this question in the appropriate manner. The recruiter will ask you to describe in detail projects you've worked on, because he or she is looking for experience. The recruiter will be looking for examples of how you approached and resolved a problem. What solutions did you come up with? How effective were they? If they were not effective, be prepared to explain why.

Career Changers: Talk about how your previous jobs and experience have naturally led you in this direction. Give specific examples of projects you have done in which you have used the same skills you'll use as a financial analyst. Talk about problems you've solved and the approaches you've used in doing so. This will demonstrate both your problem-solving abilities and your creativity in analysis. Your varied background should be a plus because you will be bringing fresh, new approaches to the company.

Q: **Tell me about a particularly difficult project you've handled.**

A: *My company knew that the consulting firm they'd hired had not done the work that was proposed and paid for. The problem was that we didn't know how or where the holes were. To discover the discrepancies, I divided all of the information into quantitative material, which included the budget and the cost, and the time and hours spent. I also divided it into the qualitative material, which encompassed all of the memos and correspondence. I lined everything up and discovered that the consulting firm had done only a third of what they'd promised. I made a presentation to my supervisor and the key financial people of the company. From there we decided how to handle the consulting firm, which we couldn't have done before we understood the whole picture.*

This is an excellent answer because the candidate focuses on the tight situation the company was in, rather than on a personal struggle he or she was undergoing. The recruiter will try to discover how strong your problem-solving abilities are. This candidate shows outstanding ability by looking at the problem from both a quantitative and a qualitative standpoint.

Q: **How do you structure your presentations?**

A: *For the consulting-firm project that I discussed, I made bar graphs. On one chart I made a bar in one color to show the projected time that the consulting firm should have spent; the second bar on the same chart had the actual time spent, so the discrepancy in proposed versus actual time was very clear. On another chart I used bar graphs to depict the disparity between the proposed charges and the actual money charged.*

The recruiter will be concerned about your ability to create presentations and your method of tackling a project. This candidate proves to the recruiter that he or she is capable in both these areas.

Q: **How important do you think qualitative concerns are to financial analysis?**

A: *I think it certainly depends on the individual case. I have found, however, that qualitative issues often raise the right questions. They can help you determine where the problem started. For example, in the consulting-firm issue, nobody*

Experienced Professionals: Sell yourself on your experience, your reputation, and your interpersonal abilities. Single out several significant achievements and discuss how you were able to deliver or produce the success. Emphasize your experience and your ability to contribute quickly to the company. Have several references ready. Choose people who are prominent in the industry to speak on your behave.

in my company had anything good to say about the consulting firm. These negative feelings may have led to my supervisor's suspicion that things were not right on the books.

The candidate has answered this question well because he or she gives a reason to support the answer. You may have a very different answer based on your own experiences, which is fine. The important thing is to have a well-balanced answer that includes an opinion supported by both a reason and an example.

Q: What publications do you read on a regular basis?

A: *I read the* Wall Street Journal *and the* Harvard Business Review *for general business. I also like to read* Forbes *and* Business Week *as well.*

What you specifically read doesn't really matter, although your answer would probably be something similar to this candidate's. The point is that you do read important and relevant business publications. Think about what you read in advance so that you don't have to "um" or think about it when the recruiter asks you this question.

Q: How did you become interested in financial analysis?

A: *I'm very prudent with personal finances, and I really enjoy solving difficult situations. So I majored in finance in college. I complemented it with a minor in history in order to develop my writing and communications skills. I also concentrated in finance when I got my M.B.A., which I really enjoyed. Starting my career as a financial analyst seemed like a natural progression.*

Explain to the recruiter why you are there taking the interview. This candidate obviously has a natural interest in finance, which he or she has concentrated on during all previous academic training. If your interests, talents, and training similarly reflect this strong interest in finance, then you're in the right place.

Q: What are your primary financial responsibilities in your current job?

A: *I manage the company's monthly and annual costs forecast. I go through an annual budgeting forecast with my supervisor, which feeds our profit forecast.*

Candidates Re-entering the Workforce: Take some refresher courses at your local community college. These should include some accounting, finance, word-processing, and presentation courses. Conduct several informational interviews to get good advice on re-entering the workforce. Thoroughly study the industry by reading industry and company reports.

The recruiter is interested in someone who has hands-on experience in financial analysis. It is acceptable to be as brief as this candidate has been. The recruiter will delve more specifically if needed.

Q: **Where do you want to be in five years?**

A: *I'd like to have a leadership role within the financial department. I'd like to be responsible for a specific financial-teams direction from a strategic standpoint.*

Of course this question is tricky because you don't want to seem arrogant or unrealistic. On the other hand, seeming undermotivated is a problem as well. This candidate took the correct approach by sharing a realistic goal, without specifically naming a job title.

Q: **What opportunities do you see in this business?**

A: *I think that businesses are becoming more and more lean, and that this trend will continue into the next millennium. So the need for excellent and capable financial analysts will be stronger than ever. Organizations will expect you to produce immediately or leave.*

First, this answer and the reasoning behind it are correct. Second, the candidate is not frightened by the importance of being the best, but is, rather, enthused. Think about where the future of your profession lies, and be able to articulate these thoughts carefully.

Q: **What things impress you in colleagues?**

A: *I admire and work best with people who are of good character and have integrity. I also think confidence and enthusiasm is positive in any business environment.*

The recruiter will want to see how developed your interpersonal skills are. More than likely, you'll be interacting not only with the finance department, but with other people in the company, and possibly colleagues. Show the recruiter that you will shine in this area.

Q: **Do you have any questions for me?**

A: *Yes, I do. If I'm hired, what would my first few assignments be?*

Be prepared with several questions. Another question you might want to ask is, "What does success look like within this company?" It would also be appropriate to ask, "Will I be expected to relocate frequently or at all?"

General Accountant

Q: **What qualifications do you have that you believe will help you as an accountant?**

A: *I have three years' experience as an accountant for a small public firm, where I did everything from generating income statements and balance sheets to assisting the controller with the preparation of financial statements. I also have a degree in accounting from the University of Vermont, and I'm a certified public accountant.*

The interviewer will want to know about your general background and how it relates to the position. A degree in accounting is typically required, since there are a number of technical aspects of accounting that can be learned only through course work. This is a quality answer since it highlights the candidate's relevant skills and education.

Q: **How did you become interested in accounting?**

A: *I've always been really interested in numbers. I remember budgeting my weekly allowance as a kid and convincing my parents to let me open my own savings account when I was eleven. In college I was immediately attracted to accounting classes; they seemed like a perfect match for my interests.*

The interviewer will want to know if you have a natural interest in accounting—if your personality seems suited to the profession. You should exhibit an affinity for numbers, as well as proof that you're detail oriented. This is a good answer because it shows that the candidate is well suited for a career in accounting.

Q: **Do you consider yourself to be task or project oriented?**

A: *I'm definitely more of a project-oriented person. I like looking at the whole of a problem, figuring out the way to solve it, and then following through on it. But, of course, if I'm given a certain task to accomplish, I certainly don't have any problem with that.*

The question is designed to discover your natural tendencies as far as your work ethic is concerned. In accounting, task-oriented workers are better suited to positions where more routine is involved, such as accounts payable or receivable. Senior-level accountants cannot be focused on just one issue; they must be able to keep the big picture in mind at all times.

Q: **What spreadsheets are you familiar with?**

A: *I've used Excel extensively in my current position for all of my budget analyses. I also use Excel at home to keep track of my personal finances.*

Today most accounting work is done using computerized spreadsheets. If you want to be considered seriously for any position in accounting, you must be proficient in at least one spreadsheet program. If you have no computer skills, most employers will not even consider your application.

Q: **What has been your experience with credit and collection?**

A: *A few months back my company experienced a temporary cash-flow problem. It was my responsibility to talk to our creditors and explain our financial situation; I arranged to send minimum payments to our creditors every month until our crisis was resolved, at which time they'd receive all their money. I also had to lean on our customers to collect some past-due funds. I managed to get some money in, and the crisis passed without any real damage to the company.*

This shows that the candidate can deal with a broad range of people, and that he or she also has a thorough knowledge of the business and industry, since it requires a familiarity with sales terms and product knowledge. This answer also exhibits the candidate's ability to handle crises calmly and responsibly.

Q: **Have you ever prepared cash-flow projections, and if so, what was the level of detail involved?**

A: *Yes, usually on a monthly basis. I've projected on a rolling twelve-month basis. I always break everything down into the smallest possible components. This helps me ensure that nothing is overlooked.*

Cash-flow projections are one of the most important tools in management and a key element in business operations. They require you to assemble information from numerous areas and summarize it in a readable and usable form. This answer highlights the candidate's experience with the task, as well as his or her ability to pay careful attention to detail.

Q: **Tell me about your experience in dealing with cash flows and variance analyses.**

First-time Job Seekers: Employers will most closely examine your school record. They're looking for accounting majors—or at least someone who's taken a number of accounting classes. Employers will also check out your computer skills; knowledge of computerized spreadsheets is essential in this field.

A: *I've prepared cash-flow analyses on a monthly basis for senior management. I've also been responsible for producing monthly variance analyses and explaining why the actual performance was different from the projections. I've worked with the appropriate department manager to correct and/or improve the negative variances.*

This question measures the candidate's skill level. The answer shows an understanding of the issues involved, the ability to determine why the actual performance differed from the projections, and the ability to work with management or operating personnel.

Q: **What has been your involvement with the actual preparation of financial statements?**

A: *I've helped the controller with all aspects of preparing our quarterly financial statements. I've also been responsible for gathering all relevant information from the staff accountants and then reporting to the controller. Then the two of us have gone through and prepared the statements together.*

There is a big difference between auditing financial statements and actually preparing them. The preparation of financial statements is one of the biggest responsibilities for any accounting position. With this answer the candidate shows the high level of responsibility in his or her current position.

Q: **Tell me about the type of cost systems you're familiar with.**

A: *I've worked with many different types, from standard to job cost. Because most of my experience has been with manufacturing companies, I've been specifically involved in the design and implementation of standard cost systems, and have had to accumulate information, then develop it into a readable and usable form for other managers.*

Cost accounting is the basis for accumulating all of the direct and indirect costs associated with a given product or service. Once they've all been accounted for, they're used to determine the sales-dollar pricing of products. The candidate's answer indicates that he or she has a high level of experience and a wide range of accounting skills.

Q: **Have you ever been involved with job costing?**

Career Changers: Employers like career changers if they're coming from another detail-oriented field. However, you still need some knowledge of the technical aspects of accounting. A few courses, at least up to the intermediate level, are essential if you want to be an accountant. Likewise, you should know spreadsheet programs like Excel.

A: *Yes, I did some job costing as part of the training program at my current company. I spent about two months doing that, as I did with all basic accounting functions. Now I simply review and examine the numbers supplied to me and give a report to the controller.*

This question expands upon the previous one. Job costing is a basic, yet key, element in accounting, since you can't run a business effectively if you don't figure out your manufacturing costs. Again, the candidate's answer highlights his or her diverse and well-rounded background.

Q: Do you have experience preparing budgets?

A: *I've prepared budgets at the corporate and department level. I've been responsible for coordinating the information with each department and converting it into a readable and consistent form for upper management to use as a decision-making tool.*

This question allows the interviewer to gauge the candidate's level of experience and highlights the responsibility in his or her last position. This answer is excellent, indicating that the candidate not only has experience in budgeting, but can deal with a range of management levels.

Q: What is the yearly sales volume of your current company?

A: *Last year the company grossed about $8 million in sales, a 20 percent increase from the previous year. This year it's probably looking at another 10 to 15 percent increase. Obviously, the company's still relatively small, but it's growing rapidly.*

This question is a roundabout way to gauge the candidate's level of responsibility and experience. A staff accountant at a medium-sized firm like this would generally have much more responsibility than a staff accountant at a big *Fortune* 500 company.

Q: What is your level of tax experience?

A: *I have experience in preparing corporate returns, both federal and state, for both "C" and "S" corporations, as well as sales-tax returns. These were generally smaller companies with up to $2 million in sales.*

Experienced Professionals: Highlight your previous work experience during your interview; employers want to see that you've held positions of responsibility in the past. Recruiters will also look at any experience you have managing or supervising people. And, of course, you should make sure that your computer skills are sharp and up to speed.

This question is also designed to gauge the candidate's level of experience in, and determine basic knowledge of, corporate tax issues. Not all general accountants get exposure to corporate tax issues so this candidate already has a leg up on the competition.

Q: **Do you have experience preparing documentation for accounting systems?**

A: *I prepared an accounting manual at my last position. The manual encompassed procedures, forms, and flow charts as well as a detailed explanation of the nature of each general-ledger account. This became the training manual for all new hires in accounting.*

This question is designed to determine not only if the job seeker understands the nature of the position, but if he or she can teach and explain concepts to others. The candidate gives a great answer here because it both highlights these qualities and demonstrates his or her ability to digest information, then enable others to learn from the experience.

Q: **Tell me about your auditing experience.**

A: *I worked for a year at a small public-accounting firm, doing mainly review-type work of all the books and records for small service corporations. I was responsible for the preparation of all papers for those clients, determining the accuracy of the records prepared by the client companies, and drafting the financial statements and reports signed by the partner. I was also involved in drafting a management report for areas requiring improvement in internal control and other procedures, as well as working with the client to implement recommendations.*

Auditing teaches analytical thinking. It also requires a broader-based knowledge of accounting principles and standards. Through this answer the interviewer learns of the candidate's extensive auditing experience.

Q: **What has been your experience with accounts payable?**

A: *I had an internship where I reviewed all invoices processed by the accounts payable department for verification of quantities received, pricing, and general-ledger coding. I was also involved in negotiating prices with suppliers as well as resolving discrepancies that could not be resolved by payable-department personnel.*

Although accounts payable is a very basic part of accounting, companies want you to have a working knowledge of how purchase information is processed. This is a good answer because it shows a significant amount of accounts payable experience.

Q: **Have you had experience with accounts receivable?**

A: *Yes. I've reviewed customers' financial statements, determined credit limits, and on occasion posted cash into the accounts receivable module. I've set up input control sheets that the posting clerks maintained to assure that all the transactions balanced.*

Accounts receivable is the corollary to accounts payable. So, similarly, it is necessary to understand how shipments, collections, and adjustments are made and processed. Again, this answer highlights the candidate's solid background in accounts receivable.

Q: **Describe some specific accounting projects you've worked on. Were you responsible for the entire project or just specific segments?**

A: *I've worked on a lease-versus-buy analysis for the acquisition of all company computer equipment. I was responsible for the entire analysis work and had to do all the research and calls to financing sources. I also had to make final recommendations to senior personnel.*

The candidate's answer illustrates his or her ability to work on one's own and the ability to reason, prepare data, come to a conclusion, and make a final recommendation. It also illustrates his or her ability to work with other people both within and outside of an organization.

Q: **What type of computerized accounting systems have you worked with?**

A: *Many different types, from mainframe systems to PC-based systems, both stand-alone and on a network. At my last position I was responsible for networking all of the PCs in the entire company. I used RealWorld Accounting systems with most of the modules.*

This is another question to measure the candidate's level of familiarity with computers. Unlike the question concerning spreadsheets, this question addresses one's experience with computer hardware. Again, the answer here shows a wide breadth of experience.

Candidates Re-entering the Workforce: If you've been out of work for awhile, be sure to brush up on your computer skills and learn a few spreadsheet programs. Also, past bookkeeping experience or accounting experience, along with a few accounting classes will help you sell yourself in any job interview.

Q: **What is the most difficult accounting experience you've ever had to face?**

A: *In my first job the company was faced with an IRS audit. I wasn't directly involved, since I wasn't working on any tax issues at that time, but we all had to go through our books and documentation to make sure everything was accurate. Luckily, the audit went well, so the whole thing turned out to be a good bonding experience for the department.*

This question addresses how well the candidate works under pressure. With this answer the job seeker demonstrates that he or she does not crack when faced with difficult situations. The answer also illustrates how well the candidate works in teams.

Insurance Underwriter
(Entry-Level)

Q: **What attracts you to underwriting?**

A: *I'm attracted by the varied functions and tasks of the position, the interaction with such a wide range of people—actuaries, sales reps, brokers, clients—as well as the opportunity to make decisions that impact the bottom line, order my work as I see fit, and set my own priorities. I understand that there may be more work than I can handle at times and that the position involves a certain amount of stress. However, no two days will be the same, and I'll never be bored. I'm a high-energy person, and that suits me just fine.*

This is a reality check. The interviewer is trying to gauge how accurate the candidate's expectations are. Needless to say, your expectations should be realistic. This indicates to the interviewer that you're likely to be satisfied in the position and will stay with the company for a reasonable period of time. Describe both the upside as well as the downside aspects of the position as you see them.

Q: **How has your college background specifically prepared you for underwriting?**

A: *My major course of study was finance with a minor in economics. I believe this background helped to increase my general business knowledge and improve my math and analytical skills, which are critical to success in underwriting. However, my course work also included a wide range of subjects, from history to literature to philosophy. These electives help to make me a well-rounded person.*

If you've done your homework, you'll understand the basic skills required to succeed as an underwriter. You should also be prepared to explain how your educational background and practical experience demonstrate those skills. If you don't have experience in underwriting and you didn't major in business, be prepared to discuss specifically any business courses you may have taken, along with practical experience that demonstrates any of the desired skills.

Q: **What were your SAT scores?**

A: *My SAT scores were 1100 combined, 550 verbal and 550 math. However, that was over four years ago. Those are respectable scores, but I believe my more recent college career is a much better indicator of my skills in the areas of math and verbal aptitude.*

If you're a recent college graduate with no experience, be prepared to answer this question. Successful underwriting requires strong math and communication skills. This is just another way to measure or cross-check these skills. If your SAT scores are low, be prepared to highlight your grade-point average and specific college courses that support your contention that you possess strong skills in these areas.

Q: How do insurance companies make profits?

A: *Generally speaking, insurance companies generate profits from providing consulting services for a fee—like mutual-fund management and retirement-planning services—from investment income—stocks, bonds, real estate, and so on—and from line-of-business operations—when premiums exceed claims, reserves, and expenses. This is accomplished by attracting and retaining quality employees, offering competitive products and services, and focusing on satisfying the needs of the customer.*

Most insurance companies provide not only traditional insurance, but a wide array of products and services. Many insurance companies are multiline, diversified financial-service institutions. This answer shows an appreciation of the "big picture" and an understanding of where and how the line-of-business underwriter fits in.

Q: What does an underwriter do?

A: *An insurance underwriter is responsible for many functions but, I believe, is primarily responsible for the assessment of risk. Underwriters determine the acceptability and premium-rate level of new and renewal business. They must also maintain customer-service standards in the service of that business.*

If you're interested in the field of underwriting, you should at least have a basic understanding of what an underwriter does. If you're not sure, do some research into the field. The answer to this question is an indication of your level of interest. The more detailed the answer, the higher the interest. Are you interested in a job or a career? Your answer to this question will tell.

First-time Job Seekers: Companies expect underwriters to have a college degree, with a concentration in business, finance, and accounting. You most likely won't be expected to have any specific experience in underwriting, but an internship in which you used some methods of financial analysis can be helpful. Many large insurance companies offer training programs that last for three or more months. A typical entry-level position would be as an underwriter assistant or trainee.

Q: **What skills do you think a successful underwriter needs?**

A: *The successful underwriter needs strong written- and oral-communication skills, outstanding interpersonal skills to interact with diverse groups of people, effective self-management skills to prioritize work and meet deadlines, good math skills to price products and services, strong negotiation skills, strong analytical skills to interpret and evaluate data, good decision-making skills, and good computer skills.*

Contrary to popular belief, underwriting is not just "numbers crunching." Underwriters perform a variety of functions and tasks requiring much more than addition, subtraction, multiplication, and division. In today's competitive marketplace and downsized economy, the successful underwriter will be adaptable, flexible, and cross-functional. Again, the interviewer will want to determine if you have an accurate impression of the skills the job requires, and how well you rate yourself in terms of those skills.

Q: **Which function is the most important to a successful group-insurance operation: marketing/sales, administrative services, actuarial services, underwriting, or claims?**

A: *All are equally important and couldn't fully contribute to the organization's success without the others. Sales couldn't attract new clients if the reputation for service provided by the administrative area wasn't a good one. Underwriting couldn't properly price new and renewal business without the help of actuarial services. Each department's performance is dependent upon the others' performance.*

Although each department must have its own set of objectives and standards, all departments must work together in support of the broader business strategy. This answer illustrates a solid understanding of how the success of an organization depends on the contributions of each and every person in each and every department.

Q: **Why is service such an important issue?**

Career Changers: If you were previously a loan officer or financial analyst, you shouldn't have much trouble making the switch to underwriting. In your interview point out that you already possess strong analytical skills and have a good eye for detail. Sound judgment is also an important trait for an underwriter to have, so point out any specific examples that argue for your commonsense decision-making. You'll also be expected to get your associate-in-underwriting certification after about a year.

A: *Service is a major contributor to customer satisfaction. Just as important as, or maybe even more important than, cost. If a customer isn't receiving a level of service that meets or exceeds his or her expectations, that customer won't be a customer for very long. In addition, that customer's experience with your company may affect how potential customers in the marketplace view your company. People do talk and share information. This may affect not only profits but future sales as well. In many instances service may be the one thing that distinguishes a company from the competition. A bad reputation for service may compromise a company's position in the marketplace.*

The interviewer is trying to determine if the candidate understands the importance of customer service in establishing a positive image in the marketplace, and its impact on new business sales. Outstanding customer service is also a great help in establishing long-term clients and repeat business—the profitable company's "bread and butter." The longer the relationship, the greater the possibility for profit.

Q: In what order would you prioritize the following tasks: (1) completing a new-business proposal, (2) resolving a service problem for an existing client, (3) renewing an in-force account?

A: *Since a "bird in the hand is worth two in the bush," I'd address the needs of my existing clients first. I'd resolve the service problem because nothing creates more "bad press" than a disgruntled customer. Second, I'd renew the in-force account as soon as possible to begin receiving any new premiums resulting from the renewal-rate increase. I'd review and complete the new-business proposal last.*

Customer service and retention of in-force business are very important in this competitive market. Service and satisfy your existing client, renew the in-force account to maintain profitability, and complete the new-business proposal in that order. This answer demonstrates the ability to set priorities based on business objectives.

Q: In general terms, what three or four demographic characteristics might distinguish a good risk from a bad risk for group life insurance?

Experienced Professionals: Continuing your education is important in underwriting. If you're interested in advancing to chief underwriter or underwriting manager, you may want to consider becoming a chartered property casualty underwriter (CPCU). This involves taking a series of ten exams, usually after you've been an underwriter for at least five years. CPCU certification is especially important if you're interested in becoming a senior manager.

A: *Age, sex, and occupation or industry are all good indicators of risk. Although I don't have any practical experience, I'd say that for life insurance a group of white-collar office employees with a low average age and more females than males would represent a fairly good risk. A group with these characteristics has a longer life expectancy and therefore may have a greater chance for profitability and be a better and more desirable risk.*

The interviewer is looking to see how well the candidate thinks on his or her feet. How well do you apply common sense and logic to situations that are new and unknown?

Q: How would you justify a premium increase to a client whose claims accounted for only seventy-five cents of each premium dollar paid?

A: *I'd explain to the client that premiums are meant to fund not only claims obligations but also any reserve requirements, as well as administrative expenses. To the extent that current premium rates don't cover claim, reserve, and expense projections for the coming year, premiums will need to be increased.*

Your answer should demonstrate that you have a working knowledge of insurance pricing, as this candidate does. Show the interviewer that you understand there is more to determining insurance-premium rates than pricing for claims on a dollar-for-dollar basis.

Q: Consider the following scenario: You're working late one evening and are the last person in the office. You answer an urgent telephone call to your supervisor from a sales rep who's currently meeting with a potential client. The sales rep needs an answer to a question to close the sale. Tomorrow will be too late. You have the expertise to answer the question, but it's beyond your normal level of authority. How would you respond?

A: *I'd get all the pertinent information, taking well-documented notes. I'd then answer the question based on my knowledge and the information provided. I'd leave my supervisor a note and fill him or her in on the details the next morning. I'd be sure to explain my decision, as well as the thought process behind it.*

Candidates Re-entering the Workforce: In your interview emphasize your work experience before your hiatus. Make sure that you have associates-in-underwriting certification, and be ready to prove that you've remained knowledgeable about the industry in general. These days the insurance industry is rapidly changing, and you must show that you've kept up with the changes.

This response shows that the candidate is confident in his or her ability and can be counted on in an emergency. Similarly, your answer should indicate that you're not afraid to be the decision maker in a tough situation, even if the situation's beyond your normal level of authority.

Q: **As a group-insurance underwriter, what alternate funding arrangements have you had experience with?**

A: *My experience with alternate funding arrangements is extensive and includes administrative services only and stop loss. Under the stop-loss arrangement, for instance, the insurance carrier provides claim-administration services and excess-loss coverages, which insure the client against higher-than-expected claims. The client agrees to fund claims up to a predetermined level, usually up to a certain level on an individual, and a certain level on a group in aggregate. In the event there are claim charges beyond these levels, the insurance funds those claims. The client pays a fee for claim-administration services and a premium for insurance coverage against claim loss.*

If you have any underwriting experience at all, you'll be asked this question in some form. Although most insurers still offer traditional, conventionally funded products, an increasing number offer alternate funding arrangements in which the client or employer accepts part or all of the claims risk. If you lack this experience, the interviewer will regard your background as limited.

Loan Administrator
(Entry-Level)

Q: **Why do you want to pursue a career in banking and finance?**

A: *I've always had an interest in the financial industry. I think that in a position as a loan administrator I could put my analytical skills and attention to detail to good use. And because a loan administrator often deals with clients, I'd also be able to use my interpersonal skills.*

In order to succeed in this field, you must be able to analyze an application as well as financial statements. You should also be detail oriented, as an error or omission could result in a loss for the lending institution. Be sure to emphasize these skills in your job interview. Demonstrating your outgoing personality will also be important, as loan administrators must be able to develop and retain a large client base.

Q: **Have you had any formal credit training?**

A: *Yes, I've taken Omega Lending Courses at the American Institute of Banking. I've also had in-house training from senior lenders in my previous positions.*

For the most part banks promote from within, so experience, performance, and education are all important criteria for the hiring-and-promotion process. Show the interviewer that you have a desire for additional knowledge, that you're interested in future growth as well as potential advancement.

Q: **What are the five C's of credit? Which is the most important, and why?**

First-time Job Seekers: Relax during the interview—this shows confidence. Keep in mind that you're applying for a customer contact position and need to exhibit confidence and the ability to deal with people. Your educational background should include courses in business, business law, accounting, finance, and taxation. A minimum of an associate's degree is required, though a bachelor's degree is preferred.

Don't expect to have any real lending authority in your first job. You'll probably start as a commercial loan assistant, helping senior loan administrators with paperwork, phone calls, and some analysis of financial statements.

A: *The five C's of credit are "credit," "character," "capacity," "collateral," and "capital." "Credit" is the most important. If a customer has a history of paying his debts, he or she will continue to do so, even in a less advantageous economic time.*

The five C's are a basic lending fundamental. Credit, followed by capacity (ability to repay), is considered the most important. Too often collateral is given too much emphasis. A correct response indicates that you have a good foundation for your decision-making process, whereas an incorrect response will most likely eliminate you from further contention. You should be prepared to answer this and other "basic quiz" questions.

Q: **If a customer was undecided about whether to have your bank or a competitor handle his loan requests, what would you do to convince that person to do business with you?**

A: *I'd stress our bank's and my own ability to provide prompt and personal service, as well as our commitment to our customers. I'd tell the client that we're a reputable institution and that we're around for the long run. I'd never try to downgrade or criticize the competition.*

This answer shows the interviewer that the candidate, too, is "in it for the long run" and not just looking at the position as a stopgap. Many people are alienated by negative advertising or competitor bashing, so be careful not to suggest that you might use this method.

Q: **Have you ever been in a situation where you had to set your own rate on a loan in order to save a deal?**

A: *Yes. I had to do that a number of times in order to be competitive with other banks. But at the same time, I didn't put the bank at risk, as the margin was still profitable. I think it's important to have some flexibility without "giving away the farm."*

This answer shows the interviewer the candidate's ability to make responsible, independent decisions necessary for the position. Your first loyalty as a lender is to your employer. However, customer relationships, business development, and maintaining business ties are also important.

Career Changers: Be prepared to explain why you want to change careers. It's not unusual for people early in their careers to switch jobs or even professions, but if you've spent twenty-five years acquiring skills that have little to do with loan administration or even banking in general, you're likely to be greeted by employers with much skepticism.

Q: How would you go about increasing the size of your loan portfolio?

A: *I'd start with community involvement in organizations such as Rotary, chamber of commerce, YMCA, Boys & Girls Clubs, and so on. I'd also network with my professional contacts, such as attorneys and accountants, who are an excellent source of referral business.*

This answer shows the candidate's willingness to make a commitment to the bank and to the community. Convince the interviewer that you have the aggressiveness necessary for this highly competitive field—that you're willing and able to go out and drum up business for the bank. A large professional network at your disposal is especially attractive, as referral business is the best type of new business.

Q: If you presented a loan to a supervisor for approval and were denied, what would you do?

A: *If I thought it was a request that had merit and would be profitable for the bank with minimal risk, I'd find out what my supervisor's concerns were and try to get additional information. I'd then re-present the loan for approval and try to make a strong case for it. But if the loan was refused again, I'd go back to the applicant and explain that our bank just couldn't do it.*

This shows the interviewer several things: that you feel a certain commitment to the customer, that you have respect for your supervisors (you should never say, "I'd go over his or her head"), and that you have concern for the profitability of the bank. At the same time, you should know when to let go and realize when a situation is beyond your control.

Q: How would you describe your thinking, and how does it affect your ability to tell someone no?

A: *I'd consider myself a moderate. The ability to tell someone that his or her loan has been declined is something I've developed over the years with experience. No one ever wants to say no, but, unfortunately, it's a necessary part of the job.*

Experienced Professionals: Be sure to bring all your experience to the interviewer's attention. Employers are looking at specific skills in relation to commercial lending. A background in retail lending that includes both direct and indirect financing, as well as equity mortgages, is considered attractive. Show that you have skills in short-term as well as long-term mortgage financing. If you have experience as a commercial-loan assistant, you can graduate to the level of junior loan officer and eventually senior lender.

Avoid presenting yourself as someone who grants loans too liberally or too conservatively, as either can be damaging to a bank. The ability to say no when necessary is a great virtue for a loan administrator.

Q: What sort of lending authority and portfolio size did you have in the past?

A: *I had a portfolio of $25,000 in unsecured and $50,000 in secured loans. I've also had a great deal of experience presenting large loans to senior management and loan committees. I've been involved in the formulation and approval of numerous other complex deals, as well.*

The interviewer is trying to judge the level of authority the candidate is able to handle. This answer illustrates the candidate's ability to handle loans even though they're above his or her level of authority, and to make recommendations regarding them. Also, it shows good analytical ability, which is a necessity in decision making. The size of your previous portfolio will certainly play a part in determining your lending authority in your new position.

Q: Would you allow an applicant to reapply for a loan with a cosigner after he or she has already been denied credit?

A: *It would depend on the circumstances of the original denial. If the applicant was denied credit because of insufficient income or inability to supply adequate collateral, and these circumstances had changed, then there would be sufficient reasons to reconsider the application. But if the applicant had a bad credit history, such as a failure to repay loans or a history of paying bills late, then I wouldn't allow it.*

This is an excellent response. A good cosigner doesn't make a bad loan good. If credit is an issue, then ten cosigners shouldn't be able to change your decision. But if the sole reason for your original denial was lack of sufficient income, then it's generally not a bad idea to consider the loan. Show the interviewer that you exercise sound judgment, as this candidate does.

Candidates Re-entering the Workforce: Be prepared to explain the reason for your absence from the workplace as well as the reason for your return. You need to show that you've thought your decision through and are ready to commit to a new job. You may have to overcome employer concerns that you'll no longer be able to withstand the rigors of a nine-to-five job. Emphasize your previous experience in commercial lending, and how you've kept your computer skills, especially spreadsheet programs, up-to-date.

Q: When you take collateral for a loan, what factors do you consider?

A: *I'd first consider the value of the collateral. But marketability, condition, and fully securing the bank's position by a chattel, mortgage, assignment, or attachment, are all additional factors that need to be carefully considered.*

Collateral needs to be looked at in a worst-case scenario—"loan values" or "quick sale values" should be used. Don't overestimate your collateral. Perfecting your lien is essential for a second loan. Closing in the proper names and using the proper documents (mortgage, security agreements, and so on) are musts.

Loan Officer

Q: **What types of customers do you lend to in your current position?**

A: *Middle-market companies with sales ranging from $5 million to $50 million. I've had experience with several companies in different industries such as pharmaceuticals, high technology, and consumer goods.*

You should give the interviewer a variety of customers in different industries, if at all possible. Of course, you should mention dollar amounts and give the interviewer a brief rundown of your lending history with the customer. It also makes sense to discuss how you first met the customer (Was it a cold call, or were you referred to the customer?) and if the customer referred you to his or her friends or colleagues.

Q: **Are you a cash-flow or asset-based lender?**

A: *A little of both, really. However, I'm primarily a cash-flow lender because that's the primary source for repayment of loans. I do look at the balance sheet to analyze my downside risk.*

The interviewer will be looking for your expertise in understanding each of these particular financial statements and how they impact the decision to lend to a prospective customer. To be given serious consideration for this type of position, you need to understand what each statement says about a prospective customer's business and how it impacts a customer's ability to pay off the interest and principal of the loan. Give an example, if possible.

Q: **How easily do you think you can make the transition from a big bank to a smaller institution?**

A: *One of the most important characteristics a loan officer can have is strong people skills, which I count as one of my best assets. No matter the size of*

First-time Job Seekers: Try to draw parallels to your academic experience, and/or to any internships or summer job experience you think best illustrates your skills and suitability for this type of position. Don't be overly concerned that you don't have real experience to draw on—bank-hiring managers often lament the fact that experienced candidates seem to lack the enthusiasm and desire for such jobs. This could be your ticket to landing your first job in banking.

the organization you work for, a loan officer always works with people, and because of my strong skills in this area, I believe that I can work for any bank, regardless of its size.

Focus on your skills in dealing with people and how you effectively interact with customers in a variety of settings. The interviewer's concern here is that the candidate might not be able to adjust to a different corporate culture, with customers whose portfolios might not sustain his or her interest. It's the candidate's job to convince the interviewer that the congenial atmosphere and aggressive nature of a smaller institution will be welcomed, and that the candidate's skills are well suited to the style and demands placed on employees at a smaller bank.

Q: Tell me about the new business you've developed.

A: *Over the past twelve months I've developed $15 million in new loan commitments, resulting in average loans outstanding of $9.5 million. These commitments have resulted in five new relationships for the bank, and in addition to the loan volume, the accounts will generate $100,000 in new fee income for the bank.*

Give examples of new customers that you've brought into your current bank and how you were able to attract them. What methods did you use to convince them to go with your bank rather than the competition? Convince the interviewer that you have what it takes to land new customers and that you thrive on finding new companies in different industries.

Q: How do you target and call on customers?

A: *I use various sources to target prospects, and employ several different calling methods, depending upon the situation. In my calling area the bank has a list of companies ranked by sales size, which I use as a starting point. I also use my contacts with accountants, lawyers, and the local chamber of commerce to come up with more prospects. But I find the best source of prospects to be my current customers. They like the job I do for them and feel confident referring me to others.*

Career Changers: In some sense you're much like the first-time job seeker, as you have no banking experience to fall back on. Here you'll want to draw on your professional accomplishments and skills as they relate to the position. Do your homework on the bank to gain a perspective on the skills and abilities you'll need to sell to the prospective hiring manager. Don't be surprised if you possess a skill or special talent that a bank would find appealing or that internal candidates cannot bring to the job.

The interviewer will want to know what methods you use to find and attract new customers to your bank. List as many different methods as possible and demonstrate that you're creative and resourceful in lining up new customers. The interviewer will be interested not only in the types of sources you use but in your approach, and your method of coming up with alternatives if your original sources fail to turn up positive leads. Give examples such as friends, colleagues, family members, association leads, directories, and so on.

Q: How do you sell your institution?

A: *I sell the bank as a financially sound, customer-responsive organization. Customers and prospects are interested in financial strength and excellent customer service. We don't just sell a commodity, we sell excellent service.*

Your selling skills will be on the line here as well as your knowledge of what your institution does best in comparison to the competition. Treat the interviewer as if he or she is a prospective customer; accept the invitation to show off how much you know about your bank's services and its competitive edge in the marketplace. Remember to match what your bank does exceptionally well to what the interviewer needs from your bank. The interviewer wants to make sure that when you represent his or her institution, you'll be thoroughly prepared to sell it to prospective customers.

Q: Is there any new business success story that stands out in your mind?

A: *Yes, as a matter of fact, I'm most proud of the recent $3 million financing package we won as one of three bidders. We acquired the package mostly because of our fast turnaround time, which impressed the prospect as much as did the content of our proposal. It conveyed that we were serious about wanting that customer's business.*

You should be prepared to give a detailed example or two, including numbers, if possible. The interviewer may be interested in the type of customer, the industry, how you landed the business, and what skills you used to close the business. You should be ready and willing to discuss all of these matters.

Experienced Professionals: You may want to highlight more than just your background. Show enthusiasm for the bank you're applying for and be prepared to discuss how the institution is well positioned to take the advantage of market opportunities. What special skills or experience do you bring to this bank that cannot be found in other candidates? Do you know companies in certain industries that might be of interest to the bank as prospective customers? Use your knowledge and experience to your advantage and find out where the bank has holes you can fill with that experience.

Don't worry about what the interviewer considers a new business-success story; jump in with any new customer that you believe made a significant impact on your bank.

Q: **What's your approach to monitoring a portfolio? What do you watch for?**

A: *I firmly believe that the real work begins once a prospect becomes a customer. To do a good job monitoring an existing portfolio, you need to be proactive, not reactive. You have to set up systems and procedures with the help of others in the commercial loan department to monitor the financial-reporting requirements and the financial covenants as outlined in the loan-approval documents. You watch to see that customers are keeping to projections. Monitoring deposit balances as opposed to historical or seasonal patterns is one sure way to uncover "red flags" early.*

You'll be tested on your methodology, analytical ability, and experience in averting possible problems when a customer starts to fall behind on payments. Here the interviewer has some definite thoughts on the subject, and it'll be up to you to demonstrate that you look for certain signals telling you when and how to act to avoid a potential problem. Do you turn to anyone for help if a situation starts to get out of hand? You must impress the interviewer with a logical sequence of actions that are intended to oversee loans and spot potential problems.

Q: **Tell me about a problem loan you helped turn around.**

A: *One of my customers, a residential-construction company, experienced problems handling rapid growth after a decision to expand into commercial construction. I met with senior management and convinced them that in order to resolve their loan problems, they should focus on their core business, residential construction. Taking my advice, they were able to turn around their delinquent payment schedule.*

Candidates Re-entering the Workforce: You'll have to be up-to-date on changes that have taken place during your absence and know how your skills and abilities can quickly be adapted to take advantage of new technologies, methodologies, or procedures. If you need additional training, don't hesitate to get it. If you're currently taking classes or seminars to hone your skills, mention that during the interview. Don't shy away from the fact that you've been out of the workforce for a period of time. Instead, focus on how you can help the bank today and tomorrow. Remember—if they called you in for and interview, they must think you can help them. It's up to you to convince them that you have what it takes to succeed right away.

What have you done to avoid a potential disaster and restore a payment schedule that satisfied both your bank and the customer? The candidate's being tested here for his or her problem-solving ability, as well as for the ability to work with customers to ensure they understand the severity of the situation and to show them how to avoid future problems. To that end you'll need to demonstrate your creativity and business sense in developing solutions that work for all parties involved. What did you first do when you noticed the problem, and what steps did you immediately take to rectify it?

Q: **In calling on new accounts, what's the main obstacle you've encountered selling your bank over your competition?**

A: *I found initially that many small businesses considered my bank cold, unresponsive, and too large to care about their needs. I countered this problem by demonstrating a sincere interest in their business, and in problems unique to their business. When they requested more information about my bank's services, I made sure they received the information within forty-eight hours.*

The candidate's being tested here not only for selling ability, but for resourcefulness in overcoming a problem and turning it into a positive situation for his or her bank. How persistent are you in assessing what a customer needs and how your bank, as opposed to the competition, can better serve the customer? When a particular obstacle appeared, what did you do to try to overcome it? If you had to do it again, would you have taken the same approach? Your understanding of your competition, as well as your ability to emphasize competitive advantages that make sense to the customer in spite of objections, will be a key to dealing successfully with this question.

Q: **Is there an industry or firm you particularly enjoy lending to?**

A: *My experience as a lending officer has put me in touch with many different types of businesses, both large and small, and from a variety of industries. I really don't have a particular favorite, but I've found that working with small companies can be very rewarding because you get to know the people behind the business and to work with them as they grow the firm into a larger company.*

The interviewer wants to know why the candidate prefers certain companies or industries over others, whether or not those companies might interest the interviewer as possible candidates for new business. He or she will also be measuring your ability and interest in going after new business, depending upon the variety of companies you discuss as part of your answer to this kind of question. You'll want to show enthusiasm for these companies, give reasons for your enthusiasm, and let the interviewer know if the relationship has been built over time or is brand-new.

Research Associate

Q: **When did you first become interested in the financial industry?**

A: *During my freshman year of college as an undergraduate, my economics professor suggested that each of us get a subscription to the Wall Street Journal. WSJ's profiles of corporate financial leaders and their firms got me really excited about this industry.*

The recruiter will want to see that you're passionate about the business. The candidate addresses the question cleverly here, describing an interest developed a long time ago as a freshman in college. In other words, the candidate's desire for this job isn't just a passing fad but demonstrates a sincere and abiding interest.

Q: **What are your primary responsibilities as a research associate for your company?**

A: *As a research associate I have a variety of tasks I must juggle at all times. I develop operational and financial models under the supervision of a senior analyst. I collect data and analyze companies. Most contact with vendors, competitors, and customers comes through me and the other research associates. I also spend a great deal of time preparing marketing materials and client presentations.*

The recruiter will want to know how much responsibility you've had, which will reveal a great deal about how much you can handle in the new position. The candidate's answer here is commendable because it gives a good overview of his or her responsibilities without going into too much detail.

Q: **What experience helps you to be prepared and qualified for this research-associate position?**

A: *I have a B.A. in economics as well as an M.B.A. I also have three years' work experience as a research assistant. I concentrated on finance during my M.B.A. studies.*

The recruiter is looking for a certain set of qualifications for a research-associate position. The candidate possesses the required distinguished academic record. An M.B.A. is not a requirement, but it's impressive and helpful.

Q: **What special licenses do you have that are helpful as a research associate?**

A: *I've earned a Series 7 license. This makes me a registered financial representative, which means I can give investment advice to the public.*

More than likely this is the answer the recruiter's looking for. There are other licenses, but a Series 7 is what's expected at this stage. Work toward this license if you haven't already earned it.

Q: **What's been your greatest challenge in your current research-associate position?**

A: *My greatest challenge has been stepping into an existing marketing program that, before I joined, wasn't successful. Lots of initiative and input were required to make the marketing program work, and I enjoyed the effort involved.*

Here the candidate must demonstrate flexibility and adaptability. An answer like this would help show how you've been able to work with a plan to achieve success, despite some undesirable circumstances. Your positive outlook and proactive approach should be apparent.

Q: **If you could work with anyone in finance, whom would you want to work with?**

A: *There are many bright individuals in the finance industry, and especially a lot of talented newcomers over the last five years. I'd like to work with top management at Morgan Stanley or Goldman Sachs because of their long-term success. Specifically, working with Warren Buffett, an industry leader, would be extremely beneficial—I'd like an opportunity to learn how he thinks.*

The recruiter will want to see if you know who the industry leaders are. The candidate's answer here demonstrates a solid interest in the industry. It also suggests that the candidate has long-term personal goals for the business.

First-time Job Seekers: Send a general resume with a cover letter specific to the job and the institution's needs, not yours. If possible try to begin your career on the firing line (nonsupport-role position). If not, start in a support role in a department that you know you're ultimately interested in. If there's one day you should look serious and businesslike, it's the day of the job interview. Be sure to have clean fingernails and polished shoes—recruiters notice! Before accepting a position, evaluate how it will help you reach your long-term career goals.

Q: **What are your career goals for finance and banking five years from now?**

A: *In five years I'd like to be a senior research analyst for a boutique research firm like this one. I'd like sole responsibility for analyzing the industry and its major companies. I'd like to be in a position where I'm making explicit recommendations to clients regarding their investments. I'd like a lot of personal contact with the firm's clients, for whom I have great respect.*

The recruiter is trying to get a sense of the candidate's ambitions for the industry and the company. This answer reflects the normal career path and is thus quite appropriate. The candidate cleverly takes the opportunity to re-emphasize his or her interest in the recruiter's firm.

Q: **What specific financial skills have you developed, and what experiences helped you build these skills?**

A: *My strongest skill is my ability to understand my "internal" clients and to prioritize. In my current job I'm responsible for managing several studies at once, so I have to give each my full attention at all times—which is, of course, impossible. I've become quite adept at dealing with the most important issue first. This means that I can look at a large number of obligations that are all screaming "do me first" and instantly realize what needs my attention the most.*

The candidate's answer is excellent because he or she names one of the most important skills of the trade: the ability to prioritize effectively. An added plus is that this candidate has management potential. Although management skills aren't required, think of a skill you have that would make you indispensable to the position and to the people you'll support.

Q: **If you had extra time to devote to some financial project, what would that project be?**

A: *I'd like to develop an in-depth database of business analyses of all the companies and industries that my firm covers. That way the research associates could keep fully abreast of each other's work, and the firm as a whole could be stronger.*

Career Changers: Thoroughly research the financial industry and the companies you're applying to by reading annual reports, industry analysis, and the *Wall Street Journal.* Network with everyone who has connections to the financial industry. Find out everything you can. Determine how you can best meet the institution's needs, and position yourself accordingly for the job. But be realistic. This is an industry that trains its own from thousands of entry-level positions.

Here the recruiter's looking for a strong work ethic and team/company orientation. This candidate's answer reveals these traits, as well as a superior analytic ability and an outstanding facility for numbers. The candidate's strong interest in analyzing businesses will also make an extremely favorable impression upon the recruiter.

Q: **What's your weakness professionally as a research associate?**

A: *I find it sometimes hard to interrupt the firm's senior research staff. They're so busy that I've found it difficult to get time with them when I've needed it. I've developed a "critical memo" system to solve the problem. I also have a lot of interaction with the other departments in the firm. I've practiced my communication skills on them and now use these skills with the senior research staff, which has really helped.*

The recruiter will want to know where you may fall short in what's expected. Having difficulty dealing with the firm's senior research staff is a problem, because this kind of interaction is one of the main responsibilities of a research associate. The candidate has resolved this issue, however, so the recruiter will be comfortable with this answer.

Q: **What career opportunities do you see in the financial industry?**

A: *Opportunities in finance seem to be changing greatly because of all the new product offerings. The greatest opportunities will be found, first, in discovering where the industry as a whole is going, and then playing a part in creating whatever products are in demand. Wall Street is now more competitive, so it is much harder to make money these days.*

The recruiter's looking for a big-picture knowledge of the industry. The late nineties were a glamorous and opulent time for Wall Street, and the candidate demonstrates that he or she is fully aware these days are over for the financial industry. Read general-business publications, as well as financial publications, so you'll be able to answer questions like this.

Q: **What books have you read about the financial and banking industry?**

A: *I've read a lot of books about finance and banking. What immediately sticks in my mind is* Understanding Wall Street *by Jeffrey B. Little and Lucien Rhodes. I've also read most of the personal testimonial books, because it never hurts to hear about someone else's experience. Of these, I particularly enjoyed* The Predator's Ball *by Connie Bruck,* Barbarians at the Gate *by Bryan Burrough and John Helyar, and* Liar's Poker *by Michael Lewis.*

The recruiter will want to know the depth of your interest in the financial industry. This candidate has read a good selection of books, which would impress any would-be employer. Why not read some of these books, if you haven't already, before the interview?

Q: What financial publications do you read on a regular basis?

A: *I definitely read the industry publications, especially* The Economist, *the* Wall Street Journal, *and* The Institutional Investor. *I also try to read the* Financial Times.

The recruiter will expect that you read the industry publications because it's almost a requirement for the job. This candidate reads a very good selection. If you don't read at least some of these periodicals, start doing so before the interview.

Q: What are the differences between financial management in private and in public firms?

A: *There's a big difference in how capital is raised. Equity can be used to raise capital for a public firm, but a private firm usually can only use debt or a more limited private equity placement.*

Building again on the candidate's specific skill and knowledge base, the recruiter is looking for proof that this job seeker understands more than does the typical research associate. The candidate gives a strong, confident answer to the question. Brush up on financial-industry basics before the interview so you'll be prepared for questions like this.

Q: You've got a great education. Do you think an education is necessary for this research-associate job?

A: *It's necessary but not sufficient. The research-analyst job requires lots of technical knowledge best developed in an educational institution. But it's also a game of nerve and wit. You need street smarts as well as book smarts.*

Although a good education is an important prerequisite for the job, recruiters know that intuitive "street smarts" distinguish the best and allow them to get quickly to the top. Use an example of how your street smarts have complemented your technical-educational background.

Experienced Professionals: In a big city use headhunters. They're often a good source of job leads, and they're paid by the company, not by you. In smaller areas try to get referrals. You should interview only for jobs that really interest you. Don't be influenced by a flashy offer. You have a lot of leverage at this point in your career, so you might as well choose a job you really want. Be sure to gauge your true worth. Salaries are high for "stars."

Q: **Do you think Wall Street got carried away with derivatives?**

A: *Well, the conventional wisdom seems to indicate that that's the case. However, all financial instruments are derivatives—even stocks. It's not the product that's a problem, but how it's used.*

The recruiter is probing for the candidate's ability to see beyond conventional wisdom and to think through the issues. It's important to demonstrate, too, that you see "the big picture" and can defend your opinions.

Q: **Would you prefer to work for a full-service or a specialty firm?**

A: *I like both but right now want to work for a full-service firm. I want to get broad exposure to all financial markets and opportunities, and a full-service firm offers the best opportunity to do so. If I find an area I'm particularly good at, then I could specialize in a division of a full-service firm or with a specialty firm.*

The recruiter is looking for flexibility because an analyst's job at this stage could lead in many directions. Obviously you should "tailor" your answer in the appropriate way depending on whether you're interviewing with a full-service or a specialty firm.

Q: **Some people say Wall Street represents the world but is a small town. Do you agree?**

A: *I think that's right. There are literally thousands of financial-services firms, but the top twenty-five represent over 75 percent of the businesses in the United States. It's important to know the key players. I've developed contacts with all the major firms.*

You need to demonstrate your knowledge and contacts in this very special industry. The financial-service industry is in many ways a "club," and you need to know its rules. Developing a wide network is important, and you should demonstrate your knowledge of key players and of the industry as a whole.

Q: **Our analysts work incredibly long hours. Are you used to long hours and lots of stress?**

Candidates Re-entering the Workforce: No matter what questions are asked, always try to work into your answer information about a skill or positive attribute that will benefit the company. Write a thank-you note after each interview; restating the main attributes you can bring to the job and how you can benefit the company. Don't get discouraged. You'll receive an offer.

A: *I thrive on them. In my current job I've often worked fifteen to eighteen hours a day for weeks on end. My spouse is an analyst, too, and we both accept the challenge and support each other. I like to get totally immersed in a project and wrestle it to the ground no matter what it takes.*

Research-associate positions are tough and demanding in terms of skills and time. The recruiter will want to be sure you've got the stamina to succeed, and that you know what you're getting into.

Q: Banks are rapidly entering into a number of areas that have been traditional fields of financial services. Do you think they can compete?

A: *Most definitely, because they bring strong client relationships. Also, the bigger banks are now quite large and well capitalized. We can be competitive, though, because of our in-depth experience and innovation with new products.*

The recruiter will be interested in your knowledge of the changing competitive dynamics of the financial-services business and whether you have an understanding of what it will take to succeed. If you're interviewing for a research-analyst position at a bank, tailor your answer to the bank's competitive strengths.

Stockbroker

(Entry-Level)

Q: **Have you ever worked in this industry?**

A: *Yes. I worked as an intern for a small brokerage firm for two college semesters. I worked for two brokers, putting together client lists and researching companies, which involved some analysis of financial reports and data. I also have a bachelor's degree in business administration.*

If you have no prior professional experience, you'll need to demonstrate an interest in the industry through an internship or some other relevant experience. Describe relevant college courses you've taken or informational interviews you've conducted with professionals in the field.

Q: **This is really a tough business to get started in. Do you have any idea what you're getting yourself into?**

A: *I have a friend in the business who first got me interested in it, and recently I've conducted informational interviews with two brokers at different houses about the brokerage business in general. All the information I've obtained from these people has helped me decide that this is the career I want to pursue. I realize it'll be tough, but if you'll give me a chance, I'll prove to you that I'll be successful.*

If you're an entry-level candidate, the recruiter may try to talk you out of getting into the brokerage business to determine whether you can think on your feet and hold up under pressure. Tell the recruiter why you're going to be successful. Your answer should reflect a genuine enthusiasm for, and a realistic understanding of, the business.

Q: **Do you have a Series 7 license?**

A: *Yes, I'm Series 7 licensed.*

Federal and state regulations require you to be licensed by the National Association of Securities Dealers (NASD). You need to be with a company for a set period of time (usually four months) before you can register for the exam. If you're just starting out, you won't be expected to have your license already. Most larger brokerage firms will pay for classes that help you study for the test, which is sponsored by the NASD. Depending on your career track, you may eventually have to get additional licenses, such as a Series 63.

Q: Do you have any experience with intangible sales?

A: *The closest thing I've had to experience with intangible sales was during my senior year, when I worked as a telemarketer for my college's alumni fundraising campaign. I had one of the highest sales records of all the telemarketers.*

Stocks and bonds are intangibles—you can't touch or feel them, which means you have to describe them without overdescribing them. It's difficult to sell intangibles, and you'll need to prove that you're capable of it, regardless of your level of experience. The interviewer will want to hear that you're comfortable selling intangibles and that you can't wait to get started.

Q: Have you had any cold-calling experience over the phone or in person?

A: *Yes. As I mentioned, I worked as a telemarketer for my college's alumni fundraising campaign during my senior year of college. So I would say yes, I'm comfortable on the phone. I also think a big part of being able to do phone sales is the ability to handle rejection—which I have.*

This question and the previous one are two of the most important questions you'll encounter. Many candidates have field experience, but not telephone experience, so a background in telemarketing will give you a strong advantage. Tell the interviewer that you're comfortable with the phones and that you can handle rejection.

Q: Do you have any connections in this geographic area?

A: *Yes. In fact, I've lived here for twenty-five years. Over the course of my career I've developed a sizable network of local professional contacts, including attorneys and accountants, who are an excellent source of referral business.*

The answer to this question is important because referral business is a great source of new business and recruiters will want to know if you have a large

First-time Job Seekers: Companies look for a bachelor's degree in business, economics, accounting, or marketing. A general liberal-arts background is also considered acceptable as long as you have the drive and desire. A big company like Prudential of Solomon Smith Barney receives thousands of resumes every year, so internships or work experience will make you stand out. If you don't have your licensure, a company may teach you the material and sponsor you so you can pass the series 7 exam.

At the job interview portray yourself as outgoing, quick thinking, intelligent, and self-confident. Don't go into the interview with the attitude that brokering is an easy way to make a lot of money. Show the recruiter you know that you really need to be smart and work hard to succeed.

professional network at your disposal. Relocating from another part of the company is a big disadvantage; having ties to the geographic area means not only that you're likely to stay in the position, but that the company's potential for acquiring new business is good. Tell the recruiter how long you've lived in the area and whom you know. Portray yourself as someone who could bring a lot of new business to the company.

Q: **Here's an example of a business plan that people have followed in the past. Put together your own business plan and bring it back to me tomorrow.**

A: *That would be no problem. Actually, I brought with me a sample of a business plan I did for an assignment in my corporate-finance class. May I show it to you?*

If you have limited experience in brokering, you may encounter this question. The employer will want reassurance that you're capable of doing this kind of work. Make sure you put some thought into the marketing aspect of your business plan. Regardless of your experience, you should consider bringing a sample business plan with you to your first interview. This is bound to impress even the toughest recruiter and give you a big advantage.

Q: **Where else have you interviewed recently, and for what positions?**

A: *I've interviewed at several other nationally known securities firms in the area, all for the position of stockbroker.*

Brokerage houses prefer candidates who express a strong interest in their company, but who still shop around. Your candidacy will be especially attractive if you have several different competing firms interested in you. Interviewing with other firms in the industry also demonstrates your commitment to a career in brokering—you're not just looking for any job to make ends meet. This is a good reason for interviewing with companies even if you're not initially interested in the positions they're offering.

Career Changers: Managers like to see a pattern of success in your work history. You should show that you're self-confident and smart. Emphasize any relevant experience you may have, especially in telephone sales or in the insurance industry, because stockbrokers sometimes deal with investments (such as annuities). You'll have an advantage over entry-level candidates because you're more likely to have a well-developed network of personal and business contacts at your disposal. But you'll have to show that you really know what you're getting into and that you have extensive knowledge of, and interest in, the business. Talk about your success with managing your personal portfolio, or perhaps about the informal financial advice you give to friends.

Q: **Have you ever heard of our firm? What are your first thoughts when you think of our company?**

A: *Yes, I'm very familiar with your firm. When I think of this company, I think of an industry leader with a solid reputation for being stable yet innovative. I also find your extensive employee-training program very attractive. I think this is a company that I could make a positive contribution to, while learning a great deal and continuously improving my skills.*

Your answer should obviously be affirmative. Discuss your in-depth knowledge of the company as well as why you're attracted to the company based on its strengths. Expect follow-up questions if your answer is vague—don't expect to be able to bluff. You'll need to be prepared to answer this question—if you aren't, you could seriously hurt your candidacy.

Q: **How well do you handle pressure?**

A: *Fine. I played sports in college and high school, so I'm used to pressure. I know the securities business is filled with stress and pressure, but I think that's part of what makes it so exciting.*

When the market becomes volatile, a stockbroker's job can get pretty stressful. Clients will call you up asking what to do, at the same time you have to worry about getting all your buy and sell orders. It's normal to get frazzled, but you'll need to convince the interviewer that you'll remain calm enough to work.

Q: **Tell me about any honors you won in college and high school, or any extracurricular activities you participated in.**

A: *In high school I was in the National Honor Society and the Spanish Honor Society. In college I was student-body treasurer my junior year, and senior year I was class vice president. I played varsity soccer all four years, and I started the last two. I also graduated with honors in my major and ended up summa cum laude overall.*

Experienced Professionals: Companies like to see winners. When you change companies, you usually bring your clients with you, so discuss the number of clients you have, your average portfolio size, how much the portfolio has grown, and so on. Show how well you've done in the past. Companies also like to see evidence that an experienced candidate can handle institutional investors like banks. Potential career paths for experienced brokers include becoming a branch manager of a national firm (like Prudential) or other management/supervisory positions.

Companies like people who are aggressive, self-confident, and have a documented history of success. Discuss the sports or clubs you participated in, or the volunteer work you did. Convince the interviewer that you're aggressive and sharp and have the drive and determination to do well.

Q: **What newspapers or magazines do you read on a regular basis?**

A: *I read the local paper every day so I can keep up with the news, and I also read the* Wall Street Journal *to keep up with goings-on in the markets, and with business news. I also subscribe to* Money *and* Worth *magazines.*

In order to be taken seriously, you must read the *Wall Street Journal* on a regular basis. You don't have to read every word, but enough to talk about it intelligently. It's a good idea to subscribe to a couple of financial or investing magazines, too, for a different perspective. Some managers like to follow up this question with others about a news item that may have recently appeared, so don't say you read something if you don't.

Q: **How do you plan on attracting a solid client base?**

A: *I think I have enough contacts in the area to start me off, but then I plan on doing a lot of phone work to attract new clients. I know I have a lot of work to do before I'll be comfortable with the number of clients I have.*

Expect this question if you're new to the business. Show you have plenty of contacts or sources for potential contacts: college-alumni associations, college or high-school friends, your parents' friends, and so on. Some companies will give newcomers clients from retired brokers. It's also important to show the interviewer that you're realistic—that no matter how many resources you have at your disposal, you know how tough it will be to get settled.

Candidates Re-entering the Workforce: This can be a very difficult transition. If you've left the business altogether, you've probably had to give up you clients (and their portfolios), so basically you'll be starting from scratch. First you'll need to make sure your licensure is still valid, and even then, with all the regulatory issues involved, companies will look at you skeptically. You'll have to answer a lot of questions about why you left your last company and why you're coming back. Presuming you weren't serving time for insider trading be totally honest. Talk about your previous experience (number of clients, portfolio size, and so on) and how you've kept up with changes in the industry (for example, by reading the *Wall Street Journal*). It won't be easy, but if you do a good job of selling yourself, you'll probably be back in the business.

CHAPTER 9
ADMINISTRATION

Administrative Assistant

Q: How does your previous work experience relate to this position?

A: *Well, I don't have any formal experience as an administrative assistant, but I feel I'm well qualified for the position. I learned excellent typing and computer skills in school, both of which I used in my last position as a part-time receptionist for a small law firm. I'm very flexible and I can learn new skills easily. For example, the receptionist position involved learning legalese in a hurry, as well as using some advanced word-processing skills. Within two weeks' time I could handle more calls and take more memos than any other receptionist in the office. I also developed excellent telephone skills as a volunteer telemarketer during a sales drive for a local television station.*

Expect this question if you're an entry-level job seeker. The employer is concerned that you may not have the skills and qualifications necessary for the position. Reassure him or her that you're just as qualified as candidates with several years' experience by showing precisely how you can use the skills you learned, say, as a part-time sales clerk or a full-time student in this new position. Most employers will be looking primarily for typing, computer, and interpersonal skills. Be sure also to emphasize your flexibility and enthusiasm to learn new tasks.

Q: What is your typing speed?

A: *I'm usually accurate at about fifty words per minute.*

This is a fairly standard question. Many candidates will greatly exaggerate their typing prowess, only to be given a typing test at the conclusion of the interview. If you perform poorly on the test after boasting lightning-fast, error-free typing, you've lost your credibility. If you're not sure what your speed is, test yourself (on a typewriter, not a word processor) so you can be prepared to answer this question.

Q: What word-processing, spreadsheet, and database management programs are you familiar with?

A: *I'm very comfortable using both Microsoft Word for Windows and Excel for Windows. I've also used ACT occasionally to do large mailings of form letters.*

It's a sure bet that you'll be asked this or a similar question about your computer skills. If you don't have any, get them fast, since they're a prerequisite for most administrative positions. If you're not up-to-date on the latest applications, a refresher course could greatly enhance your candidacy. Most employers look for sound knowledge of Microsoft Word and Excel, and some experience with a database-management application. If you aren't familiar with the applications a particular company uses, be sure to emphasize your ability to learn new software quickly.

Q: On a scale of one to ten, rate your proficiency with these applications.

A: *I'd say I'm a nine with Microsoft Word, and a seven with Excel. In fact, I used both applications on a daily basis in my last position.*

Your proficiency with software will directly affect your productivity on the job. With so many computer-literate candidates vying for jobs, employers will not consider you if you'll need to be trained on the job in basic computing. If you can't honestly say you're at least a "seven" with at least one common word-processing and spreadsheet application, you'd better take a refresher course.

Q: What operating systems are you familiar with?

A: *I'm very proficient in Windows 2000. I'm also comfortable using Mac OS.*

This question separates the techies from the computer-phobes. Answering the employer with a blank stare will do nothing to bolster your claims of computer proficiency. Most employers these days are looking for sound knowledge of Windows, though knowing MS-DOS and Macintosh operating systems is a plus.

First-time Job Seekers: A high school degree and basic office skills will qualify candidates for most lower-level secretarial positions. Knowledge of word-processing, spreadsheet, and database management programs is becoming increasingly important, and most employers require it. You should also be proficient in key boarding and good at spelling, punctuation, grammar, and oral communication. Many employers will also be looking for a pleasant telephone manner, so be sure to speak clearly and articulately on the phone and during the interview. Stress any experience you may have had in school or in part-time jobs that can be applied to this position, such as typing or interpersonal skills.

Q: **Do you have any experience taking dictation?**

A: *Yes. My last boss would often dictate long, detailed letters with lots of technical jargon. He had a habit of speaking very quickly, so I had to learn to write and type very quickly. I would also transcribe his tape-recorded notes onto disk.*

You'll encounter this question only if taking dictation is part of the job description. So if you've never done it, emphasize your willingness and ability to learn.

Q: **Can you take shorthand?**

A: *No, I can't. But as I mentioned earlier, I do have experience taking rapid dictation. My last boss never had to wait for me to catch up.*

This skill is required for some higher-level positions.

Q: **Have you ever screened telephone calls?**

A: *Yes, I fielded many calls for my last employer from some pretty determined callers. If a caller became angry or upset at not being able to get through, I would say something like, "I'm sorry, Ms. Reynolds is not available this afternoon. If you'll leave your name and telephone number with me, I'll be certain she gets your message as soon as possible." Then I would politely restate my position until the caller finally realized that he or she was not going to get past my desk. I was always polite, but firm.*

Busy executives like assistants who can handle a large volume of calls with accuracy, judgment, and tact. Speaking clearly and articulately during your interview will go a long way toward convincing the employer of your capabilities in this area. Be sure to emphasize any previous professional experience you may have had on the telephone.

Q: **Do you plan to further your education?**

A: *I don't have any plans to go to school full-time in the near future, but I do like to take occasional night courses and weekend seminars to help keep my job skills up-to-date. Last year, for example, I took a speed-typing class and attended a seminar on international business protocol. I also make a point of regularly reading BusinessWeek magazine, as well as several trade journals to keep up with the latest business news.*

Answer this question with great care. Though wanting to better yourself is certainly laudable, employers do not want to hear that you intend to quit your job and enroll in school full-time, particularly if the degree you're pursuing is unrelated to a career in administration. On the other hand, you do not want to appear inflexible and unwilling to learn new things. Your best bet is to express an ongoing interest in learning that will help you on the job, such as a weekly computer class or a weekend seminar.

Q: **What are you looking for in your next job?**

A: *I'm looking for a position where I can use my computer, typing, and interpersonal skills. I thrive in a busy environment, where I can juggle many tasks at one time. I would like to be given increasing responsibilities over time, though I'm also adept at performing lengthy, mundane tasks. I like to work hard and do the best job I possibly can, no matter what the task. For example, I really enjoyed my position in customer service at Bocca Industries. I felt continually challenged by solving customer problems and felt as if I was really making a positive contribution to the company.*

Be careful—this is a trick question. If you describe your dream job complete with lavish office and corporate jet, the employer will quickly write you off as unrealistic and unlikely to stay in the position for very long. On the other hand, if you cite typing and filing as your ultimate goal, the employer may conclude that you lack ambition. Pay careful attention to the job description. If the employer seems to be looking for a career secretary who can type, take phone calls, and greet clients, that's how you'll need to portray yourself. In general, you should express satisfaction at performing various clerical tasks and an ongoing enthusiasm to take on additional responsibilities.

Q: **Tell me about your last boss.**

A: *Ms. Winters was a great motivator—she would push people to their limits, and she was a stickler for detail. But she was always fair, and she rewarded good, hard work. I would call her a tough boss, but a good boss.*

While the recruiter realizes that most people do not adore their bosses, he or she wants to determine if you're willing to badmouth yours. After all, if you speak ill of your last boss, what's to stop you from doing the same with your next one? Avoid making any type of negative comment, no matter how justified it may be, because it will only reflect badly on you. Even if your previous employer was absolutely horrific, your best bet is to remain upbeat and diplomatic.

Q: **What type of person do you work best with?**

A: *I really get along well with most everybody, but I work particularly well with other dedicated, hardworking people. The crew I worked with at my last job*

Career Changers: Emphasize your office and computer skills, making sure they're current. You should be able to speak with authority about the industry you're interested in, as well as about the company you're interviewing with. Be ready to discuss your reasons for wanting to change careers, and how you can apply the skills you've gained to this new position.

was made up of some really terrific people; everyone was completely profes-
sional, and we all thought of ourselves as part of a team.

The employer wants to know more about your interpersonal skills, since administrative assistants must be tactful in their dealings with many different people. Name several general types of people you work well with and why. Don't give a laundry list of very specific qualities, or employers may conclude that you're difficult to get along with.

Q: **What type of person do you find it difficult to work with?**

A: *I really don't have any problems working with other people. My former col-*
leagues would tell you that I'm actually quite easy to get along with.

Again, navigate this question with care. You don't want to end up unwittingly listing traits the recruiter admires in others or embodies himself. If pressed, you should be as vague as possible, citing a dislike of employees who don't work to their potential, or some other safe bet.

Q: **How do you typically organize your work and plan your day?**

A: *I learned the value of good organizational skills when I worked for three differ-*
ent managers in a very hectic office. I had to juggle many different tasks at
one time with a constant stream of contracts and paperwork passing across
my desk. Without a concerted effort to stay organized, there would quickly
have been chaos. So I developed a system. I usually come into work a few
minutes early to get myself settled and look at the tasks in front of me. I take
a few minutes to jot down a few goals for myself for that day, which helps to
keep me focused and motivated. I have an electronic organizer, which helps
me keep track of key telephone numbers, appointments, and meetings. And
most important, I try to keep all clutter off my desk. This way I'm always on
top of my work so that I'm available to drop everything to help my boss at a
moment's notice.

Organizational skills are very important for secretarial positions. Do you use a personal organizer or planning software? Do you use a card file or a

Experienced Professionals: Your task is easy—simply emphasize all the progress you've made over the years as well as a few key accomplishments. You want to make it clear that you're building a career, not just doing a job. If you've reached a plateau in your career, you may want to consider becoming a certified professional secretary (CPS) by passing a series of examinations. For more information, contact the International Association of Administrative Professionals, 10502 NW Ambassador Dr., Kansas City, MO 64195-0404 (phone: 816-891-6600).

contact-management application? Are you a whiz at reorganizing cluttered work spaces? If so, now's the time to talk it up.

Q: **We're a company that believes that employee flexibility is crucial. How do you feel about that?**

A: *I consider myself very flexible. I'm less interested in what's on my job description and more interested in doing what it takes to get the job done. When my boss at Sanders had a baby, she was unable to work the long hours she used to put in. I helped out by taking over some of her responsibilities like generating reports and interfacing between various departments. I even represented her at some key meetings. On other occasions I helped her maximize her time by running some personal errands for her. I didn't mind, and I know she really appreciated it.*

Many employers want an assistant who is willing to go beyond the call of duty if necessary, someone who is willing to help out with an overflow of work from another department or even run occasional personal errands. Employers do not like to hear "That's not in my job description." Regardless of your true feelings on the subject, you should present yourself as enthusiastic and agreeable. Remember, your goal at this stage is to get a job offer. Once you have the job, it will be easier to renegotiate terms.

Q: **What other types of positions are you interested in, and what other companies have you recently applied to?**

A: *Well, I definitely want to stay in the clothing industry, and I'm applying only for administrative-related positions. I've recently interviewed for a secretarial position at Harcourt Clothiers and a customer-service position at Winterhill Catalog Company.*

This is not the time to mention that you've interviewed for everything from a hostess at a local burger joint to a junior exec at an advertising agency.

Candidates Re-entering the Workforce: The key to your success is making sure all of your skills are up-to-date. If they aren't, you should consider retraining, which might mean learning a new word processing program or taking a typing class at a local community college. If your skills are current, not to worry! Emphasize your previous job experience and skills, ways you've kept up-to-date during your leave (reading trade journals, doing part-time or temp work, attending seminars, and so on), and the skills you've learned at home that can be transferred to the workplace. You should also be prepared to discuss the reasons behind your leave of absence, and why you're ready to return.

Employers want to hear that you're committed to a career, that you're not just looking for another job to put in time. Mention only similar positions, ideally in the same industry.

Q: What would your references say about you?

A: *I think my references would tell you that I'm a dedicated, hardworking professional who can be relied on to get the job done on schedule. I use discretion and good judgment and get along with most everyone. My old boss used to tell me I was one of the most valuable members on his team.*

This is a great opportunity to sell yourself to a recruiter. Stress a few key qualities you have to offer, and give an example of praise you've received. Don't go so far as to misrepresent yourself, however; most employers will check your references.

Q: What do you know about our company?

A: *Farrah Fashions has a reputation for producing quality women's clothing at affordable prices. I read the June article in the* Times *about your recent growth and was quite impressed. I'm particularly interested in learning more about your new children's line.*

Because there's usually a lot of competition for administrative positions, you'll need to distinguish yourself from other qualified applicants. A great way of doing this is by doing a little background research on the potential employer before your interview. Working your knowledge of the company's products, services, and corporate philosophy into the conversation will impress even the toughest recruiter. Request a catalog of the company's products from its order department. Or check your local library for trade journals and other publications about the appropriate industry.

Claims Adjuster

Q: **Are you licensed to adjust claims in this state, or do you hold licenses in other states?**

A: *I don't currently hold a license for this state, but I've already contacted the Bureau of Insurance to inquire about licensure. I'm licensed to adjust claims in the state of Maine.*

Some states don't require a license to adjust claims, so it's important to know which ones do. Also, if you apply to a company that covers territory in different states, you must check into whether those states require licenses as well. For instance, you may apply to a company in Massachusetts that covers claims in Maine or New Hampshire, as well.

Q: **Have you taken any continuing-education classes or insurance training?**

A: *Yes, I'm currently enrolled in an associates-in-claims program. I've also attended numerous seminars, including one recently on negotiation. Continuing education is important to me, because there's always more to learn.*

The Insurance Institute of America sponsors dozens of classes and seminars nationwide. If you've taken some continuing-education classes, you'll stand apart from other candidates. Employers like to see that you have a genuine, active interest in the industry, and taking such classes proves that you're dedicated to a career in the field.

Q: **How have you demonstrated time-management skills in the past?**

A: *In my present position I'm careful to prioritize my workload. I always make the necessary phone calls as soon as I get a new claim, just so I have them out of the way. I believe it's important to follow up pending claims in a timely manner, since that allows me to close more files. If I'm well organized, then I can settle cases more quickly and, as a result, handle more claims.*

As a claims adjuster, you have many tasks to handle at once—new claims coming in, pending claims on your desk, and dozens of phone calls to make—so good organizational skills are essential. Show the interviewer that you can prioritize your duties and complete your tasks in a timely manner.

Q: **How do you see claims as functioning with underwriting?**

A: *Claims and underwriting departments are definitely related, especially in respect to reserving and the policies that you write. Setting a reserve on a claim triggers underwriting—you put that money aside, and it lets underwriting know if you need to write more business or what to do with the rates. Also, it's important to have contact with underwriters if there are any problems with claims or insureds, or if you get a claim with misrepresentation on the policy, such as an unlisted driver. It's very important to let the underwriters know of that sort of incident, so they can take care of it, adjusting premiums as necessary.*

The interviewer will try to gauge your level of understanding about the true nature of claims. If you say that the claims department and underwriting aren't related, the interviewer may conclude that you're inexperienced. It's important to explain accurately, as this candidate does, your understanding of how the two departments interrelate.

Q: **What's your theory on customer service?**

A: *I think that customer service is one of the most important areas in claims handling. You need to communicate to customers that you really care about them and their claims and that you're going to do everything you can to help them.*

Especially in a state where all of the rates are the same, customer service is what makes a company stand out from its competitors. Most customers have contact with the company only if they have a claim. If you want to keep their business, you have to handle each claim right. That means returning phone calls promptly and treating the customers with friendly, capable service. Reassure the interviewer that you understand the importance of good customer service.

Q: **How do you go about making the initial contacts on a claim?**

First-time Job Seekers: A business background is a plus, but depending on the company, a college degree is not necessarily required. The interviewer will also be looking for good writing and communications skills. Taking an Insurance Institute of America seminar or enrolling in an AIC program will give you a competitive edge over other applicants. (The AIC, or associates in claims, is a series of four classes: claims, worker's compensation, property, and liability.) Be sure to emphasize this special training in your job interview.

You may begin your career in claims customer service or in a lower level of claims, working on the easiest claims—the quick turnarounds, the claims without injuries, insured claims—but not claimant injuries. But if you're right out of college, don't expect to go straight to the bodily injury desk where you can potentially be dealing with hundreds of thousands of dollars.

A: *I think it's important to make that initial contact as soon as you get the claim. I believe that you should do it on the same day; I don't think you should wait a day or two before making it. It's essential to talk to the person right away to find out if there are injuries, and to get the accident facts. If somebody has a few days to think things over, facts are likely to change.*

Prompt calls to initial contacts on a claim are appreciated by the insureds as much as by the claimants, because they feel as if you're there for them, and that they're important. Reassure the interviewer that you understand the importance of establishing rapport with the insured or claimant; that you know to maintain control of the claim, you need to contact the customer expeditiously, so he or she isn't left wondering what to do or where to turn.

Q: **What kinds of claims have you handled, and is there one that has stood out?**

A: *I've handled all types of claims—home owner, commercial, automobile, collisions, collisions with injuries. The one case that stands out in my mind is one in which I received a claim for an alleged stolen car, and the insured had been missing for two weeks. When he reappeared, he claimed to have needed to get away for a while in a secluded cabin in the woods, but he didn't have any witnesses or any other proof to corroborate his story. This case was a real challenge, since I had to do a lot of extra investigation, including taking statements from the insured's entire family, but the claim was eventually resolved, and I think I learned a great deal from it.*

It's important to show that you have a wide breadth of knowledge when it comes to claims. In some companies claims adjusters specialize in one area, but you should still know the procedures for all types. This response is effective because the candidate proves that he or she has a good eye for what could be a fraudulent claim, and doesn't just accept a claim at face value.

Q: **What is your philosophy of handling claims?**

A: *I think you have to take a proactive approach. You can't just wait for things to come to you; you have to get out there and start gathering all the facts as soon*

Career Changers: Get experience through training: take an Insurance Institute of America seminar or enroll in an AIC (associates in claims) program. Or contact the Bureau of Insurance for information about the insurance industry. This is a very competitive field, so you'll need to offer some special skill or other qualification that will set you apart from those candidates with claims experience. Emphasize your interpersonal or customer-service skills, your negotiating skills, your attention to detail, as well as your strong interest in the field.

as a new claim lands on your desk. I always try to obtain all information at first contact, since that's when the facts are freshest in the customer's mind.

Most companies have different official "philosophies" of handling claims, but this answer touches on what they all have in common: a concern for the client and an awareness of how best to approach a claim. This answer is also effective because it shows that the candidate knows the importance of good customer service.

Q: How do you handle pressure in stressful situations?

A: *I react very well to it. I try to remain calm and focused. I believe my good organizational skills help me cope with the pressure, because I always know the status of my claims, and I don't let myself fall behind.*

A career in claims means that you'll be working in a very stressful, fast-paced environment, and it's imperative that you stay calm at all times, even when facing piles of work. This candidate shows an ability to handle pressure in a calm manner, and to deal with stressful situations proactively.

Q: How do you deal with difficult people?

A: *Well, I always remain calm. It gets hard sometimes if people start yelling at me, but I remind myself that they're just upset or frustrated—perhaps because they just got in an accident, their car was stolen, their house was burglarized—and I try to be understanding. But if a customer becomes abusive, I'll say something like, "It's difficult for me to help you when you're yelling. Please try to remain calm, and I'll help you resolve this as quickly as possible." I never allow myself to get angry or yell back at a customer.*

The interviewer will want reassurance that you understand the stressful nature of the position—that you may often have to deal with difficult customers—and that you can handle such situations in a professional manner. Reassure the interviewer that you realize you're the only contact customers have with the company, and that you strive to remain professional and diplomatic at all times.

Q: If you're not sure how to handle a certain claim, what do you do?

Experienced Professionals: Talk about the dollar amounts and types of claims you've handled. Be sure to mention big responsibilities you've been given, such as working on injury claims or at the liability desk. Discuss how you deal with working under a great deal of pressure.

A: *If it's a coverage issue, I look at the policy. But if I still can't resolve it with any of the materials I have, I consult my supervisor for advice.*

The interviewer will want to know if you use good judgment. The insurance industry is highly regulated, especially when it comes to claims. If you give customers erroneous information, you may be accused of breaking "bad-faced laws," which are strict laws governing the industry. Reassure the interviewer that you understand the importance of giving customers accurate information, and that you know when it's best to consult with a supervisor or manager.

Q: **How do you feel about taking recorded statements, either over the phone or in person?**

A: *I believe they can be quite helpful. When I take recorded statements, I know I'll have all my facts, and that they can't be misinterpreted. Especially with face-to-face statements, I can establish a good rapport with the injured.*

It's important for you to have some experience taking recorded statements, as they're required for most claims involving bodily injury, theft, fire or other potentially fraudulent claims. If a case ever goes to litigation, you'll then have recorded, accurate statements from the insured or claimant. Because claims involving bodily injury often involve large sums of money, it's usually necessary to take recorded statements in person. Discuss in detail any experience you have in this area.

Q: **Do you feel that you're proficient with policy knowledge?**

A: *Yes, I am. I know a great deal about the coverages and exclusions in homeowner and automobile policies, among others.*

With all the different policies and coverages that exist, the interviewer won't expect you to have all the facts memorized. But there's still some basic information you'll need to know—for example, the definition of an insured. Tell the employer that you're familiar with all the legal language and you know where to find any information you may need on a policy.

Candidates Re-entering the Workforce: Network with your former professional associates in order to find job leads. Before you begin interviewing, check to see if licensure is current, or, if you've moved to a new state, find out if it requires claims adjusters to hold licenses. Take an insurance seminar to learn what's new in claims. Finally, be ready to show that you're willing and able to handle the pressure of working in claims once again.

Q: Why do you want to be a claims adjuster?

A: *I really enjoy the challenge of working in claims and helping people out in difficult situations. It's a good feeling to do a thorough investigation and get the claim resolved. I also like the thrill of negotiating a claim successfully—of bargaining with a claimant or attorney for a fair settlement.*

This question is asked in virtually every job interview. The response here is particularly effective because the candidate shows that he or she understands all aspects of claims adjusting, customer service, investigations, and negotiations. You shouldn't say something generic, like "I enjoy helping people."

Executive Secretary

Q: **What are your impressions of the duties of an executive secretary?**

A: *The duties of an executive secretary vary widely from situation to situation. In most cases the executive secretary performs customary administrative duties, such as word processing, mail processing, arranging appointments and managing schedules, coordinating travel, and communication. In other cases the executive secretary develops into a valued assistant who plays a key role in advancing his or her manager's role within the organization. On the far extreme are executive secretaries who develop roles within the organization independent of their manager. I can operate effectively in any of these scenarios. My preference is to work closely with my reporting manager in the role of a valued assistant.*

This question allows the interviewer to gauge the candidate's level of understanding about the potential requirements for the position. This is a good answer because it shows a broad and deep understanding of the range of roles an executive secretary may be called on to play.

Q: **In your opinion, what kinds of aptitudes, skills, and traits are necessary to be successful in this position?**

A: *A successful executive secretary must be excellent at both written and oral communication, have outstanding organizational skills, and have a strong understanding of business processes, protocols, and etiquette. This person must be able to work independently, balance a large number of competing priorities, and have excellent judgment and strong initiative. There are many other requirements that may come into play in specific situations. However, these aptitudes, skills, and traits are, in my opinion, some of the most important.*

Here the interviewer is testing not only the candidate's knowledge about key requirements, but also his or her communication skills. Answering this broad, but specific, question effectively requires the job seeker to organize his or her thoughts and to present them in a clear and concise fashion. Make a clear, succinct statement and avoid the temptation to ramble.

Q: **Which of these required aptitudes, skills, and traits do you consider to be your strengths?**

A: *I have extremely strong skills in all the areas I just mentioned. If I had to pick a particular strength, I'd say my communication and organizational skills are especially strong.*

This question allows the interviewer to determine the candidate's level of confidence in his or her abilities. Give examples of how you've demonstrated your strengths in your previous positions.

Q: Which of these required aptitudes, skills, and traits give you the most difficulty, or offer you the greatest opportunity for improvement?

A: *I believe my record of success in the positions I've held over the years demonstrates that I'm pretty strong in all these areas. However, I never stop trying to improve myself, and I'm always seeking ways to increase my effectiveness. Right now I believe that improving my organizational skills offers me the greatest leverage. Strengthening these skills will enable me to handle more responsibility.*

Answer this question by balancing the opportunity for improvement against your already highly developed skills. There's always room for improvement. This is a good answer because it shows a receptive attitude toward self-improvement.

Q: Tell me about things you're doing now, or would like to do, to improve in these areas.

A: *I'm currently learning to use a software-based project-management tool. I find that this activity forces me to apply a disciplined thinking routine to the planning process. By using this software, I'm better able to understand what it takes to complete a complex assignment on time and within budget.*

The interviewer will want to hear in detail about your efforts for self-improvement. Speaking in general terms about improving won't be nearly as effective as speaking specifically about efforts under way or proposed.

Q: What five traits do you value most in your close working relationships?

A: *First is trust. I must be able to feel that the person I work closely with has my best interests at heart. Second is integrity. I must believe in the basic honesty and good character of the person I work closely with. I want to be able to care deeply, personally, and consistently about the person I work with and the results we produce, and be willing to do what it takes to produce spectacular outcomes. Third is respect, mutual support, and loyalty. We should be able to honor each other both personally and professionally, and sincerely value our differences. We should treat each other as professional family members. The fourth trait I value is openness. I want to work with a person with whom I can* *be open about the real issues. Last is fun and enjoyment. I enjoy working with someone who can occasionally relax and have some fun when appropriate. I find this really helps to alleviate pressure and stress.*

This is a probing question that gives the interviewer an opportunity to learn what the candidate really believes is important in working relationships. The recruiter is looking for values compatible with his or her own in order to avoid becoming entangled in a situation that will result in conflict. This answer is good, as it shows a highly developed sense of what it takes to work effectively with people.

Q: **What atmosphere and tone do you strive to create and maintain in your close working relationships?**

A: *I like to create an atmosphere that's filled with creative energy; energetically relaxed; happy, upbeat, positive, and focused; flexibly disciplined; warmly efficient; as well as friendly and determined.*

This question gives the interviewer an opportunity to learn more about what it might be like to work with the candidate—whether or not the candidate and the company would make a good match. This answer is effective because it describes a working atmosphere that would appeal to many different people.

Q: **Tell me what you try to do on an ongoing basis to create and maintain this kind of atmosphere.**

A: *First, I strive to exhibit these traits daily as I approach my work. Second, I try to inspire my associates and superiors to exemplify these traits. Again, this starts with my being happy, upbeat, positive, warm, friendly, and determined.*

The executive secretary has a huge impact on the atmosphere in an office. This is an opportunity to talk about what you would do to help maintain an ideal working environment.

Q: **How do you handle conflict?**

First-time Job Seekers: You'll probably start your career as an administrative assistant. A high school degree is sometimes considered acceptable, but an associate's or bachelor's degree is often preferred. Before you can become and executive administrative assistant, you'll need office experience, the ability to handle large projects, and business savvy. You must also have self-confidence, since you'll be dealing with many high-profile, polished business professionals.

A: *First, I think it's important to talk about how we define conflict. I define conflict as anything that interferes with having an optimized, close working relationship. Second, I believe the sooner a conflict or barrier is cleared, the better. Third, I think direct communication between the parties involved is a requirement. Fourth, I want everyone to share responsibility for making sure that conflicts are resolved as soon as possible. This means I don't feed the conflict. If I'm not a party to the issue, or there's nothing I can do about the issue, I don't communicate about the issue to stakeholders. If I'm a party to the issue, I don't communicate about the issue to people who aren't stakeholders or who can't do anything to resolve the issue. Fifth, I resolve the conflict directly with the involved parties with these guidelines in mind: be open and caring; approach the situation with the honest intent to seek resolution; speak to the real issues; engage in a mutual inquiry for truth, truth seeking, and truth honoring; be willing to honor diversity; and, finally, share genuine concern and understanding for the interests of all stakeholders.*

This answer shows a mature attitude toward conflict resolution and management in an office environment. It shows that the candidate can be looked to as a key contributor to maintaining peace in the office and resolving conflicts.

Q: Do you think it's important to maintain optimum working relationships? Why or why not?

A: *Yes, I do. I believe that an executive secretary can greatly impact the degree of job satisfaction everyone in the office enjoys. I consider it an unofficial part of my job to help maintain a pleasant and productive working environment—and I get personal satisfaction from working in such an atmosphere. I look forward to coming to work in the morning. In the evening I enthusiastically think about things I want to share with my coworkers. Going to work each day enriches my life.*

This answer is effective because it shows a mature attitude toward working and job satisfaction that could be a tremendous asset to the company.

Q: Discuss the need for confidentiality in the role of executive secretary.

A: *The executive secretary is often involved in the planning and implementation of business, organizational, and personnel matters. It's critical to the health*

Career Changers: Not many people change into this field, but if you do, you'll need to determine which of your aptitudes, skills, and competencies will translate into this new career. Be prepared to explain in detail how you plan to use your abilities in you new career. Emphasize the organizational and communication skills you've honed in your last job.

of the organization that these details remain confidential to avoid destabilizing the organization. In addition, significant sensitive information about other members of the department, such as salaries, job-performance reviews, and appraisals, all require that confidentiality be maintained.

The interviewer is trying to gauge the candidate's level of understanding concerning sensitive information. This answer shows that the candidate has an adequate understanding of the issue and handles it appropriately.

Q: **How do you approach the challenges of maintaining confidentiality?**

A: *It's critical to avoid at all costs discussions with friends, associates, and coworkers about these issues. This almost goes without saying. It's also important to exercise a high degree of care in daily work processes. For example, I take care never to print a sensitive document at an unattended printer. I stand at the printer during the printing process. I never leave documents open on my computer, and I use a password-protected screen saver to keep all information on my computer out of the view of visitors at all times. I'm especially careful in the copy room and make sure that people don't look over my shoulder.*

Maintaining confidentiality is an important and ongoing part of the daily work process of an executive secretary. This answer shows an understanding of the practical aspects of maintaining confidentiality in an office environment.

Q: **The position of executive secretary requires the ability to exercise mature judgment in sometimes difficult situations. Describe a difficult situation that you've faced in the past that required you to exercise mature judgment.**

A: *I'd just completed development of the review documents for a manager who was being placed on probation. The review was scheduled for later in the week. The manager in question came to me and asked if he could see his personnel file. I had to decide if I should show him the file or not, and if not, how to handle the refusal. I decided not to show him the file. I confirmed with him his appointment for his performance appraisal later in the week. I then told him that he should speak to his boss about getting access to the file, since the performance appraisal was still being developed.*

> **Experienced Professionals:** Never stop updating your resume! Keep a file of accomplishments on your computer and continuously up-to-date. Spend time each month reviewing this inventory and updating self-assessment of where you stand professionally. View each job as a project assignment whose purpose it to prepare you for your next project assignment.

Handle this kind of question carefully. Describe what's at stake in your situation, what your choices are, the consequences of each choice, what you decide to do, and why. Be sure to have an answer prepared, because this kind of question often causes the candidate to draw a blank.

Q: **Give an example of a situation where you faced conflicting priorities, and tell me what you did to resolve the conflict.**

A: *I've had several positions where I was responsible for the work of more than one executive. Sometimes an organizational crisis would occur that forced almost everyone to deliver a certain set of reports in a rapid turnaround. As the executive secretary I was responsible for producing everyone's reports correctly and on time. Under normal circumstances, I'd have been able to complete only half of the required reports on time. To resolve these unusual situations, though, I developed a standard format, then called a meeting with all the managers involved, explained the problem, and proposed my solution. They all agreed to a standard format, which enabled me to complete all the reports in the allotted time.*

Executive secretaries are required to manage a large number of priorities. Sometimes conflicts in priorities may arise. Show the interviewer that you have initiative, a solid command of the work process, and creative problem-solving skills.

Q: **Describe a situation in which you demonstrated independent initiative.**

A: *I like to be thought of as an independent thinker. I don't like to be spoon-fed tasks. I much prefer to be given an area of responsibility, then allowed to perform within the boundaries of those responsibilities. For example, one time in a previous position I was running out of filing space on the floor. I reviewed the files and found that five cabinets were devoted to storing a set of documents that no one had referred to in almost three years. I set out to learn why we were keeping the documents and if they could be discarded. It turned out that seven years earlier, a request had been made by outside counsel for a certain document. The document wasn't available. The outside counsel requested that*

Candidates Re-entering the Workforce: Devote part of your time to a deliberate effort to build a network of contacts who know you, like you, and respect your skills and abilities. Consider volunteering to serve as a board member for a local not-for-profit organization. You can make valuable contacts this way that can help you re-enter the workforce. You should also make sure your computer skills are up-to-date. You should be proficient in the latest word-processing, spreadsheet, and database applications.

we make these documents available in the future, and we established proce-
dures to do this. Meanwhile the law changed and there was no longer a need
to keep the documents, but the procedures hadn't been changed. I got the
procedures revised and got permission to discard the unneeded documents.

Executive secretaries need to show independent initiative. Explain your attitudes about independent initiative and give a specific example of a time when you handled a problem skillfully on your own. This answer is effective because it illustrates the candidate's initiative, persistence, and perseverance.

Office Manager

Q: **How do you see the office manager functioning within a company?**

A: *In general terms an office manager ensures that the company is running smoothly. This responsibility can include all office functions—ordering supplies, making sure equipment is properly maintained, answering phones, and overseeing the office staff, such as the receptionist or administrative assistants. Basically, if the office runs out of something or if something breaks, the office manager's responsibility is to see that the company's operations are not interrupted.*

Describe your idea of the nature of the position and its duties, and how you see yourself interacting within the office. The interviewer will want to see that your expectations are compatible with the needs of the company. Many people are attracted to the title without a thorough understanding of the realities of the position. Like this candidate, show that you know what the position involves, that it can cover a multitude of tasks—often tasks that other managers don't want to do—and that one minute you might be negotiating terms with a vendor, the next cleaning out the company coffeepot.

Q: **What kind of company are you working for now?**

A: *I work for a small, family-owned financial-services company. We have a very exclusive clientele, all individual investors with a high net worth. The company has about seventy-five employees, including an office support staff of fifteen, which I oversee.*

Office managers are often found in the professional-services field—law or architectural firms, doctors' and dentists' offices—or in small businesses, like manufacturing or construction. Larger firms normally don't have an office-manager position, because they have department managers who take on many of the same roles and responsibilities as an office manager. The interviewer is trying to get a sense of the candidate's background, to see if he or she will fit in well with that particular company. If the company you work for is not well-known, be ready to give some background information.

Q: **Why do you want to leave your current company?**

A: *I've been with this company for twelve years. When I started, the company had eighteen employees; I was hired to be the president's secretary. Through the years my duties have expanded to cover the entire office; I was promoted* *to office manager seven years ago. However, this is the only company I've ever worked for. Although I think it's a wonderful company, I feel rather limited. I'd like the opportunity to expand my duties and take on some new challenges. I want to experience a new office environment, and I believe working in the computer industry would be very exciting.*

Don't feel embarrassed if you're leaving because you were laid off or because your role is diminishing. Many offices make do without an official office manager because they find it easier (and more economical) to spread out those responsibilities among the various department managers. Like this candidate, you could also discuss your desire to challenge yourself professionally. But a response like, "I left because I had a conflict with my boss," will raise a red flag for interviewers, and they may well regard you as a potential problem.

Q: What are the major responsibilities in your current position?

A: *Basically, I'm responsible for company operations. I'm the liaison between our company and outside vendors, such as the marketing, equipment-leasing, and cleaning services we use. When we changed offices five years ago, I found the new office space, helped negotiate the lease, and managed the move itself. I supervise our fifteen-person office-support staff, including hiring and firing new administrative employees; when the company needs temporary employees, I handle their hiring. I'm also responsible for the training of all new employees on our computer system. I order and maintain our inventory of office supplies, and I also do some accounting work—handling incoming checks, booking them in, and doing bank deposits.*

The title "office manager" is quite nebulous. Some office managers can really be more like an office clerk, whereas others have dozens of high-level duties and are involved in major company decisions. Describe your role within the firm so that the interviewer will have a better idea which category you fall into.

Q: Can you describe your ideal job?

A: *That's a tough question. I'm basically happy with the kind of job I have now. I enjoy handling a variety of duties every day—I don't think I'd be happy in a position where I did the same job day after day. That's what I enjoy most about being an office manager: no two days are ever the same. I like to work in a*

First-time Job Seekers: Most office managers start as administrative assistants; for that position most companies require candidates to have a high school diploma or an associate's degree. You'll need solid typing and computer skills, including proficiency in a variety of word-processing and spreadsheet programs. Employers like candidates who show poise and have good organizational, communication, and interpersonal skills.

fast-paced environment, where I'm constantly learning and being challenged. I really enjoy being in a behind-the-scenes, support kind of position. At the same time, I like taking on special projects, and I'd welcome the opportunity to do more of that.

Don't mention specific job titles or salary levels. Try to describe a position that's close to the one you're applying for. Think about what your favorite responsibilities are—what do you like and dislike most about your current position? You could also mention the company size, and the industry, you'd like to work for. The interviewer will want to determine if your goals are compatible with the company's.

Q: **What are some of your strengths?**

A: *I have solid computer skills. I have a working knowledge of many different types of software and hardware; I'm our company's resident systems manager. Also, my supervisor has told me on several occasions that I'm an excellent negotiator, to the point that I'm now in charge of negotiating the terms of all major purchases, such as our new phone system.*

This is an excellent answer because the candidate showcases strengths that go beyond the traditional. Most candidates mention organizational, interpersonal, or communication skills. Although these characteristics are essential, they're usually considered mere prerequisites for the position. Like this candidate, discuss strengths that will set you apart from other candidates and give examples of these strengths from your past experience.

Q: **What's your greatest weakness?**

A: *I have a hard time delegating authority. I tend to take on tasks or responsibilities that could probably be handled more quickly, and even better, by someone else. But I'm trying to improve at this. Nowadays, if I have a large-scale project to work on, I'm more likely to ask for some assistance instead of handling the whole project myself.*

Many times candidates will give a litany of strengths but find themselves unable to name any weaknesses. Like this candidate, name one or two weaknesses

Career Changers: Most office managers are former administrative assistants or executive secretaries. These positions share many of the same duties as the position of office manager, so candidates with these kinds of backgrounds have most of the skills needed to make a successful switch. But office managers also have other duties, such as supervising or budget management, so be prepared to answer questions regarding your skills in these areas as well.

that some interviewers might, in fact, view positively. Be honest, but don't mention a skill that's essential for the position in question. For instance, if you're applying for an opening at a computer company, a response like, "Well, I really don't like computers and I'm not comfortable working with them," would definitely put you out of the running.

Q: What's your experience with employee relations?

A: *Because our company doesn't have a human-resources department, I have to handle many of the nonfinancial aspects of employee relations. By this I don't mean I choose benefit plans or make other decisions of that nature, but I do have experience dealing with employee grievances, both from my own staff and throughout the company. I've often been called upon to mediate and resolve employee feuding. I'm also responsible for maintaining company morale. Through the years I've started a number of employee-recognition programs, offering rewards, like movie passes or department-store gift certificates, to employees who've done exemplary work.*

Many small companies don't have a human-resources department, so some office managers handle employee-relations issues. As this candidate does, give examples of any experience you may have in this area. For instance, if an administrative assistant came to you with a problem with his or her boss, you could discuss how you worked with that person to come up with a solution.

Q: Do you have any experience managing budgets?

A: *Currently I control the administration of an annual operating budget of $500,000. I'm responsible for the negotiation and purchase of all new office equipment and supplies, as well as miscellaneous expenditures for the office. I'm also in charge of a separate expense budget; I monitor how much is spent on events such as lunch with clients.*

Not all office managers have the responsibility of managing a budget; the interviewer is simply trying to gauge the candidate's level of experience. If you do have experience in this area, try to give the interviewer a detailed answer. As this candidate does, give the specific budget amount you were responsible for and discuss what that budget covered; for instance, did it include the salaries of the administrative staff? Also, if you have a history of staying within your budget, say so. Companies are constantly looking out for the bottom line, and the interviewer will want to see that you have the ability to control costs.

Q: How do you approach multidimensional projects?

A: *I first try to get a clear understanding of the project's goals. Then I determine who's best able to give me advice and assistance, and I arrange a meeting to* *consult with those people. This group helps me identify what steps need to be taken to achieve the project goal. Once we've identified all the necessary steps, I'll prioritize those tasks and assign each step to a different member of the group, taking care to match the task with the individual's strengths and to give firm deadlines. I like to meet with the team at least once a week to monitor progress until the project is complete. Of course, I always keep my supervisor well informed of the project's progress.*

Your answer will reveal your thought processes and give an indication of your organizational skills. Try to take the interviewer through all the steps you'd follow once you're given a major project. Office managers are often responsible for large projects, such as the relocation of the company to new office space, so the interviewer will be concerned that you can handle the planning of such projects logically and responsibly.

Q: **Give an example of a problem that faced your office and how you solved it.**

A: *Our business was growing very quickly, and it soon outgrew the computer system we had. Technologically speaking, we were still in the dark ages. The president put me in charge of setting up a network for the company. With his help and a lot of research, I determined our needs and came up with a solution. I also had to negotiate terms with companies to design and install the system. Once the system was installed, I arranged a companywide training program with the engineers from the computer company.*

The interviewer will want to see if you can approach problems proactively. Demonstrate your ability to use initiative to take charge of a situation, and show how you assessed the problem and designed a plan for its resolution. Your example can be from any area; an employee-relations issue would be just as appropriate.

Q: **What computer systems and software do you know?**

A: *I've used PCs with general-office software such as Microsoft Word, Access, and Excel. I have some experience with Macintosh systems as well. And through my*

Experienced Professionals: Emphasize your strengths and discuss any special projects you've worked on. Interviewers like to see experienced candidates who can take initiative, who aren't afraid to take on responsibility. Familiarize yourself with the company's business climate—is it formal or fairly laid back? The interviewer wants to see that you'll fit into his or her organization. Finally, show some flexibility in terms of what you expect in your new job. Just as no two companies are exactly alike, no two-office managers are exactly alike either.

search for a computer network, I've gained some familiarity with local networks; the computer company we used trained me on basic troubleshooting issues.

In today's business environment computer literacy is a must. Word-processing and spreadsheet experience is essential, and familiarity with database management or graphics programs is valuable as well. Most businesses use PC-compatible computers, but many companies in the creative field, such as publishing or advertising, use Macintosh computers. If you're interviewing in one of those fields, you might find it helpful to familiarize yourself with Macs.

Q: **How do you handle staff development?**

A: *Because my staff is the most important resource I have, I always encourage their professional growth. Once people are hired, I try to pick out their strengths and weaknesses, as well as their likes and dislikes, and give them duties that allow them to shine. Say someone shows a natural affinity for technology and computers. I'd encourage that person to be more active in that area, perhaps by asking him or her to train employees on software and the network.*

Office managers are often in charge of the company's administrative staff, such as the receptionist or administrative assistants. If you're asked this question, convince the interviewer that you have an understanding of the importance of staff development. A good manager will recognize the strong points of his or her staff and develop each person according to those strengths.

Q: **Are you available to work late or on weekends?**

A: *Yes, although it's easier for me if I'm given some notice. For instance, if you want me to work late one evening, I like to know the day before so I can make alternate plans with my family. But, naturally, if something unforeseen crops up and it's necessary that I stay late, I'll make do as best I can.*

Although an office-manager position is usually a nine-to-five job, you'll occasionally be asked to work overtime. Never say you can't work overtime during a job interview. Flexibility is one of the first traits companies look for in office managers, and if you say you can absolutely work only forty hours, the interviewer might wonder if you'll be inflexible in other areas as well.

Candidates Re-entering the Workforce: The interviewer's biggest concern will be that you haven't kept up to date with the latest computer technology. If you haven't kept your skills current, be sure to take a continuing education class to learn the more popular word-processing and spreadsheet programs. In your interview, emphasize the skills and traits—organization, communication, and flexibility—that have made you a good office manager in the past.

Q: What are your salary expectations?

A: *I'd like a salary that's comparable to what I'm earning in my present position. But salary isn't my only consideration. I'm most interested in this opportunity because I think it represents a good match between what you're looking for and my qualifications.*

Salaries of office managers may vary greatly from company to company; if you've been with a company for a long time, you could be overvalued (or undervalued) and may need to adjust your expectations accordingly. Your best bet is to emphasize your flexibility. If you want to negotiate terms, don't do it now. Wait until you're offered the position.

Word Processor/Tape Transcriber

Q: Have you had experience with tape transcription?

A: *Yes, but not on a full-time basis. I work as a medical secretary in a doctor's office, where one of my main duties is transcribing case notes for the practice, which consists of five doctors. I'm thoroughly comfortable transcribing technical material, and I'm familiar with a lot of medical terminology.*

This question allows the interviewer to gauge the candidate's experience level. Most employers prefer candidates who have some experience with tape transcription. Don't simply answer yes or no here; tell the interviewer what type of transcription you've done—medical, legal, or commercial. If you have experience with technical transcription, chances are you'll adapt easily to all types of transcribing.

Q: How long have you been doing tape transcriptions?

A: *I've been transcribing part-time for three years. Generally, I spend about three hours per day working on the doctors' notes.*

Again, your answer here will give the interviewer a better sense of your skill level. The interviewer is also trying to determine how comfortable the candidate is at transcribing. If you haven't been performing this kind of work for long, the interviewer may be concerned that you don't have a precise understanding of what the job entails.

Q: What's your keyboard speed?

A: *I average about seventy-five words per minute.*

This is a fairly straightforward question. Most interviewers look for candidates who can type a minimum of about seventy words per minute. Don't be

First-time Job Seekers: Tape transcription isn't a skill that's normally taught in business classes, so you'll need to have some work experience. You can learn tape transcription while working as an administrative assistant; many entry-level word-processing positions—especially those in medical and law offices—involve transcribing tapes. In addition to work experience, employers look for candidates with fast typing speeds and a thorough knowledge of the rules of grammar.

tempted to overestimate your speed—you may be asked to prove your skills with either a typing test or transcription of a short tape.

Q: How comfortable are you with computers?

A: *I'm extremely comfortable with computers. Most of my experience is with a PC, but I've had some exposure to the Macintosh as well.*

Computer literacy is a must in this field. Virtually all transcription is done on computers these days, so the interviewer wants to know that you have some familiarity with different types of computer systems. Discuss which system—Macintosh or PC—you're most comfortable with. Most companies use PCs, but computer experience on any system is helpful. You might also mention any additional experience you have with computer systems or hardware.

Q: What software are you familiar with?

A: *I'm proficient with Microsoft Word and Access. I have extensive experience creating spreadsheets with Excel, and I've used ACT to create a patient database for each of the doctors in this practice. In my current position I'm responsible for training our new office staff to use the software.*

Employers will be most interested in your experience with word-processing software. Your answer will give an indication of your skill level and will also tell the interviewer whether you'll need additional training. If, like this candidate, you demonstrate a familiarity with a wide variety of software, the interviewer will know that you can easily be trained on virtually any program.

Q: Tell me about your educational background.

A: *I have an associate's degree in business administration, which I completed while I was working full-time. In addition to my business classes I've taken a few classes in American literature and history. Eventually, I'd like to return to college so that I can receive my bachelor's degree and round out my education.*

Most employers require candidates to possess a high-school diploma and to have completed some college course work, such as an associate's degree

Career Changers: Career changers are common in the field. Many people, who have worked as executive assistants or in law or medical offices have some experience transcribing tapes. For instance, if you've worked in a law office, you probably have experience transcribing depositions. During your interview, emphasize your typing speed and other skills, such as customer service experience, that are relevant to the position. Also, be prepared to discuss the things that interest you about this career.

from a business college. But if you don't have a college education, a high-school diploma and at least two years' solid tape-transcribing experience are usually sufficient.

Q: **How would you rate your grammatical skills?**

A: *I believe I have an excellent grasp of language. The doctors at the practice have always complimented me on the letters, transcriptions, and other documents that I produce for them. I believe the literature classes I've taken in school have improved my vocabulary, and the feedback I've received on my papers has helped me polish my grammar skills.*

Interviewers look for candidates who not only can transcribe tapes quickly and accurately, but can also construct full, clear sentences from transcribed material when necessary. To do this properly, you need solid English and grammatical skills, because the chances are good you'll eventually find yourself transcribing conversations on tape for official purposes. If so, you'll quickly discover that when we speak aloud, we usually don't speak in complete, carefully structured sentences. Transcribing a conversational tape verbatim isn't always the best choice.

Q: **Do you have proofreading experience?**

A: *I don't have any formal experience, but I always check my correspondence for errors before sending it out. I also proofread all transcribed notes before returning them to the doctors.*

This question also allows the interviewer to gauge the candidate's level of experience. You aren't expected to have formal experience in this area, but you should be able to proof your work as you go along.

Q: **Where do you see yourself in three years?**

A: *As I said, I hope to return to college and obtain my bachelor's degree. Although I'll probably work part-time, I'd like to attend college on a full-time basis. I have a strong interest in the health-services field, and eventually I'd like to work for a hospital or HMO as an administrator. However, I can't see myself returning to school for at least several years. Until then, I'll continue working full-time.*

Experienced Professionals: Employers prefer candidates with experience because they already understand the nature of the position and have honed their transcription skills. Discuss the type of experience you have—medical, legal, or other. You may also be asked questions about your future plans and goals. It's common for people in the tape-transcribing field to work for two or three years, then move on to other administrative positions.

The interviewer will want to get a sense of your goals. Do you regard this position as simply a tool to help you complete your degree? Do you want to acquire more skills and eventually move into an administrative position with more responsibility? Many tape transcribers plan to do this kind of work only on a short-term basis, so don't be afraid to discuss your long-term goals. Also, be prepared for follow-up questions, such as why you're interested in tape transcription.

Q: Have you ever worked under deadline pressure?

A: *I've never worked in a really deadline-oriented business, like a newspaper. However, I never had problems meeting deadlines for school assignments. Also, my supervisors will tell you that I always keep on top of my workload. I've often worked on projects with short turnaround times, such as case notes. The doctors usually want them available the next day.*

The interviewer wants to be sure that the candidate understands the concept of deadlines. When clients turn in tapes for transcription, they expect them to be completed by a certain date, and it's your responsibility to be sure that such deadlines are met. Show the interviewer that you can work under pressure and have experience meeting deadlines.

Q: When would you like to work?

A: *I'm available for full-time work. I'd prefer working days, Monday through Friday, but I can work some evenings as well.*

Many word-processing services offer day, evening, and weekend shifts, so if you prefer to work evenings or weekends, this shouldn't be a problem. If you're planning to work part-time for an agency, be prepared to discuss how long you'd like to remain in the job.

Q: Are you comfortable on the telephone? Tell me about your customer-service skills.

A: *I'm completely comfortable on the phone. In my current position I cover the phones whenever the receptionist is away from her desk. I also interact with*

Candidates Re-entering the Workforce: This is a good career for people returning to work from a long absence, as it's easy to begin part-time. The interviewer will be most concerned that your skills may have waned during your absence, so be prepared to take a typing test. Also, be sure to discuss any freelance transcribing you may have done during your absence.

patients on a regular basis—scheduling appointments, handling patient questions, and greeting patients and visitors.

If you work for a small company, you might occasionally be asked to handle other duties, such as answering the phone or dealing with clients. Although these tasks will be only a small part of the job, it's important for you to be comfortable performing them. Any customer-service experience you have is also a plus. Even if you've worked only at a fast-food restaurant, you'll likely have acquired some very basic skills interacting with the public.

Q: **Do you prefer working alone or with others?**

A: *Although I enjoy working with people, I don't mind working by myself. That's one aspect of transcribing that I like best. The office where I work can get quite hectic, and it's nice simply to tune out all the noise and concentrate on one task.*

The interviewer is trying to determine if the candidate will be comfortable sitting under headphones transcribing or will always want to put the headphones aside to interact with coworkers. Although it's important to get along well and socialize with others in the office, it's also important to show the interviewer that you know when to get back to work in order to meet your deadlines. Tell the interviewer you're aware that working alone is a key aspect of the job and that you're comfortable doing so. If possible, give examples of past positions in which you've worked alone.

CHAPTER 10
ART AND DESIGN

Art Director
(Book Publishing)

Q: How do you see yourself functioning as art director?

A: *Since the art department interfaces regularly with other departments, being an art director requires a lot of organizational, managerial, and interpersonal skills. The art director is really a business manager, managing a busy, high-profile department, along with a large staff, freelance designers, a sizable budget, and a stable of outside vendors. But you're also the creative director, originating concepts, encouraging creativity from the staff, implementing these concepts, and then working swiftly to produce them. Finally, you must do all of these on an extremely fast-paced schedule, constantly working under deadline pressure.*

The interviewer will want to be sure that you understand what your role will be within the company. Many people view the art-director position as a strictly creative role; they forget all of the other, less glamorous, aspects that go along with it, such as the supervision of employees and budget management. This candidate has a good, realistic grasp of the role of an art director within the company.

Q: How would you rate yourself in terms of organizational, managerial, and interpersonal skills?

A: *Well, I believe my ability to coordinate multiple tasks is excellent, and so are my interpersonal skills. But I think I still need to improve my managerial skills. I tend to see the big picture so well, that sometimes I forget my staff might*

First-time Job Seekers: Be sure that you understand the nature of the business and of the particular company you're interviewing with. Naturally, you can't expect to start as an art director; instead, you'll start as an assistant graphic designer. Entry-level applicants tend to be very centered on their concept and their ideas, so be sure to convey an understanding that the product is ultimately more important than your design. Finally, don't forget to bring a portfolio of your designs to your interview.

not understand its importance. I can also be rather critical of those to whom I have to explain the specific steps. I expect them to have a sharp instinct for what seems to me the obvious, forgetting that that instinct comes with experience. But once I realize I'm doing this, I spell things out as carefully and clearly as necessary.

This is a good, honest answer. The candidate reveals his or her biggest weakness—managing staff members—but then makes it clear that it's not a true problem. The interviewer will want to find out about your strengths and weaknesses: In which areas do you still need improvement? How do you overcome your weaknesses?

Q: **How do you respond to criticism from management, editorial, and sales?**

A: *Well, I usually take the approach that there's always more to learn about the entire process. In fact, criticism can be quite constructive when it comes to cover design. For instance, I like to hear immediate responses from coworkers outside the art department. But I believe that once I take criticism into consideration, I must use my own skills and judgment as to whether or not I should make any changes. Often the criticism helps the cover. When it comes to criticism of my management style, I'll try to adopt any suggestions that I feel are compatible with my own distinctive approach.*

It's absolutely necessary that an art director be able to take criticism well. You simply cannot become defensive or take it personally if somebody criticizes your work. This is a great answer, since the candidate obviously understands the importance of criticism in the creative process.

Q: **How do you go about giving your staff critical feedback on cover designs?**

A: *Well, I honestly say what I think, but I don't do so without offering some suggestions on how to improve the design. I understand how sensitive some designers can be when it comes to their work, so I'm always careful to watch how I word the criticism. And whether I'm criticizing their designs or their work habits, I don't do it in front of their coworkers.*

Career Changers: If you're coming from magazine publishing, the transition won't be that difficult. Discuss how your design experience is easily transferable to the medium for which you're applying. Also, during the interview, emphasize your organizational and managerial skills. And know enough about the company so that you can speak intelligently regarding its products.

Your staff's designs will ultimately reflect on you as the art director, so you must know how to give "constructive criticism." The candidate's answer shows that he or she knows how to give criticism tactfully and effectively.

Q: **How do you feel about using the latest trends in cover designs?**

A: *I think it's important to keep up with trends, because the audience, or the consumer, is also keeping up with trends. At the same time, I'm also a believer in classic designs, so what I like to do is incorporate a current look into my overall concept, which tends to lean toward the classic. But I also realize that some titles need a trendier design, so I'll always hire the appropriate designer.*

The cover is the most important aspect of book design since, contrary to the old adage, many people do judge a book by its cover. Therefore, it's important that an art director stay current with trends in cover design. This answer shows that the candidate doesn't get swept up in trends, but, rather, incorporates them into his or her overall design.

Q: **Have you ever implemented new procedures or introduced new concepts to your department?**

A: *Yes. At my last job I completely revamped the scheduling process. I created a flowchart memo, distributed it on clipboards to my staff, and told them that heretofore this chart was sacred. I also made copies and gave them to the editorial staff so that they, too, could keep track of their titles through the art department. We'd always faced the problem of getting editorial information to the art department early enough so that we could create a jacket in time for the sales conference or catalog.*

This question is designed to get a sense of the candidate's ability to innovate and to come up with new ideas. The candidate's answer is an excellent one since he or she gives an example of an innovation that streamlined the entire work process, and also demonstrates good organizational skills.

Q: **What is the difference between trade and mass-market books?**

A: *Trade books sell by the season, and mass-market books generally sell by the month.*

Experienced Professionals: You're likely to be asked just as many questions about your managerial skills as about your design experience. Be ready for questions regarding your supervising and budgeting skills, as well as more general questions about your philosophy of deign.

You may be asked this or a similar "pop quiz" question. Any experienced art director, or anybody who has worked in the art department of a book publisher, should know the differences between the two types of products.

Q: **Do you understand how the differences between trade and mass-market books affect the art department?**

A: *Yes. Trade art departments cycle three times a year according to sales conferences, whereas mass-market art departments cycle monthly, and sometimes weekly, in regard to cover meetings.*

Again, this question is designed simply to find out how much the candidate knows about the company and the industry. Obviously, the art director's role in a publishing company is crucial, so it's absolutely necessary that you understand how the various products the company produces affect you and your department.

Q: **Do you believe you're overqualified for this position?**

A: *Not at all. My experience and qualifications make me do my job only better, and in my opinion, my good design skills help to sell more books. My business experience helps me run the art department in a cost-efficient manner, thus saving the company money. Finally, I think I'm able to attract better freelance talent because of all my industry contacts. My qualifications are better for the company, too, since you'll be getting a better return for your investment. Again, I'm interested in establishing a long-term relationship with my employer, and if I did well, I would expect expanded responsibilities that could make use of even other skills.*

Most people don't expect to be asked if they have a great deal of experience. This question could quite easily catch a candidate off guard, which is exactly the interviewer's intention. The candidate doesn't hesitate in answering this question and shows complete confidence in his or her ability.

Q: **What do you know about our company?**

A: *Well, I know you publish both trade hardcovers and mass-market paperbacks, and that you've had a number of best-sellers already this year. I've long admired your books; they're always beautifully designed.*

Candidates Re-entering the Workforce: Ideally, you managed to get in some freelance design work while you were out of the full-time workforce. Employers will be most concerned that you're not current with design trends. The best and easiest way to get up-to-date is to go into different bookstores and examine the designs of books in various categories and genres. Finally, be ready to discuss your opinions during your interview.

This is about as direct as an interview question can get. With any job interview you should know about the company and its main products. The interviewer isn't expecting you to recite last year's annual report, but you should know enough about the company to speak intelligently about it. The problem with most job hunters in more "creative" fields is that they don't do that much research before an interview; they expect to get by on talent alone.

Desktop Publisher

Q: **Do you have any traditional production experience?**

A: *Yes, I worked for one summer at a printer, where I learned film stripping and masking. I also took a class on the letterpress when I was in school.*

Because computer software has been designed to match as closely as possible traditional means of accomplishing the same tasks, having experience with those traditional crafts gives a candidate a greater appreciation of the computer, as well as greater sensitivity to the tasks at hand. Emphasize that your working knowledge of these traditional methods makes you less liable to make mistakes—that is, less likely to rely on the "undo" command that computer software offers.

Q: **Do you have a background in graphic design? Have you, for any previous jobs, had any graphic-design responsibilities?**

A: *I once took a continuing-ed class on typography, and for some of the smaller pieces I've worked on I've been expected to make minor design decisions during the last phases of the project, but nothing more than that.*

This is a bit of a toss-up: On one hand, the interviewer wants a production person to be sensitive to aesthetic issues of design, because generally that person will be more careful and exact. On the other hand, the interviewer knows that a member of the production team who dreams of being a graphic designer probably won't stay on the team for very long and may be more disgruntled with the work at hand than someone who has fewer creative aspirations. In order to achieve a balance between the two, you should emphasize your creativity as well as your ability to perform more mundane production tasks. Give specific examples of how you've done this in the past.

First-time Job Seekers: Employers will expect you to have a thorough understanding of Quark or InDesign, which you could learn by taking a continuing education class or just by teaching yourself with an instruction manual. Your first job could be something like flowing text into templates for a magazine, or doing basic word-processing work (editing, cut-and-paste) on an already laid out page. Usually you'll be asked to take a basic-skills test at your interview. You should also try to have some portfolio samples to show your interviewers, such as newsletters, flyers, and so on. Any samples will give an interviewer a better understanding of your abilities.

Q: **What software applications are you familiar with?**

A: *I'm familiar with most major software programs and consider myself to be expert in QuarkXPress, Illustrator, and Photoshop. I've worked primarily on Macintosh computers but have some experience with the Windows environment.*

Computer skills are essential to a career in desktop publishing. The more programs you have experience with, the more opportunities will be available to you. Although the graphic-arts industry is still dominated by Macintosh computers, experience on multiple platforms is an asset.

Q: **Have you ever worked with style sheets in Quark? Have you ever had to create from scratch a set of style sheets and templates for use on a project?**

A: *Yes. For one job it was my responsibility to transfer traditional spec sheets to computer format. This was for a revision of a textbook series that had previously been set traditionally by typesetters, so there were over fifty pages of specs for the job. From those specs I had to create templates with style sheets that would be used for the duration of the revision.*

You may encounter this or other specific technical questions that test your knowledge about desktop-publishing software. On larger projects, especially, it's very important to be able to take advantage of the page-layout options, which ensure uniformity over what could be many pages of text formatting. Emphasize that since you know how to use these features, you can be counted on to have more accurate layouts.

Q: **Have you worked with Photoshop?**

A: *Yes. On my last job, for the first time, I needed to make several composite images in Photoshop, so I used the layers option extensively.*

Photoshop expert features are not necessarily well known. Any experience in this area would be considered a plus.

Q: **Have you done any basic Photoshop work with masques and silhouettes?**

Career Changers: If you're coming in from the publishing or printing fields, you'll have a head start by knowing the terminology of the business. Also, any computer skill you have will be helpful; Quark and PageMaker are the most popular. You could learn these programs through a continuing education class at your local college.

A: *I once worked on a catalog with 250 images to silhouette—some using a soft edge, where we'd masque and feather to clear the background; and some using a hard edge, for which I'd create clipping paths.*

These are some of the most basic, yet important, aspects of using Photoshop to edit images. In addition, the applicant demonstrates more in-depth knowledge by making the technical and practical distinction between soft and hard silhouettes.

Q: Have you ever done any color correcting?

A: *Yes. When I worked for a service bureau, I was taught basic fundamentals—checking a proof against an original and making the adjustments necessary in Photoshop.*

Color correcting is the process of checking a color proof of an image against the original artwork, and adjusting the color balance of the scanned file so that the reproduction matches as closely as possible the original. This skill is needed less and less frequently in production environments—generally designers will check proof against original and give verbal instructions to the service bureau that scanned the image. Nevertheless, there are times when it's most efficient to do color corrections in-house; having this skill is valuable and demonstrates a superior knowledge of Photoshop.

Q: Have you done any scanning?

A: *I've worked often with flatbed scanners for low-resolution FPOs. At the service bureau I was taught their drum scanner, and also how to use a good flatbed scanner for final high-resolution scans.*

Experienced Professionals: If you have enough experience (over five years), you want to look for a position as a production manager at a design firm, publishing company, publication, advertising agency, or public relations firm. Any company that wants to send out brochures, newsletters, or company magazines will need a team of desktop publishers and production workers to polish their publications. Again, you should bring plenty of samples to show the interviewer. To be on top of the field, you must, of course, know desktop-publishing software inside and out. Interviewers will expect you to have extensive knowledge of the printing process, and how to price out a job. And unless you're planning on working for a large corporation, it wouldn't hurt for you to have a grasp of computer hardware. The interviewer will probably ask you about any experience you have supervising, since you're likely to be overseeing a staff of graphic designers and other production workers.

Drum scanners produce quantitatively better scans than flatbed scans but are generally prohibitively expensive for any office but prepress service bureaus. Design studios will typically have flatbed scanners (black and white only, or color) that are used to make "low-res" scans for position only (FPO)—that is, scans that are used in digital layouts as placeholders but won't be used in the final printing. This is a common task for anyone on the production team, and a necessary basic skill.

Q: **Have you done any streamlining of existing scans in Illustrator or Freehand?**

A: *Yes. Once I had a set of twenty logos that needed to be scanned, streamlined using Adobe Streamline, and then adjusted for final EPS files. It was a very time-consuming, exacting task. We'd print out pages at 1,000 percent to make sure we didn't miss any bumps or tweaks.*

Streamline is a wonderful way to turn an existing image into an editable drawing file, but the automated software for this task is too precise for its own good—the final EPS file usually needs to be extensively edited using a wide array of illustration tools. Streamline takes a bitmap (Photoshop) file and makes it an encapsulated postscript (Illustrator) file. This is not something you always want to do: photos tend to look distorted if you streamline them, though it's conceivable that this is a style an art director might want. Usually Streamline is used for logos and signatures. This skill probably won't be required by most companies, but having a thorough knowledge of the software may work to your benefit.

Q: **Have you ever created Illustrator files from sketches, or from image templates?**

A: *I once worked with an illustrator on a project for which the final art needed a very smooth, computerized look. I don't have a drawing background, and she*

> **Candidates Re-entering the Workforce:** Software changes all the time, and if you miss a year of work, chances are you've missed a lot of new features. Naturally, you have some catching up to do. The good news is that the major programs in desktop publishing aren't changing drastically; usually the software companies simply add some new features. Also, once you're proficient in a program, the learning curve for new versions is pretty minimal. You can also keep up with new software by reading the industry journals. Even so, nothing is as good as hands-on experience, but reading about new developments in technology will at least help you sound knowledgeable in an interview. If you have a computer at home, and have kept up with the latest changes in software, you'll have a slight advantage.

had no computer experience, so neither one of us could create the final files from scratch. She made sketches from the client's specifications, and I scanned the sketches and used them as a template behind a drawing that I then created in Illustrator.

Being able to work with a human illustrator for these jobs is very important, and being able to translate his or her nontechnical, creative ideas into usable digital files is what production work is all about.

Q: Have you ever been responsible for trapping in any project?

A: *Yes. I worked at a service bureau for a year, and there we had to check trapping on nearly every job that went through. Sometimes we'd let our trapping software take care of it automatically, but often we had to go into files and set the trapping manually. Quark has some very good trapping defaults, plus the flexibility to let the user make many decisions to override defaults. Most Photoshop files don't need to be trapped because they consist of continuous tones, but once I had a file with two solid rectangles butting each other—I used Photoshop's own trapping feature to good effect. Illustrator now has some good automatic trapping functions, but I used to set trapping in versions before that feature was implemented, when each separate shape needed to be given an overprinting stroke. I still find with some files that you're better off not using the auto-trap features and doing it the old-fashioned way, to ensure you're getting the trap you want.*

Trapping is one of the more complicated issues of color printing, especially for people who have no traditional printing experience. Trapping is the process of overcompensating before printing for problems that may occur on press with adjoining solid colors. Usually trapping issues are left up to the service bureaus, so production departments don't have to worry about them, but some projects require an intimate knowledge of how trapping works for different software. Generally, this is an impressive skill to discuss in an interview, even if the job you're interviewing for doesn't specifically require it.

Graphic Designer

Q: Which software programs are you familiar with?

A: *I've worked primarily on Macintosh computers but have some experience with the Windows environment. I'm familiar with most major software programs and consider myself to be expert in QuarkXPress, InDesign, Photoshop, Illustrator, and Freehand. I'm also familiar with many word-processing programs.*

Computer skills are essential to a career in graphic arts. The more programs you have experience with, the more opportunities will be available to you. Although the graphic-arts industry is still dominated by Macintosh computers, experience on multiple platforms is an asset.

Q: What makes you an "expert" in QuarkXPress?

A: *I've used it daily for the past three years. I've designed and produced everything from business cards to catalogs to album covers on it. I know the strengths and weaknesses of the program. I know what it can and can't do. I know the shortcuts and extensions.*

Expertise in a particular software program means knowing what the software can and can't do. Precious time can be lost searching for a nonexistent feature or cobbling together an inefficient (and sometimes irreproducible) solution.

Q: What is the difference between RGB and CMYK colors?

A: *RGB stands for red, green, and blue and is the usual standard by which images are displayed on screen. CMYK stands for cyan, magenta, yellow, and black and is the process by which images are printed on conventional presses.*

Knowing the difference between how input and output devices interpret colors is essential to producing quality work. As production cycles get shortened, the margin for error is reduced.

First-time Job Seekers: Emphasize the technology you worked with in school. Be sure to visit the graphic design department and take note of how things are done there. Pay special attention to the layout of the department and the contact among the personnel in it. At the start of your career you want to be surrounded by more experienced people solving graphic-design problems rather than shut away in a private office.

Q: Suppose I gave you a piece of artwork and told you to scan it and that it was going to be used in a printed brochure and as part of a disk-based presentation. What would you do?

A: *I'd make one high-resolution scan, correct it if necessary, then save the artwork in two files: high resolution for the printed piece, and lower resolution for the disk-based presentation. The disk-based presentation doesn't need the high resolution, or large file size.*

Knowing the end use of the project determines the starting point. The resolution of the image for the printed piece would be much higher than that of the disk-based presentation. A compromise between the two would produce disappointing results.

Q: Which are your favorite serif and sans-serif fonts?

A: *My favorite serif font is Garamond; my favorite sans-serif font is Futura.*

Knowing what fonts are, how they're categorized, and what they're used for is basic to the position of graphic designer.

Q: Suppose you were setting type at 12/14 and had a 3 3/4 inch column to fill. How would you figure the number of lines that would fit?

A: *First I'd convert the inch measurement to points by multiplying by 72. Then I'd divide that number by the leading of 14.*

Most type-based graphic designs use picas and points as a unit of measure. Since a font is based upon points, it's much easier to estimate the correct size and leading of type after converting a dimension into points.

Q: Describe a trap and why it's important.

A: *A trap is an area where two different colors of ink butt. The two different colors need to overlap slightly in order to prevent a white edge between the two colors.*

The best graphic designers understand the mechanics of the printing process. In the past, trapping was done using chokes and spreads when the printer made film from the mechanical. With more and more graphic designers

Career Changers: Make sure you're familiar with the technology used in graphic design. Emphasize how your ability to solve problems in your previous careers can be transferred in graphic design. Bring only those samples of your work that are of high enough quality for a graphic-design position.

supplying disks and outputting film themselves through a service bureau, unprintable files and film are sometimes delivered to the printer. This causes delays and costly makeovers.

Q: **Suppose I gave you two sets of specifications, one on Monday and another on Wednesday, for the same piece—let's say a poster—and they were different. What would you do?**

A: *I'd bring the discrepancy to your attention and ask you which set of specifications I should use.*

The adage of "measure twice, cut once" is true for graphic design. You should always double-check specifications. A difference of a half inch in trim size can mean redoing the entire job. The difference between a job spec'd as 4 PMS versus process can be catastrophic.

Q: **How fast can you produce a thirty-two page catalog?**

A: *That really depends on the nature of the piece. Certainly, a thirty-two page catalog of one-color straight text with two head levels would be much easier to produce than a thirty-two page catalog with four-color images, multiple page designs, runarounds, and so on. I could probably give an estimate if you give me more information.*

In the long run speed is often less important than the end result. A catalog that's produced in two days but is filled with errors and inconsistent design is far less valuable than one that's done correctly in five days. Remember, what you produce may be around for years. Deadlines must be met, but speed simply for speed's sake is not the way to do good graphic design.

Q: **Have you ever missed a deadline?**

A: *No. I've worked late into the night many times to meet deadlines.*

Deadlines can be brutal, and it is often the graphic designer and manufacturer who are called upon to pick up the slack. Having solid design skills and a comprehensive understanding of the process will help you make those tough deadlines.

Experienced Professionals: Emphasize your portfolio and be prepared to analyze how your work was performed. Make sure you're aware of evolving standards and technologies. Demonstrate your ability to solve the most complex problems and work with people from many departments and backgrounds. Be candid about ongoing or anticipated freelance projects.

Q: **How do you feel when someone finds an error in a finished piece?**

A: *Horrible. I work very hard to avoid mistakes. I realize the impact they can have.*

Errors in finished pieces are public and often embarrassing. Blame usually follows and soon focuses on the person responsible for producing the piece—the graphic designer. A good graphic designer learns from his or her mistakes and sets up systems to ensure that they don't happen again (for example, additional rounds of proofreading, color proofs, or mock-ups).

Q: **How many times will you redo a piece?**

A: *I try not to keep count. I look at it this way: I'll redo a piece until you tell me it's done. I realize that many people might have input.*

A graphic designer must accept input from many sources. At times the things that make a product sell are in conflict with the "look" the graphic designer is trying to achieve. A graphic designer must be able to put ego aside and listen to the concerns of others.

Q: **How often do you back up your work?**

A: *Daily. I have a good system, and it usually takes less than half an hour to back up all my work. I've gotten into a routine, and it's rescued me several times.*

Organizing projects, backing up disks, and storing final film and mechanicals are all essential to a successful graphic designer. When it comes time to update a piece, you should know where it is, be able to get at it, and use it.

Q: **How would you deal with freelancers?**

A: *I've found that when dealing with freelancers it's important to establish certain ground rules such as payment, schedule, copyrights, and so on. Once those are established, it's much easier to focus on the creative aspects. I've also found that clear instructions are essential to define a project.*

Graphic designers are often responsible for hiring and supervising freelancers. Being organized and capable of giving specific instruction is important. The experience of hiring and supervising freelancers will give you a new appreciation of the importance of verbal communication in graphic design.

Candidates Re-entering the Workforce: If you come from a traditional graphic-design background, emphasize your willingness to embrace today's technology. Address your understanding of deadlines and your willingness to work long hours to meet those deadlines.

Q: **May I see your portfolio?**

A: *Yes. In fact, I've brought many samples of my work that I'm eager to show you.*

Don't forget to bring samples of your best work with you to all your interviews. Be prepared to analyze how your work was performed.

Staff Photographer

Q: **What interests you about this job?**

A: *Well, I love photography and I love journalism. I'm interested in communicating with the public through my images. I like being out with people, creating a visual image of an activity, and creating a story through my photographs. I thrive on being in the field. Maybe I'm photographing a rising river that's threatening to flood a neighboring town, or maybe I'm just taking a picture of a candidate for city office. Either way, I like knowing that my photographs are reaching people and helping them understand the story behind that picture.*

If you respond by saying "I just love taking pictures," the interviewer may doubt that you have any real idea of what photojournalism is all about. The enjoyment of simply taking pictures tends to wear out eventually; to be a good photojournalist, you need to have more than that. Like this candidate, you should have a journalistic urge to teach others through your photographs, and demonstrate an understanding that being a good photographer is only part of the job.

Q: **How would you react if you were assigned to photograph the dog of the week?**

A: *I wouldn't mind at all. I realize that in a city this size there are bound to be more of these types of assignments than ones like photographing burning buildings. I also think that it's often more challenging to get a good picture from simple, everyday subjects than from more glamorous kinds of shots. Besides, I love dogs.*

If you want to work for an average-sized city newspaper, this is most likely what your job will be. Basically, you'll often have to take the same kind of picture over and over again; only the subjects themselves will be different. You'll more likely be judged on your more mundane images rather than on your quick-breaking, fast-moving action shots. Essentially, that's what photojournalism is all about—observing the most ordinary scenes, then catching that one live moment that tells the story. If you're not aware and awake enough to take the more mundane picture, your editor will doubt whether you'll be able to do a good job when a big story breaks.

Q: **Tell me about your educational background.**

A: *I graduated with a bachelor's degree in history, and a minor in journalism. As part of the journalism minor, I took a number of classes in photography.*

I worked on the college newspaper for four years, where I contributed as a photographer, reporter, and editor. I also worked as a photography intern for my local paper the summer before my senior year. It was a real learning experience to see all the work that goes into getting a daily paper out, even for a city as small as mine.

Unless you're a well-seasoned assignment photographer, you'll need a college degree in most cases. Many interviewers believe it's important for their staff photographers to have a degree in journalism in order to understand the more technical aspects of newspapers. You can be a talented photographer but not have any real idea of what goes into putting a newspaper together. Journalism classes also help you understand legal issues, such as libel law. If you didn't major in journalism, you should have at least taken a few classes on the subject. For instance, if you majored in biology but took some journalism classes and worked on your college newspaper, you may be able to convince an interviewer that you can bring valuable experience to the position.

Q: **What positions did you hold on your college newspaper?**

A: *My freshman year I started as a staff photographer. By the end of my freshman year I was regularly writing feature stories. I was assistant photo editor my junior year, and then during my senior year I was layout editor. The paper was a weekly and averaged about thirty-two pages. Being the layout editor was especially challenging, but it was also a really terrific learning experience.*

The interviewer wants to know if the candidate is "just" a photographer or a true journalist. As with the question about educational background, here the interviewer is interested in finding out if the candidate has a real, nuts-and-bolts understanding of how newspapers work. The specific positions you've held—photo editor, page editor, layout editor—aren't as important as simply being involved with some aspect of the newspaper other than photography.

First-time Job Seekers: A bachelor's degree, along with some hands-on newspaper experience is required for most staff positions. Be prepared for several questions designed to test your level of dedication to photojournalism. The competition in this field is tremendous—the market is saturated and the demand for positions far outweighs supply. Often, dedication and determination are just as important as talent and skill in finding a position. And since turnover is generally quite low, especially among newspapers in smaller or medium markets, you shouldn't be afraid to apply at larger newspapers early in your career. Don't assume you have to get experience at a small newspaper first, since you might end up being there a lot longer than you think; in photojournalism, wherever you go first, you have a tendency to stay there for a long time.

That kind of involvement indicates that you have an understanding of the many different facets of a newspaper. If you didn't hold a position but still worked on the paper, you should discuss what you learned from your experiences as an assignment photographer.

Q: **Do you have a portfolio of your work?**

A: *Yes, I have it with me. Would you like to see it now?*

You should always bring your portfolio with you to interviews; it's the best way for the photo editor or art director to get a true sense of your work. The presentation of your work is extremely important. Your portfolio should be a neat package—eye-catching, but simple. Most photographers use a sheet with about twenty slides of their photographs, their best five arranged in the center. Of course, these should be photographs that were published in other newspapers or publications. Don't overwhelm the editor with dozens and dozens of photographs; have enough confidence in your abilities to display only your best work. Since most college newspapers are in black and white, most entry-level candidates include only black-and-white photographs in their portfolio. However, be sure to include some color pictures to give the interviewer a better idea of your skills.

Q: **When did you begin your career as a serious photographer?**

A: *About ten years ago. I first started taking pictures in high school, where I was on the school newspaper and yearbook. Then, as I said before, I worked on my college newspaper, first as a staff photographer and eventually as layout editor.*

This question allows the interviewer to judge the level and quality of the candidate's work. The photographs of someone with only two years' experience will be very different from the photos of someone who's been a photographer for twenty years. More advanced photographers will have a maturity in

Career Changers: Although many people do photography as a second career, it's difficult to jump in without having some experience as an assignment photographer on some level. If you have no formal education in journalism, but photography has always been a hobby, you'll need to take some classes to learn the technical aspects of photography and journalism. You should also take a few computer classes in programs like Quark, Photoshop, and Associated Press, to make sure your skills are up to date. Some people believe that simply because they've traveled extensively and take some great pictures, they can find work as a staff photographer, but you won't be taken seriously unless you have some experience in journalism. Also, be prepared for a long, tough job hunt; turnover is very low in this profession, and even seasoned professionals have a difficult time finding work.

their images that less experienced photographers lack. Again, take care how you arrange your work in your portfolio, as the way you display your photographs can also say a lot about your level of experience.

Q: **What are your interests outside photography?**

A: *I really enjoy the outdoors—hiking, mountain biking, camping, and skiing. I usually don't bring my camera with me on these outings. Although at times I do enjoy photographing nature, for the most part I prefer just to live the moment. I guess I don't feel the need to capture every scene I encounter. If I'm admiring a spectacular sunset, the furthest thought from my mind is digging around a camera bag looking for film.*

The interviewer will want to get a sense of your hobbies, of what you do in your off time, in order to get a more complete picture of you as a person. It's important for you to have a life outside photography, because to be a good photojournalist, you must be very much a part of the world we all share. The interviewer will be looking for a well-rounded person who's had varied life experiences. The only way to create real, vital images of your subject is to understand that subject. And though it's natural to love what you do, you should also demonstrate that you don't simply go through life with a camera around your neck, waiting for something to happen so you can take a picture.

Q: **Tell me what you know about reproduction photography.**

A: *Basically, it means converting an image so that it will reproduce in other mediums, such as in magazines or newspapers. This can be done through the photographic printing process, when you develop a negative and then make your print from that negative, or with the help of software like Photoshop. This technique is necessary so that you can fine-tune your image to look better in print. For instance, certain darker colors turn black when they appear in newspapers.*

This question is designed to measure the candidate's technical skills. It's a straightforward question that throws many applicants, because they expect to go into an interview and simply talk about their pictures. Reproduction photography is a very important part of the printing and developing process. Like this candidate, you should give a brief definition that demonstrates your understanding of the process.

Q: **How much computer experience do you have?**

A: *I'm very comfortable with both PC and Macintosh computers. I have extensive experience with PageMaker, Photoshop, and Associated Press, and I'm also proficient in word-processing programs such as Microsoft Word.*

Most newspapers, even those in small towns, are computerized. Although you still produce images with a regular thirty-five-millimeter camera, photographs are now digitized so they can be used with the newspaper's computerized layout software. Most interviewers will expect you to have some familiarity with desktop publishing software, like Quark or PageMaker, and with Photoshop, the most common software for image manipulation. Many newspapers also use Associated Press LeafDesk, an electronic editing system, so familiarity with that program is a plus.

Q: **Have you ever done any digital imaging?**

A: *Yes. My college newspaper was computerized, so we had to digitize all our pictures for reproduction. During my internship, when I went out into the field with another staff member, we'd often have to scan the photographs on-site, then send them back to the paper via modem.*

Since most newspapers are now produced with computers, it's essential that you have at least some experience or familiarity with digital imaging. Among other things, digital imaging is used to convert color images to black and white. Although the majority of photographs in newspapers are in black and white, few photographers shoot in black-and-white film anymore; color film is cheaper and more convenient. Usually photographers will take their photographs in color, then use software such as Photoshop to change them to black-and-white film. Digital imaging is also used to send photographs from remote sites to the newspaper. When you travel a certain distance from the paper, it's more difficult to meet deadlines, so very often you'll develop your film at a one-hour photo shop, and then scan the image, digitize it, and send it via modem back to the paper.

Q: **How would you describe yourself?**

A: *Well, I guess the words that would best describe me are "outgoing" and "upbeat." I enjoy meeting new people and working with others. And I'm not at*

Experienced Professionals: Many experienced staff photographers are eventually promoted to the position of editor; however, that usually means giving up your camera, and many photographers prefer to stay in the field shooting. If you're interested in staying in the field, be sure to present an attractive portfolio of your best work, and be prepared to explain why you want to change jobs. For the most part, your work should speak for itself. If you're applying for a position at a large-market paper after working in a small market, your work should stand out from the competition. Your experience is your biggest selling point, and in this competitive field you shouldn't feel shy about discussing your accomplishments and experiences.

all shy, I can tell you that. At the same time, I enjoy going biking or hiking by myself, since that gives me time to think and get myself together.

The minimum requirement for this position is being a good photographer. You can have all the equipment in the world and be a great photographer, but if your mind and eyes aren't open, you can't see the picture to take. The interviewer is looking for someone who's an individual—who's comfortable going out into the community and making decisions on his or her own. You should also demonstrate that you're extroverted and a positive person, since interacting with your subjects and the community at large is a major part of your job.

Q: How would you rate your writing skills?

A: *I'd say they're above average. As I mentioned before, I frequently contributed to my college paper as a feature writer, and during summers, I occasionally wrote for my hometown paper. As a history major, too, I had plenty of opportunities to hone my writing skills; I often had to write more than ten papers a semester.*

Interviewers like to see photographers with strong writing skills, so be sure to discuss any experience you have in this area, even if it's simply writing term papers while in college. Photographers are required to write explanatory captions for their photographs, so if you can write a good, clean caption, the editor will save time by not having to rewrite it. Also, many photo editors will give the best assignments to photographers who can write well. This is simply because photographers deal with a visual world, so if they can come up with a story idea and communicate it well on paper to the editors, they are communicating on the editor's level. And on smaller papers you could be called upon to write the occasional news story. Having solid writing skills will set you apart from the competition.

Candidates Re-entering the Workforce: You should try to keep up with the field by freelancing. This is easier to do in very small towns, since most small papers don't have full-time staff photographers, or large cities through the Associated Press. In you interview, focus on your experience and present the interviewer with an impressive portfolio of your work. Show that you understand the latest technical advances in photography, and demonstrate knowledge of the software—like Photoshop and Quark—that is used in most newspapers. After a long absence from the field, you'll need to prove that you still have the drive and determination to succeed in this competitive field.

Q: **How do you work under pressure?**

A: *I enjoy working under pressure. I understand that most people become really tense around deadlines, and that doesn't bother me at all. I'm used to dealing with deadlines from my days at college, from both the newspaper and my classes. And, of course, through my summer internship at my local paper, I learned firsthand about the pressures that go along with putting out a daily.*

Newspapers are a deadline-oriented business, and being able to work well under pressure is a prerequisite for any photojournalist. You must demonstrate your ability to function effectively in a fast-paced environment. The interviewer will be interested in seeing that your work is consistent, even when facing a tight deadline, and that you can continue to work through the pressure and tension. You can expect this question if you're inexperienced in photography or in the daily newspaper industry. For many photographers the most difficult aspect of the job is becoming accustomed to the pace of a daily newspaper.

CHAPTER 11

COMMUNICATIONS

Account Executive

(Advertising)

Q: **Give me an example of a great idea you've had.**

A: *When I was chair of sorority rush, I decided to have sweatshirts made for myself and all of my rush counselors that had "Rho Chi—Cornell '04" on the front. People on campus then easily identified us and stopped us to ask questions and discuss anxieties or concerns.*

The first thing that entry-level interviewees typically do is talk about a class. They may say, "In my marketing class I came up with the idea for our group project." An advertising recruiter isn't interested in that as much as, for example, your organizational skills when you had to do a fund-raiser. The recruiter is much more interested in hearing that you came up with an idea to sell T-shirts because that was the hot thing on campus.

Q: **Tell me about a time you assumed a leadership role.**

A: *This past year I was the co-fundraising director for my alumnae college class. I suggested that we have a phone-a-thon to ask our classmates for contributions. The other co-fundraising director didn't want to do it that way until I explained that we could make all of our initial contacts in one night, instead of spending weeks on it. Getting a group of Cornellians together for the phon-a-thon is also good for school spirit and morale. She instantly agreed to my plan after I explained my reasons to her.*

The recruiter may pick something directly off your resume regarding leadership. If not, you may want to answer the question by referring to something on your resume. Leadership is a crucial skill, and the recruiter wants to make sure you have it.

Q: Name three examples of leadership that I would find on your resume.

A: *I was vice president of my sorority my junior year of college. Senior year, I was sorority-rush chair. The year after I graduated, I served as the co-fundraising director for my college alumnae class. I was elected to all three leadership positions.*

It's great if you can answer the question by naming leadership positions that you've held in college. If you can't, just tell the recruiter how you emerged as a leader in different situations. You may want to consider developing your "leadership portfolio" by volunteering in the community.

Q: What's your favorite advertising campaign? How would you make that campaign better?

A: *Advertising for the United Negro College Fund is my favorite campaign. I'm thinking of a TV commercial in particular, in which a young man is told by his parents that they just can't afford to send him to college. In response the young man's little brother donates his piggy bank to the cause. This commercial works because it's a tear jerker, but it is still appropriate. It warmly and effectively expresses the point that the United Negro College Fund needs support so that more highly qualified, but financially needy, African-Americans can attend college. I think the campaign could be improved by playing this particularly poignant commercial more frequently. Perhaps it could be targeted to*

First-time Job Seekers: If you're young and have no experience in or knowledge about advertising, it would be helpful to be a member of a professional advertising organization or a professional marketing organization, in order to get an understanding of what the business is all about. Also, develop the habit of reading industry publications every week. Both of these activities can help you understand the kinds of business problems that advertising professionals deal with. For example, they don't deal with financial as much as they do, say, building a brand or selling toothpaste. These activities help if you're someone who needs to learn and get acclaimed to the field quickly. It also doesn't hurt to meet people and to network.

If possible, start preparing early for a career in advertising. An advertising recruiter is looking for skills or leadership, salesmanship, idea generation, and relationship building. In addition to your course work, get involved in activities so that by the time you're a senior, you've got interesting things to talk about. It could be anything, even a trip abroad, or a family vacation. Show the recruiter that you have well-rounded interests and that you can come up with good ideas.

air during programs that draw a strong academic audience. Also, several new commercials similar in the look and feel would be effective.

The point of asking advertising questions is to uncover your strategic and problem-solving skills. Also, a recruiter wants to see that you're genuinely interested in the industry. So as long as your answer is honest and well thought out, there is no right or wrong answer.

Q: **What is your least favorite campaign? What would you do differently?**

A: *I really dislike the Jerky Pizza commercials with the stomping elephants. In a nutshell, I get really annoyed when I see any of these commercials, and I always immediately change the channel, which is very ineffective advertising. I don't think a commercial should annoy you. I think an approach like what Pizza Pizza has done would be much more effective. I like the way they have variations of the old couple deciding how to spend a few bucks, because they're funny commercials, and the couple always concludes at the end that they should have ordered a pizza. These commercials are a bit more avant-garde and a little bit more clever.*

The recruiter will want to know that you can analyze a particular advertising campaign and uncover the reasons why it didn't work. As long as you have well-thought-out reasons behind your answer, your answer can't be wrong.

Q: **What color is your brain?**

A: *My brain is red because I'm always hot. I'm always on fire with new plans and ideas.*

Be aware that you'll probably be asked zany questions. The point is not to stump you, but to find out what makes you tick. When the standard interview questions are asked, people are prepared, and it's harder for the recruiter to get to know the real person. An advertising recruiter tries to avoid this. There is no right or wrong answer to this type of question. In fact, the recruiter won't even really care what your answer is. He or she just doesn't want to hear something like, "I don't know, I guess it's blue because that's the way I imagine it." The point is to see how creative you are and how you think. Be sure to explain why you answered the way that you did.

Q: **If you got on an elevator where everyone was facing the back, what would you do?**

A: *I think I'd face the front anyway and say aloud, "It's really much more comfortable facing forward, you know."*

An advertising interview is different from other types of job interviews. Advertising recruiters tend to have a different interview style and process, usually conducting more of a behavioral interview. Recruiters ask questions like these to figure out what your behavior might be in a particular real-life situation.

Q: **What would you do if a client asked you to design and significantly expose an advertisement on a very limited budget?**

A: *I designed an ad for a decorated-Christmas-tree show for a ladies' auxiliary group in my hometown. Their budget was extremely limited, but since this was their premiere event, they wanted to get the word out into the community. I designed a great ad, which I arranged to have displayed on the side of a building at the main intersection of town. I also had the newspaper run the ad on a full page each Sunday. The first year was a hit, and the event has been repeated for the past two years.*

Prove that you can think. Use real-life examples rather than classroom work examples. Advertising recruiters' questions will not be like more traditional business interviews that have standard evaluation forms and standard questions, but, rather, they will be designed to understand your thought process.

Q: **What do you think about purple hair? When would you advise someone to have it?**

A: *I actually don't think about purple hair, but I don't think that I would recommend it. Curly hair is another story, however. So much more interesting. As my sister's maid of honor, I was in charge of making sure she looked her best for her wedding. She wanted her hair swept up in a ponytail with long, dangling curls hanging. The rollers that we used curled most of her hair, but it left all the ends straight. My sister was practically in tears, so I quickly suggested that we*

Career Changers: Examine your desires for wanting to switch to advertising. Think about the skills that it takes and determine if you have those skills. If you have no experience in advertising and are switching careers, it's helpful to read industry publications every week. Also, join a professional advertising or marketing association to get an understanding of what the business is all about. Reading the industry publications is important to get a flavor of the business. Set up as many informational interviewers as possible, preferably in several different ad agencies. If you can shadow an advertising professional for a day, you can really begin to understand what the job is all about. Get as much hands-on experience as you possibly can without being employed in the field. Read all the advertising textbooks in the library for information on what makes a good campaign or strategy.

give her hair a loose, backward sweep, so that we could tuck the ends under. She looked great and said later that she was much more pleased with her new improvised hairstyle anyway.

Regardless of how zany the question, the things to get across in an advertising interview are times when you were in a tough situation and how you creatively handled it. Or a time when you generated a lot of good ideas—in other words, that you have a thought process that's relevant to what you're trying to accomplish. Prove that you achieve your objectives. This candidate also shows a sense of humor, which is important.

Q: **What is the story behind your pin?**

A: *It's a guardian angel that my mom gave to me. I wear it everywhere and on everything. I even wear it on my jean jacket. I definitely think it brings me good luck.*

While sticking to the traditional business dress, you'll do well to show a bit of individuality. You might, for example, wear an interesting pin that means a lot to you. In fact, try to have one creative accessory that will help the recruiter remember you.

Q: **What publications do you read regularly?**

A: *I read the industry publications, including Ad Age, Ad Week, and BrandWeek. I think Ad Age is the best, so I really study it carefully. I also read the local newspapers and the Wall Street Journal, because it helps me stay focused on what consumers want. Staying in tune with the trends and dynamics in our culture is important.*

You should make a point of reading the industry publications to stay on top of the latest. The recruiter will certainly be impressed that you take the time to do this kind of reading. It also shows genuine interest in the industry.

Q: **How did you become interested in advertising?**

A: *I'm a really creative person, so I always knew that I wanted to make a career out of my creativity. But I also love the thrill of the deal, and I've found that business appeals to me as well. Advertising is the natural blending of the two, so it makes perfect sense.*

This candidate is sharp and proves that he or she has a good thinking process. The professionalism exhibited in this interview would impress the recruiter. Equally important is that the job seeker is able to relax and be natural, traits that the recruiter is certainly looking for. It would be a turnoff for the candidate to tell the recruiter something that he or she obviously thinks the recruiter wants to hear.

Q: **What qualifications do you have that will make you a success at this company?**

A: *I have a B.A. from Cornell University, where I majored in Russian studies. I was president of the Russian Club my junior and senior years. I also worked for three years in an advertising firm in my hometown.*

What you majored in doesn't really matter, as long as you have a solid degree. This candidate has leadership skills, which are particularly important to advertising recruiters. Of course, relevant work experience is also a plus.

Q: **What do you think your primary responsibilities would be as an account executive here?**

A: *As an account executive I'd be in the client-service area, as opposed to the creative, research, or media sides of agency business. I would become an expert in the client's business so that I could fully service that client. I'd also have to be an expert in our other service areas, so that I could put everything to use for the client. Projects would probably be both executional, like creating TV and radio ads, and strategic, like writing the client's marketing plan for the next year.*

This candidate's answer would impress the recruiter because it shows a knowledge of agency business and structure. The candidate understands that as an account executive, he or she would have to help the client represent himself to society, and would also have to represent the client to the agency. Understanding how the different areas in the agency interrelate is essential.

Q: **What has been your greatest challenge in your last job?**

A: *Dealing with the amount of work and stress is really challenging. Client service is probably the most stressful and time-consuming area in an agency, because you're always working with people, whether it's your colleagues in your area, suppliers, or the actual client. There are also always deadlines that have to be met.*

The candidate understands the importance of meeting deadlines. He or she also understands that the client-service aspect of agency business means that you're always accountable, both to the other departments of the agency and

---

Experienced Professionals: Talk about your successes for past clients. Describe where you want to be in the company now, and where you hope to grow to. What can you add to the agency that it desperately needs and doesn't currently have? Do you have any clients that you can bring with you to the agency? Work on convincing the recruiter that your personality would mesh well with the company culture.

to the client. Understanding the intensity of the job and still wanting to take it will translate into a clear commitment and an ability to give your all.

Q: Where do you want to be in five years?

A: *In five years I'd like to be an account director with your agency on a medium-sized account.*

The candidate has realistic expectations about career growth. He or she is also saying to the recruiter that this job is not just a passing fancy, and that the agency will not be used as a stepping-stone for bigger things elsewhere. Long-term interest in the agency and in a career is both important and evident in this answer.

Q: Give me your ideas for selling a pencil.

A: *It's slim and will fit in your jacket or pants pocket. It's yellow and reminds me of elementary school and yellow school buses. It'd make a great last name. Infinitely more convenient than a pen because you can erase your mistakes. It's fun to sharpen.*

The recruiter will want to see that you have idea generation. The recruiter will also be looking for problem-solving abilities. What you actually say isn't as important as the fact that you can think on your feet.

Q: What skills do you think you'll need for this job? Do you think you have these skills?

A: *I think I'll need strategic-thinking skills, which I've developed from solving problems and looking at client problems analytically. I also think both formal and casual presentation skills are important. I've really developed my casual communication skills just by being in the business. And I make a point of taking a class every once in a while at the local community college to learn the latest presentation software.*

Be able to talk about specific examples of learning strategic-thinking skills if the recruiter digs further with this question. For example, if you've had to come up with specific client strategies, or write a marketing plan for a client, you could use these as examples. Presentation skills are important because you'll be making plenty of presentations.

Candidates Re-entering the Workforce: Brush up on your leadership, salesmanship, idea-generation, and relationship-building skills. Perhaps do some volunteer work in the community that will give you an opportunity to build these skills. Convince the recruiter that you're going back to work to stay, and that this isn't a short-term move.

Q: **Do you have any questions you'd like to ask me?**

A: *Yes. I wondered why you chose this company. Would you ever leave it?*

It's appropriate to ask the recruiter both personal and professional questions. Personal doesn't mean, "Tell me about your romantic life," but rather, "What's your favorite part of your job?" or "What's your least favorite part of your job?" You can also ask appropriate industry questions, like: "I read in the paper that McDonald's is really making an effort to go international. Is this a big priority? How will you accomplish this?" Ask professional questions to show that you're really interested in the business. Don't just have a page of questions ready to ask a recruiter. This seems as if you really don't care what the answer is. It's more impressive to ask a question about something you've given a lot of thought to. Once you receive an answer, ask another question following up on what the recruiter has said. This shows that you're really interested in the subject and that you'd genuinely like to have a discussion about it.

Account Executive

(Public Relations)

Q: What qualifications do you have that you believe will help you as a public relations account executive?

A: *I have two years' experience as a company media spokesperson with a $30-million-a-year company, as well as three years' account experience with a PR firm. I also have a degree in communications from UCLA.*

The recruiter will look closely at your background in terms of experience and education. This candidate has both varied and solid work experience. Majoring in communications is very acceptable, but by no means required. A solid liberal-arts background is the key, because the skills that you must have include writing, speaking, and visualizing.

Q: How did you become interested in public relations?

A: *My two biggest role models are my parents. My mother's been an editor for the local newspaper for the last twenty years, and my father's a businessman. Since I was a child, I've always wanted to combine their two businesses, and public relations does just that.*

The recruiter must feel confident about why you're in this industry, because it's demanding and takes full commitment. This candidate's answer would successfully assure the recruiter of his or her career dedication. The most common mistake made in the PR interview is that candidates say they want a PR job because they "like people." Although PR does include answering questions for the media and employee communications, it also entails a lot of writing with no human interaction. Convince the recruiter of your reasons for wanting to be in public relations.

Q: Which undergraduate courses do you think best prepared you for a career in public relations?

A: *Effective Listening was extremely helpful because we concentrated on identifying barriers to effective communication, as well as learning to analyze information critically. Understanding Mass Communication was very enlightening because it allowed us to develop a basic understanding of communication theories and processes.*

Although out of school for a while, this candidate remains freshly aware of his or her academic training. You must be prepared to answer this question, so refresh your memory by browsing over your transcript as a reminder of the different courses you took. Show that no matter what your major was, it's had an impact on your career. Courses that are relevant and important to preparing for a career in PR include sociology, psychology, history, and technical classes.

Q: What writing classes did you take in college?

A: *I took Organizational Writing, which emphasized adapting the tone to the audience and the purpose of the message. I also took Professional Writing: The Power of the Written Word, which sharpened my existing skills further and a creative-writing course, which gave me the opportunity to try both fiction and verse writing. I think effective writing skills are a requirement for success in business, and these classes helped me gain the confidence and the writing skills necessary to address most situations effectively.*

Writing is something that's held in high esteem in PR circles because there are so many people who can't write well. Possessing honed writing skills is absolutely critical, because if you can think critically on paper first, you can articulate just about anything. If you didn't take any specific writing classes, talk about other classes in which writing was emphasized. If your writing skills aren't up to snuff, take a course at your local university or community college.

Q: How do you think that new information technology will affect public relations?

A: *I think that the new technologies are already dramatically affecting the way that the PR business is conducted. A big component of PR is communication, and all forms of communicating are undergoing a revolution, you might say. How clients want information, and how we deliver it to them, are good basic examples.*

Being aware of changes in the marketplace that will affect public relations is important. Be able to discuss briefly the impact that the Internet is having on PR. This candidate is acutely aware of the impact that information technology

First-time Job Seekers: Get a job on your local or community newspaper, because it will basically be a PR job. When practicing local journalism, you must be objective as a reporter or editor, but you're also carrying the banner of the community in a close-knit situation. In this kind of environment, you'll learn an enormous amount about balancing objective reporting and serving the business needs of your advertisers. It's a great experience, and it will teach you to write fast.

is currently having on public relations. Read what you can before the interview about this trend and be able to discuss it on at least a basic level.

Q: **What challenges do you think information technology will present to public relations people?**

A: *I think that this technology is creating even greater challenges for PR people. The sheer speed in which information is transferred, as well as the staggering accessibility of information, means that we must be even more precise in our thinking and writing. I think the trend will create new and exciting opportunities for PR people.*

This is a quality answer because the candidate shows that he or she is both aware of industry trends and excited by them. The recruiter will look for someone who is embracing the changes in technology. You should think about the different implications of how information technology is affecting PR personnel before the interview.

Q: **What do you read on a regular basis?**

A: *I read all of the PR publications, especially* Reputation Management *and* Public Relations Journal. *Beyond PR I like to read the related industry publications, like* Ad Age, Ad Week, *and* Brand Week, *because it's helpful to keep up with what's going on in marketing communications. I read the journals in my clients' industries. I make a point of reading the current business-trends books. I also think it's important to read the* Wall Street Journal *every day, because in PR, it's essential to have the big-picture perspective.*

The candidate proves two things with this answer: he or she is extremely well-read and very interested in the public relations profession. Be able to give an answer similar to this one. If you don't currently read some of these publications, start doing so.

Q: **Do you read any information-technology publications?**

Career Changers: It's always hard to change careers because once you've gained a certain amount of work experience; a recruiter may be looking for a different set of skills. You must have some PR experience in order to be marketable in the field, and a good way to do this is by doing volunteer work in the PR arena or perhaps gaining your first PR work in not-for-profit. Either choice will demonstrate real motivation for making a switch. You'll have to be flexible, especially with your initial rank and status, and therefore you'll probably have to take a pay cut.

A: *I read* Wired *magazine because I consider it to be the guru of information-technology publications. There are also dozens and dozens of publications covering every aspect of information technology, but* Wired *helps me keep on top of the big picture in a rapidly evolving industry.*

This candidate is involved in every aspect of PR, which is what the recruiter's looking for. Further, he or she demonstrates an efficient use of time. Impress the recruiter by having the same habits and approach.

Q: What types of public relations projects have you worked on?

A: *When I worked in corporate PR, I was the spokesperson who talked to the media on any issue that needed comment. I also wrote the quarterly and annual reports, took care of financial communications, and dealt with analyst meetings. Currently, in my agency job, I work on the national and global accounts for both a major sports-shoe company and a photographic-film company.*

This candidate has excellent experience in both corporate public relations and the industry's side. Experience is really the most important factor to any recruiter, so try to sell yourself on any related PR work experience that you have. Practice articulating your answer to this question before the interview to make sure that the recruiter will remember your qualifications.

Q: Do you have any experience with identity-management consulting?

A: *I did a project for a college class in this area. I chose a large frozen-food company that had been aggressively diversifying its business and created a report that identified a corporate identity. I also developed branding and naming strategies and explored organizational-structure issues.*

Identity-management consulting is a sophisticated and high-level-niche side of the business. It's not important that you have experience in this particular area, because the recruiter could ask if you have experience in many specialty areas. What is important is that you can easily adapt to a new and different project if needed. Show the recruiter that you have a "can do" attitude.

Q: What has been your most frustrating experience working in public relations?

A: *I take my client accounts very seriously, but sometimes agencies do not give the attention and resources needed for their clients' accounts. In a big agency things become impersonal, and success is measured solely on the number of account time sheets and expense reports that you sign. I think it's important to stay focused on what really matters, which is growing creatively and servicing the client.*

This answer is commendable because the candidate does not get caught up in the glamour of the business at the expense of the client. Further, this candidate proves that he or she can see the forest through the trees. He or she is able to focus on the big picture without getting off track.

Q: **Do you approach your projects from a task- or a project-oriented position?**

A: *I think being able to work both ways is essential in PR. Project deadlines inevitably are stepped up, and new "emergencies" can happen at any time. I would say that I'm task oriented when I have a stretch of time to compartmentalize and get a project done. When something suddenly comes up, I switch into project-orientation mode so that I can keep several things going at once.*

Flexibility is the name of the game in PR. You have to be able to jump from project to project as client deadlines and needs dictate. This candidate has a natural propensity to work in this manner, which would impress any recruiter.

Q: **Are you comfortable with computers?**

A: *Yes, I'm proficient on both a Macintosh and a PC. I am also hooked up to a DSL line at home. I like to use a project-manager software program at the office for maximum efficiency in keeping client projects organized.*

An answer like this candidate's is important in light of the impact that information technology is having on the public relations industry. On a practical level, computer skills are important to have for many jobs in almost every industry. Further, this candidate could easily learn and adapt to new software packages as needed.

Q: **Do you have any experience with budgeting?**

A: *In fact, that's a big part of my responsibility with my two major accounts. I work with my clients to develop a budget that we must maintain, which is really a challenge sometimes. But I have a good relationship with my clients, so together we're usually able to come up with creative solutions to get everything done efficiently.*

Experienced Professionals: You've probably already developed a reputation for yourself in professions. If so, there's a good chance you won't have a formal interview, especially if you're interviewing with an agency. The recruiter will try to get you talking about what you've done and what kind of person you are, perhaps what you're like to work with. This type of discussion is often very valuable to the interviewer because you'll reveal important things about yourself, your skills, and your finesse in dealing with clients.

Recruiters will want to know that you can handle the budgeting aspect of the job. This candidate proves that he or she can, and at the same time manages to describe a positive relationship with clients. A general rule of thumb is that you move upward very quickly in agencies if you can prove that you're adept at handling budgets and clients.

Q: **What do you think your agency could do better?**

A: *I think the agency is pretty good at what it does. If anything, I think it should do a little more PR work for itself, perhaps even hire an advertising agency. You can always be bigger and better, and I think we'd have even more clients if more businesses knew what we're capable of doing.*

This candidate's answer is both thoughtful and big picture oriented. It proves that he or she can step out of the daily routine and understand how to improve the actual running of the business. It also shows a true propensity for the business of public relations.

Q: **Do you prefer to work on your projects individually or with a team?**

A: *Sometimes it's more efficient to work individually in the interest of advancing a project, but ultimately I think it's the team that gets things done. I really enjoy interacting with colleagues and clients, because if I work alone on something for too long, I start to feel isolated.*

The recruiter is really asking, "What are you like to work with?" This is important because agency work is teamwork. Positive interaction with clients is also extremely important.

Q: **Are you accredited?**

A: *Yes, I've been accredited with the Public Relations Society of America and have an APR. I'm also accredited with the International Association of Business Communicators.*

The public relations profession is always working toward building credibility, so the PRSA sets standards for the industry. The candidate's mention of the

---

Candidates Re-entering the Workforce: First, you must get over the credibility hurdle and prove that you're really intent on doing PR and prove that you're going to stay with it. Like the career switcher, you have to take a less than ideal job, or a job that you're overqualified for. You should, however, look for a situation in which you can grow rapidly. In this case an agency would be a good place; in a corporate function you might get pigeon-holed into an employee-communications role.

IABC is also quite impressive to the recruiter. If you're accredited with either or both of these organizations, that's positive. If you are not, focus your answer on your experience, the results you've achieved, and the relationships you've got with your clients, all of which are infinitely more important.

Q: **Do you belong to any other professional associations?**

A: *I belong to the American Marketing Association—the AMA. I find the association helpful because of its marketing publications. I also belong to the associations of my clients' industries.*

This is impressive to a recruiter, but certainly not essential. It simply shows that the candidate has a high level of motivation. Again, your track record is your biggest selling point.

Q: **In your opinion, what constitutes a tremendous public relations success?**

A: *Not the number of column inches of information written in the paper; true success is simply solving a client's problem. Sound public relations advice won't appear in the paper. Success is the advice to do the correct thing to avoid difficult situations.*

This candidate's answer is excellent. Public relations is not a numbers game; it's looking at the big picture.

Q: **What would you do if a client asked you to stretch the truth in a press release or press conference?**

A: *I would encourage my client to be creative in coming up with a solution to the problem. Stretching the truth may help in the short run, but it never does in the long haul.*

This question is aimed at determining the candidate's ethics and integrity. The candidate has proved to the recruiter that he or she is solid in this regard. Your answer should be something similar.

Copywriter
(Advertising)

Q: **Why do you want to leave your current position?**

A: *I've been working for my current employer for two years now, and though I really enjoy my position there, I want to add more diversity to my portfolio.*

There's no single right or wrong answer to this question. Agencies are normally very aware that copywriters jump around from one employer to another, often to diversify their portfolios. When you're locked into an agency or a corporate environment, your ads can all start looking the same because you're working for the same clients day in and day out. So listing a lot of different employers on your resume will not necessarily be a negative, as it usually is in other fields. At the same time, however, some agencies like to find writers who stay in one place. There's nothing more disruptive in an agency than constantly having to replace copywriters. Another reason copywriters tend to jump around is that creative environments in general tend to have quite a bit of internal conflict, and a copywriter may look for another job simply because he or she hasn't found the right personality mix. Most copywriters are teamed with an art director, and the relationship is like a marriage. If the marriage works, they stay together a long time; and if it doesn't, they part ways. You shouldn't admit in an interview that you didn't get along with your art-director counterpart. Agencies look for easygoing and creative writers, not prima donnas. Presenting yourself as someone both creative and easy to get along with will go a long way toward winning you a job offer.

Q: **How much of an art-director role did you play as opposed to a copywriter role?**

A: *Well, it depends on the job. I art-directed in my job at Smith and Faber, but I assumed mostly a copywriter role at Jordan Kraus. Here are some examples in my portfolio of work I produced in an art-director role.*

The interviewer will want to know if you simply wrote copy while someone else was coming up with the big ideas. Agencies would rather hear that you were also creative-directing your own copy if that was in fact the case. Show samples of your work for which you assumed art direction.

Q: **Do you have experience with a diverse client base and diverse mediums?**

A: *Yes. I've done work for agencies as well as for corporations. I've done a lot of print work, including print ads, corporate brochures, and annual reports. I also have experience writing for radio and television. You'll find all of this reflected in my portfolio.*

Two of the big things agencies look for are a diversity of client base (have you written only high tech?) and diversity of medium (have you written only print ads for magazines, or have you also written for newspapers, radio, or television?). This diversity should be clearly portrayed in your portfolio. You may want to include such things as storyboards or cassettes to strengthen your application.

Q: **Did this print campaign have a radio segment to it? If so, did you bring a tape?**

A: *Actually, it does. We ran a four-week radio campaign in ten major markets. Here's a tape of the two different radio spots that ran during this period.*

Writers often forget to bring tapes and/or transcriptions of tapes to job interviews. It's a big advantage for you to bring all supportive materials rather than saying you'll send them later. Not only does this strategy prevent delays in the hiring process, it will help give the impression that you're an organized and thorough individual.

Q: **Did you write this entire ad?**

A: *Yes, I wrote the body copy and the headline. I also came up with the idea behind it and commissioned the artwork. I especially enjoy working when I can perform several different key roles, from initially conceptualizing the idea for an ad to fine-tuning the writing.*

This is another way of asking "What did you contribute to this ad? What hat were you wearing at the time this ad was created (art director, junior copywriter, senior copywriter)?" Your answer should correspond to the position you're applying for. If you're applying for a senior copywriter position, for

First-time Job Seekers: Normally, job interviews in the advertising industry consist mostly of a portfolio review, so you'll need to have a substantial portfolio at the ready. Bring samples you've written for classes, especially copywriting classes—anything that will give the agency a good feel for what you're able to do. Educational qualifications tend not be an important consideration, as long as you have a four-year degree. Your portfolio and any relevant experience you have will be heavily considered. Hanging an advertising internship under your belt will give you a significant advantage over other entry-level applicants.

example, you should be able to say that you've done everything in the ad and perhaps also took an art-director role. If, on the other hand, you're applying for a midlevel position, answers like "Well, I only write the body copy" or "I only wrote the headline" or "I was just the art director—I came up with the idea but somebody else wrote it" are also acceptable. Vague answers like, "Well, I co-wrote this with someone—I wrote this part and someone else wrote this" leaves the interviewer wondering exactly what you contributed to the ad and whether or not you've stretched the truth a little bit.

Q: **Were you teamed with a designer for this job, or did you write the copy and come up with the idea independently?**

A: *I was teamed with a designer for this ad. In fact, I've worked with designers on several different projects.*

This is a fairly critical question. Agencies value copywriters who have experience working with designers. Such experience shows that you understand the sharing of ideas that goes back and forth between copy and design. Often it's hard to draw a line between the two. This is an especially important skill for junior copywriters looking for senior-level staff positions. If you're not a visual person or haven't worked with a designer, your experience may be perceived as limited. If that's the case, you should emphasize your potential to do this kind of work.

Q: **How much client interaction have you had?**

A: *In my last position I sat in on a lot of client meetings with the account executive and other key agency personnel. When I was working on the corporate side, I functioned as the go-between for top management and clientele.*

It's especially important for you to be comfortable and effective when dealing with clients if you're applying for higher-level positions. Agencies in general like to know that their copywriters can be, as one advertising executive told us, "dressed up and taken out"—that is, that copywriters have a professional appearance and demeanor and can be presented to the organization's most valued clients.

Q: **How did you come up with the idea for this particular piece?**

A: *Well, I based my idea on the client's three main objectives: to introduce a new arthritis medication, to establish name recognition for the product, and to emphasize its unique selling point—that it's the strongest arthritis medication available without a prescription.*

Give a brief background for every piece as you go through your portfolio; this will enable the interviewer to evaluate the effectiveness of each. It's best to volunteer this information; don't let the interviewer assume the worst—that you've created a bad solution. The recruiter may not like what he or she sees until you explain the assignment. For example, in some cases you may have had a very tough assignment that didn't have an obvious, spectacular solution, but you came up with some solid solutions that made sense based on the assignment.

Q: **Can you write lengthy copy? Do you have any corporate-capability brochures or annual reports under your belt? If so, do you have them with you?**

A: *Yes, I've produced several annual reports. Here are some samples.*

This is the weakest point for most job candidates. Agencies tend to get a lot of clever people in the door with jazzy ideas but with no experience writing longer, drier assignments. Lots of copywriters like to show highly creative, jazzy pieces and leave at home corporate-capability brochures, annual reports, and other pieces that are copy heavy. Be sure to include both types of pieces in your portfolio. Show not only that you're quick with a headline or good with a short, clever idea, but that you can elaborate on copy and big ideas. The interviewer isn't looking for highly creative, lengthy copy—he or she just wants to know if you have the ability to write it when necessary.

Q: **What environments have you worked in? How well have you worked with account executives?**

A: *I really like working one-on-one with account executives. They're the ones who are on the front line with the clients and can give me the best input, short of meeting with the client myself.*

This is a personality-related question rather than a skill-based one. All creativity aside, the interviewer will want to determine if you have the interpersonal skills necessary to fit in with the other personalities in the office. Don't say something like, "Well, account executives are really hard to work with. You just have to tolerate those 'suits.'" This is a common answer but not necessarily a good one.

Q: **Why did you choose copywriting as opposed to editorial or writing for a magazine?**

Career Changers: If your previous experience is in editorial or public relations, emphasize creative work you've done on your own time, even if it's just creative writing. This is especially important because editorial writing is very different from creative writing—like apples and oranges. Making this transition can be difficult, and you'll have to convince advertising-agency personnel that you've made it successfully.

A: *What initially interested me in this field was a copywriting class I took in college. Then I interned for three months at a local ad agency. I've also spoken at length with several professionals working in the industry and believe that I have a good sense of what the field is like.*

This question is commonly asked of junior copywriters, not seasoned ones. If you're entry level, you should be prepared to discuss a particular teacher, class, or experience that inspired your interest in the field.

Q: **What's your favorite advertising campaign, and why?**

A: *I'd have to say that the series of public-service ads that ran in the early nineties is my favorite to date. That was a great campaign because it was the first of its type, and each ad was provocative in its content as well as in its presentation. The ads hit a chord with me, and I still remember them to this day.*

The interviewer is probing the candidate's likes and dislikes here—what gets the person excited, what he or she aspires to. A really effective ad will be not only creative but memorable and inspiring. Explain why your favorite ad is effective, which will indicate to the interviewer that you're marketing oriented as well as creative.

Q: **What computer systems have you used?**

A: *I use Mac, though I'm also familiar with PC systems. Which system does your company use?*

Conversion software has made this less of an issue, but it's a bonus in your favor if you're familiar with the system the agency uses.

Q: **What are your salary requirements?**

A: *I'm really flexible. I'd like to be making a salary comparable to what I'm currently earning, but I'm willing to put some time in if it would make you feel more comfortable with hiring me. I could work on a trial three-month basis or even freelance a couple of jobs with you before you consider me for a permanent position.*

Experienced Professionals: Your portfolio should illustrate the diversity and breadth of your experience—that you've written for many different types of clients in a variety of mediums. Be sure to include many samples of the type of work that the interviewing agency does. Emphasize your extensive client-contact experience, an important aspect of the position. Present yourself as an individual who is personally, and creatively mature.

There's no right or wrong answer to this question, though your salary requirements should be realistic and in line with the going rate. If you're willing to do freelance work, you should mention it at this time. This will give you a great advantage over the competition, because it demonstrates your confidence in your work and enables agencies to "test the product" before they actually "buy" it. Saying that you're not open to freelancing will create a negative impression unless you're prevented from doing so because you're working for a competitive agency.

Q: Do you have any references?

A: *Yes. Here's a list of three industry professionals I've worked with in the past.*

Sometimes you may not be able to provide references—for example, if you've been freelancing with one of the agency's competitors. If you're able to give references, that's a plus—provided, of course, that they have good things to say about you.

Q: Would you leave some samples?

A: *Yes. I've prepared a package of samples to leave with you, including several print pieces, a tape of radio ads, and some storyboards.*

In addition to leaving samples of print pieces you've produced, you should be prepared to leave cassette tapes of radio spots and/or storyboards of television spots. Transcribed scripts of radio spots are also acceptable if you don't have a tape available. Often the first person to interview you isn't the one who'll be making the final decision, so it's important to leave these materials for the decision maker to review; they'll often have a big impact on whether you'll be invited back for a second interview. Keep in mind that packaging is also important. Bring chrome proofs of printed pieces rather than low-quality black-and-white photocopies. This can also make a significant difference. Your copy may be spectacular, but if it's not packaged well, it may be perceived as inferior to the samples left by other candidates.

Candidates Re-entering the Workforce: Show how you've kept active during your sabbatical, perhaps by taking freelance jobs, writing your child's play group's newsletter, or taking an active role within your professional association. Agencies know that once a creative writer, always a creative writer, so these activities are considered very valuable, especially when coupled with prior experience in the workforce.

Editorial Assistant
(Book Publishing)

Q: **Why are you interested in publishing?**

A: *I first became interested in publishing when I worked on my college newspaper. I began as a contributing writer, then joined the staff as a proofreader and fact checker, and was eventually promoted to a staff writer. I found it was a natural extension of my dual major in English and political science. After graduation I attended the Columbia Publishing Program. It was an intense program, and it gave me a solid foundation on which I plan to build my career.*

Most entry-level publishing candidates cite a love of books, reading, and writing. While this is an acceptable answer, it's not entirely original or inspiring. Try to distinguish yourself from the competition by demonstrating a clear and consistent interest in the field. Cite an interest derived from work you've done on your college newspaper or literary magazine, relevant courses you may have taken, works you've had published, and/or experience working in a bookstore.

Q: **What specific area of publishing are you interested in?**

A: *I'm interested in learning more about the editorial side of trade publishing.*

You should have some sense of direction. If you say, "I'll do anything," many employers will conclude that you lack depth of interest and are trying to find just any job. Cite a particular publishing area that interests you—editorial, sales, subsidiary rights, production, design, publicity, and so forth. Also, mention what kind of publishing interests you. Do you prefer children's books, textbook publishing, or trade books? Of course, if you're interviewing for a position at an academic press, for example, it would be unwise to divulge your desire to work on illustrated children's books.

First-time Job Seekers: The key to your success is to have, in addition to you liberal-arts degree, some kind of relevant publishing experience. If you don't have any, get some quick! This could include taking a proofreading course, working part-time at a bookstore, or doing an internship at a publishing company. Previous office experience and computer skills are a definite plus. Don't forget to bring multiple photocopies of your writing clips!

Q: **What kinds of books do you like to read?**

A: *I like to read many different kinds of books, though I find myself gravitating toward nonfiction more often than not. I regularly read biographies, current events, and history books. In fact, I just finished Colin Powell's* My American Journey, *which I understand is published under this imprint. I was very impressed with it, and that's one of the reasons why I chose to apply for a position here.*

Ideally, the kinds of books you cite should include the type of books published by the company you're interviewing with. If you're not familiar with that particular genre, do some research prior to your interview so you'll appear well informed.

Q: **Name three books you've read recently.**

A: *Well, besides Colin Powell's book, I've also read James Coleman's biography of Lincoln, and a book called* Rebuilding Russia, *which is an analysis of the economic and political consequences of the end of Communism.*

This is a common question. Be prepared to name (and possibly discuss) at least three books you've read recently, possibly more. Employers will assume that if you can't answer this question, you don't read a lot, and will all but eliminate you from contention on the spot.

Q: **Who is your favorite author and why?**

A: *I admire many authors, but if forced to choose, I would have to say Stephen Covey. I've adapted several of his seven habits into my daily work routine and have found that they've helped me tremendously.*

This is where you should discuss several works by the same author in some depth. Again, you should keep in mind the kind of publisher you're interviewing with when you choose which of your favorite authors to discuss. This is not to say that you should name only an author published by that company, but you probably shouldn't name a romance novelist, for example, if you're interviewing at a nonfiction publisher.

Q: **What was your major in college?**

A: *I had a dual major in English and political science.*

Career Changers: Your challenge is to determine which of your skills and experience you can transfer to an editorial position. For example, if you have experience working in human resources, you have valuable knowledge that a career publisher may find appealing. Emphasize your office and computer skills, and your enthusiasm for the position.

Most publishers look for a bachelor's degree in English, though most liberal-arts majors are considered acceptable.

Q: How fast can you type?

A: *I'm usually accurate at about fifty words per minute.*

This is a fairly standard question, since most entry-level editorial positions involve a lot of administrative work. Many candidates will greatly exaggerate their typing prowess, only to be given a typing test at the conclusion of the interview. If you perform poorly on the test after boasting lightning-fast, error-free typing, you've lost your credibility. If you're not sure what your speed is, test yourself (on a typewriter, not a word processor) so you can be prepared to answer this question.

Q: Tell me about your computer skills.

A: *I'm very comfortable using both Microsoft Word and Excel. I also have some experience using Access.*

It's a sure bet that you'll be asked this or a similar question about your computer skills. If you don't have any, get them fast, since they're a prerequisite for most entry-level editorial positions. Most publishers look for sound knowledge of Microsoft Word. Familiarity with a spreadsheet program like Excel and a database-management application can also be a plus. If you aren't familiar with the applications a particular employer uses, be sure to emphasize your ability to learn new software quickly.

Q: Do you have any relevant publishing experience?

A: *Yes. I worked on my college newspaper as a staff writer. During my senior year of college I did an internship in the sales and marketing division of Sound Reading Book Club, assisting the marketing director in direct-mail projects and ad placement. Since I graduated in June, I've been working as a clerk in an independent bookstore until I find the right full-time editorial position.*

This is a terrific opportunity to "sell" yourself to the employer. Mention any relevant experience you may have, including writing for your college newspaper, publishing internships, and/or bookstore experience.

Experienced Professionals: If you have previous editorial experience, you've already done the hardest part—breaking into the field. For job leads, talk with your contacts among literary agents, sales reps, and other editors. Once you've scheduled an interview, emphasize your professional experience and knowledge of that company's books. That's a powerful combination!

Q: **What types of writing have you done?**

A: *I wrote many news stories and op-ed pieces for my college newspaper. I also wrote occasional book and music reviews. As a marketing intern, I wrote a lot of ad copy and business correspondence.*

This is the time to bring out your writing samples. Be sure to bring samples of many different types of writing, and be prepared to explain each in depth. Also be prepared to take a writing and/or editing test on the day of your interview.

Q: **What would you say are the broad responsibilities of an editorial assistant?**

A: *Though I'm sure it varies from company to company, I think it would be safe to say that being an editorial assistant involves a lot of typing, filing, and general administrative work. I would probably be expected to read and evaluate book proposals, write manuscript-rejection letters, have some limited correspondence with authors, and generally assist the editor in whatever needed to be done.*

You will probably be asked this question in some form or another. Many entry-level applicants have a "glamorized" view of publishing and are unhappily surprised to find themselves performing mundane, clerical tasks. The employer wants to make sure that you have a realistic view of the job and will be likely to be happy in that position for several years.

Q: **How necessary is it for you to be creative on the job?**

A: *Well, I like to be creative every day and would like to integrate that into my job. But creativity can take many forms. For instance, when I was an intern at Quality Publishers, I spent a great deal of time processing book returns. It seemed like a tremendous waste of books and paper to dispose of the returned titles, as was the company's policy. I talked with a local recycling center, who agreed to pick up the books twice a month for recycling. This would also save the company several thousand dollars annually in Dumpster fees. I presented the idea to the operations manager, who really loved it. The company adopted the policy immediately, and now they're saving not only trees, but money too.*

Candidates Re-entering the Workforce: Since editorial work requires many late nights at the office, you'll want to stress your readiness to commit to a full-time position. Be prepared to discuss how you've kept up during your leave, by reading *Publishers Weekly*, attending trade show conventions like the American Bookseller's Association convention, reading *New York Times* book reviews, and perusing bookstores on a regular basis.

This is a derivative of the previous question. While you should cite an interest in using your creativity on the job, you should also emphasize an ability and enthusiasm for performing more mundane tasks. Again, you want to give the employer the message that you have a realistic idea of what the job entails.

Q: **Are you familiar with our books?**

A: *Yes. In fact, I've used several books in your Software Simplified series to help me out of a few computer jams. I noticed that the company is expanding the series outside the computer area, particularly with a new home-repair book. I'd be interested in learning more about the series, and how the company has managed to establish itself as the dominant player in this competitive niche.*

Your answer to this question can make all the difference between getting a job offer and getting a polite rejection letter. This is because there are many more qualified applicants seeking to break into publishing than there are entry-level openings. Employers must find a way to eliminate all but a small number of qualified candidates, and this question is designed to help do just that. If you take the time to familiarize yourself with a particular publisher's books, you'll have a leg up on all the other first-round candidates who skip this important step.

Production Assistant

(Television)

Q: How much do you know about what goes on behind the scenes in television?

A: *Before I began my last internship, I visited every station in town that offered tours to individuals and groups. I always asked questions and even got to talk to some of the producers and anchors. I know every station has a different philosophy about news, but in general I have a pretty good grasp of what each person's job is in relation to the newscast, from the assignment editor, who decides what should be covered, to the producer, who formats and times the on-air product.*

If you have little or no experience in television, expect this question. The interviewer is trying to get a sense of whether you have a real-life "nuts and bolts" understanding of the industry, or if you just see it as "glamour." It's important that you have, at least, the minimal working knowledge of what goes on, even if you're interviewing for an unpaid internship. Although most people in the industry are glad to help out newcomers, hand-holding is almost impossible.

Q: What do you think your typical day would be like?

A: *The first thing I'd do in the morning, before coming here, is read the morning papers and watch morning newscasts on all competing stations so I'd know what the day ahead looks like. I'd try to imagine how a particular story might progress throughout the day so I could be one step ahead. I'd meet with producers and assignment people in the morning meetings to find out what stories would be assigned to me and constantly update them throughout the day on late-breaking information. Then I'd pull together whatever file tape might be needed and any additional statistics that would be helpful for the viewer to know when the story hits the air.*

Especially for less-skilled positions, the interviewer will want to make sure you understand that there's a lot of very unglamorous grunt work involved. This kind of work can range from spending hours logging video, to getting lunch and coffee. What any person who has a desire to be in the industry should know is that almost everyone starts out this way in television. If you're unwilling to do the grunt work, somebody else interviewed tomorrow will understand that "getting in the door" is the key and will be more than willing to perform menial tasks with flourish and get noticed.

Q: **What have you seen on our station that you like?**

A: *Basically, I like your focus on the community. It's to your credit that the station seems to remain focused on the tradition of local news and what matters to its audience. The special reports that focus on town politics, that go on location each week to a different town for a live shot and tell us what big issues the community is facing make the people watching feel that this station is their station. It is, in my opinion, a great way to maintain a loyal audience.*

Going to an interview knowing nothing about the hiring company indicates an unwillingness to learn. This question is designed to see if the candidate is indeed familiar with the station conducting the interview. It's imperative that you watch every newscast you possibly can in the days before your interview, and watch competing stations as well. Read the television section in your local paper to find out about any changes the station may be making. If you read, for instance, that this particular newsroom is planning on changing its set because the news director thinks it's boring, you can answer with a criticism, but one that is right in line with the station's desire to change. Ask other people what they think, and then throw in some of your poll results.

Q: **What is something that you dislike?**

A: *I read last week in the paper that you're planning to add more consumer and economic stories. I was glad to read that because I believe the station really needs a "business beat" feature. So many people get all of their information from television—and right now everyone's concerned with making money last and making wise investment decisions. This could be a really well-watched feature—and I'd love to help out with it.*

This is the old question anybody dreads in an interview, akin to "What are your greatest weaknesses?" If you've done some research on the station, you

---

First-time Job Seekers: Be prepared for your first, and sometimes your second, TV job to be an unpaid internship. And sometimes these are very hard to get. Most stations won't accept interns unless you're getting college credit. One television professional told us that in order to get her first job, she actually registered at a local university and took one course on the way to a graduate degree. Then she was able to get an internship. Also, remember that anyone who knows anyone can help you get your foot in the door. Some people are afraid of networking, but in television that's often the quickest and easiest way to get ahead.

should be able to make an intelligent suggestion. Stations are constantly written up in local papers whenever a change is being considered. Keep abreast of what goes on in any newsroom you're interviewing with. You can preface a negative comment by saying, "Those of us with a real working knowledge of the newsroom tend to be a bit more critical, but ..."

Q: **What improvements, if any, could you make in the product?**

A: *I'm a real team player, and just by doing well any task that I'm given, I could make a very positive contribution—positive contributions on any level lead to positive changes. Though I think what you do on air is great, I know that the longer I'm here, the more creative I'll be in my suggestions.*

Again, research is the key here. Be creative! Call television reporters for the local papers and tell them you're going in for an interview with a station. They may be very helpful with inside information. Of course, this will be harder to accomplish in large TV markets, where the local critics are big stuff, but it's worth a try. They usually have great sources at the stations and know if any changes are in the works. You will pleasantly surprise any interviewer who finds your thinking about change is in line with station philosophy.

Q: **If you could have any job at a station in five years what would it be?**

A: *If I work hard, I think a realistic goal for someone with my experience would be to produce my own newscast. I'm going to try to learn everything I can to meet this goal.*

Never say "Yours!" but do display a working knowledge of the organization's "hierarchy." Also, this is a great time to pitch any creative ideas you might have for new products, or any segments you'd love to create for a newscast. Sometimes looking at stations in larger markets and scaling down their ideas to fit the station you're interviewing with will make for very impressive and creative suggestions.

Career Changers: Television people are constantly moving from station to station and town-to-town to follow better opportunities in jobs. If you're moving in from another career, remember that TV stations are businesses. They need accounting people, human-resource people, and secretaries. If you have these types of skills, you can "get in" to a station and try to make a move later into production. Don't be upset if you're still doing the same type of work at a different location. At least you're in the door and will be getting to know people who can take you where you want to go.

Q: **What are your long-term career goals?**

A: *I'm really excited about all the opportunities that may exist, with interactive TV, more cable stations, and networks evolving every day. There's no telling where I may be, but whatever my job in this business, I'm sure it will be exciting and satisfying.*

Most important, try to have a long-term goal, but keep in mind that the television industry, with the onset of cable, personal satellites, and new networks cropping up all over the place, will offer a great many more opportunities. At least try to show a knowledge of these changes by reading trade publications such as *Broadcasting*. And try to have some kind of picture of how the skills you will learn at the job you're applying for will help you reach your goals.

Q: **Why do you want to get into this business?**

A: *I know a lot of people want to get into television for the money, or they just want to be on camera. But to me, communicating well is an art. The television industry is the ultimate test of how well one can communicate. It's not like working for a newspaper, where if you miss a fact, you can go back and reread it. A television news story can go by in a flash, and the challenge is to get the audience to understand it, learn from it, and, in the broader sense, use the information to better their lives or their situations. It's the way television can evoke action that's always made me want to be a part of the industry.*

This is a question that separates the adults from the children. Make it clear that you know there are long hours, that your first job might be "assistant to the assistant," but you're willing to do whatever it takes and work as long as necessary. This is not the time to talk about how you want to replace Katie Couric. Employers tend to shy away from people who have great on-camera aspirations for production-assistant work, because past experience has taught them that these folks become bored with the menial-support work. If you do want to become Katie Couric (or Peter Jennings), remember they didn't start at the top, and it took years of hard work and patience for them to achieve their star status.

Q: **What is your impression about the industry in general?**

Experienced Professionals: You already know the game plan. Keep up all your connections: discretely let friends in other stations or markets know you're on the lookout for a new job. Do the best work you've ever done, because your potential next employer could be watching.

A: *Right now I see a medium in rapid change. Years ago, the news was just reported. Now stations and newsrooms interact with their viewers through online services, viewer-action hot lines, and shared community events and sponsorships. I see the television industry not just as an information relay, but as a vital and proactive part of the community.*

Again, research is the key. Mention any innovation you can think of that's made a positive change in the industry. It would score big points to mention something that the station you're interviewing with has done in the past few years, or even months, that's made a positive change for them. This could range from anything like new graphics and set, to the edition of a morning newscast, to going online with viewers.

Q: What do you think in your background has prepared you for the hard work and long hours?

A: *To me every experience is a learning experience. I understand there are what one could term menial tasks in this job. But a task is menial only if you treat it that way. I know that a great many well-respected journalists tell stories about getting coffee and making copies in their first jobs. I guess in some ways it could be compared to earning stripes in the military.*

Here the interviewer is not only trying to get an idea of how hard you'll work, but if you'll be a good person to work with. This industry, like any medium, is based a great deal on personality. The ideal candidate for any job must be strong, self-confident without being conceited, and fun to work with. Any experience that proves you're a team player and willing to go the extra mile should be brought up here.

Q: Is there anything about this kind of work that makes you a little apprehensive?

A: *I'm awestruck by the responsibility the writers, producers, anchors, and directors have in doing their daily jobs. But that's what makes it so exciting. I can*

Candidates Re-entering the Workforce: If you've worked in TV before, you most probably have left your station on great terms, kept up on your connections, and done at least some freelance work "to keep your hand in the business." If you're trying to break into the business from another industry, after an absence from the workforce, remember that all types of workers make a station run. But find out what changes may have occurred during your absence. Anything from a new accounting system to new newsroom computers to a new news director you should know about, and make those changes work for you. Let everybody know you're looking to get back into the business.

imagine there's nothing more satisfying for them than to break a great story or put together a flawless newscast, and knowing they've done some social good in the process. There are very few things we can be involved with in life that can bring that level of satisfaction.

Although working in television can at times be the funniest of jobs, you must be aware of the responsibility of each person. Even an intern can make a mistake that could leave an entire newscast looking bad. It's imperative you make the interviewer aware that you understand the interdependence of a team, especially a team that has a live newscast on the air. Unfortunately, hundreds of thousands of people will notice when things don't go quite right. That's why you have to convince the interviewer that he or she can expect perfection as far as your job is concerned.

Q: **You're producing the evening newscast. One day three things happen: a well-known entertainer dies, there's a huge fire that forces evacuation of a local manufacturing plant, and a drug shooting occurs. Which would you lead with?**

A: *Although in many cases an umbrella lead can encompass several stories that could possibly lead a newscast, I would say—judging from your overwhelming interest in what affects the community—you would have to lead with the evacuations and make the entertainer page two. Unfortunately—the shootings like the one you mentioned are so common—I wouldn't consider leading with it unless it was a slow news day.*

The interviewer is trying to get a sense of the candidate's news instinct. Of course, skills like picking a proper lead can be learned and improved upon, but it's great to be able to show some insight. If you get hit with this question, think of one thing: what would be most important to your audience to know about? If you're talking about a six o'clock evening show, the local lead is better, but in the later newscast a late-breaking national story should take precedence, unless local lives are at stake. This is the general rule of thumb, but there are always exceptions. If your interviewer does not agree with your choice, ask him or her why you're wrong. If you've been watching the station, though, you should have a good idea of their news philosophy, and that knowledge should lead you to the right decision. (Remember, if you've watched the station, make this answer consistent with what you've seen.)

Public Relations Assistant

Q: Define "public relations" for me.

A: *Basically, public relations is a means by which companies and individuals establish a favorable impression with a targeted audience. The audience can include the business community, potential customers or clients, the investment community, the media, and the general public.*

The interviewer will want to know that you understand the field. Do you understand what goes on in a public relations firm? Many people mistakenly believe that PR is simply about socializing or talking with people, and no interviewer wants to hear that. Like this candidate's, your answer should provide an accurate and brief definition of the profession.

Q: Time management has become a necessary factor in productivity. Give an example of a time-management skill you've learned and applied at work.

A: *I regularly use scheduling software, which helps me effectively plan for the day, week, month, or year. It also has a to-do-list feature and an alarm option, which is helpful for meeting timely deadlines. In general, though, I'm very goal oriented and self-disciplined. I like to focus clearly on one project at a time for a set amount of hours. In the past I've found that this has helped me save time, which in turn has given me the opportunity to implement new procedures that have ultimately saved the department time and money.*

When answering this question, describe a time-management technique you've applied at work that's allowed you to save time and resources. In public relations time is precious, and the interviewer will want to see that you have an idea of how valuable your time is. Try to give an example that demonstrates how you've managed to increase productivity because of effective time management.

Q: Organization and the scheduling of people and tasks are necessary functions in any account role. Give me an example that illustrates your organization and scheduling ability.

A: *In college I headed a student volunteer group. During my senior year we decided to designate a specific day for students to volunteer in the community. I was in charge of organizing student sign-ups, finding the placements, and supplying food and transportation. I clearly outlined all the steps needed to put* *the day together, prioritized the tasks, and concentrated on finishing one task before moving on to another. Through careful planning I could foresee potential challenges and was able to devise solutions for problems before they occurred. Since I managed to organize the day so well, I was able simply to enjoy it like everyone else. I didn't have to run around taking care of little glitches that I'd overlooked or forgotten.*

Your answer to this question should give an example of a systematic approach you've used for organizing and scheduling. The interviewer will expect you to demonstrate that you can prioritize tasks. This answer is an excellent example, as the candidate shows an ability to organize a large event from scratch. These types of organizational skills are essential for anyone in public relations.

Q: **Give an example of a time when you've used facts and reason to persuade another person to take action.**

A: *Recently a magazine editor refused to review one of our clients' products in an article, claiming that the product didn't suit the magazine's targeted readership. Realizing we were getting nowhere over the phone, my colleague and I faxed the editor a memo specifically addressing each one of his concerns. The following day I contacted the editor again. It turned out that the fax had made him change his mind, and he allowed our client's product to be included in the article.*

In PR you often have to overcome strong resistance to your ideas. Since "no" is often the first word you encounter when pitching an idea, it's essential that you have the ability to change someone's mind. Demonstrate that you can make an organized presentation that addresses specific concerns. The interviewer will also want to see that your action was appropriate to the situation.

Q: **Give an example of a time when you used your authority to influence another individual.**

First-time Job Seekers: You'll need a bachelor's degree, preferably in journalism, English, or marketing. Because public relations is a very competitive field, most agencies will expect entry-level candidates to have at least one internship or summer job in public relations. Candidates with internships on either the corporate or agency level will stand out from the competition. Besides needing good writing and communication skills, the ability to organize is critical. Also, be ready to present the interviewer with you portfolio, which should contain writing samples, including any press releases or flyers you've produced for school related activities or other organizations.

A: *As a resident adviser in college, I discovered that a student in my hall was steal-*
ing from her roommate. I consulted my supervisor, and upon her recommenda-
tion I directly confronted the apparent thief. I told her I knew what was going
on and explained what would happen if there were any more thefts. Soon
afterward her roommate said that her money was no longer disappearing.

Account teams are vital to any PR agency, and the interviewer will be interested in seeing how you'd fit in and what role you'd feel comfortable assuming. Even though the use of authority in a leadership role isn't popular, it's
necessary in some situations. The interviewer will want to know if you have
a sense of what's an appropriate use of authority, and if you're comfortable
using your authority to meet your professional goals.

Q: **Tell me about the last time you put your foot in your mouth.**

A: *I told my friend Lisa that I'd no longer be attending yearbook-club meetings*
because I thought the editor was a complete idiot. I later found out that the
editor was her cousin. As soon as I found out, I apologized and asked her why
she didn't say anything when I made that foolish comment. Luckily, she and I
are still friends today.

Everyone makes mistakes, and it's important for you to be cognizant of yours.
The interviewer will want to find out if you have a sense of right and wrong,
and what steps you're willing to take to provide restitution for your mistakes.
In PR leaving someone with a bad impression of you, your company, or your
client can be very detrimental to your firm.

Q: **Give an example of a time when you were asked to accom-**
plish a task but weren't given enough information. How did you
resolve this problem?

A: *At my last internship, my supervisor, an account executive, asked me to assem-*
ble 500 press kits for a mailing. I wasn't sure in what order the pages and

Career Changers: You should consider starting a smaller agency, where
there's often more latitude, and where you're more likely to have room to
develop all your talents. Also, at a smaller agency you can be exposed to
the full realm of public relations instead of just one particular aspect. Many
career changers come from a marketing or journalism background, as these
fields share quite a few characteristics with public relations, including the
need for good communications skills. Another important skill to have when
making the switch to public relations is the ability to negotiate and persuade.
This is especially true if you're looking to enter the field at a higher level,
where you'll likely play a strategic role in formulating campaigns for clients.

press releases should go, but my supervisor had already left for a client meeting. Afraid of putting the information together in the wrong order, I managed to track down her cell-phone number and called her in her car. She explained the order of the materials over the phone, and in the end I managed to prevent a mistake that would have cost hours of work and a delay in the mailing—not to mention a few headaches.

Although this example may seem trivial, the candidate demonstrates maturity and an ability to approach work conceptually. The interviewer will want to know that you understand that just getting the job done isn't enough. Your response should show resourcefulness and initiative. Public relations is a service-oriented industry, and you'll often be expected to go the extra mile to meet the needs of your clients.

Q: How did you become involved with public relations?

A: I'd taken some courses in PR as part of my marketing major. I really enjoyed learning about the industry; I found it more complex than I'd imagined it to be. Plus, I've always enjoyed writing, and I've been told that I'm a persuasive speaker. So I asked my sister's roommate, who worked in a PR firm, about summer job possibilities. She got me an interview at Schuler and Kraft, and I did my internship there last summer. Now that I have firsthand experience in the field, I want to make a career in public relations.

Convince the recruiter that you have a deep understanding of what public relations is all about. The notion that PR is a glamorous field is inaccurate, and that perception, if communicated, will more than likely turn off the interviewer. Also, don't say that you entered the industry by chance; recruiters want to hear that you're actively pursuing a career in their field.

Q: What single accomplishment are you most proud of?

A: I was one of five students from my college to be selected to participate in a three-day leadership seminar in Washington, D.C. There were to be 150 students from thirty different universities in attendance. I was very surprised when I found out I'd been selected—the faculty had received almost 100 applications

Experienced Professionals: As an account supervisor or director, you'll play a more strategic role when dealing directly with clients, so the interviewer will expect you to be able to communicate on a more sophisticated level. You should also have a solid understanding of how the business world works; if a client shows you an operating statement to use in materials targeted to investors, you should be able to understand it. Also, be ready to discuss specific examples of your work and accomplishments.

for the seminar. I attended speeches, discussion groups, and break-out activities. I learned a lot about leadership and teamwork that I think will be very useful in my career. Plus, I made some great friends that I'm still in contact with.

The interviewer wants to find out what the candidate considers a major accomplishment, in comparison with others vying for the position. Most people don't feel comfortable talking about their accomplishments, but it's a good idea for you to practice. Because teamwork is an essential part of public relations, try to use an example that demonstrates you've worked with others to meet a goal.

Q: **Tell me about a time when you were able to learn a difficult concept without the direction of another person.**

A: *Two summers ago I worked in a management-consulting firm. My supervisor asked me to set up some spreadsheets and do some expenditure comparisons. The company used Excel, which I wasn't familiar with. I turned to some junior people in the firm, hoping that they could help me, but no one had time to instruct me. So I ran to a bookstore and bought a book on how to use the software. With that book I learned how to put the project together in no time.*

If you're asked this question, give the interviewer an example that illustrates your initiative. Public relations is such a fast-paced field, there is little time to take a new person step by step through a project. You should show your ability to be self-sufficient; demonstrate that you're comfortable working independently, with little supervision.

Q: **Tell me about the last time you decided to withhold information from someone.**

A: *I was teaching my younger brother to drive. We were going down a busy street, and he ran a yellow light. A policeman pulled the car over and, when he saw that my brother had only a learner's permit, decided to go easy on him. Of course, he'd also noticed that my brother was unbelievably scared. The*

Candidates Re-entering the Workforce: Public relations is a relatively easy field to re-enter, because it's filled with opportunities for freelancing or volunteer work. To demonstrate that you've kept up your skills, show the interviewer any press releases or flyers you may have written for community organizations during your leave. Discuss how you've stayed current with technology and changes in the industry, perhaps by reading trade journals. Most important, highlight your accomplishments made before your absence and prove to the interviewer that you once again have the desire and drive to work in public relations on a full-time basis.

policeman gave him a written warning, but no ticket. I didn't think it was necessary to let our parents know what happened, because I thought my brother had learned his lesson.

Your answer to a question like this should show an understanding that, when you control information, you don't necessarily need to tell everyone everything all the time. In public relations there's no need to advance information to an inappropriate audience. The interviewer will want you to demonstrate your ability to function effectively as an information gatekeeper.

Q: Tell me about a time when you felt inappropriately reprimanded by a supervisor. How did you handle the situation?

A: *Well, in my internship last summer I made a call to an editor, and I realized that the conversation was moving more quickly than I was prepared to handle. The editor started asking me questions about the company I was representing that I wasn't prepared to answer. My supervisor was pretty angry and wanted to know what had happened; she thought that I'd jeopardized an opportunity for the company to appear in that publication. I explained to her that I'd let the editor know I was a college intern and had provided my supervisor's name and phone number for follow-up. She eventually cooled off after she received a call back from the editor, who mentioned to her that I'd handled the situation well.*

The interviewer will want to see how you cope with adversity. Do you fly off the handle, internalize the problem, or deal with it directly? The interviewer will be looking for evidence that in times of stress you're able to present your position clearly and calmly. In public relations you're often required to make phone contacts, and there are many opportunities to misinterpret information. It's important for you to realize that the best way to handle adversity is to maintain some level of flexibility and remain open to the observations of your supervisor.

Radio Program Director

Q: Why did you decide to pursue a career in radio?

A: *I minored in communications in college, and I took one class on the history of radio. The professor was an absolute fanatic about radio, and the way he talked about it really intrigued me—I thought it seemed a lot more interesting than television. So I started working at the campus radio station, and I got hooked. I hosted an overnight show during my sophomore and junior years, and my senior year I was elected program director by the rest of the staff.*

Although this may sound like a question that would be asked of an entry-level candidate, it's applicable to a candidate of any experience level. The interviewer, usually the station manager or station owner, will want to know if you simply fell into the field or if you've actively pursued a career in radio. Your answer to this question must be sincere and thoughtful. Even a basic answer like "I love music, so I wanted to work in a music-related field" is acceptable. The best program directors are the ones who have a true passion for the business, and either of these answers would demonstrate that passion.

Q: Tell me about your experience in radio.

A: *After college I started as a promotions assistant at a locally programmed 2,000-watt station upstate. After a few months I began working as a night DJ on the weekends, hosting an oldies overnight show. I eventually got promoted to music director, where I managed to talk the program director into changing the format slightly—it was an oldies station, but it played music mostly from the fifties and sixties. I thought we should add some seventies music as well. After about two months of playing more "newer" oldies, our ratings had jumped about 10 percent. It seemed the seventies music drew in some younger listeners who'd previously ignored us. So after about two years I got a job at a 5,000-watt adult contemporary station in Rochester. I've been program director there for over four years, and our market share has increased each year. Now I feel I'm ready for more of a challenge, and I want to move on to a station with a larger market.*

If you want to be a program director at a radio station in a fairly large market, you should have experience at a minimum of two radio stations. Like this candidate's answer, your answer should illustrate the greater responsibilities you held in each position. You'll also need to show proof that what you did at these stations was successful—how much did your ratings increase? Did the station's advertising revenues go up? This candidate has experience with a variety of station formats. Some station managers like this; others prefer to see people who've been in the same format throughout their career. If the interviewer seems concerned that you don't have experience in the station's own format, simply point out that, in general, an idea that works for one format will work for another. If you mention this, though, be sure to have some examples ready to support your case.

Q: What's your philosophy of radio?

A: *I believe in giving the audience what they want to hear. But I don't mean this in the sense that you should change your basic format every six or nine months. I believe in staying current with trends in music, but I think that listeners get confused if their favorite station sounds completely different every time a new style of music becomes popular. Instead of completely embracing a new genre, I believe in slowly incorporating it into the rotation. Also, I really believe in stations that are music intensive. It's good to have a strong personality in the mornings—I think people like to laugh on their way to work—but I think they'd prefer to hear music otherwise. On the more technical side, I don't believe in heavy production. I don't think music, especially rock and roll, was meant to be all cleaned up; I believe that listeners like hearing music that's raw, that sounds more real.*

This is a broad question aimed at determining your compatibility with the radio station. The interviewer wants to know what you think a radio station should sound like, in terms of type of music played or amount of production used. Do you believe in getting strong on-air personalities to attract listeners, or do you prefer simply playing music? In general, a radio station is a reflection of the program director; it's his or her creative vision that you're listening to, and the station manager wants to be sure that your vision won't

First-time Job Seekers: Most people in radio either have a bachelor's degree in communications or have completed a program at a school of broadcasting. Not all schools are reputable, however, so if you're considering enrolling in one, call your local radio station to find out which ones have the best reputations. If you worked at your college radio station, you'll have some advantage over the competition. Most people start in radio as a promotion's assistant (big-city radio stations have many such positions), or in other departments, such as news. Most likely, you'll get your first break as a weekend DJ at a radio station in a smaller market, and then simply move up from there. Your first job as a program director is always the hardest one to land; it's often difficult to convince a station manager to take a chance on you.

be in conflict with the station's mission. For instance, if a station has a nationally known personality as its biggest attraction, you wouldn't want to tell the station manager that you prefer a music-intensive format.

Q: **Tell me what you know about market research.**

A: *Obviously, conducting market research is essential for radio stations. The audience's tastes are constantly changing, and market research and listener surveys are the best ways to keep up with the listeners' likes and dislikes. On the other hand, I think that a station can be too dependent on these techniques. When I see the results of a survey, I always want to know whom they asked—what were the demographics of the group? When did the firm do the survey? I also want to see the questions. For example, if the research firm asked a random sampling of people if they liked alternative music, did the company define "alternative"? If you're forty-five years old and you usually listen to sports-radio talk shows, "alternative music" will probably be anything that came out after 1980! In short, I don't like to take survey results at face value—I always try to read between the numbers.*

A program director needs to have a thorough understanding of market research—what it is and how to use it to change or improve a radio station. Without market research it's impossible to gauge the opinions of your listeners. You should also demonstrate a strong grasp of ratings services, such as Arbitron or Nielsen, as well as a clear understanding of survey research techniques. Market-research companies will give you a mountain of information, but if you don't understand what it all means, you'll have difficulty defending your ideas to the station's management or ownership.

Q: **If market-research reports indicated that one of your most popular programs was steadily losing market share to a competing station, how would you go about reclaiming your market share?**

A: *First, I'd examine the reports. Maybe the surveyors didn't take a critical factor into consideration, or maybe they surveyed a group that wasn't our target audience in the first place. But if the results were accurate, I'd have my research*

Career Changers: Don't expect someone to take you on as program director if you have no background in radio. You'll need to have plenty of hands-on experience before you'll be entrusted with someone's station. Try to apply for jobs in which you have related experience. For instance, if you're coming from a field like public relations, you'll most likely start in the promotions department. In your interview, highlight skills that are valued in radio, such as you ability to think creatively or your organizational or interpersonal skills.

department conduct a listener survey to find out why people had stopped listening. What were they hearing elsewhere that they weren't hearing on our station? Then, depending on the survey results, I might decide to alter our format. Whether that would be a major or minor alteration would depend on the survey results. Maybe we'd just need to beef up our promotions, or perhaps add a stronger personality to that time slot. In either case I'd wait at least six months before determining if the change was a success. But I'd never drastically change the station's format based on a few months' worth of data; I think you have to wait at least a year to get the full effects of a change.

This question addresses your ability to plan strategically. If you're given a problem, how will you fix it? A program director needs to be able to identify the problem, come up with the reasons behind a drop in ratings (which includes analyzing survey data), and then develop a plan to turn things around. Your answer should demonstrate not only that you can think conceptually, but that you know how to turn vision into reality. The differences between radio stations are very subtle; there are alternative stations that lean toward the pop side, and pop stations that lean toward the alternative side. There are techniques and methods to attract listeners, and you as program director must understand what these are.

Q: **How would you rate your interpersonal skills?**

A: *I'd say they were pretty good. I have my bad days, like everyone else, but generally speaking, I think I'm pretty easygoing and good-natured.*

As program director, you have to interact with virtually every department within the radio station—promotions, sales, production, plus on-air personalities. Station managers want to see that you can get along well with others; program directors in general have a reputation for being hard to work with. Nobody expects you to be perfect, but like this candidate, you should show that you can interact well with others.

Q: **What's the greatest strength you can bring to this position?**

Experienced Professionals: Station managers will want you to show that you have a real sense of what you think the station should sound like. During your interview, be sure to articulate that clear, creative vision. Also, be ready to discuss your experience at previous jobs. You'll need to give detailed examples of how you helped improve the ratings and market share of the station. Did the revenue of the station increase after you took over? The interviewer will also ask you a number of questions about your management style and business experience.

A: *I have an almost endless supply of energy. I'm no stranger to long hours—I have no problem waking up at 5:30 A.M. to listen to our morning show, and I can just as easily wake up at 2 A.M. to see what our overnight personality is doing.*

Interviewers want to hear what you consider your greatest asset. Do you take pride in your creativity and imagination? Or in your organizational skills and business acumen? All of these are essential traits for a program director. Like this candidate, you should try to give an example of how your strength plays out in the day-to-day workings of the station.

Q: **If you could change one thing about your work habits, what would it be?**

A: *I suppose it would be my short attention span. Sometimes my mind works so quickly that I have a hard time focusing on just one task at a time. I move from one thing to another really quickly, and I might not give something as much attention as I should. When this happens, it's usually because I'm concentrating more on the big picture. But I like to think I'm getting better at this. Now I try to pay more attention to the little steps necessary to achieve the ultimate goals.*

The flip side of the previous question, this question addresses your greatest weakness. Like this candidate, try to mention a weakness that you can attribute to one of your strengths—for instance, this candidate skillfully describes the weakness by emphasizing his or her ability to see the big picture, an important skill in this field.

Q: **How would your former coworkers describe your management style?**

A: *I believe they'd say that I'm fair. I don't think I'm ever as hard on other people as I am on myself. If I believe someone's not performing up to standard, I have no trouble letting that person know. However, I try to make sure that I talk to the person in private. I remember that there was nothing I hated more than when my boss reprimanded me in front of everyone else in the office, so I try to show my coworkers respect.*

> **Candidates Re-entering the Workforce:** You'll need to convince the interviewer that you've stayed current with trends in radio. If you've continued to listen to the radio with regularity during your absence, this shouldn't be a problem. If you're interested in working for music stations, reading magazines such as *Billboard* or *Rolling Stone* will also help keep you up on trends in the industry. However, station managers will be most interested in your ability to think creatively and to come up with broad conceptual ideas.

Although the program director isn't usually in charge of the hiring and firing of personnel, he or she is still somewhat responsible for what the employees produce. As the creative director of the station, the program director has ultimate responsibility for the quality of the station's product and, therefore, must be effective in motivating the station's employees.

Q: Tell me about your experience with budgets.

A: *In my previous position as program director, I was given free rein over the budget. The station manager simply gave me a fixed amount that I could spend, so it was my responsibility to determine how that money was allocated. I had to figure out how much to spend on promotions, personalities, and the like. I'm proud to say that even though that was the first time I ever had to actually come up with a budget on my own, the station managed to come in under budget for the first time in five years.*

One of the less glamorous aspects of being a program director is dealing with administrative tasks such as budgeting. At some stations program directors are simply given a budget by the station managers or owners; they have no say in the creation of the budget. At other stations program directors are given the responsibility of developing the station's budget. In either case it's necessary for you to demonstrate an understanding of how budgeting works.

Senior Publicist

Q: **What types of jobs have you held other than publicity?**

A: *I'm currently working as an associate producer for WMBR TV's* Good Morning, Cincinnati *program. In addition to organizing all production details for studio tapings, I'm responsible for generating and researching story ideas, and booking guests and panelists. I also coordinate all local publicity, such as running ads in local newspapers. Before that I was a promotional assistant for the University of Washington's theater group. I implemented promotional campaigns for on-campus productions, which involved, among other things, writing and designing advertisements and initiating student involvement in the group.*

This type of question is designed to find out "what else you bring to the table." In other words, when you work in any type of publicity, you'll deal with all types of clients. It's good to know if you have experience in any of those businesses that would give you and your company a leg up. The key is to research the type of clients the company handles and gear your past experience toward them. For example, someone with television or a talk-show background would be a great candidate for book publicity because they have been on both sides of the media fence. If you've been a waiter or waitress, tailor your answer to the company's restaurant clients. Remember, your past job experiences are unique, and learning how to make them fit the position you're interviewing for will be key.

Q: **What was your most difficult assignment?**

A: *I was assigned a promotion project to get customers into a low-traffic store for Christmas. Research showed that this mall was a favorite with teenagers, but not parents. So to increase the adult traffic, we ran mother-daughter, father-son promotions and contests. In fact, I've brought some of the ads and press releases here in my portfolio. Would you like to see them?*

The interviewer will want to get a sense of how well you follow through with assignments no matter how difficult. Publicity jobs require a person with a take-charge attitude, someone who can deal with difficult situations and clients. This answer should be well thought out, and documented if possible. You should always have with you a portfolio of samples. Even if you're new to the publicity game, you can come up with a "make-believe" or sample product to pitch, and lay out your own campaign. Be wary of trying to improve upon a campaign conducted by the company you're interviewing with. One publicity manager we talked to described this as the worst mistake she ever made. It turned out the interviewer worked on that account and was very taken aback by her "upstart attitude." Needless to say, she didn't get the job, even though some of her ideas were incorporated into the next campaign for the product.

Q: **Tell me about a project where your input made a difference.**

A: *I was working as an intern on a promotion for a local furniture company. The owners were the spokespeople, and they were doing a series of promotional appearances for Mother's Day to bring more traffic into the store. Instead of just setting up chairs for their appearances, I thought it would be kind of fun to have the audience sit in furniture from the store. The owners thought it was great. That way more people could see and sit in their couches, love seats, and chairs, and it looked terrific!*

The great thing about any kind of job in a creative field is that anybody can come up with a great idea, no matter what level of a project they're involved in. Be prepared to share one or two creative ideas you've used on the job, even if they are not directly related to publicity.

Q: **Tell me about your telephone experience.**

A: *As a publicity assistant for Pendant Publishers, I spent at least half my time each day on the telephone, publicizing new books and authors, and booking media tours. I developed good relationships with producers at several national television and radio shows, which I maintain to this day.*

Knowing how to use telephone, fax, and e-mail effectively is crucial in publicity. Time on the phone is essential, as is developing relationships with people you're pitching to—so they look forward to responding to you. Remember, throughout the job interview you have been giving the interviewer clues to your personality. Be upbeat, amusing, and effusive—and show that those qualities will come through over the phone. Members of the media get thousands of calls over the course of the week. You have to stand out—even if you know you're pitching the greatest invention since white bread. Sometimes you read things in the paper and you wonder, "Why is that in there?"

First-time Job Seekers: The great thing about publicity is that everybody needs and uses interns and assistants. You need to be enthusiastic, personable, and hardworking. Demonstrate sound communication skills, both oral and written. Make sure you bring any writing samples you may have, even if they're simply clippings from your college newspaper. PR can be hard to break into, but if you join some local associations and keep with "who's who" in your local market, you can create your own opportunities.

More often than not a skilled PR person has cultivated a good relationship with the writer over the phone.

Q: How persuasive are you?

A: *I find persuasiveness goes hand in hand with creativity. You can keep calling someone back, trying countless times to convince that person to cover a client, and that can be very ineffective and sometimes damaging to the relationship. What you need to do is constantly come up with fresh approaches to the topic. For example, if I was trying to repitch an idea to a producer who had already turned it down, I would say something like, "I remember you said you didn't like my idea because there was no women's angle. Well, here's a great one that both of us must have missed during our first conversation." One rule I live by is that the more information you gather and the more creative work you do on a client—that is, the more approaches you tailor to each individual you're contacting—the greater your chances are of getting the coverage you want.*

This question is tricky. Depending on your interviewer, the right answer could be "I'll know when I've convinced you to hire me." But don't count on that alone. Powers of persuasion are key in publicity, so be prepared to give several detailed examples of how you have effectively used persuasion on the job.

Q: What type of writing do you prefer? How have you honed your writing skills in your other positions?

A: *I enjoy writing nonfiction, like newspaper and magazine pieces. I also have a lot of experience writing press releases and advertising copy. I've brought a lot of samples to show you, if you'd like to see them.*

Many job hunters make a mistake by saying they prefer writing short stories or poetry; it's a mistake because it does not necessarily translate into the ability to write effective press releases. Instead, emphasize any experience you may have writing nonfiction, including ad copy, radio copy, news releases,

Career Changers: Let's say you've spent ten years working for a small software company in manufacturing; this is a great time to look at the other side of the business. Contact smaller software companies in your area about getting into their PR offices. If they don't have one, maybe offer your services to that company, and several other small companies, on a freelance or consulting basis. The key here is to take whatever job experience you've had and look at them as if you have to explain what you did to someone who has no knowledge of that field. You'll be surprised to find out just how much you know that can translate into PR skills—especially friends and contacts.

newspaper pieces, and possibly some well-thought-out campaign strategies. Be sure to bring samples of many different types of writing, and be prepared to explain each in depth. Also be prepared to take a writing test. Some hiring managers have been known to hand products to job candidates, giving them ten minutes to write a sample release.

Q: **What papers and magazines do you read? What about radio and television?**

A: *I regularly read* USA Today, *the* New York Times, *the* Chicago Tribune, *the* San Francisco Chronicle, *and the* Washington Post. *I also try to keep up with People magazine, listen to National Public Radio, and try to tune in to several morning television talk shows. I don't just stick to these sources, though; I'm constantly picking up new magazines and watching whatever shows are considered "hot." In fact, I saw your full-page ad in the* Times *on Tuesday for your new line of athletic shoes. It really looked terrific!*

The interviewer is trying to get a sense of how informed the candidate is. You can't make contacts with media members if you don't know who they are, where they work, or what types of stories they write and report. Be very informed about the marketplace, and if you've done your research well, you may be able to tell the interviewer of the countless times you've seen ads for his or her clients on TV or in print, or heard the company's campaigns on the radio.

Q: **What type of events have you planned in the past? How did they go?**

A: *I've planned many different types of events, including fundraising dinners, celebrity benefits, book signings, and radio-station contests. The key to making an event a success, I've found, is creative thinking and careful planning. Once when I was working at Pendant Publishers, I was publicizing the autobiography of a major political figure who was, at the time, running for Congress. Due to some canceled speaking engagements, this politician suddenly had some free time to do some book signings. I had only two weeks to put together several signings, which are usually scheduled months in advance. It helped that he was*

Experienced Professionals: This is one field where who you know is incredibly important. The contacts you've made throughout the years of working are worth their weight in gold. Go through the old Rolodex and find just who can help you. Also, make sure you have at least one great campaign under your belt that everybody knows about. Keep all your tapes, clippings, and contacts. If you're successful and well established, other companies will be looking for you.

a hot figure in the media at the time, but I couldn't have pulled it all off without calling in a few favors. We ended up generating a lot of local publicity, and the signings were a complete sell out.

Planning an event can be anything from an in-store cooking demo to a trade convention. The best thing to do is give the interviewer a range of events that you've worked on and then be able to explain one less-complicated event in depth. If possible, bring reviews or clippings that note your involvement and make the event sound like a well-planned and greatly executed extravaganza. At this point you're doing your own best publicity for yourself.

Q: **What kind of contacts have you been able to establish in your previous positions?**

A: *I have a huge Rolodex of media contacts that I've built up over the years, though I try to focus on cultivating and maintaining relationships with a few key contacts. For instance, I'm good friends with Linda Smith at the Lauren Rickey Show, Bill Jackson at Wake Up America, and Jennifer Collins from 90 Minutes. I also have a lot of newspaper-editor friends. In fact, Josie Manning from the Post is an old college friend of mine.*

Although it's an annoying thing to do at parties, this is the time to name-drop. Mention whom you know, where they work, how you've worked with them in the past, and the great stories you've placed with them. Remember to bring clippings of articles, or any television and radio placement ads, in which a previous client has been prominently featured. If you haven't had a great deal of experience, get acquainted with local media members through your town's advertising clubs or by attending well-publicized local events.

Q: **Pretend I'm a member of the media. Make me want to do a story about this career book, The U.S. Jobline Directory.**

A: *"The U.S. Jobline Directory features hundreds of toll-free telephone numbers job seekers can call to get job and hiring information from prospective employers. At first glance, you can see that this book offers a great service for someone who's job seeking—the opportunity to find great information in almost all*

Candidates Re-entering the Workforce: Almost any kind of experience can help you toward a career in publicity. The key is finding creative ways to make it work for you! Just coming back to the job after raising a family? Look toward smaller agencies and companies that have products designed to mothers and children. Volunteer some time to state agencies that may need help planning fundraising events. Even if you don't get paid, people will know who you are and recognize your talent ingenuity in getting your job done. And a great paid position is sure to follow!

cases without cost. The U.S. Jobline Directory does all the legwork for you!"
Then, once I'd formulated this pitch, I'd have to define my target audience. The
first thing to know about any book on job seeking is that there is an extremely
wide market. A good publicist would formulate several pitches that could be
used for college students, women job seekers, downsized employees, and so
on. Next, I would target college publications, women's magazines, lifestyle and
business editors at newspapers, and career editors at mainstream publica-
tions, as well as corporate newsletters. I would also pitch the book to local
and national television shows, and radio business reporters, perhaps as a tie-in
with current stories about large-scale corporate layoffs. Obvious big hits would
be the Wall Street Journal, National Business Employment Weekly, *and*
other business publications.

It's time to sell, sell, sell! This is a hard thing to do on the spot. If you need
to stall for some time, say to the interviewer, "A well-informed publicist is
a great publicist" and then ask some key questions about the client. What
are the company's needs? Whom does it need to reach, and most important—what does it do? You can ascertain enough from these answers to
throw back a few statistics, or at least relate this client to someone you have
worked with in the past. Take a deep breath and go! You'll be surprised how
many great ideas you can think of under pressure.

Staff Copy Editor

Q: **What experience do you have with newspapers or magazines?**

A: *For the past year I've worked as an assistant copy editor for a national fashion magazine. Before that I was features editor of my weekly college newspaper. The staff was small, so I did a little bit of everything—assigning articles, writing and editing copy, and designing my section.*

Most publications don't require candidates to have experience specifically as a copy editor, but you do need experience working closely with copy. Tell the interviewer about any internships or previous jobs you've had. If you're an entry-level candidate, discuss your experience working on the school newspaper or magazine. Describe what you did, what department you worked in, what your duties were, what type of editors you worked with, and, of course, any copyediting you did. The interviewer will be looking for candidates who know the rules of grammar and of style, so show that you have the technical knowledge necessary for the position. Be careful not to exaggerate your skills or experience, as during the interview all candidates are required to take a copyediting test.

Q: **What copy styles are you familiar with?**

A: *Words Into Type is the style guide we use at the magazine, and my college newspaper followed Associated Press style. I also have some familiarity with The Chicago Manual of Style.*

The interviewer is trying to get a better sense of the candidate's skills and background. If you aren't aware that different style guides exist, your candidacy

First-time Job Seekers: Interviewers look for candidates with a bachelor's degree and a strong writing background. Although many editors have a degree in English, and degree in the humanities or social sciences is helpful, as these majors usually emphasize writing. In you interview discuss any relevant experience you have, either through internships or working on your college newspaper. Show the interviewer that you're detail oriented; interviewers prefer candidates who say, "I also notice misspellings, grammatical errors, and usage mistakes in the newspaper, that's why I want to be a copy editor." You should also demonstrate a familiarity with one or more style guides. Most copy editors will start as an assistant to an editor, but if you have solid experience from college, you may start as an associate copy editor.

won't be taken seriously. Tell the interviewer which style guides you've used in the past. Your answer will generally depend on your experience. Most magazines use *Words Into Type*, newspapers generally use the Associated Press style guide, and book publishers follow *Chicago* or other copy styles. Don't worry if you aren't familiar with the specific style of the publication you're interviewing with; most publications will train their copy editors to use their particular style. Finally, you should discuss how strictly you adhered to a particular style in your previous position.

Q: **Tell me about your computer experience. What software do you know?**

A: *I'm proficient in Microsoft Word and PageMaker. We used PageMaker to design and lay out the college newspaper. I have experience using QuarkXPress, but at this point I'm not as comfortable using it as I am PageMaker. I'm also familiar with spreadsheet programs, such as Microsoft Excel.*

Because many magazines do their copyediting online, computer literacy is a must for this position. You should at least know word-processing software like Microsoft Word or WordPerfect. Experience with desktop publishing software is also important. Most magazines use QuarkXPress, but experience with other software is just as valuable. If you have no desktop publishing experience, express an interest in learning the software; many companies offer computer training to employees.

Q: **How do you handle deadline pressure?**

A: *I'm accustomed to working with deadlines, and the pressure doesn't bother me. When I worked for the college newspaper, which was a weekly, all the editors, including myself, would often stay up until three in the morning to get the paper out on time. And at the magazine, of course, we work under monthly deadlines.*

Career Changers: Discuss any experience you have with publications—writing or editing press releases, company newsletters, or advertising copy. Freelance writing experience is also helpful. Tell the interviewer about the editing skills you've gained from working with other publications. Also, discuss any computer skills you've acquired in your previous position—word processing and desktop publishing are extremely important in this field. The interviewer will want to know that you have the required technical knowledge—that is, an understanding of style guides such as *Words in Type* or *The Chicago Manual of Style*—so be sure to familiarize yourself with at least one of these before your interview. You should also be prepared to take a skills test on the day of your interview.

It's important to show the interviewer that you'll remain levelheaded despite the stress and pressure of working under deadlines. Discuss your experiences working with deadlines, either with your school publication or in your previous job.

Q: Are you available to work extra hours when necessary?

A: *Yes. As I said, I've worked with deadlines before, and I understand that it's usually necessary to stay late when approaching a deadline. As long as I know I'll be required to work long hours for only a few days a month, I don't mind working the extra time.*

The interviewer will want to know that you're flexible in terms of your work schedule. Obviously, you should always answer this question in the affirmative; a negative answer is likely to hurt your candidacy. Show the interviewer that you understand that working for a magazine or newspaper is not always a nine-to-five job. When a magazine is closing an issue, for instance, you may need to stay until nine o'clock every night for a week.

Q: Do you have experience trafficking copy?

A: *No, the copy chief at the magazine is in charge of trafficking all copy. However, I do have some related experience. As I said before, I was features editor at my college newspaper, and as such I was responsible for all aspects of designing a five-to-six-page section of the newspaper. I assigned articles to staff members, made sure they were completed and turned in on time, chose appropriate photographs or graphics, edited the articles, laid out the section, and did whatever else was necessary to get the paper out.*

Each story that appears in a magazine needs to be reviewed by as many as seven or eight people—those in the copy department, the research department, the beauty or fashion departments, and finally the editor of the piece. Depending on the size of the staff and of the production department, you may be responsible for trafficking copy. Experience in this area can only help you. However, if—like this candidate—you have no experience trafficking copy, try to discuss any related experiences you may have. For example, the duties described by this candidate require the same aggressiveness and coordination skills necessary for someone who would traffic copy.

Q: Tell me about your experience working with other editors.

A: *The magazine I work for now encourages interaction between the copy editors and the other editors during the copyediting process. If I have a question about a certain piece, I'll discuss it with the appropriate editor in order to clear the matter up, rather than simply making the change on my own.*

The interviewer wants to learn the extent to which the candidate has inter-acted with other members of the editorial staff. Some copy editors prefer to work alone, without consulting editors. However, most interviewers favor at least some discussion between the editor and copy editor, so it's important to show that you can work well with others. Draw on your experiences working on your school newspaper or in your current position to give exam-ples of your ability to work effectively with other editors.

Q: **How far do you think a copy editor should go when editing?**

A: *I believe a copy editor should change as little as possible in a piece. Naturally, it's important to clean up the writing—correct grammar, misspellings, and so on—but you need to do this without going too far and actually changing the writer's intent. As I said before, when I encounter an issue I'm uncertain about, I'll discuss it with the editor of the piece to make sure that my proposed change is acceptable.*

Show the interviewer that you understand the role of a copy editor. This is important because copy editors should avoid making unnecessary changes to a piece. Altering the writer's voice or intent is usually a mistake; your job is simply to make sure the piece reads well and is in style. Heavy editing is more commonly the responsibility of article editors or department editors, who are the main editors of a piece.

Q: **Why do you want to work here?**

A: *I've been reading your magazine for years. I've always admired the fact that you aren't afraid to take risks and go beyond the traditional beauty and fash-ion tips that most fashion magazines offer. In particular, I learned a great deal from the piece you published recently on the dangers of holistic medicine. What I especially enjoyed about that piece—and what I like about the maga-zine in general—is that your writers don't talk down to your readers. The features tend to have a literary quality about them that I believe is unique for this type of magazine.*

Specific and informed interest in a magazine or newspaper is an issue that many people overlook when preparing for an interview. It's important that

Experienced Professionals: You'll be expected to have expert knowl-edge of issues of style. Employers are also interested in candidates who have had the responsibility of being the last person to see material before it is published, so discuss any experience you may have in this area. You should also talk about significant style changes you may have made in your previ-ous position, as well as computer skills you've acquired. Finally, discuss any experience you have had training new hires. Interviewers know that training experience ensures a greater mastery of skills on the part of the trainer.

copy editors are interested in what they're editing; no one wants to hire someone who doesn't enjoy what he or she is doing. Like this candidate, you should discuss what you like about the publication. If the magazine or paper isn't one you ordinarily read, be sure to read the last two or three issues carefully before the interview.

Q: **What are your career goals?**

A: *Well, right now I'm interested in copyediting. Eventually I'd like to work as a department editor or a managing editor for a magazine, but I believe that working in the copy department will give me a good background for that.*

The interviewer will be suspicious if you say that copyediting is your only goal. Most magazine copy editors are aspiring writers or editors who simply work as copy editor for a few years to gain experience in a particular field or magazine. At the same time, you shouldn't openly declare that copyediting is simply a way for you to "get your foot in the door." No matter your long-term goals, it's important to show that you're excited about copyediting and would like to learn as much about it as you can.

Q: **Outside of work, what do you like to read?**

A: *I try to read as much as possible. I read the* Times *every day, and I subscribe to Elle, Vogue, and Time. I pick up other magazines whenever they have topics that interest me. I also read books and novels as much as possible. I especially love the work of Toni Morrison. I've read almost all of her books, and I'm currently reading* Song of Solomon.

The interviewer wants to get a feel for the candidate's interests and what he or she is like outside the office. It's important to demonstrate that you're well-read, especially if you're applying for a position at a popular, general-interest magazine. Although there's no single correct answer to this question, you should at least mention other publications that are related to the one you're interviewing with.

Candidates Re-entering the Workforce: Changes of rules in style don't happen rapidly in this field, so you don't need to be overly concerned that your skills have become obsolete. However, if there's a new edition of a style manual out, you may want to familiarize yourself with the changes or updates. Most important, show the interviewer that your computer skills are current. If you don't know the more popular software such as Microsoft Word, QuarkXPress, consider taking a class on the subject; many community colleges and high schools offer short-term programs or tutorials on how to use different software packages.

Staff Journalist

Q: **What are some of your story ideas?**

A: *I think that a story on how the changes in health care in America today will affect women would be both interesting and useful to your audience.*

Prove that you're both creative and original. This sample answer may or may not fit the bill, but you should read several months of the publication to get a good understanding of what it does. Suggest several appropriate story ideas.

Q: **What sorts of things are you interested in?**

A: *I'm fascinated by the fashion world. I read virtually every women's fashion magazine on the market. However, I'm also interested in topics such as decorating and cooking, so I like to read things like Real Simple as well.*

Your interests should be in line with the publication. At the same time, you should not exist in a vacuum. Talk about other related interests that you have as well, if they're easily translatable to the publication.

Q: **How would you change this publication?**

A: *I'm an avid reader and have read this magazine for years, so I'm a big fan. I would, however, like to see more articles that give women tips on gracious living, like how to throw together a last-minute dinner party, or how to plant an herb garden.*

The purpose of a question like this is to find out if you have done your homework. Have you thought about the publication? Do you have any ideas about what you'd like to sink your teeth into? The recruiter's not looking for arrogant or unrealistic responses. Nor should you insult the publication. But within reason you should not be afraid to answer this question. Be honest, and give constructive criticism.

Q: **What would you like to write for this publication?**

A: *I'd like to write several articles about what to wear for different social occasions. I like to know what's happening in fashion now, but I need help in knowing what to wear to different places. I know I'm not alone, because I often get calls from my sister and friends saying something like, "I have a four o'clock garden wedding to go to. What should I wear?" I think some articles addressing issues like this would be very helpful.*

This question is similar to both the first and the third. The recruiter will want to know if you're genuinely interested in the publication. Be convincing that this publication is important to you by having lots of ideas ready to go. Further, are you savvy about what's going on in popular culture? Prove your creativity.

Q: **Why do you want to write for our publication?**

A: *I like the way you cover stories. I'm interested in building my career in writing for women, and I think you offer the best periodic literature for women. I also think that I can add something to the magazine.*

The recruiter will be interested in uncovering your motivation. Be honest, and have some good reasons to talk about. Be sure to talk a lot about what you can do for the publication, not just what it can do for you.

Q: **What books have you read recently?**

A: *I have just finishing reading an eighteenth-century English novel by Samuel Richardson called Clarissa. It's 1,500 pages, so it took a while to read. For some lighter reading I've also just read The DaVinci Code.*

Prove that you're both aware and knowledgeable about what's popular in modern culture, and exposed enough to know that there's more out there in the history of literature. Be honest, and talk about what you've read. You should have at least two or three things that you've recently read to talk about. Basically, they just want to know that you're reading.

Q: **What are your qualifications to be a staff journalist?**

A: *In terms of my educational qualifications, I have a B.A. in English literature from Vassar. I also have solid work experience. I worked for two years at a major women's fashion magazine, and I've been freelancing for the past two years.*

First-time Job Seekers: Getting a job as a staff writer for a publication is good training ground for a career in journalism and the publishing industry. It's not always easy to get these jobs, however, so take whatever's offered to you at the beginning. Work hard and learn as much as you can, and then move on to the next thing as soon as possible. It can be a real challenge to getting this first job, so stay focused on your job search and don't get frustrated. Even if your first job offer isn't in line with your ultimate interests or goals, take the job anyway, because you'll inevitably learn more about how to write. Once you learn the discipline or journalism, you can write about anything, because you will know the trade. You will learn to report.

A liberal-arts degree in any field is a great foundation. It's important that you've learned to look at things critically. Journalism school is positive, but not a must. This candidate also has solid work experience.

Q: Why do you want to go on staff?

A: *I'm very interested in specializing my writing now, and your publication offers the best opportunity for me to do just that. I've spent the last several years writing on a variety of topics in this general field, but now I'm ready to hone in on a particular aspect. I'll be able to draw on my freelance experience to quickly contribute to your publication.*

The recruiter will want to know your reasons for wanting a staff position. If you're at one publication already instead of doing freelance work, then the recruiter will ask why you are interested in switching publications. Have positive and constructive reasons ready to answer this question. Don't say something like, "Because I hear that there isn't as much pressure here."

Q: What do you do on a day-to-day basis as a freelance journalist?

A: *I try to read all of the papers and talk to people on the phone, so that I can keep in touch with what's going on out there. This way I get story ideas that I then pitch to magazines.*

The recruiter will want to understand how disciplined you are. The candidate's answer proves that he or she has a system for working every day that is successful. If you're on staff, discuss your typical day as a staff journalist.

Q: Do you find it difficult to come up with and sell story ideas as a freelance journalist?

A: *It's very difficult coming up with story ideas that are original and haven't been written about. That's a real challenge. But what's also very difficult is that when you call a magazine and say you have a great story idea, there's nothing keeping them from thinking, "That's a great story. Let's get one of our own people to do it." Or you can call with a great story idea, and the magazine might say, "We're already working on that." You can never really prove that they're not.*

Career Changers: Size up what you're currently doing and find a publication that writes about what you do know. Having expertise in the subject matter of the magazine will help you. For example, if you're working as a stockbroker, try to go to a finance or business publication. The recruiter might be attracted to the fact that you know finance. Also, conduct some informational interviews, if possible. Call newspapers and magazines and talk to editors and recruiters about how you can break into the business.

Admitting the difficulties of working freelance is fine, because it will establish trust between you and the recruiter. If you were to say that it's a breeze the recruiter would wonder if what you say in the rest of the interview is true. The advantage of the freelance writer is seasoned experience that he or she can bring to the staff.

Q: **What do you like most about being freelance? What are the drawbacks?**

A: *It's not always easy because there's no one standing over you saying, "You have to work." On the flip side, you also get a lot of freedom to do what you want when you want. The nice thing about being freelance is that you can work out of your home. So if you have pets or kids, you can spend more time with them. You don't have a lot of administrative duties that you'd have if you were on staff. When you're freelance, the editor of the magazine that you are writing for takes care of all that. There are some drawbacks to working out of your home, though. There's nothing necessarily keeping you from saying, "I think I'll take a nap now." There's also nobody telling you what time to get up. It can also be difficult not being in an office environment because you can sometimes feel as if you're in a vacuum. You have to push yourself to get out there. You have to really work the phone so you don't feel out of it. You have to make yourself go to lunches occasionally with people who are interesting and do interesting things.*

Talk about the pros and cons of freelance versus staff writing. If you're on staff now, you could talk about the differences between the two positions. You could say, "There's a lot more planning when you're a staff writer. For example, you're responsible for turning in story ideas so there isn't a hole in the magazine, and for making sure that pictures are taken." Be sure to emphasize that, for you, the benefits of staff writing are more desirable.

Q: **What has been your greatest challenge as a journalist?**

A: *While working freelance, I sometimes feel like a door-to-door salesman when I have a story idea and I'm pitching it to a magazine or several magazines. You have to call them up and say you have a story idea, and they either say they're interested or they're not. The whole process can be frustrating.*

Experienced Professionals: As a seasoned pro, you'll probably be able to write your own ticket. Emphasize that this job would be mutually beneficial: you will bring experience and a name to the publication; you're interested in having a forum that's always there for what you want to say. Have you writing portfolio on hand to show the recruiter.

The recruiter is also asking, "What are your weaknesses?" In this answer the candidate hasn't admitted to a major problem but has discussed some of the realities of the job. You could also talk about a particularly challenging experience.

Q: **Where do you want to be as a journalist in five years?**

A: *I want to be a well-known journalist with a reputation for writing interesting stories that say something and have some importance in the world. If I continue on the freelance path, I'd like to be able to write a little journalism, a little advertising, and a little fiction, just to keep things interesting and different, so that I'd never feel stuck in any one area.*

The recruiter will want to know how motivated and determined you are. What will this mean for the publication? Convince the recruiter that being a journalist is a career choice, and that you won't be moving on to other things, like advertising or public relations, for example.

Q: **What opportunities do you see in journalism and publishing?**

A: *It seems to me that right now there are a whole lot of opportunities with things happening online. People are starting up online magazines. This seems to be a frontier right now. On the downside, they haven't really worked out how you avoid being plagiarized, or how you get paid. But this is certainly an area that's being tapped right now.*

The recruiter is looking for the big-picture perspective. Do you know how information technology is affecting the journalism profession and the publishing industry, as this candidate does? Prove that you do enough reading and the right reading to understand the different industry trends.

Q: **How is information technology affecting you as a journalist?**

A: *I'm finding it very helpful being hooked up online. On numerous occasions I've gone online and downloaded articles on subjects that I was working on. It certainly is easier than having to go to the library and look up things in the Reader's Guide to Periodic Literature.*

Information technology will have a big impact on the publishing business because it's changing the way society communicates. This candidate has clearly incorporated information technology into the way he or she does business. Convince the recruiter that you're aware of the phenomenon and its effects on journalism.

Q: **What do you read on a daily basis?**

A: *I usually buy the dailies, including the New York Daily News, the New York Post, and the New York Times. These are definites because I tend to write about things that are going on now, so you need to keep up with what's going on and what's already been written about. It's interesting to compare how one newspaper covers a story with how another one does. I also usually look at the newsstand to see what's on the front page of the Wall Street Journal. If there's anything that interests me, I'll buy it. I particularly like their features about quirky subjects and human-interest stories. I think they're really wonderful. I also like to check out the New York Observer, which comes out on Wednesdays, and New York magazine on Mondays. And, of course, there's The New Yorker. Even if I can't read those cover to cover, I peruse them for a grasp of what's in them these days.*

It's very important to read the newspapers. The recruiter will expect an answer very similar to this candidate's. If you're not currently reading, before you interview, pick a minimum of two to three publications and start reading regularly.

Q: What books do you keep on your desk?

A: *I keep a good dictionary on my desk. I also keep Strunk and White, which is a good reference for looking up all the grammar rules that you learned in high school and college but forgot, or for particularly difficult situations.*

The recruiter will be interested in determining how seriously you take your profession. A good dictionary and a good reference book are typical, and necessary, books for a writer to keep on hand. Perhaps you like to keep your favorite novel on your desk as well.

Q: What specific personal skills have you developed?

A: *I think I'm a very good talker. I'm very good at getting information out of people. People feel at ease telling me about themselves. Also, I've learned to look at both sides of an issue rather than take one position. I believe there are always two sides to an issue, so a story is much stronger when you balance those two sides and then make your decision about how you feel.*

Candidates Re-entering the Workforce: Ask the recruiter several questions, showing that you've done your homework and that you know all about the publication. Emphasize your years of experience with different staff jobs. You probably have lots of contacts and know several editors round town, so make this clear without dropping names. Express that you really want this staff job because the magazine publishes articles on subjects that challenge and stimulate you.

The gift of gab is important for a journalist. You must be able to communicate with people so that you'll have something to write about. This candidate proves that he or she has this skill. Objectivity is another important skill, because presenting both perspectives is the key to good journalism.

Q: **If you had extra time to devote to some project, what would that project be?**

A: *I'd be writing fiction. I do try to write some fiction in my spare time. I first come up with the idea, then I develop an outline to see where I might need to do some research. I like to use weekends to work on projects like these.*

The recruiter is looking for an answer that relates to the profession of journalism. The candidate's answer proves a love of the trade. Your answer could be something that you're working on to help the staff journalists become more efficient, for example. It doesn't necessarily need to be another writing project.

Q: **Do you have any questions you'd like to ask before we conclude?**

A: *When are your deadlines? How much time does a writer usually have on a story? You come out every day—is it hectic? What is the pace like here?*

Not being prepared for the interview is a major turnoff to the recruiter. In a profession where you always have to do your "homework," the interview is not the place to slack off. Have several well-thought-out questions ready before you go into the interview. Prove to the recruiter that you're thoroughly knowledgeable with the publication.

CHAPTER 12
COMPUTERS AND ENGINEERING

Applications Programmer

Q: What type of degree do you hold?

A: *I have a degree in computer science.*

The interviewer will generally be looking for a computer-programming-related degree (such as computer science or management information systems) or a certificate with related work experience. It's possible to demonstrate that even though you don't have a computer-related degree, your programming experience is more than sufficient to qualify you for the position.

Q: What type of programming experience do you have?

A: *I've programmed in a variety of environments, including PCs using C/C++, and Visual Basic. Throughout my career I've been involved with the development of mission-critical applications within a variety of industries.*

This question is designed to obtain information about your background. It's important to show familiarity with a diversity of programming environments, as well as knowledge of the latest technology.

Q: Do you have any analysis-and-design experience?

A: *My last position required that I be involved with the analysis and design of an inventory control module for a stock room. I spent several months analyzing and designing the function for interfacing the new PC-based inventory-control module with the existing mainframe financial system.*

Be sure to provide an answer that demonstrates experience applicable to the position and/or a fundamental knowledge of analysis-and-design concepts.

First-time Job Seekers: Be sure to include any applicable experience with programming, including hobbies. Display a willingness to overcome a challenge, and possibly to accept a position with a lower salary to start your career.

The interviewer will attempt to evaluate your ability to analyze and design, and also how well your programming skills stack up.

Q: Have you ever programmed in a Windows-based environment?

A: *I've been programming in Windows for the last two years using Visual Basic. Some things are simpler to program in Windows, while others are more complicated.*

The purpose of this question is to evaluate the amount of Windows-based program experience you have, and to determine your comfort level with Windows programming.

Q: Do you have experience with client/server technology?

A: *I've used Windows for Workgroups and Windows NT for the last year and a half. Also, I've used Sybase and SQL Server quite extensively.*

It's vital to demonstrate knowledge of client/server technology for this question. The use of client/server databases is an excellent method for showing an understanding of the environment. It's important to realize that definitions of "client/server" vary from company to company and even from individual to individual. A good way to avoid answering incorrectly is to discuss the technology and ask the interviewer questions as you talk.

Q: Explain the concept "referential integrity" as it applies to relational databases.

A: *Referential integrity is used to enforce rules about what fields must exist in related tables before permitting the addition of a record in a table.*

This question is designed to test your knowledge of databases as it relates to programming. It's not necessary to know exactly how each database handles referential integrity, but more important, how the overall concept applies to database maintenance and programming.

Q: How much experience do you have using SQL (Standard Query Language)?

A: *I've used SQL over the last year, while developing an application database.*

Career Changers: You need to seek training through education programs or retraining opportunities at your current job. One difficulty of changing to such a career is that you'll almost certainly begin at an entry-level programming position, and companies will expect to pay you accordingly. Attempt to transition slowly while gaining educational training you'll need.

Although SQL is fairly simple to learn, it takes some time to become proficient at creating optimized SQL. Some experience using SQL is good, but extensive experience at tuning SQL is bound to get you a number of job offers.

Q: Have you ever used database triggers?

A: *I've programmed using database triggers over the last six months for a financial-analysis application. The triggers were used to improve the performance of several of the analysis modules that were too slow when using regular SQL statements.*

This question is designed to test your knowledge of database concepts and determine suitability for programming in a variety of environments. If you have not used database triggers, simply explain that you don't have any experience using database triggers, but you understand the concept.

Q: What experience do you have dealing with customers or clients?

A: *I haven't held a position where I deal with a customer or client per se; however, I've dealt with internal end users who do not have much computer experience. In general, when there was a problem at my last position, I was the end-user contact.*

In many cases you may be required to talk directly to a customer or client in order to evaluate a bug or complete a design. Even if you're not communicating with an outside customer or client, you may be talking to an end user who's not computer literate. It's important to demonstrate that you have the ability to communicate effectively with a variety of computer-knowledge levels in order to make yourself more valuable.

Q: Have you ever worked on mission critical applications before?

A: *Yes, I've worked on an application that provided billing information to a mainframe system from a PC-based client-server inventory-management system.*

The interviewer will be interested in how much experience you have with programming business applications that are vital to the continued success of the company. The importance of having applicable experience in developing mission-critical systems varies from company to company, so don't attempt to claim experience if you have none.

Experienced Professionals: Consider the position being applied for when sending a resume or interviewing and be sure to gear your answers to fit the position. Try to avoid applying for positions for which you are overqualified, but if it's necessary, don't include an excessive amount of experience on your resume or when answering interview questions.

Q: Do you prefer to work individually or within a group?

A: *I prefer to work within a group, because it's possible to get input from other programmers when a problem arises.*

This question tends to be rather tricky to answer since there are benefits and drawbacks to both work environments. Be sure to realize (and mention) that just because you prefer to work in a particular environment doesn't mean that you're not effective at working in the other environment.

Q: Have you been involved with the quality-assurance process of application development?

A: *I've been involved with the ongoing testing of programs, although I've not been involved with the quality-assurance department.*

An often overlooked but vitally important part of application development is that of quality assurance. You may not have experience in a quality control department of product development; however, if you've programmed, you've been involved with the quality assurance of programs.

Q: Have you ever been responsible for directing other programmers?

A: *Yes, I've directed a small group of programmers in the development of an inventory-management subsystem. The project lasted about four months and involved frequent communication between the end users, the programmers, and myself.*

The recruiter will want to determine how well you might fare in a management-type position. It's not necessary to have management experience for most programming positions, but such experience is a plus. You could also express an interest in supervising other programmers at this point, if you're so inclined.

Candidates Re-entering the Workforce: Depending on how rapidly technology changes within your particular area of expertise, you may encounter some of the same problems as career changers or first-time job seekers. Emphasize measures you've taken to maintain your skills while out of the workforce.

Chemical Engineer

Q: **What type of working environment are you looking for?**

A: *I prefer working in manufacturing, where I can get my hands dirty on an assembly line. I like the challenge of figuring out ways to optimize the process.*

The interviewer will want to determine if you have a preference for office work, field work, or manufacturing. Do you want to work in an office environment and wear a shirt and tie? Would you be available to travel occasionally to the field to work on projects? Or do you prefer working in a manufacturing environment, as this candidate does? There's no right or wrong answer to this question. You should have advance knowledge of the job you're applying for, and you should be able to tailor your answer accordingly. Be sure to explain the reasons behind your preference.

Q: **What are your future plans regarding chemical engineering?**

A: *I'm interested in staying on the technical side for another five years or so, then moving into management. But even then I'd like to contribute, on a smaller scale, to the technical side, since I don't want to become so bogged down in administrative duties that they take me away from being a true chemical engineer.*

The interviewer will want to know if you're interested in staying on the technical side of engineering throughout your career, if you want to manage, or if you want to get into business development or sales. Some companies are interested only in individuals who want to stay technical. Other organizations prefer people who'd like to stay technical for five or ten years, then broaden their skills. Take into consideration your own preferences as well as the position you're applying for.

Q: **Tell me about significant team projects you've worked on.**

A: *I worked on a petrochemical design project, an upgrade of an ethybenzene styrene plant. I was assigned to do a review of the piping and instrumentation diagrams. I worked with other chemical engineers and designers to make sure that we met the specifications for the project.*

In most organizations everything is based on teamwork on a project-by-project basis. You should be prepared to give a detailed example here, explaining what you worked on, what your role was, and how you contributed to the project. If possible, describe a project for which you were the team leader. On the other hand, if you're the type of person who's more interested in R&D and working in a lab, you may not be suited for a team-based-project environment.

Q: **What were the difficulties that came up in working with a team?**

A: *I think it's always fairly difficult to work on a team in the sense that you're being judged on the team's output, even though you're not responsible for the other members of the team. Even so, in the last project I worked on for which I wasn't the team leader, I was still able to rally the other workers to get the project finished on time and within budget.*

You need to be careful about how you answer this question. You should talk about what role you had in the team and how you were able to enlist the support of other team members who didn't report to you. This is crucial, because teamwork is important in any design project, where you could be working in a group with five, or 100, members.

Q: **What type of software have you used before?**

A: *I'm proficient in Microsoft Word and Aspen and Process simulation software. I'm very comfortable with my computer skills and am quick to learn new applications.*

The specific software programs the interviewer is looking for will depend on the company. In many companies you'll be expected to know some type of spreadsheet program, a word-processing program, and process-simulation software. If you're not familiar with the particular software programs the company uses, emphasize your ability to pick up new computer skills quickly.

Q: **How proficient are you with using process-simulation software?**

A: *I've very proficient in Aspen and have used it in my last position for the past four years. I've also used Process occasionally in the past.*

Strong hands-on experience with process-simulation software is often a requirement for chemical engineers working in an office environment. If you don't know this software, your candidacy for the position could be considerably weakened. However, this skill isn't usually required for positions in a manufacturing setting.

Q: **Tell me about your last project. What were you trying to accomplish? How did you optimize the process?**

A: *My last project was with an oil refinery. We were trying to decrease the refinery's toxic emissions to meet EPA standards. Because the refinery was a hydrocarbon* processing plant, it was impossible for us to eliminate these emissions completely. So we focused on keeping them to a minimum by tweaking different parts of the system, including the flow in and the flow out of emissions during hydrocarbon processing. At first we considered major design changes to the process, but then we decided that the process just needed some subtle adjustments rather than a complete overhaul. So far the project has been a success—we've reduced emissions by over 8 percent.

You should expect this question if you're applying for a position in a manufacturing or field environment. What the interviewer is trying to find out is how much knowledge you have of the entire process. Even though your role in the project may have been very narrow, you should have an understanding of the overall process. Articulate exactly what you did, how you made decisions, your role in the process, how your role interacted with the process as a whole. Emphasize what you accomplished and how you optimized the process. Your goal is to show the interviewer that you have a solid understanding of the basic concepts of chemical engineering—that you're not just throwing around a lot of buzzwords. It would be a mistake to say something like, "Well I was just responsible for this one small piece of the process. I couldn't tell you what the whole thing did." Communicating clearly and articulating the work you've done in the past will also give the interviewer a sense of how you'll perform in front of a customer. Many times, even if you're doing formal sales and business development with proposals or have only indirect contact with the client, you may be on the job site and have to talk to people who aren't chemical engineers about the processes that are going on. Show that you have strong communication skills and that you can explain technical ideas in a nontechnical language to a lay person, or to a designer or technician.

Q: Do you have knowledge of and experience with GMP, TQM, and/or ISO-9000? If so, where? What was your role?

First-time Job Seekers: "Sell" yourself during the interview by demonstrating your knowledge of the company and the type of position your applying for. You should be able to tailor your work experience, your schoolwork, and your individual accomplishments to the job. For example, no matter where you've worked, you've learned organizational skills, how to be on time, and perhaps how to work in teams. Emphasize co-op or internship experiences you've had. Talk about extracurricular activities and how you balanced part-time work while getting good grades in school. Most important, if you're applying for a manufacturing job, don't say that your career goal is to be a salesperson; make sure that all your answers reflect your interest in a job in manufacturing.

A: *I've worked with GMP for about five years, and both my TQM and GMP experiences have been derived from my last employer. I was also team leader on one of the TQM committees dealing with running effective meetings. Also, the plant at my current company has recently moved to the ISO-9000 standard, so I'm still learning about that.*

You're certain to be asked this question if you're applying for a position in a manufacturing facility. At the very least you should know that "GMP" stands for "good manufacturing processes," "TQM" for "total quality management," and that ISO-9000 is a certification. You should also have a basic understanding of each. If you're applying for a position in a production or manufacturing facility, especially if you're leading and supervising others, you'll need in-depth knowledge of, as well as experience with, some or all of these training processes. The best advice is, don't try to fake it. A lot of people try to talk up the buzzwords without really knowing what they mean. The interviewer is certain to test the depth of your knowledge and understanding with several follow-up questions, such as, "Tell me what you did and how you used the training process? Were you involved in training, or were you involved in a steering committee that put it out throughout the facility?" If you have experience as a TQM leader, you'll be able to answer and elaborate on these questions with ease.

Q: Do you have any proposal experience?

A: *Not directly, but I've been asked to write about sections of my work that have later been used to secure a proposal worth $5 million. I really enjoyed this aspect of my job and would be interested in continuing it at my next assignment.*

This question might be asked if you're a senior-level chemical engineer with at least ten years' experience, looking for a position as a project engineer. The interviewer will want to make sure that you know how to put together a proposal, which you may be called on to do. If you've written proposals before, tell the interviewer how many, and the size and purpose of the proposals. As a result of your efforts, were the proposals successful? Did you actually write the proposals yourself or coordinate a team that pulled them together? Both approaches require valuable skills.

Career Changers: In order to make a career change into floor manufacturing or design engineering, you'll need to go back to school to earn a minimum of a bachelor's degree in chemical engineering. If you're interested in getting into research and development, a master's degree or Ph.D. may be required depending on the company. Draw upon your accomplishments and skills in your previous work experience and clearly explain how you can transfer them into chemical engineering.

Q: Do you have project-management experience?

A: *Yes. In my current position I led a small design team of three engineers who were responsible for the instrumentation and control documentation of a small oil-refinery upgrade project. And though our budget was relatively small, we were able to keep costs down. The project came in under budget.*

You should expect this question if you're a chemical engineer looking for a management position. The interviewer will want to know how well you'll be able to deal with the challenges of managing a project in which you're responsible for the coordination, the overall budget, and the delivery—even though you're supervising and directing people from other disciplines. This is a skill that a higher-level person with ten or fifteen years of experience will need to move up.

Describe the projects you managed before and the size of those projects. Tell the interviewer how many people you supervised. Was it a fixed-cost or a cost-plus project? You should also be prepared to tell the interviewer (with honesty!) that the project was completed on schedule and made a profit.

Q: What products have you designed?

A: *In my current position we designed water desalination and purification products used in water desalination. Specifically, we developed in a lab membranes that enabled us to separate brackish water. In layman's terms, we filtered dirty water through membranes so that it was pure drinking water. I was involved in every step of the process, from the conceptual stage all the way through manufacturing, quality assurance, and production release.*

This is a design-engineering question that you might encounter if you're applying for a manufacturing position. Explain the process and your involvement in detail. Expect follow-up questions like "What were the challenges you faced in taking the products from concept to marketplace? Were the products successful? Are they on the market and making money?"

Experienced Professionals: Sell your experience on working on a wide variety of projects and developing various products. If, like most chemical engineers, you began your career in manufacturing and want to go into management, you should focus more on your "soft" skills in management than on your technical skills. You should also play up your accounting and budgetary experience. Give examples of how you finished projects on time and within budget, how you've developed products and took them through manufacturing and into the marketplace, and how you've used creative measures to reduce costs.

Q: **What cost-reduction steps have you taken to increase the profitability of your group?**

A: *At my current company we implemented a plan to start working on a team-based concept. There were five different jobs in the production line, and instead of each person becoming a specialist in one job, we had everyone in the company learn all five jobs. This ensured that the line wouldn't shut down in the event that one or several people called in sick. Someone else would simply rotate into that job, and the production line would continue as usual. Over time this prevented many missed deadlines and delays in production. We became more efficient and more profitable.*

This is another question you should expect if you're in manufacturing or product development. The interviewer wants to see how efficiently you've run your groups in the past. Were you merely spending money, or did you work at managing the groups in the most cost-effective way? Describe the creative ways you've increased productivity and, ultimately, profitability.

Q: **Tell me about your senior design project in school.**

A: *I did a co-op internship in a water-purification facility where we were using a lot of dangerous chemicals. These chemicals went through a process and were eventually emitted into the atmosphere. What we had to do was take a look at that process and decide how we could tweak it to cut down on the toxic emissions into the atmosphere. We solved the problem by making adjustments up front and at the beginning of the process rather than downstream and at the end of the process.*

If you have less than three years' experience in chemical engineering, you'll probably be asked this question. The interviewer will want to know if you understand the concepts that you're talking about and how they interact with one another. Describing your project in a clear, concise manner will help accomplish this.

Candidates Re-entering the Workforce: Be prepared to explain during your interview why you took some time off, and why you now want to come back. Such scenarios are becoming more and more common, and most employers will have no problems with a career hiatus if you're an otherwise strong candidate. You should reassure the interviewer that you're ready to commit to a full-time career. For instance, if you took time off to raise a family, let the interviewer know how you have day care and backup day care, covered. The employer can't legally ask you if you do, but if you bring up the topic, you may allay any concerns he or she has. Emphasize your recent relevant experience and how you've kept your skills up to date during your hiatus, for example, by taking some computer classes.

Q: **How do you feel about shift work?**

A: *My preference is to work days, but I'm fairly flexible. If the company would need me to work nights or weekends on occasion, that wouldn't be a problem.*

Expect this question if you're interested in a career in manufacturing. The employer wants to see that you're willing to be flexible. For example, if a facility is running three shifts twenty-four hours a day, will you function on a floating basis? Other times you may be asked to do weekend coverage on a twenty-four-hour-day operation. Responding negatively to this question may seriously hurt your candidacy.

Q: **Do you have any experience working in a union environment?**

A: *Yes, the workers at my current company's manufacturing plant are unionized.*

You should expect this question if you're applying for a supervisory position in a unionized manufacturing environment. Supervising in such an environment has its own special challenges that you must be prepared to overcome. For example, if the technicians on the manufacturing floor are unionized, and you, as an engineer, are not, you have to be sensitive to their concerns and to the potential conflicts that may arise. Emphasize any experience you've had working in a unionized environment, especially at the managerial level. If you don't have any experience in this area, you should reassure the interviewer that you have no problem with it.

Electrical Engineer

Q: **Tell me about your experience with transducer design.**

A: *I've spent the last five years working with Capacitive gauges. We use Capacitive probes to measure very small differences, some as little as several nanometers. The design of the transducer itself is mostly mechanical, but there are some important electrical considerations that must be observed, such as shielding the cable and probe. If the probe isn't properly shielded, nonlinearities can be introduced into the system.*

This question addresses the candidate's analog-design skills. In most interviews for this position you'll be asked a number of questions to determine your knowledge of both analog and digital design. You should explain how you've used this particular design application. Since certain transducers are specific to certain applications, discuss how your experience is relevant to the company you're interviewing with. Your answer will also give the interviewer an indication of your level of experience.

Q: **Discuss your experience with temperature-stable circuits.**

A: *The Capacitive probes that I mentioned earlier were designed to be temperature and humidity stable. The approach that was taken to maximize thermal stability was to use digital circuitry wherever possible, and analog circuitry only where necessary. In the analog sections components were selected carefully to minimize thermal drift. Part of the initial test and calibration of all circuit cards is a preliminary burn-in at an elevated temperature to age all components thermally.*

This candidate effectively describes some methods for designing in temperature stability with a specific type of circuit. Your answer to a similar question will give the interviewer an indication of the breadth of your experience in the area of temperature-stable circuits. If the company you're interviewing

> **First-time Job Seekers:** You'll need a bachelor's degree in electrical engineering for most entry-level positions. Because it's likely that you have little or no real work experience in this area, describe some projects you've worked on in your classes. Any work experience, either through internships or summer jobs, will set you apart from other applicants. Also, you'll probably be asked about some of the classes you took, and why you chose electrical engineering over other engineering disciplines.

with manufactures products that use this particular kind of circuit, you might be asked more questions to determine your in-depth knowledge of temperature-stable circuits.

Q: What kind of design experience do you have with high-power components?

A: *I spent five years working with a 10-kilowatt RADAR system. I designed a three-horsepower servo system, including the power amplifier and shunt regulator, and a variable power supply for a 15-kilowatt infrared source. I also designed all the electronics for a 100-watt pulsed LASER system.*

Again, this question addresses the candidate's design capabilities and knowledge in terms of analog skills. Your answer should include examples of particular products or projects you've worked on, as well as the kind of equipment you used when you designed those products. You could also go into more detail about how you determined the requirements for the design specifications.

Q: What's the most difficult problem you've solved?

A: *I think it was probably the time when a ten-kilowatt RF amplifier in a system returned from the field was experiencing an intermittent problem. The amplifier used fourteen tubes, basically in parallel, so a glitch with one tube could have caused the problem, but that would be something very difficult to isolate. The tubes were powered from a pulsed two-kilovolt source, which required an expensive high-voltage probe, and which also gave off lethal voltages, so extreme caution was necessary. I tried replacing all the tubes, but that didn't solve the problem, so next I checked all the tube voltages to see if they were operating as they should be. I discovered that the heater voltage on all the tubes dropped after we'd been transmitting for a while. The heaters for each tube were powered by an individual transformer, and since all of the heater voltages dropped, something had to be wrong with the AC power going to the heater transformers. After several false starts with fuses, connectors, and cables, I discovered that soot had built up under several terminal blocks, and the soot was providing a short to the chassis. After we cleaned up the soot, the problem stopped.*

This question addresses the candidate's attitude toward problem solving, his or her analytical and technical skills, and the resources called upon to solve operating problems arising after a product has been released. If you're asked this question, the level of sophistication of the problem you describe will allow the interviewer to gauge your skill level. Your answer will also tell the interviewer whether you're team oriented or independent minded—for example, whether you like to get input from others or prefer doing everything yourself. A similar question you may encounter is "What's the most difficult digital problem you've had to solve?"

Q: What type of lab tools are you comfortable using?

A: *I'm comfortable with Tektronix oscilloscopes—both digital and analog—Fluke digital multimeters (DMM), and Hewlett-Packard spectrum analyzers and power supplies.*

This question determines whether the candidate has extensive experience with different types of testing equipment. Some candidates may be familiar with only one area of the product testing, and the interviewer will want to find out where you've concentrated your work. If possible, give examples of situations where you've used all these tools.

Q: What type of simulation tools have you used?

A: *I've used PSPICE for analog-circuit simulation. I also have some experience with MATHCAD.*

Simulation tools are software packages that allow you to see how a designed product will work in the field, before it's actually released. It's important for you to know process-simulation tools, so that you're able to complete the projects at hand. This question also determines whether the candidate's knowledge of the programs is current, or if he or she will need additional training.

Q: What microprocessors, microcontrollers, or Digital Signal Processors (DSPs) do you have experience with?

A: *I've done three designs with 8051s, Zilog Z80s and Motorola 6805s. I have seven years of x86, PowerPC, Alpha, MIPS and SPARC series experience.*

These next five questions address the candidate's digital design and troubleshooting skills. With this question the interviewer will want to gauge your experience level with different microprocessors. You should also discuss in detail a specific product you've designed using one of these instruments.

Career Changers: If you're coming from an industry other than engineering, you'll need to go back to school to earn your bachelor's degree. If you have experience in another engineering discipline, you'll probably need to take a few courses to learn the technical issues of electrical engineering. During the interview be ready to give the reasons for your transition. Emphasize your skills that are related to engineering, such as have an aptitude in math, possessing strong problem-solving abilities, or being detail-oriented. Also, discuss any experience you may have in the industry, such as working in the human-resources department of a high-tech firm.

Q: **Elaborate on any high-speed communications standards you've worked with or designed.**

A: *I've worked with extensively with 10Gb Ethernet and IEEE 802.3 compliant Ethernet MAC interface to provide connectivity options.*

This question determines the candidate's exposure to certain kinds of high-speed standards. Your response to such a question will give the interviewer an indication of your comfort level with these standards. In order to design certain products, you must be comfortable using high-speed communications standards, and it's helpful to have at least some familiarity with them.

Q: **What kind of design experience do you have with FPGAs (field programmable gate arrays), complex PLDs (programmable logic devices), or GALs (generic array logic)?**

A: *I'm my company's PLD expert. I've designed every PLD that's in a product or text fixture in my company. I'm most familiar with Actel A1020B and A1280A FPGAs using 1.0 μm technology, and various GALs.*

Give examples of specific projects you've worked on using these designs. The sophistication of the products you discuss will give the interviewer a better idea of your experience level. From your response the interviewer will be able to determine in what areas you may need more training.

Q: **Describe any experience you've had with metastability.**

A: *I once had a metastability problem with a serial communications link that I designed. I took three separate serial-data streams from three different Sigma-Delta ADCs and combined them into one serial port on a TMS320C30. Unfortunately, the ADCs and the C30 ran off asynchronous clocks, and in order to meet the data rate, the C30 port had to be clocked internally. I managed to clock all of the flip-flops synchronously except for one input to a three-bit machine. I ultimately used two more flip-flops in series to "synchronize" the signal.*

Experienced Professionals: Stress the extensive knowledge you have in the field; discuss the specific projects you've worked on and the quantitative results of those projects. For example, if you've finished a project under budget, say how much you were under budget. As a senior engineer, you'll be expected to have some experience supervising a team of engineers, so be prepared to answer questions about your managerial experience. Also, since electrical engineering is such a highly technical field, continuing education is essential. Attend industry seminars so that you can discuss current advances and trends in the field. A master's degree is helpful to experienced engineers who are interested in moving to a position of greater responsibility.

Give a specific example of a situation where you've had to deal with meta-stability. Your answer will show how comfortable you're with solving these types of problems, or even if you've been exposed to this type of situation. Once more, the interviewer is trying to determine in which areas you may need additional training or experience.

Q: **What is the biggest engineering change order that you've been involved with?**

A: *I did an ECO that affected the rework of $20,000 worth of material that was in production and had a ship date two weeks away. I had to coordinate a manufacturing waiver with production to have the rework done before the ECO was complete. I also had to work with purchasing to change the material that was already on order, and during that checking we found some additional material that needed to be received and reworked.*

The interviewer is trying to gauge the candidate's communication and problem-solving skills. Emphasize your ability to coordinate tasks with a number of different departments within the company, such as production control, purchasing, and field service. These skills are essential for resolving a problem that isn't discovered until a product has already gone into large-scale production. You must have the ability to stop production and coordinate with others to correct the problem before a product is released.

Q: **Tell me about any application notes you've written.**

A: *I worked with bandwidth, thickness application, and dielectric thickness application when I was writing application notes.*

Your answer here will be specific to your company's products and will give the interviewer an indication of your experience with documentation. This question also measures the candidate's writing and communications skills; the interviewer will want to see if you have experience writing for both technical and nontechnical audiences.

Candidates Re-entering the Workforce: Interviewers will be most concerned that you haven't kept up with the rapid technological advances in the field. Emphasize any efforts you've made during your time away to keep up with those changes, either through continuing education, seminars, or industry publications. You'll want to discuss your earlier accomplishments and demonstrate and eagerness to get back into the field. Also, before your interview, ask for some information on the company and its products, and become thoroughly knowledgeable about them. Since you'll be competing with other candidates who haven't taken sabbaticals, you'll need to do everything possible to make yourself stand out from the competition.

Q: **What types of CAD packages are you comfortable with?**

A: *I use PCAD in my present job, and I have extensive experience with ORCAD. I'm also familiar with AutoCAD.*

Computer-aided design software is very common in the engineering field. It's used extensively in designing new products, as well as revising old ones. If you have any experience in the manufacturing industry, you'll most likely have some experience in this area. Don't worry if you don't have experience in the particular CAD package that the interviewing company uses; as long as you know one type of software, the others are easy to learn.

Environmental Engineer

Q: We're an environmental consulting engineering firm. What's your understanding of environmental consultancy in general, and of this company in particular?

A: *I understand that environmental consulting firms are generally involved in providing engineering, consulting, and scientific services to government and industry. Specifically, I'm aware that your company focuses on managing water resources, wastewater, solid waste, hazardous waste, air quality, and storm water.*

The interviewer must feel confident that you understand the type of work performed by environmental engineers, and by this company in particular. If you haven't worked in environmental consultancy before, you should expect this question.

Q: Do you have experience in water treatment and distribution systems?

A: *I worked on the design of the Anytown Water Treatment Plant upgrade and spent three months setting up and running a pilot plant. This plant was used to evaluate a number of water-treatment options designed to remove high iron and manganese levels in the raw water. During summer vacations from school I worked as a laborer with a civil engineering contractor, laying 10,000 feet of eight- and six-inch diameter ductile iron water mains in Newtown.*

This question is designed to gauge the candidate's technical knowledge in a particular area. The question could just as easily refer to wastewater treatment, landfill design, groundwater modeling, or air-quality monitoring. The

First-time Job Seekers: Most environmental engineers have B.S. in civil engineering, with environmental engineering as a specialty. A double major or a minor in environmental sciences would be ideal. During interviews you should show that you're flexible and willing to work outdoors in adverse weather and environmental conditions. Also, discuss any projects you may have worked on during summer breaks, or internships you may have had. You should also make sure that you take and pass the NCEES Fundamentals of Engineering (FE) examination (formerly known as the Engineer in Training—EIT—examination) in your junior or senior year in college.

candidate communicates a good working knowledge of water treatment processes. It's also beneficial to have spent time working for a contractor in the field, which demonstrates a willingness to do this type of outdoor work—something that's invariably required of environmental engineers. Point out to the employer that this kind of experience has given you a solid understanding of a contractor's perspective on environmental-engineering construction projects, which will be of great benefit to you in the design of such products.

Q: Are you familiar with federal EPA sludge regulations?

A: *As part of a team, I helped to prepare a guide to the EPA's national Sewage Sludge Use and Disposal Regulation for use by our municipal clients. While I was involved in the overall production of the guide, which required the coordinated efforts of many individuals, I was responsible for writing the section on land application of sludge. I made a presentation to representatives of the Bureau of Wastewater in Oldtown, which was instrumental in my company's being appointed to produce a report of the bureau's current sludge-disposal methods and to make recommendations on how to comply with the new regulation.*

Since much of the work of environmental engineers is driven by federal, state, and local regulations, it's important to be familiar with the impact of those regulations on clients' activities. With this answer the candidate demonstrates familiarity with an important federal regulation, and an understanding of the subsequent impact on the client. In addition, the candidate shows the ability to work as part of a team with a common goal. Most engineering-design projects are undertaken by project teams. Being able to function well in a multidisciplined team is a valuable attribute.

Q: Have you been involved in new business development?

A: *Yes. In response to a formal request for proposals, I participated in the development of a proposal for engineering-design services for a water-treatment plant upgrade. I was responsible for writing those sections of the proposal relating to the existing water-treatment facilities, and I also participated in the presentation of the proposal to the town's selection committee.*

Career Changers: There aren't many "late bloomers" in this field; most people don't decide to enter environmental engineering after spending a number of years in a totally unrelated profession. But if you don't have a B.S. in engineering, you're going to have to start from the beginning by going back to college to get a degree in civil engineering; then you'll have to compete with kids fresh our of college for the same jobs.

As an environmental engineer progresses in his or her career, it's vital to be aware of the importance of engineering services. This response demonstrates that the candidate understands something of the procurement procedures employed in municipal contracts and, furthermore, has had experience in presenting a proposal in person. Presentation and public-speaking skills are desirable, especially when you must effectively communicate technical concepts to both a technical and a nontechnical audience.

Q: Do you have experience with the use of personal computers for engineering and general-office functions?

A: *I've used personal computers for a number of years, primarily in report writing. I'm familiar with Word, and for performing engineering calculations and analysis using spreadsheet programs, Excel. More recently, I've started to use Access, a database-management program, to create an inventory of storm-water-inflow sources for a sewer-separation project that I'm working on. I use AutoCAD for computer-aided design and drafting (CAD) work and attended two training courses in the past year. I'm also investigating the use of geographic information system (GIS) technology for a landfill-sitting project.*

The personal computer is an essential tool for environmental engineers today. This answer demonstrates the candidate's familiarity with the use of computers for general-office applications and also with the more technical applications that are increasingly found in consulting engineering offices. Hands-on CAD and GIS skills are becoming less of a luxury and more of a necessity for environmental engineers.

Q: How do you envision the development of your environmental-engineering career over the next few years?

A: *For the past four years I've worked mainly in a technical capacity and have gained solid technical expertise in the water- and wastewater-treatment areas. I'm confident of my technical skills, but I also realize that these skills will need constant updating. I feel ready to complement those skills with a greater project-management role. I've had some project-management responsibility—setting budgets and monitoring costs for a number of projects on which I've worked—and would like to become more involved in this aspect of*

Experienced Professionals: After about two or three years in the business most companies will expect you to get your master's in environmental engineering. Be sure to become professionally licensed in the state in which you intend to work. During interviews highlight all of your experience. Talk about the projects that you've headed or worked on. Also, stress a desire to advance in your profession.

the business. Ultimately, I see myself in a management role rather than in a purely technical one.

A midlevel environmental engineer should be aware of choices that can affect the direction of his or her career. Be sure to demonstrate your awareness of some of the available options, and that you've given some thought to the direction you'd like to take.

Q: **Have you ever come up with a particularly creative solution to some environmental-engineering problem?**

A: *Yes. I was working on a project to survey and categorize sources of storm-water inflow from private residences to a combined sewer system, and to produce an inventory of such sources for use in a sewer-system report. Initially, the plan was to document house inspections and record other information on paper forms, which would then be collated and analyzed for the report. I customized a computer database program for use with a pen computer, which could be used in adverse weather in the field. By recording information this way, the fieldwork was completed accurately and ahead of schedule. Immediate data analysis was made possible without the requirement for additional data entry. As a result, we now use this method for most of our field-collection work.*

This answer demonstrates the candidate's use of technology to improve on a laborious and time-consuming procedure. It's refreshing to hear of a person using his or her creativity and initiative to devise new ways to look at old problems. The candidate's answer demonstrates that creativity is an effective trait for an environmental engineer to develop.

Q: **Are you a member of any professional associations?**

A: *I've been a member of the American Water Works Association for over four years. Recently, I joined the Water Environment Federation, as much of the work I've been involved in recently has been in the wastewater field. Membership in both associations has kept me abreast of developments in both water and wastewater fields.*

Candidates Re-entering the Workforce: As long as you've maintained your professional license, you shouldn't have any problems. Just be sure to emphasize everything you accomplished before you took time off. The interviewer will probably have some concerns that you're not up to speed on some technical issues, so do your best to reassure him or her. Talk about trade journals you've read to show that you're caught up with all the latest technological advances.

Membership in professional associations allows engineers to keep pace with research and development, regulations, products, and projects in the environmental-engineering industry. The candidate's membership in two of the most respected professional associations in the water and wastewater fields demonstrates an acknowledgment of the positive educational role that such associations offer and a willingness to become involved.

Q: Would you consider working abroad?

A: *Yes, I think it would be of great benefit to me professionally and personally to work abroad for a number of years. After graduation I traveled overseas, spending three months backpacking in western Europe. I enjoyed meeting people from different cultures and backgrounds. I even got a chance to try out my high-school French which, I'm afraid, gave rise to some laughs in a few train stations and supermarkets. As a matter of fact, one of the key factors in my applying for a position with this company is that you undertake design and construction work in many parts of southeast Asia.*

Many environmental-engineering firms are focusing on growth opportunities in foreign markets, particularly the Pacific Rim and southeast Asia. Often projects are undertaken as part of a joint venture with local engineering companies. It's advantageous to have engineers who are willing to travel abroad and can appreciate the diversity of cultures that will be encountered during such work. The candidate's response suggests that he or she would enjoy such an experience and would be open-minded and flexible.

Q: What are your professional goals over the next two to three years?

A: *My two main goals are to become a professionally licensed engineer and to finish my master's degree in environmental engineering. I'm currently putting together my application for licensing as a professional engineer and expect to take the Principles and Practice of Engineering examination this October. As for my master's degree, I expect to graduate in June of next year.*

For an environmental engineer working in a consulting engineering firm, becoming licensed as a professional engineer is vital to career development. Having a master's degree is a plus, though not essential. This response indicates that the candidate has set worthwhile career goals for him- or herself.

Industrial Engineer

(Entry-Level)

Q: Tell me about the most interesting manufacturing job or project you've successfully completed.

A: *When I was in engineering school, I did a project for a company where we reorganized the factory floor. I worked on the project for an entire semester, laying out the tools so that the product had a better flow. I did all the engineering drawings for the factory floor and presented them to management. They were impressed and ended up using my plan.*

Since most industrial engineers work in a manufacturing environment, most employers will want to know that you have a solid understanding of a manufacturing job. Emphasize any manufacturing experience you may have, even if it's simply a school project. Describe your accomplishment in specific and technical terms to show the employer your in-depth knowledge of the field.

Q: What excited you the most about that job and why?

A: *I found the ability to bring about change to an environment that's been static for a long time really gratifying. Also, to have that change recognized by others as positive was exciting.*

The employer will want to determine if you're passionate about your job. Don't give a "fluff" answer—your excitement has to be genuine.

Q: Why have you selected industrial engineering as a career, as opposed to mechanical or electrical or some other field in engineering?

A: *Well, I want to work with people, which is something I probably wouldn't be able to do in most other engineering fields. I also like the business aspect of engineering and get a sense of accomplishment from seeing things being built.*

First-time Job Seekers: Emphasize any relevant job experience you may have, including co-op assignments. If you don't have any real job experience, you should talk about your goals and ambition. Try to give the interviewer the idea that you're willing to work as a team member, and that you want to put your college education to work.

The employer will want to hear that you definitely want to work with people, and that you recognize this as a key component of the job. You should also be prepared to tell exactly what it is about industrial engineering that attracts you. This will assure the employer that you're likely to be happy with the job and to stay with the firm for a period of time.

Q: How do you feel about working in manufacturing as a long-term career?

A: *I recognize that manufacturing is a very broad career field. I can spend a lifetime in manufacturing and still not learn all aspects of the job. This possibility is very interesting to me.*

That's important, because industrial engineering involves wanting to work in a manufacturing environment as opposed to development or a research kind of environment.

Q: Here's a scenario I'd like you to listen to, and tell me how you'd respond to it: You've just been hired to work in my factory, and your job as an industrial engineer is to get more output from the workforce. The workforce is made up of twenty-year employees and is unionized. How would you go about implementing your ideas?

A: *The first thing I'd do is talk to each member of the workforce, letting them explain to me how they do their jobs. I'd do a lot of listening and very little talking. I've found that this helps me formulate effective solutions more easily. After all, how can I come up with a new way of doing things without understanding the old way first? Equally important, it helps me win over the workers, so that when I make suggestions to improve their jobs, they'll be willing to listen to me.*

Being a team player is very important in industrial engineering. A lot of engineers make the mistake of never asking the operators running the tools how to do the job. They suggest new ways of doing things without understanding the old way, upsetting the workers and stirring up the unions. Employers want to know that you like to be a team player with the workforce, that you're not going to create more problems than you solve.

Career Changers: Emphasize your reason for wanting to work in industrial engineering. Tell why the idea of working in this field excites you, and how your previous experience and/or training apply to the position.

Q: Have you had any co-op engineering assignments? Which assignments did you prefer and why?

A: *I was put to work helping a manufacturing line. It was a project to determine how many operators could run an automated tool using a man-machine analysis. I automated the man-machine analysis technique, putting it on my PC. It was a challenging project that involved not only a lot of engineering know-how, but computer expertise as well. It was exciting putting to work in the real world all the skills I'd learned in school.*

This is very important—especially so if you don't have any professional engineering experience. Describe in detail any co-op assignments you've had, emphasizing any accomplishments you made, no matter how small. You should also discuss what you liked about the experience, and why.

Q: Which do you prefer and why: projects in which your individual accomplishments are apparent or projects that are team oriented?

A: *I really like to work in teams. I find that a project tends to be more successful if there is input from many different people with many different areas of expertise. I was lucky in that my university's engineering program placed a lot of emphasis on teamwork, and I was able to work in groups on many different engineering projects and assignments.*

The right answer for jobs in the manufacturing environment is team accomplishments. If a person is looking hard for individual recognition, he or she may have a tough time in manufacturing because so much work is done in teams. Give examples of how you've worked effectively in groups in the past, in school or in the workplace.

Q: What kind of job do you see yourself doing ten years from now?

A: *In ten years I can see myself as a production control manager. I think that's a pretty realistic expectation for someone with my skills and experience.*

The employer will want to know if you have ambition and would place a high plus on that. This question also tests how much the candidate knows about

Experienced Professionals: Before you apply to a company, do a lot of research to determine exactly how you plan on contributing your skills and experience to that company. Be sure to outline these ideas first in your cover letter, and later in your job interview.

the company. You should know the manufacturing functions within each particular company and be able to identify which function you'd like to work in. You should also say whether you'd prefer to be in a technical or a management role. It doesn't really matter which.

Q: What software programs are you familiar with?

A: *I've done a lot of work on Microsoft Excel and Word.*

You should be very familiar with a spreadsheet program. Microsoft Excel is most commonly used. You should be proficient in a drawing program that enables you to draw flow charts and factory layouts. Most employers also require you to be able to document your work using any word-processing program, such as Microsoft Word. Depending on the position, you may be required to learn other software programs, but you can usually learn these on the job.

Q: Which industrial engineering course did you enjoy the most and why?

A: *I enjoyed engineering economics because it gave me some interesting insight into how to value engineering projects. I see this as a useful skill in my future career.*

Be sincere but also be sensitive to your interviewer. Consider choosing a course that has some relevance to the company where you are interviewing.

Q: Have you had any experience with manufacturing simulation? If so, which types?

A: *Yes, I've studied Promodel and WITNESS and have built models using Promodel.*

This is your opportunity to shine. Play up your experience to the interviewer, no matter how insignificant it may seem.

Q: What do you know about our product?

A: *To be honest, before this interview I knew very little about your product. However, I've recently done some research and was very impressed to learn that it's number one in a field of almost thirty-five competing products.*

Candidates Re-entering the Workforce: Be open and honest about why you've chosen to re-enter the field. Have a clear idea of what your goals are and be able to articulate them. The interviewer will be wondering why you left and if you heart is really in this field, so you'll have to take pains to quell those fears.

The employer will gauge from your response your depth of interest in the position and the company. Did you make an effort to find out about the company before the job interview? If you did, you've got points in your favor. If you didn't, you can be sure some other candidate vying for the job did.

Q: **Tell me about some specific technical subjects you would like to learn more about.**

A: *I'd like to learn more about logistics systems. The field is growing so fast that I didn't have time in my undergraduate studies to learn as much as I could have. I'd like to work on a master's degree at some point down the line, maybe specializing in logistics.*

Employers want to hire people who are willing to grow. Be sure to demonstrate your ability and enthusiasm to keep learning. You might also give one or two examples of how you've gone beyond the call of duty to learn more in the past.

Interactive Multimedia
Project Manager

Q: How did you become interested in interactive multimedia?

A: *My father's always been interested in the possibilities with interactive multimedia, and I guess that excitement rubbed off on me. I think it's a phenomenon that's here to stay, and that will dramatically change the way we live as a society.*

This candidate's answer is appropriate. The candidate's strong interest has been effectively expressed. Convince the recruiter that there's nothing else you'd rather be doing than interactive multimedia.

Q: What are your qualifications for being an interactive multimedia project manager?

A: *I've worked as an associate in an interactive multimedia company for close to three years. Before that I worked as a development junior executive for a television production company in Hollywood for two years.*

Having work experience in an interactive multimedia company is beneficial but not necessary. This candidate mentions his or her entertainment experience, which is a very natural starting point for interactive multimedia. If you don't have any relevant work experience, promote the work skills that you do have. Notice that the candidate did not mention his or her college major—it really doesn't matter what you majored in.

Q: How did you decide what your role within an interactive multimedia team should be?

A: *My biggest strength is my organizational ability, so being a project manager made sense. I'm also very creative, so this role allows me to use both of these skills.*

The candidate expresses that he or she fully understands the skills needed for the function of project manager. At the same time, the candidate sells his or her own set of skills. In answering a question like this, convince the recruiter that you know what it takes, and that you have what it takes.

Q: What do you think makes the ideal interactive multimedia team?

A: *I definitely think it varies from project to project, but in general, it first takes someone to come up with the idea. This is usually the producer, who often provides the funding for the project. Then you need at least one writer as well as a computer programmer. You also need a marketing person to sell the finished product. And, of course, you need a project manager to keep everything organized, on time, and within budget.*

This candidate is clearly aware of the first fundamental of interactive multimedia development—that it takes a team. The candidate seems to have a solid understanding of the different roles, as well. If you've never been on an interactive multimedia team, talk to some people who have before your interview.

Q: Did you take any college courses on interactive multimedia?

A: *I took a class called Interactive Multimedia: Design and Research Issues, which emphasized design, application, and evaluation. I got to do my first interactive multimedia project in that class.*

The candidate's been exposed to interactive multimedia, which is positive. Having taken such a course is certainly not an imperative, however. You could talk about a creative-writing course or a communications course instead.

Q: Have you been to any interactive multimedia training seminars?

A: *I go biannually to the SALT, or Society for Applied Learning Technology, seminar. It's a good way to keep up with what's going on in the industry. I also find it interesting to see what my colleagues have been creating.*

This candidate's involvement is extremely impressive. Perhaps there is a local day-long seminar that you can attend. If not, answer this question by telling the recruiter about an interactive multimedia book that you've just read.

Q: What interactive multimedia programs have you created?

A: *I've developed an interior-design aid that helps you visualize what the different rooms of your house will look like after you actually decorate them. It's been very well received in the designing circles in my town.*

First-time Job Seekers: Having work experience in an interactive multimedia company is beneficial but not necessary. If you don't have any relevant work experience, promote the work skills that you do have. Discuss any relevant courses you may have taken in interactive multimedia. Having taken such a course is certainly an imperative, however. You could talk about a creative writing course or a communications course instead. And although a casual dress code is the norm for this industry, you should wear your formal "interviewing suit."

The candidate shows creativity with this answer, proving that he or she can actually create. If you haven't developed a program, discuss a well-thought-out idea for an interactive multimedia product. Or discuss how you'd improve upon something that's already on the market.

Q: **What do you think the most difficult aspects of creating an interactive multimedia program are?**

A: *In my experience, getting to the end product without going tremendously over budget is the most difficult aspect of the project. It takes a lot of resources to create an interactive multimedia program, and most programs end up costing much more than what was originally expected or budgeted for.*

The candidate answers this question quite well, because what he or she is saying is absolutely true. On the other hand, if you have a different answer based on your experience, definitely express it. The recruiter is looking more for a level of experience than for any particular answer.

Q: **What would you like your next interactive multimedia program creation to be?**

A: *Because the interior-design program that I designed was so successful, I'd like to expand that idea a bit further. I'd like to develop a program that would allow someone to see what his or her house renovations would look like in the final outcome.*

This sounds like a creative idea. What would you do? The recruiter is trying to determine whether or not you have a creative mind.

Q: **What's your favorite interactive multimedia program?**

A: *I really think Myst is a great interactive multimedia software program. I played it over and over in my spare time. I've also really enjoyed From Alice to Ocean.*

The candidate has chosen to speak about two classics in the industry. Anything that you've truly enjoyed would be appropriate to talk about. The

Career Changers: Realize that information technology is a rapidly evolving field. It's probably one of the largest growing industries of the near future. That's both exciting, because there are and will be unlimited opportunities for many different kinds of involvement, and frustrating, because nothing is clearly established yet. There are no set career paths in information technology because the industry is only now being established. Your best bet is to figure out what's out there and how you want to be involved. Then just jump in!

recruiter wants to be sure that you actually use interactive multimedia programs in your spare time, because this indicates a high level of interest.

Q: Whom do you see as industry leaders?

A: *Although there are many brilliant minds in interactive multimedia, I think in some ways you could call Nicholas Negroponte the guru of information technology. What is particularly impressive about his book,* Being Digital, *is that it speaks to both the layperson and the interactive multimedia professional.*

Talk about whomever you think is the most influential leader or leaders in the interactive multimedia and information technology industries. You should be aware of who the most important people in the industry are, and the recruiter will make sure that you are. You can't go wrong with Negroponte for this question.

Q: Do you work better in project- or task-oriented situations?

A: *I'd say that I lean more toward the project-oriented side of things. I tend to look at the big picture, and then work from there toward a conclusion.*

In interactive multimedia, being project oriented makes sense for the project manager, who must oversee and direct the entire project to completion. Other roles are more suited for task-oriented people, like computer programming for example. If you don't think you work in a project-oriented fashion, then perhaps interviewing for a project-manager position is not the right move for you.

Q: Do you work better in a conservative corporate office or a casual office?

A: *I'm much more comfortable and productive in a casual office. Also, I find I can spend more time at the office when I'm wearing "business casual," or even jeans, than in a formal suit.*

The culture in interactive multimedia offices tends to be more creative than in traditional corporate offices. This candidate mentions the dress code he or she prefers, as well, which is also the norm for this industry. However,

> **Experienced Professionals:** Emphasize your technical competence and be prepared to relate your previous work experience to the job opening that interests you. Of course, keeping up with current technology, trends, and progress is one of the most important preparations you can make for the interactive, multimedia interview. Mention any books, magazines, trade journals, and other relevant publications that you've read recently. You should also be proficient on both Mac and PC platforms.

unless the recruiter advises you to dress casually for the interview, wear your formal "interviewing suit."

Q: Are you on the Internet?

A: *Of course! I've been on it for years. In fact, I have to be careful that I don't spend too much time surfing the Net. I can easily spend hours in one sitting in the evenings or on weekends.*

The recruiter will obviously expect an answer of yes to this question, just as this candidate has given. Being hooked up to the Internet tells the recruiter two things. First, it indicates that you're truly interested in information technology, and second, it displays a certain level of technical competence, which is also important.

Q: What do you see as Hollywood's role in the interactive multimedia revolution?

A: *I think it's a bit early to tell what the long-term outcome will be. We're seeing an increasingly large number of computer-animated films, however. I think that in some ways interactive multimedia could be called the next Hollywood.*

The candidate's answer is astute. Although answers may and should vary, the candidate demonstrates, most importantly, that he or she has thought about this very relevant and timely issue. Be sure to read a lot about the interactive multimedia industry before the interview so that you're able to give an opinion on different issues.

Q: What other industries do you think will be affected by interactive multimedia?

A: *I think every industry will be affected by interactive multimedia. Right now I'd say that the most pronounced changes due to interactive multimedia are occurring in public relations. I think that education will change dramatically, but I also think it will be resisted.*

Candidates Re-entering the Workforce: Information technology, and interactive multimedia within it, is an industry that is outdating itself every six months. You'll want to convince the interviewer that you've kept up with the industry during your leave. Have you attended any interactive multimedia training seminars such as the Society for Applied Learning Technology seminar? Perhaps you've just read and interactive multimedia book or found something interesting on the Internet that you can discuss with the interviewer. You should also mention any interactive multimedia publications that you read on a regular basis.

The answer to this question is to some degree speculation. This candidate's answer is sound. It's important that he or she is able to look at the big picture, and not just at the interactive multimedia industry. Be sure to read the *Wall Street Journal* before your interview so that you'll be prepared to answer questions such as these.

Q: **What platform do you feel most comfortable with?**

A: *I really prefer working on a Macintosh, although I'm just as proficient on a PC.*

It's acceptable to answer this question either way. Personal preference is the only issue. Be sure that you're proficient on both systems, however, because you may not know which system the recruiter's company uses.

Q: **What books on information technology do you think are particularly insightful?**

A: *There are lots. In terms of manifestos about the direction and scope of technology, I found Stanley M. Davis's 2020 Vision quite interesting. There's also Paul Kennedy's The Rise and Fall of Great Powers.*

The candidate names two very impressive books and gives a good answer. Check with your local public library or, even better, with a local business-school library for additional current and appropriate books. It's important to read the current information technology and business trends books on the market.

Q: **What direction do you see interactive multimedia taking?**

A: *I think that it's difficult to say at this point. I believe it will become a part of everyone's daily life sometime in the near future. One area that I think would greatly benefit from an increased use of interactive multimedia is education. And, in fact, I think we'll see a lot more interactive multimedia programs in schools in the near future.*

This candidate provides an appropriate and solid answer. It's difficult to answer briefly what's taken some authors 200 pages to write about. Mentioning education as an ideal target area for interactive multimedia suitably rounds out the candidate's answer.

LAN Analyst

Q: Why are you leaving your current position?

A: *Technically, the company is moving quite slowly. Its management doesn't really embrace new technology, so I don't imagine that the position is as challenging as it would be in another company. I want to work for a company that's not afraid to move ahead—where I can be exposed to all the latest advances in the industry.*

Convince the interviewer that you're leaving your current position because you want to expand your horizons, not just your paycheck. You should stress the fact that you want to work with emerging technologies in an environment where you'll be intellectually challenged.

Q: What would you consider your "perfect job" in both the short and long term?

A: *Right now I'd like to do consulting work, designing and installing local-area networks and wide-area networks. I enjoy real "hands on" tasks and working with clients. In the long term I'd like to be a project manager, overseeing a group that's designing local-area networks.*

The interviewer will try to find out about your career goals. Are your aspirations realistic and in line with what you're doing now? This is a good response, since the candidate describes realistic goals.

Q: Tell me about some computer classes you've taken.

A: *I've taken a number of classes, both in college and since I've graduated. I've taken courses in data structures, Pascal, operating systems, database design, and artificial intelligence, to name just a few.*

Through this question the interviewer is trying to find out about the candidate's computer background. There is no right or wrong answer to this question. The interviewer is simply looking for someone who will understand the

First-time Job Seekers: Along with a degree in computer science (or a comparable major), you should have some relevant work experience or internships. Even working at the campus computer store will look better than flipping burgers at a local greasy spoon. Naturally, you should have your own computer so you can discuss what systems or hardware you've used.

"big picture," and someone with a wide range of knowledge will be able to do that. This is a great answer, since it shows that the candidate has the range of skills necessary for a position as an LAN analyst.

Q: Do you enjoy programming? What are your programming skills?

A: *Yes, to a certain extent. I'm not really interested in programming full-time in the traditional sense, but I like it if it's interactive. I know C++ and Perl.*

Again, a breadth of knowledge is important in this position. You aren't going to have to program every day, but you still need to have a good understanding of it, since you may occasionally be asked to write a few codes here and there.

Q: What kind of hardware and systems have you been involved with?

A: *I've worked with Novell Netware, Microsoft Windows, Ethernet Token Rings Topologies, Cisco routers, and TCP\IP, SNA, and IPX protocols. I also have some experience with UNIX, and I have Windows NT on my home computer.*

This is another basic question intended to uncover the depth and breadth of the candidate's knowledge. The answer shows a varied background that covers a wide spectrum of systems, demonstrating that the candidate has a good grasp of computer-hardware technology.

Q: What kind of computer do you have at home?

A: *I have a PC with a Pentium III and a cable modem. As I said before, I just installed Windows NT, so I'm still learning that system.*

The interviewer asks this to see if the candidate's interest in computers extends to his or her personal life. Are you doing all you can to push your limits at home? This is a good answer since the candidate shows an interest in trying the new technologies, even at home.

Career Changers: You should immerse yourself in the field before attempting to find a job. If you don't already own a computer, you must buy one; if you already have one but it's over a year old, you should definitely upgrade your system. Play with your computer as much as possible, learning whatever you can about what makes it tick. You may want to take a class or two, or teach yourself a few basic programming languages, then write your own programs. Subscribe to trade magazines to get up to speed on all the technological advances; get an Internet connection and browse it to see what's out there. Once you're sure you know you computer inside and out, you'll be ready to look for a job.

Q: How do you manage to keep up with the latest technologies?

A: *I subscribe to a lot of trade publications, like* Internet Week, Network Computing, *and* Planet IT. *I also like to try out new software and hardware at home on my own computer.*

It's essential that LAN analysts stay on top of all the latest technology, so trade magazines are a must-read. You can also peruse others, like *Data Communications Week*, and even some standard magazines like *Business Week*, which have pretty good technology sections. If you mention a magazine like *Wired*, you won't really score any points, as that type of magazine is geared more toward popular culture.

Q: What kind of training have you done?

A: *I've done a mix of things, from conducting seminars to one-on-one training with end users for a variety of applications, including Windows, and Outlook.*

Interviewers like candidates who show enthusiasm about training and dealing with people. LAN analysts should be good with people, because a large part of their job is dealing with clients.

Q: How do you juggle tasks when you're in a stressful situation?

A: *The first thing I do is write down everything that needs to be done. Then I check with my manager and prioritize the tasks, assigning each job a level of importance. Finally, I just go down the list and do each job in its order of importance.*

Organization is an essential skill in any profession, especially one involving computers. You need to demonstrate that you can think logically and sort through tasks to decide which is most important. Also, interviewers like to see people actually using pen and paper; if you say something like, "Oh, I just keep a running list in my head," the interviewer will almost certainly conclude that you lack true organizational skills.

Q: Which thirty-two-bit operating systems are marketed today for the Intel PC architecture?

Experienced Professionals: During your interview focus on those you'd like to learn more about and on the ways you plan to stretch your abilities. You should show a palpable desire to expand you horizons. Talk about the systems at your current company and what you'd do if you had the power and resources to change it. Firms are looking for people with imagination: clients will say to you, "I want a system that can do this," and you must be able to take it from there, creating a system that will best serve their needs.

A: *Mac OS, Windows NT, and Windows XP.*

This is a pretty straightforward question designed to test the candidate's knowledge of the various products available on the market. As an LAN analyst, you must always know what products are available for which systems, so that you can recommend the best products to your clients.

Q: **Consider this situation: My PC's sound card isn't working. It's configured at IRQ 7 and I/O 220. What could be causing the problem?**

A: *Well, if there's a printer port on the machine, it could be using IRQ 7. Most operating systems won't allow coexistence of two devices using the same interrupt. Another device in the system, such as an NIC card, could be set to use I/O port 220. Again, the operating system might not permit two devices to use the same I/O port. The problem is solved by changing one or both settings on the sound card or other competing adapter if possible.*

This is a fairly basic problem. The interviewer may well ask this, or a similar question, to determine how quickly you can think on your feet. The candidate's answer here is thorough in its examination of a number of different possible causes.

Candidates Re-entering the Workforce: You must be sure that you kept abreast of all the latest technologies. Read magazines like *Network World*, and *eWeek*, and make sure your home computer is equipped with the latest systems and software so that you'll know how they work. You need to show that although you haven't been working for a few years, you've still kept up with the advances in this fast-paced industry.

Mechanical Engineer

Q: Tell me about your educational background.

A: *I have a bachelor's degree in mechanical engineering from Lehigh University, where I graduated with a 3.2 GPA. Many of my classes involved working on team-based projects, and I was voted team leader several times. In addition to my classes I interned for one semester at a small tooling company where my project involved redesigning a flange to fit a customer's product. Later I went back for my M.B.A. Much of my graduate curriculum also involved team-based projects, which have proven helpful in my experiences as a project leader.*

The educational experience described here is extremely valuable. Not only does it include the core mechanical-engineering competency, but it also includes practical, as well as business, experience. Today's engineers, especially those at the higher levels, are often called upon to do less traditional engineering tasks, such as writing business proposals or purchasing raw materials.

Q: What computer-design experience do you have and at what level of application?

A: *I have extensive experience with AutoCad and CAD/CAM and have used them in product and process redesign.*

AutoCad and CAD/CAM are software packages that are widely used in the mechanical-engineering field. Problem-solving skills are tested by using these software packages to solve part- or process-design problems. This question allows the interviewer to gauge the candidate's level of experience in using a necessary skill.

Q: Do you have experience with quality programs?

First-time Job Seekers: Conduct informational interviews to acquaint yourself with what organizations are looking for. This will also give you an opportunity to hone your technique. For mechanical engineers a bachelor's degree is always a minimum requirement. In addition, engineering internships and other practical experience gained during college add value because they expose you to a real life work environment.

A: *I have experience working in an ISO-9000 environment. My responsibilities included documenting manufacturing procedures to ensure consistent processing on three manufacturing shifts.*

ISO programs are in great demand in manufacturing. Experience in these types of quality programs will enhance your marketability. The acronym stands for the International Organization for Standardization. ISO programs have been implemented extensively in Europe and are gaining widespread attention in the U.S. A manufacturing facility that's ISO certified is identified as a top-quality supplier. All processes and systems in a certified plant are documented to ensure consistency and quality in the manufacturing of the product. You can also mention your familiarity with good manufacturing processes (GMPs), which are a set of federal regulations governing manufacturing companies.

Q: Have you had any experience in process optimization?

A: *In my last position I had to increase production in a stamping machine by 10 percent. I redesigned the equipment to combine two functions and increased production by 15 percent.*

This response shows problem-solving skills and the ability to think conceptually about processes. The goal of process optimization is to identify and implement the most cost-effective way to manufacture a product. Your job as an engineer is to redesign a process in a way that will lower costs, hence increasing profit margin.

Q: Tell me about your experience with product optimization.

A: *I've had experience redesigning an existing part to meet customer specifications. In my previous position I was part of a design team that had to redesign a part in order to meet new safety standards. This was a difficult project, as we'd originally thought the part would need a small change, but in the end the part had to be almost completely redesigned.*

In addition to problem solving, this response shows the candidate's positive approach to customer issues. The candidate should be knowledgeable

Career Changers: Without an engineering background, this is a difficult field to transition to. You'll need to return to school to get your bachelor's degree in mechanical engineering. But if you're making the transition from a different engineering field—say, chemical or civil engineering—be sure to highlight those skills that are easily transferable, such as problem-solving skills or the ability to work well in teams.

about both kinds of product optimization: revising a product to meet a specific customer's changing needs, and finding new markets and applications for existing products.

Q: **Why did you choose mechanical engineering over other engineering disciplines?**

A: *I've always liked working with my hands, and a mechanical-engineering curriculum has enabled me to enhance my innate skills. I believe that mechanical engineering is really the most "hands-on" of all the engineering fields.*

This is a good answer because it shows the candidate has pursued an area of genuine interest instead of taking a course of study just to obtain a degree. When you discuss education in an interview, be sure to give a good reason why you decided on a specific curriculum. Let the interviewer know you've given serious thought to the profession you've chosen.

Q: **Have you been involved directly with any customer-related issues?**

A: *I have experience responding to and resolving customer issues on a front-line basis. Customers feel comfortable talking with me about design issues, and I always respond in a timely fashion.*

This response reflects the importance the candidate places on customer service and also allows the interviewer to gauge the candidate's interpersonal skills. Such skills are important because in many organizations mechanical engineers have continuous contact with customers regarding such product issues as price, delivery schedule, product quality, and product applicability.

Q: **Have you facilitated any systems training?**

A: *Yes. I've trained employees in various process-control systems, including SPC (statistical process control), as well as material testing and maintaining production-control sheets.*

This is a good answer because it focuses on quality and also provides input on facilitation skills. Employers like to see systems-training experience, because

Experienced Professionals: Network with professionals within the industry to identify potential job leads. During your interview, focus on your accomplishments and how they affected your previous company. Be ready to discuss your leadership and managerial experience. For higher-level engineering positions, supervisory experience is valued as much as technical expertise, so be prepared to discuss any experience you have in this area as well.

in a manufacturing work environment systems play an important role in the way products get made. SPC is a system that monitors the quality of the product in process. A candidate with experience in SPC will be valuable to any manufacturing organization. Recent graduates should consider taking systems quality courses like SAC, as this type of training can make a candidate even more attractive to a prospective employer.

Q: Are you certified as a professional engineer?

A: *Yes, I'm a fully certified M.E. and have testified in court on engineering issues.*

To earn this certification, an individual must have at least four years of engineering experience and have passed a technically challenging test. Most companies require their experienced engineers to be certified. Like this candidate, you can also expand on this question by offering additional information that might not be readily apparent from reading your resume.

Q: Do you have experience purchasing materials and/or equipment?

A: *I have experience doing both. In my last position I participated in a material review board, which dealt with supplier-pricing issues, and I've been involved with pricing for technical expenditures.*

This answer highlights not only technical expertise, but also finance and managerial experience. Many companies today are downsizing, so employees are often given responsibilities traditionally outside their scope. In many cases engineers are hired not only for mechanical competencies but also for business acumen. A typical example would be purchasing equipment and/or materials for one's manufacturing department.

Q: Have you been involved with patenting a product or process?

A: *I've been a team leader for two patented products that went to market ahead of schedule. Both products have gone on to gain solid market shares.*

This is basically a yes-or-no question. With a positive answer you can demonstrate initiative (in that you have experience conceptualizing and developing new products), and communication and leadership skills. If you haven't

Candidates Re-entering the Workforce: Acquaint yourself with new technology by reading trade journals and other engineering material. To help get your foot in the door, call old contacts from your previous work experience and network through them. Also, attend area engineering networking groups, such as, meetings of your local chapter of the American Society of Engineers.

yet worked on a product or process that's been patented, don't say that you have. Instead, simply say you look forward to the possibility of working in an environment where that kind of creativity is encouraged.

Q: Have you had any experience supervising employees?

A: *In my last position two entry-level mechanical engineers and ten machine operators reported to me. I was responsible for hiring, training, performance-evaluation, and discipline issues.*

This is an excellent answer. Regardless of occupation, an employee's career growth is impacted heavily by his or her managerial capability. In today's work environment employees must wear many hats. In order for an employee to progress in an organization, he or she at one time or another must have supervised employees. If you're interviewing for a position that requires no supervisory experience, such as an entry-level engineer, a history of supervision on your resume—even if it was managing a shift at a fast-food restaurant while attending college—can reflect positively on your potential for growth in the organization.

Q: What's your greatest strength?

A: *I think my greatest strength is problem solving. When I'm given a technical project, I'll remove any obstacles impeding solution of the problem. The internship project I did in college is a good example. The company was having an ongoing problem with a customer in terms of product application. By stepping outside the problem and looking at it conceptually, I decided to add a flange which made the product fit the customer specs. This unorthodox approach solved the problem.*

This answer shows forward thinking, initiative, and creativity—essential traits for any engineer. What's impressive about this candidate's answer is the fact that even at a young age, he or she wasn't intimidated by the scope of the problem, or by the potential impact of the decision.

Senior Systems Analyst
(Health Care)

Q: Describe your philosophy of what would be important if you were the senior systems analyst and had to staff your organization with programmers and systems analysts.

A: *What I would look for in my staff are certain characteristics that have enabled me, in my own working experience, to be effective: the ability to conceptualize, to think logically, and to verbalize easily. When I see these skills, I know a person has the ability to talk to client groups and to translate accurately what's been said into meaningful systems design. I'd also want to see programming experience.*

This question addresses the skills that would be critical to building an organization. The candidate is smart to sell his or her personal characteristics and skills while answering the question. This demonstrates that the candidate is aware of the recruiter's perspective (that is, the recruiter is looking for reasons to hire the candidate, not merely for reasons the candidate would hire a staff).

Q: Are there certain personal qualities you believe are compatible with the information-systems profession?

A: *I like people who are eager to learn and to experiment, because technology changes very quickly in our business and you have to be able to keep up with advances. And I'd look for integrity, given the potential power analysts have to create viruses and to access information that could cause the company or other individuals harm.*

Here the candidate shows he or she can judge people's ability to stay current—critical in any technology industry where things become outdated quickly. The candidate also implies that staying current is a personal goal; similarly, another selling point is the way in which the candidate works his or her own integrity into the conversation.

Q: Tell me about your experience with hardware.

A: *I've worked with a variety of platforms, including DEC and IBM PC. I've experienced several major systems conversions in my fifteen years' experience—for example, when we moved from mainframes to servers and terminals, then to PC platforms.*

This is a skill-assessment question. It's the type of question anyone should anticipate. Logically, the next question will be about software experience, so the candidate could have improved the answer by addressing his or her software skills after addressing hardware skills. Learn to anticipate from questions you're asked what the recruiter needs to know.

Q: What software are you familiar with?

A: *I've worked with a variety of applications. Actually, one of the things that's been very helpful to me while working in a hospital-management company is my background in insurance claims, my two previous employers being insurance companies. Understanding the insurance-claim process—which has a big impact on how we do business as a health-care provider—has helped me design tracking reports and create models for various patient scenarios with associated costs of care.*

This answer is strong because it links past experience with the candidate's current experience. It builds a total story or consistent pattern of development along the lines of industry specialization as well as technical skill. If the candidate had not linked the insurance experience to the hospital experience, the recruiter might have missed an important connection between the two: the parallels might not be so obvious to someone who hadn't lived both experiences. The candidate's answer would also be appropriate if the question had been, "How has your past experience helped you in your current job?"

Q: In your early programming experiences, what did you have to be able to do well?

A: *I had to be able to solve problems and write good code. Then I also learned things like how to do more thorough research on the front end, including interviewing people and getting them to reveal what kind of information they really need as opposed to what they say they want from an automated system.*

This question has essentially the same purpose as the first question—to determine if the candidate can remember what it was like to be a programmer. Would the candidate, in charge of hiring and managing a staff, have realistic expectations about what an entry level person should be able to do? (Sometimes people with advanced experiences have difficulty stepping

First-time Job Seekers: A technical background in school, like computer science or math, provides the best entrance into this field. Demonstrate your ability to listen and to ask good questions, since that skill is critical on the job in the initial stages of research and determination of system requirements. Be ready to do a lot of programming in your first job.

back to simpler concepts.) In this case the candidate clearly remembers what it was like and goes on to explain what skills were expected and what was learned on the job, as well as how that has made the candidate more effective. Again, the job seeker brought the question back to selling his or her own specific skills.

Q: **Is it sometimes difficult to get clients to reveal what they're thinking in terms of information output?**

A: *I think that definitely can happen if you rush people. Then, also, there are the type-A personalities who immediately assume they can tell you the answer— do the design analysis. Since I know the dangers of rushing the front end of a project, I've learned how to move a conversation along and get that type of person to give more complete and thoughtful background information instead of personal conclusions. One thing that really helped me deal with these types of personalities was reading* Seven Habits of Highly Effective People.

This question hints at a potential negative or problem, so the candidate has an opportunity to turn it around (make it positive). The candidate makes a positive statement about handling adversity and even shows an eagerness to seek outside learning to master management difficulties. The candidate appears thoughtful and well read.

Q: **Describe the process you went through to develop one of the systems at your current company.**

A: *An example is an integration project we did, where many hospital departments had to share patient information. We wanted to replace the manual process of moving pieces of paper from floor to floor, or of having patients repeat name, address, and social security number a number of times as they moved from hospital department to department. We interfaced the patient information from the business-office system with patient information from the radiology system and lab system and made it available to the nursing computer system. In doing the initial work we included the director of nursing and all medical department heads and offered them various design alternatives. The goal was to get them to buy in by making a choice.*

This question addresses problem solving and accomplishments, so it demands a specific example. The candidate gives a good example and reinforces why getting good information up front from the users is critical to the users' ultimate acceptance of the end product.

Q: **How would you describe the internal reputation of the information-systems department where you work?**

A: *In general people have always considered my company an excellent place to work. We're known as a cost-driven company, which means our systems group is critical in terms of accurate data collection. I think that the goals of my job and the goals of the company are well connected—we want to save the company money. My department eliminates duplications and automates things so that people aren't manually keying in information, which is both time-consuming and error prone. One way my group has earned its reputation is by involving users in our designs so that user needs are the beginning point and end point, as I said before.*

This question concerns passion for the business, the department, and the company. The answer is thoughtful and ties in how the candidate's job supports the goals of the company and protects the consumer in a hospital. The interviewer ends up with a good understanding about why this candidate is motivated to continue working in the field.

Q: **How would you describe the realities of a systems-analyst job?**

A: *I've always understood that this isn't an eight-to-five job. There are lots of project deadlines to juggle around troubleshooting. I've been awakened at home at midnight because someone's system has locked up, and I understand that. I also understand that to each client group their project is number one. One way I've always relieved some of the inherent pressure is that I'm a good time manager.*

This question addresses the candidate's suitability for the job, and the candidate demonstrates an ability not only to handle the workload but to master it. The candidate again sells a specific skill—time management—which is a good fit with the job.

Q: **Why do you want to continue to work in systems analysis?**

A: *I'm certainly ready for more managerial responsibility; in addition to on-the-job training, I've also completed an executive M.B.A. program to build my management skills. In terms of why the systems work continues to appeal to me, there's never a dull moment. The job requires left- and right-brain thinking and a lot of intelligence as well as creativity. I remember my initial interest in learning data processing and why. After college I was a reservation sales analyst, which was my first introduction to computers. Although that wasn't a*

Career Changers: Be prepared to go back to school and learn programming and systems design from the ground up. Don't wait until late in a career to make this switch. Then stick to application in an industry where you already have experience.

challenging enough job for me to stay interested in a career there, what I liked was having all that information at my fingertips. I decided it would be interesting to be the person behind what's inside the computer. That's why I left the job to go back to school and get another degree—this time to learn systems. And I know that I want to stay in this field. Whether the company is downsizing or fighting inflation, the Management Information Systems department will provide a critical skill. Information is king in any business, and that's the value I provide.

This is another form of the motivation, or "passion for the business," question. The candidate goes back to his or her initial motivation to do systems work, and this story ties up some loose ends for the interviewer—namely, why the candidate wants to stay in the field. The job seeker has obviously thought this matter through.

Q: **Where do you see real opportunity to use management information in a new way in the health care industry?**

A: *Except for true acute care, which will stay in the hospitals, the industry will have to have a realistic handle on costs. The primary health-care transition will be the capitation model, where physicians are paid on a per-patient basis and have to figure out how to make a profit out of that within an HMO plan. Accounting and finance departments will have to allocate certain dollars to specific specialists and make them operate profitably. Individuals will pay a hospital group, which subcontracts work out to different specialists. Within health care and hospitals specifically, no one can tell exactly what a patient day costs. If you could come up with a realistic model for different patient scenarios, you could really decrease the instances of abuse in the system, ranging from insurance and claims processing to scheduling. The goal is to minimize cost and maximize value.*

This is a question of leadership and creativity in looking for new business opportunities. The candidate is able to demonstrate strategic thinking and concern for improving the business. The answer is especially important from the standpoint of understanding the state of the health care business today. The candidate has shown that he or she can address strategic issues through MIS skills.

Q: **What do you think are critical skills for an information-project manager?**

A: *You have to be able to speak well with MIS management at the client site. You also have to know when to answer questions and when to bring in a specialist. So good problem-solving and quick evaluation or diagnostic skills are really important. Technical people aren't necessarily good at some of these things.*

As you seek to add responsibility and earn promotions within systems analysis, you have to be able to serve as a project manager. This involves either selling or promoting potential projects internally (if you work in an in-house, corporate MIS group) or selling to corporate MIS groups (if you work in a systems consulting firm.) Presentation skills, finesse, and judgment are skills you will be evaluated on in interviews to determine your long-term viability.

Q: **How do you get people to embrace a new software product?**

A: *I demo it so they can see it hands-on. Then I get their input into what type of output they will need—reports and data. Then I demonstrate how that output will be presented by using sample screens before I actually develop the product. This way I avoid miscommunication.*

This answer is strong. It's direct and easy to follow because it's presented sequentially (I do this, then this, then . . .). It also explains the benefit of the method. In other words, if the recruiter hires this candidate, he or she is pretty confident that the candidate won't spend extensive time developing products until the products have been well defined, with buy-in from the client/user groups.

Q: **What have you learned about training users after a system implementation?**

A: *You have to get them involved at the front end. For example, getting a user who's worked only on terminals to use a mouse, even with a game of solitaire, is a good way to get the person comfortable with a new machine. That way you avoid information overload, because the user won't be hit with the new software and with learning how to use a mouse at the same time.*

Experienced Professionals: If you have a long history in systems design and analysis, look for your new challenges to come from a change of industries (same job function) or from leaving evolving technologies (job enrichment). Don't allow yourself to appear tied to one type of systems architecture or software. You must demonstrate a flexible, inquisitive nature so as not to appear outdated.

In terms of internal promotions, aiding a smooth transition is important; people have sometimes been held back from promotions if a company's worried about finding a suitable replacement for the position that would be vacated. One rule of thumb is to always train your replacement in advance. At the very least, show concern for not "abandoning" a position in the organization. Can you recommend someone on your staff or outside who is capable of assuming your current responsibilities?

This answer is creative. The candidate shows a fun way to get users comfortable with new hardware before learning new software. Also, the answer shows empathy for the users—an important characteristic of successful trainers and teachers in general.

Q: Describe a new system that was a great success in terms of ease of implementation.

A: *In my current company we designed our benefit-management software product on the front end, knowing it would be used in divergent businesses. We set up parameters to be table driven, so when doing implementation, our project managers can set up tailored products for different businesses without having to recode the product. A key to a good product is to have a market niche or vertical market approach so your project managers know the business; our niche is selling insurance-application products. Our document-imaging-based, operations-management product provides customer service and problem resolution for health-insurance companies and managed-care companies.*

The candidate shows strategic thinking by framing the answer around the company's market niche and how the MIS organization works within that niche. In addition, the answer demonstrates pride in the product's flexibility, so you don't get the sense that the candidate has negative feelings about his or her current employment. This is important, since no recruiter wants a candidate who's running away from something, but does want a candidate looking for something—the difference between reactive and proactive. This candidate clearly demonstrates a proactive way of thinking.

Q: When you integrate several types of systems, what types of problems do you typically run into?

A: *At my current company we have a client/server product on Intel servers. If customers have a mainframe product we have to interact with, we have to write files in a format to pass files back and forth in batch mode. Very little of it is real time. The way we've gotten around that is to use DDE—dynamic data exchange—links to be able to bring it up into the mainframe Windows environment. That way we avoid entering data into two systems.*

This answer demonstrates putting the system user's interests first. The user needs to avoid redundancy of work. And the candidate describes use of Windows, the most current application technology.

Q: What new technology do you think will be most significant over the next few years?

A: *The real trend is downsizing and going to client/server products. We still need to run applications on multiple platforms simultaneously. Specifically in the* *health-insurance environment, we need to run historical patient information on mainframes for speed. Although that information is centrally located on the mainframe, many different people, such as specialists in an HMO plan, must be able to access the current patient record and add to it using a client/server system.*

This answer demonstrates knowledge of where the industry is headed. It also demonstrates understanding of different system-user needs. Most important, the question is an opinion question, and the candidate is confident, and thus believable, in giving an opinion readily.

Q: **Data security has come into the spotlight more and more. What are your views?**

A: *It hasn't been a big problem for my current company, because insurance companies—the payers—have kept patient records all under one roof. Where it will be significant is in cost capitation, because groups will have to share patient information to control cost. The number-one thing that can make the health-care system more effective is to share information, so when someone is referred to specialists in an HMO structure, they are relying on clinical records and actual lab values as opposed to sketchy information from the patient— they can avoid duplication of tests and numerous other problems. The way to do this is to have systems that can talk to each other, so specialists and sub-specialists can talk to each other. In other words, information must become patient centered versus specialist centered.*

This answer is effective because it avoids technical jargon in favor of universally understood terms—"systems that talk to each other, so specialists can talk to each other"—giving the recruiter confidence that the technical candidate will not talk over the heads of client groups. The summary statement at the end—"patient centered versus specialist centered"—is an excellent example of making a point clear. It would be equally effective as an introductory statement to set up the answer. When people are listening to you, as in an interview, such summary statements or introductory statements are especially useful storytelling tools to help the listener follow along.

Candidates Re-entering the Workforce: Show how certain skills apply, such as ability to interview and list to client groups, skill in conceptualizing and logical thinking, relational thinking (even from such avenues as music or languages). Then pick an industry as a starting point and learn about that industry's specific information needs: what type of internal information is driving business decisions at the most successful companies in that industry, and so on.

Q: **When do you believe client/server architecture is better than hierarchical systems?**

A: *Client/server is lower cost, but you give up security, speed, and data integrity. Hierarchical provides a simple structure to link things—accounts payable/ receivable, financial info, project control, and so on.*

This questions addresses decision-making skills. The answer is quick and to the point, demonstrating that the candidate is confident of which type of system to use and when.

Q: **How does the fact that more and more people are setting up home offices and using notebook computers impact systems use?**

A: *In my last company our customers were handling the processing of 20,000 or more documents a day. When the Clean Air Act in New York resulted in more people working at home, some of them started doing data entry of claims using ISDN lines—that's a three-channel phone line with high bandwidth that allows the user to designate point-to-point voice and data communication. In a case like that, the employee can be more productive, with less interruption, at home.*

This answer demonstrates several important things: a specific (therefore believable) example; knowledge of how current events impact the business; and ability to embrace change in the workplace.

Q: **Describe an innovative software product you've offered.**

A: *For employer groups—benefit managers—providing medical-plan options for employees, one product issue was that the female population was much more likely to make physician decisions based on past relationships than were men, so the idea of HMOs with a list of approved physicians was often less attractive to women. Market research showed men to be more cost conscious. So my application group offered a transition product—a point-of-service plan—in which an individual employee can pay more, make a larger copayment, to go to a physician he or she likes outside the approved physician network. Actually, only 5 to 8 percent of people take advantage of going outside the network, but it makes the total offering more attractive to women.*

This answer gives a real example. It's also strong because it shows "thinking outside the box"—an MIS person draws upon client (individual employer) issues, individual employee (plan participant) issues, and market research to come up with a creative solution. Most important, the answer ends with a description of the success of the product, thus proving it was innovative in creating the desired outcome.

Systems Analyst

Q: **What role do you play in the design and development of the system conversion to C++?**

A: *I begin by doing a process analysis of how we'll take an application from one platform to C++. I select conversion tools and write the necessary code to convert cleanly to C++. I then test to ensure total conversion in program execution and data integrity.*

The candidate's being tested here for technical expertise, methodology, and analytical ability. Be precise and detail oriented in your answer to such questions, but don't go on forever. The interviewer will want to know that you have a logical and rational plan for handling this problem and does not want the history of programming for an answer.

Q: **When you start a project, do you prefer to create a flowchart or immediately start coding?**

A: *I prefer to break a project into components, then build timelines for completing various segments of an application. Once I have a clear overview of how the application will look, I assign responsibility to project members and start my own coding.*

The candidate's being asked to discuss his or her methodology in breaking down a problem into its component parts, and the preferred plan of attack in starting and finishing a project. What analysis do you perform immediately before launching a project? The interviewer will want to see how you approach a problem and whether you account for all variables before starting a project.

Q: **How do you structure your coding?**

A: *A code should be created so that any programmer can quickly understand the program flow. Discrete program functions should be separated and organized logically. The code itself should be systematically indented with appropriate comments.*

Again, this question is designed to test the candidate's methodology and thought process as he or she builds applications or programs. Your technical acumen as well as your logical and rational approach to problem solving will be evaluated with such a question. Keep your answer short and to the point, but don't miss any details that might lead the interviewer to question your ability to handle the position.

Q: Tell me about a time when a major project you were working on was unexpectedly running far behind schedule.

A: *The XT-14 jet project was extremely complex and involved a number of government agencies. During the project top management was reassigned, and some key modifications were pushed aside. After six weeks I realized that we could not make up the lost time and therefore could not meet the ultimate deadline.*

Demonstrate how you handle unexpected delays and how you can quickly organize, plan to avert any major downtime, and keep a project moving forward. How versatile and flexible are you? What leadership qualities have you demonstrated to take hold of a bad situation and turn it around? This candidate demonstrates a responsible attitude and an understanding of his or her limits in handling certain types of problems.

Q: How did you try to mitigate the problem?

A: *By assigning overtime and hiring fifteen temporary programmers to meet the deadline. I even canceled vacation plans to pitch in.*

What steps have you taken to turn a bad situation into a positive? This candidate is being measured for his or her aggressiveness in handling the problem, and for leadership and the willingness to assume responsibility. What problem-solving techniques have you used to eliminate a similar problem? Give a concrete solution and avoid theory or abstract possibilities.

Q: How would you describe your management style?

A: *I delegate. I let my people know what has to be done. I set goals and time frames and review progress on a regular basis. I don't tend to micromanage, but I like to be kept up to date.*

The employer will want to know how you interact with junior-level programmers. What communication techniques do you find useful in getting these employees to respond to your needs? How do you set goals and objectives for the people who report to you? If your management experience is limited, you need to draw on experiences in which you influenced or led a group or a project team and how you defined your role as manager within the team.

First-time Job Seekers: You'll be tested more for your technical knowledge than for any professional exposure, so it's wise to discuss projects you've worked on in school and what you took away from those projects. Focus on why the position is so appealing to you and why you're interested in the company and the industry. Don't get in over your head by trying to give the impression you know more than you do. Talk about why this position and career make sense given your talents and interests.

Q: **How do you benchmark the progress of a programmer who reports to you?**

A: *I look closely at how the programmer learns new methods of developing code and how quickly he or she is able to grasp and implement new concepts without my assistance.*

What are the keys to success in the development of a programmer? What standards do you impose on junior-level programmers to help them progress as systems analysts? You'll want to give the interviewer a well-thought-out program that measures a programmer's development, his or her learning curve, and the right time to encourage the programmer to go beyond past learning experiences and try new problem-solving techniques.

Q: **What percentage of your time is devoted to providing technical guidance to junior-level programmers?**

A: *I'd say about 10 to 15 percent. Because there's intense pressure to meet project deadlines, I try to limit the amount of time I spend with the junior level people. Most of them require little technical guidance, but they do need direction to meet deadlines and stay focused on the most important aspects of the project.*

How often do you take time out of your schedule to meet with junior-level employees to assist them in developing their programming skills? You should demonstrate how you manage to strike a balance between the demands of your own position and what you can contribute to the development of junior-level programmers. In that way you'll be illustrating your leadership ability as well as your willingness to share your knowledge and experience for the benefit of the company.

Q: **What's motivating you to seek a new position?**

A: *I've been in my present position for the past five years and, though I've progressed, I'm currently seeking to expand my technical knowledge along with my professional responsibilities.*

The interviewer will want to know why you're interested in his or her company and what you find so appealing about the job opening. Be candid, without

Career Changers: People trying to change careers by moving into a technical field have a long road to travel, but it can be done if you get the training you need and seek out opportunities to build your background and experience. Take any opportunity to work on a complex or challenging project no matter what your role. Discuss your relevant skills and accomplishments in such a way that any interviewer will want to listen to your story and give you serious consideration for the position.

discussing any negatives about your current position, and show enthusiasm for the challenges of working for the interviewing company, and how you hope to broaden your skills and background with this new position.

Q: Other than a lack of particularly challenging work, what are the other less desirable aspects of your present position?

A: *I'd like to explore new technologies and have the opportunity to build complex applications using the latest object-oriented tools.*

The interviewer may be trying to determine if the candidate is having problems with a supervisor or a coworker. Focus on what this new position offers and don't dwell on the past. You're not there to go in depth into what you dislike about your current position. Stay on track and zero in on what this new position offers you for the future.

Q: What do you like about your current position?

A: *I enjoy the opportunity to work on a technically challenging project and to assist younger programmers. The company has a good reputation and is a good place to work.*

You'll want to be able to assess realistically what appeals to you about your current situation, because you'll at least hope to replicate that in your new position. What you won't want to do is go on and on about how great your company is and how much you enjoy working there, as this will raise questions in the interviewer's mind about why you are talking to him or her.

Q: Let's move on to your tenure at Software National. I see that you were with the company for less than a year. Can you tell me what prompted you to leave so quickly?

A: *I worked for Software National, a small company, when I first got out of school. I wasn't all that happy there, but at the time I thought the problem was the company, not its size. I soon realized a small company was not for me because the technical capacity was too limiting. That's why I went to Brown Associates.*

Experienced Professionals: You should have plenty of examples of complex applications or systems that you've designed for a variety of clients and companies. Tap into that experience and show the interviewer how you can add value to his or her organization and that you're ready for the challenges that come with the position. Don't dwell on the age factor; use it to your advantage and show how you can influence younger programmers by sharing with them your experience and ideas on how to build dynamic systems.

The interviewer wants to find out why the candidate left the job so quickly, and if the same thing might happen in a new position. The candidate needs to convince the interviewer that the decision to leave was not a reflection of a desire to job hop or of restlessness with his or her career choice. Rather, it may have been a lack of experience or simple incompatibility with the job. The candidate wisely doesn't dwell on the subject but briefly states a reason, and would be wiser still to move on to a discussion of his or her interest in the open position.

Q: What is your present salary?

A: *My present salary is $55,000, not including benefits.*

You will do well not to dodge this question, as that will raise concerns with the interviewer that you may be out of his or her price range. Do your homework and research pay scales for similar positions at similar companies. Be honest and give only the salary figure; don't try to dress it up with additional compensation that isn't part of the base salary.

Q: What type of compensation are you looking for in your next position?

A: *I'm open. It will depend on the entire package as well as the position's growth opportunities. Could you tell me what the range is for this position?*

Try to turn a question like this around by asking for the salary range of the position if you don't already know. Do your homework and be prepared to give a realistic answer based on the size of the company, the industry, and the position you're applying for.

Candidates Re-entering the Workforce: You toughest challenge will be to convince the interviewer that you've remained current with technologies and systems that are being used today, and that you have a strong grasp of popular terminology and processes. Taking refresher courses, or courses on new techniques, systems analysis, and design and programming, will only help you in your quest to land a position. Be realistic in what you can accomplish for a company today, and convince the interviewer that you're a quick study and have the intelligence and technical acumen to get up to speed without slowing the company's or department's productivity.

Technical Support Specialist

Q: **Tell me about your most recent technical support experience.**

A: *At my last company we had eighteen specialists supporting three different products. It was a challenge to get up to speed on each product, but I thoroughly enjoyed helping customers resolve their problems and eagerly look forward to additional training on new products that we develop so I can continue to provide a high level of service.*

The interviewer will want to find out whether or not you're going to reveal anything negative that could affect her tech-support operation, for example, that you're not a good team player, you have problems sharing information, you don't communicate well with your peers, or you don't get along with the engineering staff. Obviously, your answer should be only positive. What kind of positive accomplishments you have created for yourself? What did you do that was really great that helped your company support its products? The recruiter is looking for someone who's a winner.

Q: **What was your most difficult support experience?**

A: *When I joined my last company, they were introducing a software product on a platform that I wasn't familiar with. It took longer than I expected to learn the product, and because of this I found it difficult to handle calls that were geared toward the product. But I found it to be a great learning experience, and I believe that being technically challenged like this only served to make me a better specialist.*

Be honest about something that did not go well. Not every support call is going to go 100 percent your way. There will be calls that aren't clear-cut and are difficult to handle, and the interviewer will want to know if you can handle them. What kind of personal skills did you use, what kind of actions did you take? What steps did you take to make a difficult situation manageable?

Q: **What are the three most important skills that a technical support specialist should possess?**

A: *I believe first and foremost that you have to love helping people solve their problems. If you don't enjoy listening to people in a crisis stage, you're not going to be a good support specialist. Second, I think you need patience to be able to get the customer to articulate a problem clearly so that you can make a good decision in helping that customer solve the problem. Finally, you have* *to be part salesperson in terms of selling the company and the product to the customer, because obviously the customer is distressed about some problem he or she is having with the product. So you want to make sure the customer leaves with a good feeling about the product and the company, believing that it was worthwhile to make a phone call to get support.*

The interviewer probably already has three skills in mind: people skills, analytical skills, and listening skills. He or she doesn't want to hear, "Oh, I just love people and I just love being on the phone," which are really requisites for the job, not skills. The interviewer wants to make sure that you have the skills to break down a problem and solve it.

Q: **Why do you think people with good communication skills fail as tech-support specialists?**

A: *Tech-support specialists have to be able to think through a problem logically and sequentially and understand a customer's pattern of thought. It's not just listening to a customer yell and scream about the fact that this product doesn't work right—you have to get behind that and be able to pull apart the problem piece by piece and then put it together to find the solution. That's a special skill that not everyone has, even if you're a good listener with good communication skills.*

The interviewer will want to find out if you understand all the elements necessary for being a good tech-support specialist. He or she wants to get beyond the obvious, to the core of what it means to be a good tech. You could also give an example of a time when someone with good communication skills failed to meet the needs of a customer.

Q: **Why do you think it's important for a company to have an in-house technical support department?**

A: *As a tech support specialist for my last company, I felt that not only was I helping the company by solving customers' problems, but I was learning at the same time a lot about the products and about the company. Therefore, I could*

First-time Job Seekers: Companies usually look for candidates with a computer-science or related degree, though some smaller companies like to see college graduates with a more general liberal arts background. Focus on the position. Don't worry about impressing with your academic credentials. Through your resume, the interviewer will already know that you have the technical skills necessary for the position, and is more interested in finding out about you as a person: do you have the communication skills, maturity, and patience to handle the job? You should show plenty of enthusiasm during the interview.

almost act as a quasi-sales rep in that I could really trumpet the strengths of the products and the benefits they could produce for the individual customer.

The interviewer will want to know if you understand the tech support function within the company. How valuable do you think you are within that company? Give examples of how tech support people help the company, and explain why you think the information that you get from customers is valuable to other people within the company.

Q: **What do you think is the most challenging product to support?**

A: *Probably the most difficult product that I've encountered is one that runs over a computer network, because you're dealing with different computers, different configurations, and different platforms. Not only do you have to work with your product and try to figure out anything that might be wrong with it, but then you have to get into the network configuration. But I also find this kind of technical challenge rewarding.*

You won't necessarily be responsible for knowing how a product works over a network, but if it's a networkable product specifically, you do have to be familiar with networks, and that's tough. The interviewer will also want to gauge how confident you are in your technical skills and intelligence, and your ability to solve problems. The more technical a problem you describe, the more of an impression you'll make. If you describe a problem that the interviewer thinks isn't that technically challenging, he or she may be reluctant to hire you, especially if the company has some highly technical problems to be solved.

Q: **At what point do you bring a customer's problem to your boss's attention?**

A: *I would make every attempt to resolve the problem over the phone with the customer, in the hopes that I could bring it to a satisfactory conclusion, but I do realize that a customer may be difficult or obstinate, or will simply refuse to accept what I'm trying to do to help. At that point I know there's a resolution in sight, but I still need to get my manager's assistance.*

The interviewer will want to see your skills in terms of judging the severity of problems, and whether or not you communicate with your supervisor.

Career Changers: After deciding which industry you'd like to be in (computer or financial-investor relations), you should be sure to learn as much as you can about the product or industry you'd like to support. You'll be competing with people within the industry, so you have to know the product better than anyone. Be sure you know all the relevant terms, buzzwords, and other industry-insider information.

The key is to show that you can accurately determine the severity of a problem. Give a few examples of times when you've made sound decisions about bringing problems to your boss's attention.

Q: **Have you ever been in a situation where you were unable to resolve a customer's support problem?**

A: *I do recall a time when a customer called in with a problem that was so unusual we hadn't run across it yet (and we do keep a running log of problems and issues). Rather than say "I give up" or "I don't know," I told the customer that I'd make a good faith attempt to resolve the problem, but I'd need to consult our engineers, and I'd get back to him within twenty-four hours.*

Here the customer went away feeling good even though the problem wasn't solved. The key is to be honest with the interviewer, but to try to find a case where you don't look totally incompetent. In this example, the candidate's being proactive even though he or she can't solve the problem right then and there.

Q: **Do you ever find yourself burning out from being on the phone so much?**

A: *I love being on the phone. I really enjoy talking to customers—listening to, and helping them solve, their problems. Phone work to me is very enjoyable and a great way to help a company support and sell its products.*

This is a classic tech support question: can you handle being on the phone for eight hours a day? You shouldn't hem and haw—just address the problem up front. Don't dodge it, even if you don't like being on the phone. Tell the interviewer you love being on the phone.

Q: **What are your goals beyond being tech support?**

A: *Actually, I really enjoy tech support and find it continually challenging. I'm truly dedicated to helping customers, and I love being on the phone. I really don't have any goals right now but to become the best tech support person I can.*

Experienced Professionals: If you're going for a management position in tech support, you'll have to showcase your people skills. Your technical competence will be assumed, so don't worry about that; the interviewer is going to want to know how you handle certain people situations. You'll be asked about some more strategic issues, like how tech support fits into the rest of the company. You should be able to show that you can see the big picture.

This question is asked to find out how dedicated a candidate will be on the job. There's generally a lot of turnover in the area of tech support, and it's very hard for companies to keep good people. They're reluctant to lose employees who are genuinely good on the phone, even if those employees are only trying to move to another department. You must show that you're truly dedicated to helping customers, and that you love being on the phone. Don't give job titles or mention other areas of the company. For instance, don't say, "I'd like to move into marketing in about six months." The interviewer wants to know that you're going to be completely focused on being a tech support specialist. If you mention any other job titles or departments to the interviewer, you'll be sending up a red flag that you'll leave at the first available opportunity.

Q: Do you feel comfortable sharing information with other specialists?

A: *Yes. At my last company I got a call from a customer who was having problems with a product that I'd just taken on, and that another rep still with the company had supported before I did. I wasn't totally familiar with the product at the time of the call, but I did know a little bit about what was going on. I helped the customer as best I could at that time and then went to the previous rep to get more information about how he would have handled the situation. He was extremely helpful, and the problem was easily resolved to the customer's satisfaction. Later I was able to return the favor and help the rep with a tech support problem that he had.*

The interviewer will want to see if you're a team player, but more important, if you're the type of individual who likes to have personal control over your product and customers. Does everything have to fall into your domain, or can you go to other support specialists and exchange ideas and information comfortably? Be sure to give a specific example of how you've shared information in the past.

Q: If you got a call that you knew you couldn't resolve within thirty seconds, what would you do?

Candidates Re-entering the Workforce: This used to be a lot tougher. Whether you returned to school for another degree, or took time off to spend a few years with your kids, be sure to be focused on what you want to do. You must convince employers that the time is right for you to return to work and that you're sincere. Show that you've thoroughly researched the company or industry. You must be able to prove that you've kept current with all technologies and trends in the industry.

A: *I'd be honest with the customer from the start if I knew that I couldn't support the problem. But I'd assure the caller that I'd make every effort to come up with an answer within twenty-four hours, and that if I couldn't, I'd refer the customer to an appropriate resource who could answer the question.*

The interviewer will want to know how you deal with a no-win situation. How do you turn this scenario into a positive? The interviewer will be looking for you to be creative and logical, and to come up with a good, solid, believable way to handle a common problem. The interviewer will also be testing you to see how well you think on your feet. Can you think and act quickly?

Q: How would you handle a verbally abusive customer?

A: *I'd remain calm and professional, and I'd never let my personal feelings get in the way of my job. I wouldn't respond to any abuse. I'd just make a note of it in my log, and I'd continue to help the customer as best I could. If the situation continued, I'd politely ask him or her to call back and ask for my manager, because at that point I probably couldn't resolve the customer's problem.*

The interviewer will want to find out what kind of personality you have and how you handle stress. Some people don't handle it well. Can you remain calm and professional and not lose control, even under such adverse circumstances? Reassure the interviewer that you can keep your cool.

Q: What do you find appealing about this position?

A: *What attracts me is that I know I'm able to solve customers' problems and help them become productive once again, and that I'm supporting my company and its products and services.*

The interviewer will be interested in finding out precisely why you want to be in tech support. He or she won't be looking for a canned, puffed-up answer. You should stress what makes you better than the rest of the candidates and prove that your interest in this career is sincere. Explain why you genuinely feel that the position is a good fit for you.

CHAPTER 13

EDUCATION

Elementary School Teacher

Q: **Tell me about any previous experience you've had with children.**

A: *I was head counselor at a sleep-away camp for five years, where I was in charge of campers ranging from five to thirteen years of age. I also spent two semesters student teaching at a local elementary school.*

Expect this question if you're an entry-level candidate. The interviewer is looking for experience of direct involvement with children, preferably in a leadership role—perhaps as a counselor at a summer camp, a student teacher or even a teacher's aide. If you're an experienced candidate and you're asked this question, talk about some of the highlights of your career, such as your most rewarding experience or most difficult challenge.

Q: **What has your involvement been with other teachers or counselors?**

A: *In my present position my colleagues and I meet once a week to discuss how our classes are progressing. Teachers from the same grade level usually exchange lesson plans to generate new ideas and a fresh perspective on the curriculum. And if I have any special-needs children in my classroom, I meet with school counselors so that we can discuss the child's developmental progress.*

The interviewer is looking for collegiality; many teachers have experience with children but have little experience working with other teachers. Your answer should show that you've shared ideas and materials with other teachers; try to provide examples of positive interactions with your colleagues. This question also addresses your interpersonal skills; interviewers want to see that you get along well with parents, administration, and colleagues.

Q: **Describe the reading program you'd use with your grade.**

A: *I'd use a balance of whole language and phonics-based programs. With the phonics-based program I could ensure that the class was learning specific reading skills, such as verb endings, plurals, prefixes, and consonant blends. For the whole-language aspect I'd use a combination of choral reading, charts, age-appropriate literature (like fairy tales or folktales), and trade books for the* *different units we covered. For instance, the class would read biographies and books about animals, science, or social studies. I also believe in using heterogeneous reading groups—which include all skill levels—instead of grouping according to reading levels.*

This question is designed to determine whether or not you've a grasp on the concepts appropriate for a specific grade level. This is an excellent response because the candidate shows an understanding of the latest developments in education and teaching. Naturally, your answer should be tailored to whatever grade you plan to teach (this answer is geared toward someone applying to teach third-grade students). You might also want to mention specific titles of literature or trade books that you'd use.

Q: How do you incorporate writing into your curriculum?

A: *I believe in teaching writing skills in all areas of the curriculum, not just English. For example, in science students can develop observational skills simply by writing down what they see; in math I'll ask questions like "What does multiplication mean to you?" and have students write down answers in math journals. In literature I ask students to keep a dialogue journal; after they finish a chapter in a book, I'll give them a question and then ask them to respond in writing to it. I also like my students to do free writing, where they can write about anything they'd like—their favorite sports team, what they did that weekend, or even fiction if they're so inclined. I believe that writing is the most effective way for a teacher to assess a child's spelling and grammar skills.*

Again, this question examines the candidate's approach to the standard curriculum. The interviewer will want to see if you can think of creative ways to incorporate a subject into the classroom. Many teachers delegate writing to a lesson that's taught once or twice a week, forgetting that writing skills can be developed in the context of any subject. The candidate's answer demonstrates an ability to go beyond traditional thinking to find ways of enriching the curriculum.

Q: What do you think should be included in the math programs for this grade level?

A: *Although I do feel that drill has its place, I believe in using real-world examples in lessons. For this age level I like to use manipulative, hands-on materials, such as cubes and blocks to teach counting and sorting, coins to teach money knowledge, and dice for addition or multiplication. I also like to ask children open-ended questions that they can respond to in their math journals, so that they can learn critical-thinking skills.*

The standard math program will already be established for the grade level for which you're applying. Even so, the interviewer wants to determine if you know the skills that should be mastered and introduced at this particular level. Like this candidate's answer, yours should tell how you'll go beyond the traditional curriculum to develop the skills of your students.

Q: How would you teach multiculturalism in your classroom?

A: *I'd make sure that respect was shown for human diversity, and that each child understood that he or she is a unique individual. In fact, I'd celebrate those differences. In my classroom I like to display pictures of people from different cultures working in a variety of occupations. I also provide books that reflect a wide variety of countries and cultures. Finally, we have activities throughout the school year that expose the children to different cultures and traditions. If I had Japanese children in my class, for instance, I'd organize a project, like making paper cranes, that related to their culture. I also like to invite parents in to give a presentation on a holiday or cultural event that's celebrated in their family.*

Teaching diversity is essential in today's classroom. Be sure to discuss how you'd teach children to be tolerant of those who are different from them. The interviewer wants to hear specific examples of how you'd incorporate a variety of cultures into your classroom. Describe how you'd celebrate multiculturalism in your curriculum.

Q: Today, classrooms have become much more diverse, with the inclusion of special-needs children, children from different socioeconomic backgrounds, and children from different cultures in the same classroom. How do you expect to meet the needs of all the students in your class?

A: *I'd adapt the curriculum to meet the particular needs of each student. For example, say I had one student who was having an exceptionally difficult time with spelling. If I gave the class a list of twenty-five words to learn for a spelling test, I might give this particular student a list with only ten words. Then, after he or she had mastered those ten words, I'd add another five, and so on. I always try to look for success rather than failure. If I have children with disabilities in my class, I'll be an active participant in all multidisciplinary meetings, working with the specialists to design an individual program for each child. I try*

First-time Job Seekers: Before you can begin interviewing for a teaching position, you'll need at least a bachelor's degree and state certification. Some districts may even require a master's degree, usually in elementary education, so be sure to do your research. You'll also need at least a semester of experience as a student teacher. Come prepared to discuss and additional involvement you've had with children—even any baby-sitting experience you may have—and why you want to get into teaching.

to include parents as much as possible, offering additional conference hours if necessary, and if a parent can't come in because of work or other obligations, I make phone calls to keep that parent in touch with his or her child's development. And as I said before, I always try to integrate a variety of cultures into the classroom environment.

Teachers are expected to have a classroom environment where no child feels excluded. Fewer special schools exist than in the past, and children of all ability levels must coexist in the same classroom. Many times you'll have a third-grader with the reading ability of a high-school senior sitting next to a third-grader who's still reading at a kindergarten level. The interviewer will want to hear specific examples of how you'll work with each student to ensure that his or her particular needs will be met. Make a point of discussing your experience with the various specialists involved in a child's education, such as school psychologists, counselors, or special-needs educators.

Q: **If I walked into your classroom, what would it look like?**

A: *I like to have a classroom that's alive with color and the personality of the children. I'll have student work displayed on bulletin boards throughout the room, with all children represented. I also divide my room into distinct areas—clusters of desks or tables so that the children can interact when they're working; an open, carpeted area for group meetings, where children sit for show-and-tell or storytelling; learning centers dedicated to particular areas, like science, math, computers, art, writing, or social studies; a reading center with comfortable chairs or beanbags so that the children can curl up with a good book. I also like each child to have his or her own mailbox for picking up corrected work, letters, and so on.*

Most elementary-school principals like to see a floor plan that shows specific, clear areas of a classroom. Your response should show spatial awareness, organizational skills, and attention to detail. Obviously, your classroom will reflect your own personal teaching style, and this question will be asked in part to determine your compatibility with the school. Although there's no right or wrong answer, different districts can sometimes favor one teaching style over another, so try to do some research before your interview. Remember to bring along some pictures of your old classroom, so that the interviewer can actually see how well you apply your ideas.

Career Changers: Naturally, you'll need to become state certified and acquire a semester or two of student teaching. If you're coming from a field such as day care, discuss your desire for a greater challenge. Be sure to emphasize the strengths you'll bring to the position—a love for children and an ability to get along well with parents.

Q: What computer experience have you had, and how will you integrate computers into your classroom?

A: *Well, I have experience with both PC and Macintosh computers. I have a PC at home, and I've used Macintosh computers at school for years. I like to have my students use computers in their writing workshops. I'll have them type their stories, print them out, and then put the stories together to make a class book. My students have also used the Internet to e-mail "pen pals" from other states or countries. In the future I'd like to see my class go online for discussions with other classes, and maybe even do a project with other classrooms via the Internet.*

Computers are now an integral part of the classroom, so computer literacy is almost a prerequisite for teachers. Most schools use Macintosh computers, so it's helpful to have experience with those. The Internet is especially popular in today's classrooms, so you'll want to come prepared with a few examples of how you'd use these services in your teaching. You can also mention using computers for curriculum-based games, such as science, social studies, or geography.

Q: Have you had experience leading parent conferences?

A: *Yes. At my current school we have parent-teacher conferences twice a year.*

The interviewer will want to determine your level of experience with parents. If you don't have experience leading these kinds of conferences, you can talk about your experience observing them when you were a student teacher or a teacher's aide. A detailed answer isn't necessary, but it should show that you're comfortable speaking and interacting with parents.

Q: How would you tell a parent about a negative situation involving their child?

A: *As a parent myself, I understand how hard it is to hear that your child's having problems, whether those problems are behavioral or skill related. When I talk to a parent, I start by discussing the child's strengths and then state where the area of concern lies. I'm always sure to give detailed and dated examples of what the problems are and when they began. I then ask the parent to set*

Experienced Professionals: In your interview emphasize your need for personal growth. Discuss how you feel this change will help you to improve your weakest areas, while your strengths will add much to the department. Be sure to tell the interviewer about specific skills or talents—perhaps you're multilingual or a computer wiz. But, most important, talk about your passion for teaching, and give examples of positive contributions you've made to your current school.

goals with me to help the child develop in that particular area. I believe it's important to do this with the parent, and to share the responsibility of designing a plan for the child. Once we've established goals and how we'll try to meet those goals, I schedule a meeting for a later date when we can discuss the child's progress.

How you handle relationships with your students' parents is one of the most important aspects of teaching, and this question addresses perhaps the most difficult part of such relationships. In general parents don't like to hear negative information about their children, so it's important that you also discuss a child's strengths with the parents during your meeting. Like this candidate, you should give a clear and detailed indication of what you would say to the student's parents.

Q: **With all the materials being covered in today's classroom, how do you plan to gather information for assessments?**

A: *I like to keep a portfolio of my students' work so that I can easily measure progress when report-card time comes around. I also find that I'm better prepared for parent conferences. I let the student help decide what work goes into the portfolio. Then, at the end of the year, I pass the students' portfolios along to next year's teacher so that he or she can see how the child progressed through the year.*

This question addresses the candidate's organizational skills when it comes to assessments. With many classes having as many as thirty students, it's important to have a system that will allow you to keep a careful watch on the progress of each student. Like this candidate, you should give a detailed response as to how you'll chart the development of your students. Another good system is to keep a notebook on each child, in which you can write about the child's development, accomplishments, or problems.

Q: **How do you handle discipline in your class?**

A: *I establish ground rules right from the start, so the children will immediately know what kind of behavior I expect from them. On the first day of school I read them a list of expectations, such as speaking in turn and raising one's hand. I then post them around the room, along with corresponding pictures and drawings. I try to teach respect for self, others, and belongings. But I always hold the students accountable for their actions so that they learn the concept of responsibility.*

When a problem occurs, I talk to that student or, if there's more than one child involved, I talk to both of them and let each one tell his or her side of the story. I provide active listening, by restating where each of the children thinks the problem lies. Next, I ask the children how they think the problem can be solved, and how a compromise can be reached in order to bring about a win-win situation. Naturally, I offer suggestions if the children can't figure out the solution for themselves. Finally, I ask the children how they'll handle the situation next time if it happens again. But if a situation can't be resolved, or if I notice a pattern of behavior, I consult the appropriate specialists.

The interviewer is looking for the candidate's ability to set limits and to lead a group in a responsible way. Give a detailed description of the steps you'd take if a problem occurred. It's important that teachers instill responsibility in their students; it's not enough for you to say, "Stop that because I say so." You can also describe other disciplinary techniques you'd use, such as "time-out" chairs.

Q: **How do you go about planning and developing units or lessons for your students?**

A: *Before the start of the school year I'll look at the expectations and requirements for each of the subject areas. Then I'll decide which month each unit will be introduced and how long each unit will last—six lessons, twelve lessons, or two or three months. Then I start developing the unit about a month in advance, gathering all the necessary materials, like books, pictures, and so on. Then I write up all of my lessons for each unit, taking care to provide extension materials to supplement each unit, so that there's always enough material available for those students who finish early and want an additional challenge.*

A teacher is always told what to cover; it's up to him or her to figure out how to fit all the material into that year. Again, the interviewer is trying to gauge the candidate's organization and planning skills. Be sure to discuss in detail how you plan for the school year. It's also a good idea to mention how you would determine your assessment procedures—how you'll measure the progress of your students.

Q: **In what areas of teaching would you like to improve?**

A: *Like everyone, I could probably learn to be a little more patient. But I'd say my greatest weakness is the fact that I've never worked in a multicultural environment. The community where I'm teaching now is fairly homogeneous, and I think a more diverse group of students and teachers would give me the challenge I need to grow as a teacher.*

Candidates Re-entering the Workforce: It's important for you to discuss the skills you've developed or gained during your absence. If you were out because of an injury, perhaps you've learned to be a little more patient. If you were raising a family, tell the interviewer how you can now better identify with the concerns of parents. The educational system is rapidly changing, so demonstrate that your skills, especially computer skills, are up to date.

This is a fairly straightforward question that asks the candidate to do a little bit of self-reflection. Like this candidate's answer, your answer should be thoughtful and honest. You could also mention specific subject areas—such as science or history—that you'd like to work on.

Q: Why should we hire you?

A: *I'm dedicated to working with children and watching them grow and develop. I spent a year abroad in Spain, so I'm fluent in Spanish. Also, I can play the guitar, and I like using my music in teaching; the students always seem to enjoy it. Finally, I think I have a pretty good sense of humor, and that's always helped me establish a fun relationship with my class.*

Competition for teaching positions is often keen. The interviewer will be looking for your strengths—characteristics that will set you apart from the rest of the candidates. What exactly those traits are will vary depending on the school and what the school wants, but virtually every school values teachers who have a high level of enthusiasm and dedication. Interviewers also like to hear that you've an excellent attendance record. And if you've a unique talent, like this candidate, be sure to mention it—interviewers want to hear about any special skills you could bring to their school.

Guidance Counselor
(High School)

Q: What do you see as your role as guidance counselor at the high-school level?

A: *A guidance counselor is a professional educator with a broad background of graduate-level training who attends to the needs of students' personal, social, and emotional problems, and at the same time develops a career plan to ensure that each student becomes a successful member of society.*

The employer wants to know which philosophical values the candidate attributes to the role of guidance counselor. A counselor should be a student advocate and yet ensure that school policies are followed so that issues can be resolved to the betterment of students, parents, teachers, and the school administration. Guidance-counselor candidates shouldn't give the impression that they're student advocates with little regard for established school policies.

Q: What strengths could you bring to the role of guidance counselor?

A: *I'd say that I'm a self-starter with expertise in helping students make the transition from school to the workforce. I also have a great deal of experience in the college-entrance process and have many local college and career contacts that I could use to benefit the students at this school directly. I don't think of my career as "just another job," and I try to be sensitive to the needs of all students.*

Your answer here should reflect not only your qualifications, but your eagerness and enthusiasm for the position. Portray yourself as someone who'd become an indispensable member of the school staff. Discuss how your strengths could specifically benefit the school and the community.

Q: What do you consider your major weakness?

A: *I have a tendency to take on too many projects and often find that I must work hours beyond the normal workday to help all the students I possibly can.*

Whatever your answer may be here, be sure to give it a positive spin. This answer, for example, cites a weakness that most interviewers will consider attractive in a job candidate. Answers that could seriously hurt your candidacy might indicate that you're not really interested in the position, that you have no experience or contact with the local community, or that you have a negative attitude that could easily be identified by the students you'd be counseling.

Q: **A student comes into your office. The teacher's note states that the student was being disruptive in class. The student says the teacher is prejudiced and hates him. How would you deal with the situation?**

A: *I'd explain to the student that I'd discuss the situation with the teacher and call the student to my office later in the day.*

This is an explosive issue and is best put off until you speak to the teacher involved, and to the student later. Getting into a lengthy discussion about a particular teacher's conduct will lead ultimately to the faculty's complete distrust of the guidance department. Once this happens, the counselor loses all creditability and becomes a tool for students to use when they have disagreements with a teacher.

Q: **What do you consider to be the role of parents in the school, and how would you involve them? Also, how would you promote their involvement at school?**

A: *Parents are our second-most-important constituency—the first, of course, being students. Parents should be highly involved in all aspects of the school. They can be a great ally of guidance counselors, particularly in budget meetings, where we can use all the advocacy we can get. Parental involvement can be encouraged by sending a monthly newsletter to parents, and by conducting evening meetings on specific topics, such as financial aid for college.*

Your answer here should indicate that you recognize the importance of strong parental involvement in your role as guidance counselor. In addition, you should be sensitive to parent concerns in the community and be able to address them.

Q: **What computer skills do you have regarding automated student attendance, warning notices, and report cards?**

First-time Job Seekers: A career path that has proved successful is to teach school first, getting a feel for the students, teachers, administration, and school policy. Then get the required state and local certification and volunteer to assist in the guidance office during your free classes to gain some experience that supplements your education and certification. At that point you'll be ready to start applying for guidance positions.

A: *I'm familiar with computers and can easily adapt to the specific programs needed to address the administrative need of students.*

Discuss the various types of computers, their programs, and, more important, the educational and career-oriented software you've used. You may also mention which software you'd recommend for both college and career guidance, further demonstrating your knowledge and expertise in serving the counseling needs of students.

Q: **The duties of this position include all data processing, record management, automated student attendance, and supervision of one grade level. How would you incorporate the latter component of supervision in your job description?**

A: *I'd expect the school administration to hold me accountable for these matters, if it's school policy. I'd institute measures to ensure that my office has complete control of these items.*

The interviewer will want to know what you believe your role is in a high school. Many counselors think that administrative tasks aren't in their domain. You should be prepared to discuss your feelings about the idea of teamwork in the total school environment.

Q: **Do you feel confident that you'd be able to handle this wide variety of responsibilities?**

A: *Yes. I'm used to ever-increasing responsibilities, having been in education for many years. I've always accepted, and in many cases sought out, duties that will make me better equipped to assist my students.*

This is your chance to showcase all your positive attributes in the managerial area, and your expertise and experience in education. Describe in detail the significant managerial experiences you've had. Don't indicate that you have no managerial experience—everyone has some such experience, whether it involves managing people, projects, or simply large volumes of work.

Career Changers: Many guidance counselors start out as teachers. If that's the case with you, you'll need to get the required state and local certification. You should also volunteer to assist in the guidance office during your free classes to gain some experience and further demonstrate your interest in the field. This approach will give you the education, certification, experience, and track record necessary to become a viable candidate for a counseling position.

Q: **How do the needs of the high-school student differ from those of the elementary- or middle-school student?**

A: *High-school students are, of course, older and starting to realize that at the end of high school they must make decisions that will affect their lives. There is a much more serious side to their behavior and thinking. They're entering the adult world and should be treated in that manner.*

As a high-school counselor, you need to be aware that you're dealing with adults and not with young children. The interviewer wants to be sure that your thinking and demeanor are appropriate to that level.

Q: **What do you perceive as your strengths in regard to working with racially, culturally, and ethnically diverse urban youngsters?**

A: *I was raised in a city environment and went to both a high school and a college that had diverse student populations. I've had further contact and experience in this area through my work with community agencies, which is detailed on my resume.*

The interviewer wants assurance that the candidate will be an appropriate addition to the school and to the local community. Ideally, your answer will relate to your prior experience and training. If you have no experience with diverse student populations, you should draw on your own background or discuss your own feelings about working with a diverse student body.

Q: **Do you feel that community and other external agencies should have a role in complementing what our school system has to offer?**

A: *Yes. Community and external-agency assistance can be a vital resource for developing programs for our youth and assisting our school system. It's obvious that the caseload for counselors in high schools is so high, we can use all the help we can get. In addition, the variety of expertise offered by community and external agencies is a resource that can greatly benefit our students.*

Urban areas have a vast array of social and educational agencies that can assist schools. You should be prepared to discuss your knowledge of external resources in that community. If you're not familiar with the school's local community, be sure to do the appropriate research before your job interview.

Experienced Professionals: Make sure you do research in the demographics of the particular community in which you're applying, as well as of the schools. This will not only prepare you for the specific questions you'll be asked but will further demonstrate your interest in the position.

You shouldn't say that you won't be open to accepting outside assistance, because the interviewer may conclude that you don't want to make the effort necessary to seek out and coordinate such assistance. A negative response may also indicate an egotistical personality and an unwillingness to work as a team player.

Q: **How would you go about tapping into these community and other external resources?**

A: *As a resident of this community, I'd seek out the appropriate resources through local contacts. If not a resident, I'd conduct research in the community to develop a local-resources directory.*

Discuss your knowledge of external resources in the community. If you already have contacts that may be useful, be sure to mention them. You should assure the interviewer of your ability to take the initiative to develop new resources and to coordinate services once those resources are developed.

Q: **How do you see counseling conducted in schools today, in terms of group or individual approaches? Who would be involved?**

A: *Certain areas of counseling can be better accomplished in group settings, such as filling out college board applications. In other instances individual counseling may be needed—for example, when there's a personal issue the student wishes to discuss.*

Not all counselors have the expertise necessary to conduct group sessions with students, and many have a tendency to avoid conducting them. The interviewer is trying to bring forth the candidate's own experience and preferences in this regard. If you have any special training or expertise in conducting group sessions, be sure to mention it.

Q: **"Parents as partners" is a concept we like to nurture in our school system. How do you propose to maintain communication and involve the parents on a regular basis?**

Candidates Re-entering the Workforce: Aside from discussing your previous professional experience and qualifications, you'll need to show the interviewer how you've stayed current in the field, perhaps through activity in professional organizations such as the American Association of School Counselors, the American Counseling Association, or your state school counselors' association. You should also emphasize your up-to-date computer skills and knowledge of the latest educational and career-oriented software.

A: *I like to send parents a monthly newsletter containing general information about report cards, financial aid, and college-entrance procedures. In that newsletter I also encourage all parents to seek out the service of their child's guidance counselor. I've found that this helps parents to think of me as a conduit to school services for their student.*

The interviewer will want to hear specific examples of innovative measures you've used on the job to foster school-parent communication. Another good answer might be, "In my last position I sent birthday cards to all my students and invited each student and his or her parents to my office for an informal meeting on the student's birthday."

Q: How would you reach out to students and parents in the bilingual and special education communities?

A: *I consider all students equal and would include bilingual and special-education students and their parents in all guidance activities. I wouldn't treat them differently from others, as this would only lead to a sense of being singled out.*

The interviewer wants to be assured that the candidate is sensitive to the needs of bilingual and special education students and their parents. Familiarize yourself with state and local regulations regarding bilingual and special education in the community. You should also be prepared to answer a potential follow-up question like, "What do you think is the appropriate amount of time for a student to become mainstreamed in either a bilingual or special education setting?"

Q: What's your responsibility to the school staff in terms of evaluating and developing educational or remedial strategies for students at risk? What's the staff's responsibility to you?

A: *As a guidance counselor, I consider myself the student's advocate. I must work with the school staff to ensure that the student is able to perform in school at an appropriate level. Students who are considered "at risk" must be counseled individually to determine the reason for their nonperformance. This can be accomplished by having students produce a daily note for teachers discussing inappropriate behavior.*

Counselors will spend most of their time counseling "at risk" students. Each case is unique and thus requires all the counselor's skills to ensure that every student enjoys school and becomes a productive member of the school and the community.

Librarian

Q: Why did you become a librarian?

A: *I became a librarian for several reasons. First, I enjoy doing research and gathering information. I get a sense of satisfaction from finally finding the answer to a difficult question. And I like doing different tasks every day—no two searches are ever alike. Finally, I used to be a teacher, and I decided that working as a librarian would allow me to do what I like best about being a teacher—help people. I believe being a librarian is an important, worthwhile career.*

The interviewer is trying to determine if the candidate is genuinely interested in a career or is just looking for another job to pay the bills. There's no right or wrong answer to this question, but your response, like this candidate's, should be thoughtful and honest. You shouldn't say something generic like "I just love being around books." Your answer should also demonstrate an accurate understanding of what being a librarian is all about.

Q: What are your ultimate career goals?

A: *Eventually I'd like to become a supervisor or manager. This would enable me to have more input into management issues such as acquisitions or budgeting, while maintaining contact with the public by working at the reference desk.*

The interviewer will want to see if you're committed to a career in library science. This is a good answer because it shows that the candidate not only is interested in advancement, but also has an interest in the everyday workings of the library.

Q: What are three issues that will influence librarianship in the next ten years?

A: *I believe the issue of funding will probably have the biggest impact, particularly on public libraries. In recent years budgets for public libraries have been slashed dramatically, and this has already taken a tremendous toll in terms of staff size and the services offered by libraries. If communities want to maintain the quality of their public libraries, I think they'll have to re-examine their priorities. The issue of intellectual freedom is also important. There's such pressure to be "politically correct" that it's often difficult to maintain a balanced collection that represents many different points of view, as someone is always bound to get offended. Finally, I think the issue of print versus electronic information will impact libraries in several ways. First, in terms of funding—how will libraries pay* *for new workstations? Libraries must decide what information should be kept online and what should be kept in print—magazines, newspapers, and books. Also, how does a library regulate online services? I think all these issues are interrelated, and that they'll all have significant impact on libraries now and for years to come.*

These are three important issues in library science, according to professional journals and field experience. This response is effective because it shows not only that the candidate is keeping up with developments in the field, but that he or she has actually put some thought into these issues.

Q: **What are the advantages and disadvantages of electronic media?**

A: *I'd say that the biggest advantage of electronic information is the fact that patrons can get the information they're looking for so quickly and easily. With the right system they can gain access to hundreds of sources and materials that they wouldn't normally have access to. But the biggest disadvantage is cost. These computers and workstations are very expensive, and these days when libraries are fighting for almost every dollar, the management is forced to make some difficult decisions.*

This is a tough question that forces the candidate to examine one of the most difficult issues facing librarianship today. Your answer should be thorough and should reflect a solid understanding of the issues. Demonstrate to the interviewer that you keep up with industry wide developments and pay attention to the larger issues confronting your own library.

Q: **If you were to help prepare purchasing guidelines for library materials, what would you include?**

First-time Job Seekers: Most librarians need and M.L.S. (master's degree in library science) from an ALA-accredited school. Most states require that school media specialists, or school librarians, have their teacher's certification as well. Specialized librarians, have their teacher's certification as well. Specialized librarians, such as archivists, medical librarians, or law librarians, also have a specific course of study within their M.L.S. classes. Employers like to see some practical library experience—for instance, have been an aide in a public library or an assistant in college. You also need good computer skills because many searches are conducted online now. Also, many libraries look for candidates who are proficient in a foreign language. This was once required only for academic or other specialized librarians, but now it's a must for almost everyone.

A: *I'd include the American Library Association's (ALA) "Intellectual Freedom" statement and the materials recommended by those who have ultimate responsibility for materials selection. I'd also provide a means for patrons to question purchases and define selection parameters.*

Intellectual freedom is an important issue these days. It's essential for a collection to be balanced, presenting many points of view, including liberal, conservative, and moderate. It's also important to have well-written guidelines—they may help to defuse a potentially explosive problem. Your response should show an awareness of the intellectual freedom issue and a sensitivity to patrons' rights.

Q: **Would you advocate allowing videos to be borrowed with no age restrictions? Why or why not?**

A: *I favor the restrictions used by many libraries—that is, requiring borrowers to be at least eighteen years old. Intellectual-freedom issues aside, this age requirement is practical, if only from a financial standpoint. Quite simply, videotapes are expensive! It's difficult at times to collect fines, and with the eighteen-year-old-age requirement, the library may have a better chance of recovering money for replacement.*

Age requirements at libraries are a potentially volatile issue, and many librarians believe they're a clear violation of intellectual freedom. Here the candidate effectively discusses the issue from a practical standpoint that virtually everyone can agree with.

Q: **Tell me about your experience supervising library workers.**

A: *Throughout my career I've been responsible for training and supervising library aides to shelve books, and to retrieve books from the storage stacks. As part of my young-adult-collection management duties in my current position, I supervise the aide who works for both the YA and reference areas.*

In most libraries a midlevel librarian will have some supervisory responsibilities. The interviewer simply wants to see that the candidate has some experience in this area. If you don't have any experience supervising others, you

Career Changers: It's very common these days to see people entering librarianship as a second, or even third, career. Depending on your previous career, you'll need either to take some courses in library science, or to go back to school to earn a master's degree in library science. If you were a teacher and want to work in a school library, you'll probably need to take only a few classes, but if you want to work in a public library system, you'll more than likely need your master's.

can say something like, "I haven't really had the chance to do any supervising, but I'm looking forward to the challenge."

Q: **What do you think are the most important aspects of supervision?**

A: *I believe it's important to establish a good working relationship with employees, and to treat all employees fairly and equally. It's important to treat people with respect—the way you'd want to be treated. I make a point to give praise when it's due, but at the same time, I'm not afraid to reprimand a worker when his or her work is unsatisfactory.*

The interviewer is trying to get a sense of the candidate's management style. This answer shows that the candidate is comfortable in the role of supervisor but, at the same time, knows when to use discipline.

Q: **Tell me about a management issue you recently faced. How did you handle it?**

A: *In my current position I recently discovered that one of my aides was answering reference inquiries instead of only directional inquires. First, I praised what the person was doing well. Then I explained the difference between reference and directional queries (which is normally a part of training). Finally, I suggested some appropriate responses for the aide to use when asked reference questions in the future.*

The interviewer wants to see how the candidate would approach a specific management issue. The answer here is effective because it's a specific example of how the candidate has successfully resolved a management issue, and it gives the interviewer a clear sense of the candidate's management style.

Q: **Describe one of your most significant contributions to the library.**

A: *I established an after-school storytelling program in our children's area. After reading an item in the local paper about how many children go home to an empty house and watch television every day after school, I decided to see what I could do about getting an activity started at the library. In the three years*

Experienced Professionals: If you want to work for a large university library or a big-city public library, as in New York or Boston, you may want to get your Ph.D. in library and information science. This is also true if you want to go into teaching at the college level or into a high administrative position at a large library. Even without a Ph.D. you can become the head of a department or, in smaller library systems, library director.

it's been running, it's become quite popular and has been written up several times in the local paper. Our library regularly gets letters of thanks from parents, so it's been gratifying to see an idea grow into something that's had a real impact.

The interviewer wants to see what the candidate's done for the library, beyond what his or her job description calls for. Again, there's no single right answer to this question, but you should demonstrate that you can think creatively and take initiative. You should also talk about any systems you may have implemented, such as reorganizing a collection, or an area, within the library.

Q: What would you do if another librarian at the reference desk gave a patron information that you knew was incorrect or incomplete?

A: *Well, that would depend on who the staff member was. Some people don't mind if you correct them in front of a patron, but others do. So, depending on the situation, I'd either just volunteer the correct information there on the spot, or wait until the patron was away from the desk to give him or her the information. I'd later share the same information with the librarian, saying something like, "I found this source extremely helpful in a similar situation."*

This is an important issue, since you don't want a patron walking away with incomplete or erroneous information. The candidate here shows a sensitivity and understanding of the other librarian's point of view, while at the same time making it clear that he or she would give the patron the correct information.

Q: Do you believe it's important to join and work with local community groups?

A: *Yes. I believe that community involvement helps to build good public relations for the library, and to develop local contacts who can contribute to the library both financially and culturally. When you get out into the community, you can help people understand the importance to everyone of a strong local library. Also, community involvement is an excellent way to learn about your city or town from the viewpoint of community leaders.*

Candidates Re-entering the Workforce: Show how you've kept in touch with the field, either by maintaining your membership in a local or regional library association, or by reading professional journals. It's best to keep in some contact with the field through volunteering or through memberships in a "library friends" group. Also, you'll need to give evidence that you've kept your computer skills up-to-date, as so much of what librarians do today is online.

This is an excellent response that shows the candidate's understanding of how important it is, from a public-relations standpoint, for the library to have a good relationship with its community. The community can be of enormous help to a library—either through donations and volunteers, or as a source of local cultural materials.

Q: **What are some of your strengths and weaknesses as a librarian?**

A: *I'm good at conducting reference interviews. I can help people target what they actually need. If my library doesn't have the desired information, I try my best to find an outside source; this includes asking my colleagues for assistance if I can't find an answer. Also, my supervisors have told me that I work well with "problem" patrons. One of my weaknesses is getting too involved in a search and giving a patron more than he or she actually needs.*

This question enables an interviewer to gauge the candidate's estimation of his or her skills. The answer here is effective because the "reference interview," in which the librarian speaks with a patron to determine what information is being sought, is one of the most important aspects of working at a public library. Similarly, it's important that public librarians can handle "problem" or unruly patrons in a calm and pleasant manner, without disturbing other patrons.

Q: **What skills would you most like to improve, and why?**

A: *Well, I think I have to do a better job at prioritizing, so that my most important tasks are completed first. My previous supervisors have said I should work on my ability to say no and learn how to delegate responsibilities more. I'm learning how to stop taking on more than can be reasonably accomplished, and how to stop working on tasks that another person should be doing or could do more efficiently.*

No one's perfect. Knowing your strengths and using them to your employer's advantage benefits everyone. Likewise, knowing your weaknesses and how to overcome them is important for growing, and for improving your job performance. The key to answering this question is to discuss not only your area of weakness, but how you've managed to overcome it.

School Psychologist

Q: **What are your highest priorities as a school psychologist?**

A: *My highest priority is ensuring a student's individual growth. To accomplish this, a school psychologist must fill a number of roles—providing consultation so that specialists can work as a team to meet the needs of students, helping the classroom teacher create an appropriate environment for each student, and working with each child's family to learn about any issues that might affect his or her behavior and development.*

This question helps the interviewer determine how the candidate will fit in with the district. The answer will provide the interviewer with insight into the candidate's professional philosophy. Like this candidate's answer, yours should be well thought out and reflect an understanding of a school psychologist's role in serving the student and the school.

Q: **What positive personal attributes would you bring to this position?**

A: *I've had eight years of experience at other urban sites, so I'm familiar with the various issues that impact urban students. I also have a multicultural background that includes working with a multicultural staff and student population.*

This is a perfect opportunity to sell yourself as the top contender for the job. Tell the interviewer what distinguishes you from the rest of the candidates. Why should the interviewer hire you? There is no single right answer to this question; other acceptable responses might cite general professional traits, like reliability or being a team player. Keep in mind that your response should include traits that would fit in well with that particular school system.

Q: **How would you involve parents in the education of their children?**

A: *I'd involve parents in the assessment process by asking them to provide information on their child's developmental history, and by finding out what their concerns and goals are for their child. I also like to get them involved in intervention teams and problem solving. I want their input when I'm developing and enforcing joint motivational systems. Finally, I make a point of providing parents with the names of advocacy groups that could give them support, and asking them to join in counseling sessions when appropriate.*

School districts want parents involved in their child's education, and in many circumstances it's required by law. The interviewer wants to see not only that you're comfortable interacting with parents, but that you know the proper times to consult them or include them in your counseling sessions. Your answer to this question should reflect an understanding of the importance of parents' involvement in developing an appropriate program for their child.

Q: **Select a curriculum, or an IEP (individual education plan) goal, for counseling as a related service, and tell me how you'd set up, implement, and evaluate the program.**

A: *Well, say I was working with a child who was having a hard time identifying the feelings of others. After I obtained feedback from the child's parents and teachers, I'd design a program based on the student's learning style. If this style was a visual learning one, I'd present the child with a series of pictures, each showing different facial expressions, and we'd identify those that the student knew or didn't know. Together, we would name those expressions, then go on to role-playing, and eventually move to real-life situations. This would be done through a series of group or individual meetings, depending on the particular child's needs. I evaluate this type of program based on the student's ability to identify the pictures instantly, then the ability to identify people's reactions and expressions sufficiently. If I notice improvement in the child's interpersonal relationships, I'll know that the IEP was a success.*

This question addresses your knowledge of a particular area of the job—counseling as a related service. Federal law requires that the provider, in this case the school psychologist, set up and evaluate the IEP's goals and objectives. Your answer should mention a specific goal, as well as the fact that you based this program on an assessment that you'd done on the child's social-emotional areas. Your response, like this candidate's, should include a clear, detailed description of how you'd design and implement an IEP.

Q: **Describe how you'd help teachers establish a positive classroom environment.**

A: *With the teacher's permission I'd spend a day or two simply observing the class. I'd take note of the light and decorations and check if student work was*

First-time Job Seekers: Most states have a law that clearly defines the role of a school psychologist. In some states you'll need to hold a master's degree in school psychology. But not all states have full-time psychologists in their schools—some contract for clinical psychologist in private practice. You'll also be expected to have had at least one internship while you were in school. In your interview, emphasize your tangible skills, such as the fact that you're an organized, hard worker, and be sure that you're knowledgeable about all the state and federal laws that concern special education.

displayed, as well as models of correct work. I'd also want to see that there were certain routines and procedures established, and that the children had specific places to work or play. This kind of organized system helps children know when and where to conduct activities and cuts down on confusion—and less confusion is better for children. I'd also look at the teacher's attitude toward the class. Is there a caring attitude, are successes celebrated and mistakes confronted? Is the teacher's attitude consistent? Finally, I'd offer the teacher my feedback and, if I saw room for improvement, offer suggestions on how to improve the classroom environment.

It's often part of a school psychologist's role to be a consultant, and to help teachers improve what they're doing. Part of your job is to make observations and give feedback to the teacher. Modifying the classroom environment is the easiest form of intervention a teacher can use. The interviewer expects you to address three main areas: physical set up, organizational efficiency, and emotional tone. Like this candidate, you should give a detailed response about specific elements you'd examine in a classroom.

Q: **What behavior-modification techniques could you use or share with teachers?**

A: *I believe that reward systems are one of the most effective ways to modify behavior in children. For instance, a teacher could have a reward system based on completing a contract—a student starts out with certain rewards or points, then loses them only for inappropriate behavior. Another idea is a tier system in which students could move from one level to another based on behavior. As they move upward, they receive more rewards or more freedom.*

Again, the interviewer wants to learn more about the candidate's intervention strategies. How will you help teachers work with students better? What do you know about behavior issues as they concern students? Like this candidate, describe the techniques that you'd recommend to teachers.

Career Changers: Most people who choose school psychology later in life have previously been teachers, counselors, or private-practice child psychologists. In all of these cases you must meet certification requirements. All these professions have skills that are easily transferable to school psychology, so during your interview be sure to highlight those skills. For instance, a former teacher would already have strong intervention strategies but would need to strengthen other areas—his or her knowledge of compliance and legal issues, for instance. Similarly, a counselor would have a number of behavior-management strategies but might need to strengthen intervention skills.

Q: **How would you handle a noncompliant student?**

A: *First, with the teacher's help, I'd try to identify where the noncompliance occurs. Does it relate to a special education disability the child has? Is it the child's age? All these kinds of factors should be taken into consideration when design-ing an intervention. It's my goal to create clarity of expectations and a consis-tency of response. Once I'd determined the area of noncompliance, I'd develop a motivational strategy for the child, creating a model of appropriate behavior that would be used consistently. Finally, I'd work with the student's teacher so that these methods could be implemented within the classroom.*

Here the interviewer wants to learn more about the candidate's knowledge of behavior-management issues. Working with noncompliant students can be a large part of the job, and you'll need to convince the interviewer that you're capable of doing so effectively. Your answer should give a detailed, step-by-step description of how you'd deal with this common area of school psychology.

Q: **What would be your involvement, as a school psychologist, in the identification of a student with a disability?**

A: *Before I'd even begin an assessment, I'd ensure that I had written permission from the child's parents to be involved. Then I'd complete and interpret the standardized assessments appropriate for the particular area of concern. If necessary, I'd act as case manager and bring other specialists into the assess-ment who could help determine if a disability exists. Next, I'd gather written information from the team of specialists, as well as the parents, and include that information in the assessment report. Then I'd write a summary that determined whether or not a disability was present, and if an IEP or 504 accommodation meeting was necessary, I'd present the findings to the child's parents and other participants.*

The term "disability" in this question refers to a special education disability, or 504 disability—a federal law that covers all people with disabilities. This law states that appropriate accommodations must be made for people with disabilities if the disability affects one of life's areas, such as walking, breathing, or learning. For example, a child can have a disability like asthma, which might

> **Experienced Professionals:** In your interview be clear about why you want to change jobs. Focus on your professional growth needs or the fact that you want more of a challenge. Although you should emphasize your wealth of experience, the interviewer will want to hear more about the results of those experiences. Give specific examples of your success sto-ries—the drug-addicted students you helped get off drugs, or the student you helped get back into a classroom after everyone else had given up.

affect the capacity to learn if the child can't be in the classroom because of certain allergens. A school psychologist must know how to deal with a number of compliance issues, including assessment for disabilities. Through this question the interviewer learns if the candidate is able to identify the areas, such as assessments, for which he or she is responsible.

Q: How do you measure student progress? How do you use that information?

A: *To determine what a child already knows, I use formal, standardized assessments to compare the results to reference, or "norm," groups. This allows me to measure growth against an objective standard. Naturally, when you use standardized instrumentation, it's necessary to consider any reliability or validity issues that may arise. Then I administer curriculum-based tests during the program, and by comparing the tests, I'm able to see how well a child is progressing. Based on the results, I'd do an evaluation of the child's program to determine if any further interventions are necessary.*

Part of the school psychologist's job is to help develop ways to measure student progress and to teach the instructors how to use that information correctly. Other good answers would include the use of informal assessments, such as curriculum-based measures, which many schools favor because the outcome is directly relevant to the specific interest in that curriculum. You could also mention using a portfolio assessment, which is a collection of the student's work that's evaluated against a standard.

Q: As a school psychologist in a system with more than one school, how would you balance your clinical responsibilities with your paperwork?

A: *First, I'd look at the schools' and students' needs and estimate what my workload might be; then I'd block out times each day to complete all activities, such as scheduling intervention team meetings at one time and reserving other times for assessments. I'd also set aside some time for consultation. Naturally, I'd leave free time so I could complete my paperwork and deal with all the special situations that inevitably arise.*

Before your interview you should try to talk to people who previously held the position to determine what system of organization worked best for them. Interviewers want to know that you have the ability to organize and prioritize to get your work done in a timely manner, and that you can look at the long-term view to determine what the district's needs are. Your answer should also show a realistic understanding of all that's expected of you.

Q: What would you consider to be two key variables in intervention strategies?

A: *I believe a student's motivation and the degree of support the student is receiving from his or her parents are the two most important factors to consider.*

This is a fairly straightforward question. The interviewer is trying to determine where the candidate will focus his or her energy regarding intervention strategies. Your response to such a question should demonstrate an understanding of child development. Other appropriate variables include the consistency of the strategy being implemented, the simplicity of the strategy, and the staff's enthusiasm in embracing a particular strategy.

Q: What do you believe contributes to the disproportionality of identifying certain groups of students as handicapped, and what suggestions do you have for addressing the problem?

A: *Economic issues often determine who gets identified as handicapped and who gets referred to school psychologists or counselors. I've noticed a bias against certain groups that affects who gets referred for assessment. Also, lack of intervention before referral often contributes to the identification of a child as handicapped. So does a refusal on the part of teachers or counselors to look at certain exclusionary factors, such as economics, length of time receiving education, and health or medical factors. I believe better intervention, and documentation of those interventions before referrals actually occur, would improve the situation. I also believe in using a full-blown ecological perspective—that is, looking at the child's community and family in addition to the school environment.*

The candidate's answer gives examples of key variables in assessment and intervention issues. A thorough understanding of testing, and of statistics about economics and how they affect students and evaluations, is necessary to avoid misdiagnoses. As a school psychologist, you have to know what makes a test valid or invalid and which tests are appropriate for what you're trying to do. The interviewer wants to know that you understand that rushing to an evaluation isn't always the best way to deal with a problem. Your answer should reflect a willingness to consider interventions first, as well as an understanding of the fact that interventions are usually the best way to deal with a child's problem.

Candidates Re-entering the Workforce: You'll probably need to do some research into possible changes in legal procedures. It will also be helpful to have some advance knowledge of the school district itself. For example, what's the educational system's philosophy? At the same time, realize that you do have valuable experience, and emphasize that in your interview. Talking about how the knowledge you've gained during your time off—such as how you've used techniques learned as a school psychologist to raise your own children—will help you restart your career.

Q: **What do you consider to be the school psychologist's role in an urban school district?**

A: *A school psychologist has multiple roles in any district—to be a consultant to teachers regarding intervention, to work with families and students, to work with teams of specialists in changing classroom environments. We conduct assessments to determine a child's educational or emotional needs. And, finally, we must act as counselor, to help children get through rough times, like the death of a family member or classmate.*

Like this candidate's answer, yours should demonstrate that you have a realistic grasp of all the roles a school psychologist must fulfill within a school. You'll have to convince the interviewer that you understand all the components valued and all the skills needed to be a school psychologist in this setting, especially if you're coming from a very different background, such as private practice.

Q: **Briefly summarize your knowledge of applicable state and federal laws for special education as they relate to the field of school psychology.**

A: *The Individual Disability Education Act, or IDEA, is a federal law that emphasizes the rights of students and parents. Section 504 of the Rehabilitation Act of 1973 doesn't necessarily give children entry into special education, but it does give the right to reasonable accommodations, which could include any classes or programs that the school has that are federally funded. Finally, I know that this state has a number of categories under the general heading "special education," that certain criteria must be met for a child to fall under a specific category, and that these are different from either mental-health or medical categories. These laws recognize the fact that students have civil rights and, with IDEA, parents have due-process rights.*

The interviewer will probably want to determine whether you know some of the conceptual foundations from which you're working. Your answer doesn't have to be especially detailed, but you should demonstrate a knowledge and understanding of the laws that govern your field.

Special Education Teacher

Q: What's your understanding of due process as it pertains to parents and children with respect to Chapter 766 and the IDEA?

A: *Generally speaking, I understand that these laws spell out a parent's rights of consent and notification, as well as procedures that have to be followed in a regulatory manner. For instance, when a referral is made for an evaluation, from the classroom teacher or other specialist, I know that we're obligated to notify the parents of the child within five business days. Similarly, after we meet with the parents or other specialists to draw up an Individual Education Plan, we're required to present goals and objectives to the parents within a specified amount of time.*

Your answer to this question should demonstrate a thorough knowledge of legal issues and due process as they apply to your particular state. IDEA, which stands for the Individual Disability Education Act, is federal legislation that governs special education; title Chapter 766 is the special education law in Massachusetts, but each state has its own set of laws regarding special education. Be sure you understand all applicable federal and state legislation before your job interview. This is especially important if you've recently moved from a different state. A staff member's lack of knowledge in this area can create problems for the school administration.

Q: Explain your understanding of the concept of team evaluations.

A: *A team approach ensures that the child will be evaluated from a number of different viewpoints. Each specialist has a different perspective—a school psychologist, for instance, will consider factors different from those that a classroom teacher will consider, so a team approach is better for seeing the "whole picture." And the more information and viewpoints we have, the better we can design an appropriate education plan for the child.*

Team evaluations and assessments are an integral part of designing an educational plan for a child. Whereas once a plan would be designed by one or two teachers, now a child will be evaluated by a group of professionals, which could include classroom and special education teachers, a school psychologist, and perhaps a speech-language pathologist or other specialists. This group of people will come together as a team to discuss their findings and recommendations for a particular child. This candidate's answer demonstrates a knowledge of the true purpose behind group evaluations.

Q: **What strategies would you use to consult with classroom teachers?**

A: *After I evaluate a child, I'll ask the classroom teacher if I can come in and observe for a day or two. Usually this isn't a problem, but some teachers are hesitant to have another professional come in to their classroom. If this is the case, I try to explain that I am not there to judge their abilities; I'm simply trying to determine how a given child's needs can best be addressed within the classroom setting. Then, based on the data I collect from assessments and evaluations, I'd offer the teacher suggestions on how to modify or change the curriculum or classroom setting so that a child's needs could be better addressed. For instance, if a child is off task, I'd discuss ways to get him or her back on task. Some teachers have never worked with children with special needs, so I believe it's important for them to learn how to build successes for a child within instructional activities.*

Special education teachers spend much of their time consulting with classroom teachers, rather than directly servicing a child. This question is designed to determine the candidate's approach to that role. Often you'll encounter obstacles with classroom teachers who resent someone telling them what to do. Then there are others who want to be told what to do—who want someone to critique them all day long. As a special education teacher, you need to know how to balance your consulting duties with your direct-service, administrative, or other duties.

Q: **Tell me about your most difficult experience.**

A: *A few years back a student I was working closely with confided in me that her father had been molesting her since she was eight years old. I was absolutely horrified—this was only my third year of teaching, and I wasn't sure what I should do; I didn't even want the student to go home that night. Well, I immediately reported the incident to the building principal, who reminded me that I had to follow certain established procedures. So a group of us—the principal, the classroom teacher, the school psychologist, and I—met to discuss the claim.*

First-time Job Seekers: Naturally, you'll need a bachelor's degree and usually one or two semesters' worth of student teaching. In addition to your certificate, which is required in all fifty states, some states require additional certification in special education. You can be certified as a Teacher of Moderate Special Needs, or get your Young Children with Special Needs certificate, which is for preschool- or primary-level students. Be ready to discuss the more technical aspects of the job, such as the legal issues surrounding the field. Also, emphasize your enthusiasm and commitment to the field of special education.

After the girl was examined by the school psychologist and nurse, we decided the claim was valid and filed the appropriate documentation with social services. To tell the truth, it was extremely difficult for me to maintain my professionalism throughout the whole process. But my colleagues had been through this type of situation before, and they taught me the difference between caring about a case and becoming emotionally involved.

The interviewer will learn two things from this question: what you consider to be a difficult situation, and how well you overcome difficulties. It's not enough here simply to refer to a difficult situation; you must also describe in detail how you managed to work through it. As a special education teacher, you'll have countless demands placed on you, and you'll need to know how to deal with sometimes very stressful and difficult situations.

Q: How would you advocate for a child and balance the needs of the child with the system's ability to deliver services?

A: *I understand that often a school system is simply unable to meet the needs of a child. When this happens, I try to work with what the system can realistically provide. If that help proves inadequate, I'll look outside the school system. Depending on the needs of the child, I'll look to charitable organizations, human-services agencies, or even local businesses for help. In my experience I'll eventually get the services I want if I'm willing to work hard enough.*

This situation can be a real quandary for many teachers, because you know what a child needs, but at the same time you know that your school, or even district, is limited in its resources. The interviewer will want to see that you won't get discouraged if you don't receive the help you've asked for. Many teachers come into the system with a high level of enthusiasm but give up after a few disappointments. Be sure that your answer shows creativity and resourcefulness; no interviewer wants to hear that you'll simply make do within the system and leave it at that.

Q: How would you deal with angry or upset parents?

A: *I know that usually when parents are upset about something that's happened to their child, they simply need to voice their frustrations. Once this is done, we can move forward, address the issue, and come up with strategies to resolve it. But I've also experienced a few situations in which the parents have become abusive and started using language that I found offensive or threatening. When that's happened, I've remained as calm as possible and told them that I wouldn't tolerate such behavior, and that if they wanted to help their child, they'd have to stop it. Usually the parents have eventually calmed down, and the meeting was continued.*

If you work with children, there are bound to be times when you encounter irate parents. Unfortunately, this is a part of any teacher's job. Your answer should demonstrate an understanding of the parents' need to air their frustrations. At the same time, you should show that you won't stand for abusive behavior. Interviewers want to hear that you'll establish personal parameters for parents, and that you'll stand up for yourself and your beliefs if subjected to verbal abuse. Of course, be sure to mention that no matter what the circumstances, you'd remain calm and professional at all times.

Q: **How do you integrate educational goals with a child's social or emotional needs?**

A: *Unfortunately, kids today bring a lot of baggage to school—issues that aren't related to education but nonetheless affect their ability to learn. I encourage classroom teachers to incorporate some of these issues into their curriculum. For instance, through essay or journal writing children can get a chance to voice their worries and concerns on virtually any subject. Classroom teachers can discuss social issues, such as welfare or violence in schools, during social studies or can use math to introduce economic issues like money spending, allowances, and income.*

In this day and age teachers need to recognize and acknowledge the fact that students' home and school lives are linked. The family and social issues that many children face inevitably affect their behavior and attitude in school. Especially in more urban settings, it's essential that these issues are addressed within the classroom setting. As a special education teacher, you must give examples of how you'd advise classroom teachers to do just that.

Q: **How do you react when you have a conflict between the reality of a situation and your professional beliefs?**

Career Changers: In addition to classroom teachers, many professionals from related fields, such as speech-language pathology or physical therapy, switch to special education later in their careers. If you're a classroom teacher, the transition isn't that difficult. The interviewer will assume that you're already familiar with the role of a special education teacher, as well as most of the laws that pertain to special education. If you're coming from a position outside education, you'll need to go back to school and get your teaching certification. In either case you may also need to be certified in special education, depending on the laws of the particular state in which you live. In the interview discuss why you want to change careers, and emphasize those traits, such as compassion and a love of children that are easily transferable to this field.

A: *I know full well that public education can't do everything that needs to be done for children. And sometimes going into the community doesn't help either. Earlier in my career I found this very disheartening. I thought that as a teacher, I was supposed to make everything right for my students, so I was very frustrated and angry when the system couldn't or wouldn't help. For better or worse I've come to accept that every system has its limitations, and I don't let myself become personally affected by it. I don't mean to say that I've become disillusioned or cynical; I still have the same high ideals I've always had, but now I just understand that those ideals can't always be met.*

This is similar to the question about how you'd advocate for a child, but this question addresses how you'd react philosophically rather than professionally. Your answer should demonstrate an understanding that ideals can take you only so far. The interviewer doesn't want to hear that you've simply lowered your standards. It's good to be optimistic and to have high ideals, but at the same time, it's important to be grounded in reality.

Q: What would you do if you thought you were being taken advantage of by a colleague?

A: *I'd talk to the colleague to resolve the issue. If that didn't work, or if, for some reason, I just didn't feel comfortable speaking with the person, I'd involve other people, such as my supervisor or principal. But I'd do that only as a last resort.*

This is a basic problem that many new or inexperienced teachers face. Usually the other person is a senior staff member. The situation in question could involve assessment responsibilities, paperwork, or school-building duties, such as cafeteria or hall monitoring. The interviewer wants to hear that the candidate will confront that person directly before going to the next level, such as the building principal, department head, or union representative. Interviewers like to ask this question because such issues can potentially affect your function within the building, your attitude about work, and your relationships with other staff members.

Experienced Professionals: During your interview emphasize your rich background of experiences. You should already be well versed in the legal and technical issues of special education, so be ready to answer more questions about your specific accomplishments. A master's degree in education will help you stand out from the pack of candidates. And joining a national organization, such as the Council for Exceptional Children, or the National Education Association, will help you keep up with trends in education, as well as help build your network of contacts.

Q: Say you're providing direct service to a special-needs student within the classroom. Give an example of how you'd adapt the curriculum and instructional strategies for that student.

A: *Well, I recently worked with a student who was an auditory learner. Through assessments and evaluations we realized that most of the information he gained was from listening. The student had a very difficult time absorbing visual information, such as readings from textbooks, or learning from skills sheets or from examples on the board. So after consulting with the classroom teacher we changed the way information was presented to the class. The teacher concentrated on auditory instruction and used visual information as a reinforcement. We also worked on the student's reading skills, using some whole language and other special texts to ensure that he became a good reader.*

The interviewer is looking for examples of instructional strategies that could be implemented within the curriculum. It doesn't matter what diagnosis you discuss here—it could be an example of a learning-disabled, deaf, visually impaired, physically challenged, multihandicapped, or developmentally disabled student. Whatever diagnosis you choose to discuss should be based on your personal experience, and your answer should give very specific strategies of how you'd adapt a particular classroom to meet the needs of a student.

Q: How do you formulate recommendations for services?

A: *I base my recommendations on the assessments that have been done on the child. When a child is referred to me, I conduct an assessment, then study the outcome to determine the child's needs. For instance, using the same example as before, after I ruled out any developmental disorders, I realized the child had a learning disability. Once I knew he was an auditory learner, I made the recommendation to concentrate more on the auditory part and less on the visual part of instruction, and I worked with the classroom teacher to design a program that would help accomplish our goals.*

Again, this question addresses the candidate's thought processes. How do you decide the proper course of action to take with a child? Your answer to this question should detail how you determine what's going to happen with

Candidates Re-entering the Workforce: Before your interview read trade publications such as the Journal of Learning Disability to ensure that you're current with the field. Be sure that you're familiar with any new laws or regulations pertaining to special education. You should also be ready to discuss your reasons for leaving your job, as well as your reason for returning. Most important, highlight your previous work experience and accomplishments.

the child, how and when it's going to occur, and what other specialists will be involved in delivering the service. Like this candidate, you should give a specific example of how you decide upon and design a program for a student.

Q: What's been your most rewarding experience?

A: *Well, a few years back a group of us got together and created an after-school homework center. Basically, it was an extended day program designed so that students wouldn't have to go home to empty houses. The center was open five days a week until five o'clock. We usually had around thirty kids there with teachers from different departments, like math, science, or English, to help them if the children had trouble. It was a great experience, since rather than just disciplining students for not doing their homework, we gave them an opportunity to do it at school. Parents especially appreciated the program because they knew their children were safe and were using their time constructively.*

There's no single right answer to this question. However, you should try to talk about an experience that's made a definite impact on people's lives—a situation in which you were able to take something that appeared to be a negative and turn it around positively. This experience could be an individual student problem or even a broader issue, such as helping a family cope with a family member's death. You'll want to communicate that you've had a great deal of exposure to many of the problems facing today's students.

CHAPTER 14

EXECUTIVE AND MANAGEMENT

Benefits Manager

Q: What appeals to you about human resources and benefits?

A: *I enjoy the personal contact that goes along with working in human resources; I really like working with people. Benefits in particular interests me because of all the technical knowledge, such as the legal issues, that's necessary for this position. I also enjoy the personal nature of it. We can deal with some delicate issues, and many times I feel as if I'm able to help people get through difficult times in their lives.*

This question is designed to discover if the candidate has a concrete idea of what the human resources and benefits fields are all about. Discuss how you enjoy working with and helping people, since that's always the cornerstone of any position in human resources, especially benefits. Like this candidate, you should also demonstrate a thorough understanding of the technical knowledge that the position demands. If you're changing over from a general human-resources position to one in benefits, be ready to explain why you want to specialize in benefits.

Q: What are your goals in benefits?

A: *I want to be a benefits specialist and be able to understand the full range of benefits available to employers, like medical-insurance or retirement plans, so that we can better meet the needs of our workers. Plus, I want to help others use their benefits more effectively and teach them to maximize the benefits that the company provides.*

This is a good response, since it shows an understanding of the full scope of benefits. You don't want to limit yourself to a specific area of benefits, such as health care or life insurance. Another way to answer this question would be to say that you want to understand the entire human resources field—classification, recruitment, record keeping, and employee negotiation—more fully.

Q: What's the largest check you've ever written, and how did you feel when you wrote it?

A: *The down payment on my car, about $4,000, was the most for a single check. I felt as if I were spending my life savings, really making an investment and taking on a lot of responsibility.*

The interviewer wants to know if the candidate has an idea of the magnitude of benefits. A very large company may pay over $100,000 a month for benefits, and often, the check will be written directly from the benefits office. It's essential that you have a realistic understanding of the tremendous financial responsibility that accompanies the position of benefits manager.

Q: Describe your leadership style.

A: *I believe I'm a strong leader. I don't want the people in my department to be intimidated by me, but I want them to respect my authority and position. I try to get my staff involved in the decision-making process. I like to have their input and opinions and since they're the ones who are dealing directly with the employees, they often have some great ideas of their own.*

A benefits manager is also a supervisor, overseeing the assistants and associates who actually administer the benefits, so the interviewer will also be interested in learning about your management style. Although there's no right or wrong answer to this question, it's good to show that you like to challenge your staff by getting them more involved, as this candidate does. It reflects well on your leadership and management abilities if you have a staff that's so knowledgeable you feel comfortable consulting with them.

Q: Who do you think our customers are?

A: *In HR our fellow employees are our main customers. They aren't customers in the traditional sense of the word, in that if they really don't like our product, they can go elsewhere and pick a different one—that is, unless they want to get a new job. In a smaller way the various companies we work with, like insurance companies, are also our customers.*

First-time Job Seekers: You must have at least a bachelor's degree and about five years' experience to be considered for this position. An M.B.A., or a master's degree in human resource development, is a plus. If you don't meet these qualifications, you'll probably start as a benefits assistant. In most offices an assistant answers questions from walk-in traffic, gives out general information, and answers telephones. The minimum requirement for an assistant's position is usually an associate's degree or experience in the insurance industry. But if you want to move on eventually to a management position, a bachelor's degree is a must.

You should demonstrate an understanding that in human resources your primary customer is the employee. This is unique in the sense that your customer is your peer—someone you work side by side with. You could also mention the supervisors and management of the company, who are a separate, but related, customer group. While you are teaching employees about their benefits rights, you must also reach the supervisors, who need to understand how to track and communicate with their employees to meet the requirements of the law. Outside vendors, such as insurance, financial-planning, or printing companies, are another group of customers that benefits managers will often deal with.

Q: **How familiar are you with current legislation that affects human resources?**

A: *I'm very familiar with these laws. I was the benefits manager at my last company when the Family Medical Leave Act was passed, so I'm well acquainted with that one. The Americans with Disabilities Act, as well as the ERISA, or Early Retirement Income Security Act, have had a major impact on the functions of HR.*

These are the names of some key federal laws you'll be expected to know. You should also be familiar with any applicable state laws. The interviewer is trying to find out if the candidate is aware of all the various legislation that's been passed in recent years. You don't need to describe in detail how all three have affected HR, but be prepared for a follow-up question on one of the laws you mention.

Q: **Tell me what you know about the Family Medical Leave Act.**

A: *With the passage of this law employees are now able to take twelve weeks of medical leave, without having to worry about losing their job or getting reassigned. Employees are also eligible to continue their health care coverage at*

Career Changers: Professionals from the insurance or financial industries might be interested in making a switch to the benefits management. For a non-entry-level position, you should have a bachelor's degree, as well as a few years' experience in either the insurance or financial services industries. Naturally, experience in another area of human resources, such as compensation or employee relations, would be extremely valuable. The key is to demonstrate a deep understanding of benefits. Consider becoming a certified employee benefits specialist. The certification is offered as part of a continuing education program through the University of Pennsylvania's Wharton School of Business. It's a ten-class program that could be completed either through self-study, or through classes offered through satellite schools in many major cities. Contact the Wharton School for more information.

the same rate that their employee deduction was when they were working. Although many think that the law applies only to women on maternity leave, it has many other implications as well. It's also enabled men to take paternity leave and provided for adoption and foster-care leave and it's now possible to take time off to care for a sick parent or child.

This is a law you may be asked about in detail, since it has had a big impact on company benefits policies. A brief overview of the law is fine; you don't have to have every single provision memorized. However, the interviewer will want to know if this law has actually affected your current company's policies. If it has, you should discuss the law's effects on your company in more detail. For instance, explain how twelve weeks of leave time is being tracked and how this has changed previous processes for leave. Your explanation of how you adapted old processes to administer the new policy will give the interviewer a better sense of your skill level than if you simply give a straight definition of the law.

Q: What would you do if you were dealing with an angry customer?

A: *Well, I understand that a lot of the time we have to deal with people who are going through some really tough personal situations. First I'd try to calm the customer down and explain that I was there to help with his or her problems. Once the customer was calm, I'd spell out whatever options were available, then work on resolving the person's questions or concerns.*

Sometimes employees become irate or upset because their insurance premiums have shot way up—perhaps because they've just been laid off or they have a sick child or spouse. Although you'll probably not be dealing with customers on a daily basis, it's necessary to know how to handle the situation when they get upset. Furthermore, you'll be in charge of training your staff in these situations. The interviewer will want to hear what you'd talk to the customer about, and that you'd be understanding and sympathetic to what he or she is going through.

Q: What's the difference between a defined-benefit and a defined-contribution plan?

A: *These are different types of retirement plans. A defined-benefit plan is a traditional pension plan, in which an employee receives a certain amount of money based on a formula that typically includes how many years he or she has worked with the company. A defined-contribution plan, on the other hand, is one in which employees make a defined contribution on the front end—usually a percentage of their salary. The employer may match the employee's contribution up to a certain percentage, sometimes from 10 to even 100 percent.*

You can expect this question if you're switching from a general human-resources position. Like the question on benefits legislation, this question addresses the candidate's technical skills. Many people get these two terms confused, so be sure that you're clear on the differences. You should be especially clear about the type of plan the company you're interviewing with uses. Interviewers aren't likely to base their decisions on this type of question but instead will use the question to get a feel for what kind of training is necessary.

Q: What are the differences between an indemnity/PPO and an HMO?

A: *An indemnity plan is one in which you have only major medical coverage, and a PPO, or preferred-provider organization, is a network of hospitals that usually goes along with an indemnity plan. The PPO works by offering incentives to participants to go to the hospitals in the network. For instance, if you went to a hospital within that PPO network, the plan would pay 80 percent of the costs, but if you went outside, the plan would pay only 50 percent. Most important, a PPO generally covers only illnesses or injuries; a routine physical would not be covered. The HMO, or heath-maintenance organization, is very different, as it's based on maintaining the health of the population, so things like well-care and routine physicals are covered and encouraged by the plan. The philosophy of HMOs is more proactive and preventative—that is, if you can maintain the health of the participants on the front end, they won't get sick as frequently, thus saving expenses later on.*

This is another question to assess the candidate's technical skills. Your answer doesn't really need to be this specific and detailed; you can probably simply describe the major differences between the two plans. But because the shift to HMOs is currently one of the biggest issues in benefits, you might be asked some follow up questions on the subject, such as, "What are the advantages and disadvantages of each plan?"

Q: Do you understand how long-term disability works?

Experienced Professionals: You'll be asked fewer questions about your technical knowledge and more about your accomplishments and specific experiences. You should be able to give examples of benefits programs you've designed or implemented. If you have many years experience, you may be applying for a director-of-benefits position. In many larger companies, the director of benefits may go on to the director of manager of human resources. Also, if you're seeking an upper management position in HR, you might find it helpful to get your mater's degree.

A: *Yes. Basically, the employee needs to have been disabled for a certain period of time before he or she is eligible to receive benefits. Those benefits are a certain percentage of what the employee's income was before he or she was disabled. The waiting period will vary by company; so will the percentage of income that a person receives.*

Your answer here should show a general understanding of long-term disability. This is another question designed to assess the candidate's skill level and what, if any, training will be necessary.

Q: **How would you rate your communication skills?**

A: *I have excellent writing skills and substantial experience with public speaking. In my previous position I often gave presentations to large groups of employees when our company changed or added benefits. I also had a regular column in our company newsletter on how to make the most of what the company has to offer.*

One of the primary goals in benefits is to ensure that the employees clearly understand what can be some very complex issues. This often involves using both written and oral communication skills. The interviewer will want to see that you're not hesitant to make group presentations, and that you have the necessary skills to write newsletters and notifications for employees. On a smaller scale you need to be comfortable working one-on-one with customers, including helping people who are going through difficult situations.

Q: **How would you contribute to the mission of this organization?**

A: *I'd bring strong communication and interpersonal skills to your company. I think I relate well to employees, and I really enjoy being able to help them. I'm always happy to assist them when they have questions about their benefits, and I like to see them take advantage of all the great benefits the company has to offer.*

Candidates Re-entering the Workforce: It's most important to show that you've kept up with changes in the insurance industry during your leave of absence. The shift among insurance companies from favoring PPOs (preferred-provider organizations) to HMOs (health-maintenance organizations) is the biggest news in recent years, so be ready to discuss the effect this change has had on company benefits programs. Also, the interviewer will be concerned whether you've stayed current with legislative changes that have affected HR, such as the Family Medical Leave Act. You may want to consider becoming a certified employee benefits specialist—this is a highly respected certification, which will prove to employees that you've maintained an interest in human resources and benefits.

Again, there's no single correct answer here, but the interviewer will be looking more for intangible attributes, such as your interpersonal skills. Your answer should also mention how well you relate to your customers—employees. If the interviewer doesn't offer the information, this would be a good time to ask him or her to explain the mission of human resource services and how it connects with the organization as a whole.

Q: Tell me about a project you headed.

A: *About a year ago I was in charge of putting an entirely new health-care package together for the company. With the help of a consultant I looked at the various packages offered by insurance companies and evaluated bids. In choosing a package I determined what the cost savings would be, and over what period of time we could expect to see those cost savings. I also took many other factors into consideration, including the overall climate of the workplace at the time. After management approved my choice of packages, my office began a campaign to inform all employees of the change, including putting notices and articles in the company publications and giving all employees an information packet, which included newsletters, enrollment forms, and brochures. We also held an open-forum presentation for the whole company, then went around to present the information to the larger individual departments. I was also in charge of deciding all the details—such as how we'd receive enrollments, what the time line was for having these changes implemented, and getting ID cards for the employees. After the enrollment period was over, we asked employees to fill out evaluations to help us improve the process for next time.*

The interviewer is looking for the candidate's organizational skills, as well as his or her ability to take initiative. A good response would describe a project of significant length that affected a fairly large group of people. Be sure to show that you're not afraid of challenges, that you have no trouble diving right in. Like this candidate's answer, yours should include a detailed description of how you determined what changes to make, how you communicated the changes to the company, how well these changes were received, and what you would have done differently if you had to do it over again.

Controller

Q: **What positions have you held in finance and accounting?**

A: *During the past twenty years I've held the positions of staff accountant, accounting supervisor, accounting manager, regional controller, and, most recently, controller.*

This is a fairly typical career path for a controller. Interviewers like to see a candidate, like this one, who demonstrates a steady career progression. Discuss the progressive responsibilities you've held throughout your career, stressing specific accomplishments you've made. You should place special emphasis on your responsibilities and accomplishments in your most recent position.

Q: **Tell me about your management experience.**

A: *I have experience hiring, training, and firing accounting personnel. In my current position as controller, I oversee a twenty-five-person staff. Furthermore, I've worked extensively with members of upper-level management, including the CEO.*

In addition to the main responsibilities of preparing a company's financial reports and data, controllers also generally oversee the company's accounting and finance departments. Interviewers like to see evidence that you have experience managing personnel and have done at least some hiring and firing. You should also discuss any experience you have interacting with upper management, since in many companies the controller reports to the chief financial officer.

Q: **What type of companies do you have experience with? What were their sizes in terms of sales revenue?**

A: *I've worked with three companies in the manufacturing, marketing, and service industries. These companies were both publicly and privately held, with revenues ranging from $10 million a year to over $500 million.*

Your answer to this question will help the interviewer determine the degree of difficulty and volume of work you're accustomed to dealing with. A privately held manufacturing company will be run much differently from a publicly held services company, so having experience with both types of companies will give you valuable perspective. If you have a wide breadth of experience in terms of the types of companies you've worked for, be sure to discuss it in detail.

Q: **What involvement have you had with lawyers, insurance companies, or banks?**

A: *I always consult with experts before finalizing legal matters, including fire-, liability-, and property-insurance issues. In conjunction with our company's lawyers I negotiated a lease for our organization's new location. I also have experience negotiating with banks and insurance companies for lines of credit or insurance premiums.*

As controller, you'll often have to consult with other professionals to resolve problems for your company. Assisting in lease negotiations and securing loans from banks are just a few examples of this. Interviewers like to see that you have the experience and savvy necessary to negotiate deals for your company successfully. Be sure to articulate any experience you have dealing with outside professionals.

Q: **How many years have you had responsibility for month- and year-end closings? Was there ever a year when the year-end audit adjustments were unfavorable or exceeded acceptable levels or standards?**

A: *I've been responsible for the month- and year-end accounting closings for fifteen years. For twelve of those years I had a hands-on role, and for the last three years I oversaw the whole process. I can remember only one year when the year-end audit adjustments were unacceptable.*

Figuring the month- and year-end closings are a fairly routine part of accounting; when you get to such a high level, most of that work will be handled by the accounting-department staff. Even so, the controller is ultimately responsible for the results of the closings. Your answer here will give the interviewer an idea of your accuracy when faced with pressure and deadlines. If, like this candidate, you had an inaccuracy one year, the interviewer will most likely ask you what role you played when the slip occurred. Did it happen the first year you were in charge, or was it the year you were simply a junior accountant with a small role in the end results?

Q: **Do you have experience with acquisitions, leveraged buyouts (LBOs) or initial public offerings (IPOs)? Do you have experience with 10K filings?**

First-time Job Seekers: To qualify for most controller positions, you must have at least three to ten years of progressively responsible experience in either the public or private sector. In addition, you'll need at least a four-year degree with a major in accounting of finance. Larger companies will also be looking for a CPA of M.B.A.

A: *Yes. I participated, on a small scale, in the acquisition of a European sister company. I also played a large role in completing the company's plans to raise capital through a large public offering. So far both of these endeavors have proved successful. Also, ten years ago I participated in a leveraged buyout that required extensive documentation and restructuring of all accounting operations to comply with the lenders' agreements. Finally, in my first job I assisted in the preparation of 10K filings.*

With all the takeovers, buyouts, consolidations, and downsizing happening in corporate America, employers like to see candidates who have a full range of experience in these areas. This question is more likely to be asked of experienced candidates, as they're much more likely to have played a substantial role in such deals.

Q: Have you had direct involvement establishing company benefit programs, including insurance, 401(k) plans, or SERPs?

A: *I researched and recommended a supplemental executive retirement plan to senior management, which they unanimously approved. I also was a member of a number of steering committees that provided input for company programs and strategies.*

Your answer to this question will give the interviewer some insight into your involvement with other areas of the company. If you're interviewing at a smaller company (i.e., under $10 million in sales), you're more likely to be asked this question. In smaller companies the controller has a large role in determining the company's benefits programs, as insurance and other benefits can have an enormous financial impact on the company. A larger company will probably have a separate benefits manager to handle such programs.

Q: Do you have experience with systems management? What hardware and software are you familiar with?

A: *Most recently I directed PC network coordination. I also have experience working with Mac hardware, and accounting software.*

Once again, the smaller the company, the more likely you'll need computer and systems experience. In many small companies the controller is the highest-ranking financial officer and, consequently, has a say in all decisions that will impact the company financially, including computer purchases. Of course, if you're applying for a position at a company that has an MIS manager, this question is less likely to be asked.

Q: Briefly describe why accurate financial reporting is important to any organization.

A: *Accurate and timely financial reports, whether daily, weekly, or monthly, can have an enormous effect on a company. Senior management depends on these reports to make the business decisions that control the direction of the company. For instance, a company's financial forecast can affect how many new employees the company will hire, or what products are introduced or discontinued.*

The interviewer wants to determine if the candidate understands the significance of the role the controller plays within the company. Like this answer, your answer should demonstrate a knowledge of the ramifications of accurate or inaccurate financial reporting.

Q: What experience do you have with annual budgeting and monthly forecasts?

A: *For three years I directed all aspects of budgeting and forecasting—including profit-and-loss statements, balance sheets, and capital-asset purchases—for a $10 million company. I also coordinated the budget process for two $100 million companies, one at the corporate level and the other at the regional level, which had twenty-five budget centers.*

Since budgeting is an integral part of a controller's responsibility, the interviewer will need to determine your level of experience. Your answer should include some specific numbers, such as annual sales revenue, that will alert the interviewer to the level of responsibility you've handled in the past. You could also mention the number of cost centers, profit centers, or locations the company has. If your answer indicates that you have extensive experience in this area, the interviewer will probably ask you to elaborate, and to give some specific examples of budgets you've worked on.

Q: Do you have experience preparing tax returns or managing tax audits?

Career Changers: Understand that you need to spend at least three to ten years in the accounting/finance field before you qualify for a position as a controller. Also, if you lack a business degree, you may want to look into taking an accelerated evening program at a top accounting school. This will allow you to qualify for a staff accountant or an entry-level auditing position while you complete your studies. Once you receive your four-year degree with a concentration in accounting, you may have enough experience to move up to accounting supervisor or manager. A controller's position would be the next step, possibly after two to three years as accounting supervisor of manager.

A: *Yes. One year I managed a staff of three who were responsible for filing all tax returns, including state, federal, sales, and payroll returns. I also have experience working with outside auditors, and I coordinated one IRS audit and three state-sales-tax audits. All of these audits resulted in minimal exposure.*

Most companies rely on an outside auditing firm for consultation on the latest tax laws, book and tax treatment, or filing returns. Even so, the controller needs to understand the tax laws and to work with auditors to determine the most favorable tax exposure for the company. Also, the controller is often the company's point person during federal, state, or other audits. Your answer should demonstrate some knowledge of tax and auditing issues, although extensive tax experience isn't usually required. But if tax issues are a major concern for the company, the interviewer may be looking for public-accounting experience or, in some instances, require that you be a certified public accountant (CPA).

Q: Why is it important for most companies to exercise strict inventory controls? What experience do you have with inventory management?

A: *A controller's primary objective is to protect the assets of the company. Inventory is a major element, usually the largest asset on a company's balance sheet; therefore, it must be given significant attention. In the past I've used physical-inventory cycle counts and ongoing system enhancements to maintain inventory management.*

This is another question to determine how well the candidate understands his or her role within the company. Like this candidate's answer, yours should demonstrate recognition of the role you must play in inventory control, as well as some important controls that can be used. Depending on your background, the interviewer may ask you to expand on your answer. For instance,

Experienced Professionals: Apply for positions that will realistically meet your expectations and career goals. Because there may be severe competition for a position, the recruiter may select on the basis of one small point; therefore, you must be as prepared as possible. Don't let yourself walk away saying, "I should have done this or that." Because most candidates for this position will have similar experiences, try to emphasize a skill that will set you apart from the rest. For instance, having a good understanding of the Internet will make your application stand out among most candidates. Recent surveys have shown that very few managers have a working knowledge of the Internet and the World Wide Web. As a result, experience with the Internet will be an extremely valuable commodity in the future.

if you're coming from retail, what procedures did you document or improve upon to control store losses? Be ready to give specific examples of the processes you've used to control inventory and how well those processes worked.

Q: **What experience do you have in managing accounts receivable, and credit and collection?**

A: *I have over five years' experience directing the accounts-receivable and credit-and-collection functions. I've established credit policies, developed policies for in-house collection procedures, and designed criteria for third-party interventions. For example, one policy I instituted was that bad-debt write-offs shouldn't exceed 1 percent of sales. In managing accounts receivable, I've always focused on timely billing and daily application of cash.*

Again, the interviewer wants to gauge the candidate's experience level and determine what he or she thinks is important in controlling these particular functions. Be sure to give specific examples of your experiences—don't just give a yes or no response. You could also elaborate on your answer, describing the steps you took to establish a credit policy, and the procedure for getting it approved.

Q: **Why is it important for companies to require accurate and timely cash-flow projections?**

A: *Cash is the lifeblood of a company. Identifying sources of cash flow on a consistent basis allows you and senior management to make better financial projections. Similarly, careful monitoring of cash outlays guards against disruptions in ongoing operations.*

This question is similar to the question regarding financial reporting. As controller, you have ultimate responsibility for your company's cash flow, and you must therefore demonstrate a knowledge of how your work will affect the rest of the company. The interviewer could also ask you a follow-up question about a time when cash flow didn't meet projections and you were unable to meet your credit obligations for a period of time. In that case you should give specific examples of the steps you took to resolve the problem.

Candidates Re-entering the Workforce: If you've left a controller's position due to a pregnancy, illness, downsizing, or even burnout, the interviewer will be most concerned with your commitment level as you re-enter at the same level of responsibility. Before you even begin interviewing for jobs, you may want to consider taking a step back into a position with less responsibility and until such time as you're mentally and physically able to move up.

Q: How often do you review FASB, AICPA, or other technical publications or bulletins?

A: *Our outside accounting firm normally alerts us to any major changes that are happening that could affect us. Still, you never know when something that seems like just a minor change will have a major impact on your financial statements or tax treatments, so I do read these bulletins on a regular basis.*

Changes instituted by governing bodies, such as the financial accounting standards board, may have a material impact on your company's operations. Because the candidate regularly reads these publications, he or she shows initiative and an attention to detail that's an essential trait of a controller. You should also mention that you often discuss issues and changes with other colleagues; often, changes of a technical nature aren't always clear, and you may discover gray areas that are left open to interpretation.

Q: What's your educational background? Have you ever worked for a public-accounting firm? Are you certified as a CPA, CIA, or CMA?

A: *I have a B.S.A. degree from Bentley College and one year of public-accounting experience with a big-six firm. I'm certified as a CPA and am currently studying for the CMA certificate.*

The minimum educational or technical requirements for a controller position will vary among companies. This candidate's education level is excellent but at some companies a master's degree in business administration may be necessary to meet minimum standards.

Director of Operations

(Manufacturing)

Q: **Describe in detail improvements you've made in manufacturing, both in operating efficiency and in cost reduction.**

A: *By combining one operational product line with another, we were able to increase efficiency by 80 percent while reducing the amount of labor required by 20 percent.*

The interviewer is looking for a specific example of a project the candidate has inspired and worked on that had a positive result. If you're asked a question like this, be prepared to defend your project—you should be clear in your own mind that you really did institute the project and that it really did have a successful conclusion, because you're likely to be asked a follow-up question about further details, such as, "An 80 percent improvement in efficiency is a huge improvement. How was that possible?"

Q: **There are a number of different management styles, from authoritarian to team oriented. In a position of director of operations, you have many different kinds of people reporting to you. In your experience what management style do you find to be the most effective and why?**

A: *I always try to get the maximum input from people who report to me, and I use the best of that information to come up with a decision that everyone can agree with.*

Although different people prefer different management styles, there's no right or wrong answer to this question. Whatever your style is, however, you should be prepared to back it up and explain why you believe it's effective. Most employers in operations management prefer a teamwork-based management style with one caveat: you still need to be able to make a decision, even sometimes when that decision is unpopular. So although you may want to involve others in your decision, ultimately people need to know that the decision is yours and that they must support it.

Q: **What's your opinion of the value of training at all levels of the organization? Describe any training programs that you either initiated or participated in.**

A: *In the incoming-inspections department we installed a statistical process control program that involved the training of fifty individuals in the basics of SPC and resulted in a 10 percent improvement in the yield based upon their work in that area.*

Training is an area that's becoming increasingly important. You should be ready to talk about a specific training program you've had experience with and its effectiveness.

Q: **Describe your experience in both U.S. and offshore manufacturing. How could you effectively manage in either environment?**

A: *In my previous employment we had operations in three different countries. We found that having cross-functional groups dealing with each of the issues at each of those locations was helpful in communicating new ideas among the plants, and the results were positive.*

The employer is trying to judge the candidate's feelings about manufacturing in the United States as opposed to offshore. With more and more companies manufacturing in other countries, experience in offshore manufacturing is becoming increasingly important. Reassure the interviewer that you understand the differences between these two environments and can function well in either.

Q: **Describe the biggest problem you faced on the job in the last year. What was the solution you came up with and what was the ultimate resolution?**

A: *We had a continual shortage of raw material in a certain area, and it was causing us downtime and lost efficiency. By meeting and developing a relationship with the supplier, we were able to ensure that we'd have the supply of raw materials that we needed on hand. We were then able to cut two weeks off our lead time.*

First-time Job Seekers: Sell your lack of job experience as a positive. Emphasize that you're willing to learn, and you have no preconceived notions about how things ought to be done. When asked about your lack of experience, you should say something like, "I do have a lack of experience. But I also have the willingness to learn, a lack of preconceived notions, and absolutely no rigid ideas about what's good or bad. I'm willing to try hard. I'll make some mistakes, but in the long run I believe I can become a very effective worker." Entry-level candidates often start in a supervisory role at a fairly low level, supervising a small group of people in either a department setup of a product-line setup.

The interviewer will want to know about your problem-solving skills and your judgment. The key to this question is the effectiveness of the solution you came up with.

Q: What elements of the ISO do you think are most helpful to you?

A: *The element of ISO that requires we have training on a regular basis has been helpful to me. Using that element, we set up a training program that's had a positive result.*

Again, the interviewer is trying to gauge the candidate's depth of knowledge about ISO. If you don't know the different elements of the ISO standard, you'll betray yourself here.

Q: Consider this hypothetical situation: One of the senior managers who reports to you has reached the top of her salary grade and you're not able to give her a salary increase. How would you explain to that person that she's important to the company, and keep her motivated in the face of the fact that she's not getting a raise this year?

A: *I'd say something like, "If a person's at the highest pay grade of his level, that means he's being paid as much as or more than any of his peers. Obviously, the company thinks very highly of your work, or you wouldn't be the highest-paid person at your level of experience and knowledge. The company's present inability to pay you any more than that should not take away from the fact that you're highly valued, and that your continued employment here is important and critical to our success."*

This motivational question may appear in various forms. The interviewer wants to know how the candidate keeps employees motivated in the face of difficult management situations.

Career Changers: You'll have to convince the interviewer of a couple of things. First, is that you're serious about getting into operations and that you have well-thought-out reasons for wanting to do so. For example, you could say that you think it's something you'd enjoy doing, that you'd be effective at it. Don't say. "I need a job and it's what you're hiring for." Second, you need to show the interviewer that you're well prepared for a position in operations even though your past experience is not directly related to operations. For example, if your past experience is in a quality control/ assurance position, you could say something like, "In the ever-competing world, product quality is more and more important. By having a solid background in quality assurance, I'll keep quality issues uppermost in my mind to improve the quality of manufacturing."

Q: Tell me about the last course of educational study or seminar that you attended on a particular business issue. What value did you get from it?

A: *I recently took a course on leadership skills. I learned five areas in which I could be more effective as a manager and adopted several tools to become more effective in those areas.*

Lifetime learning is now a common practice. The interviewer will want to know if you're continuing your education even while you're working. This answer shows that the candidate hasn't stopped learning, even though he or she is well established in a career.

Q: In your experience what type of organization is most effective in driving improvements and allowing you to manage effectively? For example, what managers ought to report to you, how would you relate to people in other departments, and so on?

A: *In my past employment we had a departmental structure that wasn't very effective. Under my assistance we went to a product-line management style, which enabled the departments to deal more closely with each other and to solve production problems at the earliest possible level, rather than waiting for them to become a problem at the end.*

Organizational design can have a very real impact on a business's efficient operation. This question is aimed at discovering what organizational systems the candidate believes are effective and how he or she has managed the change from one organizational structure to another. It also gives the recruiter insights into the level of decision-making authority the candidate gives to other people.

Q: We ask more of people, at all levels, than we used to, so it's becoming more important every day to understand how they're

Experienced Professionals: Your best bet is to present yourself, in a positive way, as the solution to a company's needs. When human resources people or hiring managers have a job to fill, they want you to be the right person for the job, because it makes their job easier. They don't want to have to spend four more weeks interviewing ten other people. Understand that the person interviewing you wants you to be right for the job. Many people who enter interviews are insecure about their weaknesses, and that can come across quite clearly. Suggest to the hiring manager that you're positively the right person for the job and that you'll exceed his or her expectations.

feeling. What method do you use to make sure that you're aware of the feelings or concerns of those in your work force?

A: *I make sure that I walk through the plant once a day and talk to as many people as I can. I also have a staff meeting in which my managers report to me on any issues.*

The interviewer wants to know how you deal with employee relations— whether you're the kind of person who likes to sit in an office or who likes to get out and do things. Other appropriate answers include, "I've put in place a suggestion and reward system to encourage people to give their responses" and "I've put together worker's committees to get feedback."

Q: **Describe your biggest accomplishment in bringing raw materials to the production process in a timely and cost-effective manner.**

A: *We installed a restocking program, which allowed manufacturing to continue without concern for material availability. It was automatic in its replacement so that there were always adequate raw materials on hand.*

A big part of operations deals with raw materials, since manufacturing means taking something and making it into something else. Increasingly, manufacturers and their suppliers form working partnerships to insure appropriate delivery and competitive price. Your response should illustrate your understanding of the interrelationships between customers, the company's own manufacturing processes, and its suppliers.

Q: **We have half a dozen qualified candidates for this position. Why would you be the best choice for this company?**

A: *I believe that I've proved over the past five years that I can be a very effective manager and that I'm forward thinking. I've given you examples of projects I've instituted that came to successful conclusions. I'd bring that same energy*

Candidates Re-entering the Workforce: First you'll need to convince the interviewer of your seriousness about returning to the workforce. Be prepared to give some fairly significant reasons about why you want to go back to work. The employer's biggest concern may be that you'll soon find yourself unhappy with the nine-to-five grind. Second, you should show that you bettered yourself in some was during your absence. For example, if you were out of the workplace for two years due to an injury, you could say, "Well, I was injured and the insurance company offered me a course of study. I took it, and made sure I completed it, so that I could keep my work skills intact while I was off. Now, with my injury behind me, I think I'm well prepared to rejoin the workforce and be a positive addition to your company.

and leadership to this position, and your company would be better off in both the short and the long term by having me work for you.

This is another way of asking, "Why should we hire you for the job?" There's no right or wrong answer to this question. The key is to be prepared with a positive, straightforward, and future-oriented response.

Q: Do you have any questions?

A: *Yes. If you hire me for this job, what would I have to accomplish for you to look back a year from now and say, "This is the best person I've ever hired?"*

You should prepare one or two questions in advance of your interview. This answer is particularly effective because it expresses the candidate's interest in the job and shows that he or she is goal oriented.

General Manager

Q: **How many people reported to you in your last position?**

A: *Four people reported to me directly, but there were also some other groups that consulted with me regularly. For example, I had an advisory relationship and interacted regularly with the marketing group. I was also on several different committees and chaired one on employee safety in the workplace.*

Particularly if you didn't have a large number of people reporting to you in your last position, you should discuss other people you interacted with or had some kind of influence over in the organization. Remember: in the job interview your emphasis needs to be on selling yourself and putting your best foot forward rather than being matter-of-fact and abrupt in your answers.

Q: **Compare managerial styles of people you've reported to.**

A: *I worked for a warehouse for a long time where the manager was an ex-marine and everything was extremely regimented. Although people were treated fairly and were occasionally praised when they did something well, they were usually simply given instructions to do their job and never told how that job fit into the big picture. Then there was a change in the company's management structure, and a new supervisor was assigned to the warehouse floor. This new supervisor had a very different management style. For example, if the workers were given a work change, he'd explain how that work change fit into the company as a whole. This made a huge difference to people, to see how their work contributed to the company's overall objectives. Furthermore, this supervisor would go out of his way to motivate people and make them happy. On the other hand, some people took advantage of him by regularly showing up late for work and taking two-hour lunches without explanation. I'd say that this person's managerial style was better than the first manager's, but he didn't know how to draw the line with people. I think that can be done in an increasingly firm way without people resisting.*

The interviewer is trying to determine what the candidate's management style is and whether or not it will mesh with that of the company. Ideally, before your job interview you should try to learn about the managerial styles that exist at the company so that you can structure your answers accordingly. If that's not possible, your best bet is to speak approvingly of a management style that encourages people and is supportive; at the same time, however, you need to demonstrate that you know where to draw the line and be firm with people, including dismissing people when necessary.

Q: How do you establish yourself when you're assuming a new management position?

A: *As a new manager, I think it's important to try to get a feel for the norm, both in the group you're managing and in the company as a whole. I think it makes a big difference if you're going into a group that's in tough shape and needs to be turned around as opposed to a group that's extremely successful. With a group that's doing things well I'd tend to have a hands-off approach for a while until I really understood the team dynamics. In a less positive situation I'd try to obtain everybody's input, but I'd do so very quickly, and perhaps with no formal meetings, to get to the heart of how people interacted.*

This is a very tough question because different interviewers will want different answers. No matter what your answer is, you should be decisive. If you're unable to answer this question, or if your response is ambiguous or hesitant, the interviewer may conclude that you don't have the personal qualities or the experience necessary for a management position.

Q: How closely do you tend to monitor your employees' work?

A: *With professional people I think it's important not to micromanage others' work—not to feel the need to be continually updated about every minor step they make. You need to give people a little room to grow, including occasionally making mistakes. At the same time, you need to keep the risks within acceptable bounds so that when a problem develops, you're on top of it before it becomes too severe. I also believe it's important to make clear to your employees that you expect them to come to you with a problem before it gets out of hand, and that you're available to them as a coach when they'd like some input or are dealing with something new to them.*

Your answer to this question needs to take into consideration the type of work people will be doing for you. Is it work you can set up a standard for, such as requiring assembly-line workers to produce a certain number of units per hour? Or are you dealing with professional employees whose work is more difficult to quantify? Regardless of your answer, you should be sure to emphasize that your approach involves a balance between supervising people too closely so that it creates tension and results in lower productivity, and undersupervising people so that they lose motivation and take advantage of the situation.

Q: How do you get people who report to you to give you their best performance?

A: *I like to use positive motivation to get people to give their best performance. This might involve showing employees how their work ties into the company as a whole, dishing out praise when praise is appropriate, not undermining or criticizing them in front of others, and building an esprit de corps. Another way to motivate people is to be sure that the stronger performers are given challenging projects, and that everyone has some say in the kind of work they're going to be doing. When managing people, you need to woo and entice them. You can't just push them to do things. This is even truer with bright and talented people. Furthermore, when you've successfully wooed and motivated people and got them excited about their work, the resulting performance can be terrific!*

The key here is creating an environment that encourages people to give their best work, and doing what you can to marshal the resources necessary to free them from unnecessary hindrance. Although goal setting may play a role in your answer, you should emphasize even more the things you do to motivate people positively, as this candidate does.

Q: What techniques have you used to bring an underperforming employee up to speed?

A: *Assuming the issue is quantity of work, I'd set up goals and benchmarks for the person to strive for. If the problem is with an hourly employee, I'd set up a standard for the quantity of work I expected the person to produce in a given time period. For example, I'd give somebody in a typing pool a certain number of pages that needed to be typed every hour, or somebody in telemarketing a certain number of phone calls that needed to be made on a given day. With a professional employee I'd use a parallel approach without setting a specific standard. I wouldn't try to micromanage every single hour, but I'd set up goals or deadlines for specific projects or other objectives. For example, the goals I'd*

First-time Job Seekers: Although you may not have a lot of experience managing people, you've probably formed attitudes about how people should and shouldn't be managed. This is certainly something you should expect to be questioned about at length in a job interview. One of the keys that you want to keep in mind in your discussions is balance: you're not going to do too much yelling at people and bossing them around, but you'll motivate people to do their best, perhaps by explaining why their work is important and giving a lot of praise.

At the same time, especially at the entry level, employers want to know that you'll able to change hats from a nonmanagerial to a managerial role. You'll need to convince the interviewer, for example, that you know where to draw the line with people, that you can critically evaluate them and decide when a person's work must be fixed or brought into question. Additionally, interviewers want to be confident that you have in mind what's best for the company, without being too dogmatic about it. In other words, they want to hear you spout the company position at the same time that you exhibit a health degree of respect for the individual.

---

give to someone in marketing might be to increase awareness of the company among retailers and consumers by a certain percentage, or to complete our catalog by a certain date. I'd follow up with regular meetings and discussions, emphasizing the importance of the person's giving me feedback on his or her progress.

It's important to show the interviewer that you'd vary your methods according to the employee involved and the kind of work he or she does. This kind of answer indicates that you have a solid understanding of basic management principles—that different kinds of people have different needs and must be motivated accordingly. If possible, give examples from your previous experience of how you've successfully managed to bring underperforming employees up to speed.

Q: **When do you think meetings are an appropriate use of time?**

A: *On the one hand, I'm aware of many companies that hold no meetings, or very few meetings, and I know it's worked for them. On the other hand, I've worked for companies that have lots of meetings, and I know it's worked for them as well. I think I could work in either environment. What's the environment here?*

Different interviewers will look for very different answers to this question. Some companies place a great deal of emphasis on meetings and have many, whereas others place little importance on meetings and have very few. Try to get this matter out into the open, to gauge the kind of answer the interviewer is looking for. If you're not sure, you may want to give a relatively ambiguous response, as this candidate does. If the interviewer then persists in asking for your preference, you can say something like, "Although I don't think that people should be in meetings all the time, I do think that there's a need for meetings for different reasons. Meetings are typically held for the following purposes: to disseminate information (these meetings should be quite short), to brainstorm ideas (which can be long and highly productive,

Career Changers: One of the biggest concerns the interviewer is going to have is how earnest you are in changing to a new career. And if you're changing to this new career today, are you going to want to change to another career tomorrow? To alleviate these concerns, you'll need to demonstrate some in-depth interest in a career in management. You might want to emphasize, for example, that though you've never worked in the interviewer's field, you've had a long-term interest in it, then offer proof, such as different trade publications you read, or exposure to the industry through your current work or through schooling. If you're asked in the interview about other positions you may be considering, be sure to emphasize those positions that offer further proof of your strong interest in the field.

but they shouldn't be too frequent), to resolve problems, and to establish common direction and a feeling of togetherness in the company."

Q: Have you ever had to let an employee go?

A: *Yes, I had to terminate an employee at my last company. This individual continually argued with other people in the office and created a great deal of tension and discontent. I didn't want to lose him because his productivity was high and he made very few mistakes. I tried to counsel him several times, but he continued to have problems. I finally sent him a written warning that documented his behavior and said something to the effect that the negative behavior would have to cease or we would have to part ways. When that didn't work, I made one last attempt to save the person by temporarily suspending him. After that I was dismayed to find that the person's behavior didn't improve, so I terminated his employment, carefully documenting everything in writing. Meanwhile, I'd made plans so that if I did need to make a change in staff, I'd have a replacement immediately available.*

The question here isn't how many people you've fired. The interviewer is probably more concerned about whether you have what it takes to fire somebody. By asking this question the interviewer might be signaling to you that he or she thinks your approach toward management is too soft. However, it's also possible that the interviewer simply wants to verify that you're cautious when it comes to terminations. Companies today look for managers who favor taking the appropriate steps first, trying to get an employee up to speed, before terminating the employee. Terminations involve legal risks in

Experienced Professionals: The interviewer is almost certain to associate you with the management and the goings-on at the company you're currently with. This could work for or against you, depending on the person's perception of the company. Throughout your interview you should clearly indicate how your skills and work philosophy are compatible with the company you're interviewing with.

Questions will generally be highly specific and involve some discussion about current trends in the industry and about the management at your present firm, particularly if there have been problems. If that's the case, you need to find some way to separate yourself from those problems and discuss how you'd prevent similar problems from occurring at your new company.

You'll also need to find out before your interview as much as you can about the hiring company so that you can readily discuss how your skills might fit into that organization. Additionally, you'll be expected to know about the financial performance of your current firm as well as the financial performance of the recruiting company.

almost all cases and are a morale issue for those employees who remain. On the other hand, one employee can spread disruptiveness and be a demoralizing factor to others. So you'll need to show the interviewer that you have sound judgment about when a termination is warranted, that you'd be able to fire the employee if necessary, and that you'd take the appropriate precautions in doing so.

Q: **Tell me about the biggest challenge you've experienced as a manager.**

A: *I was moved to the magazine division of my last company because articles were being delivered at the last minute, and there was a tremendous amount of tension among the employees there. Furthermore, some of the people who were responsible for the problem were becoming increasingly unproductive, and their work was falling further and further behind schedule. So I had to motivate these people to a higher productivity level while replacing some of our writers who weren't up to speed. At the same time, I found that there was some hostility and distrust from other parts of the organization directed toward that division. I spent a lot of time remodeling my own staff to give them confidence and to change their perspective about what "on time" meant. What was most crucial was that I worked a heck of a lot of hours, and I prioritized my goals. My first priority was to get the articles moving. My second priority, which had to be accomplished at the same time, was to rebuild staff morale. And though I knew rebuilding roads with the other departments in the organization was important, I had to consider this a lower priority—at least until I'd whipped my own department into shape.*

When answering this kind of question, you'll need to discuss a situation that involved a great deal of conflict and challenge and placed you under an unusual amount of stress. Describe in detail what the problems were and what you did to resolve them. Avoid discussing a situation in which the outcome was less than satisfactory.

Candidates Re-entering the Workforce: You'll need to show that you're up to speed on the latest trends in management and in the relevant industry. You may also have to overcome an assumption that you might have been "softened" by years out of the workforce. Emphasize that you plan on making a long-term commitment to the profession—which you're not going to leave again in a few years. This is a particularly important point for a position in management because managers often take a significant amount of time to reach their maximum output, and because they're difficult to replace.

Q: **What do you find to be the most rewarding, and the most frustrating, aspects of managing people?**

A: *I find it rewarding to see people grow in their careers, perhaps moving on from my department to another department because their work is excellent. I like to encourage my employees to strive continually to take on new or additional responsibilities and to achieve their goals. While I give people space to grow, I let them know I'm available as their coach when they need me. One of the things I find most frustrating is managing a person who's really trying hard but in the end just doesn't have what it takes—someone who's simply not qualified for the position he or she occupies.*

With this question the interviewer seeks to unearth any problems or weaknesses the candidate may have managing people. This is also a good way for the recruiter to get a handle on the candidate's attitude toward the people he or she supervises. Do you view the people in your division as machines that need to be kicked into gear, or do you see them as individuals with thoughts, concerns, and emotions? The interviewer is also trying to judge the candidate's empathy and determine what kind of satisfaction he or she gets from seeing people perform. Are you excited about people's successes? Are you really supportive of them? Or are you interested simply in seeing them carry out the basic duties of their job?

Human Resources Director
(Manufacturing)

Q: What area have you concentrated on the most in your current position in human resources?

A: *When I took my current position, I wasn't familiar with the state's labor laws or federal mandates such as the Family Medical Leave Act and COBRA. Although knowing these regulations inside and out was not the most exciting part of my work, becoming very familiar with them was an absolutely necessity for succeeding in this job. For a year I attended every course I could find related to labor laws and took manuals home to study at night. The knowledge I now have in this area is one of the strengths I could bring to your company.*

This answer is excellent because it shows that the candidate is knowledgeable in one of the most important aspects of personnel. Discuss your areas of expertise in detail, emphasizing how you're willing to learn more, even if it's on your own time. You'll want to communicate to the interviewer, as this candidate does, that you'll do whatever the job requires, whether or not you find the effort enjoyable.

Q: Do you think the human resources field uses your abilities well?

A: *Definitely. When I was hired for my current position, I didn't have the extensive background that many of the other applicants had. What earned me the position was my background in a laboratory, in direct mail, and in market research. I had a broader knowledge of both our company and competitive companies than the other applicants had. As people both inside and outside the department have come to realize the value of this broader perspective, the number of decision-making opportunities I've been involved in has increased. I've also seen a great increase in the demand for my writing expertise. Executives at all levels consult with me, or actually use me to ghostwrite speeches or wordsmith important documents. I've earned their confidence with my high level of confidentiality.*

A broad background is an important asset for an HR candidate to have. This question is an excellent opportunity for an applicant with no direct HR experience to turn this perceived negative into a positive. Notice in this answer how the applicant also manages to speak to one of the most important qualities in a position in HR—the ability to maintain confidentiality.

Q: **How has being in the human resources field prepared you to accept increased responsibility?**

A: *The very nature of human resources gives a person a great deal of exposure to employees at all levels. I've observed traits common to people who hold positions of high responsibility: they're typically well prepared and, as a result, have confidence in their opinions. When I communicate factually, insightfully, and concisely, I'm respected. When I am ill-prepared, I sense that I'm wasting people's valuable time. I know that increased responsibility requires an increased effort to be knowledgeable. I've always been eager to put that kind of effort into my job.*

Give concrete examples of how your position in human resources continually provides you with opportunities for additional responsibilities. Show that you've been aggressive in going after new assignments or responsibilities. What new duties have you assumed in the past year that would add to your effectiveness in this new position?

Q: **What do you particularly enjoy about your current position in human resources?**

A: *In human resources I interact more with other departments than anyone in the company. This is particularly true because I'm involved in the interviewing process and have to understand the nature of each position very well. I really enjoy learning about my company's new products and services, and I think that this makes me a more effective recruiter for the company.*

There's no right or wrong answer to this question. You might say that interviewing or screening resumes or designing benefit programs gives you the most satisfaction. Your answer should also indicate that you're willing to go beyond your job description and learn as much as you can about the company and its departments in order to be a more effective recruiter.

Q: **Why would you leave your current position?**

First-time Job Seekers: Everyone's done something that paints a compelling picture of his or her personality. Although you may have no job history, make sure to think carefully about a couple of things you've done that make you interesting or that show an appreciation or passion for something in life. For example, if you love to fly kites, the interviewer may perceive that you're a free spirit, a person who enjoys nature, or one who enjoys figuring out the scientific effect of natural phenomenon. If you held a part-time job for several years during high school, you may be viewed as dependable.

A: *Unless the company was to grow very quickly or acquire another company, I foresee no opportunity for advancement. The company has a well-developed senior-management layer in place, and I don't see a management opportunity for me in human resources unless I change jobs.*

The interviewer is trying to discover the circumstances under which the candidate would leave any company. He or she is looking for confirmation that the candidate isn't just shopping for another job and would leave an employer at the drop of a hat if someone else offered a more attractive financial package. Explain your desire to change jobs in positive terms; you should never bad mouth your current company or supervisor. You should also be prepared to articulate your reasons for believing that this position would hold your interest for a significant period of time.

Q: **Tell me about the person to whom you report. What do you like or dislike about him or her?**

A: *My boss is very comfortable with herself, more concerned with respect than with popularity. Rather than being threatened by the success of those who report to her, she views the success of each person in her department as a shared success. Because of this attitude she always strives to educate me and others in the department, and to share the spotlight. Not only have I learned a lot about the human-resources field from her, but the management philosophy on which I intend to base my future has been greatly influenced by her example.*

Be especially careful with your answer to this question. Even if you've had problems with your current manager, your answer should paint an overwhelmingly positive picture of that person. You don't want to be perceived as having problems with authority.

Q: **What does your boss give you high marks for?**

Career Changers: Be positive. Don't give the impression that you're sick of what you're doing, but rather that you want to change your path to enrich your remaining work years, or to provide greater service to humankind. You might emphasize the positive by arming yourself with a couple of interesting examples or people you know who have changed careers and have been very pleased with their decision. When answering questions, use every opportunity to illustrate how the experience you can bring with you will enhance the position for which you're interviewing. Experience in other areas is particularly valuable when moving in human resources because no other field so clearly involves a working knowledge of other departments in the company and the positions within those departments.

A: *My boss has complimented me several times on my contagious enthusiasm. She also values my writing ability, usually coming to me first when she needs some assistance in editing or writing important business memos or letters.*

The interviewer wants to know what the candidate's supervisor would say about his or her strong points. If you're asked a similar question, describe a few areas where you shine, both inside and outside your job description. Tell the interviewer what areas of human resources you'd make an immediate impact on if you were hired tomorrow.

Q: For what aspects of your job are you criticized?

A: *My boss often expresses concern that I become too involved in my job. She's a real advocate of separating one's work from one's personal life. When I shared with her that I hadn't done my usual amount of reading lately because I was spending my spare time familiarizing myself with labor laws, I was surprised at the degree of anger she expressed in my having chosen work over pleasure.*

With this answer the candidate responds positively to a negative question. Suggesting that too much of a good trait can be a negative trait is an effective way to answer this type of question.

Q: What books or publications do you read on a regular basis that help you with your job?

A: *I always read the current-event capsules on the front page of the Wall Street Journal. They give me a quick idea of what's going on in the country and the world. I look forward to reading the Sunday business section of the New York Times, saving it for a weekday if Sundays are too frantic. And though I don't always read it as thoroughly as I'd like to, I enjoy Time magazine.*

Your answer should include several business publications and certain trade publications that demonstrate knowledge and interest in the industry and the company. If possible, give a specific example of how your reading has positively impacted your job. What was the outcome?

Q: Why is this job important to you now?

A: *I want to affect the lives of the people with whom I work. Although I've enjoyed other jobs I've held, I just wasn't as satisfied as I am in human resources,*

Experienced Professionals: Realize that though you have a great deal of experience, each company has its own way of doing things, and flexibility and adaptability are keys to success. In an interview, the experienced professional needs to demonstrate the he or she can still listen and learn.

where I know I impact people's lives. I felt a true sense of satisfaction several weeks ago when I helped an employee who was having problems with another employee. We worked together to resolve those problems quickly and to everyone's satisfaction.

The interviewer is looking for the candidate to emphasize a commitment to the department and the position. Be prepared to give solid reasons why the position would fulfill your current goals. What do you want to accomplish at this point in your career? Convince the interviewer that there's a good match between what the job has to offer and what you're seeking in a new position.

Q: How do you feel your company treats its employees?

A: *In recent years management has really been dedicated to having a satisfied workforce. Their efforts, however, often rekindle past upheavals, when employees made sacrifices for the company and received little in return. In human resources we spend a lot of money trying to break down the walls between exempt and nonexempt employees. If "the company" is management, I would have to say management is making a conscious effort to mend fences and to do right by our employees.*

The interviewer wants to see if, as part of your position in human resources, you can walk the fine line between loyalty to management and concern for the employees. Although there's no right answer to this question, you should try to avoid bias and to comment as objectively as possible on your company's attitude and approach toward employees. Be prepared to give examples that reflect your company's view toward its employees.

Q: This job may occasionally require weekend work with little notice. Can you vary your schedule as the job requires?

A: *Not a problem. I often come in on weekends to make sure I stay on top of all pending and future projects so that my work week proceeds as smoothly as possible.*

If you can't work outside normal business hours, now is not the time to discuss it. If you truly can't work on weekends, you'll have to take that into consideration when and if you're offered the job. Remember, your goal at

Candidates Re-entering the Workforce: Don't apologize for the time you've been away from the scene. Before going to the interview, think of several ways in which the period you've been away has made you a more interesting person. You may wish to inquire about some training that would bring you up to date if you're in a field that's changed a great deal during your absence.

this point is to get a job offer, and a negative answer will automatically take you out of the running.

Q: **Because this job requires you to be responsible for both our locations, there will be a considerable amount of travel required. Do you have any problem with being away from home a couple of nights each week?**

A: *Not at all. My family has various commitments during the weekday evenings when I'd probably not see them anyway, so working weeknights is not a problem.*

As travel is a hot button for many candidates, the interviewer wants to make sure you have no reservations about being out of town during the week. Again, this is not the time to bring up any problems you might have with the schedule of the job.

Q: **Frankly, we've received many impressive resumes. What's unique about you that makes you the best candidate for this opening?**

A: *My background includes positions with small, midsize, and Fortune 500 companies in a variety of roles where I've gained insight and knowledge about the company's' products and services. I've been able to communicate that knowledge effectively when charged with the responsibility of bringing in new talent. My communications experience includes writing articles for newsletters, position-statement speeches, and interdepartmental communications. Finally, I have an innate ability to recognize how individuals from different backgrounds and experience can make a significant contribution to the overall success of a company.*

Expect this question in one form or another. Your answer to it is crucial and can make or break your candidacy. Needless to say, you should be prepared to give clear reasons why you'd be a more valuable hire than anyone else the interviewer is considering at the time, and not just because you happen to fulfill all the job requirements. Give examples of special skills or experience you can bring to the company that would make an immediate impact. You should avoid answering in bland generalities like, "I get along well with people," or, "I'm a very dedicated worker."

Labor Relations Manager

Q: **Tell me about your educational background.**

A: *I graduated with a B.A. in labor relations, and a minor in psychology. My course work included classes in collective bargaining, labor law, and human-resource management. For the psychology minor I took a number of classes in human behavior.*

The candidate's response is ideal for someone interested in pursuing a career in employee relations. Like this candidate, you should name specific classes you've taken that are related to the position. An education that includes classes in specific employee-relations issues will set you apart from other candidates who are less focused. A background in psychology is also important because it fosters a better understanding of people and their behavior.

Q: **Give examples of your experiences outside college that prepared you for the position of labor relations manager.**

A: *I worked this summer in the warehouse of a large automobile manufacturer and gained, I think, a good understanding of the concerns of people who work on the shop floor. I also spent a summer managing a fast-food restaurant, where I learned a number of effective approaches to managing people.*

Expect this question if you're an entry-level candidate. Interviewers look for people with some practical experience, because these kinds of candidates generally have a solid understanding of what to expect from the position, as well as the necessary skills to be a successful employee-relations manager. Discuss any relevant work experience or internships you've had, such as working in the personnel department of a local company. Any experience you've had in an industrial or manufacturing environment is also helpful, as most employee relations-positions are found in this kind of setting.

Q: **This position is all about interacting with people. What are your best skills in this area?**

A: *I believe I can handle conflicts quite well. I'm a great listener, and people seem comfortable talking to me. I have a reputation for being patient and objective, and many times our employees will come to me with their problems, then put faith in me to resolve their conflicts or difficulties.*

Strong interpersonal skills are essential for anyone in the position of labor relations manager, as duties will involve direct interaction with others. Interviewers look for candidates who can communicate effectively, and who are naturally sympathetic and diplomatic. Be careful how you answer this question, as many skills considered effective in other areas aren't appropriate for this position. For instance, someone who's extremely authoritative wouldn't make an effective employee-relations manager: you can't simply walk into a room of angry employees and announce what you're going to do for them without first listening to their complaints and showing empathy with their problems.

Q: **Labor relations can be a thankless position. How do you plan to stay motivated?**

A: *I understand this isn't a very glamorous position, and that doesn't bother me. When I'm not getting noticed—when people aren't stopping me in the halls to discuss some issue or problem—that's when I know I'm doing my job effectively. But when problems arise—and they inevitably do with a workforce this large—I can listen to the complaints and show sympathy without taking every complaint personally. I guess I'm lucky in the sense that when I leave the office, I'm always able to do so without taking the problems and the pressure home with me.*

A production-line supervisor might get rewarded for reaching 110 percent of his production goals; an accountant might receive a pat on the back for finding a new way to reduce costs; but in employee relations, if the workforce is happy, no one says a word. It's important that you understand this, because the last thing a company wants is an employee-relations manager who'll end up more stressed out than the employees. Show the interviewer that you can maintain a pleasant demeanor even when dealing with employees' complaints and problems, and give examples of the ways you cope with the pressures of the job—whether through exercise, religion, motivational seminars, or some other activity.

Q: **How important is recognition to you? What do you feel are the most and least effective ways to recognize people for a job well done, and why?**

A: *Employee recognition is extremely important, but I don't believe there's a single most effective way to recognize employees. Basically, I think that the form of recognition should depend on the type of accomplishment you're recognizing. Monetary compensation is always effective, but it's not the only way to reward people. You also need to consider other factors, such as the employees' quality of life or the quality of the working environment. By the same token, you need to tie certain achievements to monetary rewards. For instance, if the company's goal is to set an all-time sales record, and that goal is met, the owner can't simply pat everyone on the back and say "Nice job." This is likely to be construed as negative reinforcement. If, on the other hand, the company meets*

*a goal of 100 consecutive days without an injury, and the owner goes out onto
the shop floor and congratulates people—that's positive reinforcement.*

The interviewer will want to know how you reward people for exceptional
achievement. Suggesting that money is the only effective motivator is not
only a shallow approach to employee relations, it will turn off many interviewers. Show that you're willing to dig deeper to determine the needs
of your employees. Demonstrate an understanding that each workforce is
unique and will respond to different stimuli. You may have an extremely
young workforce to whom money may indeed be the most important thing,
or you may have an older workforce, with different needs and wants. If
employees have been performing the same job for twenty years, they might
respond more readily to new challenges, in which case you might consider
setting up a production contest between different shifts or divisions, or setting new quality or safety goals.

Q: **Tell me some of the ways you might motivate the employees
where you work.**

A: *At my company we use a number of different methods to recognize outstanding
work and to motivate employees. Generally, we try to tie benefits to specific goals,
so that every week, month, and so forth, the employees have something to shoot
for. For instance, we'll announce a sales goal, and when that goal is met, we'll have
a company-sponsored lunch. In the shop we'll give out awards for safety. One
time the company put $10 into a pot for every day the shop went without an
injury. After thirty days without an injury, we drew names and gave $100 to one
employee on each of our three shifts. We also sponsor periodic company events,
such as golf outings, simply to keep up the employees' morale. And once a quarter
the CEO and I will bring in breakfast for the overnight shift and eat with them.
We'll also have contests in which employees can win different prizes. For the
office workers we once had a "keep your desk beautiful" week, then gave prizes
to the people who kept their desk the neatest. We also have an annual contest
in which the top-producing shop employee got his car washed by the CEO.*

First-time Job Seekers: The typical entry-level position in this field is
assistant to personnel director or labor relations manager. You could also
start as a human resources assistant, in which position you'd handle duties
such as benefits administration. A bachelor's degree in personnel management, labor relations, or business management, along with a heavy concentration of classes in psychology and communications, is a prerequisite for
this position. In you interview, stress your educational qualifications and
your exposure to the newest theories in labor relations. Emphasize the fact
that you'll come into the position without preconceived paradigms about
the job, the company, or its employee.

Employee morale is an important issue that an employee relations manager must deal with every day. As with the previous question, the interviewer wants to see how the candidate might encourage employees to enjoy and take pride in their work. Discuss how you create a positive working environment for your employees, remembering to add how you look beyond money to other methods of motivation. Finally, give specific examples of programs or events you've planned that have improved employee morale and performance.

Q: **A large component of labor relations is negotiation. What are your thoughts on the subject?**

A: *Well, negotiation is simply a part of life. Whether you're buying a new house or a new car, or trying to get a date for the weekend—it all involves some give-and-take. I realize that I won't always be right, and I'm not always going to be able to get my way. In order to coexist with others, you need to find a happy medium, and negotiation is the way to do that.*

You'll need to demonstrate to the interviewer that you have a good understanding of the importance of negotiation. Show that you realize that negotiation means more than simply getting labor and management to agree on a contract. Unless you're willing to mandate a solution, negotiation is the only way to get two conflicting parties to reach a settlement.

Q: **How would you describe your negotiating style?**

A: *I'd say I'm a win-win negotiator—I can't walk out of a negotiation unless I know that both parties are able to go back to work feeling good about what's happened. Though I realize this style isn't appropriate for every situation, I believe that a resolution is virtually worthless unless all parties involved are fully satisfied with its terms. I've also used power negotiating, mediation, collective bargaining, and binding arbitration in a variety of situations involving negotiation. There are definitely times when it's better to use one particular style over another. For example, I use the win-win approach in labor negotiations or in any situation where there's a contract or agreement that's going to be binding and that everybody will have to live with. I also find "good cop/bad cop" negotiating*

Career Changers: You should possess at least a bachelor's degree in a related field, such as business management, as well as experience with team building and negotiations. Discuss any experience you have with issues related to human resources, such as dealing with employee benefits. Remember that strong interpersonal skills are a must for anyone in this field. Be ready to give examples of your ability to communicate effectively, both one-on-one and with groups of people. For example, you might discuss your experience making presentations to large audiences.

useful in many situations, especially those involving minor employee conflicts. When I'm negotiating with two parties, I'll ask both sides for possible solutions, which, of course, are always contradictory. So I'll tell them I need to go over the solutions with my boss and will simply leave the negotiating room. Regardless of whether I actually consult with someone or not, this tactic gives me time to consider the solutions. When I return to the negotiation room, I can say either, "Well, my boss liked this idea, so why don't we give it a try?" or "He didn't like either idea but did suggest this." I've found this method to be a good way to introduce new ideas without angering either party. Bringing in a real or fictitious third party puts the pressure on that third party and takes the pressure off me, as well as off the two opposing parties.

This question helps the interviewer determine the candidate's experience with negotiation. Show that you're familiar with the various negotiating styles. If you're an entry-level candidate, you probably won't have firsthand knowledge, but be ready to discuss the theories you've learned in your labor relations classes. If you're an experienced candidate, give examples of situations in which you've used different negotiation styles. Although everyone has a preferred negotiation style, demonstrate a willingness to use the style that's been proved most effective in a given situation. Similar questions you may encounter are: "What negotiation style do you believe is best?" and "What negotiation styles are you familiar with?"

Q: Do you think it's best to use one negotiating style all of the time, or should the situation dictate the style?

A: *Without a doubt, I believe the situation should dictate the style. For instance, if two people were about to come to blows on the shop floor, I'd use a very powerful, authoritative style. But if I was dealing with a more delicate situation, I'd take a softer approach.*

This is a follow-up to the previous question. Interviewers are concerned about candidates who hold absolute views. For example, you shouldn't say, "I'm a win-win negotiator and that's all I ever use." Many people enter this field thinking they have all the answers, believing they possess the ability to get two opposing sides to agree to anything. Although this idealism is commendable, it's simply unrealistic. Again, show that you understand that the same solution or style won't work for every situation. Any answer that fails to recognize the variables in every situation will seriously hurt your candidacy.

Q: What are your feelings toward labor unions? What's the best way to handle unions?

A: *Unions, whether you like them or not, are a way of life in many businesses, especially in manufacturing companies such as this. In my opinion unions and management can work together for the benefit of all through mutual cooperation and* understanding. When it comes to dealing with unions, I believe in communicating directly with employees, while at the same time keeping the union informed of what's going on. Regardless of one's personal feelings, if the employees elected to have a union represent them, I believe it's the obligation of the employee-relations manager to alert the union to any changes within the company that could potentially affect the workers or the stability of the company. By the same token, you can't lose sight of the fact that the company is paying the people, and that the people are employees of the company, not of the union.

Again, interviewers are wary of candidates with extreme views. A recruiter wants to hear neither that unions are the worst thing that's ever happened to this country, nor that they are absolutely essential to the nation's economy. This is an extremely important issue because when you work for a company with a large blue-collar workforce, as most employee-relations managers do, you need to deal with unions on a regular basis. Try to present a balanced, open-minded view of unions. Demonstrate your ability to establish a good working relationship with them, without allowing your personal opinions to affect your work.

Q: How important are communication skills to this position?

A: *Communication skills are extremely important. An employee-relations manager needs to feel comfortable speaking to employees, either individually or in groups, to introduce policy changes or to negotiate a contract, for instance. You also need to have strong listening skills, so that you can really understand what employees have to say and then react appropriately.*

Excellent communication skills are absolutely essential in this position. If you can't communicate effectively, then you're not right for this field. Like this candidate, you should show an understanding that communication means more than simply talking to someone; it also involves active listening. Also, watch your body language when you answer this question. If you come into an interview with a defensive posture—if you can't look the interviewer in the eye while you discuss the importance of communication skills—you won't be taken seriously.

Experienced Professionals: To qualify for the position of employee relations manager, you should posses five to ten years' experience in the field, as well as a college degree. A master's degree in employee or labor relations is a big plus. Emphasize specific accomplishments from your past experience, such as the successful negotiation of a labor contract. Also, discuss any improvements made by the workforce in the areas of productivity, safety, or morale. Some experienced employee relations managers will eventually move to operations or to other senior-management positions.

Q: How do you stay current with changing labor laws?

A: *I subscribe to a few labor periodicals, including the Labor Relations Bulletin. I also have a contact at the National Labor Relations Board, whom I talk to on a regular basis, and she sends me periodic reports that keep me up-to-date on changes in labor laws and their ramifications for businesses.*

Labor laws are constantly changing, and it's essential for you to keep current. Show that you stay up-to-date on all new and pending legislation that could potentially affect your company. Besides the Labor Relations Bulletin, many independent labor firms publish newsletters and periodicals regarding the latest changes in labor laws and other labor relations issues. Another appropriate response is to say that you correspond regularly with your professors from college, who keep you informed of new theories and laws.

Q: How much do you know about employee-assistance programs?

A: *Because an employee's mental health is just as important as his or her physical well-being, I believe it's essential to have an outside resource that provides employees with counseling for their problems. We recently implemented an EAP at my company, and the employee response has been tremendous. In such a big company I simply didn't have the time or energy to listen to, and then work through every employee's problem. The EAP has allowed me to do my job—now that I no longer have to act like the company's resident counselor. And since the program promises confidentiality, employees with more serious problems, such as alcohol or drug addiction, can seek help without fear of jeopardizing their jobs.*

Show the interviewer that although you realize it's important to be sympathetic about employees' personal problems, an employee-relations manager has too many other issues to deal with to make them a main concern. Many people come into this position expecting to play the role of staff therapist, and the interviewer wants to determine if the candidate falls into that category. Like this candidate, you should describe what you perceive as the benefits of an employee-assistance program. Also, be sure to emphasize the importance of keeping your workforce in good health.

Candidates Re-entering the Workforce: Emphasize your experiences and successes before you left the workforce. Because labor laws are constantly being written and rewritten, you must demonstrate that you've kept current with developments in the field during your absence, perhaps by meeting with former peers, subscribing to related periodicals, or taking continuing-education classes. Finally, be sure that your computer skills are up-to-date.

Q: **How valuable do you find teams and teamwork? Give me an example of your involvement with teams.**

A: *I recognize the importance of people working together in teams. Through teamwork everyone—company and employees—can succeed. I like having employees work on teams because I believe it really helps morale, and it also makes the employees more effective in terms of job performance. For instance, an employee who runs a standing press all day may feel as though his work isn't valued, but if you make him a part of a quality or safety team that reports back to management, he'll feel as if he's actually being listened to. I've been personally involved with teams on a number of levels. I played varsity basketball and baseball all through high school and college. In fact, I still play in a basketball league once a week. Then, during my internship with the automobile manufacturer, I was part of a quality-control team that reported to the manufacturing supervisor. This experience made me realize how easily being part of a team can boost the morale of workers.*

Here the interviewer wants to get a sense of the candidate's philosophy regarding this important employee-relations issue. Emphasize that you understand the importance of employees working together in teams. Discuss specific examples of the positive effect that teams have had on your company. Workers usually have the best understanding of what's really going on in a company, and if you tap into that reality, you'll get an overwhelming response not only from employees, but from recruiters impressed by your wisdom.

Manufacturing Manager

Q: What is it about this company that caused you to apply for this position?

A: *I've seen your Polarfleece products in the marketplace, and I've been advised that this company wants to grow. I believe that my own willingness to help a company expand and improve will also give me a personal opportunity to excel.*

This answer tells the interviewer that the candidate has some knowledge of the company (that he or she took the time to check), is a "team player" first, and believes that the company offers an opportunity to grow.

Q: What type of working organization do you feel most comfortable with? That is, where are the levels of responsibility in your ideal manufacturing model?

A: *The key to the most efficient manufacturing department is to move all possible decisions to the basic levels in the department. The best decisions will be made by properly trained people who are directly involved in the process.*

This answer tells the interviewer that the candidate wants to use all the abilities of all employees to be successful. The candidate also makes it clear that he or she believes the "vertical" organization of the past has no place in the future of improving businesses.

Q: What is your management style? By that I mean your overall management technique in the guidance of, and contact with, those people who report to you.

A: *The most effective management technique, I believe, is to establish mutually agreed upon goals for each person who reports to you in his or her area of authority, and to describe how those goals fit into the overall goals of the department. The formal monitoring of employees' progress toward those goals will be on a periodic schedule, assisting when required. At the same time, I'd be able to advise my superiors of my progress toward the department's goals.*

If you give an answer similar to this one, you'll have established with the interviewer that an organized approach allows for your people to exercise and develop their own management skills to reach their own goals. At the same time, you'll be telling the interviewer that this approach will enable you to advise upper management of your progress toward the goals that have been assigned to you. This is a thorough, self-confident, and very reassuring response.

Q: **Upon taking over the manufacturing functions of this facility, what's the first thing you'd look for, or put in place if not in evidence?**

A: *I would immediately track the decision-making chain, to determine if it's centralized or disseminated throughout the manufacturing operation. Bringing the decision-making process down to the lowest level in the organization includes all employees in the decisions that will affect their workplace, and will, at the same time, give me a chance to discover employees who may have potential for promotions.*

It's important for you to let the interviewer know that you're not only concerned with the everyday problems of any workplace, but that you also want to look to the future of the company. There are many things to look for at the outset of your responsibilities, but none of them can be efficiently undertaken without a proper decision-making process.

Q: **Consider this hypothetical situation: An important shipment for a key customer is ready and loaded on the truck. Just before the trailer is to be taken away, one of your supervisors reports to you that he or she believes there is possibly a defect in some of the product in the trailer. This defect may not be immediately noticeable but has been mentioned by the customer in a previous complaint. What would you do?**

First-time Job Seekers: Don't try to dazzle the interviewer—he or she knows that experience is not on your resume. Emphasize your strengths (willingness to work hard, ability to learn quickly, and so on) and give concrete examples of each. Be sure to express specifically and clearly your interests in the company. The best way to impress an employer is by learning as much as possible about the company before your first interview. Find out what the company makes, who buys it, how many people it employs. And any other general information you can easily obtain. Any knowledge you demonstrate you have of the company will be remembered by the interviewer.

You should also bring your education transcripts or the address of your school with you. Personal references will be useful. In short, be ready to provide whatever information you might reasonably anticipate being asked. Keep these documents neatly filed in a briefcase of folder.

A: *I would immediately stop the shipment and ask the supervisor responsible to be ready to inspect the product for shipment the next day. In addition, I'd personally call the customer to explain the situation and the action I was taking to resolve the problem. I would also immediately review the production process with the employees involved to determine how the defect occurred and what changes in the process they would suggest to eliminate recurrence. We'd go ahead with the investigation even if the customer told me to ship the product anyway.*

With this answer, the interviewer learns that the candidate wouldn't hesitate to make a difficult choice, would consider the reputation of the company as the most important thing, would have a plan ready to correct the problem, and would be willing to bring in all the involved personnel for their help. It's critical that the interviewer learn that you're honest and wouldn't attempt to blame someone else for what might very well be a system problem. These are important qualities for any managerial position.

Q: **What type of quality-assurance system are you the most comfortable with?**

A: *Every person in the organization is responsible for quality products. Therefore, quality decisions start at every workstation and continue throughout the manufacturing process, right up to shipment. This requires training of all people in the process, with appropriate updating. Therefore, a quality department does no inspection. Its role is to maintain records of standards and keep them as an integral part of the production process. With this type of system surprises are rare and, if they do occur, will be caught at the source.*

Here is an answer that reflects thought as well as experience. The interviewer learns that the candidate believes that the "old ways" of assuring customer quality—calling on the quality department to inspect the product after it's ready for shipment—are no longer adequate. The message to the interviewer is that the candidate's ideas will immediately conserve labor costs. Only those products that meet the customer's expectations will go through the normal production process. Others, caught during the process, will be salvaged immediately and will re-enter the process. As improvements are made, these off-line salvage operations will diminish noticeably.

Career Changers: Determine what specific experience and skills you have that are transferable to a career in manufacturing. There is always at least some common ground between careers. Your job is to find it and convince the employer of it. You should also learn as much as you can about the company before your interview. This is important, because your knowledge of the organization, along with your transferable experience and skills, will be one of the strongest selling points.

Q: **What comments do you have regarding ISO-9000?**

A: *ISO-9000 is the wave of this country's quality future. It was started just after World War II, in order to provide common standards and dependable quality to all European nations as they built up from the devastation of the war. Essentially, it provides twenty elements that must be not only followed, but documented, to assure that customer expectations are met for every product shipped. ISO-9000 does not tell a company how to run its business—it merely requires that the elements be satisfied. The businesses of the United States are just beginning to achieve ISO certification. This will be critical for U.S. companies that want to do business in Europe in the next century, because certification will be required by these potential customers.*

This is a possible question, and any interviewer who asks it is representing a company with more than a passing interest in the ISO-9000 quality approach. Your answer must show that you're an advocate of this system, and that you've at least studied the principles. (An interviewer cannot expect that every candidate will have working knowledge of ISO-9000, because of its limited, but growing, use in the U.S.) Your answer will show that you look ahead and maintain contact with the major developments affecting business today.

Q: **Consider this hypothetical situation: You arrive at work one morning to find that all of your manufacturing people are standing in a group outside their department, refusing to go to their workstations. They're protesting the firing of a coworker on the previous day. What would you do?**

A: *I would immediately approach the group and tell them to go to their workstations. This would probably bring out the leaders, who would tell me their protest concerns. If I wasn't involved in the termination, I'd tell them that I'd look into the situation, but before I did anything, the group would have to disperse and go to work. Then I'd talk to the supervisor who fired the worker, find out the details, and report back to my people the basic reason for the dismissal, without jeopardizing the ex-employee's privacy. I'd also use this opportunity to remind them that we're all in this together, and if one employee, suitably warned, doesn't care about any of his or her coworkers, then we're better off without him.*

Experienced Professionals: If you've been invited to a job interview, you can assume that you fulfill the basic requirements of the position. Now it's simply a question of which candidate out of a group emerges as the best. Rather than reiterating the information on your resume, try to distinguish yourself from the competition by focusing on two or three major accomplishments throughout your interview.

This can be a situation with many pitfalls. There are other ways to handle such a crisis; but this method is direct and honest, and the candidate makes clear that the workers can depend on their boss to answer their questions. The interviewer also learns that the candidate is not likely to invade another person's privacy. The key to handling this situation is to get the employees back to work first. Next is to get the facts without leaving the impression that you're second-guessing another supervisor. The interviewer who asks this question is really looking for your reaction to a pressure-filled situation (while knowing, of course, that you're already under pressure in the interview). Giving a measured response under these conditions will show your "coolness under fire."

Q: **The manufacturing environment seems to allow, in most companies, a different type of person to come to the surface. What do you look for in your manufacturing people when assessing them for potential promotion, and how do you bring them along?**

A: *I look for intelligence, an interest in the process, and leadership qualities. Then I look for one more attribute—a good attitude. I consider this to be the most important trait. If it's present, along with the first three, then this person can move along in the organization. If a person shows a positive approach to his or her work, and a willingness to solve problems, then this person can be tested, trained, and promoted in the future. I'd begin the process of "testing" this person by assigning tasks outside his or her regular duties, monitoring performance, and increasing the complexity of the tasks over a period of time. It won't be long before a profile of the person's abilities will become obvious, and promotion can be seriously considered. I wouldn't discuss my plan with the individual at the outset—I'd just want the person's natural inclinations to take over.*

This response tells the interviewer that the candidate considers the process of employee promotion as vital to the organization's future, and that he or she has a general plan to put people who qualify into a promotion cycle. It will reflect well on the person being interviewed and will demonstrate a wide vision of your manufacturing responsibilities. Many managers, unfortunately, do not routinely consider the overall welfare of those who work for

Candidates Re-entering the Workforce: Emphasize your past work experience, skills, and education. Are there also some skills or qualities you've gained in your absence that you can use on the job? If so, be sure to point them out. Also, tell the interviewer how you've kept your skills current during your leave—for example, by attending a management seminar or reading your industry's trade journals.

them; these are the people who are always surprised and unprepared when someone decides to leave the organization. The wise manufacturing manager thinks beyond just his or her own manufacturing area, knowing that many future company executives come from manufacturing. This message will be clearly understood by the interviewer, and the absence of this message from other candidates will be noticeable.

Pharmaceutical Executive
(Business Development/Strategic Planning)

Q: What did you expect out of your pharmaceutical sales job?

A: *I wanted a managerial role in the industry, and I knew the only way to be truly valuable in that role was to learn the business from the ground up. I knew from my research of pharmaceutical companies that they like health-care sales experience. Now I see how that sales experience will be invaluable in strategic planning, because I know what kinds of product lines are complementary.*

Most people in this industry have started in sales, because the technical-product training is critical. This job-assessment question covers two points of interest to the interviewer: (1) Did the candidate learn from the sales experience? and (2) How does the candidate make job decisions? (Remember: past decisions are often indicative of how future decisions will be made, including the candidate's decision criteria for this particular job prospect.) The candidate shows a solid commitment to the industry and demonstrates considerable thought in how he or she has previously arrived at the decision to take a job. The recruiter has every reason to expect the candidate has thought through this job just as thoroughly.

Q: What were the keys to your success in pharmaceutical sales?

A: *I'm disciplined enough to manage my own business on my own time and am able to focus my resources on what I know will help the business grow. I also have an easy time meeting new people and networking.*

This question is logical, since a candidate's reasons for success in one job are likely transferable to the next job. The answer reflects that the recruiter's needs are foremost in the candidate's mind because the candidate explains the reasons sales was a good personal choice, and why he or she has a good track record. All the skills mentioned are important skills in business planning.

Q: What interests you about business analysis and strategic planning?

A: *They take advantage of my industry knowledge and my academic training in finance. In planning you need the quantitative skills to analyze deals, but you need the instincts that sales experience in health care teaches you. For* *example, I understand how the long distribution channel affects my company's ability to market a specific product when we're not dealing with end users.*

The candidate provides a good, logical, easy-to-follow summary of what he or she learned. This is accomplished in the context of how the candidate fits the criteria the company wants. Again, this answer is a good example of keeping the recruiter's perspective (why the candidate is a good "fit") in mind.

Q: **What have you learned in your time within the pharmaceutical industry?**

A: *Certainly the industry has become much more competitive. All the major play-ers are now in cardiovascular, anti-infectives, and so on. Now they're partnering and looking toward licensing agreements. That's why I'd like to be in the middle of that action, in business analysis. The movement in the industry seems to be to serve as true health-care companies rather than just as drug companies. I know I want to be able to tell my customers that we can help them manage their diseases. The concept of "disease state management" is the big issue in our industry now. We don't just want to supply a drug for the rest of someone's life; we want to help manage the customer's underlying physical conditions.*

This question seeks, and the answer shows, problem-solving ability and indus-try knowledge. Again, the recruiter wants to determine the candidate's stra-tegic fit with the company. This is critical since the new job will bring the candidate to the corporate offices to determine which businesses are bought and sold; the job seeker shows promise here as a corporate thinker rather than just as a career salesperson.

First-time Job Seekers: In most of these companies, sales is considered the best starting point. Look at people at the top of the organization for an indication of whether sales background in the company seems to be a common denominator for getting promoted. Often corporate profession-als rely heavily on their time in the field, and on their technical product knowledge, to perform the work.

Sales training throughout the pharmaceutical industry is among the best, so entry-level jobs are highly sought by new college graduates. Because of the industry's popularity and draw, the companies screen candidates very carefully and often use GPA cutoffs to reduce the pool, but they'll look at most college majors. A sales-oriented personality, evidence of self-direction, and some academic preparation on technical courses or sciences are posi-tive attributes in the screening process.

Compensation is generally good, with a combination of salary (about 75 percent) and bonuses, plus a company car.

Q: **What's your background in finance?**

A: *Well, I have an M.B.A. and took a graduate-level course in corporate finance. I also took a strategy course, which will be very relevant, I think, since the goal in business analysis is to figure out what products you should sell or what new products you should acquire to enhance the product mix. I've also managed the profit and loss for my sales territory, which was $1.5 million in sales annually—one of my company's largest territories in the country.*

This is a skill-assessment question. The candidate does a good job of showcasing the best possible proof of financial ability, given the fact that he or she might have said, "I've taken only one finance course." But the candidate is honest and smart about pointing out all relevant information to the question.

Q: **What specific skills provide the background for your job in planning?**

A: *A pharmaceutical sales track, as a starting point, gave me a basic knowledge of our product lines. I also learned a lot from the pharmacists about compatibility of our products, which would help in considering which products to sell or try to purchase. The sales experience I had gave me a general knowledge of the pharmaceutical industry. I also learned how to deal with customers because I heard their feedback right there on the spot. I learned from that how to negotiate to play fair, make my customers happy, and still protect my company's primary business interests. Negotiation skills are what I would rely on heavily to arrange deals in a job in business development.*

This is a skill-assessment question, so the candidate should pick the most relevant skills developed in a recent job. This candidate begins with background—how the sales track is a good foundation for business analysis. The answer manages to convey what aspects of prior sales experience will particularly help in the negotiation part of the job. Negotiation skills are critical in strategic planning.

Q: **Tell me about your negotiating skills.**

A: *I believe in walking up to the table with a best alternative, plus a backup plan. I also believe in separating the people (and their personalities) from the problem. That can be difficult when you've investigated a deal for a long time and have gotten to know the players well.*

This is a skill assessment and problem-solving question. Negotiating skills are critical in strategic-planning jobs, where analysts often decide on entering into new business deals, or divesting themselves of them, and then represent the company in those business negotiations. This candidate gives a quick, but strong, response indicating an easy confidence with the negotiations process.

Q: **If you led a business-analysis group, why might you decide you want to sell rather than actively market a particular product?**

A: *I believe the goals are to get rid of products that don't fit into the therapeutic classes you're focusing on as a company, and to move cash flows into the near-term future to help cover R&D costs for something else.*

This is a problem-solving question. The candidate clearly shows strategic-thinking orientation, as well as an aptitude for understanding where the company might want to make financial trade-offs. The candidate also manages to bring up R&D, a function that drives the pharmaceutical industry.

Q: **What gross margin do you think is reasonable in the pharmaceutical industry?**

A: *This is an incredibly high-margin business, and has to be, because of the development dollars necessary to create one successful product. I believe the gross-margin percentage runs around 80 percent. That allows for money to fuel additional R&D efforts until another winner can be found. And I'm interested in working in planning because I want to help figure out other ways to free up funds for R&D.*

This question tests the candidate's industry knowledge. If you did not know the gross-margin percentage, the recruiter would still expect you to assume that the number would be high, to cover the costs of unsuccessful R&D. This candidate does some self-promoting at the end by bringing the role of the planning area into the discussion. Use every opportunity you can to drive your points home, to tie each answer specifically to your interview.

Q: **What skills will help you perform in business analysis?**

A: *I have a very analytical mind. My engineering training is technical, much like the science that drives the pharmaceutical business. That technical framework*

Career Changers: If you're trying to break into a pharmaceutical or healthcare company, consider your current skills base and use it as leverage in a related department within the pharmaceutical company. For example, if you've work in controllership, contact the controller's office within a pharmaceutical company. However, look carefully at the top of the organization (and at the top of the specific department) for an indication of whether sales background in pharmaceuticals seems to be a common denominator for people who advance. Choose organizations where your lack of industry sales background isn't going to be a major drawback down the road. Or consider working for a regional or field office before applying to the corporate location.

has helped me understand disease states quickly. Also, the heavy engineering math background was good quantitative preparation for a career that relies heavily on a person's comfort with numbers. I have no worries about my ability to perform the financial analyses necessary to make good business decisions in this job.

The recruiter is undoubtedly comparing the skills mentioned by the candidate to the skills required for the job. Here the candidate effectively relates each skill to industry relevance or job relevance. The last part of the answer is a vote of confidence in the job seeker's own abilities to perform the work. This is good strategy, because the most compelling person always gets the job.

Q: **If you were attempting to value a business, how would you start?**

A: *I would start by analyzing historical sales. Then I would look at existing sales projections. I would want to carry those out for the next ten years.*

This is another skill question. Specifically, it addresses the candidate's approach to problem solving and his or her general knowledge of financial-performance measures. The candidate decides on ten years, assuming that any returns would probably happen within that time frame or would no longer be relevant. In terms of a planning function, this is a realistic choice.

Q: **How much of an investment does it take to develop a typical pharmaceutical?**

A: *The typical pharmaceutical costs about $350 million to bring to market. This includes discovery of one that works, clinical testing, and submission of the New Drug Application to the FDA.*

This is a question of industry knowledge. Any person applying for a finance or strategic planning position in the business would want to have an idea of how to answer such a question. This candidate goes beyond the required answer and demonstrates production knowledge.

Q: **What would you consider a reasonable discount rate in an NPV (net present value) calculation?**

A: *Today I'd assume 13 percent based on the market value of the money if you invested it elsewhere.*

Experienced Professionals: Presumably, your resume shows a solid commitment to the industry, as well as extensive experience. Be prepared to explain your reasons behind your pending job change. Emphasize your sales experience and business-planning skills, and explain how those credentials have helped you in your career.

This question tests the candidate's theoretical knowledge and knowledge of current interest rates. It's also a reality check. (The candidate should not be stumped by any of these simple finance questions.)

Q: **What types of line items would you add when doing a cash-flow statement?**

A: *I would add up-front costs, such as the cost of purchasing a product.*

This answer is very specific to the planning function's role. The major pharmaceutical companies acquire existing products they want in their product line while avoiding the heavy R&D costs. Since this is the main reason for such acquisitions, the candidate's answer zeroes in on the most important point.

Q: **What would you subtract when doing a cash-flow statement?**

A: *I would subtract operating expenses, cost of product or goods sold, and taxes.*

This is the opposite of the previous question. The recruiter addresses the planning function and the candidate's abilities with financial statements. The candidate might respond to either question with both answers, thus giving a more thorough response at the outset.

Q: **Describe the distribution channels for pharmaceuticals.**

A: *Obviously pharmaceutical companies do not sell directly to end users. They sell to wholesalers and pharmacies. Physicians write prescriptions that drive the sale of the product to consumers, and they also dispense a few samples to patients. The physicians and pharmacies have the patient information, so they drive the demand.*

Here the recruiter is testing industry knowledge. The distribution chain in this business has major impact on the way sales are made, as well as on how product education is delivered. The candidate appropriately identifies physicians as the primary target for prescription drugs.

> **Candidates Re-entering the Workforce:** Be ready to start in sales, but consider those companies that do not hire strictly from the college pool. Some industry players are more inclined to hire experienced candidates. Sales positions, in which you work out of the home, can offer a great start to people re-entering the workforce. Although you must assure the potential employer that you can schedule uninterrupted time to work at home, you do have the advantage of a more flexible schedule. For this reason, many people who start in sales never want to leave the field for a corporate position.

Q: **How can you get closer to the end users of pharmaceutical products?**

A: *One answer is through acquisitions of pharmaceutical benefit managers so that we have access to patient information, which is now controlled by physicians. Another is to buy intervention—for example, you could buy a diabetes clinic. Both of these methods allow us to get closer to patients and manage their diseases, so that we can move into health-care management. The planning function would be very involved in such acquisitions, which I think are essential to the long-term viability of players in the industry.*

This answer demonstrates several important things: first, it shows knowledge of the business; second, it shows a strategic-thinking orientation; third, it ties the discussion directly to the role of planning, and thus to the job the candidate is seeking.

Q: **How do you see the role of strategic planning changing in the next few years in the pharmaceutical industry?**

A: *We have to stop thinking of pharmaceutical companies simply as manufacturers. We need to think of them as health-care-solutions companies. What that implies is that these companies need to be more involved with the whole patient—not with an isolated incident that is treated by one of our drugs. Patients and their insurance companies are demanding prevention and disease management as opposed to treatment. The net result will be to spread the overall business risk, much the same way a railroad company wisely repositions itself as a transportation company so that it's not dependent on one technology that can become archaic. Planning departments will obviously be involved in any acquisitions that make this happen.*

This question of opinion is critical. The recruiter must determine if the candidate's philosophy (and thus business instincts in planning) are compatible with the company's goals. In a question like this you cannot fake good research and preparation; company insiders' knowledge will help you orchestrate a response that fits the company's objectives. This answer is strong because of the analogy used, as well as the ending, which ties in the role of the planning function.

Quality Improvement Project Leader
(Insurance)

Q: Describe your experience with a management-control system.

A: *I have extensive experience with performance-based software. I've also developed a measurement system for a claims processing team.*

In response to this, or a similar question, discuss your knowledge of controls that ensure a process is completed successfully. The key word here is "control."

Q: Describe a project that you've managed.

A: *I was responsible for a project that improved customer service/claims processing. My role involved leading a team to improve the process over a six-month period.*

Your discussion should center on the extent or scope of the project, the length of the project, and your role in the project. Be specific, and be sure to mention your successes.

Q: Are you familiar with performance-measurement techniques?

A: *Yes. I established measurements for a customer service/claims processing team that continues to be measured over an extended period of time.*

The recruiter is looking for knowledge of performance-measurement tools and techniques. What was the measurement? How did it contribute to the success of the team?

Q: This job requires superior written and oral communication skills. Please describe examples from your previous experience that demonstrate the use of these skills.

First-time Job Seekers: You'll find that any experience you might have had in an operations environment—whether it's processing claims, answering telephones, or responding to customer mail—is invaluable. And although it's easier said than done, try not to act nervous. You'll want to come across as confident, capable, and eager to learn.

A: *I was a customer-service representative for two years while I worked at ABC Company. I was responsible for responding to customer inquiries over the telephone and in writing. I've received many letters of commendation from customers regarding the service I've provided to them. Through this experience I enhanced my communications skills with both internal and external customers.*

The recruiter will be looking for evidence of these skills in addition to those specifically mentioned in your job interview and on your resume. Bring examples of letters from customers commending your service, if possible. You should also be prepared to provide samples of your writing.

Q: **What is your educational background?**

A: *I've obtained a bachelor of arts degree from Bates College. I'm also attending Northeastern University's part-time M.B.A. program. I'm committed to improving my education on an ongoing basis.*

Whatever your background is, be proud of it. Don't become defensive or embarrassed. If you don't have a college degree, emphasize your experience and any courses you've taken recently. These can include in-house corporate training or courses at local colleges. You should also emphasize your commitment to continuous self-improvement.

Q: **Consider this scenario: You're on your first day in this position, and I'm traveling and unavailable. A call comes in from our customer requesting information by the close of the business day. What do you do?**

A: *I'd check the information at my disposal, then check with one of the managers in the area for guidance.*

The interviewer is looking for an ability to make sound decisions and to take decisive action, and doesn't want to hear that the candidate would wait for a supervisor to return before resolving the problem. In response to a question like this, give examples of creative, decisive actions you've taken in the past.

Q: **What project-management software have you used?**

A: *I'm very proficient with Microsoft Project.*

Career Changers: Be very clear about your reasons for wanting to make a career change. Any hesitation on your part may cause the employer to doubt your loyalty to a company or manager. Emphasize your experience, if any, in an operations environment, even if it's been with other industries, such as the manufacturing or services industries.

Most project-management software packages are very similar to one another, so don't worry if you aren't familiar specifically with the company's software. For a project-management position bring a copy of a project plan you've developed or used in a previous job.

Q: **How do you achieve your objectives on a project when you're leading people who report to other managers?**

A: *I set simple, established objectives that are clearly communicated to all those involved. When we start to approach deadlines or milestones, I confirm completion with the group. If any problems exist, I deal with the individual involved directly, one on one.*

The recruiter doesn't want to hear that the candidate would go to the other person's manager—this is not an indication of a team player, but rather of a person who prefers taking shortcuts. In fact, unless you're the CEO, most of the time you'll have to influence those you have no control over.

Q: **Have you facilitated a training session or a continuous-improvement team?**

A: *Yes, I've facilitated meetings frequently. In fact, I've received facilitator training and frequently use the techniques I've learned, incorporating them into every aspect of my business interactions.*

For this position interaction with others is critical. Give specific examples of how you've used facilitator techniques in the past. Mention any training you've had in this area. Speaking skills are also a definite plus.

Q: **Have you charted work flows or developed a flowchart? How has this helped improve the quality of your area?**

A: *Yes, I have extensive experience developing flowcharts. In my last position charting work flows allowed us to identify duplicate steps and reduced the cycle time of a particular process. The more detailed the work flow, the better.*

Knowledge of work flows is critical to any quality-improvement process. Give detailed examples that demonstrate you know what you're talking about.

Q: **What is causal analysis?**

Experienced Professionals: Your expertise and years of experience are your greatest assets. Describe in detail your experience with management-control systems, projects you've managed, and your knowledge of performance-measurement tools and techniques. Talk up your successes. How have you contributed to the success of your teams?

A: *Causal analysis is also known as root-cause analysis. It means analyzing outputs of an operation to identify opportunities to improve that operation.*

Indicate to the interviewer your familiarity with this type of analysis and any on-the-job experience you have with it. Good examples include analysis of claim-defect rates and customer complaints.

Q: Do you have any experience in an operations area such as insurance claims or customer service?

A: *Yes, I have several years' experience in an operations environment processing claims, answering telephones, and responding to customer mail.*

In order to lead quality-improvement projects in an operations area, you should know how some operation has worked. This can apply to manufacturing as well as to service industries.

Q: Do you have examples of work you've done on quality improvement projects?

A: *Yes, I've brought some presentation handouts, project summaries, and performance appraisals to show you. I think these will give you a clearer picture of the kinds of work I did at my last job.*

Be sure to bring copies of your best work, taking care not to reveal trade secrets. Always try to leave something with the interviewer other than your resume—a brief sample that will leave an impression.

Q: This position requires the ability to work independently. What does this mean to you? Have you done so in the past?

A: *Working independently means being able to get the job done effectively with minimal supervision. In fact, in my current position I pride myself on my ability to comprehend a situation and resolve problems with minimal interaction from my leader.*

Confidence is an important trait to display here. To lead projects successfully, a person must feel confident in his or her decisions and comfortable working with minimal supervision. The recruiter does not want to hear that working independently means being able to get the job done alone. In order

Candidates Re-entering the Workforce: Be enthusiastic. What you lack in recent experience you can make up for with your desire and ability to learn. Make sure you're current with the latest trends in the insurance industry and proficient in the latest project-management software.

to achieve your objectives, you must be able to influence others and seek assistance when needed.

Q: Are you comfortable in a team environment? Define what it means to be a team player.

A: *I believe that in the past working on a team has increased my effectiveness. I was able to access additional resources—my teammates—and improve the end result. In order to be a team player, you must be able to value others' differences and capitalize on your teammates' strengths to achieve the team's objectives.*

Demonstrate convincingly your familiarity with the team concept. Throughout many businesses teams are being formed to accomplish business objectives. You should also become familiar with the "self-directed teams" concept which many businesses are currently experimenting with. Research the abundant literature that's been written recently on this topic.

Senior Strategic Consultant

Q: **Why are you interested in our firm and in this particular practice?**

A: *I'm attracted by the quality and quantity of projects you're working with here. Among Big Six firms that have developed strong manufacturing consulting reputations, this office was one of the earliest to develop a unique reputation without relying on leads from the audit side. I think that audit and strategy work need to remain separate in terms of their images being different. What you're selling to a client is very different. In audit or tax work one considers the past, but in strategy work one contemplates the future.*

This question addresses motivation as well as job assessment. The candidate speaks to the difference in cultures and business engagements, explaining which appeals to his or her own sense of managing and developing new business. The candidate doesn't argue that one approach is right and one is wrong; rather, the statement remains positive, but demonstrates he or she has considered the issue of compatibility carefully.

Q: **Why do you want to continue a career in consulting?**

A: *When I first started consulting, I wanted the intellectual stimulation of working with lots of different clients, industries, and project teams. I also wanted to learn more, faster, and nothing accomplishes that like consulting. Finally, I wanted to be involved in proactive business decisions. Now I don't want to leave because of the respect I have for consulting professionals in general, and because I'm surrounded by peers who are so intelligent, they push me to my limits. In a corporate environment you find that level of intensity with some of the employees, but not with most.*

This question addresses the candidate's aspirations about why he or she wants to stay in consulting. The candidate makes an interesting comparison between consulting and working in a corporate environment. The recruiter has probably asked this question because he or she is concerned about burnout, which is common in the industry, or about whether the candidate, already in the field at a different firm, is being pushed out of a job. The candidate's answer here should cause no alarm.

Q: **What's your biggest concern about a consulting career?**

A: *For any consultant who thrives on the quality of the projects you get to work on, I think the real fear is that you'll either get stuck "on the beach"—(not* assigned to a project)—or that you'll get a project that isn't particularly challenging. I'd like there to be as little downtime or in-office time as possible, and more time with clients. That's why I'm interested in your firm and in this office in particular, because of the projects you've secured and reassurances from consultants who work here that they're always busy._

This is a negative question, and here the candidate wisely avoids a negative response. The recruiter may be looking to weed out people who are concerned about excessive travel or long hours—two givens in this industry. This candidate turns hard work into a selling point and also indicates that he or she has talked to insiders in the firm; that is, the job seeker has done the required homework and probably has very realistic expectations of the workload.

Q: Describe a project you've run or managed. What was your role?

A: _Nothing gives a client greater confidence than a consultant's knowledge of how some other company is proving the merits of a particular strategy. Here's an example: I had a client in the medical-supplies business, one of my most recent projects. I ran across an article about a transportation company that was outsourcing distribution for a company, and this was exactly what my client needed. I also ran across an article about how a computer-manufacturing company was reorganizing its sales force, and this was another issue my client was facing. So I got the project team started rather quickly by talking to them first about these two companies and how they'd introduced changes. We all had a clear idea of where our project was headed then._

This question addresses leadership and management style. The candidate's answer is solid because it gives a specific example of how to draw from other project experiences and outside reading to solve a client's problem. The candidate also gives the interviewer a strong sense of what client groups or consulting teams would say about his approach.

Q: How would you, as an engagement manager, motivate a team under the pressure of aggressive deadlines?

A: _I've learned a lot about managing project teams, including the fact that if you select the best people for your team, you can delegate easily and leave them alone to do their work. I remember a team that I didn't have much time to devote to, because I was managing another team that really needed my knowledge and skills on a steady basis. What I learned to do with the first team was to get caught up on their progress over lunch or dinner, asking them then if they needed any help from me. That worked out great because they didn't feel abandoned, and we all had to eat anyway. I've found that talking about stressful issues over a meal helps people to open up but also helps to keep things in perspective. And the casual environment helps me communicate that I'm there as a resource, not as someone checking over people's shoulders—they know I trust their work._

This is a problem-solving question as well as a question of management style. The candidate shows good time management (how to spread management responsibility over two teams) and effective decision-making skills (determining which group needs the most guidance), as well as confidence in his or her people and enough consideration to afford them the latitude to make decisions. Given the fast pace of consulting work, this savvy ability to delegate is critical.

Q: In what ways is your personality or your set of skills suited to consulting?

A: *Well, one thing you need to be comfortable with in consulting is dealing with ambiguity. There's always more you can do, more data you might collect, but you have to make progress. This idea underscores everything and explains why you have to stay focused on your deliverable, end product. That's something, with experience, I've learned how to do. I've seen how companies in different industries often share the same types of problems. So my strength is the ability never to seem lost, the ability to establish confidence with the client and to move a project forward.*

Here the interviewer is determining the candidate's personality on the job— his or her cultural fit with the consulting environment. Consultants are effective if they understand the end point (what they're trying to accomplish) in any situation and if they use that understanding to remain focused on what's deliverable. This candidate shows an ability to do just that. People who don't make it in consulting often have trouble remaining focused at the client site;

First-time Job Seekers: Strategy firms don't hire inexperienced candidates, and almost all require an advanced degree (typically and M.B.A., sometimes a Ph.D.), with exemplary grades and several years' prior work experience in a corporate environment. However, an alternative type of prior work experience at an entry level is the highly competitive business-analyst position in a strategy firm, where you're hired straight from college to do analysis/support for consultants, and you're expected after two or three years to leave the firm and enter a master's program. In other words, there isn't a promotion after the B.A. without an advanced degree. Some types of consulting firms—for example, systems-consulting practices—hire college grads and train them for technical positions. However, this isn't a typical career path into strategy work.

Many younger candidates from M.B.A. programs are brought in as "new hires." Consulting with a major firm (with the experience and reputation) offers a way early in a career to build experience at a fast pace. Once you're in a firm, the way to move up is by brining in new business—that is, by selling consulting engagements, which is what is expected, after all, at the senior levels.

there are always more problems to uncover than the ones you were hired to fix. Straying from the goal means money lost to the firm, because the firm carefully bids each engagement based on the hours reasonably required to complete a specific task.

Q: **What's the most difficult aspect of consulting for you?**

A: *I'd say that I wasn't always as good as I am now at making quick decisions. A quick decision is better than a decision that's made too late; you simply have to collect information fast, count to ten, and think. You also have to bring to the table everything you've learned from other engagements; it's amazing how often different companies have similar core problems.*

This is a question designed to determine the candidate's greatest weakness. The interviewer needs to feel confident that this candidate isn't trying to hide anything. The answer here is a positive statement, implying "I'm good at this now but wasn't always." The candidate's final statement is a soft sell of his or her relevant experience, reminding the recruiter that the candidate has worked with many different companies.

Q: **What new opportunities do you see in the consulting business?**

A: *I see all the firms moving toward specialization. In other words, they're collecting a group of consultants with detailed functional knowledge in an industry or type of business process. Clients are less and less willing to deal with young, smart people; they want the track record. So the big firms like the Big Six are moving toward industry specialization in their internal divisions, and boutique firms are springing up that play to only one or two specializations. As far as my own interests are concerned, I want people to think of me when they have an issue regarding international business development.*

This question addresses the candidate's skill level and passion for the business—how will this candidate fit in with the new opportunities in the field? More important, the recruiter gets a sense of whether the candidate is potential partner material—how would he or she seek new clients? The candidate effectively relates ideas about where the business is headed to his or her personal ambitions. The answer could be improved with a description of how the candidate has developed specific skills in international firms.

Q: **Would you be willing to do an extended assignment overseas?**

A: *Yes, I would. In fact, I've discussed that possibility with my spouse, who's trilingual and who could easily find employment abroad if the project lasted longer than a few months. I spent six months at a manufacturing plant in Spain on my current job. Unfortunately, my family wasn't able to accompany me at the time, and we've always regretted that.*

Most consulting jobs will eventually have overseas projects, so the recruiter needs to make sure that won't be objectionable. It's illegal for the recruiter to ask about marital status, so the candidate has offered some helpful information here that puts the recruiter's mind at ease. Usually, when people have objections to faraway projects, it's because of family commitments. If overseas projects are short-term, typically the family won't go along. Most firms are open to paying for family travel or expenses in lieu of costs that would be incurred flying the consultant home every few weeks.

Q: Describe a business process that you determined wasn't value added.

A: *We had a manufacturing client whose warranty program had experienced skyrocketing costs due to excessive administrative time. We looked into it and found that 90 percent of all administrative time in the program was spent investigating claims of less than $30. So we instituted a policy of paying those warranty claims automatically, which created goodwill with customers and allowed the company to reduce administrative staff in the customer-service department drastically.*

The recruiter wants evidence here that the candidate can make tough decisions. A consultant, looks to eliminate non-value-added processes, not people—but one often leads to the other. This answer is strong because it's specific and quantifiable.

Q: Describe your project management skills.

A: *I've learned how to treat members of my client team differently from members of my consulting team to help move a project along. In general, consultants are self-directed and highly motivated—you can point them in a direction, and they go. Members of a client team generally have more of an eight-to-five mentality, so I spend more time interacting with them and doing a little more hand-holding. That way information is ready for my consultant team when we need it.*

The reality of the business is that consultants work exceptionally long hours and are usually on the road, so they're not in a hurry to get back to a hotel

Career Changers: Many people consult during the latter part of their careers, but most often as independent consultants, selling their experience to the same people they worked with while they established their professional expertise over the years. The advantage of independent consulting late in life is the ability to accept as much or as little work as you want—that is, as a retirement income. However, the burden of travel may be more tiring than in one's younger years.

room at night. Clients, however, have families and homes to go to at the end of the day. Motivating either group can be difficult. This candidate shows a realistic way to handle both so that project milestones are accomplished on time.

Q: **Tell me how you might employ best practices in a new engagement.**

A: *Perhaps I've read in a Forbes article, for example, about a sales-incentive program created by a player in the telecom industry. If my new engagement at an insurance company involves problems motivating the sales force, I might look for ways to modify the telecom sales incentive program to fit the insurance-sales reps.*

A consultant must be knowledgeable about best practices and use that information to teach the client something useful that translates to his or her business. Thus consultants are voracious readers of the popular business press and various industry journals. That, combined with personal consulting experiences across various industries, informs the consultant's knowledge of best practices.

Q: **Describe a business-process re-engineering engagement you've worked on.**

A: *I did a project for a billion-dollar health-care company. We re-engineered the entire supply chain for one business unit. The core problem was the manufacturing infrastructure strategy.*

This is a question designed to assess the candidate's skill level. One buzzword in the consulting environment is "business-process re-engineering." This candidate, without divulging the name of the client, provides a good example.

Q: **What are the most critical success factors in domestic manufacturing?**

A: *Today's companies need flexible manufacturing to be more consumer driven. As the U.S. has become more consumer oriented, part of being "closer to the customer" has meant being physically closer—that is, building plants near product-demand points. The alternative is flexible manufacturing, by which manufacturing-line changeovers are easy, and by which numerous products can be produced efficiently in one plant.*

This skill-assessment question tests the candidate's operations knowledge. The candidate demonstrates marketing, manufacturing, and logistics knowledge with this answer. The hint of wit is appropriate and effective at making the concept clear.

Q: **What are the most critical success factors in international manufacturing?**

A: *Multinational corporations—MNCs—are aggressively establishing global sourcing policies—that is, to maintain competitive prices, they buy parts all over the world. The move toward global quality standards is important in effecting this trend, and we also have to continue to work toward reducing trade barriers and isolationist policies among countries.*

This is another skill-assessment question. The candidate demonstrates knowledge of international standards (like ISO-9000) and why they're important and also offers an opinion on how politics and government affect MNCs.

Q: **What advice would you give to a consumer-products company having trouble with distribution in certain regions of the country?**

A: *I'd first examine demographics in various locations around the country to determine different demand levels for the company's products. Then I'd examine the location and product of various manufacturing sites. The goal is to produce in proportion to local demand. This is especially critical if shipping costs are a major component of total cost, such as in the case of bottled soft drinks.*

This question tests the candidate's problem-solving skills. The answer offers a good, logical (i.e., sequential) approach to the problem and defines the goal or end result, an important element in the problem-solving process. A specific example makes the candidate's point very clear.

Q: **If you could work with someone—perhaps a particular client— who you think exhibits best practices in a lot of ways, who would that be?**

Experienced Professionals: Consulting is an excellent springboard into industry, as often consultants are hired by their corporate clients—and hired at higher levels, typically, than they could achieve through internal promotions with the corporation. In fact, consulting firms often refer to consultants who have resigned to accept offers from clients as "alumni" of the firm. Consulting firms consider it advantageous to have a former employee, who left the firm on good terms, within a client organization.

Experienced corporate candidates can turn to consulting. Because consulting firms pay well, people from industry with a particular expertise (such as restructuring, logistics and transportation, high technology, product development) may join consulting firms as "industry hires." Typically, they'll join the firm at a managerial level.

A: *I'd work with Herb Kelleher of Southwest Airlines. I'd want to study him to learn firsthand how he motivates his employees with things other than cash. I have little doubt that whatever I learned from him would help me deal with clients who have people-motivation problems—and most do.*

Many strategic-consulting engagements involve general organizational effectiveness, so this example is a good one. This question is a different form of the question "What are best practices in the XYZ industry?" You should always have several ready examples of companies that have been newsworthy because of recent successes or failures. Read the popular business journals to stay current.

Q: How might you advise a client to speed product-development cycles?

A: *First of all, I'd advise the client not to rush the phase of determining customer requirements. I'd put lots of time and people resources into making sure the up-front assumptions are valid. That way you avoid costly redesigns. I'd then advise the client to create a lean development team. What I've found is that companies tend to throw more people onto a project when they want something done quickly; ironically, the greater the size of the group, the more that's usually lost in cohesiveness and in assigning responsibility.*

This is a problem-solving question aimed at an area in manufacturing often needing improvement—time-based competition. The candidate gives a clear picture of things to watch out for. The answer would be even stronger if the candidate indicated a specific example.

Q: How do you keep up with cutting-edge business practices?

A: *I read the* Harvard Business Review, *the* Economist, Forbes, Business-Week, *and the* Wall Street Journal. *I also read various trade publications relevant to my specialty, for example, the* American Production and Inventory Control Society (APICS) *magazine.*

Any consultant who doesn't read constantly will quickly fall behind. In order to stay current on best practices, reading is a must. In addition, strategic consultants often read in the papers about the engagements they're working on,

Candidates Re-entering the Workforce: Consulting within a major firm is unlikely, as firms actively sell the expertise of their consultants, including resumes in their business proposals. Gaps in a person's work history would indicate a weakened knowledge of a current cutting-edge business practices—and of course, that precisely what consulting firms sell.

and partners and senior managers looking for new business get leads from reading the business press.

Q: **Let's go through one short business case. I have a new client in the architectural and environmental consulting business. They want to figure out how to spend their time most profitably. They've lost a few key people recently, and they don't want to lose ground. Assume that they sell their services in similar fashion to our type of firm, with a project estimate up front and an agreed-upon price for the project.**

A: *Well, I'd say that the scarce resource here is the persons at the highest billable rate—that is, the partners and senior people. So what they need to do is focus on carefully budgeting the time involved with each project to ensure that they don't exceed the amount of estimated time for any partner to spend on a given project. We all know that the project will get done; it's a matter of making sure that the client is as happy as possible with the least amount of partner time being spent. Then the partners can be out selling new business, and the firm won't have to eat into its own profits. Basically, they'll make only what the agreed-upon price was, whether they spent too many hours or not delivering the project to completion. Allocation of scarce time resources is the main issue.*

Almost all strategic-consulting interviews have case questions, and some may consist entirely of case questions. This is just one brief example. Note how the candidate frames the answer logically, them summarizes logically. In this case logic is a framework for discussion of the allocation of scarce resources. Although it may be appropriate when answering a case question to ask first for clarification about the frame of reference, in this case the candidate's frame of reference is given by the recruiter—namely, the assumption that a set price is agreed upon up front. This assumption is critical to the candidate's conclusion that careful allocation of resources ensures the expected profitability

Staffing Manager
(Computer Industry)

Q: How is our staffing opening consistent with your long-term career goals?

A: *I look at what this company does and consider what it takes to manufacture computer products. I admire the fact that you have the fastest product-development cycle in the industry, which is a major reason for your rapid market share gain in the PC world. I also admire the quality of people that you hire, which is where this job comes in. You have to have phenomenal manufacturing people, planners, designers, financial people to make it work, and HR people to pull these groups together. Getting the right people in the right jobs at the right pay and with the right rewards would be my job. I'd love being a part of an organization that's known for having the highest quality of people.*

This question addresses whether the candidate's career aspirations can be satisfied at the company. The candidate does a nice job of expressing interest in the company's current business. Then he or she explains how the role of staffing manager would fit into that.

Q: Why would you be interested in getting into a generalist role?

A: *I see your rapid growth as a real opportunity for HR people to be generalists, wearing many different hats. I believe that having one's hands in planning meetings, helping to manage and hire and train for growth, will be the best way for me to use the mix of skills I have to be an asset to you in senior management.*

This question examines job compatibility and career aspirations. An HR generalist's job is typically a good path to senior management. The candidate's answer is realistic. He or she also effectively adopts the recruiter's perspective with the phrase "to be an asset to you"—in other words, the candidate's saying (without sounding arrogant) that the company will benefit by giving him or her this opportunity.

Q: What kind of organizational structure do you believe is effective?

A: *Actually, one of the reasons your company appeals to me is the fast pace and informal structure in general. My work in executive search was fast and furious, so I think that background matches well with the culture here. As I've dealt with HR generalists over the years, one thing they've always said is* *that the job is as boring or exciting as the pace of the group you work with. I wouldn't be excited if the division I worked in was out of the mainstream or out of the priority list within the company.*

HR generalists may be called upon to assist with restructuring various groups or entire divisions of a company, so the question addresses the candidate's professional opinion. Certainly your answer should not be incongruous with the structure of the hiring organization (unless you know that organization is changing its structure). The candidate draws comparisons between the pace of the company and the pace he or she has gotten accustomed to in executive search. This is a good example of clarifying a tie-in that may not be obvious to the recruiter.

Q: **What are your specific strengths for this staffing position?**

A: *Related to the unprecedented growth you're experiencing in U.S. operations, I think that what you need is a staffing person who knows how to look for people who think out of the box. In other words, you can't just fill seats. And certainly you aren't going to steal from other players in the industry as much, because many of those candidates are accustomed to working in highly bureaucratic, established organizations, where pace and structure differences would clash with your informal culture. My executive-search background, specifically the ability to locate candidates from different sources, would be critical.*

The candidate answers this skill-assessment question by tying his or her own strengths to the company and its growth objectives. The candidate is keeping the interviewer in mind with each answer. That's good, because the burden is on the job seeker, as a hiring expert, to be a good interviewee.

Q: **What was your initial interest in HR management?**

A: *Part of the intrigue for me was being the first to know what group is going to grow or downsize. Although downsizing plans can be unpopular, I'd rather be the person with knowledge than the person without it. The pulse of the company is always up front in your work priorities. That would be hard to walk away from. And I love knowing that, when the business is thriving, I had something to do with making sure the best people were hired into the right jobs, with the right incentives to perform well.*

This is a question of aspirations and job compatibility. The candidate explains how he or she is personally motivated by the work. Recruiters always like to hear a candidate's personal opinion or feelings, because they really want to get through the surface material to know the person. Remember. if they think you've held back from giving sincere answers, you aren't likely to get to the next interview.

Q: What do you see as your role as a staffing professional? What would you like your role to be?

A: *I think that all aspects of staffing—from selection to training to motivation to succession planning—make a big impact on the company's success. The key in any business is execution of a good idea, and it's the people you hire, plus their motivation, that determines success. There are many good business ideas that fail—usually because of the way people within the organization handle the situation. So I see myself as having a major role in providing an environment that rewards training and allows people to be productive. To me that means not giving them a lot of rules and constraints and procedures.*

This question is a career-aspirations question as well as a job compatibility question. Assuming the company is loosely structured, this is an outstanding response. It combines personal philosophies with a practical way (minimizing procedures) to create the right environment.

Q: What's your approach to managing costs per hire?

A: *Well, I wouldn't sacrifice quality—quality comes before cost. The goal is to hire the best if the company wants to stay number one in the industry. I try to foster positive employee referrals and things that are relatively low cost or no cost. I also believe in staying up on your industry. If a major competitor changes its benefits plans and its people revolt, you can use that to your advantage to point out the quality of your own benefits plans; that way you can pick up some employees with solid industry experience. I use all angles and overlap and integrate all my approaches: advertising, college relations, affirmative action, getting creative in relocation strategies, and so on.*

This is a skill and problem-solving question, and the recruiter is specifically testing the candidate's decision-making skills. This question is typical of what a staffing interviewee should expect. The candidate ties in lots of ideas, then summarizes by saying he or she uses all angles. The thoroughness of the answer makes it very believable.

Q: When you have an opening, do you tend to search for a candidate within the industry or outside it?

First-time Job Seekers: Consider pace in the industry. Some high-tech organizations move very fast, whereas established companies move more slowly but probably have more mentoring support or training programs. HR people should seek a combination of staffing specialist roles and generalist roles in the first few years of a career. You're then well rounded to go either way down the road—which means promotions will be easier.

A: *I've never believed our competition was within our industry but outside of it. So I ask myself where the best people would be who could thrive in a relatively unstructured, very fast-paced company. I've learned how to go out and find new sources for candidates—I go to top business schools, and I find out where the best companies are hiring people, regardless of the industry. Our growth means that our business is changing fast enough that prior industry experience isn't that critical; having the right job skill, like sales instincts for a PR job, is critical.*

This is a question of creativity and problem solving. The recruiter may be searching for whether the answer is predictable, or whether the candidate brings something new to the table. Skills in creativity become more critical when attracting senior people away from other leading firms or when searching for a rare skill set for which you might be willing to pay top dollar, but for which the potential hire's current employer will likewise be willing to pay a high price to retain.

Q: **You could do staffing at any type of organization. What appeals to you about the high-tech industry?**

A: *The hierarchy within the high-tech field, and the demand that field places on staffing people to be really creative, make the job more interesting. Also, my engineering background gives me validity in this business. To some degree people in HR are still fighting the "personnel" image. In this company, when I talk to engineering groups or development groups, I'll be able to talk their language and more easily understand what they need in prospective job candidates in terms of technical skills. And I'll be more effective at screening candidates because I have that technical orientation.*

Why is passion for the industry so important for a staffing professional? Staffing people are front-line salespeople in a way. They have to represent and sell the company to many people. In a sense they have to talk a potential employee into the job and then negotiate as low a salary as possible to get the candidate to accept. Therefore, staffing experts should have compelling answers to this question, and a sales-oriented personality.

Q: **Suppose you had a new PC delivered to your office. How would you learn to use it?**

Career Changers: A successful career switcher will have background in an industry that changed rapidly and/or quickly. The candidate would be aided by some technical background—academic or otherwise. Proving passion for the business is a major requirement.

A: *I've always been a self-starter. When I don't know something, the first thing I do is jump in and give it a try. Then I figure out who the experts are within my company, and I get their advice or get a dialogue going, so I have someone to share things with, like neat features of a software application I might discover or they might discover.*

The recruiter wants to see how resourceful the candidate is, and to test the candidate's need for structure and passion for the industry. A PC company should have staffing professionals who are excited about the industry and generally inquisitive about new technology—this is the same expectation of any potential employee applying for a position within the industry.

Q: What differentiates you from all the other staffing people out there?

A: *I'm more resourceful than most people. I use all sources simultaneously when searching for a particular type of candidate. I also make it a point to know my business, industry, and competitors. And although I know what I'm looking for, I keep my mind open about where I'm going to find the person with the right background. Here's an example: I know that you're trying to improve your market position in the government, and I know that no one in the PC industry is doing a particularly good job at that. I know you've been searching unsuccessfully to fill a top position as VP of Government and Education. If you hired me in staffing, I'd start looking at retired officers from the U.S. military. What you really need is someone who knows Washington, who's a leader and knows business. There are ex-military guys who've run military commissaries all over the world. So if you hire me, you won't get a "me too" approach to staffing; you'll get someone who helps you break the mold to hire the best people.*

This is a great wrap-up or introductory question in particular, allowing the candidate to summarize his or her most important points. The candidate does a thorough job and gives a good example—with advice—about a current issue the company is wrestling with, then ends by clarifying what his or her contributions will be if hired. (Good way to ask for the job.)

Q: Suppose you've really got to find a candidate and you aren't having success. What would you do?

A: *I'd look at two things. First, I'd re-examine the skill set I'm looking for to make sure I've got realistic objectives and expectations of the position. Assuming I did, I'd expand my search geographically. I'd also tap into resources like schools or trade associations and see if I could find candidates through word of mouth. A last resort, if the job is senior enough in level, is to turn to an executive-search firm that specializes in that type of placement.*

This is an issue of tenacity. The candidate shows several indications of perseverance, listing more than one idea. The initial suggestion to re-examine the position objectives indicates that the job seeker has the humility to question and adjust his or her thinking. This is a sign of maturity.

Q: **What is your interviewing style?**

A: *I've always believed in the behavioral interviewing style. That way you start by identifying how the specific question you want to ask will help you evaluate some important aspect (or behavior) of the candidate—like teamwork or leadership or management style. This alone keeps inappropriate questions out of the interview. I also believe that this method, during which you insist on examples of each behavior, helps you weed out people who can't support the buzzwords they've used. They have to be able to offer proof.*

This question tests a staffing professional's operating philosophy. Whether or not the recruiter prefers the same style, he or she must nonetheless see the reasoning behind this staffing candidate's approach. The candidate gives two good arguments (the method keeps inappropriate questions out of the interview and weeds out fakes). "Behavioral interviewing" is the process of asking questions like, "Tell me about a situation where you ..." or "How have you handled ... ?" which force a specific response or example.

Q: **Describe a situation in which you were involved in recruiting and had to use outside search firms.**

A: *In my last company we often hired scientists with business experience for our R-and-D management. I turned to a search firm for directors and vice presidents. I felt that the important thing was to find a firm specializing in natural-science candidates and to let that firm get to know my company. Over time I retained a firm that helped us locate numerous people; I spent a lot of time early on helping them understand our company and the type of person we were looking for.*

Experienced Professionals: Within high tech, there's a lot of movement of candidate's among competitive companies. However, within fast-growth companies that are top industry performers, there is less of a tendency to hire from competitors. Therefore, people with specialized skill sets and other industries have a good chance—provided they feel culturally compatible with a fast-changing, unbureaucratic organization. Experienced candidates with long histories at traditional companies may have a hard time convincing a fast-growing company that they will do well in a fast-paced environment where rules and systems aren't as formal.

It's generally not cost-effective to use a search firm for less-than-senior positions; after all, the in-house staffing professional should be able to locate and attract candidates for the majority of positions. However, senior positions often require use of outside firms. Here the candidate indicates a history of using these firms successfully and provides insight into how he or she has accomplished this.

Q: **How have you used salary benchmarking?**

A: *I've always believed in benchmarking. In my current company I prefer to look outside our industry rather than within it. I'm more interested in what a financial analyst is making with x years' experience in lots of different industries. In our low-tech industry we tend to employ people with higher levels of education than many of our competitors; we're known as the premium employer. That, again, is a reason I believe I'd be effective working for your PC division, because you're known for hiring the best people regardless of prior industry experience, as long as they're "PC junkies" at heart.*

Benchmarking allows staffing professionals to research whether salary packages are competitive. This candidate shows knowledge of the two choices—in-industry and cross-industry comparisons—and also relates why his or her experience is consistent with the environment at the new company. Good example of selling and translating one's experience to the job.

Q: **Suppose several job candidates you made offers to turned you down. How would you react?**

A: *Handling rejection is something you have to get used to in this business. At the same time, you want to make sure you're doing an effective job. I always follow up to find out why someone didn't accept. One reason is for learning. The second is that I feel I'm a PR representative for my company whether I get the candidate to accept or not; I want people to have a good impression of the company. This can help you later—I've had candidates later become customers or refer other job seekers to me.*

The candidate is realistic (you don't always win). This trait is critical because a staffing person should be a salesperson to a point but should not beg or coerce someone to accept a job; this will only cause problems later, including setting up unrealistic expectations. At the same time, the recruiter wants some proof here that the candidate doesn't lose more often than not after making an offer. This candidate exhibits resourcefulness and a desire to seek continual improvement in the process.

Q: **Describe a time when a staffing situation required confidentiality.**

A: *Confidentiality is always the rule in our business. For example, I take certain precautions, like never leaving things out on my desk when I'm gone. However, there have been times when an employee has come to me to complain about a manager. Rather than tell that manager, I'll follow the case carefully to make sure someone else doesn't make the same complaint or that the manager's boss does not mention a related problem during the manager's performance review. Then what I do is offer the employee practical suggestions on ways to try to improve his or her position without alienating the manager.*

This is a question of business ethics. The recruiter will want to know specifically what steps you take—for example, clearing your desk and discreetly advising the employee. Note that finesse as well as communication or negotiation skills play into this situation.

Q: Suppose you were trying to attract a candidate to a small town. What would you do?

A: *First of all, I'd never use enormous pressure. People have to make their own decisions, or you'll end up sorry if their fears later turn out to be true. However, these are some practical things I've done in the past: show cost-of-living adjustments to demonstrate the increased buying power in a small town; arrange one or two visits, including the candidate's family, to that town to look at housing, schools, and social life; and provide names of several employees—who've also relocated there—as contacts for questions and concerns.*

This is a problem-solving or process question. The answer is excellent in its logic and organization. First, it explains potential dangers or limitations of the situation. Then it provides some logical steps to take. Last, it indicates that the candidate has successfully recruited other candidates to accept jobs in remote locations.

Q: How would you plan and organize a campus recruiting program?

A: *Assuming I'm starting from scratch, I'd first determine entry-level salary benchmark, and I'd call some of the comparable companies to see where they recruit; then I'd look at starting salaries from the various schools. That would give me a long list of schools. Then I'd pick schools where we have regional needs, and I'd visit. I'd want to meet some students by floating around, perhaps at a*

Candidates Re-entering the Workforce: Trying to re-enter a fast paced high-tech organization may be difficult, unless you can point to ways you've kept up with the changes during your leave. Emphasize your technical background in academics and/pr job related experiences.

career event like a speakers' series, to determine if the school's culture seemed compatible with our company's. Then I'd set up interviewing schedules where I thought there would be a fit. Long term, I'd use alumni from each school to help me recruit and maintain a presence on campus.

This is a leadership/creativity question as well as a problem-solving question. The candidate lays out a good, logical process that brings in diverse issues, from salary to location to cultural fit, then finishes by explaining how to shift to a development strategy using alumni. This is a well-developed answer covering the process from start-up to maintenance.

Q: **How do you calculate your annual salary plans and projections?**

A: *I look at past year's data primarily, because my current company has had steady growth for four straight years. For any high-level openings we anticipate—for example, setting up a new division—I plan to use search firms, which will cost 25 to 33 percent of the first year's salary. For attrition openings I expect to bring in people at the salary midpoint for that position classification. For general raises I believe that average performers should simply get cost-of-living adjustments at the rate of inflation; so I generally set the total adjustment for the year at that rate and ask each department manager to hold to that. Then they can determine for themselves who outperformed and who underperformed, as long as the total departmental increase doesn't exceed that percentage.*

Here the recruiter will want to see your planning skills and process. The candidate gives several ideas. Each company is likely to have very different philosophies on the process, so the important thing here is just to have some ideas.

CHAPTER 15

HEALTH AND MEDICINE

Dental Hygienist

Q: **What are your educational credentials?**

A: *I have an associate's degree in science from Northeastern University. I'm a registered dental hygienist, and I've also received my certification in dental assisting.*

In order to be eligible for licensure, a hygienist must be a graduate of an accredited dental-hygiene program that's at least two years in length. Your education should include classes in dental pathology, periodontology, oral anatomy, and oral radiology, as well as more general classes such as chemistry, anatomy and physiology, and pharmacology. During your second year you'll need to complete a clinical internship.

Q: **Are your licenses and certifications current?**

A: *Yes, my license is valid, and I just renewed my CPR certification. My physical-examination certificate doesn't expire for another three months.*

Before you can receive your license, you must pass the National Board Dental Hygiene Examination, as well as a clinical and written examination in the state where you want to practice. This license must be renewed every two years. You must also be certified in radiology and CPR. You initially receive these certifications your first year in a dental-hygiene program, but you must periodically renew your CPR certificate. You can contact your local chapter of the American Red Cross for information on how to renew your CPR certificate. The federal regulatory agency OSHA (Occupational Safety Hazard Administration) has additional health requirements. You'll also be asked

First-time Job Seekers: An associates is the minimum requirement for most hygienist positions. There are also master's level programs for those interested in education, research, or administration. Once you graduate from a dental-hygiene program you'll be required to pass the state-board examinations and apply for your license in the particular state or jurisdiction where you want to work. For more information contact your state's Board of Dental Examiners or the American Hygienists Association.

to furnish a physical-examination certificate, which should include the date when the examination was completed, and the name of the physician who performed the examination. The physical examination also requires that you be tested for hemoglobin, hematocrit, hepatitis serology, rubella titer, serology, eyes, hearing, and tuberculosis. You must also receive immunizations for hepatitis B, MMR, polio, tetanus, and diphtheria. Your certificate must provide documentation of dates received.

Q: **Why did you choose the field of dental health?**

A: *During high school I worked part-time in a general dentist office. During that time I was exposed to different phases of dentistry: restorative, periodontic, endodontic, and prosthedontic. I also got a feel for the basic business aspects of the dental office, and for patient interaction. I decided to continue my education to become a certified dental assistant. After working as a dental assistant for two years, which I greatly enjoyed, I continued my education to become a hygienist.*

Be sure to discuss any prior experience you've had as a dental hygienist, as well as any other work you may have done in a health-oriented field. This demonstrates a depth of interest in, and a commitment to, a career in the health field.

Q: **Do you feel that you're a "people person" and why?**

A: *In this field you have to be confident not only of your clinical skills but of your interpersonal skills as well. I've found that giving a patient a big smile and carefully listening to his or her concerns help to make that patient feel at ease in the dental chair. I believe that part of my job is to make the patient feel as comfortable as possible.*

Being a "people person" means that you enjoy people, and patients can sense that. Remember: a dental practice is also a business that relies heavily on referrals; small talk with patients can be a real benefit to the practice. Even the most subtle people skills keep bringing patients back to the practice and generate new business through positive word of mouth.

Career Changers: You'll need to go back to school for your associate's degree, pass the state-board examinations, and apply for your license in the particular state or jurisdiction where you want to work. If you're coming from a medical background—for example, if you've been a dental assistant or physician's assistant—you may not need to go through the entire two-year associate's program. For more information contact your state's Board of Dental Examiners or the American Hygienist Association.

Q: Have you ever worked with children?

A: *Yes, I have. The office I worked in as a dental assistant specialized in pediatric dentistry, so I'm accustomed to dealing with children and their parents. I have a number of nieces and nephews, so I think that's helped me relate to children rather well. Do you have many child patients?*

Some dentists specialize in treating children; others may have only a handful of child patients. In either case it helps to have had experience with children, as the approach used to treat them is different from the approach used with adults. Show the interviewer that you understand this difference, and describe any experience you've had with children, both professionally and personally.

Q: How do you feel about patient dental education?

A: *I believe that it's a must on someone's first visit. I try to teach new patients about good oral hygiene and the importance of regular checkups. I also like to demonstrate proper brushing and flossing techniques, because I'm often surprised by how many people don't do them correctly.*

Although this may seem like an obvious question, it's important to show the interviewer that you don't ignore the issue or intimidate new patients with a lengthy lecture. Finding the right balance between the two can make all the difference between someone's becoming a regular patient and that same person never returning. Demonstrate that you know how to be tactful while communicating your concern that a patient keep his or her mouth in a healthy condition. Describe how you make patients aware of procedures that are available at the practice, such as sealants, implants, crowns, and bridges, as well as how you teach the proper ways to brush and floss.

Q: Describe your responsibilities in your last job.

A: *My duties included prophylaxis, patient instruction, fluoride treatments, caries screening, periodontal evaluation, exposing and developing full-mouth series, panorex, bite-wing radiographs, nutritional counseling, oral-cancer screening, scaling and root planing, ultrasonic scaling, and sealant placement. I also pitched in*

Experienced Professionals: Emphasize your experience and your flexibility. Many dental hygienist hold positions in more than one office, so the interviewer will want to know if you're available for full-time work. Also, show the interviewer that you've been keeping your skills current, either through industry seminars or continuing-education classes. If you want to go into research or teaching, you'll need to earn your bachelor's degree, or even your master's degree in dental hygiene.

at the front desk when the office was short-staffed, helping with calls to patients, new-patient files, daily reports, office billing, collections, and so on.

The interviewer is evaluating not only your clinical capability as a dental hygienist, but also your broader understanding of what's involved in running a dental practice. You should demonstrate a willingness to help with administrative tasks when necessary, including scheduling appointments or filing.

Q: Do you prefer to work independently or as part of a team?

A: *I believe you have to be a team player in the dental field. Everyone must work together to ensure that patients receive the best care possible in a timely manner. For example, as I mentioned earlier, on my last job I routinely pitched in at the front desk when the office was short-staffed.*

Although it's important to be able to work without someone looking over your shoulder, you should also be able to function as a team member. Teamwork is essential to making an office run smoothly. Give examples of how you've enjoyed working as part of a team in the past, and emphasize your flexibility.

Q: Are you willing to work evening hours and some weekend hours?

A: *Yes, I am. I regularly worked evening and weekend hours in my last position.*

These days most dental practices have "people hours" for the convenience of their patients. Most dental hygienists are expected to work nontraditional hours. A negative answer to this question may hurt your candidacy.

Q: Do you have any academic honors or awards?

A: *Yes. I was on the dean's list of the ADHA (American Dental Hygienists Association), and I was an ADA (American Dental Association) scholarship recipient. I'm also an honorary member of Sigma Phi Alpha Dental Hygiene Society.*

Candidates Re-entering the Workforce: First, you'll need to make sure your license to practice is current, and update your CPR (cardiopulmonary resuscitation) certificate. Get a complete heath physical with all necessary tests and immunizations in order to renew your physical-examination certificate. Consider auditing classes you think you need to review at your local dental-hygiene school. If after doing all of this you find you're having trouble getting back into the field, try working at a temporary agency in your area. Working temporary positions gives you the opportunity to build up your confidence and speed. The agency will be able to place you in varied types of dental practices (large, small, clinical, hospital, or institutional), as well as in specialty practices.

Awards, honors, and participation in professional associations indicate that you take your profession seriously. Show the interviewer that this isn't just another job to you, but a lifetime career that's important enough for you to pursue even outside the workplace.

Q: Have you taken any continuing-education courses?

A: *I believe it's important to update my skills continually and to stay abreast of the latest changes in the industry. Recently I took a course called Infection Control and Barrier Precautions at the state university's dental school. I also attended an OSHA training seminar last month, which I found particularly informative.*

The dental field is ever changing. New procedures are continually being introduced, and infection-control procedures, as well as sterilization practices, are always changing. It's imperative that you keep abreast of these developments. Describe any courses you've taken, including the ones that are mandatory in order to renew your license.

Q: Do you volunteer your professional skills?

A: *Yes. Twice a year I join a team of dentists, along with assistants and hygienists, to help underprivileged young adults and children get much-needed dental treatment. I also volunteer at the local elementary school once a year in the "Tooth Fairy Program."*

Although doing volunteer work probably won't be a requirement for most positions, it will give you an edge over other candidates. The above answer indicates a strong commitment to the dental field, extra initiative, and valuable experience working with children.

Q: What are your long-term career goals?

A: *Well, if I were to choose a career other than working clinically as a hygienist, I'd earn my bachelor's degree and go into research in the hygiene field.*

This is an effective answer, because it indicates a commitment to the field as well as a desire to keep learning and growing. If your goals are to make a career as a dental hygienist, that's okay, too. You shouldn't, however, tell the interviewer that your long-term goals lie in a completely unrelated field.

Home Health Aide

Q: **Are you a state-certified home health aide?**

A: *Yes, I am. I completed a seventy-five hour certification program sponsored by the American Red Cross. The program met all state and federal regulations for home health aides.*

The federal government has strict guidelines for home health aides who work through agencies that receive Medicare and Medicaid reimbursement. Check with your state's board of health to see if your state requires certification. If it does, you'll need to complete a certification program, which will most likely involve both classroom and clinical training, and to pass a state-board examination. Remember to bring a copy of your certificate to your job interviews.

Q: **Tell me about your experience as a certified home health aide.**

A: *I have more than two years' experience working as a home health aide for a local health-care company. I've worked with a variety of cases, including elderly and physically handicapped patients. On a few occasions I also worked with children with severe handicaps. I've worked both long- and short-term cases, including one elderly patient whom I worked with three times a week for a year and a half.*

Many agencies require employees to have one year of recent experience. Like this candidate, you should discuss what type of patients you've treated, and what kind of cases (long- or short-term), you've worked with. You can also discuss in depth a specific patient you've worked with—the diagnosis, treatment method, and what you did for that person. If you don't have home health aide experience, you can discuss any related experience you may have. For instance, many home health aides are also certified nursing assistants, who perform many of the same duties but in an institutional setting, such as a hospital or nursing home. Also, be prepared to give the interviewer references from either former clients or other employers.

Q: **Are you currently employed?**

A: *Yes. I'm working for another health-care agency, but the work has been slow. I told them I'd work on a per-diem basis, which will keep me on their current-employee list. I've been averaging about twenty-five hours per week there.*

Don't be afraid to say you're working for another agency. In fact, most employers will take this as a sign of dedication. Many home health aides work for more than one agency in order to receive as many assignments as possible. However, be sure to tell the interviewer if you have an ongoing case that will restrict your availability.

Q: Are you available to work nights?

A: *I'd prefer to work during the day or early evening, but I'm willing to work nights on occasion. I had one short-term assignment in which I stayed overnight with an elderly patient twice a week while her daughter traveled for business.*

Being a home health aide is not a nine-to-five job. Interviewers like to see candidates with flexible schedules. You should also tell the interviewer if you're available for weekend work. This is important because many home health-care cases are available every day of the week. Keep in mind that a negative answer to this question could seriously hurt your candidacy.

Q: Are you able to travel outside your hometown if necessary?

A: *Yes, I have a fairly reliable car. However, I'd prefer to stay within ten or so miles of the city.*

It's important to cite a willingness to travel. Having a car will mean that you'll be available for a wide variety of cases; you won't be restricted by location. However, don't worry if you don't have a car. The agency will simply know to send you only on cases that are convenient to public transportation.

Q: Will you be willing to pick up several clients and maintain them on an ongoing basis?

A: *Yes. As I said before, I have experience with long-term cases. In fact, I prefer those cases and believe that a long-term relationship benefits the patient. It's important for patients to feel comfortable with and trust the aide who's working with them, and a long-term commitment will allow for this.*

First-time Job Seekers: Educational requirements will vary according to the agency, but most require a high-school diploma and the successful completion of a home health aide certification course. During your interview, show that you're cheerful, compassionate, and dedicated. This work can be very difficult, and the interviewer will want to see that you have the emotional stability to handle it. Mention any volunteer work you may have working in a hospital, nursing home, or hospice. Even experience such as caring for a sick grandmother should be discussed in the interview.

This is a terrific response that emphasizes the candidate's dedication to the field, the job, and his or her clients. It also shows the candidate's understanding of the importance of the relationship between the aide and the client. It's fairly common for home health aides to pick up clients and then work with them for several months, or even years. For instance, you could have a client with a broken hip and work with that client for months until the hip heals.

Q: **Have you had experience using Hoya lifts?**

A: *Yes. I originally learned how to use a Hoya lift during my certification program. I've also used them in my experience with clients with handicaps. I've worked with several patients with partial paralysis and used the Hoya lift to help them out of bed and into their wheelchairs.*

Hoya lifts are used with handicapped people and people who are very weak— a patient suffering from multiple sclerosis, for example, or an elderly patient who lacks mobility and agility. Experience in this area isn't usually required, but it's a big plus. If you don't have any experience with this machine, discuss your eagerness and your ability to learn new tasks quickly. Most certification programs and some employers will offer training for this and other machines.

Q: **Tell me about your experience working with quadriplegics or paraplegics. Do you have a particular specialty?**

A: *I've never worked with quadriplegics, but I've had several clients who were paraplegics. Most of these cases were short-term; I was only temporarily replacing their regular caregivers. Using machines such as the Hoya lift, I'd help these patients out of bed, help them with some simple exercises, and bathe them. As far as specialization goes, I feel comfortable working with all types of patients. However, most of my experience has been with the elderly, and I really enjoy working with them. But, naturally, I'm willing to take on a wide variety of cases.*

Treating patients with partial or full paralysis is extremely difficult, both physically and emotionally. Agencies like to see candidates who are both experienced and comfortable working with quadriplegics and paraplegics,

Career Changers: This position involves both health-care and social-work skills, so any experience you have will be helpful. Any type of aide position—nurse's aide, hospital volunteer—requires the same compassion and love of people that a home health aide needs to demonstrate every day. You'll also be required to receive some specific training in home health care and, if applicable, pass a state-board examination. In your interview demonstrate a caring attitude and dedication to the field.

so be sure to discuss your experience in this area. Also, most home health aides don't specialize—they simply have a general understanding of all types of cases. Show a desire to take on a wide variety of cases. But if you believe you're particularly strong in one area, such as working with children, be sure to mention it. The interviewer will want to know this so you can be offered the appropriate cases.

Q: **As you know, this position often requires some light housekeeping. Does this aspect of the job bother you?**

A: *Not at all. I feel that a home health aide's job is to comfort patients and make life easier for them. And if this means occasionally washing their dishes or doing a load of laundry for them, then I'm willing to do that.*

The purpose of home health aides is to provide complete personal care to patients outside an institutional setting. This can include everyday chores such as changing bed linens, bathing patients, and preparing meals, in addition to health-related tasks. Although not all cases require you to perform household chores, you must demonstrate a willingness to do so. If you don't, the interviewer might question the strength of your commitment to your work.

Q: **Are you up-to-date on your CEUs (certified education units)?**

A: *I try to stay on top of my credits. I have four credits left to maintain my certificate for this year, but I've already signed up for a class on working with patients with severe handicaps, which will provide me with those credits.*

The interviewer wants to find out if the candidate is careful in maintaining certification. In states where certification is required, home health aides must have twelve CEUs to maintain certification. Show the interviewer that you're aware of how many credits you have and are taking steps to ensure that your certification won't expire.

Q: **Are you available for live-in assignments?**

A: *I'm available for short-term live-in assignments. As I said before, I once had a short-term assignment where I stayed with a patient overnight twice a week. However, the longest assignment I could commit to is one month.*

Experienced Professionals: Portray yourself as a compassionate, responsible, and self-motivated individual with the understanding and ability to give the best quality of care to patients. You can also talk more about specific cases so the interviewer can get a better idea of your skill level. Many home health aides will continue their education to become a nurse or physician's assistant.

Like this candidate, you should demonstrate that you're flexible in terms of availability. Interviewers prefer candidates who are willing to take on virtually any case, regardless of length or type of assignment. The majority of live-in cases are short-term. Usually these are cases in which an aide will help a client—for instance, an elderly patient who has broken a hip—until he or she becomes independent once again.

Q: Would you be willing to take on more than one case per day?

A: *Yes, I want to work as much as possible. In my previous position I'd often work with four or five patients per day. I understand that this is usually how the cases come in—most of the patients we treat need help for only a few hours a week.*

You should give more than a simple yes or no answer to this question. Here the candidate demonstrates a solid understanding of the position and industry in general. It's common for home health aides to work multiple cases in a single day in order to put in eight hours. Many times you'll work with a patient for two hours, then move on to the next client. Show the interviewer that you're willing to work many different cases in a day. This is particularly important for inexperienced candidates because longer assignments—those that last an entire day—will often be assigned to employees with more experience.

Q: Have you ever worked with terminally ill cases?

A: *I've cared for several patients who were dying of cancer. Although these cases can be difficult, I do find caring for terminally ill patients rewarding. If on any given day I can make their lives just a little easier or help ease their pain, I feel as though I've accomplished something important and meaningful.*

Again, the interviewer wants to get a sense of your skill level. Working with terminally ill patients can be extremely difficult emotionally, particularly if you don't have experience with such patients. If, in fact, you don't have prior experience in this area, show the interviewer that you're willing to do this kind of work. Employers like to see candidates who have enough confidence in themselves and their abilities to be comfortable with seriously ill patients.

Candidates Re-entering the Workforce: In order to refresh your skills, try volunteering in a hospital or nursing home before re-entering a homebound environment. You'll also need to go through another training program to renew your certification. Once you've received your certification, consider working part-time at first to ease your way back into the workforce.

Medical Technologist

Q: **Why do you want to leave your current position?**

A: *I've had experience with, and learned, every bench and feel that I've become stagnant in my job. I believe that it's best for me to leave so that I can move upward and increase my knowledge and skills, as there's little room for advancement in my current position.*

Whatever the reason, be honest! If there was a personal reason behind your decision to leave your previous job, that's all you have to say. But if you had problems at your last place of employment, they will more than likely be uncovered at a later point in the interview or personal-reference process. If you aren't forthcoming initially, your candidacy for the position could end abruptly. Above all, be careful not to criticize your current supervisor, coworkers, or laboratory, or say anything else that would suggest you'll be a problem employee.

Q: **You're coming here from a laboratory where you rotated through various specialties: hematology, chemistry, blood bank, and microbiology. Do you think you'll get bored doing only chemistry and STAT lab?**

A: *Frankly, I'm looking forward to specializing. STAT lab and chemistry work have always been my favorite areas, so I'd enjoy having more exposure to them. I'm also interested in learning more about a variety of chemistry analyzers.*

It's common for candidates to come from smaller laboratory settings where technologists are rotated through all specialties. In larger and midsized

---

First-time Job Seekers: Interviewers will look for candidates with either a bachelor's degree in one of the biological sciences, or a degree in medical technology. Medical-technology programs are usually four to five years in length and are extremely rigorous; candidates with this kind of background will immediately stand out from the competition. Internships or other clinical experience is a plus, but not required. If you have no relevant experience, discuss additional activities you may have participated in while in school or during the summers. This will give the interviewer an indication of your work ethic and sense of responsibility. Don't worry about your lack of clinical experience; many employers prefer candidates with no experience because they can be trained all the more easily in the employer's procedures.

hospitals, however, a medical technologist is more likely to specialize in a particular area and will simply rotate through the various functions in that area. As this candidate does, be sure to demonstrate a genuine interest and excitement for the type of work you'll be doing. Be prepared for follow-up questions regarding how much of your total bench time was spent in chemistry, what kind of equipment you used, and other details of the area. If you can answer these questions intelligently and with confidence, the interviewer will know that your interest in the specialty is genuine.

Q: **You've been a supervisor in another job. How do you think you'll work as a bench tech here, with someone supervising you?**

A: *When I applied for this position, I knew that I'd be a bench technologist, and that I'd be supervised. This fact doesn't bother me. Having been a supervisor, I understand some of the problems that can arise between a supervisor and the bench workers. In fact, I think that knowledge will help me be a better worker.*

This situation will come up more often as laboratories—especially those in hospitals—universally downsize and consolidate. Be prepared for this question. The interviewer is trying to determine whether or not you'll fit into the institution's laboratory setting, and if you'll resent losing the authority of your previous position.

Q: **How do you rate your ability to work with equipment and to troubleshoot problems?**

A: *I believe I have solid troubleshooting skills but will never try to solve problems that I think are outside my realm of knowledge. If I have a problem I can't solve, I feel perfectly comfortable consulting with other technologists or taking the problem to my supervisor.*

Career Changers: Career changers are rare but not unheard of in this field. Some candidates who may be one of two years out of college want experience as a medical technologist to help them get into medical school. But if you're coming from an unrelated field, you'll need to bolster your scientific knowledge by taking classes in areas such as biology and chemistry. Once you have the necessary background and get an interview, be prepared to discuss why you're interested in changing careers. You'll need to reassure the interviewer that you're truly committed to making the change. In your interview discuss skills that are transferable to the position, such as computer experience, and demonstrate a track record of success and accomplishments in your previous jobs.

The ability to solve equipment problems is a necessary skill in most laboratory settings. Show the interviewer that you have a healthy confidence in your abilities; at the same time, the interviewer will be concerned if you seem to be overconfident about your skills. It's important to show that you recognize your limitations.

Q: **What is the length of commitment you're planning to give this job?**

A: *I want to work at this lab for at least three years. By that time I should be finished with my graduate degree in biology. I may decide to continue my education and go for a Ph.D., in which case I'd probably stay here for longer than three years.*

This is an important issue because training new hires in a multitasked environment is a time-consuming investment. Employers look for candidates who are interested in making at least a three-year commitment to the position. Don't expect to be seriously considered for the position if you say you'd like to stay only one or two years.

Q: **In a STAT laboratory setting you'll be making important decisions and handing out results in a timely manner. The reputation of this lab is such that a doctor may decide to change treatment based solely on the numbers we hand out. Do you think you can work well under these circumstances?**

A: *I'm confident I can perform effectively under these conditions and am looking forward to the challenge. Though I haven't worked in a laboratory setting exactly like this one, I'm sure that the high quality of my work will transfer well to this environment.*

Laboratory environments will differ, and the interviewer is trying to determine here if the candidate will fit into this particular lab. For instance, a STAT laboratory is a fast-paced and stressful environment, and a technologist who works in that kind of setting must have the ability to work effectively under

Experienced Professionals: Your experience is your strongest selling point. You bring an in-depth knowledge to the position that less experienced candidates lack. For example, you have the ability to look at a reading and determine immediately whether or not the results make sense. Discuss any special projects you worked on at you last position, such as installing a new computer system or performing instrument evaluation. Also, mention any professional associations you belong to or seminars you've attended recently. Interviewers look for candidates with a demonstrated, active interest in the field, and who approach their work as a career instead of "just" a job.

pressure. This would also be an appropriate time for you to ask specific questions about the institution and laboratory where you'd be working.

Q: **Are you able to handle multiple tasks at once and prioritize work in an appropriate manner?**

A: *Yes, I can handle a variety of duties and prioritize my workload accordingly. I've worked offshifts on my own, and on very busy nights I've been responsible for cross matches, as well as for the other hematology and chemistry work.*

In a fast-paced laboratory environment you'll often be juggling a number of duties at the same time. You'll constantly be running tests, receiving samples for new tests, and giving out results—all at the same time. Again, it's important to show the interviewer that you can handle the pressure of the laboratory and have the ability to work on several projects simultaneously. Like this candidate, you should describe a situation in which your ability to handle this kind of stress has been successfully tested.

Q: **Can you tell me what equipment is used in the laboratory in your current position?**

A: *We use the Kodak ECTACHEM as our primary chemistry analyzer, the Coulter as our primary hematology analyzer, and the Clinitek to do our UAs. Also, there are other analyzers on which we do some of the smaller-volume tests. We usually send any esoteric, or very small-volume, tests out to a reference lab.*

This question seeks to determine the candidate's level of knowledge regarding the equipment used in previous jobs. Was the candidate trained simply to push buttons, or to have a deeper understanding of the equipment and its functions? The interviewer may also ask you more specific questions about particular pieces of equipment, so don't try to discuss equipment that you're not familiar with.

Q: **You've just finished training, and this is the first week you're "on your own." The supervisor is on break and you receive a call from OB asking for a STAT magnesium. Your control is out low. What would you do?**

Candidates Re-entering the Workforce: Show that you've kept up with the technological developments in the field. If you're a member of any professional organizations, such as the American Association of Clinical Chemists of American Medical Technologists, ask them to send you publications they may offer. Attending seminars sponsored by these and other professional associations is also helpful. And because virtually all labs are computerized now, computer literacy is a must. Discuss any experience you have with computers; even experience on your home computer is helpful.

A: *I'd recalibrate the instrument to save time, instead of rerunning the control, in case it was out again. After the instrument was calibrated, I'd run the controls, and if they were in, I'd run the patient sample and report the results to the physician.*

There are a few different ways to answer this question correctly; the proper way may simply be a matter of opinion or protocol. For instance, you may come from a setting in which the situation was handled one way, whereas the laboratory you're interviewing with may follow a different protocol. The interviewer will try to gauge your judgment in difficult situations. Show that you have the ability to assess a situation and make appropriate decisions; many technologists will run the control right away simply because a doctor ordered it, without considering extenuating circumstances.

Q: **Tell me about an activity you're involved in outside of work.**

A: *I'm very interested in the martial arts. I've been studying karate for about eight years. I currently have a brown belt, but I expect to receive my black belt within the next six months. Karate has taught me many things, including the value of self-discipline and self-control. It's also taught me to stretch myself and to stop underestimating my abilities.*

With this question the interviewer is simply trying to get a better picture of the candidate as a person. Whether you have a passion for gardening, do volunteer work, or are an amateur painter, show that you have some interests outside your professional life. Interviewers want to see well-rounded candidates who are interesting and active.

Nutritionist

Q: **Are you currently registered with the American Dietetic Association?**

A: *Yes, I am.*

A positive answer indicates that the candidate has completed the requirements to become a registered dietitian—earned an undergraduate degree in nutrition or dietetics, completed an accredited dietetic internship, and passed the national registered dietitians' examination, as well as met continuing educational requirements. If you're not registered, emphasize your experience in the field and your possible goals to become registered. Registration is not always a requirement; an undergraduate degree in nutrition or a health-related field may be adequate. However, as employers and the public become aware of the importance of a strong background in nutrition, registration may soon become necessary.

Q: **What did you enjoy the most during your dietetic internship?**

A: *I particularly enjoyed working in the outpatient nutrition clinic. I was able to educate people on a variety of diets and use my clinical knowledge, obtained during my internships, to give sound nutritional advice. I think patients are more receptive and attentive to nutritional advice when given outside the hospital setting.*

This question allows the interviewer to determine areas of interest and/or specialty. The interviewer may also be interested in the type of internship program you participated in, for instance, clinically based, community based, and so on.

Q: **Do you have any experience counseling patients on an outpatient basis?**

First-time Job Seekers: In order to become a registered dietician, you must have an undergraduate degree in nutrition or dietetics, complete an accredited dietetic internship, and pass the national registered dietitians' examination. You'll also be expected to meet continuing-educational requirements. All of this aside, be sure to show your eagerness and flexibility—traits that can go a long way toward compensating for your lack of experience.

A: *Yes, I've counseled patients individually on different diets, and I've educated clients in a group setting, as well. For instance, I once counseled a client who was able to decrease his cholesterol level significantly because of the diet I'd designed. I feel very comfortable teaching people.*

Employers look for candidates who feel confident of their ability to educate the patient or client, as the field of nutrition is very education oriented. Emphasize specific diets you've used when counseling clients. Give examples of your successes due to your counseling, such as a time when a client was able to maintain weight loss.

Q: Do you have experience with enteral and parenteral nutrition?

A: *Yes, I've provided recommendations for both enteral and TPN feedings. I'm very familiar with formulas and with providing nutritional intervention for patients with NG- or G-tube feedings, as well as those receiving either partial or total parenteral feeds.*

The interviewer is trying to gauge the candidate's experience with, and knowledge of, enteral and parenteral feedings. If you're going to work in a medical setting, these skills are absolutely necessary.

Q: Describe a positive work experience you've had with a physician.

A: *I've been able to work closely with physicians as a team member in the care of patients. I've provided recommendations based on my nutrition assessment and discussed them with physicians who have then implemented my recommendations.*

It's essential for the nutritionist to be able to communicate well with the physician in order for nutrition care to be provided. Give a specific example, stressing your strong communication skills.

Q: Describe a negative work experience you've had with a physician. How were you able to cope with the situation?

A: *I can recall a negative work experience that involved a physician who disregarded my recommendations, arguing that nutrition wasn't integral to patient care. I then took the time to provide the physician with more information and eventually persuaded him to see the benefits of my recommendations.*

Career Changers: Make sure you're familiar with the requirements and experience the employer is looking for. It may take a while to get the job you want if you're not a registered dietician or at least have a master's degree in a nutrition-related field.

Again, dealing with physicians is an important aspect of a nutritionist's job. Give an example of how you dealt effectively with, or managed to turn around, a negative situation. Emphasize how you used assertiveness and diplomacy to resolve the problem.

Q: **What's your position on the use of vitamin and mineral supplements?**

A: *I'd recommend a supplement in certain cases, such as for a malnourished or medically compromised patient, and would not discourage use of certain vitamins. However, I always encourage a balanced diet to obtain adequate vitamin and mineral intake.*

This answer reassures the interviewer that the candidate would provide sound nutritional advice rather than misinformation. Demonstrate your knowledge of vitamin and mineral supplements with specific circumstances that may require dietary supplementation. It's okay and sometimes necessary to recommend a vitamin or mineral supplement, but you want to emphasize that the best way to obtain adequate vitamin and mineral intake is through a balanced diet.

Q: **Do you feel comfortable lecturing on the topic of nutrition to a group?**

A: *Yes, I feel very comfortable lecturing to a group. I've provided many presentations on a variety of topics in nutrition to different populations.*

This question allows the interviewer to determine the candidate's teaching ability, as well as organizational, interpersonal, and communication skills. Sometimes it's necessary for nutritionists to give a general lecture to a group of patients, so you should convey the sense that you feel comfortable in front of a crowd.

Q: **Describe how you perform a typical nutrition assessment of a patient. What type of progress notation do you use?**

A: *I obtain a detailed diet history including the usual eating pattern and diets previously followed, as well as height, weight, usual body weight, and medical history. I prefer the SOAP format; however, I can adapt to any format.*

Experienced Professionals: Get involved with local dietetic associations. You can make good contacts this way, as well as discover job openings that aren't advertised in the newspaper. You may also want to consider jobs in teaching or administration.

The interviewer wants to determine how thorough the candidate is in obtaining nutritional information. You need to show that you take all factors into consideration when making a nutrition assessment. Like this candidate's answer, your answer should be specific and complete.

Q: Are you familiar with current nutrition-reimbursement practices?

A: *Yes, I realize that most cases aren't reimbursed for nutrition; however, some insurance companies offer partial reimbursement. Given that, in combination with other services, nutrition services may be reimbursed.*

Your answer should reassure the interviewer that you're aware of current reimbursement and payment procedures. Your knowledge of reimbursement demonstrates that you practice cost-effectively. You also need to become familiar with these policies if you're interested in working in private practice or outside an established company

Q: Do you have experience developing patient-education materials?

A: *Yes. I've developed nutrition-education materials for a variety of diets. I've used some desktop-publishing and word-processing programs to obtain a more professional look.*

It's important to show the interviewer that you're able to work independently to develop appropriate materials for use in teaching clients. The employer wants to see that you're able to develop educational tools that are effective, and that you're aware of the need to use good written materials to help patients understand information and to encourage good compliance with the diet.

Q: How do you keep abreast of current nutrition research and information?

A: *I belong to the American Dietetic Association, I read current journal articles, and I attend several conferences a year.*

Demonstrate how you've kept your knowledge current and how you've built on a current clinical base. Show your ability to apply research to clinical practice in this ever-changing field. Also, show that you always keep an eye out for the latest studies on nutrition.

Candidates Re-entering the Workforce: Keep up with your continuing-education requirements. Be prepared to explain how you can use the experience you've gained during your leave. For example, if you took time off to raise your family, you can use this experience to help counsel pregnant women and new mothers.

Q: **Are you familiar with nutritional therapy for wound healing?**

A: *Yes, I'm familiar with pressure ulcers and providing essential nutrition therapy to increase wound healing. It's important to be sure that the patient's receiving adequate calories and protein, as well as zinc, vitamin C, and a multivitamin.*

Patients with pressure ulcers can be found in many types of settings—long-term care, nursing homes, acute-care hospitals, or the home. Nutrition plays a vital role in the healing of such ulcers. Therefore, the nutritionist is important in these cases and should have the background providing the right care to patients with skin breakdowns.

Q: **Describe your undergraduate and/or graduate work relating to nutrition.**

A: *As an undergraduate, I had a heavy course load in science, nutrition, management, and education. I completed four semesters in chemistry, as well as semesters in zoology, microbiology, and human physiology and anatomy. My last two years concentrated mostly on nutrition—clinical nutrition, nutrition education, and so on. My graduate work strongly emphasized nutrition and allowed me to focus on my particular area.*

This answer gives the employer more insight into the candidate's background and knowledge of nutritional science. It's important to have a good foundation in the sciences as well as in management and education, since many nutritionists work in a medical environment educating patients or managing staff.

Pharmacist

Q: **Tell me about your professional aspirations.**

A: *I've decided to make retail pharmacy my future. I love working with people, and I'd like the chance to build relationships with customers.*

Many young pharmacists work in retail for only a short period of time, then move on to other areas of the profession. It's important to find out if the candidate is looking at retail only as a way to move into other areas of the profession.

Q: **Do you have any experience working in a retail pharmacy?**

A: *Yes. I began working at a pharmacy my junior year in high school. I eventually was promoted to pharmacy technician. I thought I'd like to try it as a career, so when I was choosing a college, I looked for one that offered a pharmacy degree.*

The interviewer will want someone who has experience working in retail. Ideally, you'll already understand the nuances of working in a retail environment. In a big company it's very costly to train someone.

Q: **In the past have you had to direct a group of professional technicians?**

A: *Yes. In my current position I supervise a group of three technicians.*

Usually, a retail pharmacy has two or three pharmacy technicians. These aren't licensed pharmacists, but they act as liaison between customer and pharmacist. It's important that you have at least some experience directing technicians, because you'll need to deal with them constantly.

Q: **What business experience have you had?**

A: *I have two years' experience working in a pharmacy and have thorough knowledge of inventory control. I was also responsible for billing third-party insurance claims.*

First-time Job Seekers: A.B.S. in pharmacy is required of all pharmacists. You must also have passed NAPLEX, which is a board-of-registration test, and be a certified pharmacist in your state. Almost 75 percent of all pharmacists start at the retail level; others might go into different areas, such as hospital pharmacy.

A big problem with retail pharmacists is that often they don't have any real business knowledge. A pharmacist must know how to deal with insurance companies and how to control inventory. At the very least the interviewer will want to make sure you have some common sense when it comes to business. Business classes in college are a good start.

Q: **Would working long shifts cause you to lose concentration?**

A: *Oh, not at all. I'm quite used to working long hours, and my concentration rarely suffers.*

This question is important because most retail companies expect you to work twelve-hour shifts. Many pharmacists dislike the long hours, but if you want to work in retail, they're just something you have to get used to. Consequently, it's imperative that you're able to maintain a high level of concentration at all times, from the first hour of your shift until just before you leave eleven hours later.

Q: **This job requires working a lot of nights and weekends. Is this a problem for you?**

A: *No, not at all.*

This requirement will be part of the job description. Like anyone in retail, pharmacists should be willing to work nights, weekends, and holidays. Other pharmacists, like those who work in hospitals, work regular eight-hour shifts, but retail pharmacists are required to work some nights, and generally one or two weekends a month.

Q: **Are you interested in being promoted to management above store level?**

A: *Yes, eventually. For the time being, though, I'd like to devote all my energies to working in retail. I see management as something I'd be interested in later on.*

The interviewer will want to see if you're ambitious. At most larger pharmacy chains almost all people in management started as retail pharmacists, in order to become familiar with the working of the pharmacy.

Q: **Do you mind working with the elderly?**

Career Changers: Because pharmacy is such a specialized field, requiring a five-year degree and certification, it doesn't attract a lot of people from other fields. But anyone entering this field would be expected to obtain a degree and certification.

A: *No. I get a great deal of satisfaction from working with elderly persons. I really do enjoy helping them out.*

Working with the elderly is definitely a big part of any retail pharmacist's job. In many cases this requires a lot of patience, since you must get them to tell you about any other drugs they're taking, and you must also carefully explain the medication you're giving them. Sometimes they'll be taking as many as ten medications, and you have to have the patience to explain each one.

Q: **Do you feel you're good at making quick decisions?**

A: *Yes, I do. I really have no problems with making quick decisions.*

Pharmacists must be able to analyze a situation and make decisions quickly. You need to look at a prescription that someone brings in and decide if it's good, if it's forged, if you think it's the wrong medication, or if it will conflict with something else they're taking, or if it's the wrong dosage. Give specific examples of how you've made good decisions quickly in the past.

Q: **Do you have any problem delegating authority to technicians?**

A: *No, not at all. The pharmacy is often so busy that I appreciate having the extra hands around whenever possible.*

Many pharmacists have a hard time giving responsibility to technicians and often perform the tasks themselves. For instance, technicians will normally do all the legwork on insurance claims, and the pharmacist need only check it over and give final approval. If you're working in a busy store, you can't do everything, and you must learn to delegate authority.

Q: **How would you handle a situation in which you thought a client was handing you a phony prescription?**

A: *If I thought there was a good possibility the prescription was forged, I'd immediately call the doctor to verify it. If for some reason I couldn't get hold of the doctor, I'd tell the customer that we were out of the medication and to come back at a later date. If I reached the doctor and was told the prescription was indeed false, I'd immediately call the police.*

Experienced Professionals: Many pharmacists move out of retail after a number of years. Some may go on to pharmaceutical sales or research, and others may go into more specialized areas in hospital or nursing homes. In retail chains many experienced pharmacists move up to management. Still, experienced, seasoned pharmacists are always in demand in retail chains.

People coming in with phony prescriptions is a common occurrence, especially since identification isn't required to pick up prescriptions. Pharmacists must quickly develop a keen eye for which prescriptions are real and which are false and must know the proper course of action.

Q: **If you thought the dosage on a prescription was wrong, what would you do?**

A: *If there were other pharmacists around, I'd consult with them first. Then, I'd call the doctor to check the dosage.*

Although pharmacists should know what the proper dosages are for most drugs, from a legal standpoint you just shouldn't rely on your own knowledge. You're legally responsible for the prescription, so you have to cover yourself.

Q: **If you don't know the proper dosage of a drug, where would you turn?**

A: *I always keep copies of* National Formulary, Facts and Comparisons, *and, of course, the* Physician's Desk Reference *on hand.*

With more than 10,000 prescription drugs available, it's virtually impossible to know the proper dosage for every single one, though you should have the proper dosages of more common drugs memorized. Therefore, it's essential that you keep one or more of these reference books available and handy at all times.

Q: **How would you rate your professional skills?**

A: *I'd rate myself pretty highly. I always manage to keep abreast of all the latest advances in drug development, and I've a thorough knowledge of the proper use and dosages of the most common prescription drugs. On a more personal level I enjoy working with the public and giving people the help they need.*

Although you should never misrepresent yourself, a job interview is no place for modesty. The interviewer wants to hear about what you view as your strengths, so you should highlight those in your answer.

Candidates Re-entering the Workforce: If you've worked on the retail level for a number of years, you can either move back into retail or into management, sales, or research. Whichever you decide, you should make sure your certification is current and that you've stayed in touch with all the latest developments and medicines within the pharmaceutical industry.

Q: **Where do you see yourself in ten years?**

A: *By that time, I wouldn't mind being out of retail and working at the corporate office in management.*

This is a good answer, since it shows some ambition. However, there's nothing wrong with saying that you'd still like to be in retail. There's a shortage of retail pharmacists right now, so the interviewer probably wouldn't mind if you were in it for the long haul.

Physical Therapist

Q: **What are your qualifications as a physical therapist?**

A: *I'm a licensed physical therapist with a bachelor's degree in physical therapy. I've also done several internships in both hospital and clinical settings.*

All states require physical therapists to pass a licensure exam after graduating from an accredited physical-therapy program. A master's degree is recommended for those interested in an administrative position and is required for research and teaching jobs. Experienced physical therapists should expect to continue to develop professionally by participating in continuing education courses and workshops from time to time.

Q: **Which of your clinical affiliations did you enjoy the most?**

A: *During one of my internships I worked with an elderly man whose left side was paralyzed by a stroke. When I first started working with him, he didn't like me very much, to say the least, and he never cooperated in any way. At first I took it personally, but then my supervisor pointed out that he acted that way toward everybody, and that he was probably just frustrated and upset about what had happened to him. Well, from that point on I stopped acting so defensively around him and started to joke with him more, and he eventually warmed up to me. By the time I left, he was fully cooperative and beginning to make progress. That was one time when I really felt as if I'd made a difference in someone's life.*

This question is geared toward entry-level physical therapists. In a nonintrusive way it allows the interviewer to determine what really interests the candidate and to gain some insight into specific strengths or weaknesses.

Q: **Do you embrace a specific approach to physical therapy?**

A: *No. I think I have a really eclectic approach to clinical care. I don't believe that any single approach is best 100 percent of the time; different situations call for different methods.*

In a hospital setting physical therapists will encounter a wide variety of patient cases, so the interviewer doesn't want to hear that you favor one approach over the other, or that you think some new, yet-to-be-proved technique is the answer. This is a good answer, as it shows that the candidate uses a varied, pragmatic approach to physical therapy.

Q: **Upon what do you base your clinical decisions?**

A: *I'll always look at the nature of the patient's diagnosis, his or her medical history, age, and so on. I'll consider the goals of the treatment as well. I also consult with other physical therapists. I'll consider all this information before I determine a course of action.*

This question addresses the candidate's critical thinking. The interviewer wants to know what factors the job seeker considers before deciding on a particular treatment. Your answer to such a question should demonstrate a methodical, step-by-step approach to making sound decisions.

Q: **What would you do with a patient whose expectations for treatment outcome were unrealistic?**

A: *Well, I'd carefully go through the case with the patient, explaining what treatments have or haven't worked in the past, gently explaining the success rates of similar cases. I'd explain all the options that were available, and I'd hope the two of us could eventually come to an understanding regarding the outcome of treatment. But if this didn't work, as a last resort, I'd offer alternative resources, and conclude that I was unable to meet the patient's expectations.*

This question targets the candidate's problem-solving ability; the interviewer wants to discover what steps he or she would take to resolve the situation. An ideal answer should also show a recognition of patients' rights and an understanding of one's responsibilities as a clinician to recognize those rights. It's imperative that a physical therapist achieve collaboration with a patient; a patient can't simply be abandoned just because expectations can't be fully agreed upon. You should never say, in response to such a question, that you would call the patient's doctor and ask what to do.

Q: **What would your supervisor say is your greatest strength?**

A: *Well, at one point I had the opportunity to treat a very difficult patient, and it required a great deal of interdisciplinary coordination. Later on my supervisor complimented me on how well I could facilitate the coordination of the various disciplines that were necessary to manage the case.*

First-time Job Seekers: The interviewer will ask you about your various clinical internships or experiences, or if you're licensed. Be sure that you're ready to explain why you want to go into physical therapy, avoiding general statements like you just want to "help people." Read the professional journals so you're ready to discuss the latest developments in physical therapy; such as preparation will likely set you apart from other entry-level candidates.

The interviewer wants to hear some specific attributes, in particular, professional attributes. Don't just say something like "I get along well with patients"—everybody says that. In physical therapy establishing rapport with patients is absolutely essential, so such an answer won't shed too much light on your true strengths. This candidate's answer is effective because it highlights a unique skill.

Q: In what area would your supervisor say you need to improve?

A: *Well, I tend to be a perfectionist. My supervisor pointed out once that I'd probably get things done a lot faster if I could learn to accept some details that weren't absolutely perfect.*

Give examples, not just broad characteristics. The interviewer is trying to find out what the candidate considers his or her weakest characteristic. Don't offer something trivial or claim that your supervisor never told you to improve anything, because if you do, the interviewer will know you're not being honest.

Q: What strategies have you used to improve those skills?

A: *In general I now let more imperfections go by. I'm still a stickler for details, but I realize that everything doesn't need such a high level of accuracy. As a result, I get more accomplished in a day, since I'm not poring over every little detail.*

Your answer here will reveal how you respond to critical feedback and how you use that feedback to make adjustments. Can you take criticism well and institute those changes to improve your work?

Q: Describe your ideal work environment.

A: *I like to take a team-oriented approach to physical therapy, so I like an environment in which everybody works more or less together. When people with a variety of experience levels and specialties join forces, everyone wins, because we can always learn from other people's experiences.*

The interviewer wants to gain insight into the candidate's thoughts on the ideal workplace. There's no right or wrong answer here, but a good answer will closely match the profile of the department. The interviewer is looking to see how well the candidate's work philosophy will match up with the department's philosophy.

Career Changers: There's no shortcut here. If you want to get into physical therapy, you're going to have to start from scratch. Go back to a licensed, accredited school to get your degree. Secure internships so you can get practical experience. Keep in mind that in the interview you'll be asked why you decided to change careers. And try to highlight any transferable skills or abilities from your previous profession.

Q: Tell me about a difficult experience in your life. How did you overcome it?

A: *Well, physical therapy is my second career. Before this I was in human services, so I had to go back to school to pursue this new career. I was also married with a small child at the time, so it was difficult just to start all over again. I often had many doubts as to whether I was doing the right thing, and I actually thought about dropping out a few times, but I finally realized that my desire to be a physical therapist outweighed everything else, and I just persevered. Today I have no regrets about what I did.*

Your answer to a question like this will give the interviewer insight into how well you've managed a trying situation, and what types of situations cause you stress. Depending on the situation you describe, the answer may provide further information about how you'd react to a similar problem on the job. Your answer can be drawn from either your personal or your professional life.

Q: What kind of patient situation do you feel most comfortable with?

A: *I feel most comfortable with cases for which there's a clear diagnosis and course of treatment. Although I like working in a team environment, it's just less draining, both emotionally and physically, when there's a clear course of action for a case.*

This question is designed to give the candidate a chance to emphasize personal strengths—the areas in which he or she feels most confident. There's no right or wrong answer here—simply state your preferences. The situation you choose to describe could be a certain clinical environment or diagnosis, or a combination of the two.

Q: What type of situation would make you most nervous?

A: *I've treated only a few patients with above-the-knee amputation, and I'm always afraid that the patient will sense my inexperience.*

Again, be honest. You could give an example of a diagnosis you haven't encountered very often, or a case that's just outside your range of experience. Don't

Experienced Professionals: Emphasize the types of environments in which you've worked—in a hospital, for insurance, or in private practice. Since you're more likely to be interviewing for a role that requires some supervision of other therapists or interns, you'll probably be asked questions regarding your supervisory or management skills. Also, most experienced physical therapists eventually pursue advanced degrees, so you may want to consider getting at least a master's to stay competitive.

give an answer that addresses client behavior, like "I hate dealing with unco-operative patients."

Q: Why are you interested in our facility?

A: *I'm attracted to your hospital because of its outstanding reputation. I also know that your department is one of the best in the region. But, more specifically, I feel as if I need more varied experience, both in terms of patient cases and in different experience levels like those you have within the department. I want to work someplace where good mentoring is available. I also like the fact that you're a teaching hospital, so you always have new students coming in.*

This answer demonstrates how thoroughly the candidate has investigated the facility. The interviewer wants to see how much thought has been put into the kind of environment the candidate would like to work in. The answer also indicates what the job seeker thinks is important in a facility. An answer like this can set you apart from those candidates who are blindly sending out hundreds of resumes.

Q: Where do you see yourself in five years?

A: *Well, I really want the opportunity to get more experience so that I can make better decisions about whether I want to specialize in a certain aspect of physical therapy or just continue doing clinical work.*

An interviewer is more likely to ask you this if you're a candidate with little or no experience. Here is an opportunity to show the interviewer how much thought you've put into the direction you'd like your career to take. Your objectives should be focused, but at the same time, try not to rule anything out. If you mention that you're likely to go back to school for an advanced degree, be prepared to talk about what you want to specialize in.

Candidates Re-entering the Workforce: First of all, make sure that your license is current, and if it isn't, take the appropriate measures to rein-state it. You'll be asked hard questions about why you left the workforce and why you're ready to come back. Medicine is constantly changing, so the interviewer will question your knowledge of the latest developments. Read the medical and trade journals, and be prepared to discuss recent develop-ments in the world of physical therapy.

Registered Nurse

Q: Are you a U.S. citizen or permanent resident, or do you have unrestricted employment authorization granted by the U.S. Immigration and Naturalization Service?

A: *I was born in Canada, but I've lived in the United States for fifteen years and I am now an American citizen.*

Nurse recruiters ask this question because some years ago hospitals were doing a lot of recruiting outside the country, making the job search difficult for nurses in the U.S. At the time, it was not easy to find qualified nurses within our borders, whereas there were some very good nurses in Canada. Also, hospitals on the upper East Coast and the West Coast needed nurses who were bilingual. Then the U.S. government stepped in and imposed regulations requiring that hospitals have a vacancy rate over 7 percent before they recruit outside the country.

Q: What are your nursing qualifications?

A: *I have worked for ten years as a staff nurse with experience in all areas of nursing. I've also worked in quality assurance, and I currently work in ambulatory medicine.*

The recruiter is looking for both solid experience and a wide range of experience. This nursing candidate has both. The candidate's answer is also well articulated. Practice your answer to this question so that your answer is a brief summary of relevant work experience only.

Q: What are your primary responsibilities in your current nursing job?

A: *I run the ambulatory medicine facility. This means I make sure the actual logistics of the operation run smoothly on a day-to-day basis. It also means that I spend a lot of time rolling up my sleeves taking blood, for example, or whatever is needed.*

Experience is extremely important in nursing. The recruiter is digging to be sure this candidate has significant work experience. Prove to the recruiter that your job is more than a mere title, just as this candidate has done.

Q: What did you do before your current nursing job?

A: *I was the hospital quality assurance manager. I oversaw a team of nurses, although I spent most of my time determining patient releases as well.*

Of course the recruiter will know what a quality-assurance job entails, but the candidate has cleverly slipped in a definition nevertheless. Because this job requires significant nursing ability and knowledge, the recruiter will undoubtedly be impressed. This candidate also shows breadth of experience.

Q: What nursing degrees do you have?

A: *I have a master's in nursing administration. I received a B.S. in sociology before that, and an R.N. previous to that.*

This nurse is extremely educated in the field and has described some extensive training without seeming arrogant. If your highest level of education is an R.N., this is perfectly acceptable. You may want to consider continuing your education at some point, however.

Q: Who do you think are particularly important nurses in the medical industry?

A: *My personal role models are Virginia Henderson, who started the first nursing index, and Florence Nightingale and Martha Rogers, the two most important nursing theorists. These women have set important standards for the industry and have made the profession what it is today.*

This answer is commendable. The nursing candidate has knowledge of the industry and, furthermore, has chosen excellent role models. Read about current industry greats in nursing journals, or take a history-of-nursing class at your local community college.

Q: Why did you want to be a nurse?

A: *My mother was a nurse because, in her day, it was one of the few options open to women. I decided I wanted to be a nurse from an early age because, of all*

First-time Job Seekers: Many hospitals will first have you submit your nursing credentials, which they will verify. If you have the required skills, you will then have a general screening interview with a nurse recruiter, who will ask you a set of basic core questions. If you "pass" this section of the interviewing process, you'll then interview with the nurse manager in a specific unit of the hospital—like the cardiac unit, for example. He or she will judge you based on how qualified you are and according to a grading scale. The candidate with the highest "grade" will get the job. Be sure to dress appropriately and professionally for the interview.

the careers open to women today, it's the job in which I can make the biggest contribution.

This candidate's answer shows a commitment to the profession. The recruiter is looking for serious nursing candidates only—those who are making a career of it. Think about why you're taking the interview and about why you're in nursing at all. Be able to articulate these ideas clearly to the recruiter.

Q: What nursing publications do you read?

A: *On a regular basis, I read the* American Journal of Nursing *and* Nursing 96. *I also believe it's important for nurses to remain aware of what's going on outside of our profession, so I skim through the* Wall Street Journal *every day.*

Your answer should be something similar to this candidate's. The recruiter is looking for someone who's always trying to keep his or her knowledge and skill level up to date. In an industry where technology is always changing, it's important to keep extremely aware of the profession.

Q: What do you think about managed care?

A: *I think it's an important development in nursing. People are spending less time in the hospital, which is positive for the patient. And it keeps the rising costs of the health-care industry in check.*

The recruiter wants to be sure that you're aware of current trends in the nursing and medical profession. This nursing candidate's answer is exemplary because he or she is aware of changes in the medical profession and, is not resistant to that change. Be prepared for inevitable questions like this by reading current nursing journals.

Q: Do you think high technology will play an increasingly important role in the medical industry in the future?

A: *It absolutely will. Information technology will mean to nurses that they'll be able to care for their patients more quickly and efficiently. I think high technology has already played an enormous role in the efficiency of the medical industry. The laser used for surgery is a very good example of this.*

Career Changers: You should have your goals clearly in mind. Be able to articulate what it is that you want. If you're making a change, be able to explain why. You need to be able to sell yourself to the organization. Obviously, the more experience you have, the more desirable you are. At the very least you'll have to take some preparatory classes at your local community college.

The recruiter wants to see that this nursing candidate has a big-picture perspective of the industry. The candidate's answer is excellent because it demonstrates an understanding of the scope and impact of technology in the medical industry, and even provides an example. The importance of reading nursing publications cannot be stressed enough.

Q: **Do you see much opportunity in health care in the future?**

A: *I think that because the industry is changing so dramatically, there will be plenty of opportunity. Drastic change always creates opportunity. For example, doctors will probably spend 80 percent less time in hospitals, so more nurses will be needed to staff the hospital.*

This candidate's answer is good and is what the recruiter expects. The recruiter wants to be sure that the nursing candidate does not exist in a vacuum. Understanding the direction that health care, and thus nursing, is taking is essential.

Q: **What do you think is the greatest problem with the way hospitals are run today?**

A: *Hospitals are extremely understaffed. The result is that we are not able to give as good a quality of care to our patients as we might.*

The recruiter wants to be sure that the candidate is aware of industry standards, and at the same time is asking, "What frustrates you most about your job?" This candidate's answer shows genuine concern about the profession. The recruiter is not looking here for personal concerns about the job seeker's current position—like not getting enough vacation time, for example.

Q: **What would you do if you found a friend and coworker stealing medical supplies?**

A: *That would be an awful position to be in. I'd immediately go to my supervisor once I was sure I knew what was really happening.*

Experienced Professionals: You should have a good idea of what your overall goals are for the remainder of your career. Concerning the job you're interviewing for, however, you should be flexible in terms of where you want to work and what hours. Don't walk in and say, "No nights or weekends," for example. Know that it's possible to get a job, but it may not be the perfect job the first time you walk in the door. Flexibility to work in more than one setting, such as willingness to work in the SICU (surgical intensive care unit) and the MICU (medical intensive care unit) as you're needed, is also attractive to recruiters. However, your experience is the biggest thing you have going for you, and it will mean a lot in the interview.

This question is designed to determine the candidate's morals and ethics. This nursing candidate handles the situation correctly. It's also significant that he or she expresses remorse for the situation rather than enjoying power over a colleague.

Q: What is your biggest priority as a nurse?

A: *Tending to my patients has always been my biggest priority. I also really try to make the patient's family feel as comfortable as possible.*

It's important that you give an answer similar to this. The recruiter always wants to hear you talk about your patients first. A bad answer would be something like, "advancing my career."

Q: Have you read any fiction set in the medical profession?

A: *I've read the novel* The English Patient *by Michael Ondaatje. It made a big impression on me because a young woman becomes an ad hoc nurse with no training or supplies, simply because she's desperately needed by a burn patient. I try to read this book once a year because it inspires me and it reminds me of how important my job is.*

The candidate's answer is very strong here. It certainly isn't necessary that you read medical fiction. The recruiter, however, would undoubtedly be impressed with such a genuine interest in the nursing profession.

Q: What do you do when you encounter nursing procedures that you're unfamiliar with?

A: *I immediately see if the hospital offers any classes in the area. If not, I find a class at the local community college so that I can get up to speed.*

Candidates Re-entering the Workforce: People who have been out of circulation for any length of time, especially more than three or four years, need to take refresher courses. Such classes are available in every community and are usually listed as refresher courses for nurses. This course work is essential because the technology and medications change so much. And patients in hospitals these days are pretty sick. So nurses really need to be as prepared as they can from the minute they walk in the door. Hospitals don't have time to do extensive training programs anymore. In fact, many hospitals won't even hire someone re-entering the profession if they haven't taken a refresher course. You may even have to get some kind of experience before working your way back into a career in nursing again.

The recruiter is determining how proactive the candidate is. The importance of continuing your nursing education as needed cannot be stressed enough. This answer demonstrates a strong "can-do" attitude, which is another plus.

Q: Do you prefer to spend most of your time working alone or with others?

A: *One of the things I like the most about being a nurse is the constant interaction with other people.*

Nursing is a team effort. You'll always be working with other nurses, as well as with doctors and hospital personnel. You will also, of course, be interacting a great deal with patients and their families. If you prefer to work alone, then you might want to become involved in another aspect of the medical profession instead, such as research.

Q: What is an HMO?

A: *A health maintenance organization is a gatekeeper, so to speak. It's an efficient way of organizing a certain set of doctors for the company's health-insurance customers.*

You should be aware of what an HMO is and how it works. This nursing candidate understands what an HMO is and has given a brief and acceptable answer.

Q: What would be your ideal nursing job?

A: *I think I'd like to reach the next level of nurse management. I'd like to oversee a bigger clinic, with more interaction with the resident doctors.*

This answer shows ambition and commitment to the profession, and is also realistic and appropriate. Carefully think about your answer to this question before the interview.

Q: Do you have any questions for me?

A: *Yes. How many patients do you see on an average day? How do you structure the work day for maximum efficiency?*

The recruiter will want to answer any questions you may have. You should be prepared with several intelligent, well-thought-out questions. Remember, though, that the interviewer will find it a real turnoff if, this early in the hiring process, you ask questions like, "Will I be able to leave on time every day?" or "How much vacation time will I get?"

Speech-Language Pathologist

Q: Tell me about your education and clinical training.

A: *I received a master's degree in speech-language pathology. My clinical experiences as an undergraduate and a graduate student gave me exposure to most job settings and a variety of age groups. My clinical-fellowship year was spent in a hospital, and my primary focus was the evaluation and treatment of swallowing disorders.*

In most states a master's degree is the minimum qualification to work as a speech-language pathologist in hospitals, rehabilitation centers, or other settings. To work in a public or private school, you may need additional certification. Many states have a licensure law that requires you to have a master's degree in speech-language pathology and at least nine months of supervised experience in a clinical setting. You may also be required to pass a national examination. The American Speech and Hearing Association issues a Certificate of Clinical Competence with similar requirements, but this certificate doesn't supersede state law.

Q: What type of disorder do you feel most comfortable working with?

A: *I've had the most experience working in hospitals, treating adults with swallowing disorders. My clinical fellowship allowed me to work closely with a radiologist while performing and interpreting videofluoroscopy diagnostic evaluations. As part of my work I also had to plan and implement feeding programs for the patients.*

This is a fairly common question designed to address what the candidate considers to be his or her greatest strength. Although there's no right or wrong answer, you're more likely to encounter certain disorders in particular types of settings. For instance, if you're applying for a position in a hospital, you're likely to encounter a large number of patients with dysphagia, as these types of cases represent the majority of hospital in-patient referrals. Therefore, you'll want to be sure that your answer is compatible with the hospital work setting.

Q: What type of disorder do you feel least comfortable treating?

A: *That would probably be the area in which I have the least experience—working with fluency and voice disorders in both children and adults. I haven't had much exposure to these disorders.*

Here the interviewer is trying to determine what areas the candidate will need to improve. Again, be honest in your answer, but try to discuss a disorder that you'd be less likely to encounter in the job setting that you're applying for.

Q: How well do you get along with coworkers, and if you had conflict, how would you resolve it?

A: *I have a strong commitment to teamwork and realize how important it is to the success of our mission. I've often worked with other specialists in treating a patient. I also realize that it's equally important to work with the families of clients so that they understand the goals that have been established and can assist the patient in meeting those goals. I've never really experienced conflict in the workplace. If I did, I suppose I'd try to resolve it directly with the person involved. If that was unsuccessful, I'd turn to my supervisor and ask him or her for advice.*

Teamwork is extremely important in the workplace. Speech-language pathologists often work with doctors, teachers, or rehabilitation counselors as part of an interdisciplinary team. It's helpful to understand the goals of people in other disciplines and to have them understand yours. Also, a client's success and speed of recovery may be greatly influenced by the support you have, or don't have, from colleagues and family members.

Q: How did you become interested in speech-language pathology?

A: *I knew nothing about the field when I entered college. I was originally a pre-med major, but during my freshman year I took a linguistics class that I found fascinating. Then, as part of my anatomy class, I had an opportunity to visit the speech-language-pathology clinic on campus. The work really seemed rewarding, and after that I was anxious to learn more about the field and the career opportunities it offered.*

The interviewer is simply trying to learn a little more about the candidate. Again, your answer to this question should be honest and thoughtful. Many people become interested in the field because of something that happened in their own personal experience, so it would also be appropriate for you to discuss an incident from your life that inspired you to enter speech-language pathology.

First-time Job Seekers: Employers will be most concerned about your education and clinical experience. In your job interviews emphasize your desires to get started in the field, and discuss what you think you could contribute to, and learn from, that particular job setting. A master's degree is highly desirable, but as an undergraduate you could receive a degree in communications sciences and disorders, or speech pathology and audiology. Also, be sure that you have the licensure and certification required in your state.

Q: When assessing children younger than three, do you believe it's better to separate them from their parents or have the parents present during the evaluation?

A: *I want the child's parents to be comfortable with the testing situation. If the parent wants to be present during the evaluation, I have no problem with that. I also believe that it's sometimes traumatic to separate a small child from a parent—the child may not respond the way he would if a parent was present.*

This question is designed to discover the candidate's approach to treating small children. Most speech pathologists agree that it's useful for parents to observe the testing process, as they'll have a better understanding of what's expected of their child, as well as a better idea of the child's progress. Also, parents will be able to explain whether the child's responses to treatment are typical or out of the ordinary.

Q: If a child refuses to cooperate, what techniques would you use to encourage him to interact?

A: *I'd try to engage his interest in a toy he could manipulate, or in age-appropriate puzzles or artwork.*

This is another question that addresses the candidate's approach to treatment. It's sometimes difficult to request verbal responses in the initial stages of establishing rapport with a child. Starting with some fine motor activities, such as block building or drawing, will often take the pressure off the child, and he or she will begin to participate verbally while becoming more comfortable with the situation. If you're going to be in a position where you'll have frequent interaction with children, it's essential that you understand this concept.

Q: If a parent expressed dissatisfaction with your discipline procedures or with your therapy expectations, what would you do?

A: *I'd try to make clear the goals of the session, as well as my long-term plans for achieving those goals. I'd also give the parent opportunities to make suggestions that could help accomplish these goals.*

Career Changers: A career change to this field requires significant commitment. You'll need a master's degree and a year's supervised clinical experience and will most likely be required to pass a national written examination. Because of the clinical hours required to obtain a degree, even those with a bachelor's degree may need to take several undergraduate courses before becoming eligible for a master's program.

Many speech-language pathologists are quick to dismiss parents' input simply because they believe a parent is too emotionally involved in the situation to give objective advice. However, it's best to show that you'd involve parents in developing realistic goals for their child.

Q: **In job settings where parents aren't always present, would it be important to communicate with them, and how would you do that?**

A: *I believe it's extremely important to keep in close contact with a child's parents, even if this can't be done in person. It's often impossible to have personal contact with parents on a consistent basis, especially if you're working at a school. Sending a child home with written progress reports is one possibility. Also, I'm always sure to give the parents my work phone number, just in case they have questions or a specific issue to discuss.*

No matter what setting you're working in, it's always important that you maintain some contact with a client's parents. Make it clear to the interviewer that you'd keep the parents informed of the goals of treatment so that they could measure the progress of their child. Also, a child might be progressing quite well with you but regress once he or she is back at home. A parent needs to know what's happening at the therapy sessions to maintain that progress at home.

Q: **What's the most difficult child you've worked with, and why?**

A: *During a clinical practice I had to work with a child who had a terminal illness. This was the first time I'd ever been exposed to what was—to me—a tragic situation. It was very difficult for me to think of him as a normal child; I felt so sorry for him that I had a hard time getting past those thoughts. My supervisor helped me see that I was being unfair by treating the child differently from the others. Most children want to be treated the same as everyone else; they want to feel as if they fit in. My performance improved, but it wasn't easy. If it happened again, I'm sure I'd have to work very hard at my behavior.*

It's natural to show sensitivity toward and empathy with your client, but not to the point where your emotional attachment has a significant impact on

Experienced Professionals: You'll want to emphasize the job settings you've had experience in as well as the types of caseloads you've had. You will also want to discuss the varied experiences and strengths that you'll bring to the job. Show how you're able to take initiative and work independently on projects. Also, you may want to consider getting your Ph.D. in speech pathology if you wish to enter private practice, conduct research, or teach at college or university.

your work. In a field where you're likely to encounter terminal patients, it's important to be realistic—a therapist must be a source of strength and hope to clients. You could also choose to discuss here a child with behavioral problems who was hard to manage, or even a child whose disorder proved especially challenging. Be sure that your answer demonstrates how you managed to overcome a difficult situation.

Q: Have you found your age to be a problem when working with elderly patients?

A: *At first I was a little uneasy about it because I felt that they had so much more life experience than I did. It was easy to grow out of that, though, because of the specific knowledge and experience that I was bringing to their problem.*

Especially working in a hospital setting, you're likely to encounter a number of elderly patients. It's important to show confidence in yourself, regardless of the age group you're working with. An employer likes to have a staff that's able to meet new and challenging situations with ease, and doesn't like to be restricted to assigning certain employees to certain types of disorders.

Q: If you were doing an adult voice evaluation and the patient had been referred to you by his physician but had not seen an otolaryngologist, would this be important?

A: *Yes, I think it's very important. In this case, I'd contact the patient's doctor and explain that I think the patient should be seen by an otolaryngologist before I began working with him, so that I could better develop a course of treatment.*

It's often difficult for a general practitioner to give an adequate diagnosis on voice disorders. These types of disorders should be diagnosed by a specialist after a thorough examination. Treatments based upon an incorrect or incomplete diagnosis could be virtually worthless. Of course, every organization will have its own protocol in these situations, so be sure to inquire as to the established procedure in that facility.

Q: If you were seeing a lot of the same type of disorder, would you lose interest and become bored with your caseload?

Candidates Re-entering the Workforce: You should familiarize yourself with current requirements for certification, and be sure that you meet those requirements. It will be useful to show how your life experiences can help you become a better speech-language pathologist. For example, if you left the workforce to raise a family, you'll have gained a lot of knowledge in child development as well as increased insight into family counseling.

A: *I don't think so. If I enjoyed the type of disorder I was working with, I'd probably be very happy. For example, in my previous experience I worked primarily with swallowing disorders, but the challenge was terrific.*

This is a potentially sensitive area. You're more likely to encounter the same disorders in a specialized environment, such as a school, than you would in a private-practice or hospital setting. In many cases, especially in private practice, your job could be tailored to suit your specialties. For now, however, your primary goal is to get a job offer, so you should emphasize your ability to do repetitive work. If possible, give an example of how you've worked with many of the same types of disorders in the past.

Q: Paperwork is a constant demand, and timeliness is important. How well have you managed to fulfill your administrative obligations?

A: *I try to manage my time so that I don't get too far behind on my paperwork. I always make it a practice to write my clinical notes each day. I never go home before I finish my administrative obligations, because I like to do the paperwork while the cases are still fresh in my mind.*

Careful documentation is crucial to the job. Employers like to see that you can write clear, concise reports on your cases. Sloppy or incorrect documentation of cases can be potentially damaging to an employer, especially in a private practice. You may want to bring some samples of your written reports to share with the interviewer.

Q: Why should we hire you?

A: *I believe I have the clinical skills to be an asset to this organization. I think I'm a good team member and would be able to make a positive addition to your practice. In turn, I believe that if I was hired, I could benefit from my colleagues and from the supervision I'd receive. I enjoy learning and broadening my experiences.*

It's important to show confidence in your abilities, but it's equally important to demonstrate that you're eager to learn and to improve your skills. Your answer here should give primary emphasis to what you could contribute specifically to the organization. Show that you're knowledgeable about the organization, and, based on this knowledge, explain how your strengths and experiences will fit in with the organization.

CHAPTER 16
LEGAL AND PROTECTIVE SERVICES

Director of Security

Q: **Do you have any experience preparing budgets?**

A: *Yes, I do. As security director for a large department-store chain, I managed an annual budget of almost $1 million. I was responsible for all aspects of administering the budget, including negotiating with outside security firms for services such as alarm systems and monitoring.*

As head of the security department, you'll be responsible for the department's operating budget. Show the interviewer that you have some experience in this area, even if you were responsible for only a limited aspect of a budget process, such as choosing security devices for a particular store.

Q: **Tell me about a time when you saved the company money through security measures.**

A: *When I started my current position, the organization was using six different companies for six different services. In other words, our fire alarms were monitored by one company, burglar alarms by another, and so on. Through some careful research I found that we could have two companies servicing all our outside security needs and pay 40 percent less than we had been. I presented my findings to the vice president, and my recommendations were implemented within six weeks.*

Your answer here will depend on whether you're going into retail or corporate security. If you're interviewing with a retail company, you should discuss your experience lowering shrinkage rates, or programs you've implemented to discourage employee theft. In corporate security you're more likely to discuss situations in which the savings came from the consolidation or automation of services.

Q: **What kind of interview and interrogation skills do you possess?**

A: *I've taken the Wicklander and Zulawski courses on interview and interrogation. I've also attended two seminars on effective interviewing, which were sponsored by the American Society for Industrial Security.*

It's not enough to say you've conducted hundreds of interviews and inter-rogations; the interviewer wants to see candidates with formal training in this area. Like this candidate, you should mention one or two specific classes you've taken that have taught you how to conduct more effective interviews. For instance, you can learn specific techniques on how to obtain the truth from subjects without falsely accusing or threatening them. You might also give an example of a particularly difficult interview you've conducted, and how your training helped you through it.

Q: **How would you rate your supervisory skills?**

A: *I'd say they're top-notch. I believe the skills I've learned through my work in the security field—such as diplomacy and patience—have made me a tough but fair supervisor.*

A security director for a large corporation or retailer will usually supervise a staff of guards, investigators, or assistants. Show the interviewer that you're authoritative and effective in dealing with your staff; the security department isn't usually very popular within a company, and it's often difficult to keep your staff upbeat and motivated. You must also demonstrate your ability to work effectively with others throughout the organization to achieve the company's goals.

Q: **Tell me about your educational background.**

A: *I graduated from Northeastern with a bachelor's degree in criminal justice and a minor in sociology. I've also taken numerous seminars and continuing-education classes to keep my skills current and sharp.*

Education is becoming increasingly important in the security field. Today interviewers want to see candidates with college degrees. Some colleges have programs in security administration, but a major in criminal justice or classes in psychology or sociology are usually sufficient. You should also dis-cuss any specific training you've had in security, such as seminars or other classes.

First-time Job Seekers: Whether you start in retail or corporate secu-rity, your first position will most likely be as a security officer, hotel or store detective, or investigator. For this kind of position you'll need a bachelor's degree, preferably in criminal justice. Because it's unlikely that you'll have any professional experience in this area, be prepared to discuss why you're interested in the field. You'll also be asked a number of questions to deter-mine your skills in diplomacy, as well as how deftly you think on your feet—essential characteristics for someone in security.

Q: **What kind of employee-awareness training have you done?**

A: *I've regularly participated in employee-orientation programs, speaking to new hires regarding personal and workplace safety, the protection of confidential information, and computer security. When I worked in retail, I coordinated seminars in shrinkage prevention, which all sales associates were required to attend.*

The security director is often called upon to educate employees on a variety of security issues. Again, your answer will depend on whether you have a background in retail or corporate security. A retail company will be more interested in your experience with shoplifting prevention, but if you're interviewing for a position in corporate security, a response that emphasizes training in the protection of propriety information will be more appropriate.

Q: **How are your skills in safety or fire-prevention programs?**

A: *I'm thoroughly knowledgeable about all OSHA regulations that affect this industry. I've had specific training in emergency-evacuation procedures and have also attended seminars on fire prevention sponsored by the National Fire Prevention Association.*

The interviewer will want to determine your familiarity with the safety issues that are important for your type of company. The Occupational Safety Hazard Administration (OSHA) is a federal agency that strictly regulates all industries. If you're interviewing with an industrial or manufacturing company, you'll be expected to understand specific issues of regulation, such as the proper use of heavy machinery, or how to store hazardous chemicals and substances. You should also discuss your experience with fire prevention and awareness programs.

Q: **Do you have any experience with executive protection? What would you do if your CEO received a death threat?**

A: *Yes, I do. I've been trained in identifying potential threats against our top executives, including training their executive assistants to identify suspicious mail, phone calls, or visitors. The CEO's driver receives training in areas such as evasive driving*

Career Changers: Many directors of security are former state and local police officers, or former federal officials, such as FBI or Secret Agents. If you fall into one of these categories, you already have the intelligence and basic security skills that hiring managers look for in security directors. The interviewer will be most concerned with whether you'll be able to adapt to the corporate office after spending years in the field. You'll need to demonstrate that you have the unobtrusive demeanor and diplomatic skills necessary to succeed in corporate security.

and also has experience as a bodyguard. Our company has a detailed action plan, which I helped develop, of what should occur if an emergency arises regarding the CEO. If the CEO received a death threat, I'd first determine the likelihood that it was genuine. I'd secure the office, restricting both phone and personal access by visitors, and ensure that his home, as well as his routes to and from the office, were secure. And if it was necessary for the CEO to travel, I'd secure those destinations as well, making sure that he traveled with a bodyguard, and I'd take other precautions as appropriate. Naturally, I'd inform the police or FBI in accordance with the wishes of the CEO himself.

The interviewer wants to get a sense of the candidate's decision-making and planning abilities. The top executives of high-profile corporations are often the targets of threats, either direct or indirect. Although most threats originate with disgruntled employees, or others in the community, and aren't serious, some are indeed genuine, and it's important to be able to distinguish between the two. Discuss any experience you have in this area, and demonstrate your ability to think clearly and remain calm in such a situation.

Q: **What would you do if an employee threatened the safety of another employee and no witnesses were present?**

A: *I'd first identify whether or not the threat was genuine. If I thought the situation was serious, I'd take precautions regarding the safety of the person who was threatened—escorting him to and from his car and so forth. I'd then speak with the employee's supervisor, as well as with the human resources department. Maybe this person had a history of instability and violence and was a true threat. If this was the case, I'd contact the proper authorities and have them intervene, then continue to protect the threatened employee as long as a perceived danger remained.*

This is a follow-up to the previous question, designed to see how well the candidate thinks on his or her feet. The interviewer wants to know if the candidate has the ability to react effectively in high-pressure situations. Like this candidate, you should be prepared to give a detailed plan of what you'd do in a similar situation. A large part of a security director's job is to identify and evaluate threats against the company and its employees and to address them properly, and you need to demonstrate your ability to do so.

Experienced Professionals: Most people advance to director of security after five to ten years in the field. Interviewers look for candidates who have a proven ability to protect a company's interests, assets, and employees. Be sure to discuss your experiences and accomplishments in this area. Also, some companies require candidates to be a certified protection professional, a certification offered by the American Society for Industrial Security.

Q: Have you ever dealt with protection of proprietary information?

A: Yes. As I said, I have experience training employees in these issues. I've also made recommendations about what should be considered proprietary information, and I've instituted policies regarding the handling and disposal of this type of information.

The interviewer wants to determine the candidate's experience with managing sensitive information, and if he or she has a good sense of what's confidential or proprietary. Demonstrate your ability to handle discreetly company or trade secrets, research, and future business plans. Obviously, no interviewer will expect many details in your answer; if your response is too specific, the interviewer may wonder if you're truly trustworthy.

Q: What experience do you have with liability prevention?

A: I've educated sales associates and other floor employees on the liability issues of false accusations or imprisonment for shoplifting. I make sure that employees are following the law and aren't being overzealous.

This question seeks to determine the candidate's level of knowledge of civil-liability and civil-law issues, particularly insofar as the candidate can identify the issues relevant to his or her company that could create potential liability issues. If you've worked in corporate or industrial situations, you should discuss security issues, such as what would happen if an employee was assaulted in the bathroom or parking lot. Show the interviewer that you can identify threats, take steps to minimize the impact of those threats, and ensure that they won't reoccur.

Q: What do you consider your greatest strength?

A: I get along well with others. I believe I'm a very fair, diplomatic person. People seem to trust me quite easily, and I believe that's really helped me succeed in this field.

Security professionals have a reputation for being intimidating and difficult to get along with, so interviewers like to see candidates who are skilled in

Candidates Re-entering the Workforce: In your interview emphasize your previous accomplishments. The interviewer's biggest concern will be that you've lost the ability to think and react quickly in critical situations. If you've been out of work for a number of years, consider taking some courses in criminal justice at your local college, or enrolling for classes or seminars sponsored by the American Society for Industrial Security. These efforts at continuing your education will show the interviewer that you've kept up with the field during your absence.

diplomacy and interpersonal relations. You could also try to identify the company's weaknesses, then answer appropriately. For instance, if you were interviewing for a position with a retailer, a good answer might be, "I'm really good at reducing shrinkage in order to maximize profits for the company."

Q: What do you consider your greatest weakness?

A: *I really don't have much patience dealing with dishonest employees. I've never been able to understand people like that, and I firmly believe they should be dealt with severely—I don't believe in second chances.*

Like this candidate, you'll do well to respond with a weakness that many employers would consider a strength. Be honest, but don't give an answer that will make the interviewer believe you're the overly aggressive, bad-cop type of security director.

Q: Where do you see yourself in five years?

A: *Actually, this position would put me where I've always wanted to be, and from all that I've learned about the company, I think I could be happy here for a long time. It's conceivable, though, that after I've been here for a while and I know the operations well, I might find another aspect of the company that interests me. In either case my main goal is to be effective in whatever I do.*

Be careful how you answer this question. You don't want to look too aggressive, but you don't want to appear too passive, either. If you're at a junior level, you could mention specific positions you'd like, such as assistant director or regional or district security manager. This is a great answer if you already have some experience at the top level; companies like to see consistency at sensitive positions, like security manager or director.

Emergency Management Specialist
(Ex-Military Officer)

Q: **What specific strengths could you bring to this job?**

A: *I could help this organization be better prepared for disasters before they happen. With my knowledge of existing federal and state relief programs, we could use these programs as resources for careful emergency planning. For example, my knowledge of federal response would help us pinpoint whom to go to for a certain resource (like a generator, or damage-assessment support, or fresh water). I've worked within the government, and with its various agencies, for a long time.*

This is a skill-assessment question. The candidate sells the resources he or she has acquired in terms of people and agencies. This point is important to government organizations with limited resources; making the most of available help is critical, so the answer here addresses what the recruiter wishes to know.

Q: **Do you feel that your government experience as a military officer gives you certain advantages?**

A: *Definitely, from the standpoint of knowing where to access help and being flexible on the job. In the military you always have to figure out a way to do the assigned task; you can't look for excuses not to complete it. Failure isn't one of the options, so you learn to be creative to solve problems. Also, the military provides the kind of field-validation experience you don't get in many other places. I've had to test my skills in emergency planning, as well as the strength of my plans in action.*

This job-assessment question attempts to determine what leverage the candidate's military background really has with this job opening. The candidate draws important parallels and also offers a distinction that someone who has no military background can't offer—field-validation experience. In other words, this person's disaster plans have been put to use and proved valuable.

> **First-time Job Seekers:** Any college program in emergency management is helpful. State and federal course work is also available; you can check with federal and state offices to learn about these course offerings. Make sure you are familiar with the *Disaster Recovery Journal* and with publications by IAEM (the International Association of Emergency Managers).

Q: **What did your field experience in the military teach you?**

A: *It taught me that a plan on paper that seems reasonable may not work when put into action. Field validation teaches you to keep the plan simple, especially since people have to follow the plan when they're under severe stress. When I look at a plan, I want to know if anyone has used it effectively. In the military we studied an officer named Clausewitz who used to refer to the Fog of War concept. He warned against getting into the heat of battle and realizing too late that a plan falls to pieces when put to the test. The military is still the best place to get true practice, which over time helps you build plans from the start that will work the first time they're actually used.*

This question simply calls for more detail. You should prove that your field experience relates to the position in important ways. Although this candidate's answer is clear, one example related to disaster planning could have helped, such as, "This would be especially important when you design an alternate energy or shelter plan for a community, knowing what problems surfaced in test trials."

Q: **How can you develop a new plan that you know will work when put into action?**

A: *I really believe in the KISS (Keep It Simple, Stupid) approach. Also, I make as many decisions in the clean environment as can be made; that is, I make decisions in advance, so that fewer decisions have to be made when things are frantic.*

The interviewer is obviously interested in this topic because he or she asks another question. The important thing here is not to let the probing make you nervous. This candidate keeps the answers clear and his or her convictions strong.

Q: **Can you give a specific example?**

A: *Sure. Next winter, before the potential occurrence of damage from severe ice storms, your disaster planners would want to make contingencies for worst-case scenarios of losing electrical lines during a freeze. This might include an extensive list of relief organizations and contacts outside each geographic area, alternative energy sources to electricity, lists of potential temporary shelters for helping displaced families, potential food supplies, and so on. When the 2004 freeze hit the Midsouth, some of these planning decisions had not been made in advance. The consequences were widespread confusion and a sense of helplessness while the electric utilities struggled to restore downed power lines. Some people, who were out of power for days, might have been more comfortable with better planning and better communications before and during the disaster.*

Now the interviewer wants an example and gets a good one. The candidate could have anticipated and volunteered the example when answering the previous question. The example is specific and draws upon a real event—in other words, it proves that the candidate has done some investigating before the interview.

Q: **What interests you specifically about a job here?**

A: *First of all, I have family in this state, so I remember that 2004 freeze quite well. One of my interests in relocating is that I have family in the area. Within this organization, specifically, I see potential for real improvements—the emergency management program is in its infancy and is looking for people to move it forward. For example, in your recent case of planning after the 2004 ice storm, you'd have to plan for the negative impacts on businesses that were shut down for days. And you'd need someone familiar with other government programs who could identify agencies to help quickly in such cases.*

This question addresses aspirations as well as passion for the business. The candidate provides some information that would be awkward, bordering on illegal, for the company to ask—"Do you have any ties to this state?"—yet companies naturally might wonder whether a candidate with no obvious roots in a particular geographic area might adjust or enjoy the area. Also, the answer focuses on the right perspective—the organization and its goals. The candidate's goals are relevant only as they fit with the goals of the organization, which they obviously do.

Q: **Tell me about some of the emergency management activities you have actually participated in.**

A: *I've been involved in planning activities and response in the field. I've had to evaluate other disasters, which is where I got a lot of my experience, especially hurricanes and earthquakes and the Midwest floods. I reviewed After Action Reports, which are case studies conducted immediately after the fact, in which we would identify weaknesses in planning or in execution of disaster relief and look for improvements of the process. In a nutshell, I could help this organization develop solid plans to cover earthquakes, floods, or hurricane and tornado damage.*

This question concerns accomplishments. The candidate is wise to point out those accomplishments relevant to the organization he or she is interviewing with.

> **Career Changers:** If you're getting out of the military, make your military experience work to your advantage. Emphasize your management skills and your good management track record. What has the experience taught you? How have you handled stress? Be sure to avoid using jargon that pinpoints you as military: try to adopt lay terms like "meeting" (not briefing) and "employees" (not "personnel" or "subordinates").

Q: How does your vision of emergency management fit in with our business plan?

A: *Well, I can tell you my vision. I really do believe in the value of planning in emergency management. Mitigation is critical; you have to build structures to avoid disaster, including choice of location, building codes, and other careful measures of prevention. Then you have to have lists of the most likely resources needed and ways to contact them. Developing relationships in advance with those resources is also important, and I know many of those resources at the federal level. My career interests here at this organization would be to help build a fully operational program. By "operational" I mean eventually having a full budget with current plans in place, with an emergency-exercise program containing both a training and an exercise component, with preparedness for buying resources, and with fully staffed emergency-operations centers. Now, I realize that might be a far-reaching goal for now, but I believe you start by educating other decision makers about the potentially catastrophic risks of having underdeveloped plans in place. How does that fit in with your goals for your emergency management function?*

This question addresses problem solving, motivation, and aspirations. The candidate provides a logical summary and then asks a good question. What he or she is really asking for is confirmation of whether there is a potential fit.

Q: What important contacts and resources could you bring to the job?

A: *Knowledge of available federal programs, knowledge of organizations with similar interests as this organization. The most notable are FEMA—the Federal Emergency Management Agency—and the Central U.S. Earthquake Consortium. I've worked with both of these organizations.*

This question addresses problem solving in the sense that the organization can realize some benefit from the candidate's contacts. The government programs and other help organizations that the candidate describes are very critical, so they are good attention-getters.

Experienced Professionals: Start by looking at similar industries, like major utilities and other government agencies at the federal level (because pay is better at federal than at the state and county levels). Emphasize your field experience, your academic training specific to emergency management, and your familiarity with existing programs at federal and state levels. Solid knowledge of applicable regulations and statutory requirements, like what to do with hazardous chemicals, is considered a plus. Be prepared to explain specifically why you want to work for the organization you're interviewing with.

Q: How would you improve emergency management at all levels within this organization?

A: *I would promote sound policy, encouraging everyone to do certain things, to offer suggestions, and to pursue training. The training is critical so that an emergency isn't the first opportunity for people to learn. I'd also offer periodic reviews to make user-friendly plans and continual plan improvements.*

The interviewer is now getting a sense of how problem-solving skills will play out in this candidate's personal set of priorities. The recruiter gets a good feeling about how others would be impacted by hiring the candidate.

Q: Is there anything else you'd like to talk about?

A: *Yes, there are a few things. The first is that I bring an unusual background to training. I was a music major in college, and I still teach music and voice as a hobby. One of the things I know is that people learn in very different ways; some people are visual, but most learn by trial and error. The more vivid and concrete the training, the faster they will learn and the more they will retain. By applying that at work, I've found that teaching someone at the computer to use emergency management software works well, whereas lecturing about it does not. And trial and error in the context of emergency response is something you have to avoid. The cost of errors is too great, so I look for real opportunities to practice or to train prior to emergency conditions. I have found that most plans that break down do so because of inadequate training. That's why I've spent so much time today talking about how field validation is critical. The second thing I'd like to mention is my real interest in this job. I see potential for real improvements, and an interest on your part in making that happen. I'd like to be involved in an emergency management program in its infancy. If you want to move the program forward, I know I can help you do that.*

This is an excellent sales summary, in which the candidate reiterates key points and provides some specific examples that will help the recruiter remember this interview. And the candidate asks for the job.

Candidates Re-entering the Workforce: Emphasize your academic training specific to emergency management, coupled with field experience and your familiarity with existing programs at federal and state levels. You'll have to overcome the recruiter's concerns that your skills are outdated by explaining how you've remained current during your leave, for example, by reading the *Disaster Recovery Journal* regularly.

Lobbyist

Q: **How did you become interested in lobbying?**

A: *Both my father and grandfather were lawyers because they believed it was a way they could make a difference. But I've always been fascinated with American history, and I always knew that I'd work in some relation to the federal government. A particularly important undergraduate professor of mine really encouraged me to be a lobbyist because of my strong communication skills.*

This recruiter will want to know how interested you are in the profession. Is lobbying your true vocation, or just something you consider a glamorous stint? The candidate has answered the question well by giving a strong answer with some personal history, demonstrating long-term interest. The candidate has also emphasized that lobbying is a good match for his or her particular skills.

Q: **What are your primary responsibilities as a lobbyist?**

A: *The primary responsibility of the Washington office is to address legislative and regulatory issues that affect the company. On a day-to-day basis I deal with any number of issues that come up in the business setting, trade associations, government agencies, and on Capitol Hill.*

The recruiter will want to know how much responsibility you currently have and if you know what a lobbyist's job requires. The candidate gives a quality answer that highlights the most important points.

Q: **What experience and qualifications do you have that have prepared you for a career as a lobbyist?**

A: *I have a B.A. in political science from George Washington University and an M.P.A., or master's in public administration, from American University. After graduate school I worked for three years in the U.S. Department of Health and Human Services. I'm now a government relations associate with a major electronics corporation.*

For a government-relations function there is no specific route for preparation, but you must understand the issues and the impact of those issues on the entity you are representing. You must be able to advocate a position in the public policy arena that makes sense on the merits of the issue being addressed, and that also matches the politics of the legislative arena. Thus the recruiter is looking for solid work experience and an educational background that provides a deep knowledge of history and politics.

Q: **Do you have any licenses or memberships that are helpful to you in your career as a lobbyist?**

A: *I belong to the American League of Lobbyists, which is a membership organization designed to help address the issue and business of lobbying. I find it quite helpful in my job.*

The recruiter will want to know your level of involvement and commitment to the lobbying profession. Although the ALL is not vital to your success as a lobbyist, your involvement will impress recruiters. Talk about any other business organizations you belong to, particularly those related to your employer or clients.

Q: **What is your greatest challenge as a lobbyist?**

A: *My greatest challenge is to advocate successfully a position for my company, and then to have that position taken up in Congress and ultimately passed and signed by the president. This requires complete understanding of the substance of an issue and the realities of the political process.*

The recruiter will want to know if you understand how the actual logistics of lobbying work. The candidate's answer here is exemplary because he or she astutely summarizes the position. Prove to the recruiter that you understand the big picture of lobbying.

Q: **If you could represent anyone as a lobbyist, who would that be?**

A: *I like the business world, and receiving my lobbying training with my current company has been a great experience. I like working for a major corporation and advocating its interests in Washington, which is why your company is my top choice.*

The recruiter will want to know what your ideal lobbying job might be. There are many interests represented by lobbyists in Washington, but this candidate is correct to emphasize an interest in the business world. The best way to answer this question is to emphasize your interest in both the industry and the company with whom you are interviewing.

First-time Job Seekers: Be prepared to answer questions about your qualification for the position, including any relevant course work you may have taken. Be ready also to discuss relevant skills, personality traits, and/or experience you've acquired outside academia. You may be asked questions pertaining to your career goals, your motives for wanting to enter politics, and your understanding and perception of what it's like to work in the field, and in Washington, D.C.

Q: **In five years, where do you see yourself in the lobbying profession?**

A: *I see myself still in government relations and, I hope, with this company. I'd like to be responsible for a greater area, though, perhaps for the relationship between this company and governments at all levels—federal, state, and local.*

The recruiter will be interested in learning your motivation, and what that will mean to the company. The candidate has answered this question well, by expressing his or her desire, first to remain in the business of lobbying, and second, to earn increasing responsibility within the company. Convince the recruiter that you are interested in lobbying as a permanent career choice, and that this job is not just a stepping stone to other jobs.

Q: **What specific personal skills will you bring to work as a lobbyist?**

A: *I have really developed my interpersonal and communication skills, both of which are very important. And I've also really worked on developing my writing skills because I believe that's the third essential skill to effective representation in Washington.*

The recruiter will want to be sure that you're aware of what skills it takes to be a successful lobbyist. The candidate has named the three most important skills for successful lobbying: interpersonal, communication, and writing. Insist that you have finely honed these skills, just as this candidate has done.

Q: **If you had extra time to devote to a project at your lobbying office, what would it be?**

A: *I would like to work on enhancing the corporation's role in the arts, for the mutual benefit of the arts community and our company. Such a role could offer the corporation a public profile in D.C. that would attract the attention of key political policy makers.*

The recruiter will be interested in determining the extent of your commitment to your job and your profession. This candidate has answered the question quite effectively, offering a well-thought-out and important project idea.

Q: **What is your major weakness as a lobbyist?**

A: *I don't know as much about some of the members of Congress as I would like. I don't mean personally or in terms of socializing, but I'd like to have more in-depth knowledge of their background and interests as well as an acquaintance and face-to-face recognition. I'm working hard at this and have developed a program to improve in this area.*

The recruiter will ask you this question, and the candidate's answer here is certainly better than saying something like, "I have very weak writing skills." The recruiter wants to know if the company's in for any surprises if they hire you. Convince the recruiter that you're a "good buy." In this answer the candidate hasn't admitted to a major problem, but a desire to know more and a plan to achieve the goal.

Q: What opportunities do you see in the future of government relations?

A: *The government-relations profession will always be an important activity in Washington. Unfortunately, lobbyists as a group are not always viewed as positively as they should be for the role that they play. But there will always be a role for lobbyists, because it's essential for public policy makers and government regulators to have somebody from whom they can learn all sides of an issue. Members of Congress certainly can't know all of the issues they have to deal with. The important role of the lobbyist, therefore, is to inform them of the key decisions they have to make, and what the impact of those decisions will be.*

The recruiter will want to know if you have a realistic understanding of the big picture. The candidate shows the recruiter that he or she is aware of the realities of the profession from all angles. This is a good time to emphasize the importance of the field, which translates into your commitment to the position.

Q: Why do you want this particular job?

A: *It's an opportunity to work for a major global corporation. This is a good, solid company with an excellent reputation—it's been around for 104 years. It's also a leader in technology and innovation. It's in some exciting industries, including consumer electronic products that people use on a daily basis. To be with a company like this would be very rewarding. And I can translate your concerns and problems in ways legislators and bureaucrats can understand.*

The recruiter will want to know how interested you are in working for the company. Do you believe in the company? Are you excited by the things the company does? This is probably one of the most important questions you will be asked in the lobbying interview, because if you're not excited by the company, how can you effectively and successfully represent it in Congress?

Q: What do you consider important reading for a lobbyist?

Career Changers: People with business experience who later develop an interest in public policy can make the transition to lobbying very well. Advocating positions for business is a plus. Articulate why you are interested in working in the public-policy arena. How is this different from working in your previous business environment?

A: *There are several things that I read on a day-to-day basis, like the* National Journal, *the* Congressional Daily, *and the* Role Call. *And I read the major business publications as well, like the* Wall Street Journal. *I believe it's important to have a balance between what's going on in business and what's going on in the public-policy arena. I also read numerous books by politicians and academics.*

The recruiter will want to determine if you keep up with important ideas and trends. This candidate reads the *Wall Street Journal* because he or she represents a business interest, as well as books that keep the lobbyist broadly aware of new ideas and concerns. Your answer should sound something like this as well. Supplement your lobbying reading with publications aimed at the group you're representing. For example, if you're representing the AARP—the American Association of Retired Persons—you should also be reading some publications geared toward the interests of the elderly.

Q: **What impresses you about your lobbyist colleagues?**

A: *I like working with fellow employees and lobbyists who have a clear idea of what they want and why they're in this job. I find I work best with people who are dedicated and determined.*

Lobbying is hard work and long hours. Good teamwork is essential to successful lobbying. The candidate's answer tells the recruiter that this is a lobbyist who has a team attitude and can build coalitions, so necessary today for successful lobbying.

Q: **What issues have you been involved in?**

A: *Interestingly, I've been involved with a wide variety of issues, from financial and industrial issues that require detailed knowledge of my client's business, to issues that affect all companies in general, such as minimum wages. Sometimes I've been involved with all these issues at once.*

Lobbyists need to be prepared to represent their clients on an extremely wide variety of issues, from those requiring in-depth technical or financial knowledge to those requiring a broad understanding of general business and economics.

Experienced Professionals: Obviously, experienced professionals will need to demonstrate their "first-name basis" contacts with key officials. Recruiters will be extremely interested in real success stories. The more experienced you are, the more you will need to demonstrate your ability to manage internal lobbying organizations, external consultants, and budgets. Your skills at managing client expectations will be of concern as well.

Q: **Whom, specifically, have you lobbied?**

A: *Fortunately, my work so far has required me to get to know a lot of people in the executive and legislative branches, as well as bureaucrats in various departments of the government. I've lobbied politicians, political appointees, and professionals in a variety of departments. I've developed all of my contacts by knocking on doors and providing real value-added information.*

The key for lobbyists is whom you know, and your network which can lead you to meeting even more people. However, no one can know everyone, so instead of "name-dropping," focus on the breadth of your contacts and the value you create for them.

Q: **What coalitions have you been involved in?**

A: *In the short time I've been in D.C., I've been involved in a number of coalitions, and it seems that they become more important every day. They bring real value and credibility to my work. I like to take leadership roles in these coalitions.*

Today coalitions are a key aspect of lobbying at all levels of government. The recruiter is looking for not only your experience with coalitions but your attitude toward them, and your team skills. This is a good answer because it succinctly responds to all of the interviewer's concerns.

Q: **Could you lobby for something you didn't believe in?**

A: *Yes and no. I can separate my personal political views from those of clients I represent and still be persuasive. I can't, however, represent a client whose issue is potentially illegal, immoral, or unethical.*

The recruiter needs to be convinced you can represent the company even if you're not personally convinced of the merit. The recruiter is also testing for your personal integrity, which should be unequivocal. A major corporation cannot afford anything but ethical conduct in such a sensitive position.

Candidates Re-entering the Workforce: Be straightforward. Say that you're returning, that you're keenly interested in public policy, and that your work experience before leaving the workforce included various human-resources roles, or whatever that experience may have been. Management is becoming a bit more open to situations like this. Don't be afraid to ask about work sharing, part-time, or flex-hours arrangements.

Q: **Are you in compliance with the latest lobbyist legislation passed by Congress?**

A: *Yes. In fact, I'm responsible for the supervision of compliance for all the lobbyists in our office. Consequently, I have to stay abreast of all the lobbyist rules and regulations at both the federal and state level.*

Lobbying today is a complex matter in terms of rules and regulations. Demonstrate your knowledge of and compliance with all applicable state and federal regulations.

Q: **Do you have any questions for me?**

A: *Tell me a little bit more about your company's investments in China. How did you get to this company? How long have you worked here? I understand your company has a "team culture." Is it true?*

A recruiter is impressed when a candidate has some questions. It indicates a high level of interest and awareness. Prepare your questions in advance so that they come in a fluid and conversational manner. Other questions you may want to ask include, What do you think I should do to enhance my chances of employment? When will you make a decision about this job? Is it okay if I call you back in a couple of weeks? What is the next step from here?

Paralegal

Q: Why do you want to be a paralegal?

A: *I'm interested in the law as a career, but I'm not ready to go to law school, at least not right away. My friend's brother is a paralegal, and I've talked with him about the field at great length. From what I've learned I believe the position would be an excellent way for me to learn more about the legal profession, as well as allowing me to use my strong research and organizational skills.*

Expect this question if you're an entry-level candidate. For many people this is a transitory career, so the interviewer won't be offended if you say you want to be a paralegal for only a few years and then move on. On the other hand, you should demonstrate a solid understanding of what being a paralegal entails. Like this candidate, you'll want discuss how your skills are suited for the position.

Q: What are your expectations of working in a law office?

A: *I'm looking forward to the various challenges I'll be faced with. I understand this particular position requires a great deal of legal research, which I find exciting. I'm also aware of, and respect the special nature of, the attorney-client relationship that exists solely in law offices.*

The interviewer will expect you to demonstrate an interest in, and genuine respect for, the profession. The problems and challenges you'll encounter in a law office are very different from those you'd face in an accounting firm, and you must show that you understand those differences. The interviewer will also want to know that you appreciate the confidential nature of the work you'll be doing. You might also talk about other aspects of working in a law office that you find interesting. Keep in mind that your answers should be geared to the type of firm you're interviewing with.

Q: What is your educational background?

A: *I have a bachelor's degree in political science from the University of Rochester. I also took a number of classes in law, including the American Legal System, Business Law, and The Constitution.*

The paralegal field is filled with people of all educational backgrounds—from high-school to college graduates, and everything in between. Depending on the size and type of the firm you're interviewing with, educational requirements will vary. Large firms and government agencies prefer college graduates, whereas lawyers at smaller firms generally prefer candidates with hands-on legal experience, such as former legal secretaries. You can also take a paralegal certification program; most are two-year associate programs, though some require a bachelor's degree for entrance. Also, a handful of colleges offer a four-year program in paralegal studies.

Q: What was your favorite class, and why?

A: *I really enjoyed a political-science class I took on the history of American politics. The course covered everything from the governing of the American colonies by Britain to the most recent presidential election. I found it fascinating to study how our government has evolved in the past 200 years. It really made me wonder how our founding fathers would react if they arrived in Washington today.*

Your answer should be tailored to the type of law firm you're interviewing with. For instance, this response would be appropriate if you were applying for a position in a government agency. But a real-estate or tax lawyer would want to hear more about classes such as statistics or accounting—classes in which you learned skills important to that particular type of law.

Q: Tell me about a long-term project you've worked on.

A: *During my senior year in college I took a class in medieval history. We were each assigned to construct a biography of an everyday person based primarily on public records and a few secondary sources. When the professor assigned the project during the first week of classes, he assured us it would take the entire semester to do the research and complete the biography, and he was right! After doing some reading about my subject in secondary sources, I turned to the primary sources—bound copies of the public rolls from that period. Basically, perusing these documents would be the equivalent of going through modern public records and looking for birth, marriage, or divorce certificates, deeds of property, building permits, lawsuits, and so forth. Needless to say, it was an extremely difficult task. It took me two months of steady research to find all the references to my subject in the rolls. Then it took me another*

First-time Job Seekers: Educational requirements will vary, but most firms prefer candidates who have a bachelor's degree or associate's degree. Most paralegals have no legal experience prior to landing their first job, so if you've had related experience, emphasize it during the interview. The interviewer will be looking for candidates who are intelligent and able to think and work independently. Organizational skills and the ability to manage large projects are also important. Questions may differ depending on the type of firm you're interviewing with, so be sure that you understand the particular area of law that the firm practices.

month or so to put all the pieces together and come up with a rough life sketch, and the rest of the time to polish up the biography. The whole project was a real learning experience. I learned a lot about how to pace myself and prioritize tasks; obviously, this wasn't my only class, and I had to fit the research in between all my other assignments. Because the volume of information I had was so substantial, I quickly learned the importance of organization. Without good organization this project could have easily become a nightmare.

The interviewer may want to get a sense of how you approach projects of significant length—if you think conceptually and can see the broad picture. Discuss a project you did in college or at your last job. Like this candidate, you should include a fair amount of detail in your answer. Describe how you put the project together and what you learned from the assignment. Be prepared for follow-up questions like, "Did you work with a supervisor, a group, or independently?" Your answer will also tell the interviewer if you're task or project oriented.

Q: What do you like to do when you're not working?

A: *I do a lot of reading, mostly nonfiction books about politics. I also enjoy sports— I like tennis and try to play at least twice a week. And this past winter I took up cross-country skiing, which is great fun—and really challenging.*

Your answer gives the interviewer a better picture of you as a person. Do you sit around watching television, or do you like to read? Do you like sports, such as golf or hiking? You should try to mention activities that require some thought and concentration. Interviewers also like to see that you've maintained a particular interest for a long period of time. Paralegals often have to work on long-term projects, and the interviewer is concerned that you'll become bored with a project after a short while.

Q: Tell me about your previous work experience.

A: *During the summers after my junior and senior years of college, I worked as a research assistant for a national financial-services company. Basically, I looked up information on different companies, researched stock-performance history,*

Career Changers: Many people take up paralegal work as a second or third career. If you're a former legal secretary or clerk you'll already have many of the skills necessary to change careers. Especially if you're interviewing for a position in a small firm, a secretarial background will be extremely helpful, as you might be occasionally asked to do some administrative tasks. Because most firms train their paralegals, interviewers are simply looking for intelligent candidates who have project-management and organizational skills, as well as experience with research and investigation.

and did some financial analysis. One major project I was involved with was creating a database from the representative's client list.

If you have no prior legal experience, discuss the skills you have that are valuable in the paralegal field. For instance, you could talk about your ability to handle complex, detailed assignments, which is a highly desirable skill in paralegal candidates. Like this candidate, you should mention any research or investigative experience you've had. Your answer will tell the interviewer that you understand what the position is really about. You could also discuss any skills you have that are related to the particular practice of the firm you're interviewing with. If you've worked for an accountant, for example, you might have some knowledge that would be of interest to recruiters in a tax-law firm.

Q: **What was your favorite part of your last job?**

A: *I really enjoyed the research aspect of the position. In order to find information on companies, I needed to consult the Standard and Poor's directories for basic company information, and I looked through old magazines and newspapers to find relevant news of the company, such as market share, personnel changes, and so forth.*

Again, try to discuss an aspect of the job that's related to the practice of the law firm you're interviewing with. Most law firms like to see candidates who are project, not task, oriented. But real-estate or tax offices are generally more business oriented; therefore, describing numbers-oriented tasks might work better here. Try to give an example of a time when you worked without heavy supervision—most paralegals are expected to work independently. You should also be prepared to discuss what you liked least about your job.

Q: **Do you prefer to work independently or under supervision?**

A: *I like working independently; I think it's important for a supervisor to have some faith in an employee's abilities. Of course, if I come across obstacles or have questions, I won't hesitate to ask my supervisor.*

Experienced Professionals: A large firm of the public sector is the best bet for experienced paralegals. In large law firms you may decide to specialize in a particular area, such as litigation or corporate law. And because government agencies are under such severe budget restraints, experienced paralegals are in high demand. Many firms also have paralegal coordinators—experienced professionals who supervise teams of junior paralegals, and who organize case and litigation, then assign them to attorneys. In your interview be prepared to discuss why you're interested in continuing in this field. To determine your level of experience, the interviewer is also likely to ask you questions about specific projects or cases you've worked on.

Demonstrate your ability to work on your own. Most lawyers are busy people who won't have time to watch carefully over you; they must be able to trust that you'll do the work you're assigned efficiently and accurately. Portray yourself as someone who can work with minimum supervision and, when given an objective, has the ability to determine how to reach that objective and present the results in a clear, and organized fashion.

Q: Do you have any experience or training in legal research?

A: *I have some informal experience. As part of my class in American Legal Systems we had to research a case and do a mock trial, using the same evidence that was originally used. We all had roles in the case, and I was the prosecutor. We also had to write briefs for cases we studied.*

Don't be worried if you don't have experience in this area; most firms offer extensive on-the-job training to new employees. However, because most candidates don't have this kind of background, any such experience that you do have will make you stand out from the competition.

Q: How would you rate your writing skills?

A: *I believe I write well. I always received excellent marks on my papers and essays in college.*

Many times you'll need to write brief summations of all the information you've gathered in researching a case. The ability to express yourself orally is important as well, because you'll often be asked for oral summaries of cases. It's essential that you can succinctly and clearly explain any information you find in your research.

Q: Describe your familiarity with computers. What software programs do you know?

A: *I'm very comfortable with PCs and most Windows-based software, including Microsoft Word, Excel, and Access.*

Candidates Re-entering the Workforce: If you've done paralegal work in the past, you already understand the nature of the position and what a firm expects. Be able to explain why you left your last job and why you're now interested in returning. If you're having trouble getting interviews, consider working in a law firm on a temporary basis; many firms hire paralegals part-time or for special long-term projects. Make sure that your computer skills are current; interviewers want to see candidates who have at least some experience with word-processing or database management software.

Knowledge of word-processing software is essential so that you can generate documents such as letters, summations, briefs, and pleadings. Experience with database management is becoming more important, as many law firms, especially the larger ones, use litigation-support software such as DB/Textworks, LexisNexis, and WestLaw. Litigation-support software is basically a database of hundreds or thousands of summarized legal documents, with which you can locate in minutes information and documents relevant to a particular case, instead of spending hours going through old law books. Unless you have previous experience in a law firm, the interviewer won't expect you to have specific experience with litigation-support software, but experience using or creating databases will be important.

Q: What do you see yourself doing in five years?

A: *My plan is to work as a paralegal for two or three years and then return to law school. However, I know many people who've started out with that same plan, then eventually lost interest in law school and in becoming a lawyer. But I've done my research, and I believe I have a solid understanding of the field. Though I can't predict the future, at this point I'm committed to a legal career.*

You can expect this question regardless of how much experience you have. Like this candidate, you may want to enter law school eventually and so consider being a paralegal a short-term career. Or maybe you're a secretary or clerical worker, you want to advance professionally, and you consider paralegal work a lifetime career. It's important to have a feel for what the interviewer is looking for; some firms like new graduates who are preparing for law school, whereas others are looking for candidates with longer-term commitments.

CHAPTER 17

MARKETING AND SALES

Brand Manager
(Consumer Packaged Goods)

Q: **Where are the new snack-product opportunities, in your opinion?**

A: *The whole wave of wellness—like your new reduced-fat cheese balls with 33 percent less fat, and cheese curls with 50 percent less fat—represent terrific new opportunities in snack products. I understand you're coming out with a reduced-fat peanut line now.*

This question addresses the candidate's motivation as well as leadership and creativity in looking for new business opportunities. The candidate's answer is well stated, drawing upon new lines that are already in the market, and well supported with opinions picked up from working in the business.

Q: **What do you imagine is different about working on new products as opposed to working on an established brand?**

A: *When you work on an existing brand, the product's positioning within the company's portfolio is already well established. New product introduction, on the other hand, involves everything from brand management to coming up with an original idea and positioning it. The thinking is more strategic. You have to consider how the new product fits into the overall portfolio for the company.*

This is a job-assessment question. The recruiter needs confirmation that this candidate's personality is suited to the job, and that his or her job expectations are realistic. The candidate shows an ability to look beyond one product to the overall interests of the company—a more strategic outlook, which would be required for the product-development function.

Q: **What are the big challenges with your current brand?**

A: *My peanut products fall into the salty-snack category. Our challenges with consumers purchasing our product are awareness (people think of baked chips rather than peanuts in this category); health (peanuts offer protein, folic acid, and other benefits not found in other salty snacks); and price value (because peanuts aren't bulky like chips, we have to work hard to show value per serving when the serving is visibly smaller than a typical serving of, say, chips).*

This question addresses skill and problem-solving ability. The answer is well organized so that the recruiter can easily listen and follow along. The candidate builds a good explanation of his or her knowledge of the brands and the challenges facing new products.

Q: What have you learned in your various marketing positions that will help you in new product development?

A: *One of my product-manager roles was on the flagship-brand peanuts. Therefore, a lot more cash flowed into it. We look at our company name as a franchise with one brand identity, so the peanut-brand person does the big promos. Basically, whatever peanuts do affects the rest of the trade calendar. I learned to make decisions and feel confident about them. I also learned a lot from working in retail, especially about how customers in different store locations go for different things. That's helped in my decisions about regional promotional adjustments.*

This is a job-assessment question. The recruiter wants to know how past job experiences are most relevant to the job under consideration. The candidate explains how he or she has learned to make decisions and move ahead, which would be critical working in new products. The knowledge about regional consumer differences would also be critical with new product roll-out.

Q: If you had to describe brand management as more creative or more financial, which would you choose?

A: *In a company like yours, which is more performance driven, it's definitely financial. With long-established brands, less creativity is needed to support the business because awareness is established and habits keep the business alive. With new products more creativity is needed to build initial interest and bring about a new behavior pattern with consumers.*

With this job-assessment question the recruiter wants to be sure that the candidate is realistic about the challenges in the job. The correct answer, which the candidate gives, is that it is a combination, depending on the age and other market factors of a particular brand. More creativity is required up front in new products, with financial support from the flagship brands.

First-time Job Seekers: One or more summer internships in a brand-management capacity are critical, as competition for brand-assistant jobs is considerable. Most major companies recruit from a select list of schools and typically target students with strong grades and strong evidence of leadership in school organizations. The M.B.A. degree is often a requirement; some knowledge of marketing and basic accounting is also important.

Q: Here are some packaging changes we implemented. Take a look and give me your opinion on what we wanted to accomplish.

A: *This was obviously a special pack in a convenient one-serving size. I think you were trying to get people to think of a reduced-fat item in reasonable quantity as a healthy snack they can carry with them. Peanuts are compact. I would think it's much more convenient than carrying around a bag of chips, but you had to remind people of that. It seems as if the packaging is helping to establish the healthy characteristics of peanuts compared to other salty snacks like chips, but you're also suggesting that the peanuts are just as convenient as a candy bar for quick energy. That's my impression. Do you mind if I ask how close my answer was to your actual goals?*

The candidate is being tested on creativity and problem-solving ability. The most important thing here is to have an opinion, which the candidate does. And the candidate exhibits the curiosity fitting a brand manager, and the social skills to ask a question.

Q: Tell me about a time you test-marketed a product.

A: *Last month we tested a different package size in several major markets. The special pack worked as we'd hoped—mostly to remind people that peanuts can be a healthy snack. But, of course, special packs aren't really money makers like our regular-size containers, so building awareness was our primary goal.*

This question helps to determine depth or variety of marketing experiences. The recruiter wants a specific example and gets one. The answer is effective because it includes the purpose and the result.

Q: In the context of brand management, what do you think are the differences between a leader and a manager?

A: *A leader is a visionary, whereas a manager is a coordinator. A good brand manager has qualities of both. I don't think you coordinate people effectively unless they have a good idea of where their contributions will make a difference and what the possibilities are.*

This question attempts to determine the candidate's management philosophy and personality on the job. The candidate not only explains how both relate to brand management, but also how he or she prefers to work for, or work with, people who have an idea of the future direction of the company and brand.

Q: Tell me what you've learned in trade marketing.

A: *I held a trade-marketing position involving a six-month assignment as liaison between marketing and sales. It helped me understand where salespeople* *are coming from, especially when they have bizarre requests. I took the job because I thought I needed some perspective I didn't have. It definitely helped me learn to be more diplomatic and more thorough in getting everybody's buy-in to my decisions. I suppose it helped me be a little more visionary.*

This type of question, which may be drawn from resume information, examines both career accomplishments and aspirations. (The recruiter realizes that past decisions are often a good predictor of future decisions.) The answer is positive in that it shows acquisition of an important new skill—sales perspective. Clearly this person makes job decisions based on what he or she may learn that will round out the candidate's skill base for a successful long-term career in brand management.

Q: **Which of your skills and what part of your work background do you find difficult to translate into brand management?**

A: *That's not an easy question to answer—I find that almost any life or work experience is translatable somehow. For instance, I think the variety of non-profit experiences I've had really helped me with persuasion, and I've figured out how to get people throughout the marketing organization to rally behind an idea even when they aren't my employees. But because nonprofit isn't the typical brand-management experience, I really have to explain to people sometimes why the experience is relevant. I think I'm a good brand manager because I can get all the various departments that support my brand to share my commitment to what's best for the brand—even when they have many brands to support. These are the same skills I used to persuade people who weren't being paid to help in the nonprofit.*

This is a skill-assessment question asked in a negative way. Here the candidate chooses wisely to put a positive twist on the answer, drawing a parallel between how nonprofit experiences have helped him or her manage and motivate people who aren't directly responsible for the brands. This parallel is the kind of thing that, if left unsaid, would not be apparent to the interviewer.

Q: **What personality characteristic is a weakness in brand management?**

Career Changers: You will generally have to start at the bottom—brand assistant up. Typical career switchers are consumer product salespeople who decide to move to a corporate job. The sales experience provides the leverage. Night courses in accounting and marketing could help.

A: *Lack of diplomacy. I've learned how to wait, then come back with information to explain my reasoning for something, rather than just make a quick conclusion. I haven't always understood why you need everyone else's buy-in on decisions that are rightly your own to make. Now I'd say I'm very careful about it.*

This is a variation on the weakness question. The candidate does not have to list a personal weakness, but he or she is strong and direct in doing so, therefore it's believable. The answer also shows that the candidate has been careful to keep that weakness in check, so the recruiter is reassured that it poses no major disruption to work.

Q: What growth opportunities do you see in the casual-dining category?

A: *Health consciousness is here to stay. But when you look at the opportunity in the eighties with the movement away from red meat, and how quickly steak has regained popularity, you realize that not much else is certain. The real opportunity is to take advantage of the fact that consumers are more educated and more disciplined about what they eat. Providing more information (like nutrition facts) on menus is an example.*

The recruiter is asking the candidate to demonstrate creativity and leadership through an understanding of the industry. The candidate points to trends in consumer activism and health consciousness, which show that he or she is up on current prevailing attitudes. The specific example given is a good way to clarify the candidate's point.

Q: What qualities are important to brand management?

A: *The ability to link together pieces to see the big picture that moves your brand along, the ability to juggle and reprioritize a number of responsibilities, and the ability to get the teamwork going to support your brand throughout the departments that affect it.*

Experienced Professionals: Experienced corporate candidates in brand management tend to move from company to company or from brand to brand within a company, as the skills are relevant regardless of the product category. Many of the brand companies have consolidated, and brands are often bought and sold between the major parent companies. People often change positions as a result of these changes of ownership.

Some account executives from ad agencies, after working with a client's specific brand over a period of time, might switch to the brand company. Such moves are often motivated by better income potential on the corporate side than on the agency side.

This question addresses job skills. The candidate's response is brief but thorough. Next, the candidate should present strong examples of how he or she has used these skills on the job.

Q: **How is your management style suited to product management?**

A: *Somehow I learned how to link everything together to see the big picture, which is why I think I make good judgments for my brand and why I anticipate problems before they arise. So I work hard to make sure people who work with me see the big picture too. And I'm a great believer in getting everybody involved in a specific project together, meeting every other week to talk about problems that exist or are likely to arise.*

This is a management-style question. The answer is effective because it shows an ability to conceptualize and to help others conceptualize and coordinate. The comment about biweekly planning meetings demonstrates how presenting a specific example or idea in an answer makes the answer more believable and concrete. (You get the sense that this really happens.)

Q: **Tell me how you've mentored your marketing assistants.**

A: *I write down all of my marketing assistants' development goals and update these goals on a quarterly basis. I want them working on a variety of projects— like trade promotions, consumer promos, advertising, packaging, product (that is, optimizing, research, repositioning) and personal development. I always make sure there is a project in each of these areas.*

At the brand-manager level and beyond (category manager, director, and so on), you will be managing new marketing assistants and, later, other brand managers. The ability to supervise and direct these people, without handholding, is critical. This candidate lays out a specific plan for how she delegates and stays in touch with people she manages.

Q: **Tell me about an ad campaign you think was effective.**

A: *I've always thought that the commercials by the Beef Board are effective. People are more likely to consider red meat in their diet if they know how to put it in a meal rather than to have an entire steak as a meal. The commercials show recipes that are made in twenty to thirty minutes, like steak stir fry. That appeals to the more health-conscious person, as well as the person on the go.*

This is an opinion question that also tests the candidate's general awareness and knowledge of what other marketers are doing. The candidate gives a good response because it is specific and describes an ad that's not likely to be chosen by lots of candidates. (Choosing a very popular ad is probably not going to lead to a unique answer.) The answer is thorough, as well, because the candidate explains why he or she believes the ad is effective.

Q: **How do you use in-store promotions?**

A: *I rely on in-store promotions to help me with several things: promote new products, for instance; introduce a new package size or complementary marketing with another product; advertise seasonal promotions. In general, they help us get the consumer's attention for something we think the consumer may otherwise not know or notice.*

This question determines the candidate's depth of knowledge and experience. It also demands an opinion, to some degree, rather than a textbook response. The candidate might want to follow up by describing a particular in-store promotion that was very successful.

Q: **Describe how you can use off-seasons to expand a seasonal product's use.**

A: *One example I've always seen missed opportunity in is barbecue sauce. If barbecue sauce were my brand, I'd be concerned about how to increase use when people are no longer outdoors using their barbecue grills. For example, in the winter I might advertise recipes that use barbecue sauce as a base for holiday appetizers.*

This question examines creativity. The answer works because it's specific, and because it mentions a topic outside the candidate's experience. (This job seeker hasn't worked on the brand, but has thought about how they're missing out.) This approach demonstrates that the candidate thinks and applies his or her marketing skills, whether on the job or not.

Q: **If you had to recall a product, what might you do?**

A: *Well, that's certainly happened to a number of good companies with good products. The nature of the recall would affect my action. For example, in the case of a safety concern I'd immediately recall and replace products with some sort of assurance campaign to follow. I might establish an 800 number for people to call with questions or concerns. One manufacturer of a baby product*

Candidates Re-entering the Workforce: Make sure your marketing and basic accounting skills are up to date; if not, night courses could help. In addition to your previous work experience, emphasize your passion for the job and your curiosity—how you've made a point to do informal research every time you shop at the grocery store, for example. Be sure to relate how your experiences during your leave can help you on the job. For instance, if you've been on maternity leave and are interviewing with a baby-food company, emphasize your new perspective as a consumer of the company's products.

actually had a press release on an 800 number. That's a very effective way, with less manpower, to reach consumers.

The recruiter wants the candidate to discuss a problem and show some problem-solving skills. This is a negative question as presented; the candidate is wise for not dwelling on the problem that caused the recall, but, rather, on the solution. The specific example helps this answer, too. But the answer would be improved—more thorough—if the candidate also explained what he or she might do in a less serious recall.

Q: **This is your thirty-second commercial. What else do you want to tell me?**

A: *I would say that nothing beats an unending curiosity for the brand business. That means when I go to a store, I never go just to shop for myself. I constantly watch what people are putting in their shopping carts, how long it took them to pick something off the shelf, what they say if they're shopping with someone else—and I learn something every time. I also notice what people are eating at the park, what people bring to work for lunch, what my friends and family have at home. I don't think you can teach someone to be curious. They either are or aren't, and curious people are good at this business. That's what you'll get, in addition to my skills and experience, if you hire me.*

This summary question will give you a perfect opportunity to prove that you know how to position products—by showing how you position yourself. (If you cannot market yourself, no company will want to hire you to be in charge of marketing their products.) The answer here is direct and provides that "something extra"—passion—beyond simple ability to do the job.

Insurance Agent

Q: **What are your primary responsibilities in your current job as an insurance agent?**

A: *My primary responsibilities are mainly sales and marketing. I handle all the insurance needs of my existing clients, whether it's for car, health, home owner's, or other types of insurance. I also solicit new customer's life, casualty, and the full range of insurance that our agency provides.*

With this question the recruiter is determining the depth of the candidate's experience. This answer would satisfy the recruiter because it demonstrates the different areas in which the candidate has worked. Show the recruiter that because of the varied experience you've had, you could work in any area in the company.

Q: **What are your qualifications to be an insurance agent?**

A: *I've a B.S. in education. I also have four years' experience as an insurance agent for a national life-insurance company before joining a general-insurance agency three years ago.*

Any discipline that you studied in pursuit of your B.A. or B.S. is acceptable to the recruiter. The recruiter is primarily looking for a bachelor's degree from a solid college or university. You'll need three to six years' insurance experience to be eligible for a position as a senior agent.

Q: **How did you become interested in the insurance-agency business?**

A: *I was general manager of a car dealership for two years before I became an insurance agent, so I was used to marketing and managing, and things of that nature. But I really wanted to use my education in my work, and becoming an insurance agent seemed like the perfect way to combine my education and experience. My B.S. in education has really helped me because a lot of what I do involves educating people. I enjoy meeting with people and teaching them about our products and services.*

With this question the recruiter is determining how well suited the candidate is for a career in insurance. The recruiter wants to hear an answer like this that shows true interest in the industry. Explain to the recruiter why you'll be dedicated to your job.

Q: **What organizations do you belong to that help you to be an insurance agent?**

A: *I don't belong to any insurance-industry associations. However, I'm quite active in the local chapter of the Kiwanis Club, and in the United Way.*

The recruiter won't require you to belong to any industry associations, although it would be impressive if you did. However, it's helpful to be involved in a number of service clubs because they allow you to interact with different people from time to time, which is a large part of an insurance agent's job. Community involvement of any kind is a good way to meet new clients.

Q: **What's been your greatest challenge in the insurance agency business?**

A: *I think my biggest challenge is to stay consistently focused. It's easy to get down and let adversity take the wind out of your sails. Also, there can be a lot of freedom and flexibility in the insurance business. You have to be really disciplined, because your friend might call and say, "Let's go play golf." There's no one there to tell you that you can't. But at the end of the week you have to ask yourself how many people you talked to this week and how many bought policies. Over the years I've taught myself to be disciplined but flexible. However, I did meet my biggest client on the golf course!*

There are many challenges in the insurance-agency business, and the candidate has certainly identified an important one. What's impressive about this answer is that the candidate stresses the steps taken to work on the challenge. Think about one or two things you find particularly challenging, and be sure to discuss how you're working on improvement.

Q: **If you could work with any company in the insurance industry, would you still be interviewing with this company?**

A: *I really would. This company is one of the five strongest insurance companies in the world right now. The products and services are good, the mutual funds are the fastest growing in the country, and that makes me excited. Also, I've been doing a lot of reading, and I really feel good about the company and the direction it's going in.*

First-time Job Seekers: Honestly assess your strengths and weaknesses. A career in insurance has unlimited potential in many ways, but it's not for everybody. An insurance agent should be strong in both sales and marketing. Additionally, you should have strong interpersonal skills. Conduct as many informational interviews as possible so that you understand what's involved in being an insurance agent.

The recruiter is looking for a natural and sincere interest in the company. Appropriate comments might include, "I'd feel fortunate to be with this company because there are more than 2,000 insurance agencies out there." Or, "I've met some tremendous people who work in this company."

Q: **Five years from now, what do you hope to be doing in the insurance industry?**

A: *In five years I'd like to have earned my CLU, or chartered life underwriter. I know it's a fairly involved process, but I still hope to have earned it. I want to be the best-qualified person to help my clients with their needs. They have lots of choices, and I want to be at the top of their list.*

Earning a CLU involves taking a series of ten exams. The candidate's desire to earn this certificate shows determination and ambition. The recruiter will be impressed with a desire to be flexible and to increase one's skills for the agency.

Q: **What specific personal skills have you developed?**

A: *I think I'm much better equipped to manage myself and others than when I first started out in the business. And although I had already had lots of experience in sales, I think I'm an even better salesperson now—maybe I'm from the old school, but I believe that virtually everything we do in life involves sales and selling. One of the things I've learned to do is listen a lot better. That's probably the biggest problem with salespeople. They want to tell their story, and that's fine, but the client might not want to hear it. They may already know your story. I try to ask questions more than just make statements, which is just good commonsense selling.*

The recruiter will want you to discuss your strengths. What specifically do you bring to the recruiter's company? The candidate discusses two very important skills for the insurance business—being able to manage people, and being a good salesman.

Q: **Do you like dealing with people?**

A: *I find that dealing with people is one of the biggest bonuses of working in the insurance business. I also prefer being out in the field, rather than doing paperwork back at the office.*

This is a people business, so good people skills are important. You can't answer by simply saying, "I'm a people person." You have to "sell" the idea that you are. The candidate's answer shows a natural propensity for working with people.

Q: **If you had extra time to devote to some insurance-related project, what would that project be?**

A: *In the fall I'll be teaching several seminars at two community colleges. Not only am I looking forward to being a college instructor, I think it'll also be good for my business. I do want to enhance my business, but I also want to do something for the community that's not being done. I've found that lots of people have questions about saving for retirement, so this will be the focus of my seminars. I expect I'll get some new clients too!*

This candidate shows a natural altruism, which will impress the recruiter. At the same time, the recruiter will be looking for a candidate who's always trying to find new clients. If you're not currently working on some extra project, have an idea for a project ready to share with the recruiter.

Q: **Professionally, what's your biggest weakness?**

A: *As I said a minute ago, one of the things I find hardest to do is manage my paperwork in the most efficient manner. Because I spend a lot of time on volunteer activities, community service has proved to be a two-edged sword. I have to make sure that I take care of my business, too. So I've hired a part-time assistant at my own expense. This ensures that the paperwork gets done in a timely fashion and allows me the extra time I need to build my business.*

The recruiter will want to be sure that you don't have any major professional flaws that will affect his or her company. The candidate's answer here is honest without being too negative. In your answer include some ways that you're trying to overcome your particular weakness, even if it means you don't have all the answers yourself.

Q: **What career opportunities do you see for the future in the insurance business?**

A: *I think the opportunities are really unlimited. It's a matter only of my deciding where to focus. I'm interested in doing more group work and more seminars. But, in general, I think that if I work hard and apply myself, I can have a solid business and do a lot of service for people. We in insurance are going to com-*

Career Changers: Be honest with the insurance recruiter about why you're making a change in careers. Talk about the sales and marketing experience you've gained from your previous career. Also, if you have experience in related fields such as the brokerage business or banking, the transition into insurance will be easier. Start reading the insurance-industry publications and be prepared to learn the basics. It's a complicated field and demands real time attention to learn the ins and outs.

pete increasingly with brokerage houses, banks, accountants, financial plan-
ners, and even lawyers. The potential is unlimited, but all the new competition
means constantly having to upgrade your skills.

The recruiter is looking for an awareness of the big picture and the new competitive pressures in the industry. You can answer this question in terms of opportunities you might encounter within the insurance business, as this candidate has chosen to do. Or you may also wish to discuss ways in which the insurance industry as a whole is developing new products to meet the competitive challenges ahead.

Q: **What skills or attitudes impress you in your insurance coworkers?**

A: *I like working with energetic people, but I don't want them so nervous and fidg-*
ety they're squirming out of their chair. I don't want them falling asleep, either.
I like a happy medium. I like to say that I can tell if their "lights are on"! I like
people who are articulate because in this business we do a lot of talking. And
though I don't want coworkers talking the whole time, I want them to be able
to express their thoughts and ideas clearly. They should be clear and concise
in their answers because that's important when they're dealing with a client.

The recruiter is interested in the types of people with whom the candidate works best. Your answer will also tell the recruiter a lot about you. Think about what positive things you find essential to the makeup of a good insurance agent.

Q: **How important are ethics among your coworkers in the insurance business?**

A: *I like working with honest people. I also like to see that someone has accom-*
plished some specific achievement in his or her life. You don't necessarily need
to be an all-state athlete or valedictorian, but you should have some milestones
in your life, other than just showing up for work. I want my coworkers' suc-
cesses to be important but only if they achieve them within the accepted value
system. In other words, I think success is important, but not at any cost.

This question is designed to help the recruiter understand the candidate's ethics. Do you put your own interest or the client's interest first? There are

Experienced Professionals: A demonstrated interest and track record will stand you in good stead moving up the ladder in insurance. Most agents will spend their entire careers "in the field," as they are excellent salespeople but less proficient at managing. If you want to get into management, consider some advanced training, such as an M.B.A., or some on-the-job experience like coaching new recruits.

many ways to interpret and answer this question, but the bottom line is that having a strong moral fiber is important in the insurance agency. Give the recruiter proof that you're in this category yourself.

Q: **What would you say is the biggest challenge in the industry today? How do you deal with it?**

A: *As I mentioned earlier, a lot of different industries that weren't competitors before are competing with one another now. We've long since passed the stage where each of these businesses had their own little protected niche. The insurance business today is becoming wide-open to competition, but no one has all the answers to a clients' needs. I have a two-part strategy to deal with this trend. First, I'm learning as much as possible about the product lines that other industries can bring to the client. Next, I've formed very tight alliances with key representatives of these areas so that I can take the lead in bringing their skills to bear for my clients under my leadership. So far, it's proved to be a winning strategy.*

This answer tells the recruiter exactly what he or she is really after—assurance that the candidate is aware of industry challenges and changes and has a proactive strategy for dealing with them. The answer also tells the recruiter that this candidate can be counted on to initiate new ideas rather than waiting to be told what to do.

Q: **But don't you run the risk of some of your alliance partners getting some of your clients' business that you should get?**

A: *Quite possibly, yes. But my clients need the best, and when I can't provide it for them, I get people who can. Sometimes I lose a little in the short run, but my clients like my approach so much that they've given me tremendous referrals that I never got earlier. Also, my network of alliance partners has also produced a whole new revenue stream I had never had before.*

What the interviewer is interested in is the candidate's long-term perspective rather than just the short term. The insurance business has always relied on referrals, and the candidate has demonstrated how to build a strong long-term referral network. Today, as well, the insurance business is very much one of solving client problems with creative solutions. The candidate has demonstrated an effective way to do that while increasing his or her basic business.

Q: **Would you say that your job is almost like being a consultant?**

A: *That's exactly the way I approach it—as my clients' financial consultant. I know that clients' problems and concerns are getting more complicated by the day, and I can't be an expert in them all, so I really try to help them put the problem in perspective, then bring the proper resources to bear on them.*

The recruiter is digging to ensure that the candidate has thought through his or her unique approach and has the depth of understanding necessary to carry it through and be successful. By sharing the "theory" behind the strategy, the candidate is showing conclusively an awareness of the major industry trends and of how to make those trends work in his or her favor. The candidate is also demonstrating genuine care and concern for the client.

Q: **In many ways an insurance agent works for himself as well as for the company. Do you have difficulty balancing those two?**

A: *No one could balance them perfectly all the time. Frankly, my company's been extremely fair to me, so when there's a problem, I err on the side of the company. They've always taken care of me in the end, so I have no hesitation putting them first.*

An agent has many opportunities to favor his or her own well-being over that of the insurance company or agency. It's important for the candidate to demonstrate concern about this issue and an understanding of how to balance his or her own interests with the company's interests. This answer is an effective way of communicating that concern.

Q: **Would you recommend the insurance industry to a new graduate just finishing college?**

A: *This business is not for everyone. But if a young person is interested in a career that provides an opportunity to help people and at the same time is totally open-ended in terms of financial rewards, then I can think of no better industry. This is a business where you see the results of your labors very quickly. It doesn't take years to find out whether or not you can "cut it" in this field. And, basically, it's up to you! I like that!*

The recruiter is looking for real conviction about the insurance business and a realistic appraisal of what it takes to succeed. This industry is at heart a people-oriented business, and real commitment to one's clients is a critical success factor. The desire for financial success is important, too, because so much of the business relies on personal motivation.

Candidates Re-entering the Workforce: Think about your requirements in terms of your home life. Why are you returning? Is it a good time for you to return to the workforce? If you're someone who has to be at certain places at particular times, perhaps because of your children, then perhaps this isn't the right career for you now. You must be able to be flexible with your schedule, because there's always the possibility of several evening or weekend meetings a week.

Market Researcher

Q: **Do you consider yourself to be left- or right-brained?**

A: *I believe I'm naturally right-brained. Math, science, and analytical skills have always been my strengths. Still, I really enjoy the arts and work hard at developing my imaginative and creative sides.*

In market research you need to tap into both your analytical and creative talents. First and foremost you need to be able to interpret and analyze pages of data, but you should also have the ability to develop custom research conceptually to meet your clients' needs. Although it's acceptable to say that you lean more in one direction, you should also discuss how you incorporate both styles of thinking into your work.

Q: **What's your perception of this business?**

A: *My internship and my conversations with people in the business lead me to believe that advertising and market research are hectic and challenging, but rewarding. I understand that working for clients is very demanding and often requires long hours. I also believe that client contact—and of course the work itself—is exciting.*

Expect this question if you're an entry-level candidate. The interviewer will want to ensure that you have a realistic idea of the industry. Many people decide to go into advertising because they see it as a high-profile, glamorous

First-time Job Seekers: Talk with your professors. Often, professors freelance with local companies, and they may be able to offer you invaluable advice and, possibly, introductions. If a company isn't hiring, request an informational interview. The advertising industry is heavily connected and if you impress one person, he or she may recommend you to an agency that's looking for someone. A typical entry-level position in marketing research would probably include designing, coordinating, and analyzing research projects. You may assist in some of those aspects or manage the entire project; this will depend on the magnitude of the project and the number of people in the research department. You must have a bachelor's degree, preferably in communication, marketing, or statistics. Any other major would be acceptable as well, as long as you can demonstrate your analytical and organizational skills. In your interview emphasize your determination and your time-management skills.

profession—and it is, on some days. But most days, you have to work long, and often grueling, hours. Employers want people who understand that they'll be working hard.

Q: **Describe a market-research project you were involved in, either for a class or during an internship.**

A: *During my senior year in college I was a member of a four-person team that was presented with the task of developing a new product and marketing it. We developed the new product and set objectives in terms of product introduction. We researched related products, developed a target market profile, and designed an advertising and marketing campaign. Finally, we presented the entire project to our class for their reaction.*

Basically, the interviewer is testing the candidate's ability to articulate information in a clear and concise manner, an essential trait for this job, and is also examining how the candidate breaks down a research project. There are three phases to a research project: design, implementation, and analysis. Be sure to discuss each distinct stage if you're asked this question. You should also want to discuss such details as the name of the product, what it was, and who your target market was.

Q: **Discuss the main difference between secondary and primary research. When is the best time to use each?**

A: *Secondary research is extracting data from published resources—using data gathered from polls, omnibus studies, information listed in directories. Primary research is designing a research study in which the data is collected, analyzed, and interpreted to provide custom answers for the clients. The nature of the proposed study dictates what type of research can best serve a client's needs.*

This question taps into whether the candidate has a basic grasp of research terminology. Other similar questions you might encounter are, "Describe what an omnibus study is and when it's appropriate," and, "What are the

Career Changers: For someone interested in changing careers, you may have options: If you're applying for a market-research job with an organization, experience in that particular industry will be helpful. Also, any sales or management job in which you've marketed a variety of projects and had to rely on numbers would be a plus. Emphasize professional skills if your career is unrelated to market research. Strong presentation, customer and client skills, computer skills, or sales experience is very desirable. Whatever advantage or benefit you have to offer, emphasize it. And if you have minimal transferable skills, take some continuing-education classes on marketing.

advantages and disadvantages of a mail study or telephone study?" Your answer should simply be a brief summary of your knowledge of basic research concepts.

Q: **What's the difference between qualitative and quantitative research?**

A: *Qualitative research is based on people's feelings. It involves no numbers and usually has a smaller base sample than quantitative research. Quantitative research is scientific, with large sample sizes so that results from the sample base can be projected onto the population. It involves numbers and statistics and most often has closed-ended questions instead of the more open-ended, free-flowing questions and answers that define qualitative research. For example, focus groups are used in qualitative research, whereas a telephone or mail panel study would be used in quantitative research. Generally, the research question dictates which method is more suitable.*

Once again, this question tests the candidate's familiarity with industry jargon. If you don't know a term, simply ask the interviewer to define it for you. You may be familiar with the concept but know it by another name. As with the previous question, summarize your knowledge of the concept.

Q: **Here's some data from a research study. Take a few minutes to review the cross-tab table. What do the numbers say to you?**

A: *I'd say the key information here is that service centers are the primary source of metal purchases at 63 percent. Although service centers are the most popular source overall, mills are the primary source with larger corporations—those with employees exceeding 1,000.*

This question is designed to gauge if the candidate's experienced in data analysis and familiar with cross tables. If you've taken a class in market statistics, you should be familiar with these types of analyses. Don't panic if an interviewer asks you to interpret data—it will usually be a very basic cross-tabs table. You won't have to interpret every number—just point out the significant findings.

Experienced Professionals: Your experience within the industry is your biggest selling point, so don't be shy about highlighting your successes and accomplishments. If you've been in marketing research for a number of years, you may be applying for a position of greater responsibility, such as strategic planner for an advertising or marketing agency. Many market researchers also move to the corporate side to become vice president of marketing or product manager. In these positions, having the ability to read numbers and interpret market research accurately is invaluable.

Q: Consider the following scenario: A client has sunk a lot of money into a product. Your research indicates that the product wasn't well received by consumers. In fact, it's a total failure. How do you present your findings and still please the client?

A: *Well, research is what it is and you can't fudge with numbers. It would be totally unethical to massage the data or not report all the findings, no matter how many egos are involved with the design of the new product. I think I'd look on the bright side and explain to the client that it's better to sink, let's say, $30,000 on research to find out if the product's a failure than to sink $2 million in product introduction/advertising costs to find out it doesn't sell. Also, depending on the design of the original study, I might suggest doing additional research.*

This question examines the candidate's professional ethics. In market research, one walks a fine line between presenting one's findings and pleasing the client. That is, often the research simply doesn't give the answers that the client wants to hear. Despite this reality, it's important that you present your findings in a professional, unbiased manner so that the client can always feel confident in your professional integrity.

Q: What type of experience do you have with computers? What programs do you know specifically?

A: *I've worked with both IBM and Macintosh computers. I currently use Microsoft Office, including Excel and Word, and I have experience with Harvard Graphics and the data-processing program SPSS. I have a high comfort level with computers and software, and I'm confident I can be trained on any program.*

You can probably expect this question to come up if you don't have computer skills listed on your resume, or if your skills are limited. Name the various computer programs and systems you've worked on. You may want to differentiate whether they were from classes or work experience. If you're

Candidates Re-entering the Workforce: Many agencies find themselves swamped from time to time, and you might work your way into a company by doing freelance jobs. Capitalize on your career related skills: raising a family definitely enhances organizational skills, and if you want to enter consumer research, "moms" definitely keep their fingers on the pulse of the market. You'll want to make sure your computer skills are up to date. To keep up with the industry, read periodicals such as *American Demographics, Advertising Age, Journal of Market Research,* and local business weeklies. You could also join local chapters of national advertising and market research clubs, such as the American Marketing Association——virtually every major city has one.

not familiar with the specific software programs used by the company you're interviewing with, don't worry. Although companies like to recruit applicants who are familiar with the programs used in their office, they also know that someone who has used computers and comparable programs can be taught new programs with minimal training. Simply reiterate that you're very comfortable with computers, and though you haven't used their specific program, you're confident that you can learn any program, given your experience and comfort level.

Q: Where do you see yourself five years from now?

A: *I see myself starting out in a position similar to this position and growing in the company. I'd like to stay in market research and perhaps eventually take on a supervisory role. Does your company generally promote from within, and what are the other positions in the department?*

This question gauges the candidate's commitment to the field of market research as well as to the company he or she is applying to. Most interviewers don't expect that you'll spend your entire career with them, but they do expect at least a two- to three-year commitment. Companies invest a lot of time and money in each employee—wasted resources if an employee ends up leaving the company in six months. Your answer should accurately and honestly describe your desired career path. Of course, try not to mention any specific job titles. This is also a good opportunity to demonstrate your interest in the company by asking a question or two of the interviewer, as this candidate does.

Q: What interests and/or strengths do you possess that would make you a valuable asset to our market research team?

A: *I believe my strengths lie in my ability to articulate ideas both orally and on paper. My organizational skills are solid and I'm very detail oriented. I understand that this position requires a lot of juggling of a variety of projects, and I think I'm organized enough to do that. I'm also a good listener, which I believe is an invaluable trait to have in this business.*

If you've made it to the interview, you probably have the analytical and math skills required for the position. The interviewer will most likely be concerned about your writing skills. Most positions require that you summarize your research projects in written reports; therefore, you must be able to articulate your ideas in a clear, concise manner. Be sure to emphasize your writing skills in addition to a few other key strengths.

Q: Now that you've heard my description of the industry and I've outlined your job responsibilities, are you still interested in the job and why?

A: *Yes. I'm even more interested because I have a clear view of exactly what I'll be doing if I'm hired for the position. I understand that the work is demanding and the hours often grueling, but the job itself is exciting, and I know I'd really enjoy it. I'm confident that my qualifications closely match what you're looking for, and that I could really contribute to this company and to your clients. My only question is, When can I expect to hear from you?*

This is an excellent opportunity to prove that you understand the job and the industry, and to express your enthusiasm for both. Be sure to summarize quickly how your qualifications match the job description.

Marketing Manager
(Transportation and Logistics)

Q: How did you become interested in the transportation and logistics industry?

A: *My great-grandfather started a small but successful trucking company. Unfortunately, my uncle ran the company into the ground by mismanagement. I've always regretted that a family business was never sustained. Although I don't want to create another family transportation business, I've always known that I wanted to work in the transportation and logistics industry.*

The recruiter will want to be sure that you're interested in the transportation and logistics industry as a career. What are your reasons for wanting to work in the transportation and logistics industry? Be able to articulate clearly your reasons for attending this interview and for wanting to work in this industry.

Q: What are your primary responsibilities in your current transportation and logistics marketing-managerial position?

A: *I'm in the marketing-management program of a major corporation. It's a two-year rotation and development program. Essentially I have four six-month job assignments in different marketing and sales positions. Indirectly, I'm responsible for a $500,000 budget. The purpose of the program is to establish working relationships with different cross-functional groups within the company. Also, we're testing to see how well we balance and manage several diverse projects simultaneously. On a day-to-day basis I do a variety of things. Specifically, I perform market analysis in order to develop marketing strategies and implementation alternatives. I prepare and present recommendations, based on my findings, to senior management. From there I develop and implement marketing programs and projects based on my approved recommendations.*

The recruiter will want to know the breadth of your experience. How qualified are you for the position you're interviewing for? This candidate's answer would impress any recruiter because it highlights the significant experience and responsibility that he or she has.

Q: What experience prepared and qualified you for work in transportation-industry marketing?

A: *Having three years of solid marketing-operations experience with a major gasoline company prepared me for this position. Additionally, I've found that having an M.B.A. from a high-quality business school is extremely beneficial. Both my previous work experience and my M.B.A. have enabled me to develop strong analytical and interpersonal skills.*

In other words, the recruiter is asking, "What are your qualifications?" Summarize your work and educational background. Be sure to include all relevant personal, work, and academic experience. Ideally, the recruiter is looking for two to three years' work experience in marketing, sales, or other closely related work. Having an M.B.A. is also very important.

Q: What was your undergraduate major? Has it provided a useful basis for your career in transportation and logistics?

A: *I earned a B.A. in American history from the University of Tennessee. The amount of writing I did as an undergraduate has helped me tremendously in transportation and logistics because it honed my communication skills.*

The recruiter will want to know about your academic background. Having a liberal arts undergraduate major is acceptable, but it's stronger if you supplement it with an M.B.A., as this candidate has. Otherwise, recruiters will be looking for strong undergraduate majors like finance, business, or labor relations.

Q: What specific professional skills have you developed that have helped you in transportation and logistics?

A: *My past work experience includes lots of teamwork and the opportunity to make formal presentations. I also have highly developed communication skills, which have proved essential in my current job.*

The recruiter will want to know what you will bring to his or her transportation and logistics marketing team. This candidate discusses the professional skills necessary for transportation and logistics marketing. Tell the recruiter specifically what you will bring to the team.

Q: What personal skills have you developed that have helped you in transportation and logistics?

First-time Job Seekers: Do as many informational interviews as possible, so that you have a solid understanding of what kinds of jobs there are in the transportation and logistics industry. What areas are you specifically interested in? If there are several, don't be afraid to try to work in different areas. Having a breadth of expertise in the industry will only make you more marketable for future positions.

A: *The biggest learning curve I've experienced is realizing how much I really do know. Letting others know it, as well, has been the challenge. In other words, I've gained a lot of self-assurance about my abilities in the workforce, and I've learned how to present that knowledge to coworkers. I've also learned the value and importance of networking, and working the halls, so to speak. And, finally, I've learned how to be very patient.*

What are you like to work with? The recruiter will want to know how your personal skills will benefit the marketing department and the company. Are you comfortable with immersing yourself in the fray without being abrasive, as this candidate is?

Q: What professional weakness do you have that may affect your productivity in transportation and logistics?

A: *My greatest professional weakness is not being assertive enough. I've recognized that my knowledge base is valuable, which has given me more confidence to be assertive. I work hard to communicate my ideas effectively.*

Being assertive and confident in transportation and logistics is extremely important, chiefly because you'll deal with so many different types of people. You must be able to communicate with the VP of marketing one minute, for example, and perhaps one of the company truck drivers the next. The recruiter will appreciate the candidate's answer because a recognition of areas that need improvement is positive.

Q: What has been your greatest challenge in your current transportation and logistics job?

A: *My biggest challenge has been trying to implement changes that I feel are necessary in an organization with a strongly established history and company culture. It's difficult to get coworkers to grasp the strategic benefits of marketing, and how it will benefit them as well as the company. On a larger scale, it's been difficult to gain management consensus across many different divisions and field-marketing units.*

The recruiter is looking for an individual who is deeply involved in his or her job. This candidate cares about the position, as opposed to someone who simply clocks in from eight to five. Additionally, the recruiter will be interested in uncovering your problem-solving abilities.

Q: If you could work with anyone in the transportation and logistics industry, whom would you want to work with?

A: *I'd like to work closely, on a day-to-day basis, with the executive vice president of marketing for this company. I think I'd learn a lot from this experience because he has a very strong, clear vision. Further, he has the courage to make* changes in an organization with a strong operations history. I think he's successful because he has strong people skills which make him a natural leader.

The recruiter will be interested in how motivated you are. Your choice here will probably be someone you consider a professional mentor, which will tell the recruiter a lot about you as a person. Think carefully about whom you would want to work with, and whom you might consider a professional mentor.

Q: **What are your transportation and logistics career goals for five years from now?**

A: *In five years I'd like to be a marketing director for a specific marketing unit within your company. As an alternative, a director-level operations-management position is attractive.*

This question is tricky because you want to express to the recruiter how motivated you are, but at the same time, you do not want to seem unrealistic. This candidate's answer is realistic and achievable. Try to focus on the responsibility you'd like to acquire instead of listing job titles.

Q: **What opportunities do you see in transportation and logistics?**

A: *There are lots of opportunities in this industry because it encompasses a huge market. Specifically, there is opportunity to improve the technology and the processes that drive the transportation industry, because the transportation function has not been studied the way other industries and functions, such as manufacturing, have. I think logistics is the next battleground for competitive advantage.*

The recruiter will want to know how aware you are of the big picture. This candidate's answer is excellent because he or she intelligently outlines the next phase of the transportation and logistics industry. Read the industry publications, as well as business journals, to prepare for questions like this.

Q: **Why do you want this transportation and logistics marketing-manager job?**

A: *I want this job for several reasons. First, working with this company in marketing would allow me to build on my previous marketing positions, so I'd be continuing to develop a certain skill set. Second, this company is an industry leader. Taking this job, if I'm offered it, is the right thing to do.*

Career Changers: Discuss previous experiences, emphasizing positions that have given you the most relevant experience. Talk about how these skills will be effective and useful in the transportation and logistics industry. Demonstrate your problem-solving ability and creativity in past situations, and relate these skills to the position.

The recruiter will want to understand your reasons for attending this interview. The candidate's desire to continue developing his or her marketing portfolio within the transportation and logistics industry will make sense to the recruiter. Further, the candidate wisely reaffirms an interest in the company.

Q: What transportation and logistics publications do you read?

A: *For transportation and logistics, I think reading Transport Topics is a must. I also try to skim now and then through old marketing textbooks as a refresher. Other important journals that I read include Newsweek, Forbes, and the Harvard Business Review.*

The recruiter will want to know if you're reading industry publications, as well as more general business materials. These examples show the recruiter that the candidate is aware of what's happening in the world, and that he or she doesn't just exist in a vacuum. If you are not currently reading at least some of these publications, start now.

Q: Tell me about a time you worked on a team.

A: *In business school there was a lot of teamwork because we did a lot of group projects in most classes. In some cases I would assume the leadership role, and in others, perhaps in a situation I didn't have much expertise in, I would assume a support role. It's important to be adaptable to the situation. Some groups are more effective than others, but I learned that you have to make the most of a less-than-positive group situation because the ultimate goal is to get the job done.*

The transportation and logistics industry involves a lot of interaction with people of different educational levels and job ranking. You must show the recruiter that you interact well with different types of people. A good way to do this is to describe a time when you worked on a team.

Q: What things impress you about colleagues in transportation and logistics?

A: *I'm impressed with a solid work history and pattern of development. In marketing I think some of my colleagues with sales experience are especially effective in their jobs. I like working with people who have the same willingness that*

Experienced Professionals: Sell yourself on your experience. Demonstrate your abilities with several examples of how your problem-solving abilities and creativity have led to success. Capitalize on any prominent success stories, and emphasize your ability to make a contribution quickly. Have references ready.

I have to work long, hard hours. I also like working with colleagues who have a strong work ethic, and who talk in terms of the team.

The recruiter will want to explore further how effective you are working on a team. Your answer will tell the recruiter what types of people you work with best. Try to make your answer flexible, because in the transportation and logistics industry you'll be dealing with a wide range and variety of people. Also, the qualities you admire in other people are likely qualities that you yourself possess, so your answer to this question will give the recruiter some insight about what you're like to work with.

Q: **What things would be turnoffs about your colleagues in transportation and logistics?**

A: *The biggest turnoff is someone who is always saying, "I, I, I." Being confident and doing a little self-promoting is fine, but being conceited is not. It just doesn't do anything for the team.*

Again, this question further explores the candidate's ability to work on a team. The candidate probably doesn't have the qualities that he or she disapproves of, so this gives the recruiter further insight into what it would be like to work with this person. Interpersonal skills are important to teamwork in transportation and logistics, and the candidate seems fully aware of that.

Q: **Why do you think the logistics industry has grown exponentially over the last ten to fifteen years?**

A: *Outsourcing expertise is commonplace in the U.S., because of the impact of global competition. By outsourcing, a company is able to focus on its core competency. The company can then make sure it stays ahead of the competition.*

The recruiter will want to know if you're aware of the forces shaping the industry. You should have a thorough understanding of industry dynamics before the interview. Be prepared to discuss the significance of the current industry forces.

Candidates Re-entering the Workforce: Brush up on your computer and presentation skills. Conduct several informational interviews to get good advice on re-entering the workforce. Develop a good understanding of the transportation and logistics industry by reading industry and company reports.

Q: What are some of the benefits to hiring a logistics firm?

A: *Outsourcing transportation needs to a logistics company saves the company the time and money of running the transportation operation itself. This way the company is assured that the job will be done efficiently and professionally.*

The recruiter will want to know if you understand the benefits of logistics. You should be able to articulate how outsourcing benefits the customer. Be prepared to discuss the monetary and qualitative reasons a customer should consider outsourcing.

Q: What is the difference between an OTC, or an over the road carrier, and a dedicated fleet?

A: *A dedicated fleet works only for a particular customer. An OTC uses the same trucks for different vendors.*

The recruiter will want to know if you have a solid understanding of the transportation and logistics industry. You should be able to discuss the differences between a dedicated logistics company and an OTC. Be prepared, as well, to discuss the pros and cons of doing business with different kinds of logistics companies.

Q: Is there anything you'd like to ask me?

A: *Yes. I'm wondering what this company's marketing strategy is. What are the priorities of marketing here?*

Coming to the interview with prepared questions is a good idea. If the recruiter doesn't give you an opportunity to ask questions, volunteer some. Other questions you might want to ask include, "What do you like most about your job and this company?" "What frustrates you the most about your job and this company?" "What do you or my potential supervisors want to get accomplished over the next two to three years?" "What is the job interviewing process from this point?" "Is there anything I can do to assist in the process?"

Marketing Representative/Risk Analyst
(Energy)

Q: **What opportunities are you most interested in within the energy industry?**

A: *The big opportunities I see are for providing multiple energy sources like gas, electric, and other sources. I'm interested in managing people and managing a larger profit margin at the regional level. My track record in bringing in gas-supply and transportation deals shows I can grow the business and take advantage of the new revenue opportunities as alternative energy sources undergo deregulation.*

This question tests the candidate's industry knowledge. The important thing is to have a ready, educated opinion and show how you fit into that picture. The candidate here shows an interest in taking on new responsibility coinciding with the new business opportunities.

Q: **Why are hedging strategies logical in selling energy services?**

A: *Large buyers of natural gas want to lock in prices for planning and budgeting purposes. And they want a hedge against weather turns. If you buy during a cold snap, when gas heat is in great demand, you'll pay top dollar whereas with a futures contract you've locked into a lower price. Natural gas prices are very volatile, so buying for futures allows for better planning.*

This question helps the recruiter determine whether the candidate understands the core nature of the business. It is likely to be asked in a screening interview, especially of entry-level analysts.

Q: **Why do you think you could be an effective trading manager?**

A: *I have strong financial skills and intuition for the market because of the year I spent on the unregulated side. I've learned a great deal about what affects pricing on the exchange and when to lock in a price. In general, my relationships with customers show that I know how to listen, which is the key skill among successful trading managers I've known. And because I've built pipelines as an engineer, I understand capacity issues. I also understand how transportation customers want deals put together, and how realistic those desires are from a capacity standpoint.*

With this kind of question it is critical for the candidate to come across confidently. It's also important to make statements that can be supported. (For example, the candidate's intuition is aided by knowledge of what affects price changes, so the recruiter would most likely explore a comment like this with a follow-up question like, "When might you lock in a price quickly?")

Q: What would you look for if you were recruiting entry-level risk managers to trade gas?

A: *Obviously, I would look for someone with an interest in finance, trading, and futures contracts. This work requires people who can handle the pressure and fast pace of that environment. During bid week each month, when companies lock in their prices for the following month's energy prices, you barely have time to breathe. For new hires in marketing we look for economics, finance, and sales skills. I consider these more important than energy industry knowledge, which I could teach them.*

This is the type of question you might be presented if applying for a managerial position in which you would be expected to hire additional staff. Be prepared to outline what criteria you consider important and how your own strengths factor in.

Q: What has been difficult about trying to get into energy management with an engineer's background?

A: *Many professional employees in energy companies start as engineers, so I've found the technical skill to be an advantage. After all, our business is technically based. My personal weakness in terms of moving into management is that my business training in marketing and economics has all been on the job rather than formal. But I don't think I'd trade my time in the business as a project engineer for time sitting in business classes. Following nine years on the engineering side of the business, the year I've spent very successfully in marketing shows that I've learned the business side well.*

The recruiter is concerned about the candidate's lack of management training. The only solution is to address the issue head on and remain positive. The candidate presents engineering as an asset, not a liability, then sells on-the-job training. The answer might be improved by showing some interest in, or recent history of, course work in some of the management topics.

> **First-time Job Seekers:** Demonstrate knowledge about the industry—the changes, big players, and competitive factors. A finance and economics background is also desirable for energy marketing. Demonstrate knowledge as a consumer of various power companies you have relied on.

Q: **When you're selling transportation of fuel, what do you do when you've a bad margin month?**

A: *I try to determine where it went wrong. Our deals are on penny margins—zero to five cents per unit—but we're dealing with millions of units—big money. I've learned how to make hard decisions fast, especially when I'm slightly down. I think it's human nature not to lock in on a price when you're losing a penny, so you wait for the market to turn around, which it may or may not do. I learned quickly when to lock in at a penny loss rather than wait until it gets worse.*

This is a specific problem-solving question requiring a specific response. Here the candidate does a great job. His or her comments on timing show quick thinking and decisive behavior. These characteristics are highly compatible with trading environments of energy traders and even of traders in the major stock markets. Clearly, the candidate's personality is a good "fit" for the realities of the job.

Q: **Tell me about your cold-calling experience with some of the energy suppliers and exploration companies.**

A: *I've learned how to keep the conversation open and ask open-ended questions. I always find out how my competitors are successful. I ask what the competitors do that my prospect likes and doesn't like, and the prospect is more often than not receptive to answering. So the worst thing that happens is that I pick up competitive feedback, and people are usually willing to talk to me the next time I call, because I listened the first time. When I talk to them again, I'll have a deal to offer that's structured the way they've indicated would be acceptable. That's why I've been able to grow my business this past year.*

This is a skill-assessment and diligence question, and the candidate does several things well. He or she shows not only listening and conversation skills, but an ability to get people to open up and discuss competitors' strategies. Even more important, the candidate describes using that kind of information to come back later and secure business.

Q: **Suppose you had to hire transportation staff to support you in managing a regional gas-transportation business. What things would you look for in candidates?**

A: *If I was trying to hire an experienced marketing rep, I'd want good knowledge of derivative products, a good customer base of suppliers and end users, like local gas companies, and good working knowledge of the industry, on top of people skills. With a new hire I'd look for good people skills, communication skills, and a background in finance and economics. I always like to see an engineering background, although that's not a requirement, but it helps to know about the technical aspects of our business.*

Here the interviewer is assessing the candidate's management potential. Could he or she help select and develop people? The candidate does a good job of breaking the answer into two logical parts—experienced versus new hires. The description here of an ideal marketing rep is most likely how the candidate views him- or herself, and the recruiter will draw conclusions based on this.

Q: **Why are you interested in marketing energy products rather than working on the technical/exploration side?**

A: *I'm motivated by the fact that the marketing group has the most growth potential in your company, which started pouring money into marketing two years ago. I knew my engineering background would be a good complement to the rest of the management here, and I do enjoy marketing aspects more. Some of that is my personality. I'm very outgoing and determined, so when potential customers say they've already got their energy contracts for the next month or year, I don't just give up. I also would find it hard to go back to the regulated part of this business. I see great opportunity for additional services on the unregulated side.*

This is the motivation question that is always on an interviewer's mind. Here the candidate ties corporate strategy to his or her own accomplishments and decisions. The candidate shows passion as well as suitability for the job.

Q: **What do you see as the five-year growth potential in energy transportation?**

A: *The energy-transportation business is driven by those who can provide the most value-added services, plus reliability, creditworthiness, and other factors. Your next opportunity is to do in electric-power marketing what you've done in gas marketing. Suppose power marketing does take off the way natural gas has; you could serve all the energy needs of a customer—gas, oil, and electric services.*

This answer is strong in that it shows initiative and aspiration from the company's perspective. The answer shows marketing skill, or the focus on what customers need in services. The candidate's behavior is very consistent with the skill required for this marketing job opening.

Career Changers: Concentrate on skills that are transferable—marketing, financial, and negotiating. Compatible prior business experience would be financial services, including work in derivatives. Other industries undergoing similar regulatory changes are pharmaceuticals and airlines/transportation.

Q: **Do you think third-party transportation business makes sense?**

A: *Sure. Third parties are often without their own marketing staff because they devote their resources to energy exploration. Therefore, they're willing to pay for value-added transportation services. Often a transportation service will be able to offer a more competitive premium than the open market could provide, anyway. In that sense everybody wins.*

This opinion question requires a confident response. The candidate demonstrates knowledge of the business, and the recruiter easily gets the sense that, if this were a sales call and he or she were the third party, the candidate would be very convincing on the mutual benefits of a business relationship.

Q: **How do you keep up with what other energy companies are doing?**

A: *The Federal Energy Regulatory Commission produces several publications I rely on. I also read* Gas Daily, *so I know who's bought what, yesterday's prices, and other information that will help me with my next bids.*

The recruiter wants to know how actively this candidate seeks industry information. The answer here is strong. The candidate not only lists specific reports, but also explains how to use the information to his or her own (and the company's) advantage.

Q: **Do you think electric power presents good opportunities for growth?**

A: *Yes, because electrical power is about to go through deregulation the way natural gas has. If you look at how companies have capitalized on natural-gas transportation, you see good opportunity for similar value-added service on the electric side. I think that a power-marketing group seems logical for your company, and I'd enjoy being part of it.*

This opinion question also requires a strong response. The candidate presents a solid argument based on the history of the deregulation of gas service. The next part of the answer suggests a new department or division for this company and an offer to help develop that new business. If you make a suggestion during your interview, show how you would fit into the picture—create a job need.

Experienced Professionals: The best opportunities will come from the emerging deregulated businesses, so it would be best to align yourself with such a company. Also, after working in a deregulated area, you'll have obtained valuable skills for breaking back into regulated businesses.

Q: **How might a pricing strategy shift with a particular transportation client?**

A: *During bid week each month the Verizon contract closes the middle of that week for the following month. Early in that bid-week cycle people are trading gas relative to where the Verizon screen is, but after it closes, you lose that screen as a tool. The major pipeline deadlines are later that week, so not everyone has bought gas yet. When you have to buy gas on a cash price instead of on a futures contract, you hope that the weather gets really warm and the price of gas falls.*

This is a business-knowledge question. The candidate simply demonstrates knowledge of the market dynamics—cause and effect. The answer indicates that the candidate would be able to anticipate when a customer might panic and when customers are likely to lock in their prices.

Q: **What situation might force you to tell an energy customer that you cannot deliver what he or she wants?**

A: *If a company wanted to buy gas right at the well, we could not deliver value-added service. The customer would have to be willing to take what's actually produced rather than the ideal volume. Where we provide service is when we manage volume fluctuations at the delivery point (the end user's facility) after we have pooled an aggregate supply of gas from many wells.*

This question is a reality check, aimed particularly at candidates for sales and marketing jobs. The recruiter wants to establish whether the person would understand the company's limitations or would promise more than the company could deliver. The candidate might cite a specific example of where he or she presented a customer with an alternative in order to be able to deliver the result the customer wanted.

Q: **What do you consider an ideal balance of business in terms of transporting your own energy products versus transporting those of a third party?**

A: *I believe that any equity production you control allows you to more than double the amount of business you can bring in, because many customers want to deal directly with the producer. Then you can turn to third parties and leverage your position. Otherwise you have to sell gas only when you can find someone to buy it. That's why I want to work for a company like yours, because you have your own exploration and production.*

Here the candidate does not directly answer the question, if we assume the recruiter wants some sort of percentage breakdown. However, the candidate's position is very clear. And he or she ties the answer directly to genuine interest in this company—a good sales message.

Q: **What skills do you think will help you the most in this industry?**

A: *For sales and trading of energy commodities, risk-management tools and general finance and negotiating skills are the most critical. Some technical or engineering knowledge is also helpful, to understand the physics of the various energy forms and the limitations of the transportation system.*

This is the time to "sell" your skills, which this candidate does effectively. You might also present some weakness in your own skill set, provided you also demonstrate some plan of action to compensate for it. Otherwise, you should anticipate a follow-up question like, "What personal weaknesses have impeded your career in the energy business?"

Q: **After being a marketing representative for a period of time, where would you want to go next?**

A: *I might move into risk management or management of a trading group.*

The beauty of the energy-marketing business is that it changes rapidly, so frequent moves to new positions are expected. However, don't look for those moves to be to loftier titles, but to lateral positions that build complementary skills.

Q: **What are the drawbacks to working in an energy company?**

A: *There are geographic limitations—we don't produce energy in every city. Also, the industry is high risk, high reward based on the volatility of the product. Natural gas started trading in the futures market only in the early nineties, and it's still quite volatile.*

This question is another reality check. In particular, the recruiter may be concerned about whether the location would satisfy the candidate long term. Or, if the candidate already works in the local market in the industry, the question may help the recruiter determine whether the candidate is running away from a current job (negative/reactive), or looking for a good new job (proactive).

Q: **How might you secure fixed gas costs for one year for a customer who fears rising prices?**

Candidates Re-entering the Workforce: Prior business experience is critical, especially sales, negotiating, or pricing expertise. Share observations as a consumer and manager of your household about the responsiveness of various power providers.

A: *I'd try to sell the customer a futures contract so that if gas prices go up, the customer nets the gain. This allows us to help customers on a budget. For example, a steel company whose product is made up of about 50 percent gas needs the price locked in so it can control product costs and make its own reasonable projections.*

This scenario tests the candidate's sales skills and tells the recruiter how he or she would respond in a similar situation. The answer helps to demonstrate the candidate's level of experience, because the example shows the candidate's understanding of a typical natural-gas customer.

Q: What type of jurisdictional restrictions might you expect in a regulated industry?

A: *Most regulated companies have to pass the profits on to customers; they have fixed rates of return. The cost of gas transportation is regulated, but the cost of gas itself is not. That's why we can make good profits buying and selling gas, shipping it, and storing it. And that's why I'm interested in the marketing and trading aspect of the energy business.*

Expect this question if you're applying for an entry-level management/professional job. It tests your knowledge of the regulated and unregulated aspects of the business. Despite previous experience in the industry, you should understand issues of regulation if you keep up with current news events.

Q: What percent of your business would you be willing to risk by not hedging it?

A: *I would hedge up to 50 percent to have 50 percent upside potential. But that way I've guaranteed that at least half of my business (based on fixed costs of production) is covered. This means that I'll make my budget, except in an extraordinary circumstance.*

This question tests your gut instincts. It also tests your ability to handle and manage risk and uncertainty—critical in any sales and trading environment.

Product Manager
(Retail Athletic Shoes)

Q: Why do you want to work for this company?

A: *Because I'm a runner, and I think you make the best shoes in the market. I think most people want to work doing something they enjoy—even if they aren't getting paid. That's the way I feel about working in the running business. I think my field-sales experience in retail as a district manager will be invaluable. For my own reasons I'd like to learn more about product development, so the opening in product management would be great for my career growth. The specialty running-shoe business drives the technology for all the other athletic shoes out there, so I'd like to know more about how that happens.*

The candidate clearly demonstrates passion for the business by explaining that, as a customer who has used the product, he or she believes in the quality of the shoes. The fact that the candidate's already successfully worked as a retail territory manager is a good example of offering "proof" of skills that transfer to a new industry that is also retail related. And an interest in how the product development drives the industry is proof that the candidate thinks strategically (as a corporate employee should think) and is sincerely interested in the current opening.

Q: Where do you think we're headed as an industry?

A: *The industry has plateaued in terms of technology—it's a very mature business. That puts even more pressure on the development department, and it means that the information that people share from field sales and from runners is even more critical. Companies will have to focus on operational excellence as the retail-store brand name becomes the name consumers go to rather than the shoe manufacturer's label. And a recent industry conference I attended touched upon the need for a return to customer service. I'd very much like the opportunity to head up that organization for your company.*

The candidate voices belief in the role of product development, demonstrates suitability for the job, and exhibits problem-solving skills by describing how his or her role in providing input from the field will be critical to ideas for the product-development professionals. And the candidate asks for the job.

Q: How do you think athletic-wear companies can return to customer service?

A: *A big issue here is cooperation with the retailers in the use of computer technology for sharing information. We need a better sense of what's moving off the shelves. It hurts us even to sell the shoes to retailers if the retailers have to discount them to move them. As a product technology leader, the company can't afford too much discounting because it hurts the brand image. We want customers to notice that the product offers the features they need from a design and use standpoint.*

This opinion question is aimed at measuring the candidate's problem-solving ability. Can he or she think strategically? The candidate's answer addresses both issues. Note the use of "we" which effectively reminds the recruiter that the candidate is an industry insider if not already a company insider.

Q: **It can be challenging to work with field-sales reps who manage their own time and have home offices. How might you manage a group of reps?**

A: *You need to use technology to its fullest—for example, E-mail and other efficient, time-saving tools. You have to hire people capable of being their own secretaries. People at home offices often work seven days a week, especially with so much travel during the week to stores in their territory. So you also need to recognize that fact, and reward it by offering aggressive upside commission potential.*

Here's a management-style question. The technology suggestions show creativity and the ability to stay current with other business professionals, and they also hint at good time management. The candidate also offers a strong opinion about commission structures—this is important, because if the job seeker's philosophy and the company's are not in sync on this point, both parties need to know up front.

Q: **What experiences helped you to be prepared and qualified to manage national accounts?**

A: *A few different things: I'm a runner, so I understand your consumers and what they want from a performance shoe. I have running retail experience. And my prior jobs have allowed me to do lots of different things, including running sales for the entire southeast region of my current company. I've learned how to coordinate and manage reps in a large territory. Although I have no formal*

First-time Job Seekers: Any part-time experience is a plus. Be willing to start out free as an intern. Show your interest as a consumer in sports products.

academic degree in marketing, in some ways I feel as if I've completed an "apprentice M.B.A." in athletic-business strategy. Our ability to think long term is going to be critical, especially since consumers are becoming less sensitive about manufacturer names and more so about retailer names. I'm sure you want to groom people who think that way, and change as needed. I'd like to become part of senior management here, and the national sales manager job is well suited to my previous experience.

The candidate's answer to this classic skill-assessment question is clear, succinct, and well organized. And the candidate offers something extra—comments about the changing nature of the market—asking again for the job, in a pleasant way.

Q: What has been the greatest challenge for you in the athletic industry?

A: *For most people in our business, knowledge comes through experience, starting from the ground up. Sometimes I wish I had the business theory to back up those decisions I intuitively know how to call after ten years in the business. Where the lack of formal business training hurts is in strategic planning and finance, but I've made a commitment to attend seminars to learn those things. And I'd consider any executive education that doesn't interfere with my travel schedule.*

The candidate's humble answer to the weakness question is realistic, without being self-condemning. Instead the candidate points out how he or she has compensated for some lack of academic-management background by attending seminars and pursuing an interest in self-improvement. (Lack of formal business training is, in fact, common in this industry; industry experience is considered more critical, so the candidate picked a "safe" weakness to talk about.)

Q: What do you know about our company and its athletic footwear?

A: *First, I'll say what I would say if I were representing your company. I know that you're a company with a technology commitment to running shoes and, as a runner, I find that commitment admirable. With the market and technology mature, I think athletic-footwear companies will have to return to operational excellence. This company never abandoned that concept because it focused on running*

Career Changers: Look for transferable skills that the athletic industry needs right now, like technology/MIS skills, or an accounting or management background in a different retail industry that's already gone through major consolidation. Any good retail-sales background is a plus. Show personal interest in sports. Fast trackers are on the marketing and product sides (break-in is possible but limited).

technology all along while others went after fashion trends. Consistent product quality is critical now, since there are fewer instances of technology revolutions.

This question examines the job seeker's passion for the business. The heartfelt answer demonstrates loyalty to the company, and driving motivation. It also provides evidence of the sales skills that make this candidate believable and clearly compatible with a marketing and sales organization.

Q: What internal structure is necessary to achieve operational or technological excellence in footwear?

A: *The flat structure at your company is one of the things I like. It makes sense, because you're lean and can make a faster response to demand shifts. Larger, more bureaucratic organizations will take longer in responding to feedback from the sales force. And if you take too long, customers will have shifted to a new product.*

This question requires an educated opinion. The candidate delivers, without having to be a technical expert. (The question has more to do with organization design than with manufacturing strategy, which is why careful listening is critical. Another candidate might have panicked and claimed, "I haven't worked in the manufacturing organization.") In a case like this the recruiter wants to determine how a marketing person seeks and uses information.

Q: How would you get started as a national sales manager?

A: *I'll want to start by learning more about strategic marketing, sourcing, and production at your company specifically. For example, I'll want to go to your manufacturing sites to learn costing of materials and construction, so that I'd have a better understanding of how you share parts like soles and uppers in different shoe lines. That way I can give sound information to your existing major accounts. Simultaneously, I'll want to review historical account information to see where accounts have grown, been lost, and so on. And I'll make an immediate effort to meet the major accounts and the sales reps supporting them. I'm not concerned about the management of the sales reps, because I've got a good track record of field experience in training. Our top sales performers in my current company are people I trained. I hope you'll take that into consideration when you decide who should become your national sales manager.*

This is a process question, addressing problem solving and organizational abilities. The three-part answer is effective—learn product development, review accounts, meet the players. Notice the candidate's positive bias through use of "I will" versus "I would." The ending includes a strong sales message.

Q: You deal with independent sales reps in this business. What is your experience with them?

A: *These reps are as critical as the corporate salespeople, but you have to make sure they're giving your brands a fair shake. Earlier in my career as a manager, I fired an independent rep for good reasons, but I almost ended up in court. I learned that there is a statute in that particular state which gives special protection to independent sales reps. An experience like that teaches you to ask a bunch of questions before you proceed with certain actions, even though the actions are warranted. There's a safe, thorough way to do everything. I've just learned to take the extra time to figure out that safe way, but I won't tolerate unproductive people in my organization.*

This answer is revealing and humble, therefore effective. The candidate describes learning through a mistake—in other words, explains that this is one mistake the new company will not have to worry about in this case, because it won't happen again. The ending is effective in that it indicates the candidate's own strong work ethic.

Q: What athletic-industry contacts do you have that could help in this job?

A: *I've made efforts to get to know the editors of the major sports magazines; I try to take them to dinner when I can. Also, I know many independent sales reps—there's lots of crossover there in terms of people they get to know in noncompeting sporting-goods lines. That helps me stay current on the larger retail industry we operate in. Some of my biggest customers are my current company's oldest customers. Many of them have told me they buy from me because of my service level, not because of which shoe I represent.*

This question aims to determine what benefits the candidate brings beyond his or her ability simply to perform the work tasks. The answer is thorough, covering PR contacts, independent reps, and possible new account business for the company. Note the last sentence: it is always effective to report what others have said, rather than simply to promote yourself, which is, of course, just "your opinion," and more suspect.

Experienced Professionals: Your chance to move further up the career ladder may come through changing among types of retail products while maintaining a functional specialty (such as technical product development in apparel). Or it may come from reputation within a targeted sport.

By now you should know that the athletic industry is very closed. The same people switch around among players. Major trade shows are attended by everyone, so you do meet peers at competitive companies. Meet them and network; make mentors where possible. Remember not to burn bridges, especially in an industry like this.

Q: How will your business background be relevant to the athletic industry, which isn't terribly sophisticated in the way we conduct business?

A: *You have to want to be in the sporting-goods industry from the start. For example, when I studied economics, I would think about how it related to this industry. The way I communicate is through examples in this industry, not through business jargon. Quite simply, I'm not the kind of person who's going to walk around with college and graduate-school transcripts on my shirtsleeve.*

This question addresses management style, teamwork, and suitability for the position. Because most people have come through the business from the ground up, the company is obviously concerned about whether this candidate is too slick and would irritate or intimidate others. The candidate picks up on this concern.

Q: Tell me how you conduct market research.

A: *Here's an example that comes immediately to mind: I'm doing consumer research about kids playing basketball. So I play basketball with the kids. I pick up games all over town in my spare time. Then I ask myself, "How can what I heard today fit into the picture and bring our marketing to the next level?"*

The answer shows creativity and enthusiasm, since the candidate is using nonwork time to think about work. It also quite effectively indicates a passion for the business. As reinforcement, the candidate might want to share something he or she learned from playing ball in the streets that was then used in a marketing decision.

Q: The cultures of various athletic companies are vastly different— from really loose to really conservative. What environment is right for you?

A: *I'm a very spontaneous person by nature, as opposed to structured, which is why I believe I'm a good fit with this company. I understand your presentations here are very MTV oriented. I've also noted that you use basic overheads, not fancy graphics. That suits my personal style; I tend to believe that paperwork is best used to record historical information and that productive time is time spent actively. That seems consistent with what various managers at your company have said to me.*

Candidates Re-entering the Workforce: Play up any retail background, and your own consumer behavior as a retail customer. If possible, work part-time in a retail sporting-goods store while waiting for interviews, or offer to work for free for a short period of time. Show a personal interest in sports.

Many of the companies in this industry are very loosely structured. Obviously, the recruiter's concern is whether the candidate has a structured or a nonstructured personality. The best part of the answer is at the end, where the candidate mentions having talked to company insiders and investigated the work environment and structure. The recruiter understands that the job seeker has done his or her homework and made a careful selection based on company "fit." In other words, the candidate is saying, "I've worried about this already, so you don't have to."

Q: **Tell me about a particular consumer insight you learned from playing basketball in the street.**

A: *In the big cities I've talked to numerous street kids. I've learned the importance of neighborhood role models to them—people who are working hard and doing well. Their aspirations aren't so long term; they don't aspire to be Michael Jordan. They're trying to get through next week, and they relate to the guy who has gotten one or two steps beyond them—maybe someone who's just bought a first new car, or just got into college. So now our advertising is about neighborhoods, in school yards, backyards, and so on. We aren't focusing on the superathletes to attract these kids, because they can't relate—the superathlete is not a realistic goal.*

This answer is real—you can almost picture the candidate talking to neighborhood kids, then going home and making notes. He or she takes firsthand consumer research and brings it to decisions at the office. You definitely get the sense that this candidate understands the consumers.

Q: **What marketing shifts do you think some of the athletic-shoe companies will go through in the next few years?**

A: *Women and men who grew up with our company are now forty to fifty-year-olds. We're trying to get to twelve to seventeen-year-olds. We must figure out what our forty to fifty-year-olds like and how to make it appeal to the younger group. So we're weaving a thread through our advertising and in our product that we're a family brand.*

This is a question of industry insight, and the candidate provides a good observation. As the population ages, how do we attract the young consumer? The answer offers an attractive solution—appeal to whole families. The candidate thus shows creativity and problem-solving ability.

Q: **How can household panels from Nielsen—pretty sophisticated research—be useful in this industry?**

A: *One way is through cross promotions with a product like a popular cereal brand. You can then recontact end users and learn about their likes.*

The athletic-footwear industry has brought people up through the ranks and has not historically relied on sophisticated research information. This question seeks to determine if the job candidate could help bring the company up to speed with other industries (and perhaps ahead of the industry competition). The answer is decisive and strong because it is specific.

Q: **How do you manage the creative nature of the people who are predominant in this business?**

A: *I can support creative goals by providing a complement to back up quantitatively what they do. I have a lot more accounting and financial-modeling skills than many of my peers. When they have a good idea, I say, "Let me run some numbers based on that idea." Then I can give them real ammunition to get the idea approved. So my answer to your question is that I look for a way to balance their creativity with my own skills.*

This answer is very specific in selling the job seeker's distinctive competence—financial skills. It also gives the impression of a team orientation, suggesting that the candidate enjoys helping others garner support for their ideas. In closing, the candidate provides a good summary.

Q: **What would you say is the price breakdown on athletic footwear?**

A: *The factory probably makes up about 50 percent (let's say it costs manufacturing $10 or less per pair of shoes). There is about a $20 markup between the factory and your company, assuming you don't do your own production. You might charge the wholesaler about $40, and the retailer is likely to sell the product for about $80. So you make about $20 per pair and have to take all your costs of sales and advertising out of that.*

This question is a reality check. Does the candidate understand the supply chain or distribution channel? This kind of knowledge is critical in a marketing job. The candidate has a good, solid answer.

Q: **What current ad campaign of ours is your favorite?**

A: *I think your printed ads at school gyms are effective. More consumers can relate to that kind of advertising than to a superathlete. For a time I thought your pro athlete commercials were effective, but some of those guys have gotten greedy in the eyes of consumers. The personalities of the athletes and the schools your company sponsors should be compatible. For example, because your brand has an irreverent youth following, its association with the University of XYZ is appropriate.*

Know the current ads and endorsers. Do you think a particular athlete or sponsorship is good for the brand? Why or why not?

Real Estate Property Manager/
Leasing Agent

Q: **Why are you interested in moving to our company after years in another commercial real estate firm?**

A: *I'm interested in taking on leasing and management services for third parties who own commercial buildings. I think those opportunities are primarily in the major market cities like Dallas, where your company has a strong presence. And I believe my experience shows a steady increase in client development over the years, which shows I can be an asset.*

This answer turns the question into the right point of view—the company's. (Candidate's might fall into the trap of acting selfish in their response—"I want" rather than "The company needs . . ." The candidate here offers an opinion on why Dallas is such a good market for the company and why he or she could capitalize on it (to the company's advantage), given the job seeker's background.

Q: **Are there real estate positions you've had in the past that were less than ideal?**

A: *I had one staff position at the corporate office that took me out of dealing with clients, and I found I wasn't happy. The experience taught me I needed to be dealing with people—with tenants—rather than sitting alone at a desk. I'm interested in remaining a generalist, with responsibility for sales, finance, and operation for commercial sites.*

This is an issue of the candidate's suitability for the job but is asked as a negative question. The candidate does not dwell on negative issues, although he or she politely answers the questions, ("I wasn't happy" is a more positive statement than "I hated.") The candidate emphasizes effective interaction with clients in a recent job, rather than why a job in the past was a bad job.

Q: **How did you develop your general-management skills in order to be the "CEO" of a large office building?**

A: *One of my first bosses was not good at motivating in a positive way, which is damaging in a business where we have to be upbeat with tenants. At the same time, I did learn from him to manage by walking around. With so many tenants in a large building, many problems can arise. You have to be readily available and make sure that your limited staff appears to be larger than it is. That give tenants a comfort level that problems will be handled quickly, and it keeps them calm.*

This answer to a management style question is both sincere and positive. By pointing out how a previous boss demonstrated what to do as well as what not to do, the candidate shows the influence of that supervision on the management style he or she has today. The candidate does not get caught bad-mouthing a former employer, but rather, makes that employer sound human. This answer also implies that employees react well to the candidate's own "walking around" philosophy.

Q: **What day-to-day responsibilities in your past jobs helped you become a good property manager?**

A: *I think it's more the variety of experiences I've had over the past fifteen years. Development of my presentation skills and supervisory skills has been critical. I'm very good as doing client development—selling an idea, marketing, leasing negotiations, and even recruiting. I know that you're interested in solid management skills. Even in my first experiences outside the industry, I gained supervisory experience over telephone-repair clerks and unionized craft employees. I also got P-and-L (profit-and-loss) experience very early on, including budgeting and tracking variances. And I've had presentation experience, because I've had to talk to company groups and participate in a company speakers' bureau to explain to telephone-company subscribers why we had filed for a rate increase. This really isn't so different form telling a lease tenant that the rent is going up.*

This answer is a good, succinct summary of relevant skills. Furthermore, the candidate shows clearly how work in an unrelated industry is relevant to the job in property management. This is critical, because what's obvious to you is often not obvious to someone who hasn't worked in both environments.

Q: **Why haven't you managed large commercial sites such as downtown skyscrapers?**

A: *I admit that my past interest in smaller cities has kept me from taking on some major development projects in the major markets. Now I feel I'm ready to go to a major market like Dallas, where I see really strong opportunities for third-party management on a large scale.*

The candidate offers a positive reiteration of where the business is headed and how he or she is prepared to adjust to be part of it. Note that the candidate

First-time Job Seekers: Since a generalist orientation is preferred, take a well-rounded set of courses. You should also take a real estate course offered through your school or possibly through a local organization. Often centers of adult learning offer courses toward various real estate licensing requirements. These courses provide good proof of your interest and give you good information to talk about in interviews.

does not give a negative answer or make excuses. Often interviewees will become defensive when presented with a question like this; the best way to handle your answer is to tell it fast and straight, then make a positive statement, as in the example above.

Q: **What is the most difficult problem for you in property management? How have you attempted to overcome it?**

A: *My weakness is saying no to people, especially long-term tenants. I recognize this and try to prepare control the environment by practicing what I need to say and putting a positive spin on it. When I'm explaining bad news to a tenant, like why the rent is going up, I always go over what I have to say once or twice before I go into the actual meeting. Because I overcompensate, I think that my conscientiousness and caring shows, which is why I can sometimes get away with giving bad news while still retaining a client's trust. And this is why I'll be effective in major new business negotiations.*

The candidate turned this negative question around with an example of overcoming a personal weakness and was even able to turn the need to practice into an asset. Most important, this answer is very specific to the job.

Q: **Tell me about any sales or marketing experience you have. How have you gone about selling an idea.**

A: *One thing I've really sold within my current company is better use of PC technology. I've done that by demonstrating, and by training people so that they see the quick, positive impact of working smarter with systems. Before, I used to argue with people who weren't willing to invest a little time in learning. Now those same people come to me because they want to know more, and they understand now the positive impact systems have on performance. With anything you market, you start by proving the benefit to the bottom line. Another example is if you're trying to move a potential tenant to a new location under construction. Is it worth the disruption to the tenant's business, and can you sell the idea by bringing the space alive in the tenant's mind?*

This is a good, specific example that demonstrates going above and beyond what is required to perform the job. The effort has brought added value to the company, plus it demonstrates leadership. By summarizing his or her marketing approach and relating it specifically to real estate, the candidate provides an extra sales message.

Q: **Consider any property you had to sell. Would you prefer to sell it orally or in writing? Why?**

A: *Well, I'm fanatic about proper use of the English language, so I'd always fall back on good writing skills. But some combination is usually most effective. In real* *estate you have to persuade someone orally to pay attention; then, once you have that person's attention, you need to come up with something convincing—for example, a solid lease proposal.*

The answer develops a specific sequence of events related to a property-management proposal (an excellent example to tying each answer to the purpose of the interview and making it relevant to the recruiter who is interviewing you).

Q: Describe a tough situation you've experienced with a tenant. How did you handle it?

A: *I've become very skilled at representing a property owner's best interests without alienating tenants. I remember very clearly one time I had an angry client. We had lost air-conditioning for two hours in a building I managed. The client demanded one-fourth of a day's rent back in cash, because he declared the building uninhabitable during that period. Well, I responded on the spot, whereas now I'd ask him to give me a day to look into it, and then I'd come back with a well-constructed solution. And I'd have information about whether the tenant's business really was interrupted that particular day, even if the facility was warm. I'd also emphasize times when we'd provided extra services without demanding compensation.*

This is a problem-solving question. The candidate provides a good sense of his or her judgment in dealing with tenant complaints, as well as a specific example, as the question demanded. The answer also provides evidence of humility, and a willingness to learn from mistakes, making the candidate seem real, confident, and believable (because people with something to hide don't usually volunteer information about mistakes they've made).

Q: Where do you see the newest opportunity in real estate?

A: *I see it in managing or developing properties for third-party clients, which mitigates our risks. Of course, the risk is that the third party learns to do it and takes property management in-house. For example, I know that at one time your firm managed most of downtown Denver, which was still owned by a third party; the client later decided to do his own property management. I still think*

Career Changers: Property management is truly a generalist's job, requiring skills in sales, negotiation, financing, operations, and human resources or supervision. Therefore, a generalist's background including most of these skills is desirable. Target real estate management companies that emphasize these skills over prior real estate work experience. Also, consider real estate and property management courses through adult learning programs, vocational schools, or the Board of Realtors.

the third-party fee-management business is a real safe way to make money and provide an added value.

This question tests business acumen and knowledge of the industry and specific company. The answer is strong, assuming it is consistent with the corporate philosophy—that is, if the company is growing its fee-based business. The candidate cleverly shows that he or she has done the necessary homework on this company's Denver business.

Q: What do you bring to the table beyond asset-management experience?

A: *I believe that ethics and a sense of fair play are critical to being a good property manager, and mediator, even beyond the real estate generalist skills required for the job. And to grow this business, you need a property manager with a reputation that's clean in terms of tenant referrals, financing relationships, and other aspects of networking within the business community.*

The candidate demonstrates personal convictions and ethics, and manages to related how these convictions can enhance this company's reputation through contacts and professional reputation. Use the phrase, "to grow this business" shows that the candidate keeps the recruiter's perspective in mind.

Q: What's your understanding of this city's market, and how would it affect the way you work with tenants on a day-to-day basis?

A: *I have a couple of years' experience in this market, so I know what the major industries are in town, how the local government dictates terms of small businesses, what new properties will be coming available, who the big players are in town and with what types of product—retail, heavy industrial, or whatever. This knowledge would enable me to talk intelligently with potential tenants, property owners, and other property managers in town.*

This question tests specific skills. A sense of the local economy is crucial in real estate. So is a network of contacts. Knowledge of the market dynamics within a particular city allows a candidate to make realistic decisions about what to do in negotiations, what contacts to make, and so on. This answer is strong because it captures many of the factors that influence real estate decisions and bargaining positions.

Q: If you got back to your office and had three very hot phone calls—one from one of your property owners, one from a building tenant, and one from your manager—and all of them said, "Call me immediately!" in what order would you return the phone calls?

A: *I'd call the owner of the building first; second, the tenant; third, my boss. My reason for this is simply in order of where we make the most money—first in management fees, second in tenant commissions. I expect my boss would want me to take care of protecting that revenue first.*

This question tests decision-making and problem-solving skills. The answer is decisive and, therefore, strong. Most commercial real estate companies depend on management fees, and the second lifeline is tenant commissions.

Q: Talk about your build-out experience to date.

A: *I've done general construction for build-to-suit projects, with heavy construction experience. I've also done finished build-out in a retail environment. I've done competitive pricing and bidding of projects; worked on material specifications and usage, applicable material codes, and building codes; and I selected among local general contractors and finish-out contractors.*

With this type of question the interviewer is attempting to discover the depth of the candidate's knowledge: can the candidate point to the right issues? The interviewer wants a candidate with enough experience to make life easier for the company and for building owners this person would manage properties for. This answer demonstrates that the candidate would be self-directed, and would know what to do in many different situations.

Q: Give me an example of your ability to meet with people and interact, where you've had to lead a discussion.

A: *Recently I had to bring together neighboring tenants for a discussion. One tenant had voiced concern over several loitering customers who had repeatedly turned up. After my second tenant mentioned the same thing to me, I became concerned about a possible robbery. Rather than cause everyone alarm, I called*

Experienced Professionals: Experienced candidates should have solid accounting skills, a leasing/sales background, and marketing experience in areas such as advertising, development of brochures, and proposal writing. Negotiation skills are critical, so be ready with numerous examples of how you've managed expectations of various client groups. Real estate experience in major-market cities (with high-price-per-square-foot lease space) would be a plus.

As you progress in real estate management, expect new job responsibilities and additional pay to result from taking on larger buildings or groups of buildings in larger cities. Remember, as a property manager you are already acting as a CEO of a building or a group of buildings, with significant autonomy. Most job growth will come from taking on more and/or larger properties and from moving to major markets with higher-priced lease space.

together the tenants of my shopping center for a "holiday season theft preven-
tion" program. I arranged for a local police officer to be there, to give tips and
answer tenants' questions. This was a value-added service that also built good
relationships among my tenants.

Because real estate is a face-to-face, handshake business, the recruiter needs
evidence that candidates have finesse. This is a great example. It is specific,
and it shows a creative solution that gets the real estate manager out there
with tenants but shows an overriding concern for tenants' well-being at the
same time. You get the sense that these tenants must trust this candidate.

Q: **How do you manage your time day to day, to deal effectively
with your various tenants and to develop new business?**

A: *I spend about 20 percent of my time planning and working on proposals; I*
spend about 40 percent of my time on the phone, typically answering tenants'
and owners' concerns, and also cold-calling; the remaining 40 percent of my
time I'm out with people—showing space, meeting with contractors, and cold-
calling face-to-face. During that time I also walk around my properties to see
what sort of clientele is visiting the stores and observing the behavior.

This question seeks to determine organizational skills and serves as a "reality
check": does the candidate know what's involved in the day-to-day job? The
candidate's answer demonstrates that he or she can prioritize and understands the various tasks involved in managing properties. The last statement
hints to the recruiter that this person keeps a careful watch on rental properties and would be on top of such concerns as the compatibility of stores in
a strip mall, based on shared shopper demographics.

Q: **What do you believe is the ideal mix between new and existing
business?**

A: *I would say fifty-fifty. I generally organize my schedule to deal in the mornings*
with new tenants, new proposals, and cold calling. The afternoons I dedicate to
dealing with that day's calls from existing tenants, plus renewal contracts, and
so on. Sometimes I'll tailor that percentage in terms of the type of client I'm
working with. For example, retail tenants are interested in getting settled by
November for the major holiday shopping season; retailers do about 50 to 60
percent of their sales in November and December. Office space has a sum-
mer seasonality because of HVAC concerns. And industrial property provides
the most constant demand and is most tied to the general economic strength
of the community.

This is an opinion question, so the most important thing is to articulate a quick
response and back it up with industry knowledge. Here the candidate does a
nice job of explaining why he or she shifts time management to capitalize on

the seasonality of new business opportunities with various types of tenants. The recruiter gets the sense that this candidates has worked through several seasons and understands how the economy and cyclical factors influence tenant behavior.

Q: **Discuss how your listening skills have been important in dealing with a tenant.**

A: *The thing that comes to mind right away is prospects. In dealing with potential tenants, listening is critical. I want them to tell me as much as possible before I start offering a rate of terms. For example, a large retailer has concerns very different from those of a mom-and-pop store. After I get the tenant to talk, then I can tailor a proposal based on the financial strength and business strength and consideration of my tenant mix in a shopping center. For instance, I'm much more willing to offer aggressive terms to store that I really want—like a game arcade in a center where I have a movie theater. My motto is to know the tenant's concerns before I start voicing my own.*

The candidate immediately reveals his answer: "prospects," as opposed to current tenants. This is wise, because if the recruiter objects, he or she can do so up front. It also assures the recruiter that the candidate has not misunderstood the question. The answer is carefully developed and provides a clear example. The closing statement is very effective at driving the point home.

Q: **Do you use any type of contact-manager programs for better phone and time management?**

A: *Actually, I do. I use ACT! It's a contact management application that allows me to schedule appointments and reminds me when to write letters. I use it extensively for prospecting and for following up on proposals.*

In the real estate business, use of office-management tools is important. Often professional real estate managers serve as their own support staff, so knowing how to organize oneself is critical. This answer's strength lies in the explanation of how the candidate uses tools to be more effective.

Candidates Re-entering the Workforce: Your best bet is to target companies that place a high priority on training. However, you must be able to prove your generalist skills and some interest and knowledge of commercial property management. Consider real estate and property management courses through adult learning programs, or the Board of Realtors. Realize also that the real estate business is very tied to the state of the economy, so people may exit the industry in bad times and re-enter it in good times.

Q: **Prove your willingness to go beyond your job description to get your job done.**

A: *Even asset managers at the top are at times going to have to roll up their sleeves. We all call on delinquent tenants. I've had to go to construction sites, sit there, and make sure a contractor hooks up power on time for new tenants. Sometimes our jobs don't sound glamorous, but the variety is what makes it all so interesting to me—and the fact that we get to see whole projects through.*

This answer works because it proves motivation. The candidate turns the question into a positive statement about why he or she likes to have to roll up those sleeves. (This question could easily have evoke a negative response—"I have to do X, and I don't like it.")

Q: **Tell me about your negotiation skills between tenants and owners.**

A: *I've learned to spend the time up front to understand the different hot buttons of my building owners and tenants, and to expect the give and take that's likely to occur between them. I'm representing two groups with different interests, and I have to balance their interests in a way that satisfies both. And I've learned that I'm representing the building owner first; if I can't satisfy a tenant within reasonable parameters set forth by my owner, I have to be willing to lose the tenant. Most often I can keep both happy, and everyone wins.*

The question tests a skill necessary in the real estate profession—negotiation. The candidate does a good job of explaining trade-offs. The answer would be better, though, if followed by a specific example, perhaps one in which the tenant did not stay, and a better tenant was found to satisfy the owners' requirements.

Retail Buyer

Q: Why do you want to be a buyer for this department store?

A: *I've always shopped at this department store as opposed to the other two main stores in town. I remember my mother taking me here to shop when I was a child. My grandmother shops here as well. I think that the attitude and style that this store has, especially since it is a family-owned and operated business, sets it favorably apart from all the other stores in town.*

The recruiter is looking for genuine interest in the company. An additional plus in this candidate's answer is that he or she is also very familiar with the store and has been for a long time. Think about why you specifically chose this store and company to interview with, as opposed to others.

Q: What is your academic background?

A: *I majored in textiles and apparels at Cornell University College of Human Ecology, where I received a B.S. I spent four years studying the fashion industry in depth from an academic standpoint. I also minored in accounting.*

This candidate's academic background certainly is impressive. However, any liberal-arts background is acceptable. In fact, some clothing-store recruiters will prefer that your undergraduate major is not related to the fashion industry. You should be prepared to explain how whatever you studied gave you solid background for buying. For example, if you were a communications major, you could talk about how the verbal communication training helps you in dealing with suppliers.

Q: What experience do you have?

A: *I spent all of my holidays and vacations from Cornell working as a sales associate in a variety of different departments and stores. I also spent two years after college in a buyers' training program in a major northeastern department store, and an additional two years as a buyer for boys' better sportswear.*

Experience is the most important factor to the recruiter in deciding whether or nor to hire you. Discuss all retail experience you have. If you don't have any, get a job on the sales floor somewhere before you start interviewing for buying positions.

Q: In the long run, if you could work with anyone in this field, whom would you want to work with? Why?

A: *Down the road I would really like to work with Tommy Hilfiger Sportswear. My sister is a merchandise coordinator for Tommy. She works closely with the stores, as a liason between Tommy and the merchandising people. She hosts seminars on the product and things like that. It's a really neat company, and it's growing by leaps and bounds. They also treat their people well. For now, however, I enjoy doing what I'm doing, although at some point, I'll need a change.*

It is acceptable to indicate that you will not make buying a career, although if you intend to, that's perfectly acceptable to say as well. This candidate's answer describes a realistic and typical career-path option to retail buying. Think about this question before the interview so that your answer seems spontaneous and honest.

Q: What are your primary responsibilities in your current retail buying position?

A: *I am a buyer for boy's buyer sportswear and collections, so I buy sizes 4 to 7 and 8 to 20 in Polo and Levi's. When buying collections, I buy things as a group as opposed to classification buyers, who may buy six or seven vendors for a knit top. I'm in charge of selecting merchandise and negotiation prices with vendors. I go to market four times a year to do that. Merchandising collection clothes involves looking at a table and figuring out how it can tell a story that the customer can recognize and understand. I make sure everything I buy can coordinate on the sales floor. I'm also in charge of floor distribution, inventory control, and markdowns. I spend most of my time on my computer crunching numbers. The department's computer system is fantastic because we have the capability to see immediately if something's really selling well. We can then call up the vendor to see if they've got any left, then buy whatever we need right away.*

The recruiter wants to be sure you know the ropes. Discuss your retail buying responsibilities in detail, just as this candidate has done. If you're not yet a buyer, fully discuss your current retail job, emphasizing the responsibilities that you have, as well as your successes.

Q: How does taking markdowns work?

A: *When you take markdowns, you get the vendor to help you make up the difference in the price of the clothing. It's what buyers refer to as "vendor money." When you take a markdown, that's going to affect your gross margin, which is what your review as a buyer is based upon. Many vendors, Liz Claiborne for one, will guarantee your gross margin. If you do not attain that gross margin, they'll kick in money to make sure you get there. They're not going to give you the money unless you ask for it. It's hard to ask for money, but if they don't give it to me, they'll give it to someone else. They budget for markdown money, and when it's gone, it's gone.*

The recruiter is looking for both skill and knowledge. This candidate understands both how the procedure works, and the ramifications, from different perspectives. If you can, do an informational interview with a buyer before your retail buying interview, so that you can learn as much as possible. Be prepared to answer questions like this.

Q: What has been your greatest challenge as a buyer?

A: *Growing up, I was fairly shy. Having to come out of my shell has been a big challenge. I learned while working for this store that they're not going to come looking for you unless you speak up and say, "Hey, this is what I want to do." If you sit back and wait for them to come to you, it isn't going to happen. And, in a position dealing with vendors, you can't be shy. When I went to my last market buying for October and November, my purchase totaled $2.5 million. I deal with a lot of money. My review is based on whether or not I have increasing gross-margin dollars. In order to increase gross-margin dollars, you've got to be good at negotiating with vendors and convincing them to break prices on certain things, and to give you vendor money.*

The recruiter will be concerned about your personal weaknesses and how they could affect your performance as a buyer. This candidate has given an excellent answer, honest and up front. Of even more importance is that the candidate has successfully overcome this weakness.

Q: What specific personal skill do you think is the most important for a retail buyer to possess?

A: *Speaking from experience, I believe my most developed personal skill as a result of being a retail buyer is my ability to negotiate. I think it's the most important skill to have anyway, because you do it every day. I wish I had taken a negotiations class during college—but on the other hand, I don't know if a class like that really helps you in the real world.*

The recruiter is, of course, looking for the answer that the candidate has given. Negotiating ability is the single most important skill that a retail buyer possesses. Consider taking a negotiating class; even if it doesn't compare to actual experience, your awareness of its importance, as well as your preparatory efforts, will impress the recruiter.

First-time Job Seekers: Be honest and specific about why you want this job. Talk about any previous experience, either work or academic, that you think has given you the skills you need to succeed. If you've never worked in retail before, you may want to consider getting a sales position before you apply for a buyer position.

Q: What professional retail buying skills do you concentrate on improving most?

A: *Number crunching is my weakness, even though I've got an accounting background. A lot of the stuff we do is so different from anything I've done in the past. So learning the system, along with understanding why we use the numbers we use, is one of the things I've tried to improve upon. I was an assistant buyer for only three months, so there are a lot of things I didn't learn, like dealing with stock projections, projecting a 10 percent increase, and things like that. But I'm becoming more and more comfortable with the numbers. Ninety-five percent of my day is sitting in front of a computer crunching numbers, doing recaps, and so on. Being a buyer is not the glamour of constantly being at a market and going to New York, as people think. Instead, I look at my computer every hour to see how much I've sold in each department. I also look to see what I've sold the previous day. A lot of stores don't have a computer system that's capable of doing that. Working numbers is pretty much what my day is, which is also probably my one weakness. I'm getting more and more comfortable with all the different numbers and systems that we use.*

Another way the recruiter might ask this question is "What professional buying skill is your weakness?" Unfortunately, this candidate's weakness is probably the second most important retail buying skill to posses. However, the positive things about this answer that you should try to emulate are that the candidate is aware of the importance of accounting skills, and he or she is working hard to improve in this area. Further, the candidate gives actual examples of how accounting is used on a daily basis.

Q: If you had extra time to devote to some project at the buying office, what would that project be?

A: *I definitely don't have time to work on extra projects at the office, but at home on my computer I've been working on a back to school promotion, because it's really a big time for us and because Tommy Hilfiger is introducing boys 4-to-7 sizes. There's a lot of opportunity and growth in that market. So I'm putting together a little packet or brochure to send out to all the store managers and area sales managers, giving them Tommy merchandising and display guidelines. Other guidelines would not be applicable to Tommy. Polo, for example, would want 4-to-7 and 8-to-20 housed in the same place. So I'm putting together a brochure to send to all of the stores giving them guidelines and tips and letting them know what kind of deliveries they can expect. I think this is an important project for us to have a successful back to school and a successful introduction of the new Tommy line. I don't think the stores will know what to do without these guidelines. They have a hard enough time merchandising what they have, let alone getting a whole new line. I can almost hear them saying—because I'd say the same thing when I was out in the store—"Where do we put it? We* *have a problem with space to begin with, so now what?" This should help ease the anxiety. And everyone's excited about this new line because it's going to be a lot of plus business for us. It's business we didn't have last year.*

The recruiter is looking for initiative because he or she will hire the candidate that goes the extra mile. This candidate's enthusiasm and initiative is very impressive. What extra and self-initiated project are you working on in your retail job?

Q: What opportunities do you see in retail?

A: *The biggest opportunity for current retail stores is expansion by takeovers. Fortunately, the store I work for is big enough that we're the ones doing the gobbling, instead of being gobbled. We're expanding very quickly. In New York state we're opening eleven new stores in the next two years, and we're going to Atlanta for the first time. Although I'm in a more mature division, there's a lot of opportunity as we get bigger. The opportunities aren't going to come as quickly as they have in the past four or five years, but it will still happen. Eddie Bauer and The Gap have eaten away at department-store business because they carry just the basics. Department stores can't carry just T-shirts and jeans. We're supposed to offer a variety of goods. But we still do an awful lot of business, and we just keep getting bigger and bigger.*

The recruiter is looking for the candidate's ability to see the big picture. The candidate's answer certainly indicates that he or she understands the industry trends. Read the *Wall Street Journal* or other business publications so that you can speak confidently about trends in the retail industry.

Q: Do you think mail-order catalogues are threatening business of department stores?

A: *I don't think there's a big threat, because people will always want to touch and feel a piece of merchandise before they buy it. Perhaps this is not a function of the competition of mail order, but I do think department stores, as a whole, have had to reduce costs to be able to maintain their margins and to remain*

Career Changers: Before interviewing, walk the mall and see what's going on from the perspective of the consumer. Check out the competition. Then spend a good amount of time in the store and, specifically, the department that you're applying to. Be able to talk about your observations and ideas. Draw upon skills from your past experience—either at home or previously in the job market—that are relevant to this job. Prove that you already have the skills needed to be successful, and most important, that you're really interested in the position.

competitive, because customers have become so price conscious. People have more than one option now, and they'll go with the best value.

You're not expected to have cold, hard facts and figures with which to back up your answer, and this question is somewhat subjective. The recruiter wants to see if you have the basic knowledge about the retail industry as a whole, and if you think in terms of the big picture. The candidate backs up this answer with reasons and proves that he or she has thought about this issue.

Q: What do you know about kids' shows?

A: *Vendors set up different booths, and it's a time to mill about and see what's hot and what's not. It's not the same as going to the market, because when you go to the market, you have appointments with vendors and they're showing you specific things. With kids' shows, it's an informational thing. I look for kids' show announcements in the retail publications that I read and I go as often as I can.*

The recruiter wants to be sure that you know the difference between shows and market. This candidate's answer is good because he or she does understand this difference and, further, thinks that the shows are important enough to attend. Do some research on the shows that occur for the area of buying you're interviewing for.

Q: What kind of computer skills do you have?

A: *I'm PC literate. I've worked a bit on Macs as well, but I'm much more fluent on Windows-based machines. I'm also very adaptable in terms of learning new applications. For example, while in a summer corporate-retail job during college, I had to learn to use several graphics and spreadsheet programs.*

The recruiter will want to be sure you're comfortable with computers. As a buyer, you'll spend most of your time in front of your computer in your office. Take a seminar in familiarizing yourself with computers if you don't feel as comfortable as this candidate does.

Q: Do you enjoy interacting with people?

A: *While working as a sales associate in New York City, I found that interacting with people was probably the most important part of my job. Although I*

Experienced Professionals: Your positive reputation in the industry will probably speak for itself. Explain that you're truly interested in the retail buying position, and that you're not just using this as a stepping-stone. Explain how your extensive experience will help the store with all the changes in the industry.

needed to be knowledgeable about the product line and to keep my area neat, interacting with customers was almost more important. Our clientele was quite elite, but also extremely varied. I had to be flexible and adaptable, because there were so many different types of people who shopped with us. Generally, we had repeat business from an established clientele, so relationship building and maintaining was a very big part of the business. After time I continued to work with certain customers, so I kept a notebook of each of my clients, including their clothing preferences and needs. I even kept a record of an event they bought clothes for, so I could say something like "How did the black dress work at your cocktail party?" I think the reason I was so successful as an associate at the boutique was not only because I enjoyed our clientele, but because I was also very good at interacting with them.

The recruiter will want to feel good about your interpersonal skills. One of the biggest mistakes made in the retail interview is the candidate answers this question by saying, "I'm a people person." This candidate uses a real example instead of simply uttering cliché statements.

Q: **Do you mind sitting at a desk for long periods of time?**

A: *I think it's difficult for anyone, initially, to sit in front of a computer or at a desk for long periods of time, but I find that I accomplish more when I do. Like anything, you get used to it.*

The recruiter wants to be sure that you're able to spend eight hours in front of your computer. Further, it's important that you demonstrate that you're a worker and not interested in the job because of its glamorous reputation. Prove that you can handle the harsh realities of the job, and that you're prepared to experience and endure what's affectionately known as "buyer's butt" in the industry.

Q: **What basic advice would you give to an assistant area sales manager about selling your line?**

A: *Don't mix different sale items together on the same rack. For example, don't put 25-percent-off and 50-percent-off merchandise together on one bunker, because it confuses the customer. Also, you don't get credit for the more greatly reduced merchandise. And when you look at a table, it should tell a story, so use imaginary color palettes when you're arranging displays. With Tommy Hilfiger,*

Candidates Re-entering the Workforce: Discuss your previous experience and success. Emphasize your particularly well-developed skills, such as your ability to negotiate. Take a refresher computer course to make sure your computer skills are what they should be.

for example, the group color code is on the hang tag with the UPC code, so it's almost like painting by numbers. Put all the same group codes on a table and make it look good. Straighten and fluff frequently.

Prove that you have the basic knowledge about displaying and selling merchandise in a store. Also, convince the recruiter that you're interested in the business even at its bare-bones level. This is one reason why it's helpful to have sales associate experience prior to the retail buying interview.

Q: Describe your last week as a retail buyer.

A: *Right now my supervisor and I are concerned because last month we took some markdowns. We got a lot of money from The Gap from the year before because we cut it back in a lot of stores and helped clear up a lot of inventory. Vendors guarantee your bottom line, so The Gap gave us $50,000 worth of merchandise at cost, which is the equivalent of $100,000 at retail, all of which goes directly to my bottom line. That's like another $100,000 in gross margin last month. So we're really pushing this month for that money from The Gap. For the last three or four days I've spent most of my time on the phone negotiating with vendors to guarantee my gross margin. You've got to get in line for vendor money and hope that you're at the top of the vendor's list. I'm lucky because I'm with this store and we're fairly big. We've got a lot of buying power and a lot of clout. But there are seven divisions, and there's a lot of competition between each division. So we're competing against each other for markdown money. The whole buying business gets kind of cutthroat, but I like it.*

The candidate describes a typical practice in the business. The recruiter will expect a slice-of-life scenario like this one. Be prepared to summarize a typical and busy week as a retail buyer, to convince the recruiter that you fully understand what the realities of the job are, beyond the glamorous image of retail buying.

Q: Do you have any questions for me?

A: *What kind of market share do you expect to gain in the near future with new product lines? What do you see as some of the major trends in the industry, and how do you see them affecting this department store? Also, in reading BusinessWeek, I saw that this store is aggressively expanding. How will it achieve that growth? Will it just be opening new stores, or will it expand through acquisitions?*

Before the interview do as much research as you can on the company to find one or two interesting things that you can bring up. You may want to wait until the end of the interview to ask your questions. The recruiter may or may not prompt you, but if not, you should feel free to ask.

Retail Manager

Q: **What has been your most positive retail experience and why?**

A: *I'd have to say that my most positive experience was right out of school as a sales trainee with Carter's Stores. I knew from my first day on the job that retail was where I wanted to be, because I enjoy customer contact, problem solving, and helping customers find what they need to make their lives more productive. That experience has only been confirmed with each position I've held in retail.*

Give at least one or two examples of how you've successfully impacted a store or a chain of stores in some capacity. Has there been one position where you felt that all your hard work and effort paid off? Show that the position you're applying for will enhance your career and add to the positive experience you've enjoyed working in retail.

Q: **What is the size of the store you're managing and its sales volume?**

A: *When I was responsible for the clothing department at Walker Stores, I had a total of 15,000 square feet. My average yearly sales volume was $2.8 million.*

The interviewer is testing the candidate's level of experience in handling large department or store space and significant inventories. You should be prepared with more than numbers; it's imperative that you demonstrate increasing responsibility for handling larger store space and more unit volume. This way the interviewer will feel comfortable that you can grow with the demands of the position you're applying for.

Q: **How do you motivate your sales associates?**

A: *Keeping turnover low is a high priority for me, and one of the best ways to do that is to make the associate feel as if he or she is contributing to overall store*

First-time Job Seekers: Before you'll be seriously considered for a sales management position, you'll need actual experience on the sales floor and/or participation in a management-training program. The key is to demonstrate a keen interest in a particular aspect of retailing, such as clothes or music stores, and to explain why you'd be a top-notch performer in this area. Demonstrate that you're responsible, customer oriented, and enthusiastic about working in retail.

management. I've regular meetings during which each associate is able to discuss what he or she feels might improve store performance. That includes everything from store displays to the physical appearance of certain departments, as well as what we can do to serve the customer better. In addition, I have monthly private one-on-one meetings with each of my associates to discuss any personal or employment issues that they feel hamper their effectiveness in the store.

Your people and communications skills will be tested with this question, as well as your creative instincts for getting the most out of your workers. High turnover in retail is common, so you should be prepared to demonstrate that you can successfully encourage sales associates to give top performance, and at least keep any turnover to a minimum. What techniques do you employ to get your workers to give their best effort every day?

Q: **What criteria do you use in evaluating candidates for the position of sales associate?**

A: *I look for someone who's enthusiastic, hardworking, and has genuine people skills. I also want someone who can quickly address a customer's needs so that we don't lose a sale because of an indifferent or lazy attitude. I look for candidates who can display patience and listen attentively to the customer no matter how trivial the request or problem.*

Try to get a feel for what the interviewer is looking for in sales associates so that your answer will align closely with his or her thoughts. Since the position of sales associate is customer oriented, you should focus on skills that involve communication and problem solving, and more general qualities such as enthusiasm, an upbeat personality, and so on.

Q: **When do you decide to add additional people to checkout counters?**

A: *If more than two people are waiting to purchase items, I'd move to open another register and assign someone register duty until traffic abates. During the holiday season I often find myself not only pitching in to help out at the register but doing double duty in customer service as well. My philosophy is to do whatever it takes to satisfy the customer and keep the store operating at peak efficiency.*

Career Changers: Emphasize your communication skills and your organizational and planning ability. Describe situations in which you've managed large unit volumes or inventories. Any selling or marketing experience is helpful and, if possible, mention any volunteer experience you've had that's directly related to retail. Expect that making a switch will cost you in terms of salary, but if you have strong customer-oriented skills, you should quickly advance.

This question focuses on the candidate's ability to gauge store traffic, organizational and planning skills, and aggressiveness in jumping in to help should the need arise. You'll do well to emphasize not only your knowledge of retail peaks and valleys but your concern for the customer and your willingness to do what needs to be done to keep customers moving in and out of the store.

Q: **If a customer had a complaint, would you prefer to handle it directly, or would you refer the call to customer service?**

A: *Because I pride myself on a hands-on approach, I'd handle the complaint on the spot. I think it's critical to listen to a customer and respond almost immediately so that the customer feels that he or she is being treated with respect. There's no more certain way to lose a customer's business than to treat a complaint with an indifferent attitude.*

Again, this goes directly to the heart of customer-service skills and willingness to take on a problem rather than passing the buck. Can you appropriately evaluate the nature and urgency of a problem? Do you demonstrate leadership by seeking out a solution so that the customer walks away happy instead of frustrated? What's your immediate reaction when the customer comes to you with a problem, and how do you determine if the problem is beyond your ability to resolve it?

Q: **What was your shrinkage relative to other stores in the chain?**

A: *For the last two years my shrink percentage ranked in the bottom 20 percent of the chain.*

You must convince the interviewer that you've had experience handling and reducing this problem and show him or her what steps you've taken to make the problem malleable. Go beyond numbers here and discuss what you look for as indicators that shrinkage is rising beyond the norm for comparable retail outlets.

Q: **How do you account for such a low percentage?**

A: *I instituted rigorous controls during peak traffic times, such as after school and on weekends. I gave extensive training to all exempt and nonexempt employees. We focused on making sales associates more visible—such as having an associate greet customers as they entered the store.*

Experienced Professionals: Emphasize how you can use your experience to help the company improve its operations. Look for opportunities to move up in a retail operation such as at the home office of a retail chain. Demonstrate what you do best and show how you've significantly improved a retail operation from the ground up.

What steps have you taken to reduce shrinkage in your store, and what indicators tell you that it's becoming a problem? Why have you been successful in reducing shrinkage, and do you think that your methods could work in the interviewer's store? This is a great chance to show off your ingenuity and creativity as well as your problem-solving skills.

Q: **If your corporate office advertised an item in error, should you explain to the customer that it wasn't your fault?**

A: *I don't believe that's a wise move. Store personnel are often on the firing line when operational mistakes occur. However, the customer doesn't distinguish you from the company you work for. To the customer you're the company, and you should apologize and offer an alternative solution.*

Demonstrate that you can take responsibility for a problem, and give the interviewer a clear-cut, logical plan to satisfy both the customer and the home office. The interviewer is clearly interested in whether the candidate's customer-service skills are such that he or she can balance a customer's request without putting the company in an awkward position of having to pay more than it should for an oversight.

Q: **What excites you about this position and why?**

A: *Your stores have always represented top-dollar value with a professional attitude and a proactive approach to store management. I'm very attracted to the cooperative-team approach of the regional managers and the individual store managers. Knowing that my input will be taken seriously and that my ideas will eventually materialize in the form of store improvements is a motivating factor for me to seek out opportunities with your chain.*

Point to several aspects of the position that truly motivate you, and show your enthusiasm for retailing in general. Convince the interviewer that you want to work for his or her company and that this position makes sense for you at this time in your retail career. Demonstrate commitment to retailing as a career, and draw parallels to your experience showing why you'll be successful in this new position.

Candidates Re-entering the Workforce: Retail is a good area to pursue for individuals who've been out of the workforce, as the skills that are most demanding involve dealing with customers, organizing and planning ability, and sales skills. In your job interviews emphasize your accomplishments that reflect these skills and abilities, and discuss how you can add value to the organization.

Sales Manager

Q: **Tell me about the product you are currently selling.**

A: *My primary focus is on our flagship product, a fully integrated accounting soft-ware package for middle-market size manufacturing firms. Designed exclu-sively for manufacturing firms, it gives particular focus to cost accounting and inventory control.*

The interviewer is trying to determine if the product you are now selling has any relevance to what his or her company is selling, and if you have any inher-ent skills that would be helpful in selling the company's product. Be careful that you don't "oversell" in your answer. Your response should be simple and direct. A good salesperson needs to be very knowledgeable about his or her product, but should convey that knowledge in a casual manner and tone that is appropriate to whomever he or she is dealing with.

Q: **How much of your time is spent cold-calling new accounts ver-sus servicing existing ones?**

A: *At this point I spend about 70 percent of my time working on new accounts. I have trained my assistant to the point where he can handle routine requests and issues regarding existing accounts, although I also keep in regular touch with clients by phone and periodic in-person visits.*

Virtually all sales positions require some combination of these two skills. Be honest, and don't exaggerate your skills. This is a terrific answer because it shows that the candidate has done cold-calling, which is very difficult, as well as the fact that he or she doesn't neglect existing accounts in order to gain new ones.

Q: **How many new accounts did you acquire last year?**

A: *I opened seven new accounts last year and already have commitments for four this year. Out of the five-person sales force, I ranked second in the number of new accounts, but first in the dollar volume of new accounts.*

Like this candidate, be sure to show how you ranked, since your ranking gives a better indication of your skills. At the same time, you should also relate your answer to the business as a whole. For instance, opening seven new accounts would be virtually meaningless in a company with 2,500 existing accounts, but would be outstanding in a company with only forty existing accounts.

Q: **What is your biggest difficulty in selling?**

A: *Lack of recognition of the company name makes it challenging to get presentation time at major accounts. Our main competitors have much broader product lines, larger market shares, and much more visibility. This can also lead to some difficulty in closing the sale.*

The interviewer is trying to get a sense of what you consider to be a major obstacle. You could also discuss the difficulty in convincing potential clients that your company actually has something that other companies can't offer. Be prepared to discuss how you overcome this problem.

Q: **How do you overcome it?**

A: *Since our company doesn't have instant name recognition in the marketplace, I emphasize the companies that are using our products that the prospect may be familiar with. I also try to have a strong physical presence at the account's headquarters while they are testing the product, in order to build their confidence level with our organization.*

While this is a reasonable answer, it is also important to discuss money issues. When you are selling any type of product, the bottom line of what you are doing is trying to convince the buyer that your product will save his company money. For instance, you want to tell the client that although he may not be familiar with your company's products, you have sold the product to other companies that are similar to his, and these companies are now making 10 percent more money with your product. Show that you are able to convince the buyer that you can both make money if you do business together.

First-time Job Seekers: Since you don't have much experience to put on your resume, the interviewer is more likely to evaluate your personality and other intangibles to see if you have what it takes to succeed in sales. Interviewers look for candidates who demonstrate intelligence and affability. Also, show that you're flexible and willing to learn new skills. Employers look for candidates with a solid liberal arts background. A business background is usually helpful, but at the same time, a business degree does not necessarily mean a candidate has the ability to sell. Because sales is a personality-driven field, it's important to emphasize any experience you may have interacting with the public, such as public speaking, acting in college theater, or working as a radio DJ. The idea is to demonstrate that you aren't shy, and that you can communicate effectively with the public.

Q: **In an ideal job, would you like to spend more or less of your time cold-calling?**

A: *Cold-calling is my job. I enjoy it, and I'm good at it. But I'm looking forward to the chance to sell for a company like yours, because it has such tremendous name recognition.*

Virtually all sales positions require some cold-calling, so do not leave the interviewer with the impression that you dislike doing that. Cold-calling is generally considered to be the toughest part of sales. Like this candidate, you should show the interviewer that you aren't intimidated by cold-calling. At the same time, demonstrate an eagerness to employ other sales methods.

Q: **What lead sources have you found most productive?**

A: *While referrals from existing accounts are my best lead source, I also call some accounts whose names I find in industry directories.*

The interviewer wants to see how you develop leads. The candidate mentions two popular options, but you should also talk about your networking capabilities. Discuss your experience within the industry and how that experience has enabled you to build up an extensive network of contacts. Emphasize the fact that if you're hired, the employer will not only gain your wealth of experience, but your extensive network of industry contacts.

Q: **Tell me about some of the most extreme lengths you have gone to in order to close a sale.**

A: *I spent eighteen months trying to land an automotive parts manufacturer after successfully landing two of its competitors. The MIS manager would not even see me, however, because as it turned out, he was very friendly with the account executive from another software firm. I tried everything from sending e-mail to trying to corner him at trade shows. Finally, I went into my college alumni book and saw that the executive assistant to the MIS manager had been a couple years behind me at school. I arranged to meet him through mutual friends, convinced him of the superior value of our product, and then he basically sold his boss on bringing the software into the company.*

Career Changers: Emphasize your performance in your current job, and how you have progressed in that position. Employers like to see a track record of success, regardless of what field you are in. Be sure to discuss any skills you have that can be transferred to sales, such as dealing with people, phone work, negotiating, or problem-solving. Most important, show that you're committed to a career in sales, and that you won't simply switch careers again a few months down the road.

The interviewer wants to see how innovative you can be when faced with difficult situations. Discuss your ability to persevere in the face of adversity. It is important to show how you would rise to meet the challenge and come up with a creative way to land the account. However, be wary of giving examples of situations where you went over the buyer's head. Many times, doing that can anger potential clients, and you may end up losing an account for good.

Q: How have you performed relative to your goals or quotas?

A: *Last year I was 27 percent over my sales quota for new accounts, the highest in the firm. Sales to my other existing accounts were strong, but because of a shortfall at my largest account I came in slightly under my goal. My largest existing account made a strategic decision to narrow their supplier base and we were dropped as an approved vendor. I'm still working on getting that account back.*

Be sure to discuss your performance with regard to both new and existing accounts. Like this candidate, try to give the interviewer exact figures; don't simply say you finished a little higher than your goals. Also, if you did finish under your goals, be sure to discuss the reasons why. Don't simply say you didn't meet your goals and then leave it at that.

Q: Did you meet your goals during the previous year?

A: *I was a little under my goal the previous year, but only one person met their goal that year because the product update we were selling hadn't been carefully debugged and the trade press really panned it. However, I still led the firm in new accounts opened last year.*

The interviewer is trying to get a sense of your sales track record. Again, be honest. Explain your reasons for not meeting your set goals. It is also important to show that you understand the importance of having goals.

Q: What sales angle might you use in selling our product line?

A: *I would emphasize your leading position in the inventory management software market, as well as in manufacturing MIS systems as a whole.*

Experienced Professionals: Discuss your experiences within the field, while emphasizing the financial aspect of the business. For instance, you could discuss how much money you made for your previous employers, either through your sales record, or by instituting new programs or sales techniques. Discuss how the company's sales or profitability increased because of your work. Employers like candidates who show a solid belief in their abilities. Naturally, you should have numbers to back up your claims.

While the candidate discusses an important point, you should never forget the bottom line. Discuss how the company's product can either save or make money for the buyer's company. Emphasize what makes the product better than similar products—for example, is it more profitable, and does it engender fewer returns and fewer problems than the competitor's product?

Q: **How do you feel about overnight travel?**

A: *Travel is no problem. I've done a lot of it, and know it comes with the territory.*

Many sales positions include at least some traveling, either to visit existing accounts or to meet with potential buyers. If this question is asked, the position most likely requires some travel, so be sure to give a positive response. If you really don't wish to travel, you can take that into consideration when and if you get a job offer.

Q: **In comparison to other salespeople, what do you see as your strengths and what do you see as your weaknesses?**

A: *I'm probably strongest in person. Frankly, I enjoy selling and consulting on new systems or major upgrades more than being a coordinator for service or billing issues. However, in all of my jobs I've done well in getting my assistant or a staff person to help coordinate such day-to-day issues.*

The interviewer wants to see how well you can evaluate yourself. Like this candidate, show that even though you prefer one aspect of the position more than others, you don't neglect your other duties. You should also discuss one or two aspects of your performance or personality that you'd like to improve. Never say anything like, "Well, I'm really good at everything, and I have no real weaknesses."

Candidates Re-entering the Workforce: Discuss what you have done during your absence that could be helpful to the position you are applying for. For instance, coaching your daughter's Little League team would teach you organizational skills and patience. You should also discuss any reading you've done to familiarize yourself with the industry you're interviewing in. If you were applying for a position selling automotive parts, for instance, you could discuss what you have learned by reading *Car and Driver*. Also, demonstrate that you're current in terms of technology. Tell the interviewer how you have kept up with the newest spreadsheet software, or how you taught yourself to navigate the Internet.

Salesperson

Q: **What were the last five sales-related learning tools that you either read, listened to, or attended?**

A: *Since keeping motivated and showing initiative—being a self-starter—are crucial in the field of sales, I always have a Brian Tracy sales tape in my car that I listen to, and lately I've read books by Stephan Schiffman and Anthony Parinello. There's always something to learn.*

The interviewer will want to know that you're dedicated to the field, not just dabbling in it. The best salespeople are constantly learning new techniques, trying new ideas, and expanding on tried-and-true sales programs.

Q: **Why are you pursuing a career as a professional salesperson?**

A: *I find that when I believe in a product or an idea, I get very passionate about it, and my excitement and momentum builds, easily convincing others to follow suit. I enjoy finding new and different ways to reach people, helping them achieve their goals with products that I represent.*

This is a common question that you're likely to encounter. The interviewer wants to hear that you enjoy your work, look for ways to help customers find what they need, and believe in the company's product—which results in a win-win situation for both the employer and you. The recruiter also wants reassurance that you're interested in a career, not just another job. You should be prepared to discuss your interest in the field and demonstrate that you "have the knack" for sales.

Q: **What do you know about our product line?**

A: *I've been following your products for the last six months now, particularly your magazine, Careers and the M.B.A. I've noticed that your high-quality product, combined with the Fortune 500 clients who use it year after year, is an excellent way for top companies to get their message to top M.B.A. candidates.*

The interviewer will want to be sure that you practice what you preach. Just as you'd prepare ahead of time for a sales presentation, you should also prepare to answer specific questions about a company's product line in a job interview. This kind of advance preparation shows the interviewer that you have what it takes, and the passion to represent the company's products.

Q: As you may be aware, this company has a web site. Sell it to me.

A: *Here's a web site that helps users find employment. It's clean, has fast access, and is easy to get around. It can get confusing knowing what the best available option is for your company right now, but let me tell you some of the ways we can make your job a bit easier. First of all, our company's been in the business of helping job hunters find suitable employment for more than fifteen years, and we've earned a great nationwide reputation. Second, because there are so many places a user can get lost on the Web, we've set up more than 125 mutual links with search engines, and other Web sites to help people find us—and because these sites are arranged in alphabetical order, we typically come up on the first page of someone's search. But most important, we have more than 2,500 current job listings, with links to many other job-hunting sites, essentially bringing the number of current job listings to well over 25,000! What is it that you're trying to achieve on the Web for your company?*

The interviewer will want to know the extent of your knowledge about the company's products. More important, however, he or she will probably test how well you think on your feet. Although it would be impressive, it's not critical that all your facts be accurate—what's more important is that your sales pitch has a believable, logical progression. In this example the candidate finishes by asking the client about his or her company's needs. This approach is effective because it shows that the candidate believes it's important to respond to the client's objections and concerns before trying to "close" the deal.

Q: Do you prefer tangible sales or intangible sales?

A: *I've actually had the opportunity to sell both concrete items and image advertising. Although I believe I can do both well, I find that my ability to grasp elusive concepts and present them in an easy-to-understand format helps me to enjoy the intangible sales more.*

You should be prepared to discuss what you feel most comfortable with—selling something that someone can touch, see, and feel, or selling something that's harder to quantify, such as image advertising. If you have no previous experience, you should at least know the difference between the two types of sales, and speak to why you think you'd be better suited to one over the other.

> **First-time Job Seekers:** A positive attitude can make a tremendous difference for you. Many times companies are willing to train someone who's willing to learn, seems to fit in, and won't complain about whatever tasks he or she is asked to do during the day. Emphasize these qualities in your job interviews, and remember, think positive!

Q: How do you deal with rejection?

A: *Well, although I certainly like getting to yes more than getting to no, sometimes rejection helps me understand how I can improve my technique with a particular type of client. Actually, this tougher learning experience can help eliminate wasted time. I prefer honest customers who actually come out and say no. I find that I can then go back and learn a lot from them. And, of course, moving on to the next client always brings with it renewed hope of another yes.*

In all sales positions, no matter how great you are, rejection is a way of life. Being able to handle these inevitable disappointments is an important role you must be able to take on. As a matter of fact, if you're not getting a lot of rejection, you may not be trying hard enough or taking enough risks. Explain to the interviewer that you manage this kind of stress well.

Q: How do you keep yourself motivated?

A: *I find that there's more to making a sale than just phone work. There are other elements, such as research, follow-up—faxing, e-mailing, and so on—and I find that sometimes varying my tasks helps keep me motivated. And, of course, it's very motivating to move closer to the sale, and that keeps me going. I also find that good planning, knowing how much time I allot to certain tasks, helps me move toward my goal as well.*

Because many jobs can become monotonous and repetitive, especially a phone-sales job, it's important to show the interviewer that you can switch tasks and plan your day to compensate for when phone times are slow, or when you're simply in need of a break.

Q: Do you work better with people or alone in a sales environment?

A: *Although I've successfully worked from home completing projects on my own, I also work very well in a high-energy atmosphere, bouncing ideas off others and keeping up the enthusiasm with my clients.*

This can be a tricky question to answer unless you have some advance knowledge of how the interviewer's office is set up. If the sales office encourages teamwork, the interviewer will want to hear that you work better with people. You might further explain how you believe it's important to get along not only

Career Changers: Your biggest challenge is to show the interviewer how you'll apply your past experiences, specifically skills you've gained, to the new environment you seek. Don't assume that employers will take one look at your resume and instantly understand how you are going to fit in—that's your job. After all, they're hiring you for your abilities and skills, not for their abilities to find the right job for you.

with all clients, but with other salespeople as well. On the other hand, if the sales environment is set up mostly so that salespeople work independently, you should emphasize your ability to flip back and forth easily between the two environments and to keep motivated while working essentially alone.

Q: **What do you think will be most difficult for you to overcome or get used to in sales?**

A: *As I mentioned earlier, sometimes the rejection rate can be pretty challenging, but I find that this is often the best way to uncover clues as to how I can become a better salesperson.*

Especially if you're new to sales, you should expect this question or a question like it. The interviewer will be anxious to hear what your perceived weaknesses are because this will help him or her determine if the issue is something the company can help you deal with. Your answer should be honest, but it's best to frame the negative in a positive way, as the candidate does in this answer. You should specifically avoid needlessly revealing any unattractive habits or tendencies that may make the interviewer conclude you really aren't the person for the job.

Q: **How do you plan your day?**

A: *Well, I usually begin planning each day the previous evening as I wrap up my work. This way I find that when I get in the following morning, no matter what may take precedence at that time, I won't forget to do something crucial. I use a daily planner to record each contact, conversation, and follow-up item so that in the future I won't have to rewrite or rekey the entire scenario for each client. I know exactly when I need to have certain sales materials to clients, what their concerns are, and the best times to reach them.*

In sales fast turnaround is crucial in order to leave the impression that the organization you represent is a leader, is responsive to the client's needs, and is willing to go the extra mile to get the client's business. The client places his or her trust in you by doing business with you; therefore, your organization and timeliness as a sales professional are crucial in maintaining old business as well as developing new customers. Your answer should convey to the interviewer that you believe it's important to remember what you promise so that clients will see you as a competent professional, standing head and shoulders above the crowd.

Q: **What do you think may slow you down during the sales cycle, potentially impeding your sales?**

A: *I know that there are a lot of important facets that go into a full sales cycle— not all of them focusing solely on "getting to yes." I'd imagine that any time* spent off the phone or not prospecting may have the appearance of slowing down the sales cycle. However, I believe that good preparation and follow-through can be important to "getting to yes," as these things can help the potential customer feel more secure with the product and the company.

There's always work, like research and paperwork, that can distract somewhat from the business of making sales. These tasks seem to be necessary evils for a sales professional. Knowing what they are, or recognizing in advance what they can be, helps you overcome them. The interviewer is looking for an honest answer, but also an awareness of the importance of these functions, and a recognition on your part that these tasks are often considered part of the salesperson's workload.

Q: How do you keep yourself going when everyone else around you is complaining and having a bad day?

A: *Sales can have its ups and downs, but that's what I find challenging. Many times the good energy is intoxicating, and I love sharing in that—but I do recognize that slumps will occur. The worst thing in a sales organization is to have to deal with people who complain a lot. If those around me are having a bad day, I might try to cheer them up by relating a similar experience that I've had myself. If that doesn't work, then my job is to concentrate on my sales, hoping to improve projections and the way the day is turning out for the whole department. When things seem to get beyond my immediate control, I find it helpful to get up from the desk in order to clear my head and my voice, and I'll try to take a walk outside or away from my colleagues in order not to affect their day.*

No one likes to have an employee who is moody and complaining. However, people occasionally do have bad days. The interviewer may try to find out how often you do, so reassure him or her that you're not easily influenced into a bad mood, thereby affecting the sales of the company, and that when you do have a bad day, you know how to deal with it in a professional manner.

Q: What kinds of rewards do you find most satisfying?

A: *Well, frankly, I'm in sales because I've found that with a lot of well-placed effort, the high-income potential is there. So money is definitely a motivator. I also find that what satisfies me on a day-to-day basis is the challenge of being able to discuss a new idea and either present enough information to cause potential*

Experienced Professionals: The greatest challenge here is not to intimidate the interviewer by talking about how you know it all. Humility goes a long way—let your story and experiences speak for themselves. And realize that no matter what job you take, there are always things to learn. Embrace the idea of learning from others, and this will help you more than you know.

clients to change their mind, or educate them with a new idea that might help their company and their job.

The interviewer will want to hear that in addition to being motivated by the almighty dollar, you also have deeper motivations. For example, if the week or month isn't producing exactly the money that you'd hoped, the employer still wants you to gain some satisfaction from your work—not only for your own benefits, but for the benefit of those who work around you.

Q: What are your strongest sales skills? Is there one that could be improved upon?

A: *I think that among my strongest sales skills is the ability to stay focused on the sales project or product at hand, even when the going gets tough. Because sales is a dynamic environment, the best way to improve is to try new things. Perhaps a skill that could be improved upon is determining which of my ideas is the most viable before trying them all at the same time.*

The interviewer is looking for someone who's ambitious and who continually focuses on self-improvement. That means you should be prepared to discuss an area you could improve upon, though you should present it in a very positive way, as this candidate does. Show the interviewer that you have ideas and that you're not afraid to talk about them and try new things, which is crucial to a strong sales effort.

Q: Give me an example of a recent difficult sale. How did you overcome it?

A: *Well, I don't like to think that there's any sale I can't make, but I do know when to quit and move on to the next potential client. There was one client whom I must have originally reached on a really bad day. No matter what I said or suggested, I got the feeling that I wasn't getting through to him. I tried modulating my voice, calling at a more convenient time, finding out if there was someone else he'd rather I speak with, and, finally, acting surprised at his continual standoffishness when I was just doing my job. After six conversations with him, and trying to go around him twice, I concluded I'd learned all I could from that situation and that it was time to move on. In fact, I never did get that sale, but I did learn a few things for my next contacts.*

Candidates Re-entering the Workforce: Be clear about why you left the field and why you're coming back. Sometimes directly addressing these issues does the trick to waylay any suspicions and let the interviewer know you have nothing to hide. A simple statement should do it. There are a lot of good reasons why people take a hiatus, so there's no need to worry unduly about what the interviewer will think.

Everyone will have at least one sale (and probably more!) that for some reason is simply unobtainable. The interviewer will want to know that you have enough self-esteem not to shut down after this kind of experience. Discuss the different tactics you used to try to make a sale, that indicate your solid base of sales knowledge. Tell the interviewer that you realize there may be reasons beyond your control for not making a sale, and that sometimes it's best just to move on rather than waste time pursuing dead ends.

Telecommunications Consultant

Q: **What attracted you to sales?**

A: *Well, I enjoy working with people and I'm very outgoing—I've always been told I'm a great communicator. Sales seemed like a perfect match for my personality. Also, I was attracted to the challenge of being a salesman. I enjoyed the fact that, for the most part, I'd be responsible for my own well-being. If I didn't succeed, I'd have no one to blame but myself.*

The interviewer will want to know why you became a salesperson. Like this candidate, you should discuss one or two aspects of the profession that particularly interest you. Employers prefer candidates who can explain their career choice logically. Don't say something to make the interviewer believe that you simply fell into the field rather than actively choosing it. If you do, the interviewer will question whether you have the aggressiveness needed to succeed in the business.

Q: **Who inspired you the most to do what you're doing now?**

A: *My mother. She's a real-estate agent, and she's really the person who encouraged me to go into sales. Growing up, I could sense her anticipation as she was about to close a deal, and I could also feel her excitement whenever she finalized a sale. My mother absolutely adores her job, and her enthusiasm is contagious—as long as I can remember, I wanted to be in sales so I could feel that same excitement.*

This is a follow-up to the previous question. Your answer will give the interviewer a better sense of your personal motivation for choosing sales as a career. Again, demonstrate a true commitment to the field. If no single person inspired you, you could discuss a book or movie that inspired you to become a salesperson.

First-time Job Seekers: A college degree is required for most sales positions. Candidates should have a general liberal-arts background, as well as class work in marketing and business administration. Show the interviewer that you have the self-confidence and determination to succeed at this position. A beginning sales position can go slowly at first, and you need to be able to demonstrate that you won't get discouraged after your first few negative responses.

Q: Tell me about your sales background. What types of products or services have you sold?

A: *I've had five years of sales experience. I started out selling property and automobile insurance. The position consisted mostly of cold-calling. Our supervisor would buy lists of contacts from professional associations and distribute them to the agents. We would simply go through each list and call every name. I worked there for about a year; by that time I'd become less dependent on lists and was using networking and professional contacts more. For the past four years I've worked at radio station WPAW, selling airtime to advertisers. This involves less cold-calling and more reliance on contacts.*

The interviewer will want to get a sense of your experience level, as well as determine what type of sales you have experience with. This is a service-oriented field, which is different from selling tangible products, such as stocks or machinery. For example, salespeople in the service field will often take on the role of problem solver for their customers. If, like this candidate, you don't have experience with service sales, be ready to discuss why you want to change to this area. Demonstrate an eagerness to widen your breadth of experience.

Q: What's your greatest strength?

A: *I'm a very enthusiastic, upbeat person. I believe that these traits have helped me tremendously in my career, because customers are more open to someone who's positive. Many times when I get calls at home from telemarketers, I get the sense that they'd rather be doing anything else than calling me, and that negative tone really turns me off. They could be representing the most fabulous product on earth, but I won't be interested. I believe that a potential customer will sense a salesperson's enthusiasm and, in turn, is more likely to become enthusiastic about what that person is representing. Finally, a positive attitude helps me get through bad calls. If someone tells me he's not interested, I'll simply move on to the next call without dwelling on the last one.*

Career Changers: Any previous sales experience—even if it was only a minor part of your job—is helpful. Employers like to see candidates with experience in related fields, such as marketing or public relations. These fields require many of the same skills—for example, the ability to persuade and communicate effectively—as does sales. In advertising, for instance, you design ways to sell a product. Experience in the same field as the company you're interviewing with is also a big plus. For instance, if you designed computer systems for another company and are interviewing for a position selling computer systems, you might have, simply because of your technical expertise, an edge over a candidate with years of sales experience.

The interviewer wants to see how self-confident the candidate is. Like this candidate, you should discuss one of your strengths and how you've used it to your advantage. Don't simply name a strength without offering a professional example to back it up. Other good traits to mention are determination, motivation, and organizational skills.

Q: What's your greatest weakness, and how would you go about changing it?

A: *I'm not as proficient as I'd like to be with computers. Many people from my office use a database to keep track of their clients or appointments, while I often have trouble formatting a document in my word-processing software. But I've recently bought a home computer, and I'm becoming more comfortable with different software programs. Soon I hope to start handling all my personal finances with the computer.*

Try not to mention a characteristic that's directly linked to your job performance. For instance, don't say, "I have a hard time staying motivated," or "I don't follow up on leads as quickly as I could." Discuss a weakness that's more general, and not necessarily directly related to the position. Like this candidate, you should show that you're taking positive steps to address your weakness.

Q: Sell me this stapler.

A: *This is a professional-quality stapler, designed to be functional as well as attractive. It will help you reduce clutter on your desk by enabling you to fasten pages together. And since papers relating to the same subject will now be attached, it will make you more efficient and save you the time of searching for papers. Finally, the sleek shape and black color are coordinated to match the rest of your office furniture.*

The interviewer wants to determine how quickly the candidate thinks on his or her feet, as well as how effectively and succinctly the candidate communicates. This type of question is common in most interviews for sales positions, so be prepared to give a thirty-second speech on the benefits and advantages of virtually any object, from a paper clip to a telephone.

Experienced Professionals: Sell yourself and your experience. Be prepared to discuss all of your sales experience in detail. You may be asked specifically about your total average sales volume, and how that compared to the rest of the company, or if you ever had trouble meeting goals or quotas. Many experienced salespeople move up to supervisory or management positions, taking on more administrative duties in addition to sales responsibilities.

Q: What do you think is the best way to approach a potential customer?

A: *Well, I like to approach a potential customer with as much knowledge as possible. For instance, if the customer is a business, I'll do research to find out about the industry and its products, so that I can speak intelligently about them. If the customer is a person, I'll follow a similar approach—find out what he does for a living, if she has children, and so forth. Obviously, with cold calling, research is more difficult, so instead I'll concentrate more on my technique. In any case, I immediately identify myself, my company, and what I'm selling. I understand that time is valuable, so I try to take up as little of the customer's time as possible.*

Every salesperson has a different technique—the interviewer will probably try to discover yours. Like this candidate, you should discuss your own personal philosophy of selling. Because some companies do favor one style over another, careful research will help you prepare for this question.

Q: If a customer already had other representatives from long-distance carriers calling, how would you get him or her to listen to you?

A: *If a customer is constantly getting calls from other telephone companies, he or she is probably sick and tired of discussing phone service, and most likely tired of salespeople in general. I'd explain that I wasn't representing any particular phone service, and that my company had no interest in which phone company the customer eventually chose. Once customers understand that you're offering a service, not a particular product, they become more open. Of course, I'd never criticize another company.*

The interviewer wants to learn about the candidate's approach when dealing with negative customers. You'll often encounter customers who are simply sick of talking to salespeople. When this happens, you must be able to turn a negative situation into a positive one. And because the question here describes a situation specific to the hiring company, the interviewer will get a good idea of how much you researched the company before your interview.

Candidates Re-entering the Workforce: If you were a successful salesperson once, it's relatively simple to regain your form. Be sure to discuss in detail why you took time off—otherwise, the interviewer might question your motivation and desire. Although, for the most part, changes don't occur rapidly in the sales profession, you may want to discuss some recent books or magazine articles you've read that have kept you abreast of any new techniques or sales methods being used.

Q: What's your least favorite part of sales?

A: *I don't enjoy cold-calling. I realize that some cold-calling is necessary in any sales position, but I work especially hard at networking and getting referrals so that I won't have to rely on cold-calling as much to make my sales.*

Be careful how you answer this question. You don't want to mention a particular task only to discover that that task will be a large part of your job. Your research before the interview should give you an idea of the general nature of the position. As this candidate does, try to put a positive spin on your answer.

Q: How do you respond to the word "no"?

A: *That depends. When some people say no, that's it and the call's over. I'll simply move on to my next contact with the confidence that I'll make the sale. Especially if I sense that someone is irritated or anxious, I'll simply thank the caller for his or her time and hang up. But at other times a no means simply that I may have to work a little harder to get an appointment or make a sale. If I sense this is the case, I'll try to find out the reasons behind the no and then address those concerns. Of course, if I still don't get a positive response, I won't pursue the matter any longer.*

The interviewer will want to see that you can be patient with, and understanding of, the customer and his or her needs. Show the interviewer that you won't let rejection discourage you and, at the same time, that you won't give up too easily. Like this candidate, you should demonstrate an understanding of the fine line between being aggressive and being pushy.

CHAPTER 18

SCIENCE

Analytical Chemist

Q: **What is your level of experience with HPLC?**

A: *I've used HPLC for R-and-D testing using established protocols. I've also been involved with methods development and hardware and technique trouble-shooting.*

This answer shows that the candidate not only has HPLC-use experience but can go beyond the "follow the recipe" scenario into developing unique procedures and respond to changing conditions.

Q: **Are you familiar with gas chromatography?**

A: *Yes, I have extensive experience using gas chromatography for short-chain, fatty-acid microbial identification.*

This answer demonstrates that the candidate is not only familiar with a good analytical tool (gas chromatography) but also knows for what applications it's typically used.

Q: **Tell me about your experience with spectroscopy abilities. What are some common problems associated with spectral analysis?**

A: *I've used UV/VIS specs extensively for characterization of many compounds and have had to generate summary data reports based on these analyses. Common problems could be associated with the use of improper wavelengths or lack of a blank or interference.*

Specs are very common in certain kinds of chemical research. The fact that this candidate can identify potential problems demonstrates that he or she

First-time Job Seekers: You should stress any hands-on chemistry experience that you may have. Someone applying for an entry-level position would not be expected to be able to design experiments but should at least be able to "follow a recipe" and do a chemistry experiment from beginning to end.

has had a good deal of experience. The candidate's answer also shows the ability to gather, interpret, and report data.

Q: **What do you know about fluorescence chemistry?**

A: *I understand fluorescence is the emission given off after an excited molecule returns to the ground state. I've used fluorescent-detection equipment as a means for monitoring or analyzing many compounds. I've then used that information, coupled with other spectral data, to generate spectral profiles.*

This question is significant since fluorescence is widely used in chemical applications. A basic understanding of what fluorescence is and how to monitor it demonstrates a chemist who is using current and relevant technology. This answer also shows that the candidate has the ability to combine data gathered from two different sources.

Q: **Using spectroscopy, describe a simple experiment to validate the accuracy of a delivery system, such as a pump or pipette.**

A: *First, using a known concentration of a solution, prepare a standard curve of absorbency versus concentration. Second, using a valid sample size using the delivery system in question, determine the absorbency. Third, convert to concentration and then volume using the standard curve and a linear regression.*

This is a fairly advanced answer and demonstrates practical spectroscopy skills. Through this answer the candidate also shows that he or she is a quick thinker, creative, and has good interpretive skills.

Q: **What do you perceive as the similarities between microbiology and chemistry? What about the differences?**

A: *Chemistry is a more exact science than biology. Whereas a strict chemical reaction may require a tight set of conditions (pH, concentration, temperature), a biological reaction may have more latitude. Biological data does not always respond as expected. A similarity is that data is data and must be treated objectively no matter what the discipline.*

This answer shows a fundamental understanding of similarities and differences between the two disciplines, and how that may translate to an experimental

Career Changers: Unless you have work experience in a closely related field such as chemical engineering, agriculture science, or biological science, you may have to go back to school for at least a bachelor's degree in chemistry. You may be able to apply your understanding of other disciplines, including business and marketing, to a career in research and development, as these chemists are increasingly expected to work on interdisciplinary teams.

approach and interpretation. This answer may also shed light on how the candidate will work with others, especially those with a background in biology.

Q: **Tell me about your experience with statistics.**

A: *I've had to gather and analyze experimental data and prepare summary reports using valid sample sizes. From that I would report with a certain confidence level the statistically significant observations, such as mean, median, or mode. I've used commercially available statistics packages in these analyses.*

The appropriate buzzwords in this answer demonstrate the candidate's familiarity with statistics. Other good buzzwords are "anova," "regression analysis," and "probability." The answer also shows that the candidate has the ability to gather, interpret, and present data using computer applications.

Q: **Which chemistry courses do you think you apply most at work?**

A: *I find that my biochemistry and organic chemistry course work and labs have been especially useful in my experience doing classical wet chemistry. I've also learned proper experimental design.*

The interviewer will not be expecting to hear you name any courses in particular. It doesn't matter if you say biochemistry, organic chemistry, or inorganic chemistry. The questioner will just want to see if you're able to relate what you learned in school to real-life, practical experiences.

Q: **What personal qualities do you feel are important in an analytical chemist?**

A: *Perseverance, curiosity, the ability to concentrate on details and to work independently, are all important qualities in analytical chemists. Of course, they should also like to work with their hands.*

You may encounter this question if you're applying for an entry-level position. The employer wants to make sure that you understand the requirements of the position and that you are a good "fit" for the job. You should also give

Experienced Professionals: There are two basic career paths—technical or administrative. During your interview you should try to emphasize both of these qualities, since the two paths generally converge at one point or another. Also, scientists tend to resent administrators who don't have a scientific and technical background. Employers want to see that you belong to professional organizations, that you are staying current with the latest developments in chemistry. They also want to see if you have made presentations of data, since this would generally mean that you're using current techniques.

examples of how you've demonstrated these qualities in the past. If you're interviewing for a research and development position, you should cite leadership ability and solid oral and written communication skills as important qualities.

Q: **You notice a drift in pH readings over a three-day period. What might you attribute this to?**

A: *I can think of four possible problems. First, it could be an electrode problem, in which case I would try a different one. Second, the standards could be off. I would then ask if the unit was calibrated and the standard solutions were valid. Or it might be a matter of temperature. In this case I would check to see if the solution was temperature dependent. Finally, I would consider the possibility that it was a true shift, and I would examine the solution to see if it was changing or had gone through a breakdown.*

This answer demonstrates a basic understanding of the concept of pH and its importance to a chemist. It also demonstrates analytical thinking in response to a problem. By discussing these four possibilities, the candidate shows that he or she is thorough and detail oriented.

Q: **Have you had to make defined molarity concentration solutions? Tell me how to do it.**

A: *Yes, I'm quite familiar with the formula for a defined molarity concentration solution. Molarity equals moles solute divided by L solution. The weight calculation equals moles times molecular (formula) weight equals weight of chemical per liter of solution.*

The significance of this question is that all chemists should know how to make specific solutions. Although making a molarity concentration solution is pretty basic, the candidate still demonstrates for the interviewer a knowledge of chemical-solution preparation.

Q: **How do you see GMP—good manufacturing practices—as it relates to the role of an R-and-D chemist?**

A: *Detailed record keeping that documents a paper trail of design history is critical in order to adhere to good manufacturing practices. Another person must*

Candidates Re-entering the Workforce: The biggest concern of most employers will be whether or not you're up to date on all the latest technologies. During your job search and interviews you must try to convince employers that although you've been out of circulation for a while, you've still managed to stay current by reading industry journals and magazines.

be able to understand and duplicate my experiments from reading my lab notebooks, as well as other documented procedures.

This answer displays a critical industrywide philosophy. A goal of industry today is ISO (International Standards Organization) certification, which involves periodic auditing for recertification. Through this answer the candidate also demonstrates a feeling of ownership for his or her part within an entire project.

Q: **Listen to the following experiment and draw whatever conclusions you can: Customers are reporting that a particular lot of test panels are not performing to specifications. They believe stated concentrations are not in tolerance when they follow the package insert exactly. You are given the responsibility of finding and fixing the problem.**

A: *I would first try to duplicate the problem, running the experiment at least three times. If I encountered the same problem, I would attempt to isolate the problem with tools such as HPLC. I would ask myself, Is the raw-material assay correct? If it is, I would continue backward through the manufacturing process until the problem could be isolated. Once this was done, I would start from the beginning and work on the problem until it was resolved.*

Too often hearsay is taken as fact and, as a result, unnecessary and costly testing is done. Recognition and isolation of variables is the key to identifying any problem in chemistry. This well-thought-out answer shows the candidate's ability to respond under pressure in a logical and sequential manner to a potentially chemistry-related problem.

Q: **Are you affiliated with any professional societies?**

A: *I'm an active member of the American Chemical Society. When I can, I like to attend local and national meetings. Also, I read* Chemical and Engineering News *and* Chemical Week *regularly.*

This answer demonstrates that the candidate, through association meetings and journals, has exposure to the latest technologies and chemistry advances. The answer also shows initiative and a desire to learn.

Biotechnology Manager

Q: **What qualifications do you have that you believe will help you as a biotechnology manager?**

A: *I have five years of experience in chemical process and design engineering with a major player in the industry. I also have a bachelor of science with a double major in science and chemical engineering from the University of Alabama.*

Because the biotechnology industry is so specialized, a scientific and/or engineering background is a must. A recruiter will make sure, before anything else, that your background is in this area. This candidate's response is appropriate because it's crisp and to the point, without going into too much initial detail. You can be sure that the recruiter will ask you to go into much more detail further into the interview.

Q: **What science courses have you taken that have prepared you for your career in biotechnology?**

A: *I took a variety of science courses in physics, biology, and chemistry. To give you a general idea, in the physics department I took General Physics; War and Peace in the Nuclear Age; and Thermodynamics and Statistical Physics. I also took Biological Principles; Biotechnology: The New Biology; Food, Agriculture, and Society; and Special Topics in Biology, all in the biological sciences department. In the chemistry department I took General Chemistry; Organic Chemistry; and Physical Chemistry.*

Although this is a mouthful, it's important that you be able to catalog the different science courses that you've taken, just as this candidate has done. There's a very strong possibility that the recruiter will ask for your specific grades in different courses. Also, he or she will probably expect a solid GPA.

Q: **Have you taken any significant engineering courses that are relevant to your career in biotechnology?**

A: *I have a strong engineering background. I focused on chemical engineering classes, including Introduction to Chemical Engineering; Mass and Energy Balances; Chemical Engineering Thermodynamics; and Chemical Process Design. However, I also took a couple of general engineering courses, such as Technology in Western Society; and The Laser and Its Applications in Science, Technology, and Medicine.*

The recruiter will be verifying that you have a technical background. What your specific academic background is doesn't matter. Just be prepared to verbalize a list of the appropriate courses that you took.

Q: Which class was the hardest? What did you particularly learn from it that's applicable to biotechnology?

A: *I thought physical chemistry was the hardest class that I took at Alabama. It was really a conceptual course, which taught me both how to think conceptually and to look at the big picture.*

Physical chemistry is generally considered the hardest undergraduate class in any major, and at any school. The recruiter will expect that you've taken this course, and he or she will ask what your grade was. If you please the recruiter with this answer, you will have passed the first big hurdle in the biotechnology interview.

Q: What do you currently read to keep on top of what's happening in biotechnology?

A: *There are, of course, a large number of very specific scientific trade journals. Although it's fairly expensive, I think it's important to read* Biotechnology and Bioengineering, *because it's one of the oldest and most established journals, and it's excellent for keeping abreast of original research in the industry. I also read* Biotechnology and Applied Biochemistry *for international news. I try to skim through* Biotechnology News *and* Biotechnology Progress, *as well.*

This candidate knows what's out there, which is what the recruiter wants to hear. If you are truly interested in biotechnology, you should be reading the different industry rags. Know what they are and be able to tell the recruiter about them.

Q: Did you participate in a cooperative work-study program?

A: *Yes, I did a co-op for four years at a pulp-and-paper company in Mobile, Alabama. My college is set up on the quarter rather than the semester system, so it was easy to schedule my co-op every year.*

If you didn't do a co-op, the recruiter will ask you why not. If you did summer internships instead, talk about that experience. Remember that you're

First-time Job Seekers: The recruiter will be looking at your educational and co-op background. He or she will expect a solid technical background, preferably science and engineering majors. You will probably be asked for your grades and your GPA, both of which should be strong.

selling yourself on two things in the biotechnology interview: solid educational background, and experience, experience, experience.

Q: **What did you learn and/or enjoy most about your co-op (or internship) experience?**

A: *I really enjoyed being involved in the actual process of converting wood pulp to paper. I spent a lot of time on the factory floor. I found the hands-on experience a rewarding complement to the academic side of my training.*

Recruiters generally think that you've wasted your time in college if you've not done some type of co-op or internship. Saying that you did it, you liked it, and you still want more translates to the recruiter that you're a low-risk candidate, that hiring you and training you won't be a waste of his or her company's money. Positive discussion about your co-op or internship experience indicates that you have a proven track record. If you didn't enjoy the experience, however, it's okay to be honest about that. You would then say that you learned that sales, or research and development, for example, is more for you.

Q: **Have you ever taken a technical writing course?**

A: *I took Writing in Engineering and Engineering Communications, both of which concentrated on technical and professional writing, supplemented with oral and visual presentations. These were two of my favorite classes at Alabama.*

Recruiters will be looking for writing classes in your background. You'll have to be able to write well in even the most technical jobs. If you can't express yourself, the accomplishment of your work dies with you.

Q: **Do you consider yourself to be a good communicator?**

A: *Yes, I do. I've developed my writing skills with those two writing courses, and even more important, I think, is that I feel very comfortable giving presentations to my department.*

The need for good communication skills is something you can't get away from in high-technology jobs. You have to be able to express your wealth of knowledge and ideas both orally and in writing. A recruiter will want to be

Career Changers: If you're not scientifically trained, you should look for jobs in more traditional areas of business within the biotechnology industry. For example, you may want to look into product marketing or sales. To prepare, read every article from the *Wall Street Journal* for the last six months about your prospective company.

sure that you can effectively explain what you do to a layperson, for example, and that you're comfortable in the process.

Q: What types of projects have you worked on in your current job?

A: *I've done a wide variety of projects, such as preliminary process and detailed design engineering for a wide range of air-pollution-control equipment, including bed and venturi scrubbers, baghouse-type dust collectors, and thermal oxidizers. I was also responsible for construction administration, site engineering, and start-up and assembly of the operation-and-maintenance manuals.*

This candidate's answer is solid because it strikes the right balance between the general overview and the details of his or her projects. Additionally, the candidate has made it clear, without seeming arrogant, that he or she was essential in the functioning of these projects. The recruiter wants to hear that you have been extremely involved in important and difficult projects.

Q: Have you worked on any other types of projects?

A: *On the flip side, I've done air-emission audits and material-balance calculations for different industries across the U.S. and Canada. This involved constructing and operating air permits, and Title V air permitting.*

The candidate has shown the recruiter that he or she has worked on different types of projects in the specialty area. The recruiter will be looking for this type of versatility. Additionally, the candidate's answer displays a strong level of professional competency.

Q: Do you belong to any professional organizations that are biotechnology related?

A: *Yes, I'm a member of the American Institute of Chemical Engineers.*

It's not essential that you have a professional-organization affiliation, but it is a plus. This candidate's membership in the AIChE would be a plus to the recruiter. Simply state which, if any, organizations you belong to.

Experienced Professionals: You wouldn't be in the interview if the recruiter wasn't impressed with your resume and track record, so don't try to sell your resume. Instead, try to connect with the recruiter to prove that you'll make a good personality fit with this company. Discuss how your management and work style will both complement and enhance the company.

Q: **Do you have any professional registrations or certifications that are relevant to biotechnology?**

A: *I do. I'm registered as a CHMM, or a certified hazardous material manager. I've also been a Level II First Responder—Hazardous Materials Awareness and Operations for the past three years.*

Professional registrations and certifications are not essential. If you do have any, however, do tell the recruiter. This candidate has very appropriate qualifications in this area for his or her experience level, which would be well noted by the recruiter.

Q: **How proficient are you with a computer?**

A: *I feel equally comfortable on a Macintosh and a PC. I'm proficient in Microsoft Word and Excel.*

Solid computer skills are expected by recruiters in almost every industry, and biotechnology is no exception. This candidate knows some good basics. Furthermore, the variety of the programs that he or she feels comfortable with indicates to the recruiter that this candidate could easily pick up a new program if the job required it.

Q: **Can you complete projects on time and within a budget?**

A: *Yes, I can. Although there can always be special circumstances that are beyond control, my team has been known to work until 3 A.M. to meet a project deadline.*

As a biotechnology job candidate, you must "play the game," so to speak. You have to tell the recruiter what he or she wants to hear, which is yes, in this case. No matter if you are in R&D, or replacing pumps at a plant, you will have a budget and time restraint.

Q: **Describe the most difficult crisis in a work situation that you've experienced. How did you resolve it?**

A: *I had a project to design and build an on-site waste and water treatment site that went way over budget. I immediately went to the owner of the site, who felt comfortable enough with the production that he increased the initial budget to meet the current project needs.*

Candidates Re-entering the Workforce: Brush up on what's going on in the industry by reading all the industry journals. Practice interviewing by actually speaking aloud, before going in for the real thing. Be sure your resume is current and in good shape.

This candidate handled the situation correctly by not keeping the problem to himself or herself. A recruiter will want to see if you can deal with a problem effectively. Prove that you can make the best of a difficult situation, as this candidate has.

Q: How do you feel when things go wrong with a project?

A: *Well, of course I would prefer that my projects run smoothly at all times. However, the very nature of the biotechnology industry means that many changes can and probably will happen to any plan at any time. I try to realize this from the outset and cross each bridge when I come to it.*

This question is tricky. Yet the candidate understands this and has convinced the recruiter that he or she can deal with project setbacks without losing professional composure. The recruiter probably will not ask directly, "Can you work under pressure?" although this is what he or she is after.

Q: How did you get interested in biotechnology?

A: *You could say that biotechnology runs in my family. My father's been interested and involved in biotechnology from its early stages, so I was always exposed to it while growing up. Also, I've always excelled in science classes, so I think pursuing a career in biotechnology was, and is, a very natural progression for me.*

The candidate has both a long-time interest and a background in biotechnology. Further, there seems to be a good match of career and skills here. The recruiter wants to hear an answer like this because it shows that the candidate is well suited for a career in biotechnology.

Q: How do you see biotechnology changing the way consumers perceive fresh produce?

A: *I think that when the FDA approved the injected tomato, consumers were forced to alter their perceptions about their groceries. Certainly it will be difficult for the public to get used to ideas such as tomatoes with a four-month shelf life, but I think that with more and more biotechnologically improved products in grocery stores, the public will accept these advances as second nature. Just as with any technological advance—from the flu vaccine to electricity to the radio, for example—quality of life is improved, which the public accepts, whether or not there was any initial skepticism.*

The candidate is able to separate himself or herself as a scientist and see biotechnology through the eyes of a layperson. A recruiter will be looking for this quality in a candidate. It shows that the candidate can look at the broad spectrum, and not just his or her specific function in the scheme.

Q: **Consumers are becoming increasingly educated about the use of pesticides. Do you think this will affect the biotechnology industry?**

A: *I don't think there's any doubt that increasing consumer knowledge will affect the biotechnology industry. As a result, I think that the industry will have to be very careful about marketing strategies. To that end I think the industry will rapidly expand in terms of the types of jobs within the industry as well as the number of people involved.*

Again, the candidate proves that he or she does not exist in a vacuum but has a good idea of the different angles involved in the industry of biotechnology as a whole. The candidate is also able to succinctly express him- or herself in such matters. The recruiter is looking for someone who is well-rounded in approach to the issues of biotechnology, beyond his or her specific role.

Compliance Specialist
(Pharmaceuticals)

Q: **What kind of validation experience have you had?**

A: *I've had some equipment-validation experience. I've also had validation experience in a number of processes, including large-scale cell culture, large-scale column chromatography, and aseptic small-volume parenteral fills.*

Validation for the production of human drugs is mandated by the Food and Drug Administration. "Validation" means documenting that a piece of equipment is installed properly, operated properly, and can perform consistently over the long term. This is experience that's very much in demand in pharmaceuticals right now. The interviewer asks this question to gauge the candidate's level of experience in specific areas. This experience can be either as a participant performing validation tests or as a study director/manager, overseeing the execution of the tasks per a preapproved protocol.

Q: **What kind of training experience do you have, either as a trainee or a trainer?**

A: *In my current position, I'm in charge of training over twenty-five quality-control personnel. I make sure that everyone has thorough knowledge of all good manufacturing practices.*

The FDA requires by law that all individuals who participate in the manufacture of drugs be trained in current good-manufacturing-practice regulations (Gimps). Quality assurance, the department that's typically responsible for providing this type of training to all other personnel, must demonstrate that these people are proficient. You'll want to communicate an understanding of

First-time Job Seekers: Compliance specialists aren't typically hired right out of college, but entry-level candidates can begin a career in quality assurance as documentation specialists. The one exception may be an individual with an academic background in biotechnology that has a GMP course as part of the required course work. Recruiters want candidates to have a strong science background, with course work that includes classes in biology, chemistry, cell culture, and biotechnology. Depending upon performance and interest, a documentation specialist may begin moving up in quality assurance within eighteen months.

Gimps in the interview. The interviewer will also need to know your training background to determine where you would fit in with the rest of the group.

Q: What kind of auditing experience do you have?

A: *I've performed as an in-house auditor for QA inspecting standard operating procedures, quality control data, and manufacturing. I was also involved, to a lesser degree, with FDA audits on our facilities.*

The Food and Drug Administration closely monitors all drug companies. That scrutiny starts, to a limited degree, during the research and development stage and culminates when the FDA must provide a drug approval before it can be sold commercially. Part of the FDA's monitoring includes unannounced audits during which it has the legal right to arrive on-site to inspect a facility against its standards and Gimps. As a preventative measure, companies usually run periodic internal audits. The interviewer wants to see that you have legitimate experience in dealing with FDA audits and inspections, and/or that you've participated in an in-house audit program.

Q: Tell me about your documentation background.

A: *We use a tracking database. My standard operating procedures are signed by my manager. I also have a periodic review function in my standard operating procedures, and we use batch records and lot numbers in our documentation system.*

The interviewer will want to know the documentation systems that you use in your current position. Do you know the difference between standard operating procedures and validation protocols? The interviewer will also want to find out the software you've used. Your answer should demonstrate an understanding of control practices and traceability, as well as a working knowledge of documentation as a whole.

Q: Describe the batch-record review and product-release systems you use in your current company.

Career Changers: Recruiters like candidates who come from related industries, like bulk pharmaceutical chemicals, diagnostics, or medical devices. Candidates with experience in regulated industries, like defense or nuclear, are highly prized for their familiarity with the complexities of regulations. Naturally, you should get additional training and thoroughly familiarize yourself with the industry in general and the company in particular. Recruiters also look for stability and character in a candidate, as quality assurance typically interfaces with all departments in all kinds of situations.

A: *We review my batch records for GMP discrepancies and deviations. There's a deviation and investigation system for any follow-up we may need. For my product-release system, once we receive completed paperwork from manufacturing, we collate it, then evaluate the collated package to determine whether that product meets all internal as well as government requirements. Once this process is complete, we put a label on the product, then sell it to the public.*

Batch records are essentially fill-in-the blank procedures that document each step in the drug-manufacturing business. A product-release system is the vehicle through which the product is released for sale: Have all records been reviewed? Has all labeling been performed correctly? Have all deviations been investigated? and so on. The interviewer will want to know the systems you use in your current position, and how you go about reviewing the records and releasing products.

Q: What experience do you have with on-site investigations?

A: *I've headed several on-site investigations. Mainly, I've been responsible for ensuring that the proper protocol was followed when we failed to meet FDA specifications.*

Again, the interviewer is looking for the candidate to describe the system in his or her current company that kicks in when data or testing specifications aren't met for any system. In response to such a question, articulate clearly how you identify the problem and sort it out. Take the interviewer step by step through a typical investigation, explaining how you follow through and see the investigation to its conclusion.

Q: Describe the product-complaint system at your current company.

A: *I receive an adverse-event report from either customer service or the clinical department; then I go to manufacturing to investigate where the root of the problem lies.*

The interviewer will want to know how the candidate handles a product complaint, whom he or she talks to, and how the complaint gets resolved. Again, the interviewer wants to see that the candidate can achieve closure. As

Experienced Professionals: Emphasize the maturity and supervising experience you can bring to the work group. In quality assurance a highly valued asset is the ability to remain calm, rational, and discerning when making judgments, especially regarding investigations, audits, or the like.

always, your answer must meet all the FDA requirements. In this and other questions the interviewer is looking for the right terminology—buzzwords that show you have a real familiarity with the industry.

Q: **Do you have a stability program at your current company? Tell me about it.**

A: *Yes, we have a program that makes sure our products have the shelf life they're supposed to have. We use accelerated stability intervals with stability intervals that are defined by our group of engineers.*

Drug manufacturers need to show that their drugs have a shelf life. You should describe the system and how a stability study is set up (the protocol, how stability intervals are defined, where the testing is done, where samples are stored, who coordinates testing, how final reports are written up, and where those reports get stored). How does your current company do quality-control testing, and who coordinates it?

Q: **Describe the change-control system at your current company.**

A: *Our standard operating procedure for change control is written to define how we control changes in our major utilities, our drug-manufacturing processes, and our assay and test procedures. We carefully document each and every improvement or change that's made to our equipment.*

The FDA requires that drug manufacturers maintain a history of any change that's made to any system or process. Companies must document and explain every step they go through for change control. The interviewer wants to know what kind of documentation requirements the candidate's company uses to report change control, and how changes are tracked and monitored. Explain how every change-control item is individually identified and how the system is controlled. Again, you should be sure to describe how you close out each item.

Q: **Why do you want to be in quality assurance?**

A: *I enjoy the challenge. I think it's a great opportunity to learn about a company. I like the fact that I get exposed to a large number of aspects of the pharma-*

Candidates Re-entering the Workforce: Thoroughly familiarize yourself with current trends in the industry and with each particular company you plan to interview with. Depending on how long you've been away from the industry, you should also consider getting additional training; many colleges have eighteen-month to two-year biotech certificate programs.

ceutical manufacturing business, compared to a laboratory or a manufacturing-operator role. More specifically, I enjoy the steps I go through when conducting investigations, since I have to interact with personnel from many of the company's departments.

The interviewer is looking to gauge the candidate's level of motivation and interest. If you give a generic answer, the interviewer will think that your interest in the position is superficial.

Research Technician

Q: Tell me a little about your duties and responsibilities in your last research position.

A: *I've been responsible for running enzyme-characterization assays and large-scale bacterial isolations over the past nine months. Additionally, I'm responsible for coordinating, monitoring, ordering, and inventory of laboratory supplies.*

Here the interviewer is attempting to get a feel for the level of responsibility the candidate had in his or her last position. Don't overwhelm the researcher with too much detail, but give a feel of the last position you occupied and emphasize any major responsibilities you had within the lab. If you had multiple responsibilities, be sure to stress this point.

Q: Have you ever had any experience writing research or grant proposals?

A: *Yes. I've helped draft a research proposal for the isolation and identification of bacteria near a known contaminated groundwater source. We were interested in the effect of the pollution on the type of bacterial populations found in the region.*

Be prepared to discuss any experience you may have in the proposal of a research project or grant funding. Grant and research proposals are the life of the laboratory, and any experience in this area is a definite plus.

Q: This position requires experimentation with animals. Do you mind working with laboratory animals?

A: *No. I understand the need for the use of laboratory rats in the brain-chemistry study you're performing. I had experience doing surgeries with hybrid mice in genetic studies several years ago.*

This question determines how well the candidate understands the requirements of the position he or she is applying for. Does it require work with animals or hazardous materials? This is something you must seriously consider before applying for any position. If your ethical or personal makeup is not suited to performing certain work, it's better to find out now than for the job to cause you misery later.

Q: Have you had any experience lecturing or presenting research material before?

A: *Yes. I recently presented a poster board on a new enzyme-isolation technique at the university's molecular-biology lecture series. I fielded questions from research colleagues within the university.*

For a mid- to upper-level position, presenting findings and organizing materials for presentations and talks is expected. The ability to communicate effectively and to interpret your findings to your peers is essential within and outside the laboratory.

Q: Have you ever supervised and trained anyone before? If so, tell me a bit about that experience.

A: *In my last position at the university I supervised an undergraduate student in the isolation and mutation study of antibiotic resistance in Streptococcus bacteria. I made sure she stayed on track and helped her evaluate the results of her mutation studies.*

Here the interviewer is trying to determine how well the candidate works with others. Can you assist an entry-level person in learning a technique? Also, if you've had supervisory experience, this implies that you can learn and act independently. A senior researcher may not have significant time to invest in training a mid- or upper-level technician in methods and techniques.

Q: What is the research environment in your present position like? Do you prefer a flexible or a regular schedule?

A: *The last lab I worked in had ten people with five projects going simultaneously. It wasn't unusual for me to come in at nine in the morning to start an experiment and not leave until ten in the evening. Basically, I'm flexible about my schedule as long as I can get my work finished in a reasonable time period.*

It's not unusual in active research labs for hours to be extremely varied at times. Often an experiment will finish late or be dependent on someone else's work. Flexibility and patience within reason will go a long way, especially in a small, intimate research environment.

First-time Job Seekers: Since you've probably just graduated college with a B.S. or B.A. in a scientific discipline, stress the pluses in your background: any courses or labs you've taken that taught specific techniques; any independent research projects or internships you worked on as an undergraduate; any presentations, talks, or reviews you had to write in the context of a class. Try to draw a correlation to how this experience pertains to the specific position for which you're applying.

Q: **Tell me about your research experience characterizing DNA.**

A: *I have experience synthesizing small oligonucleotide probes. I was also required to label these radioactively with P32 for hybridization experiments. From the results we determined the relatedness of a community of wild finches. Because of this I was trained in the proper handling techniques of radioactive isotopes.*

Any special training in hazardous materials is a definite plus. Showing that you have successfully worked with these materials reflects positively on your research abilities. That you have experience with very widely used or sought-after techniques such as probing or radioactive material handling can only register positively with the interviewer.

Q: **Have you published any articles in a scientific journal?**

A: *Yes. I co-authored an article in Science with seven other research assistants. We published a piece on a new rapid DNA sequencing technique to be used later in a human genome project.*

If you've been published anywhere in a scientific journal, be sure to mention it! That you have a research project to which you significantly contributed is a major accomplishment. Do not be shy about this, but be very certain that you don't overstate your contribution, either. Published credentials in the scientific research community are extremely important and are taken very seriously.

Q: **How much experience have you had with microscopy techniques?**

A: *When I was a technician in my last position, my duties included freezing and staining samples for one of the graduate students in the laboratory. I understand that you will be taking cross-sectional views for your internal-structural studies of mitochondria. I would be very interested in this aspect of the project.*

The interviewer will be interested in your in-depth knowledge of a specific technique that may be of importance to his research. Any experience you've had with the various techniques should be mentioned. The more detail you can give here, the better.

Career Changers: It's not unheard of for people to switch scientific fields of research. Because science disciplines tend to be narrowly defined, the researcher will naturally be worried whether you have the background for the position you're interested in. Reassure the employer that you have the basic required knowledge for the position. Don't be afraid to apply for a position that's different from your previous one; just be sure you're current and knowledgeable about the field.

Q: How familiar are you with electrophoresis?

A: *I'm very comfortable running both extremely large and small gels. In my past two positions I used this technique almost daily to isolate DNA fragments and determine approximate sizes, and have isolated fragments for further study. I've run and prepared thousands of gels in the past.*

Here the interviewer is asking about a very commonly used technique in molecular biology. Though the techniques vary widely depending on the scientific field, you should be conversant with techniques like this and probably will have had at least some experience with them. If you assure the interviewer you can perform a specific technique, you probably will not be asked to explain it in great detail. At the midlevel the interviewer will assume you're familiar with, or can quickly pick up, details for commonly used techniques.

Q: Tell me what it is about this research project that interests you.

A: *After having read your last two papers on the analysis of the partial crystal structure for this enzyme, I'm very interested in the structural studies you and your colleagues at Brookhaven are pursuing. With my background in the structural and functional study of E. coli endonucleases, this enzyme is of definite interest to me.*

Here the interviewer wants specifics. It's always a good idea to read the latest articles or to review papers on the topic, if they're available. If possible, head to the local university library and do a search for some of the researcher's latest articles. The more knowledge you know about the project, the easier the interview will be for you. Always try to do your homework beforehand.

Q: Have you ever had any unexpected or unpredictable results with your research? If so, what happened and what did you do to defend your position?

A: *Yes. As a graduate student getting my master's degree, I was working with a group on analysis of a protein crystal structure, and our analysis disagreed with a popularly held theory on the mechanism of the protein. Our group was grilled by senior researchers in the department. As it turns out, several of the senior professors and researchers were most impressed and surprised. Also, two months later a paper corroborating our theory was published.*

Experienced Professionals: The most important advice is to research the researcher! Know as much as possible about the current project you would be working on and what your duties would likely be. Do a literature review of the specific group or researcher if possible. The more specific your knowledge, the better your chances of getting the position.

This is the time to demonstrate your confidence in your research abilities. If you show that you can stand firm even in the face of disagreement from "experts," and can logically support your findings, you'll be of immense value to any researcher.

Q: **Tell me about any future plans you might have for schooling or furthering your scientific career.**

A: *Presently I'm enrolled part-time as a graduate student in biology at the local university. I plan to work for several more years while earning my master's degree. Eventually I'd like to complete my Ph.D. in neurobiology.*

The interviewer wants to determine how active an interest the candidate takes in the field. How interested are you truly in this field? It's extremely common for research assistants to take courses relevant to the work they're doing. It's common to attend lectures or classes to keep current on the latest research and theory. With the dynamic nature of scientific research, this is almost a job requirement for such a position.

Q: **How long do you expect to commit to a position here?**

A: *Though I've worked within three laboratories over the last several years, the main reason for changing has been due to the moving of the primary researcher or the loss of grant funding when results of the research project weren't as expected. I've been in my last position for almost three years now. I expect to remain in my next position for at least two more years.*

The researcher is trying to determine if there were personality conflicts or insufficient skills in the candidate's previous position. In the often intimate environment of research, personal conflicts can adversely affect an entire project. Because grants and funding can be very unpredictable, it's rather common for research funding not to get renewed, or for a researcher to move to a different company or university as funding shifts. This makes

Candidates Re-entering the Workforce: The interviewer's major concern will be how well you've kept up with the field. Scientific research changes so rapidly that a three-year absence may be like twenty years in some other fields. Do a review of the literature before interviewing for a specific position. A few days in the library catching up with the latest developments will go a long way toward putting you at ease in the interview. Try taking a course or two at the local university if you think it's warranted, or pick up a textbook at the local campus bookstore. In this case the more knowledgeable you appear, the better you and the researcher will feel about your ability to pick the work back up again.

research at times a highly mobile profession. If you can give a reasonable explanation for rapidly shifting positions, this kind of history should not adversely affect your career.

Q: **I see that previously you were doing work in physics. Tell me why you're thinking of switching fields to molecular biology. Isn't this a rather large leap for you?**

A: *I originally got my degree in biochemistry. While I was an undergraduate, I did a research project with a professor in the physics department. Though I like physics a great deal, I miss biology. My previous job was actually a cross-over pertaining more to biophysics than to classical physics. If you look at my resume, you'll see I have experience with many techniques that will be helpful to you. I have extensive experience in handling and preparing DNA. Additionally, I have excellent analytical skills because of my detailed spectrographic studies of DNA-protein binding in the physics department.*

Often formal training in a different scientific discipline can be invaluable to a researcher. But, especially at the midlevel, the researcher must satisfy him- or herself that you have the basic required knowledge for the position. This question can make or break your candidacy, so make sure you're prepared with a convincing response.

CHAPTER 19
SERVICE

Customer Service Representative

Q: **Do you believe that the customer is always right?**

A: *Yes. I do whatever it takes to assure that the customer is satisfied and will continue to buy from the company.*

This is an important question, as it gets to the heart of the matter in regard to dealings with customers. Employers look for a person who will bring forth the extra effort required to assure that the customer is satisfied, and that all appropriate action has been expended. An outgoing personality would be most desired for this position, as voice intonation and attitude are readily conveyed to the person on the other end of the phone. Try to demonstrate these traits in the interview.

Q: **How do you handle unruly or demanding customers?**

A: *I try to talk in a calm and even voice, in order to get the person to talk in a businesslike manner and not vent his or her anger.*

Here the employer is really looking for clues to the candidate's personality and his or her method of dealing with tough customers. Besides an outgoing personality, the customer service representative must have the maturity to determine quickly the nature of the customer's frustration and to be able to remove the anger from the conversation so that the problem can be resolved. Give an example of a difficult situation you've encountered in the past, and how you successfully resolved it.

Q: **What level of decision-making authority have you had in your last two positions?**

A: *I was able to make decisions up to $1,000 in value. This would include the issuing of credits, replacement of merchandise, or offering of price adjustments.*

This question determines whether or not the individual can make a decision in order to satisfy a customer without having to go to the next level of authority. Most customer service representative openings require someone who has at least three to five years of experience.

Q: How did you handle a situation when the customer was totally wrong?

A: *I recently had a situation in which a customer returned merchandise for credit that was not purchased from our company. I explained to her that the item was not one of ours and that probably someone in another shipping department put the wrong label on the box.*

The employer is trying to determine the thought process that the candidate would use in trying to diffuse a difficult situation. It takes someone who has the patience and ability to explain the nature of a problem, rather than merely pointing a finger at the customer and affixing blame. By using this approach, the customer service rep will be able to convince the customer that the problem was human error by an unrelated third party in their organization, and avoid having to take a hard line.

Q: Why did you go into the customer service department of your company, as opposed to sales?

A: *I like the challenge and satisfaction of dealing with customers, problem resolution, and the fact that every day is different. In reality most of the job is, in fact, sales.*

This is a somewhat negative question. The employer will want to know how you feel about your job. Try to portray yourself as someone who's at ease on the telephone, who talks in a calm and nonintimidating manner, and who's seeking self-satisfaction knowing you've done everything possible to aid or assist the complaining party.

Q: After a difficult day, how do you handle the stress associated with your job?

A: *I usually go for a ten-minute walk. This allows me to relax and unwind and forget about the day.*

Customer service can, of course, be a stressful field to work in. The employer will want to determine whether you're likely to burn out. Do you hold all your problems inside, or do you seek a healthy release so that you're ready to go on the next day? If you exercise on a regular basis, say so. Tell the

First-time Job Seekers: Look for a company that has an existing department in place with approximately two to three other people. This will provide you with a formal training program and resources to aid you in performing the job on a daily basis.

employer that you recognize the importance of using sports or some other physical activity to vent your frustrations.

Q: **What was the most difficult situation you had to face at your last company?**

A: *I had to recommend that we stop doing business with one of our oldest customers, who claimed there was a problem with every shipment, even though we triple-checked each order with signatures on all of the shipping documents. Apparently, that customer was belligerent with all suppliers and used these means to get additional price concessions.*

One of the most important characteristics a customer representative can have is an ability to assess sensitive issues and make recommendations and/or decisions regarding customers. The customer service representative is the provider of key information regarding accounts, which is valuable to all other areas of the company. The ability to provide this type of insightful information separates the strong candidates from the marginal ones. Be specific, and describe a situation in which you implemented sound analytical thinking and good judgment to resolve a problem.

Q: **What type of industry do you prefer to work in?**

A: *I prefer to work with a consumer-oriented type of product. The exact nature of the industry is not that important to me.*

Your answer will reveal the type of customer you're most skilled at dealing with. Those buying a product have different kinds of issues from those buying a service. Where a product is involved, one's experience and judgment levels need to be more acute, as the problems are generally more complex. Also, when dealing with products, the representative is more likely dealing with a reseller than with the ultimate consumer. The reseller will voice complaints down to the manufacturer's level. The customer service representative, therefore, must be aware of the problems affecting both types of consumers.

Q: **When you start work with a new company or industry, how do you go about gaining an understanding of that company and its products?**

Career Changers: Look for a company that affords you an opportunity consistent with your new career goals. For example, if you're changing from an accounting position, the new job should offer you challenges and diversification via decision making that was not present in your previous career path. Be sure to emphasize these goals to the interviewer.

A: *The first thing I generally do is get a copy of the most recent catalog, order forms, pricing lists, and any other marketing literature. I also try to look at the company's sales reports and/or receivable aging in order to find out what the products are and to whom they're sold. Additionally, I speak with the sales manager to find out what concerns he or she may have in handling any given account.*

Try to portray yourself as someone with a lot of initiative, the type of person who will, on your own, assume responsibility to learn all that you can about the company, its products, and its policies. Give examples of how you've spent a fair amount of time with the other departments in order to learn about the ways and means the product is developed, produced, marketed, and sold. The interviewer knows that this kind of experience and initiative will make you more effective in dealing with the customer.

Q: **What was the pace of the company at your most recent position?**

A: *We were extremely fast paced. Being a multimillion-dollar, consumer-oriented company, we faced constant demands and issues that needed to be resolved each day.*

The interviewer will want to know about your ability to handle many issues, and many types of calls. The demands in a fast-paced environment require a person who does not get easily flustered and can handle multiple tasks. Your answer should convey that you have an even temperament and the ability to prioritize tasks and be straightforward with customers.

Q: **How are you able to interact effectively with others in your most recent company?**

A: *I'm an even-tempered individual who believes in treating everyone on a professional basis. I feel that I'm a good listener, and I help or assist everyone I can in order to resolve the problem at hand and not worry about who gets the credit for the decision.*

An effective rep must be able to deal with diametrically different influences in the company. The ability to communicate effectively with internal personnel is indicative of how you'll be able to communicate with external sources. You should have strong written and oral presentation skills.

> **Experienced Professionals:** Your best bet is to find a company that has formal systems and procedures in place, and that also offers you a significant decision-making role. The company should be open to new methods of performing the function, by using your extensive knowledge and experience.

Q: **What do you feel are the personal qualities necessary to make a success of this job?**

A: *My experience has taught me that the most important personal qualities in this field are the ability to listen to the customer's complaint, to deal with people on a professional and somewhat sympathetic level, to talk to people, and to make decisions that placate all parties.*

First and foremost, the most important personal quality for a customer service rep is a professional demeanor. You should have decision-making skills and be able to execute them in a mature manner. You should also be comfortable dealing with all levels of an organization. A sense of urgency is also a must, as customers expect that issues will be resolved on a timely basis, both fairly and accurately.

Q: **What types of decisions are difficult for you?**

A: *The decisions I find most difficult are ones where there are no formal guidelines or policies in place, when I have to spend a lot of time trying to figure out what's happened and what should have happened.*

Customer service representatives must have the ability to respond to questions from customers, make decisions at their level of authority, and exercise judgment in their application. The ideal candidate can handle complaints and issues as they arise using his or her best judgment, even when no formal policies exist. By setting a dollar-value decision-making limit, the rep can deal with a situation in the absence of formal guidelines.

Q: **At your most recent position, what were some of the things that you spent most of your time working on?**

A: *I spent a lot of my time researching paperwork for bills of lading, copies of invoices, and credits. I was also responsible for obtaining proofs of delivery and mailing customer statements. I would spend the remainder of my time in correspondence and phone calls.*

Organizational skills and time management are key to this type of position. Stress your ability to think and act in a clear manner in order to avoid duplicating efforts or, worse, not performing the task at all. You should have the

Candidates Re-entering the Workforce: Look for a company that offers a formal training program and the opportunity to work with an experienced individual. You may be asked to start out doing research work in order to learn the company's systems and procedures.

ability to delegate lower-level tasks (for example, securing proofs of delivery, photocopying invoices, or shipping documents), and be able to focus on the major issues.

Q: **If you were head of the customer service department with authority to effect changes, what three things would you change?**

A: *First, I'd get a new computer system that would allow us to call up all relevant information on the screen without having to dig through files for the data. Then I'd hire an additional person to help with the workload. Last, I would clearly state our returns and claims policies in our catalog, on our order form, and on our invoices. This would eliminate at least two-thirds of the calls from customers who claim that they don't know what our policies are.*

An appropriate response to this question would be something to the effect that changes would be made to computer systems, work flows, or forms, or that procedure flows would be formalized in order to handle and resolve issues. You should limit the mention of personnel to how to train or use them more effectively.

Flight Attendant

Q: **Why do you want to fly for our company?**

A: *I'm attracted to Ace Airlines because it's a stable carrier with an excellent reputation in the industry. Of all the turboprop airlines operating out of the Midwest, Ace offers the best safety record as well as superb customer service—even in coach—all with competitive ticket prices. I'd like to be a member of that winning team.*

Your answer should demonstrate a strong interest in and specific knowledge of the company you're interviewing with. Do your homework and learn plenty about the airline and the industry of which it's a part (see Chapter 2 for more information on this). The minimal knowledge you should have going into an interview is the location of the flight-attendant bases, the make of at least some of the aircraft in the company's fleet, and the route over which the airline operates. Knowing some of the company history, who the company president is, the standing of the company in the industry, and other company-related matters will also impress your interviewer favorably and set you apart from the competition. A similar question you may encounter is "What do you know about our company?"

Q: **Aside from company benefits and travel advantages, what makes the flight-attendant position attractive to you?**

A: *Well, I've always enjoyed working with the public, and this position offers the opportunity to meet new and interesting people every day. I have a lot of the other qualities that are important in flight attending, such as maturity, responsibility, and strong interpersonal skills. I understand that a career in flight attending demands some sacrifice, but I like to think of it as high adventure and a great calling.*

The interviewer will want to hear that you have realistic reasons for seeking a career as a flight attendant. Express your personal satisfaction in working with and serving the needs of other people while displaying no reluctance about accepting the responsibilities and lifestyle of a flight attendant. Be sure you know how flexible your lifestyle will have to be, and how great the demands, before you show up for an interview. You must give the impression of being able to offer all of the requisite skills and concessions without hesitation or regret.

Q: Tell me about your educational background.

A: *I have a high-school diploma as well as two and a half years of college work. Though I enjoyed college and got good grades, I had to put off getting my degree for financial reasons. I do hope to return and get my bachelor's degree in business someday.*

Airlines look for an adequate general education and prefer some college study. The interviewer may also want to determine how committed you were to school work, which is often a good precursor of commitment to a job or career. Your answer should convey a sense of stability and maturity. If you're a recent graduate, you should also anticipate follow-up questions like "What was your grade point average?" and "How did you finance your education?"

Q: What are your future career plans as a flight attendant?

A: *My goal is eventually to work in management, but I understand that I'll need to spend some time first working my way up the ranks.*

To answer this question appropriately, you must know what's important to you and how to express it in a concise way. Having clearly defined career goals is a strong indication of initiative as well as dedication to flight attending as a career. If you think you may want to make a career of flying, that's okay, too. Remember—wanting to be the best in your job is a commendable quality.

Q: Have you ever had a problem dealing with a fellow employee or boss?

A: *I'd say that I'm pretty easygoing and can get along with most people—and I think my previous employers would attest to that. However, in my last position there was one coworker I found difficult to work with. He'd often arrive late*

First-time Job Seekers: Be forewarned: the hiring process for flight attendants is rigorous. In addition to a resume and cover letter, you'll need to complete a flight attendant application form long before you get to the interview stage. If your application passes muster, you'll undergo a series of three different types of interviews: a group interview/personnel briefing during which you'll be given a series of language, aptitude, personality, and physical tests to determine if you meet the basic criteria of the airline company; a screening/initial-impact interview, which will be a one-on-one session designed to explore your character and personality in relation to the flight-attendant position; and a personal interview conducted by a panel of three or more interviewers, designed to determine how you react under stress.

and leave early and was constantly behind in his work. Because of this the rest of our group had to work that much harder to make up for lost time. Besides that, this particular individual tended to be belligerent, making him very difficult to work with as part of our team. I tried to steer clear of him when I could, and tried to be patient when I had to interact with him concerning various work-related issues. Eventually, the company recognized the problem and let this person go.

Your answer should portray how well you've worked with others in previous situations. You should never denigrate or blame your current, or a former, employer. Instead, accentuate the positive. The interviewer is trying to find out if the candidate has been prone to conflicts with, or resentments toward, the people he or she has worked for in the past. The same holds true for relations with fellow employees in past jobs. If you think you may get an unfavorable reference from a previous employer, be sure to explain the situation as dispassionately as possible. Other, similar questions you might encounter include "What do you think of the people you work with?" and "Why did you leave your last job?"

Q: **Tell me about a time when you had to deal with an irate customer or fellow employee. How did you handle the situation?**

A: *My customer service position at the telephone company involved dealing occasionally with irate customers. When that happened, I'd try to talk in a calm, even voice, in order to get the person to respond in a businesslike manner and focus on trying to resolve the situation. Most times I was able to rectify the problem and pacify the customer, but I remember one incident in particular in which the caller became verbally abusive. I tried to remain calm and professional, and not to let my personal feelings enter into the situation. I didn't respond to the abuse, I just made a note of it and continued to help the customer as best I could. When the abuse persisted, however, I politely asked him to call back and ask for my manager, because at that point I knew I couldn't resolve the problem.*

Career Changers: You'll need to consider carefully whether or not flight attending is the right career for you and if you're right for it. Aside from travel advantages and other benefits, there are numerous potentially negative factors to consider, including irregularity of work schedule, strictness of dress codes and work rules, and the base system, which may well mean that you'll have to move to another city in order to accept employment. If, after careful consideration, you decide to forge ahead, you'll also need to convince the interviewer of your interest in and dedication to a career in this field.

How you react when others lose their temper or become upset is very important in a flight-attendant position. The interviewer will be looking for evidence of your aptitude for work that involves a great deal of contact with the public. Give an example of a time when you were faced with a difficult person and how you handled it. Your answer should illustrate your maturity, diplomacy, and awareness of the needs and feelings of others.

Q: How many days were you absent from work last year? Why?

A: *I was absent four days last year, three because I came down with the flu, and one due to the death of a family member.*

A history of absenteeism or tardiness, or any indication of a weak work ethic or poor performance standards, will disqualify you from most airlines. Convince the interviewer of your willingness to take responsibility at work, your punctuality, dependability, and solid attendance record. If you think you may get poor references because of attendance or undependability, you'd better be well prepared to give a detailed and exonerating explanation. A similar question you may be asked is "Are you punctual?"

Q: What are your leisure-time activities or hobbies?

A: *I'm an active person who enjoys many different outdoor activities. In the summer I like to swim, bike, and go camping. In the winter I enjoy cross-country skiing.*

Flight attending is an active profession that requires a great deal of vitality. You'll need to convince the interviewer that you have the energy needed to become a flight attendant. Discuss your hobbies and leisure time activities, especially those that help keep you in good physical condition. If you're a

Experienced Professionals: If you have experience working as a flight attendant, it's probably safe to assume that you'll meet most airlines' broad requirements. Your best strategy, then, is to find some way to distinguish yourself from the competition. A great way to do this is to learn a good deal about the airline before your first interview. Usually, information about the company, together with a job description, is sent to you along with the application form. Read this information! Consult your local library to complete your preinterview education on a particular airline. Take a field trip to the airport and talk to some of the airline's employees. They'll share the good and the bad with you and tell you exactly what you need to know about the job itself. The knowledge that you gain in these ways will give you an edge over other candidates vying for the position. Potential employers are always pleased when you know a good deal about the company—and are always displeased when you know little or nothing.

recent graduate, any extracurricular activities you may have participated in will be relevant.

Q: Would you mind moving?

A: *Not at all. I moved here a year ago for a job and have no family or other significant connections to this area. Also, I don't own a home, so I'm pretty mobile.*

Expect this question if you have no prior experience in flight attending. Because this position requires at least some initial sacrifices, the interviewer will be curious about your ability to be flexible. The job will probably require you to move away from home, family, and friends. Give examples of your ability to make concessions—for example, you might describe how well you've adjusted to living away from home in the past. If you've never lived away from home, you should describe how you've demonstrated flexibility in other areas—for example, by coping with a difficult work schedule or conforming with a company's rules and policies.

Q: When would you be able to start training?

A: *I'd have to give my current employer two weeks' notice, but I'd be available immediately thereafter.*

Uncertainty about when you can start training can hurt your candidacy, so make sure your answer is specific and firm. Don't hesitate to say that you must give your present employer a two-week notice. The airline will expect the same courtesy from you someday and will respect the consideration you're showing those who currently write your paycheck. If, on the other hand, you're available immediately, this could give the airline an opportunity to hire you sooner. A word of caution: an offer of training usually is valid for three to six months, depending on the carrier's policy. If you're unavailable until some time afterward, you most likely will have to begin the hiring process all over. If you have an availability problem, consider waiting until it's

Candidates Re-entering the Workforce: Because flight attending is a demanding career that requires a great deal of flexibility on your part, you'll need to overcome the interviewer's concerns about why you left the field and why you feel ready to return. Emphasize your independence, flexibility, and ability to adapt to change in lifestyle. If, for example, you left the workforce to care for your family, explain how you plan to accommodate the demands that a flight-attending career will place upon you and your family. Your response should indicate that you've carefully considered these issues and that you've come up with workable solutions to the problems you may encounter.

cleared up before you begin the interview process. In any event, check with the airline beforehand to make sure you're not spinning your wheels.

Q: Why should I hire you?

A: *My five years' experience working in the customer service department of the telephone company, as well as my years of experience as a restaurant server, gives me an excellent background in customer service and dealing with the public. And since Ace Airlines places such strong emphasis on providing superb customer service, I think that makes us an excellent match. I'm responsible, loyal, and eager to learn. I would take pride in representing this company if you should hire me.*

Although this question can seem a bit daunting, it's really a wonderful opportunity for you to reiterate the skills, experience, goals, and personal qualities that set you apart from other candidates. Take some time prior to your interview to examine your strengths, weaknesses, what you have to offer, and why you'll be a valued employee. Then practice expressing your thoughts in a concise statement: "I want to . . . for your company as a flight attendant. And I've acquired the skills, abilities, and experiences that will be of value in this line of work." Then list examples of each. Keep in mind that your answer should place more emphasis on what you can do for the company than on what the company can do for you. And, as with any good sales presentation, always finish with a strong close.

Hospitality Manager

Q: What are your primary responsibilities in your current hospitality job?

A: *I handle our guest-satisfaction tracking system. It's a $300,000 customer-satisfaction tracking system in which we talk to 300 customers every month at every one of our sixteen resort and spa locations. It enables the company to edit and improve our service continually.*

The recruiter will want to determine the magnitude of the responsibility that you've held. Talk about your current work experience in the most impressive terms possible, without becoming untruthful. This candidate gives a quality answer because he or she explains what the job is as well as its importance.

Q: Why did you want to go into the hospitality industry?

A: *I wanted to do something that was interesting and different. I had an opportunity to work with a telecommunications company, but I couldn't see myself getting up every morning and talking about bits and bytes and modems. But I could see myself getting up every morning and talking to people about something they do with their free time, something they get really excited about. People love to gamble and vacation, and I love to help them have fun.*

The hospitality industry requires long hours and can be quite stressful. The recruiter will be looking for candidates who display a true love for the industry. This candidate demonstrates that he or she has a natural propensity for the profession.

Q: Tell me about how you manage the many conflicting demands on your time.

A: *In my last job there wasn't a time when I didn't have ten projects going at once. I was in charge of the front desk, the restaurant, and the housekeeping staff for our biggest hotel, as well as serving on the corporate-wide team for developing new products. Additionally, I oversaw our company's college-intern program. I keep a tight schedule, carefully prioritizing, and I was able to achieve good results in all of these functions.*

Working in the hospitality industry means that you'll always be juggling many different projects at once. Prove that you can handle this. The recruiter wants to hear that you're experienced and adept at prioritizing. The recruiter doesn't want to hire someone who can't handle the stress of dealing with several things at once.

Q: Everyone talks about managing people and managing the people that work for you, but nobody ever bothers to talk about managing the people who manage you. Do you have the ability to "manage up" within an organization?

A: *I work directly for three bosses, and they all want all of my time. And, of course, the customers invariably think they're my boss! So it's really up to me to make sure that all of their needs are met, without letting anybody down.*

In the hospitality industry, in addition to having too many projects on the go, you'll also probably have several bosses who expect you to devote your full time and attention to each one of them. Of course this is an impossibility, so you must know how to handle it. Prove that you've been in similar situations before and that you know just how to deal with these conflicting demands on your time.

Q: Speaking of customers, tell me about a time in which you've had to deal with a difficult client or situation.

A: *I've had to give a lot of bad news in my previous job as a casino client-service manager, and I've dealt with many difficult clients. I learned that you've got to be straightforward, and you've got to be honest. You can't sugarcoat the answer so that they miss the point, but you've got to phrase it or position it in a way that makes sense to them, and so that it's believable. One time I had to explain to a board member why his daughter, who was earning an M.B.A., didn't get hired for an intern position. Although she was working toward a higher degree and had excellent grades, she just didn't have the "people skills" that were necessary for the position. She wasn't the most qualified person, and I simply had to tell him that.*

The ability to deal with difficult people often comes from experience. No amount of preparation or education can help you here, but you'll want to prove to the recruiter that you're more than capable in this area. In hospitality the customer is everything, so it will be extremely important that you can handle all customer interactions, particularly difficult ones, with grace and ease.

Q: Do you have any market-research experience?

A: *I majored in marketing in business school, and I specifically concentrated on service quality marketing classes. In my second year a professor hired me to research all the case examples for a book he was writing on total quality management.*

You should be able to give some example of work that you've done in market research. This work doesn't necessarily have to be in a job; class work is fine to talk about. Or perhaps you've done some market research while volunteering in your community, so you could talk about that as well.

Q: How do you think high technology will affect the hospitality industry?

A: *We're breaking into a new business in our casino division, which is called in-flight gaming. On long-haul or international flights many of the major airlines have added seat-back displays with a multichannel system, where you can choose to listen to music, watch a movie, or shop. We're going one step further and adding a channel that allows you to gamble in-flight. You can play casino games and actually bid on them.*

High technology is affecting virtually every industry, and hospitality is no exception. This candidate gives an excellent example of technology's influence on his or her company. Read current business journals so you can answer this question in general terms.

Q: What are your qualifications for an advanced career move in the hospitality industry?

A: *I've a B.S. in Psychology from UCLA, as well as an M.B.A. from Vanderbilt University. I've also worked four years with my current company. I spent two years in the casino division, and I'm finishing my second year in the spa-and-resort division.*

Having an advanced degree like an M.B.A. is very helpful for managing in the hospitality industry. Other options are an M.P.S. (master of professional studies) or M.S. (master of science) from a hotel and restaurant management school. The recruiter will also be looking for solid industry work experience.

Q: What's been your greatest challenge in the hospitality industry?

A: *My greatest challenge has been handling the market research for all of our new properties. We've grown from five casinos to sixteen in a three-year period. We expect to continue that growth throughout the decade. By the end of the decade we plan to have thirty casinos. My challenge has been to see my client base expand dramatically and to still win these people over. We're really an internal-service provider. I have to sell my services to the marketing team at*

First-time Job Seekers: Be flexible in your job search. You probably won't get the exact job, rank, and amount of money that you want in the beginning. Working in hospitality often involves paying your dues, and you should be willing to do this. Get your foot in the door and work your way up diligently. Be sure to step back every few years or so to make sure you're on the right path. Have an industry mentor, and if possible, conduct an informational interview with this person. Have people that you can touch base with every once in a while to make sure your career is on the right track.

each of our properties. And each property is staffed just as you'd see at a large corporation, with a finance group, a marketing group, and so on. Everything has to happen at the property level because we have different competitors within each market and different customer bases.

Talk about a particularly challenging experience by giving a specific example. The recruiter will be interested in your problem-solving ability. The candidate gives a quality answer here because he or she discusses the issue, as well as how it was handled.

Q: **Five years from now what do you expect to be doing in this business?**

A: *My five-year goal is to move into operations and become a vice president, then eventually a general manager of a casino.*

In an industry that heavily stresses paying your dues and climbing up the proverbial ladder, giving specific job titles is acceptable. With this question the recruiter is ascertaining the candidate's determination and motivation. This candidate is obviously interested in hospitality for a career, which would impress the recruiter.

Q: **What specific personal skills have you developed over your last several jobs, and what experiences helped you build these skills?**

A: *The skill that's helped me the most is the ability to act as a consultant internally. My job sometimes involves going out to clients in the field and giving them news that they don't want to hear. And they immediately have to be suspect of my purpose, because I don't work every day in their market. I've spent the last three years learning how to tie pieces of information together to help build the client's trust in the best plan. I've found that in conferences, if I approach the issue of where the company's headed and what the situation is with the competition—which is what everyone is truly concerned about—I'm a lot more effective than if I try to sell myself. It's a matter of understanding my client's mind set and the issues that are truly going to impact them in the near future.*

Career Changers: The hospitality industry is a tough one to break into beyond the entry level because there's so much emphasis on "paying your dues"—that is, working in all areas of the business. It's not impossible to break in, however. You need to demonstrate clearly a solid reason for wanting to do so. Show skill development (for example, working with large numbers of semiskilled workers) in a related field and offer something special—knowledge of new technologies that will impact the hospitality industry—that's hard to duplicate within the industry.

The recruiter will be interested in the specific skills you can bring to the company. The candidate's answer here is excellent because he or she discusses one of the most important attributes in the hospitality business—excellent customer-interaction skills. The answer also demonstrates that the candidate has the ability to grow, learn, and innovate. This is critical in the hospitality industry as it undergoes much change.

Q: **If you had extra time to devote to some work project, what would that project be?**

A: *I'd develop internal company seminars to hone our employees' abilities to serve our customers. We spend a lot of time and money on a guest-satisfaction tracking system, but I don't think we incorporate the results as fully as we might. I'm trying to free up some time from my current responsibilities to do just that.*

The recruiter will be interested in where your job focus lies. The candidate's answer is excellent because he or she focuses on the customer, and on how the company can continually improve customer service. Demonstrate to the recruiter that you're concerned about and aware of the company and its operations as a whole, rather than just your assigned responsibilities.

Q: **Do you have any weaknesses that I should be aware of?**

A: *I'd have to say that earlier in my career I was often too quick to jump to conclusions. I'd hit the boards running sometimes before actually sitting back and thinking about the five or six ways to handle a problem. I'd see one way and run with it. I realized this when I went to business school and starting working on teams. I learned that getting input from several other people really had an impact on the quality of the end decision. So what I do now is discuss really big decisions with three or four trusted associates, trying to get others' perspectives on the conclusions I'm drawing and the solutions I'm considering.*

Prove to the recruiter that your professional weakness won't be a detriment to the company. This candidate's answer is very good because he or she clearly articulates both the recognition of a weakness and an effective solution to it. No one's perfect, so have a ready answer for this question and turn a negative into a positive.

Q: **What future opportunities do you see for the hospitality industry?**

A: *There are incredible opportunities. It's a cyclical business, and public opinion continually changes. But I believe that people will always need to relax and escape. So it's up to us to be even more creative so that customers choose our resorts, restaurants, and casinos over the competition's.*

The recruiter is looking for a candidate who has a good sense of industry dynamics as well as of the big picture. This candidate proves that he or she has a positive "go get 'em" attitude, which is especially needed in today's competitive times. Read the *Wall Street Journal* as well as the hospitality-industry publications to prepare for this question.

Q: **Do you think TQM, or total quality management, is a relevant issue in hospitality?**

A: *I think it absolutely is. There's always a lot of talk in the hospitality industry about customer service, but I believe that hospitality leaders should think about how and why they incorporate different customer service strategies into their company policies. Often customer services are wasted or unappreciated by clients because they're targeted at the wrong area. There's an excellent book on this topic that I've found extremely helpful—Return on Quality by a group of university professors. It demonstrates how to make quality work for you and the customer. For example, I used the techniques in the book to help me decide on a staffing pattern for our cash window office. I was able to cut down the cost of staffing and improve service to our clients.*

The recruiter is looking for a candidate who understands the finer nuances of hospitality issues. This candidate gives a good answer because it ties in the major issues of quality and customer satisfaction to the specifics of the industry and to a particular issue for the company. The answer demonstrates that the candidate initiates positive action after careful investigation. And, of course, the payoff is in the improved program that saves money and improves customer service.

Q: **Have you had to supervise people? How many? When?**

A: *Currently I manage a small group of ten professionals, all with degrees and half with M.B.A.s. One has a Ph.D. This is a small but creative, demanding group. We work cooperatively and well, but I'm the leader as well as the manager. Our work output is ranked among the top in the company. Earlier, in a previous position, I supervised nearly 100 hourly people in a hotel. It was quite a different management situation.*

Experienced Professionals: Hospitality-industry executives at the senior level are often experienced professionals who are reasonably familiar with others in the industry. Networking is a key part of your job-search strategy, and you'll want to ensure that you have several big name contacts who'll allow you to use their names in a search, and especially in an interview. If you don't attend one of the "clubs" (Cornell University Hotel School, for example), be prepared to demonstrate your successful track record with hard facts (for example, increasing occupancy rates by 35 percent).

Midlevel jobs in the hospitality industry often mean managing everyone from highly trained, educated, and skilled professionals to hourly workers with few job skills. You need to be flexible and to adopt different management styles for different situations. Although you're interviewing for a particular job now, the recruiter is interested in your ability to handle different management situations in the future.

Q: **Obviously, working with a large group of semiskilled, entry-level employees is difficult. How did you handle it?**

A: *I have a well-defined management philosophy and style. And it's pretty simple. We had a set of goals, and everyone on the team knew what their responsibilities were. We dealt with any confusion about them at the outset. Also, we had a set of rules and worked within them. However, with such a large group problems did come up—like baby-sitters, sick time, and other things. So everyone was flexible within reason. I was willing to give people a chance and believed in them and their integrity until they gave me a reason to doubt. When there was a problem, the employee knew about it quickly. I wanted no surprises from them, and they got none from me. It was a very successful way to manage.*

This is a well-thought-out answer. In the hospitality industry middle managers have huge responsibilities and often less than adequate staff, or staff that aren't well trained. The response indicates three things: a focus on results, flexibility to ensure good working relationships with staff, and success with the management style.

Q: **Gambling is somewhat controversial. Do you have any ethical problems with it?**

A: *I've no religious or ethical dilemmas with gambling, personally. But I understand the legitimate concern some people have. I think they have a right to express their concerns, but we simply follow the law—and we're very careful about following both the letter and the spirit of the law. We also look out for people who are obviously in over their heads and try to lead them into more productive areas. This philosophy of mine extends to other areas as well.*

Here the recruiter is probing much deeper than the ethics of a single issue. The answer is good because it deals specifically with the question but presents

Candidates Re-entering the Workforce: It's certainly possible to return to the hospitality industry after an extended absence. However, you may have to take a job at a slightly lower ranking than when you left. You probably won't be able to return at a higher level. With persistence and time, however, you should be able to continue building your career. Start your job search by networking to reacquaint yourself with old contacts.

a more general framework about ethical issues. It's important that you both demonstrate an understanding of the issues and have a positive philosophical perspective when handling other issues.

Q: **Do you have any questions for me?**

A: *Yes, as a matter of fact. What attracted me to your company was its recent moves internationally. I'm quite interested in that, actually, but I'm curious as to why you picked Asia as your first area for expansion.*

This answer is preferable to asking about salary, company benefits, and so on. Although these are legitimate areas of interest, and the recruiter will expect you to ask them eventually, you should first establish your deep interest in, and knowledge of, the industry and the company. Once you've sold the recruiter on your suitability for the position, you can then move to questions about compensation and benefits.

Hotel Manager

Q: **Why do you think some people prefer to stay at smaller hotels?**

A: *It's a matter of personal taste. Different people look for different qualities in a hotel. Basically, guests look for a hotel that meets their particular needs. One person might want to stay downtown, as close to the action as possible, whereas someone else might want a more peaceful atmosphere and stay in a small hotel on the outskirts of the city. Although smaller hotels might not offer such services as gyms and room service, they do have individuality and personality.*

Show the interviewer that you understand the appeal of small hotels. Large chain hotels may offer competitive rates and a wider range of services, but small hotels offer atmosphere, personality, and image. Your answer will also tell the interviewer if your personality is compatible with the hotel's image. For example, if you project a corporate and business-oriented persona, but the hotel you're interviewing with is quaint and homey, the interviewer may conclude that you won't be a good choice to run the hotel.

Q: **Tell me about your strengths and how they relate to this position.**

A: *All of my professional experience has been working exclusively with the public, so I truly understand the importance of customer service. I have experience dealing with people both face-to-face and over the telephone. As an inside sales representative in a busy office, and then as manager of a ten-room hotel in San Francisco, I've always taken initiative and been proactive in my approach to my position. Whether working independently or supervising others, I've always managed to improve sales for the companies that have hired me.*

Here the interviewer is looking for someone who understands the nature of the position, particularly the importance of dealing with people. Your customers are your guests, and it's essential that you understand the importance of that idea. Like this candidate, you should emphasize your experience working with people. The interviewer is also looking for someone who's detail oriented and who can motivate the staff to make sure that the hotel runs smoothly.

Q: **Business has been good, but your clientele isn't what you'd like it to be. You're trying to create an image of a romantic hotel for couples, but most of your bookings have been for student tours. What would you do to change your customer base?**

A: *I'd try to find out what it is about the hotel that's appealing to students and not to couples. Is it the location of the hotel, the rates, or the style of the rooms? I'd find out how the students are learning about the hotel—maybe I need to change where we advertise. Or it might be that our rates are too low and we have a reputation as a budget hotel. If that's the case, we could appeal to a more upscale crowd simply by raising our rates.*

The interviewer is trying to determine the candidate's understanding of marketing and advertising and is looking for a creative approach to selling the hotel. It's easy for a hotel manager simply to sit back and say "Well, we're making money, so what's the difference?" But it will be your responsibility to help create an image for the hotel. The interviewer will want to see that you understand why a hotel appeals to one group but not to another. Discuss what changes you'd make, based upon what your target group typically looks for. If you understand your customer base, you'll be able to help reach the long-term goals of the hotel.

Q: **No-shows are costing your business. How would you reduce no-shows without risking overbooking?**

A: *First, I'd review our reservations system to determine if it's appropriate for the hotel, and, if needed, I'd modify the reservation policies to ensure that there'll be fewer no-shows. I'd also make certain that everyone on the staff is clear on our cancellation and no-show policies and is conveying this information to guests.*

This question addresses the candidate's problem-solving abilities. If you're asked a similar question, demonstrate your ability to devise effective solutions to potential problems. A hotel manager must be able to make changes as growth of the business warrants. It's important to show that you'll take initiative, and that you'll adapt and enforce policies that will make the business more successful.

First-time Job Seekers: Most large corporate hotels prefer candidates with a college degree in hotel management, or a college degree and some experience working in a hotel. In large hotels, these candidates would start as assistant managers or management trainees. Small hotels don't have strict educational requirements—these employers look more for personality and solid interpersonal skills. Discuss any relevant experience you have—working at a reservations desk during school breaks, for instance, or in a customer service department. Knowledge of computer-reservations systems is also helpful, as is experience with accounting or bookkeeping.

Q: What if a few of your employees didn't have the background and experience to recommend good restaurants or other activities for guests? How would you try to improve their skills?

A: *I believe it's important for all employees to be on equal footing, so that all of our guests receive the same level of service. Naturally, I can't send my entire staff to every restaurant in town to get firsthand experience, so I'd put together a file that would be accessible to all employees. I'd include reviews from newspapers or magazines, along with recommendations from other guests. I might also ask local restaurants for copies of menus to have on hand for guests, or call the local chamber of commerce to see if it had any tourism materials available. Once I'd gathered all the information, I'd ensure that all employees were familiar with the file, and that they kept up-to-date as new information was added.*

You'll often face this problem in a small hotel, because employees don't have the formal training they'd have in a large chain hotel. Personalized service, such as recommending area restaurants, helps enhance a hotel's image, which is why guests come back to small hotels. The interviewer is also trying to determine the candidate's skills in relation to managing and developing staff.

Q: A new employee is great in some aspects of the job, but not in all. How would you get this person to excel in all aspects of the job?

A: *Employees in small hotels have more responsibilities than employees in large hotels. Whereas large hotels have separate departments for sales, reception, and registration, in smaller hotels employees are expected to work in all three of these areas. So I couldn't allow an employee who excels in sales, for example, to perform only that function. First, I'd try to pinpoint the employee's strengths and weaknesses. I might spend the day with the employee to see exactly where he was having trouble. Then I'd talk to him and discuss ways we could improve on his weaknesses, offering suggestions on how to enhance his skills. If employees have the right attitude, they can work through their problems and be successful.*

Career Changers: Discuss your experience in other service fields. Managing a restaurant, for instance, requires many of the same skills—flexibility, creativity, resourcefulness, and organization—that interviewers look for in a hotel manager. Customer service experience is also a definite plus. Large hotels generally have more requirements than do small hotels, so if you don't have hotel experience, it's easier to start your career in a smaller establishment. Interviewers for small, independent hotels look for excellent interpersonal skills before they look for formal experience in hotel management.

This is another question that enables the interviewer to determine how well the candidate manages staff. Small hotels don't have separate departments, and all employees are expected to handle all basic duties. The candidate shouldn't suggest that one person work in only one area, as this approach might create problems with other employees. Like this candidate, you'll want to show the interviewer how you'd work with the employee and encourage his or her professional development.

Q: **How would you handle a situation in which the guest was upset about everything—room, decor, location—and angrily demanded that the manager rectify the situation?**

A: *I'd hear the guest out, listening to all complaints to determine what the real nature of the concern was. I've found that guests are usually upset about only one thing, and will simply build on that complaint until they're upset about everything. I'd try to accommodate the guest in any way I could—obviously, I can't change something like the location of the hotel, but maybe I could put the guest in a different room with a better view. But if I couldn't find a way to pacify the guest, I'd offer to find a different hotel that could.*

Demonstrate your ability to defuse a potentially volatile situation and to work with difficult customers. The interviewer will be looking for someone who's skillful at reading people and has excellent interpersonal skills. Guest relations are extremely important for any hotel, especially a small one, and the interviewer needs to know that you'll act appropriately toward all guests, even difficult ones. Because they set the tone for the other employees, most small-hotel managers are hired for their personality as well as for their skills.

Experienced Professionals: If you have experience as a hotel manager in a large, or chain hotel, don't expect to have the same duties in a small hotel. Although, in general, the two positions are similar, the manager of a small hotel is expected to have a more hands-on role in the day-to-day running of the hotel. The jobs in a large hotel are well defined—there might be separate front-desk and housekeeping managers, for instance—whereas in a small hotel the hotel manager handles all aspects of hotel operations. Regardless of your background, however, the interviewer will expect you to demonstrate good people skills, resourcefulness, and versatility. If you're switching from a small hotel to a corporate one, you'll probably be interviewing for a position as an assistant or department manager. Then, once you're more familiar with the corporate structure of the hotel, you may be in line for the position of general manager.

Q: **A guest you can't stand comes into the hotel. He hasn't done anything wrong; he just rubs you the wrong way. What would you do?**

A: *Well, I pride myself on my professionalism and make a point of treating all guests with the same excellent service. If I find a guest simply irritating, I might try to minimize my contact with him. I'd be courteous, but I might avoid engaging him in small talk, or I might ask another employee to take care of the guest's check-in or checkout.*

Much of the selling of the hotel begins when guests check in. You must ensure that the hotel lives up to its guests' expectations as much as possible. Let the interviewer know that your personal feelings won't color your professional attitude, that you're polite and courteous to all guests, even those you personally dislike. As hotel manager, you have a responsibility to make all guests feel at ease.

Q: **One afternoon a guest comes back from lunch intoxicated and acts loud and obnoxious as another guest—who appears to be offended—checks in. What do you do?**

A: *I'd apologize to the guest checking in and explain that what's happening in the lobby isn't a normal occurrence. It's important for the guest to understand this, because image is so important for a small hotel. I'd then ask another employee to check in the guest while I took care of the person who was intoxicated. I'd also make sure that the two guests were staying in rooms far apart from each other.*

Tact and diplomacy are a big part of a hotel manager's job. In this situation the intoxicated guest isn't really doing anything wrong, but he may make the other guest feel uncomfortable. Like this candidate, you should describe how you'd make both guests feel comfortable without embarrassing anyone. Answering this question quickly and satisfactorily will also show the interviewer that you have the ability to think and react quickly in difficult or awkward situations.

Q: **A boisterous group checks into half the rooms of the hotel. They're not rude, but they're very loud and are disturbing the other guests. What would you do?**

A: *First, I'd find out if the group had a leader. If it did, I'd talk to that person, making sure he or she understood that the group's behavior wasn't tolerable. Then if their behavior didn't improve, I'd ask them to leave immediately. If there isn't a group leader, it's more difficult to talk to every member of the group, so I might try to separate the group, assigning it to its own wing of the hotel, if possible.*

The hotel manager sets the tone for the hotel. Show the interviewer that you have good judgment and the ability to act with authority and to maintain control in difficult situations. Give examples of how you've had to take tough positions with guests in the past in order to preserve the best interests of the hotel.

Q: **You're working alone. Two guests are waiting to check in, calls are coming in for reservations, and the lights suddenly go out in the rear of the hotel. How do you resolve the three situations?**

A: *First, I'd take the calls, quickly explain the problem, then offer to take the callers' numbers and get back to them. Then I'd explain to the guests waiting to check in that I had an electrical problem and that I'd be right with them, maybe giving them registration forms to fill out in the meantime. Then I'd attend to the electrical problem; if I couldn't solve it, I'd call the electrician or the electric company. I'd return to the guests, thank them for their understanding, and get them checked in. Finally, I'd call back those people who had called earlier.*

Demonstrate your ability to think clearly and remain levelheaded in times of stress. The interviewer will want to know you have the ability to prioritize and juggle tasks. Most important, show you understand that in a small hotel you're selling personality and atmosphere, and that guests patronize your hotel because of the attention they receive there. A hotel manager must make guest satisfaction the highest priority.

Q: **You have only one housekeeper. She comes down with the flu and will be out for a week. How do you ensure that your rooms stay clean?**

A: *For this one week the hotel would have to get by with bare-minimum cleaning. I'd have a staff meeting and tell the employees that I expected everyone to pitch in while the housekeeper was gone. If an employee had Tuesdays off, for instance, I'd ask him or her to come in and help clean that day. If necessary, I'd pick up a cleaning brush and clean the rooms myself.*

Candidates Re-entering the Workforce: If you've been out of work for a long time, it's fairly difficult to make a direct transition back into hotel management. Especially if you want to work for a large chain hotel, you'll need to start at a lower level, such as working at the reservations desk. Though most of your skills, such as your creativity and your ability to relate to others, should still be fresh, you may need to take a continuing-education class or two to update your computer skills. You may also need some time to adapt once again to the frenetic pace of a hotel.

Resourcefulness is a major aspect of hotel management. A hotel must run twenty-four hours a day, seven days a week, without interruption. Show that you'll take the responsibility of ensuring that necessary work is completed, even if it means doing the work yourself.

Q: **Give me an example of a time when your actions helped change a customer's attitude.**

A: *A couple had found a coupon in a magazine for a tour with a company I'd never heard of. They booked the tour, but the tour bus never showed up. They were very upset and were starting to believe that one thing after another was going wrong and they were going to have a terrible vacation. So I called the tour company that our hotel uses and asked them if they'd please take these people on the next tour at the same, lower, price that the other company was offering. The company agreed, and the guests took their tour. They were so happy that throughout their stay they kept coming into my office to tell me what a wonderful time they were having.*

If a customer was unhappy, how would you go out of your way to change that? Show that you're willing to be flexible to meet the needs of guests. A good hotel manager is always bending over backward to help guests, and passes this attitude down to the other employees. This candidate also mentions another important point: a hotel manager should maintain a network of contacts that can potentially contribute to a hotel's success. Large chain hotels might have their own resources, but in a small hotel the manager has to be able to anticipate the guests' needs to make sure that the services they want are easily available.

Restaurant Manager

Q: **Name the top three states you'd like to live in.**

A: *I'm pretty flexible, but if I had to choose, I'd like to live in the Virginia/Washington, D.C./Delaware area because I have family in that region.*

You may encounter this question if you're applying to a restaurant chain, particularly a national one. Your answer will give the interviewer an idea of where you want to be geographically, and of how mobile you are. If you name a region in which the company has openings, you may have a greater chance of getting the job, as well as better opportunities to advance.

Q: **Did you participate in any extracurricular activities when you were in school?**

A: *Yes, I was a member of the intramural soccer club and a catcher on the school softball team.*

The interviewer wants to hear that the candidate participated in extracurricular activities, which indicates initiative. If you participated in team sports, be sure to mention it. Some employers place strong emphasis on teamwork, and knowing what it's like to be a member of a team will work to your advantage.

Q: **Why do you want to leave your current position?**

A: *Well, I've been working at this particular restaurant for over five years. It's been a very positive experience for me, but I no longer feel challenged. I'm particularly interested in this position because it offers an increase in responsibilities, which I find exciting.*

Although you should be up front and state your true reasons for wanting to leave, you should never bad-mouth previous employers or colleagues. Even if you're entirely justified in your point of view, making negative statements will reflect poorly on you and put an unfavorable tone on the entire interview. Your answer should be honest, but diplomatic.

Q: **What was your base income at your last job?**

A: *I made $35,000 annually.*

Base salary means no bonuses and no benefits. The interviewer will want to know what value your previous employer placed on your work and your level of experience. And if you make it to the job-offer stage, your answer to this question will give the company an idea of the ballpark salary you'd require. Don't exaggerate or misrepresent your salary, because the employer may verify the information before offering you a position. Any false or misleading statement you make in a job interview, if discovered, will cost you a potential job offer or may lead to immediate dismissal after you're hired.

Q: **What was the sales volume, food cost, labor cost, and ticket average for the last restaurant you managed?**

A: *The restaurant was doing $2 million, with food cost of 32 percent, and labor cost of 16 percent. The ticket average was $17 to $18.*

The interviewer is trying to probe the depth of the candidate's experience. Having a working knowledge of the numbers that restaurant managers must work with indicates solid knowledge of the restaurant business. "Sales volume" indicates the number of customers a restaurant services during any given period; "food cost" refers to the percentage of sales that the food costs; "labor costs" refers to how much a restaurant pays its employees; and "ticket averages" indicates the average amount a customer spends on a single meal.

Q: **What would your employees say about you if I asked them?**

A: *I think they'd say I have an upbeat, positive attitude and that I'm a hands-on manager—meaning I'm willing to jump in and help bus tables, seat customers, or help out in the kitchen when necessary. I work well with people, and most employees feel comfortable coming to me to discuss problems. At the same time, I think they'd tell you that I'm a demanding boss—but that I'm always fair.*

The interviewer wants to know more about the candidate's management style. Are you more like a dictator or a team player? Try to portray yourself as having an upbeat attitude, taking initiative, and leaning toward a teamwork management style with the ability to make firm, difficult decisions when

First-time Job Seekers: Although some larger restaurant corporations recruit managers straight out of school, most require actual hands-on experience in the restaurant business. Some national chain restaurants offer internships on a limited basis. Barring that, your best bet is to prove yourself by working in a restaurant, perhaps as a server or cook, then being promoted from within.

If you're applying to a large restaurant chain at management level, you'll most likely be hired from a central, national office. You may be asked to take a personality profile and a values test before your job interview, and subjected to a criminal, credit, and employment-history check before receiving a job offer.

appropriate. Confidence is another important trait to display. As one executive in a leading international restaurant chain told us, "People who feel good about themselves produce good results."

Q: Have you worked with profit-and-loss statements?

A: *Yes, I regularly work with P-and-L's in my current position as restaurant manager. I think this experience has given me a good sense of how every expenditure and every sale affects the bottom line, which in turn has helped me to make better decisions in running the restaurant.*

Restaurant managers, even in chain restaurants, have a great deal of control over the ultimate success of that restaurant—and the bottom line—by controlling costs and creating a positive atmosphere in the restaurant itself. Because of this, employers look for solid management skills. Ideally, you should have experience working with figures on a weekly, monthly, and long-term basis.

Q: How have you controlled costs in your previous position?

A: *Well, I've found that one of the best ways to control costs is to control loss and waste. For example, I'm careful to control the loss of operating supplies, such as glassware. Glassware is heated when you wash it. If you don't let it cool off before you use it again, it'll likely break when you add ice and a cold beverage. So it's important to rotate the glasses and have enough in stock at all times so you don't have hot glasses going on the line.*

This is really a follow-up to the previous question. Give at least one detailed example of how you've negotiated lower prices, controlled loss, or minimized waste in your previous management positions. No example of cost control is too insignificant to mention. For example, though you may not have control over big-ticket items such as administrative fees, rent, amortization, and restaurant improvements, you probably have control over linen costs, in that you can make sure you don't create too much waste, and janitorial and cleaning expenses, in that you can see to it that these services aren't overused.

Q: What's your biggest weakness?

A: *I have a tendency to take on too many different jobs, and find that I must work hours way beyond the normal workday to deliver the highest-quality food and service that we possibly can. For example, if a line cook calls in sick for a particularly busy shift and I can't find a replacement, I don't hesitate to put aside my task at hand and spend the day cooking in order to deliver speedy service to customers.*

Whatever your answer to this question, be sure to give it a positive spin. The candidate's answer, for example, cites a weakness that most interviewers would consider attractive in a job candidate. Answers that might indicate problems serious enough to affect your job performance, especially problems that can't be corrected, may cost you the job offer.

Q: Tell me about the toughest termination you've ever had to make.

A: *That would be a situation in which I terminated a server. It was tough because the district manager told me to fire the person after getting some negative feedback from the head office. I told the district manager I didn't believe the feedback was representative of the person's work. And though I thought it wasn't just, I had no choice but to terminate the person.*

When answering this question, describe how you handled the situation and what the complications were. Keep in mind that your answer shouldn't breech the confidentiality of the company or of the individuals involved. The interviewer is trying to gauge the candidate's level of management experience and expertise. You'll need to convince the interviewer that you have the ability to make firm and difficult decisions when necessary.

Q: Describe the biggest mistake you've ever made, or the biggest regret you have.

A: *I'd have to say that my biggest mistake was leaving a previous job because of a lack of opportunity and taking a position that wasn't suited to me. It wasn't long before I knew I'd made the wrong decision and wished I hadn't left that other job.*

How bad was the mistake? Was it easily fixable? Is it a problem that's still ongoing? You should give here an example of a relatively minor mistake, focusing your discussion on how you promptly resolved the problem.

Q: What's the toughest feedback you've ever received, from either your supervisor, another manager, an employer, or a guest?

A: *I remember one particular guest who was disgruntled and didn't like the service or the food. I found it difficult to satisfy him, no matter what I tried. I felt bad about it because I can usually make amends to irate customers, but this customer never came back. After that experience I made some minor adjustments in our service as a result of the customer's feedback.*

Career Changers: Emphasize your interest in the industry. Companies want to hire the best people and retain them—they don't want to hire candidates who are just hopping from job to job. Get some restaurant experience and stay with that restaurant for a while to show that you're willing to make a commitment to a career in the industry.

The interviewer is looking for maturity in the candidate's answer. Show that you've learned to handle difficult situations from experience, and that you correct mistakes immediately so they aren't repeated.

Q: How would somebody best manage you?

A: *I'd say that I'm pretty flexible and can work with many different types of managers. My ideal manager, though, would be a teacher—someone who would give me both good and bad feedback so I can hone my skills. This person would have a positive impact when he or she came into the restaurant, building people up, patting them on the back, creating a positive team atmosphere.*

The interviewer wants to gain insight into how well the candidate would fit into the company and whether there would be potential personality conflicts. From this information the employer will also know how to best manage the candidate to avoid those conflicts in the event he or she is hired.

Q: If you were hiring servers for your restaurant, what characteristics would you look for?

A: *I look for outgoing, personable people with flexible schedules. Experience in the restaurant field is important, as is having a neat, clean appearance. I also look for people who seem as if they'd work well with the others in the restaurant.*

Describe here the basic characteristics of your ideal candidate. The interviewer will want to determine if you have good judgment in hiring and if you'd look for the same traits the company would look for in an employee.

Q: What characteristics are most important to you in evaluating performance?

A: *I look closely at the employee's attitude toward customers and staff members, productivity, the ability to work well without close supervision and to take initiative, going above and beyond the call of duty, and the willingness to help and teach others.*

The interviewer wants to know how the candidate would judge employees, and what aspects of their work he or she would expect to improve. Would the review process be a positive growth opportunity for all concerned, with manager and employee working together to create a better situation? Would the candidate encourage the worker, or use the opportunity to barrage the person with negative feedback? Your response here should indicate that you carefully examine the same performance issues that the company believes important.

Q: What are your recommendations for lowering employee turnover in restaurants?

A: *I like to use team meetings and incentives—things that get the crew excited— to keep a positive atmosphere where people want to come to work.*

The interviewer is looking for ideas to retain employees. Employee turnover is very expensive, and companies want to hire and retain the best people. Show that you can create a positive, fun atmosphere where the employees want to work.

Q: How would you develop teamwork within the restaurant?

A: *First, I think it's important to set a positive example for the staff by acting like a member of the team who's willing to go beyond the call of duty when necessary. I try to hire people who also have that "team spirit" and I foster that kind of atmosphere by regularly holding team meetings.*

This is a follow-up to the previous question. Describe how you've developed teamwork in your previous positions. Your answer should reflect experience and ability in this area, as well as mature management skills.

Q: Consider the following scenario: You approach a table and ask the couple sitting there is everything if satisfactory. The gentleman replies that his steak was not cooked properly but he ate it anyway. How would you handle the situation?

A: *I'd acknowledge the problem by introducing myself as the restaurant manager and restating the guest's concern. I'd apologize and take responsibility without making excuses. I'd then fix the problem and follow up with an appropriate action. For example, in this case, I wouldn't charge the customer for his dinner and I'd give him a gift certificate for his next visit. I think it's important not only to fix a problem but to exceed the customer's expectations in order to create "raving fans" who'll keep coming back and who'll generate tremendous word-of-mouth publicity.*

In the competitive restaurant business service can often make or break the best of companies. Of course, each company will have its own policies for handling situations like these. Before your interview you should visit the restaurant and try to determine its philosophy on issues like pricing, service,

Experienced Professionals: Shining stars in the industry have tremendous experience and valuable management skills. Many companies look for a good mixture of "hard" and "soft" qualities, so you should try to convey yourself as someone who can hold employees accountable yet can be compassionate as well. You should be professional, honest, and straightforward in your demeanor. Recruiting firms, networking referrals, and direct (or "cold") contact are the best method of job hunting for you.

convenience, atmosphere, and so on. Try to take these factors into consideration when formulating your answer. For example, this candidate's answer may be appropriate for a company that emphasizes service over price, but may not be appropriate for a fast-food company that gives low price and convenience first priority.

Q: **As a guest is leaving the restaurant, you ask her if everything was satisfactory. She replies that she was offended when her waitress sat down with her to take her order. You've given instructions to the servers that it's okay to sit down to take orders from guests when it seems appropriate. What would you do?**

A: *I'd listen to the guest, take ownership of the problem, apologize, and find some way to bring that customer back for another visit. As far as the employee goes, I'd counsel him or her about reading the guest properly—that is, about knowing when it's appropriate to sit down and when it isn't—in order to prevent the situation from reoccurring.*

Again, your answer to this question should be in keeping with the particular restaurant's philosophy. Regardless, you should always acknowledge the problem, apologize, and try to fix it. Restaurants don't want to hear that you'd tell the customer something like, "Well, our policy is that servers can sit down with guests," which really tells the customer that her concern isn't valid and that the restaurant doesn't care to cater to people who feel the same way she does. That would be a great way to ensure that the customer would never return.

Q: **You have a chief rolling cook who continues to fight and argue with the servers. You don't want to lose him because he keeps ticket times down and makes very few mistakes. You continue to counsel him, but he continues to have problems. What do you do?**

A: *I'd make one last stab at counseling the person. If that didn't work, I'd send him a written warning that documented his behavior and included something*

Candidates Re-entering the Workforce: Be up front and explain why you left the workforce, and why you're ready to get back in. In other words, what's changed in your circumstances since your leave? If you've been out of the restaurant business for several years, it may be beneficial for you to refresh your skills by working as a server or cook and seeking promotion from within. Recruiting firms, networking referrals, and direct (or "cold") contact are the best methods of job-hunting for you.

to the effect that either the negative behavior would have to cease, or we'd end up parting ways. If that didn't work, I might make one last attempt to save the person by temporarily suspending him. Barring that, I'd plan in advance for a change in staff before terminating the employee, or if I had to, I'd replace the person myself until I found a permanent replacement.

There are many different ways you could approach this issue. The interviewer is looking for a good solution to the problem in which the candidate ultimately finds a way to change the person's behavior or terminate him. An important component of your answer to this question would involve showing that you'd keep appropriate documentation so the company wouldn't be liable if you did terminate the employee.

Travel Agent

Q: **Why do you want to work in travel?**

A: *Because I love to travel and want to see as much of the world as possible. I also enjoy the sales aspect of the position. And I think I can be a better salesperson if I'm enthusiastic about the product I'm selling.*

This seems like a very simple question with a correspondingly simple answer. However, this answer is one that job candidates rarely give. Don't conclude that the interviewer will think poorly of your motivations—wanting to travel is the best reason for working in this field. Don't say something generic or insincere like, "Because I'm a people person!"

Q: **As a leisure-travel agent, would you consider yourself a salesperson or a customer-service representative?**

A: *I think of myself as 51 percent salesperson and 49 percent customer-service representative. I consider selling travel very similar to selling cars or clothing or sporting goods. In order to get the sale, I must first be a salesperson. After the sale I must provide exceptional service in order to keep the client for the long term.*

Without sales a travel agency will quickly go out of business. Too many leisure-travel agents forget they are salespeople above all else. On the other hand, a corporate-travel agent should focus on customer service before sales. Most large corporate agencies have a distinct sales force that rarely handles customer service. The sale is usually made before the business traveler calls.

Q: **How do you feel about rote paperwork?**

First-time Job Seekers: You must get some basic knowledge of the major computer-reservation system in your area. It's not necessary to go to an expensive travel school to acquire this skill. Most continuing-education programs offer shorter, less expensive classes usually taught by moonlighting agents. These courses can be a wealth of knowledge and a real insight into the agency without some computer experience. Once you have computer training, you'll at least be of some value to the agency while your training is completed. Destination knowledge is not as important, as it can easily be learned or self-taught.

A: *With every job there's paperwork—it's simply a fact of life. And because travel involves so many different suppliers and wholesalers, a paper trail is not only important, it's essential. Travel is a very subjective profession. Once the product is sold, you no longer have control over the product's performance. A flight can be late, a cruise ship can have unusually poor food or forget to provide airport transfers. I've found that having everything clearly described in paperwork can be a client saver.*

This response turns a negative question into a positive answer, and the candidate also emphasizes his or her attention to detail and concern for the elimination of errors. Assure the interviewer that you understand the true nature of the position—that it involves some necessary but not so glamorous tasks—and that you're willing to perform these tasks.

Q: **Consider this scenario: One of your clients, Mr. Johnson, calls to say that the tickets you just delivered were issued for Cleveland and not for Columbus, as he'd asked. You're absolutely positive he said Cleveland. How would you handle the situation?**

A: *I'd calmly and politely say something like, "I'm very sure you asked for Cleveland, Mr. Johnson; however, I will be happy to change your tickets to Columbus. Do you want to leave at the same time?"*

The interviewer wants to see how the candidate reacts in a role-playing environment. Your answer should show confidence and gentle firmness. In travel a simple mistake can cause the agent to lose a very large account. It's important to affirm that a mistake wasn't made if in fact it was not. In addition, this answer, which ends with a question, immediately and gently leads Mr. Johnson away from an argument.

Q: **Consider the same scenario with one difference: This time Mr. Johnson is right. He did ask for Columbus, and you made a mistake. What would you say to Mr. Johnson?**

Career Changers: Include a mission statement at the top of your resume, explaining your reasons for wanting to enter the travel industry. Also, try to extrapolate any experience that might pertain to the travel industry. If your resume is loaded with experience that's not associated with travel, the employer might think you're only looking for perks. Enroll in a continuing-education program to learn the basics of the major computer-reservation system in your area. To find out what system is used by most agencies simply call them and ask.

A: *I'd say, "You're absolutely right, Mr. Johnson. I sincerely apologize for the error—it's not something that happens often. I'll have a new set of tickets delivered to you immediately."*

Mistakes will be made. And when they are, it's important for you to admit the error and correct it immediately.

Q: Would you consider yourself a specialist on any particular destination?

A: *I'm not a specialist, but I did some research on Morocco for this interview. What would you like to know?*

If you don't have in-depth knowledge of a particular destination, you should research one or two destinations before your job interview. Although this won't enable you to claim specialist status, it will show the interviewer how you can turn careful research into a successful client/travel conversation. If you do believe that you have an average or above-average knowledge of a destination, then say yes, but be prepared to answer specific follow-up questions about that destination.

Q: In travel we're always looking for new ways to get business in the door. What would you do to increase my business?

A: *The first thing I'd do is create an announcement and send it to all my friends, relatives, and acquaintances, enthusiastically letting them know about my new job. I'd tell them that I'm looking forward to hearing from them, and that I'm available to serve their future travel needs.*

Most travel agents get started building their clientele through their family and friends. However, some agents simply use word of mouth, whereas the most productive agents let their contacts know in writing, regularly. Once a few of your friends start booking through you, your business will grow from referrals.

Experienced Professionals: Be sure to mention on your resume and in your job interviews the specific accomplishments you made in your previous travel jobs. This shows that you know what it's like to work in travel and that you're ambitious and will grow in the industry. One hiring manager told us of a job candidate who created a chart documenting her sales increases over time. Needless to say, she got the job. If you can't show a list of sales increases, show a list of time savers you created or some other accomplishments you've made.

Q: What do you think is the most important skill for a travel agent?

A: *Speed is a very important skill, especially with the computer. Speed without errors.*

Travel is a volume game. In order to stay in business, agencies must process hundreds of transactions while keeping mistakes to a minimum. Because correcting errors is the most expensive time that an agent can spend, you should give details about your speed, and especially about your accuracy.

Q: Consider the following: It's ten minutes before closing time and a partner in your second-largest account is waiting for her tickets, which you haven't yet printed. Meanwhile, a gentleman walks in, sits at your desk, and starts to ask questions about Cancun. All the other agents are on the phone. What do you do?

A: *I explain to the gentleman that I can't help him at the moment, that I need to finish helping another customer first. I'd tell him that if he doesn't mind waiting, I'll be able to help him in a few minutes. Otherwise, I can make an appointment with him for the following day at his convenience.*

Although you'll often be called upon to do many things at once, it's important to prioritize your clients when necessary. This gentleman may never make a purchase, but the partner has spent thousands with your agency.

Q: How would you feel if I offered you a position that gave you the option of salary plus commission?

A: *Great! I'd love the opportunity to increase my salary by selling more.*

Although this may seem like the only obvious and correct answer, many people are scared by a commission income. Even if the interviewer plans to offer you straight salary, he or she may ask this question because it reveals how confident you are about your own selling ability. If commission income scares you, you might want to consider a different occupation.

Q: What computer-reservation systems are you familiar with?

A: *I've used SABRE exclusively for the past five years for both corporate and leisure travel. I'm extremely proficient in it. In fact, I was the fastest, most productive agent at my previous company.*

Candidates Re-entering the Workforce: Your strongest qualification is your previous work experience in the travel industry. Be prepared to discuss it in detail, along with your up-to-date computer skills. Stress the potential business you can bring to the company, including possible business from associations you made while on hiatus. In travel, contacts are key.

You should be prepared to discuss in detail your experience with the major computer-reservation system in your area, beginning with the number of years you've used it and for what types of travel. To find out what system is used by most agencies, simply call them and ask. SABRE, Apollo, Worldspan, and System One are the most common, but there are others. Don't claim any expertise you don't have—it's very likely that you'll be given a computer test, with the interviewer playing the role of the most difficult client in the world.

Q: What did you like least about working at your last agency?

A: *I worked reservations, and we were never given the opportunity to make marketing suggestions. I had great ideas for getting new business, and though I tried several times to voice them, the people in marketing made it clear they didn't want my input.*

There's something about every job that people dislike, and if you say, "I liked everything, I had no complaints," you may be perceived as insincere. However, you should take into consideration the particular agency you're applying to. For example, this answer wouldn't be appropriate if the interviewing agency also frowns on marketing input from reservation agents. It's important, as well, that you don't present yourself as someone who complains a lot without trying to do anything about it. Explain to the interviewer what you disliked and a valid reason why it was a problem. What steps did you take to try to correct the problem?

Q: What did you like best about your last position?

A: *I got a great sense of satisfaction from seeing my sales grow. The job itself was fair, but getting that sales report and seeing my increase every quarter really kept me going.*

Every manager loves a salesperson. And as a travel agent, you're a salesperson before anything else. Show that you enjoy the challenge of sales and are highly motivated, which tells the interviewer that you'll begin making a contribution to the company your first day on the job.

CHAPTER 20

SOCIAL AND HUMAN SERVICES

Case Manager

Q: **Do you have experience working with children or adolescents who are technologically dependent?**

A: *Yes. I worked as a hospital case manager with children who had multiple handicaps. I coordinated the implementation of educational plans.*

This question allows the interviewer to gauge how relevant the candidate's background is to the position. A good answer will relate the population needs the candidate previously served to the population needs of the new position. You could also discuss some of your experiences serving a particular population in more detail than the candidate does here.

Q: **What skills do you believe are important for dealing effectively with young children?**

A: *I've found that patience and honesty are most effective when working with young children. I've also found that children respond better to adults who are willing to engage in activities and discussions that young children are involved in. And because children can get nervous around adults in a clinical setting, I believe it's always important to clearly define my role to the children I'm working with.*

Basically, the interviewer wants to see that the candidate is capable of relating to children. You could also tell the interviewer about your specific experience in working with children of different ages and different emotional needs.

Q: **Do you have any additional skills to deal specifically with children who are medically fragile or technologically dependent?**

A: *No. I believe that children are children, and that you need little more than the basic skills of patience and honesty in dealing with them all. The only real difference with children who are technologically dependent—who, for instance, are not mobile or have lost the ability to speak—is that they may need to find different ways to communicate.*

This question is designed to determine if the candidate sees the disability before the child. Responses that concentrate heavily on medical terminology are inappropriate. Like this candidate, you should show the interviewer that you realize that all children, regardless of any disabilities, will respond positively to the same kind of treatment.

Q: What skills do you believe are important in dealing with the families of patients?

A: *I believe good interviewing skills are essential for getting a good history of the patient, and for unearthing parents' needs and concerns. With a good initial interview you can also discover if the parents have complaints about current and past treatments, or about case management. It's important, as well, to have the ability to empathize with all the work they've done in the past and the difficulties they face in the future.*

The interviewer will want to know that you can balance the needs of the child, the caretaker, and others in the case-management process. Even if you have no personal experience in dealing with families, you should demonstrate an understanding of the skills necessary to advocate effectively for parents.

Q: Tell me about a time you needed someone's cooperation to complete a task and that person was uncooperative.

A: *I was assigned a new child to treat, so I met with her mother to try to learn some background information, including the patient's case history. She was very reluctant to tell me anything beyond her daughter's name, age, and diagnosis. I spent a great deal of time explaining why I needed the information and told her specifically what the information was going to be used for—but she was still wary of me. Finally, when she told me she was concerned with the confidentiality of our conversation, I made sure she understood that I was the only person who would know of her daughter's history. Once I explained that I wouldn't be sharing what she told me with anyone, she felt better about giving me the information, and completely opened up.*

Cite a personal or professional example that shows your ability to sway opinion and overcome resistance. Emphasize your ability to solve problems proactively,

First-time Job Seekers: A typical entry-level position would be as a case-manager assistant. This position requires at least a bachelor's degree in psychology, special education, rehabilitation, or social work. You should also have some experience working with people, either through volunteering at a community organization or working at a summer camp for children with disabilities. During your interview, show that you have realistic expectations. Many people right out of college say that they want to do consulting, but this is almost unheard of in the field—you need to get plenty of hands-on experience before you can consult.

before the person's uncooperative behavior creates problems, rather than simply reacting to existing problems as they occur. You should discuss what techniques you used in this situation, and what the outcome was.

Q: **How do you evaluate conflicting information or intervention approaches?**

A: *I like to collect all points of view and then get professional outside advice to help me evaluate those differing opinions. I also believe that an outside opinion helps me gain perspective and balance the conflict. That way, when I go back to the conflicting parties, I'm able to set up a positive negotiating approach.*

Professionals involved with children who are medically fragile can often have conflicting diagnoses and treatment strategies for the same patient. You'll need to demonstrate your tolerance for conflict and for opposing views, and show your ability to evaluate each situation thoroughly in order to mediate between parties.

Q: **Discuss your knowledge of handling confidential information while advocating for a client's needs.**

A: *I've never knowingly breached the confidentiality of a client. I'm very familiar with the rules of permission and the guidelines of the state. I've attended specialized training in this area and am familiar with the things that can be legally and ethically discussed in public regarding therapeutic situations.*

The interviewer will want assurance that you understand the seriousness of the policies, rules, and guidelines that govern the conduct of case managers. Like this candidate, show the interviewer that you've taken extra efforts to educate yourself and have stayed up to date with these policies. You can also ask the interviewer whether the job in question has additional guidelines and opportunities for future training.

Career Changers: Many people enter this field mistakenly believing that it's enough simply to say they want to help children. You'll need to acquire some relevant experience in the field, which is easiest to do through volunteering. Even with that experience, however, be prepared for your first paid position to be an entry-level one. In the interview, mention any medical-care experience you might have, as well as skills that are more easily transferable, like negotiating or computers. Since you'll have less experience than most candidates, try to bring something extra to the interview. For instance, try to find out how the organization's programs are funded. The interviewer will be impressed if you can speak knowledgeably about the funding source and how the organization works.

Q: Discuss your methods for documenting your case-management work in individual case files, as well as for reimbursement purposes.

A: *Generally, I take notes during or immediately after a phone call, meeting, or other patient encounter. At the end of each day I put these notes in a folder for each client. At the end of the week I compile and transcribe this information on the required forms.*

Good documentation is crucial for supervision and billing issues, and also for external clinical review. Even if your other work is satisfactory, poor documentation can create potentially serious employee-performance problems. It's crucial to demonstrate an understanding of the importance of careful documentation.

Q: Discuss your experience with, and knowledge of, medical terminology, developmental stages, and disability groupings.

A: *I have extensive experience working with many different disability groups, particularly children with cerebral palsy and spina bifida. I regularly attend conferences offered by associations supporting these particular groups.*

You don't necessarily need to have a medical background, but you must be comfortable with medical terms, diagnoses, methods, and treatment modalities. Cite your work experience, the classes you've taken, and any special training you've received in this area. Professional conferences are an excellent way to educate yourself and update your professional skills.

Q: How do you manage multiple concurrent deadlines and demands on your time?

Experienced Professionals: In the interview, emphasize your skills in areas such as negotiation, case documentation, and multitasking. You should also have solid experience working with the population that the organization serves; be ready to discuss some of the positive things you've accomplished working with that population. Demonstrate a thorough knowledge of the organization's funding source and show an understanding of the changes in the field of managed care.

A wide range of opportunities exists for case managers, including private case-management companies, employee-assistance programs, and private and public social service agencies, such as the Department of Mental Health. Possible career paths for the case manager include moving up to case-manager supervisor, director of clinical services, program manager, or director of client services.

A: *I maintain a well-organized appointment book and diary of my work. I begin each day by reviewing the work I need to complete and prioritizing those tasks. Occasionally I'll consult with my supervisor in deciding deadline order and program priorities.*

The ability to manage conflicting responsibilities is an important part of the job. Demonstrate that you have an established system of organization and that you're able to operate in that organizational structure.

Q: What's your familiarity with computers and electronic client-record-keeping systems?

A: *I've used word-processing programs in college and at various jobs. My last company was a pilot site for an electronic client-record system, and I was involved in providing feedback to the managers implementing that system.*

Even though electronic client-record systems are in their infancy, many programs and companies will require at least the ability to word-process client-progress notes. In most cases secretarial resources aren't available for routine dictation or the transcribing of notes and files. Many organizations will be moving to specialized electronic records in the future, and interviewers like to see candidates who are comfortable with computers and can easily learn the new programs.

Q: What do you consider to be your most beneficial assets in your professional work?

A: *I enjoy work that's within my level of expertise while providing me opportunities to learn and grow professionally. I'm creative in my thinking and enjoy sharing ideas with my colleagues. I'm supportive of my professional colleagues, and I don't hesitate to solicit supervisory and technical assistance when necessary.*

A proved ability to work in teams, solid case-management skills, and a willingness to learn are all attributes that any interviewer will be looking for in

Candidates Re-entering the Workforce: Be sure to emphasize your past experience and accomplishments. Most important, demonstrate that you've stayed current with the human-services field, which has experienced some major changes in the past five years. Make sure you're familiar with available community resources, medical and payer trends, and philosophical trends within the population you're going to be serving. To find out about changing trends in the field, talk to former colleagues and network with people in your field. You can also attend conferences sponsored by service groups, or by organizations like United Way, that cover the specific population you are interested in.

candidates. You might also wish to discuss in depth your area of expertise and how it relates to the position.

Q: **What are your future goals, if any, in advanced educational training?**

A: *I'm interested in pursuing a graduate degree in rehabilitation. I'm also interested in pursuing specialty courses of study such as assistive technology, acquired brain injury, early intervention, and spinal-cord injuries. I'd like to be introduced to a variety of disciplines so that I could work on interdisciplinary teams.*

Medical technology is constantly changing, so the interviewer will want to see that you're interested in continuing your education. It's important to remain open to a variety of opinions and schools of thought, as a wide breadth of knowledge is important for any case manager to have. If you already possess a graduate degree, you can say that you're seeking your advanced certification in a given field, such as rehabilitation.

Q: **What's your experience in dealing with individuals who exhibit inappropriate behavior?**

A: *I have substantial experience in this area through an internship and my last job. I'm familiar with a number of behavior-modification techniques, including reinforcing behavior through direct feedback, as well as nonaversive and supportive methods. I'm particularly skilled at modeling appropriate behavior as a general course and have had a number of experiences in which I've used role-playing to reinforce a more appropriate behavior pattern.*

It is important that the interviewer sees you as a professional who won't be punitive or negative in your dealings with difficult persons. Demonstrate that you're able to handle difficulty in your daily work with success. You should also show that you can determine when a situation has reached a point that's beyond your capability to handle, and that you'll seek outside help when necessary.

Clinical Social Worker

Q: **Are you able to perform a mental-status assessment?**

A: *Yes, I'm trained to use DSM-IV assessment tools. I'm familiar with all the codes and the criteria for diagnosing any presenting problems that I'd face in a clinical setting.*

The interviewer will want to know if you'll be able to discern the typical symptoms and signs of psychiatric illness—a key role of any clinician. A clinical social worker must know the symptoms of all psychiatric illnesses, including chronic syndromes such as schizophrenia, clinical depression, and any of the mental illnesses that fall into the category of thought disorders. If you've been trained to use the Diagnostic Statistical Manual assessment tools, be sure to say so at this time.

Q: **What do you believe is your true mission statement?**

A: *I want to work to work with people with substance-abuse problems, to help them function the best they can in society.*

Given that all human-services professionals should have some altruistic goal, it's important for you to have developed a clear mission statement. Keep in mind that the position you're applying for should correspond with these goals.

Q: **Do you know what to do and what to ask of a patient or client who announces that he feels suicidal, or who's making suicidal ideations or gestures?**

A: *I'd immediately ask him what his plan is, how he plans to do away with himself. If the plan is practical, direct, immediate, and workable—for example, if he says, "I have a knife and I'm going to cut myself," that person needs to be hospitalized because he is a danger to himself and others. If the person has any type of complicated or vague plan like stealing an airplane and crashing into a building, it usually means that person is crying out for some kind of attention or help. It doesn't necessarily mean that the person needs to be hospitalized.*

It's important for a clinician to be able to distinguish real suicidal threats from a cry for attention or help. If you have experience working with suicidal patients, this would be a good opportunity to discuss it. If not, you should be able to articulate clearly how you'd handle such a situation.

Q: How do you determine when it's appropriate to use treatment modalities such as cognitive behavioral intervention, insight therapy, or transactional analysis?

A: *To reinforce positive behaviors and deter negative ones, I'd use cognitive behavioral modality with clients who present with oppositional defiant behavior, passive-aggressive behavior, or substance abuse. I'd use transactional analysis for nonaggressive people with limited social skills in order to teach them to be more assertive. I'd use insight therapy with a person who's situationally depressed—for example, due to the death of a close family member or the loss of a job.*

These three major types of treatments give social workers specific guidelines for treating patients. This is a basic "quiz" question that the interviewer is using to test the candidate's knowledge and skill. If you're a licensed social worker, you should have no problem answering this kind of question.

Q: How do you determine when a client needs to be referred to a psychiatrist for medication?

A: *I can usually diagnose a client within the first three sessions. If the client presents any disturbance in thought, such as auditory or visual hallucinations; any impairment of state of awareness, such as disorientation regarding time, place, and person; any clouding or disturbing of consciousness; or any disturbance in reaction to outside stimuli, I'd refer him or her for medication. Also, disturbances in attention, such as attention-deficit disorder; clinical, nonsituationally triggered depression; anxiety; and mood disorders are all criteria for medication.*

This is another basic quiz question with only one correct answer. Therapeutic milieus currently consider the most successful and best approaches to any mental-health patient those that provide the least restrictive medical and psychopharmaceutical methodologies. In other words, they emphasize treatment over medication. Show the interviewer that you want to avoid overmedicating patients. At the same time, you must be aware that certain presenting problems, such as the ones described by this candidate, create a

First-time Job Seekers: A master's degree in social work is a prerequisite for this position. Work experience in hospital settings or advocacy work in community organizations (such as volunteer work with the homeless) is also very valuable. Not only will this type of experience help you get a job, it will help you determine which areas you do or do not want to work in. For your first position in the field, look for support-staff positions, such as research assistant. Positions like clinical office manager or billing clerk provide enormously enriching contact with all facets of clinical practice.

direct dysfunction that affects the activities of daily living and requires the use of medication in treatment. It's also important for you to emphasize that your primary interest in treatment is the health and safety of your patients.

Q: How do you best distinguish organic from emotional disturbances?

A: *I'd observe the person's behavior and determine whether his or her problem is a temporary adjustment disorder or a chronic syndrome. For example, clinical depression is different from situational depression in that it's a chronic, organic emotional disturbance.*

Most individuals with organic disorders—that is, neuropsychological or brain damage—usually exhibit one or more typical disturbances in form of thought, such as tangential thinking. This organic disturbance is evident in persons who are prone to seizures such as aphasia, or who show loss of ability to comprehend the meaning of words common to the average person. An extreme symptom of organic disorder is intermittent fugue state, such as amnesia. It's important for you to be able to distinguish between organic and emotional disturbances because the two disorders have different treatment modalities. Show that you'll rule out the possibility of any physical causes of the disturbance before diagnosing the patient and determining a treatment method.

Q: How do you feel about working with clients with personality and character disorders?

A: *I don't have a problem working with people with personality or character disorders, but I do take extra precautions with them. For example, I wouldn't close the door to my office when I'm in session with a character-disorder patient.*

People with personality and character disorders are people who commit violent crimes without pangs of conscience. Working with this type of patient is very different from working with people who are suffering from emotional and organic disorders, such as depression or anxiety. Many clinical social workers won't work with personality- and character-disorder people. No matter what the client's character and personality flaws, it's important for a professional to find, and work with, a client's strengths in order to create what's known as a therapeutic alliance. Let the interviewer know that you feel ethically and

Career Changers: For most positions in social work you'll need to go back to school to earn your master's degree. In the meantime you should consider doing basic case management or direct social work services, such as recruiting resources for alternative housing or for foster or adoptive parents. This experience will give you a good indication of whether or not social work is the right career choice for you.

professionally obliged to treat a client with empathy and with as much positive regard as possible. These are the hallmarks of a skilled therapist and are essential if the patient is to be helped and supported in the therapeutic alliance. Keep in mind that for some positions this type of work is required—for example, working in a prison setting. If you have a problem working with this type of patient, you should ask if it's a required part of the job.

Q: **What psychological theories do you believe have weathered the decades?**

A: *I'm a systems theorist. I believe in treating both individuals and families.*

The interviewer will want to know your school of thought. Are you a proponent of Ericksonian developmental theories, Eric Burn's theory of transactional analysis, William Glasser's reality therapy, or Freud's theory of psychoanalysis? You should avoid citing off-the-wall, trendy theories that haven't yet been proved.

Q: **How would you treat a dysfunctional family system?**

A: *I'd treat each person in the family as an individual. I'd look for any signs of scapegoating particular members of the family and identify the role of each family member. For example, let's say a mother in a family of five comes in with a young child who's acting out in school, hitting the teacher, and getting into fights. She says, "Fix this kid, he's messing up my whole family." I'd say, "Okay, we'll fix Johnny," but rather than focusing on the one child, I'd really be looking at the family system. The family may have problems with alcoholism or violence. That kid is usually just a symptom of the dysfunctional family system.*

The term "dysfunctional family" is a popular buzzword in mental-health circles, and it's important to know how to treat this type of family. Like this candidate, you'll want to show that you'd treat the entire family, not just one person. The basis of family-systems theory is that the dysfunctional family strives toward a point of homeostasis, or a steady state—that is, the highest possible level of functioning for that family to stay together. This level is achieved and maintained usually at the expense of the weakest or most vulnerable member of the family. Some good systems theorists can be referenced in a book

Experienced Professionals: Expect detailed questions about your clinical skills and your general philosophy of social work. Be sure to emphasize the areas in which you have experience as well as your area of specialization. You should also stress your familiarity with specific innovations in the profession, for example, updated skills in providing monitoring and support cognitively and behaviorally for patients being treated with psychopharmaceuticals like Prozac.

entitled *Systems Consultation: A Perspective in Family Therapy*, by Lynman, Wein, and Weber. If you can discuss this theory in-depth, then the interviewer will know that you keep current with the trends in treatment modalities.

Q: Where do you feel your talents lie?

A: *My specialty is in family therapy, but I also have experience in substance-abuse cases, adolescent counseling, and couples counseling.*

Every clinic wants to have a couple of good family therapists, adolescent workers, substance-abuse therapists, and so on. Ideally, your area of expertise will fill a need in that clinic.

Q: How would you fit into an interdisciplinary team in a clinical setting?

A: *I work best in a team that utilizes the individual skills of each clinician. If, for instance, I'm treating a client in crisis with severe anxiety and panic attacks, I'd want a good psychiatrist with state-of-the-art knowledge of psychopharma-ceuticals to co-treat the case initially until I can work with the client in more extended sessions, teaching anxiety-management skills.*

Like this candidate, you should demonstrate flexibility in terms of working in interdisciplinary teams. The interviewer will want to see that you understand the importance of teams in providing the most thorough and accurate diagnostic evaluations of a patient. Assure the interviewer that you won't be argumentative or in any way try to disturb the delicate balance of the team. An interdisciplinary team must work together in order to meet the individual needs of a patient.

Q: What do you feel are good clinical social-work ethics?

A: *I think it's important to have a positive regard for patients, strict confidentiality, and the desire to treat a patient in a positive way.*

Social-work ethics evolve and change over time, so it's important to stay up-to-date with the latest trends. Most interviewers will immediately look for the three ethics that this candidate discusses, but you may also mention other important aspects of your philosophy of social work.

Candidates Re-entering the Workforce: Discuss how you've remained up-to-date on the latest clinical and intervention theories, perhaps by reading professional journals. Be prepared to explain to the interviewer why you left the field and why you're ready to return.

Q: **What do you think are the best safeguards in a clinical agency to ensure that safe clinical interventions are being used?**

A: *I think that a good quality-assurance system, such as clinical reviews of methodology on a monthly or weekly basis, is an important safeguard that should be used in a clinical setting.*

Sound, consistent supervision of staff is very important in an agency. All approved state providers have an internal checks-and-balance system known as a utilization-review team, as well as a quality-assurance team. These are multidisciplinary review boards, consisting of a licensed psychiatrist, psychologist, and clinical social worker. All cases are reviewed to ensure that the diagnostic treatment plan, and progress toward the goals for the client, are being achieved. Basically, the interviewer will want to be sure that you'll respect these safeguards and that you won't damage either the clinic or the patient. In response to this question, discuss how the safety of the client, both clinically and emotionally, is of paramount importance. You could also mention the importance of excellent supervision, which includes a high level of peer supervision.

Mental Health Therapist

Q: **What motivated you to become a therapist?**

A: *I was always interested in psychology, but I knew I didn't want to work in clinical psychology. I wanted to get out in the field and actually try to help people who were having personal difficulties. In choosing this particular area I reviewed the values that the field tries to promote and found that they're compatible with my own values. I believe in self-determination, empowerment, and treating people with dignity and respect, and being a therapist allows me to put those values to work by helping others.*

Discuss the particular philosophies and values that attracted you to this field. Each discipline in the mental-health field, whether it's social work or psychology, has its own code of ethics, and the interviewer will expect you to talk about those ethics and how they relate to you. Be sure that your answer addresses your philosophical, rather than your personal, motivations. This question helps the interviewer determine if the candidate has healthy or unhealthy reasons for choosing the field of mental health. The interviewer isn't looking for someone who wants to "save the world." Like this candidate, you should show that you have reasonable expectations of what therapists actually do and the role they assume with patients. Demonstrate a desire to teach people how to be healthy, rather than simply to take care of them.

Q: **Identify and describe relevant issues when you were growing up that have been significant in understanding your life.**

A: *When I was thirteen years old, my best friend was diagnosed with advanced stage leukemia. She died two and a half years later. Needless to say, this had a tremendous impact on me. First of all, I'd never had to deal with death on any level; my grandparents were still alive—even my family's ten-year-old Labrador was in perfect health. Death was this very foreign, distant thing that happened only to other people. But then, all of a sudden, the girl I'd grown up with was dying, and things that I once thought were important didn't seem to matter as much. The whole experience forced me to grow up much faster than I would have under normal circumstances. I learned early to stay grounded and keep life in perspective, and to remember what's truly important.*

This question allows the interviewer to gauge the candidate's level of insight into him- or herself. A popular industry philosophy states that therapists can help patients as much as they've helped themselves. If you haven't engaged in introspection, you won't be able to help other people much with their lives. The particular issues you discuss here can be either negative or positive, because the interviewer will be more concerned with your ability to recognize those issues and understand how they've affected you. Show the interviewer how you were able to learn from experience and gain insight into, and empathy with, other people's problems.

Q: **What kind of messages did you receive from significant adults when you were growing up?**

A: *I believe I was quite fortunate, because when I was growing up, all of the adults in my life—my parents, grandparents, and teachers—were basically happy and positive individuals. They all gave me the sense that they were quite content with how their lives had turned out. Without ever pushing they encouraged me to stretch my abilities and to really challenge myself. Though my parents may not have liked all the choices I made growing up, they respected me enough to support me and let me learn from my own mistakes.*

If you're acting out your life based on messages you received when you were younger, you need to understand why. If you don't understand why you behave the way you do, then you won't have the ability to help patients. This question also helps the interviewer gain insight into how to best manage you as an employee. For instance, if you received messages from your parents that you were inadequate, then the interviewer might pay special attention to how to approach you with criticism of your job performance. Again, the messages you describe here aren't as important as your ability to demonstrate an understanding of how those messages impact your life.

Q: **Are there any issues from your personal life that might potentially have an impact on your professional career?**

A: *I'm always careful to separate my personal life from my professional life. I believe it's important to remain objective when treating patients. A therapist should always be able to take an emotional step back in order to make an*

First-time Job Seekers: An entry-level therapist should have a master's degree in psychology, social work, guidance counseling, or divinity. You're also required to have 500 hours of field practicums. The programs are usually divided into two 250-hour practicums. In addition to your practicums, try to acquire some volunteer experience to demonstrate your commitment to the field. Employers look for caring individuals with solid communications skills, which means more than the ability to talk to people; it also involves active listening and the ability to ask probing questions. Finally, be prepared to discuss why you want to be a therapist and why you're interested in serving a particular population.

unbiased assessment of a patient. It only hurts the patient when you try to project your own issues and feelings onto that patient.

Assure the interviewer that you can sort out personal opinions from professional behavior. The interviewer wants to determine how well you've integrated yourself as an individual. If you have personal issues that you've been unable to work through, they could easily interfere with your relationships with your patients. These issues could also affect your judgment in assessing patients, as well as how you approach treatment planning and recommendations. For instance, if you've experienced a crisis that you haven't dealt with positively, you might not be willing to help your patients face really traumatic issues because that would bring up too many of your own intense emotions.

Q: How did the dynamics of your family of origin influence the development of your personality?

A: *As I said before, I have a wonderful family. As boring as it may seem, I love and respect my parents completely, and I know they have just as much love and respect for me. My parents always encouraged my sister and me to talk openly with them. My parents didn't believe in holding hurt or anger inside. And I'm still this way today—both with my family and with others. I believe in being completely honest and open with people; I don't hide my feelings. It's been hard for me to learn that complete honesty isn't always appropriate. But I now realize that in certain situations discretion is better than total disclosure. At the same time, I always treat people courteously and with respect, and that's how I expect to be treated by others.*

This is another question designed to gauge how insightful the candidate is about him- or herself. Again, you should demonstrate self-awareness as well as an ability to treat your patients objectively. Your answer will also allow the interviewer to assess your knowledge level of the theories regarding family-of-origin issues.

Career Changers: You'll first need to go back to college to obtain your master's degree. You should also focus on doing volunteer work in your chosen area. Volunteering within your community—For a Big Brothers/Big Sisters organization, a crisis line, or a homeless shelter—will give you valuable experience and help you break into the field. It will increase not only your knowledge base, but your networking contacts as well. Communications skills you've learned in a previous position are easily transferable, as are any interpersonal skills you've picked up while working in other caretaking roles, such as nursing, case work, or as a parole officer.

Q: How do you view a supervisor's role?

A: *I don't think that a supervisor should be someone who simply tells you what to do and when to do it. I believe a supervisor is someone who's there to support and guide you and help you grow. A true supervisor is someone who's able to use the strengths of his or her staff, and to help develop those strengths. In my past supervisory experience that's the approach I've always taken, and I know that I work best under that sort of nurturing supervision.*

Describe the characteristics you look for in a supervisor. By finding out what you expect from your supervisor, the interviewer will have a better indication of what to expect from you as an employee. Staff morale is extremely important in any treatment facility, and the interviewer may hesitate to hire you if he or she feels that you'd bring negative views of supervision to the center.

Q: What does leadership mean to you?

A: *Leadership is a natural ability that someone is born with. I believe that a good leader is someone who can inspire and direct people with ideas, and is able to use his or her influence effectively to make changes within a system. In my opinion a good leader won't necessarily make a good supervisor; similarly, someone could be an excellent supervisor without having any true leadership qualities.*

This is another question to determine the candidate's views about supervision. Demonstrate here that you recognize the differences between leadership and supervision. A candidate who can show that he or she understands this is more likely to require less supervision. If you exhibit signs of being self-directed and assertive, the interviewer will have a better idea of what you can contribute to the organization.

Q: What do you know about this organization's philosophy and mission?

Experienced Professionals: Employers look for candidates with at least three to five years' experience in each position they've held as therapist. This is important because building relationships with your patients is crucial, and if you're unable to sustain a long-term relationship with an organization, chances are you can't build one with a patient either. Experienced professionals should also have an area of expertise, either a special certificate in testing or art therapy, or a specialization in an area that most people don't want to serve, such as domestic violence or chemical dependency. Also, be prepared to run through a "mock" case study during your interview. The interviewer will want to determine the sharpness of your assessment and evaluation skills, as well as get some general feedback regarding the level of your knowledge.

A: *I know you are a values-based treatment center for adolescents. I'm interested in joining your organization because though other centers use therapies based strictly on cognitive or psychodynamic theories, your therapists add the component of teaching patients values and ethics. I completely agree with your philosophy that although traditional theories are necessary in treatment, you also need to give these patients the capacity to make their own moral choices about what's right and wrong.*

Describe the framework and philosophy of the organization, then discuss how your personal and professional opinions fit in with the program. The interviewer will want to be sure your philosophy regarding therapy is compatible with that of the treatment center. If the two philosophies are contradictory or incompatible, neither you nor the organization will be content with the match. Most important, the interviewer will want to ensure that you won't be entering a situation in which you can't ethically condone the treatment methods being used.

Q: Tell me about your experience relating to treatment planning, discharge planning, and case management.

A: *I have experience in all these areas. In the treatment center where I'm currently working, the therapist is responsible for all aspects of a patient's treatment. In other words, we don't work with a separate case manager. So when I'm assigned a case, I must coordinate the various treatments and services for the patient, contact the appropriate agencies, and so forth. Naturally, I do all this after I've conducted an assessment and identified the patient's specific needs and problems. I formulate individualized treatment plans for my patients, deciding which therapies to use and consulting with other professionals when necessary. I also handle the discharge planning for my patients; the treatment center has criteria to determine when a patient is ready for discharge, but it's up to the individual therapist to decide exactly how to finish services for a patient.*

Candidates Re-entering the Workforce: Don't worry too much if you haven't practiced for several years, because life experience is often the best determination of what kind of therapist you'll be. You will, however, need to explain how you've kept up your skills, for example, through volunteer work. Even if you worked only five hours a week, the interviewer will know that you maintained an interest in the field during your absence. Attending continuing-education classes and industry conferences are other excellent ways to keep current in the field. Show the interviewer that you've kept abreast of the latest trends and theories by reading trade journals such as the *Journal of Social Work* and the *Journal of Psychology.*

All therapists, whether they work in a public, private, or residential setting, will need experience in the three basic areas of treatment planning, discharge planning, and case management. Your answer will tell the interviewer how much training you'll need during orientation. For instance, not every therapist has experience as a case manager, which requires fewer clinical and more administrative skills, such as time management and organization. Although it's important to give a general overview of your skills in these areas, be prepared to answer more questions regarding specific cases you've treated and your approach to treating them.

Q: **What knowledge do you have of eating, personality, attention-deficit, and disruptive-behavior disorders?**

A: *Patients with eating disorders suffer from a severe disturbance in eating behaviors, as well as a distorted perception of their body shape and weight. This disorder is most commonly found in women, usually ranging in age from adolescence to late twenties, but men may occasionally suffer from the disorder, too. Personality disorders are distinguished by enduring patterns of inner experience and behaviors that deviate markedly from the expectations and norms of society. If gone untreated, they may cause significant functional impairment or subjective distress to the individual. Lastly, patients with attention-deficit and disruptive-behavior disorders exhibit a pattern of inattention and/or hyperimpulsity that interferes with everyday functioning. However, when I come across patients who exhibit symptoms of a disorder, I always first rule out the possibility that chemicals, such as drugs or alcohol, or an undiagnosed medical condition are causing the symptoms. I'll also make sure that the patient isn't simply "faking it" in order to get attention or medication.*

These are just a few of the many diagnoses you may come across in the mental-heath field. The interviewer is trying to determine the extent of the candidate's knowledge regarding the illnesses that the organization serves, as well as how much supervision the candidate will need. Many centers will give you a questionnaire that lists over twenty different diagnoses and ask you to write about your knowledge of, or experience with, each disorder. Even if you haven't practiced in every area, you should at least have a general understanding of the identifying characteristics of the various disorders.

Program Director

Q: **What's your personal or professional philosophy of helping people?**

A: *I've always been committed to a community-based approach, serving people in the least restrictive environment possible. I've worked in settings that moved people from hospitals into community residences, teaching community-based skills.*

Saying "I just like helping people" is not enough. The interviewer will want to get a sense that you've thought about it, and even if your commitment is, for example, to teach dangerous people in restrictive settings, he or she will still be interested in hearing why you think that works and why you think it's important. Some other key words are "empowerment"—that is, teaching people to do things for themselves instead of doing tasks for them—and "self-determination"—teaching people self-worth and how to make their own decisions. It's important to determine your philosophy before deciding which area of human services to enter.

Q: **How do you think the services we provide can best be delivered?**

A: *For a residential program like yours, I think these services can be delivered best in small groups, where a sense of community and commitment to each other can be encouraged. I think peer support is very important; teaching people to be independent in the community means teaching them to identify community-based supports, rather than relying on staff.*

The interviewer is looking for someone who has a philosophy and has thought about how to implement that philosophy. If you're going to empower people to make their own decisions, then it's important for the interviewer to hear that you're going to teach them how to be independent. Again, how have your experiences shaped a larger, guiding view of how you approach your work? This question can also give you an opportunity to discuss how your life and work experiences have helped shape your philosophy—for instance, raising a child, caring for a pet, or whatever.

Q: **Tell me about your previous experiences in managing programs.**

A: *Well, in college I was the arts editor for our school newspaper. I was responsible for assigning articles, seeing that they were completed, and doing the layout. In my two previous positions I was responsible for all of the recreational programming for consumers, and I also helped create a community volunteer program.*

The purpose of a question like this is to get a better understanding of how you've approached a coordinating and planning project. Your answer should give the interviewer a sense of your level of creativity, what your experience is, and how well you work under pressure. How do you make something happen out of nothing? If you're given an assignment, and not a lot of guidelines, how do you reach that goal?

Q: **Please share some of your experiences and thoughts regarding evaluations.**

A: *I helped design and implement a program evaluation in my last job, which looked at the consumers' progress in acquiring skills. We also looked for consumer satisfaction. I believe that an ongoing and targeted evaluation program is crucial to ensuring the effectiveness and usefulness of a program.*

The ability to evaluate both program and staff is becoming increasingly important in this field, especially as the accountability of the human-services field grows. Your answer need not be extremely specific here, since the interviewer is mainly interested in gaining an understanding of your thoughts about the evaluation process, and assurance that you'll use the information you acquire to make changes, implement new programs, or implement a model that you're developing. This is a great answer since it shows that the candidate understands that accountability and evaluation are critical attributes of any program director.

Q: **Tell me about your experience with budget management.**

A: *When I worked for the school newspaper, we paid our stringers and I was allowed to spend only a certain amount of money, so I had to monitor our funds carefully. Also, when I was organizing recreational activities, we had to develop a fee structure when we wanted to do special projects, so I had to keep an eye on the money we were budgeted. When I coordinated volunteers, I was given a limited budget for training.*

The interviewer will want reassurance that you pay attention to money and budgeting issues. You should show that you can make sound decisions when

First-time Job Seekers: Most people start in human services through volunteering, so be sure to stress any experience you've gained through volunteer work or internships. You also might want to discuss any relevant course work you may have taken, such as classes in public health. And don't be afraid to talk about leadership or organization experience and how you can adapt the skills you've gained from such activities to this new position. For example, if you were sports editor of your high-school newspaper, you can clearly handle a significant amount of responsibility.

it comes to spending your budget. If you've worked as a case manager, you can also describe how you've helped consumers develop their own budgets.

Q: Tell me about your supervisory experience.

A: *I managed a staff of three at the school newspaper, and as the recreational coordinator, I was responsible for managing a staff of five. I did the hiring and all of the staff evaluations. Also, in high school I was head counselor at a camp for children with physical disabilities.*

The interviewer will want to hear about your leadership experience and your management skills. He or she will want to see evidence that you've experienced a full range of tasks, including supervision and going through the entire hiring process, as well as promotions and dismissals. Any experience, whether formal or informal, is valuable in this situation.

Q: What was the most difficult staff problem you've faced?

A: *I had to put an employee on probation, and then eventually fire him for not following program protocol. That person had been with us for two years and was a very popular employee, so it was an extremely difficult situation.*

The interviewer is simply trying to find out how the candidate has dealt with a difficult staff situation and is also trying to gain some insight into his or her management style. Have you worked with staff to identify and change the behavior that was problematic? If you needed to terminate an employee, could you do that?

Q: What has your experience been with team building and staff development?

A: *In my last position I worked with staff at staff meetings to identify good training methods, then put together a monthly training manual that covered different topics each month. And I always asked the staff for any suggestions or ideas that they thought would make our programs better.*

Career Changers: Again, volunteer experience is key here—anything to show that you've had an active interest in the human services for a period of time. During your interview highlight your transferable skills, such as experience supervising a large group, or the ability to plan and develop projects. If there's a personal reason why you're changing careers, it may be appropriate to mention it in the interview. Although potential employers won't be interested in hearing a sob story, they will want to know why you've suddenly decided to change careers. Addressing the matter honestly and directly will help to alleviate any concerns they might have.

Give a response that includes working directly with staff to determine their needs and to discover a way to get beyond whatever challenges they're struggling with. Teamwork in human services is crucial, perhaps more so than in any other field. You simply can't have five different staff members using five different approaches with an individual who's struggling with an issue. Continuity and consistency of philosophies among staff members is essential.

Q: **The human-services field works with divergent populations, and each of these has different needs. What is it about this particular area that interests you?**

A: *I've always been interested in public-health issues and how they affect the community. The issue of addiction has been a part of my work and personal life for years. I grew up in a home that was disrupted and disturbed by an alcoholic father, so I learned from an early age the various issues that such an addiction could affect, from job to home life. Since then I've volunteered for many years at a center for recovering alcoholics.*

This question lends itself to a very important moment in any interview—self-revelation. Although no employer should ask you directly about your own personal history (that's illegal), this question does create an opening for candidates to share a piece of their lives with the interviewer. Many human-services workers become interested in the field because of something that's happened in their own lives, and they want to share this with the interviewer. However, the interviewer is simply trying to ascertain your familiarity with the target population. If you do choose to reveal something about your own personal history, don't simply leave it out there—you must relate how it's increased your knowledge and understanding of the issue. And most important, you must convince the interviewer that you've already worked out your problems with the issue, that you're not going to try to work through them within your job.

Q: **What do you know about the system for delivering services for that population?**

A: *Well, from my understanding of people who have addiction problems, the treatment continuum can involve detox, postdetox, or a residential program that lasts*

Experienced Professionals: You'll probably be asked a number of questions about your general philosophy concerning human services, as well as about supervision experience or budget management. The interviewer will also want to know about your availability. In most areas, crises can strike at any time of the day, and you must show that you're available and able to help people, even at three in the morning.

as long as six months. Then you're usually working with people independently in the community, and you might want to consider some community twelve-step programs.

This answer tells the interviewer that the candidate has done a little bit of research, and has thought the matter through. You should tell enough to show that you're familiar with the field. The interviewer will want to be sure you're not just sending out resumes blindly to hundreds of organizations.

Q: What has been your experience with crisis intervention?

A: *I've volunteered at a suicide hot line. As a recreation coordinator, I was faced several times with crises that involved people acting out in public. When clients left the recreational activity, I'd have to figure out what happened to them and how to find them.*

Anybody applying for a position as a program coordinator should have some crisis-intervention experience. Regardless of what population you're working with, you're eventually going to face a situation in which you have to think on your feet. Many people in human services have had training in crisis management, so be sure to mention it if you have. The interviewer will need to be assured that you can recognize a crisis and respond appropriately and effectively.

Q: What has been your experience with substance abuse and addiction?

A: *As I said earlier, my father was an alcoholic, and often on the hot line, I'd field calls from intoxicated people. I've received training on the effects of alcohol and drugs, and at the recreational center I worked with a population of individuals who viewed substance abuse as a primary problem. I also have some familiarity with twelve-step programs.*

The interviewer will want to see that you have some familiarity with the specifics in question. This answer shows that the candidate understands some of the dynamics surrounding addiction, the behavior of addicts, and the characteristics that one could expect from people struggling with addiction. You

Candidates Re-entering the Workforce: Naturally, the interviewer will want to know why you're suddenly interested in rejoining the workforce, so you must prove that your interest is sincere. You'll be asked about any volunteer work you've done in the interim, as well as about your experience before your absence. The biggest area of concern for the interviewer will be if you've kept abreast of the trends in the various areas of human services, so advance research into whatever area you're interested in is essential.

should also show knowledge of the various resources available to such a population. Substance abuse can affect virtually any area of human services.

Q: What has been your experience with assessments?

A: *When I worked on the hot line, we did suicide- and validity-assessments for people. While I was at the recreation program, I had to design individual service plans with people to determine their recreational needs.*

You should demonstrate that you have the skills to analyze a situation and develop an appropriate response. This kind of experience can range from being an emergency medical technician, who must immediately decide what the appropriate medical treatment is, to something as simple as working with an individual to design a recreation program that fits his or her needs.

Q: Tell me about your experience representing programs in the larger community.

A: *As a recreation coordinator, I was in constant touch with community members to arrange for recreational activities such as a night at the movies or theater. I also did a lot of fund raising for my old organization.*

Many program directors nowadays have to deal with the public not only around a crisis, but also simply to raise funds and to keep the public informed. Program directors must increasingly reach out to the community to discuss or gain support for the programs an organization is promoting to get volunteers. You should address this concern directly, as this candidate does, by telling the interviewer that you're accustomed to dealing with members of the greater community.

CHAPTER 21
TECHNICAL

Architecture Project Manager

Q: What were your responsibilities in a professional project that you've worked on?

A: *I worked as an intern for a small firm, so I did a little bit of everything. For example, we designed a house for a very famous science professor who was retiring, and I was responsible for developing a preliminary overall basic design concept for the building from scratch, and later I was responsible for picking up red lines (which means making small changes to drawings).*

A recruiter will ask you a question like this because he or she wants to know what you've done architecturally. How involved have you been? What was your level of responsibility? Having experience doing many things, just as this candidate has, is essential to being a successful project manager.

Q: What construction responsibilities have you handled?

A: *I have not had as much direct involvement with administering the construction process, but in the firm where I previously worked, I was mentored by a job captain on-site. This was a tremendous learning experience, because I was able to observe this process firsthand.*

Following from the first question, the recruiter will continue to find out exactly how much expertise you've developed. This answer is fine, because the candidate does not over-sell him- or herself. At the same time, the candidate clearly has developed the necessary skills and has had the right experience to be a project manager.

Q: How much client contact have you had?

A: *In the same firm I also got to sit in on all phases of client meetings. This allowed me to get a good understanding and foundation of how to project myself professionally with the client. I really learned by observing.*

Again, the recruiter will want to understand more about your level of exposure in the business. In all of these types of questions, express what you have and have not done. Don't be dishonest and say that you've had more responsibility than you really have had.

Q: **Which of your strengths are particularly important to architecture?**

A: *I think I develop good rapport with my coworkers. In my last job I really tried to stay grounded and focused, while some of the other architects would get wound up and stressed out near deadlines. I emerged into a sort of leadership role in the projects that I worked on.*

Sell yourself. This is a very convenient question, so without being arrogant, tell the recruiter what you do particularly well. Specific skills and abilities such as this candidate describes having are particularly important to architecture. The recruiter will be looking for them.

Q: **What things hold you back as an architect?**

A: *I sometimes find it difficult to ascertain what a supervisor really wants. In my last job I had a supervisor who didn't explain fully what he wanted. He gave vague instructions. When I tried to assume or guess, I went in the wrong direction. I learned to take a extra few minutes with my supervisor to clarify what he was asking me to do.*

This candidate is very discerning. The recruiter will want to know what your weaknesses are, but he or she is also saying, "Tell me about a time when you learned something." Show that you've improved in one of your weaker areas.

Q: **Are you computer literate?**

A: *Yes, I am. In architecture school we were required to take a computer drafting class, which gave me an opportunity to learn the program cold.*

There are probably a dozen different CAD systems in the business, so if you don't know the system that the firm currently uses, assure the recruiter that

First-time Job Seekers: Bring in a portfolio of your design work from college and, if you have any, from professional work. You should be able to speak technically correctly in an interview. Know how details are put together and how to manage a project or solve difficult problems. If you want to be a draftsperson, know how to discuss putting a drawing together. For example, what is the first step in putting a drawing together?

Demonstrate that you are willing to do anything it takes to learn your profession. An architect literally has to start as an office boy (or girl). If you come out of college thinking you know anything, you are absolutely wrong, and the people you work for will go out of their way to show you. Tell them in the interview that you plan to go in as a sponge so you can learn as much as possible, and then do it.

you can quickly learn to use it. Or do your homework before and find out which one the firm uses, then get familiar with it before the interview. Tell the recruiter which programs you're fluent in, and which ones you're currently trying to master.

Q: **How competent are you at drawing and drafting?**

A: *I find that many of the younger architects spend less and less time honing their drawing and drafting skills because they can rely on computer-generated drawings. Although I use both methods, I think having these skills is extremely important. They're the basic tools of the architect. I try to practice if I think I'm getting rusty in any area.*

This is a quality answer because the candidate understands and expresses the recruiter's underlying motivation in this question. Further, the candidate has certainly supplied the answer that the recruiter wants to hear. Excellent drawing skills are by far the most important skill an architect can have and, therefore, should be the most developed.

Q: **Do you like dealing with clients?**

A: *I actually find it to be one of the most rewarding aspects of the business. I think it's important to relate to a client in layman's terms. You have to speak to clients on their level, so that they can communicate what they want. Transforming their ideas to a working plan on paper, and finally to an actual structure, is extremely rewarding.*

Without clients there'd be no architecture firms, so the ability to work well with clients is obviously something the recruiter is looking for. Expect several questions digging for this kind of information. You should convince the recruiter of your interpersonal skills through both your discussion of examples and your interaction with the recruiter him- or herself.

Q: **How do you think dealing with contractors differs from client interactions?**

Career Changers: This is certainly possible to do, but be aware that it is a long process. If you have a liberal-arts degree, get the necessary architecture schooling and technical training. You don't have to have a college degree, however. If you don't have a B.A., take a technical drafting course at a community college or technical school. After ten years' professional experience, regardless of your educational experience, you can sit for the test in some states. There are several different tracks. Remember that a varied experience makes a good architect.

A: *I think they come from different angles. While clients are excited or possibly focused and serious, contractors are more laid back. Although this can clearly differ from contractor to contractor, they are often well-educated individuals who are doing what they love. Treating them with respect goes a long way toward getting an excellent end product.*

Dealing with contractors is another big part of the architect's job. The recruiter will certainly be looking to see that you can do this well. As the candidate mentions, the manner of dealing with contractors is often quite different from that of dealing with the client.

Q: Show me three of your best drawings.

A: *My best drawings include my final project for a class in college, a drawing I did for my internship, and one from my last job.*

Being the project manager or the job captain requires technical skill. The recruiter will therefore ask you about details on your drawings. Be prepared to explain how things fit together. The recruiter will be sure that you really do know how to do this job technically.

Q: Were you able to earn your requirements for the AIA's IDP?

A: *Yes, I logged my hours in the internship I had after college. I passed the test on the first attempt.*

The American Institute of Architects's IDP, or Intern Development Program, requires all interns to log a certain amount of time in different tasks before taking the thirty-two-hour architectural test. Passing this test is essential to having a career in architecture.

Q: What do you think the job of project manager would entail?

A: *I would probably be the primary contact with the firm's clients. In fact, being a project manager would probably mean that I'd be in contact with clients on a day-to-day basis, starting with initial contact, working through development, and following through to completion.*

The project manager is the contractor's direct contact with the client. The candidate understands that his or her job would include the design of the

Experienced Professionals: Your experience in the industry will practically speak for itself. Emphasize the variety of your experience and your particularly successful projects. Be sure to be helpful if the recruiter needs to research any of your past projects.

building from the documentation phase, to administration during the construction phase. Showing that you have a realistic and clear-cut understanding of what the job encompasses is important and necessary.

Q: What experience do you have that qualifies you for this job?

A: *I have an architecture degree from the University of Tennessee. I have also interned, as I mentioned earlier. Furthermore, I worked as an assistant job captain for two years. I have also passed my licensing exam.*

Becoming an architect is a long process. First you must get an architectural degree, followed by an internship, which can vary in length. After passing your thirty-two-hour licensing exam, you can work as an architect. The candidate has met all these requirements.

Q: What did you get out of your architecture-school training?

A: *I think majoring in architecture in college really gave me the opportunity to learn design and history. It gave me the background of what has gone before. It also taught me how to go through the whole design process.*

This candidate has gleaned the appropriate information from his or her formal education. Being an architecture student gives you the proper foundation upon which to build your experience. A good understanding of the benefits of each step is what the recruiter is looking for.

Q: What do you think one lacks after graduating from architecture school?

A: *I didn't really learn the technical side of architecture in school. For example, I don't think I learned how parts of a building fit together. Once I had my internship and my first architecture job, however, I started to pick these things up.*

Architecture school may touch lightly upon the technical side of things. But no student who comes out of school is ready to draw complicated details for a contractor. Although this candidate would certainly have developed these technical skills in an internship and a previous job, he or she shows humility rather than arrogance, which is what the recruiter is looking for.

Q: Why did you want to become an architect?

A: *I read a book when I was very young, The Fountainhead, by Ayn Rand. Although the novel is essentially a philosophy book, it uses architecture as its vehicle. The awesome importance of the architect made an impression on me that never went away.*

The specifics of your answer really aren't important here. Proving to the recruiter that you have a deep-rooted interest and desire is important. A recruiter will understand your commitment based on the amount of work and experience you already have, but drive home the point with an answer like this.

Q: **What publications do you read?**

A: *I think* Architecture *is a very important publication. I also flip through* Architectural Digest, *just to see what currently interests the public.*

Reading the industry publications is important in order to stay on top of recent trends and developments. This candidate adds an unusual touch by referring to *AD.* Interest in the industry, as well as motivation to keep up, will impress the recruiter.

Q: **What licenses do you have?**

A: *Well, of course I passed my licensing exam with the NCARB in Tennessee. I also belong to the AIA.*

Each state has a licensing program that is held collectively under the National Council of Architectural Registration Boards umbrella. The American Institute of Architects is also an important organization to belong to. You should belong to at least one of these organizations.

Q: **If you could work on a special project for this firm, what would it be?**

A: *I would like to develop an advertising or public-relations campaign for the firm. I think it's arguably the best architecture firm in the southeast, and it deserves to be recognized as such.*

This candidate would clearly be proud to work for the firm. A recruiter likes to hear something like this because he or she sees someone who will be productive for the firm. This candidate would also be concerned with soliciting more work for the firm, which would impress any recruiter.

Q: **Is there anything you'd like to ask me?**

Candidates Re-entering the Workforce: Try to bring yourself up to speed in terms of where the profession is currently. Get back to the books and see what's being done today. What are the trends in design? Try to get an understanding of the market you're going into. One region may be in recession while another is not, for example. What type of building projects are being done? Look for the right type of firm to get a job with. Find out what firms are looking for people and demonstrate that you have what they need.

A: *Can you describe more of the job? What is the development track? How long would I be in this position?*

You should have several questions prepared to ask the recruiter. Having a list is perfectly acceptable. Show your intuitiveness and interest by asking several well-thought-out and intelligent questions. Other possibilities might include: "Is there any kind of exposure to what other staff members in the firm are doing, and to other projects in the office?" "What is the firm's philosophy in terms of approach to design?" "What is the firm's business approach in terms of the steps taken to do a project?"

Drafter

Q: **Tell me about your educational background relative to drafting.**

A: *In high school I took a heavy concentration of math and drawing classes. After graduation I attended a two-year technical college, where I took classes in trigonometry, calculus, and drafting. I also took some beginning engineering classes.*

Expect this question if you have little or no experience. A drafter should have a solid background in math and drafting technology, as all sketches are drawn painstakingly to scale. A high-school education is all that's required, provided you took some vocational classes to learn the necessary technical skills. An associate's degree from a two-year technical school is a plus, but not a prerequisite.

Q: **Tell me about your previous work experience.**

A: *My first job out of high school was at a small manufacturing company in Maine. The company produced parts, such as spindles, for the machine-tool industry. I started as a detailer, doing component and machine drawings. I also have some experience working with engineers to come up with initial designs based on client specifications.*

The interviewer is interested in hearing about any drafting or related experience the candidate might have. Your answer here will allow the interviewer to gauge your skill level. If, like this candidate, you have some solid drafting experience, you could also discuss in depth some specific projects you've worked on.

Q: **Do you have any samples I can see?**

First-time Job Seekers: A typical entry-level position would be as a first-class drafting technician. To qualify for such a position, you'll need to have some experience with basic drafting, through classes either in high school or at a technical college. Interviewers like to see candidates who demonstrate a natural affinity for this kind of work. Since you won't have any real experience, the interviewer will be looking for three basic traits: an inherent mechanical ability, solid math skills, and manual drawing skills. Interviewers want candidates to be detail oriented but, at the same time, to have the ability to see the broad picture of what they're working on.

A: *Yes, I brought a number of drawings with me.*

Always remember to bring samples of your work with you to the interview. Basically, the interviewer will be looking for attention to detail and the overall neatness of your drawings—if you have good line work, for instance. The interviewer will also analyze your drawings for basic design skills—for example, do they have the proper symbols and dimensions? By looking more closely at your designs, the interviewer can better assess your technical and mechanical skills.

Q: Have you taken any courses in geometric tolerancing?

A: *Yes, I have. In college all students concentrating in drafting and design were required to take a class in geometric tolerancing.*

Knowledge of geometric tolerancing is critical in drafting. Basically, it's a method of standardized symbolism for comparing parts, such as squareness of surfaces to each other, or concentricities of diameters to each other. Geometric tolerancing allows the workers who are going to make that part to look at your drawings and see how accurate you want that part to be. Again, this question allows the interviewer to measure the candidate's level of experience and determine how much, if any, training will be needed.

Q: Tell me about your training in the proper use of drafting symbols.

A: *I learned drafting symbols as part of my regular drafting course work in college. In my previous position I had to use drafting symbols regularly on my drawings to communicate with the engineers and other workers who used them.*

This is another question to determine the candidate's technical abilities. To qualify for even an entry-level drafting position, you should have some basic knowledge of drafting symbols. Depending on the type of company you're interviewing with, you might need to know symbols for hydraulic, electrical, or pneumatic designs. Each type of industry has its own series of symbols. For example, in construction you'd use symbols to give workers instructions on welding, such as where to weld, or the width of the bead. You should

Career Changers: You'll need to take a class or two on drafting to learn technical issues, such as geometric tolerancing and drafting symbols. In your interview emphasize your math and drawing skills, essential skills for any drafter. Again, employers will be looking for candidates with an inherent mechanical ability. The technical issues can be taught, but the natural ability cannot. If you have tranferable skills, such as your ability to read blueprints, discuss them. Not many people choose drafting as a career later in life, so be prepared to answer questions about your reasons for wanting to change careers.

have some training in, or understanding of, the use of these various symbols, because in many manufacturing companies you'll be called upon to use them at some point.

Q: **Give an example of a project you've worked on.**

A: *Picking out just one is pretty tough, but this is one of the most memorable ones: I was given a project that was fairly complicated. My supervisor gave me a deadline for the planned product release, and then I was given the responsibility of analyzing the job and putting together a schedule for the release of the drawings to manufacturing. First, I sat down with my supervisor to go over the written customer specifications; then I looked at some similar units to see how the procedure had been done in the past. The project had a number of components, so I had to work with the engineers to figure out such issues as how long each part would take to manufacture. Once I had this information, I could schedule drawings so they could go through the proper flow in the plant. For instance, one part was a long lead item, and absolutely critical to the project, so I decided that part was the first drawing I'd release. I enjoyed working on this project because it gave me a broader perspective of the whole facility. It was really the first time I understood the entire manufacturing process, from conceptualization to finished product.*

If you're an experienced candidate, you can expect this question. Describe for the interviewer how you approached a particular drafting job, explaining what role you played in the process. If, like this candidate, you have about one year of drafting experience, your answer should indicate that you had some responsibility in the actual planning and designing of the product. The more experience you have, the more you'll be involved with designing specifications for the projects. The interviewer will also be interested in how you prioritized your work to meet a deadline. If you have less experience, it's likely that you'd simply be told by your supervisor how to approach a given project. In that case you can discuss the specific part you played in the drafting and manufacturing process for that project.

> **Experienced Professionals:** If you have years of solid experience, you might be interviewing for a supervisory drafting position, or maybe an assistant engineering technician. Show the interviewer that you can work independently on projects—an experienced drafter shouldn't need much supervision. You should also give examples of specific projects you've worked on and discuss your role in them—have you ever been responsible for an entire project? Also, be prepared to show samples of your drawings. Interviewers will be interested in your communications skills as well, since at a higher level, you'll often be interacting with other drafters or engineers discussing design issues.

Q: How do you work under pressure?

A: *I have no problem working under pressure. In fact, I'm very used to it. At my last company we were always working under tight deadlines; the company was growing so fast that we had more than enough work to keep us busy.*

The interviewer wants to find out if the candidate can work effectively within a tight schedule. You should demonstrate that you're comfortable working under deadline pressure. Be ready to discuss one or two specific projects you completed under a tight deadline in case you're asked to give an example.

Q: Are you comfortable working alone, or do you prefer to work under supervision?

A: *When I first started at my last job, I preferred having someone there to watch my work and answer all my questions. But now that I'm more confident in my abilities, I feel very comfortable working without supervision.*

Most likely your answer to this question will depend upon your level of experience. The extent to which you need supervision largely depends on how much experience you have. If you're an inexperienced drafter, it's natural for you to have questions and need reassurance that your work is correct. But if you've been in the field for a while, you should be able to work independently.

Q: Are you available to work nights or weekends when necessary?

A: *Although I try to get all my work done within the regular workday, I understand that there will be times when I may have to put in some overtime. If we're trying to meet a tight deadline, I have no problem staying as late as necessary to get the job done.*

The interviewer will want to see if you're flexible in terms of when you're available to work. Many times when a job has to be completed, you'll be asked to work late, or on weekends. Like this candidate, you should show a willingness to put in overtime when necessary. If you're interviewing for a position in which you'll be frequently faced with deadline situations, you should expect that you'll occasionally be required to work late.

Candidates Re-entering the Workforce: Read trade journals to keep up to date with industry news. If you're a mechanical drafter, magazines such as *Design News* and *Manufacturing Engineering*, published by the Society of Mechanical Engineers, will keep you abreast of trends within the industry. Naturally, if you're an electrical drafter, you should read journals appropriate to your field. You might also find it helpful to take a refresher course in drafting, both to polish your skills, and to learn about new technologies, such as computer-aided design systems.

Q: Tell me about your long-term goals.

A: *I'm interested in going back to college part-time to get my degree in mechanical engineering. I want to stay in a manufacturing environment, but I believe I'm ready for more of a challenge. And since I'm going to school only part-time, I want to continue working.*

Don't be afraid to say you want to continue your education; it's not unusual for drafters to move on to positions as engineers. On the other hand, maybe you're looking for security and more advancement within the drafting field—for instance, as a drafting supervisor. Whichever path you choose, it's important to show the interviewer that you have a desire to grow professionally. At the same time, it's important to have realistic goals. If you say, for example, that you want to be an engineer, you have to be willing to go back to school and get your degree.

Q: Why do you want to work for this company?

A: *Well, I grew up here, so I know that you're the biggest manufacturer in the area. Your company also has an excellent reputation for how well you treat your employees. Your products are also intriguing—I'm a real car enthusiast, and I know you manufacture engines for the automotive industry, as well as aircraft—so I think it would be very exciting to work in this environment.*

Before the interview learn as much as you can about the company. You should be able to speak knowledgeably about the products it manufactures. Discuss what you know about the company and the reasons for your desire to work in the company's particular industry.

Q: Do you have any experience with computer-aided drafting systems?

A: *Yes, I do. In my previous position I used AutoCAD regularly in the product-design process, both for development and detailing.*

Most drafters use CAD systems in addition to regular paper drawings. CAD systems make it easier to create mathematically precise drawings, as well as to revise existing designs. Again, your answer will give the interviewer an idea of how much training you'll need if hired.

Prepress Operator

Q: Why are you looking for a new position?

A: *I've worked for a large printing company for more than twenty years. I have experience working in all areas of the prepress process, but I've worked primarily as a stripper for the past ten years. Unfortunately, the company's been going through some tough times, and last month it was forced to lay off more than fifty workers, including me.*

Don't be hesitant or embarrassed to say that you were laid off, if that's the case. This circumstance is becoming more and more common in the industry. The growing popularity of computerized desktop publishing has taken a lot of business away from small printing shops. Many companies now do in-house what they would once send out to a printing shop—brochures and newsletters, for example. The decrease in business means fewer jobs for traditional prepress workers, so downsizing is common in larger shops. Whatever the reason you're looking for a new position, try to put a positive spin on it. For example, if you've had problems with your previous employer and fear you may get an unfavorable reference from that company, be sure to explain the situation accurately, and as dispassionately as possible. You should never denigrate or blame a former employer for anything that's happened in your past. Otherwise, the interviewer may conclude that you're prone to conflicts with others, or that you easily hold resentments.

Q: What experience do you have operating a Mac?

A: *I have made the transition to the digital workflow and have been operating a Mac for the past five years. I have been working with all the major applications and have some experience with color retouching.*

First-time Job Seekers: Employers look for candidates who are neat and detail oriented, and who have graduated from a vocational or technical institute. Depending on the school, these programs can be anywhere from two to four years in length, and will teach you the technical skills necessary to work in a printing shop. Most entry-level prepress workers will start in the prep department of a printing shop making proofs. Once you have experience, you'll be exposed to other areas of prepress work, and if you work in a large shop, will specialize in one particular area.

Mac operation is a key skill that every prepress worker should have. The sophistication of your answer here will give the interviewer an indication of your experience level, and of what additional training you'll need, if any. Computer skills will continue to play a major role in the trade as more and more equipment becomes integrated into the digital workflow. For instance, this candidate demonstrates a high level of experience, as color retouching is relatively specialized.

Q: **How would you increase the resolution if you needed to enlarge an image?**

A: *You can only gain resolution by sizing an image down. In this case I would have to go back and rescan the image at a higher resolution to accommodate the intended size.*

Here the interviewer wants to test the candidate's skills. As this candidate rightly says, you can't gain resolution when increasing the size of an image. If you can't answer this question satisfactorily, the interviewer will have serious doubts about your knowledge of camera operation.

Q: **How would you eliminate banding on vignettes?**

A: *I'd simply recreate the vignette and save it as a .tif. After that, I would add some noise to the image and replace the gradient blends with the .tif files in the layout application. This method should solve the problem.*

Again, if you have any experience with color correction software, you should know this. Banding will sometimes appear on one- or two-color blends and vignettes. This is a common problem and this is the only way to correct it.

Q: **Do you know how to maintain the proofing system, log materials, and do all the required maintenance?**

A: *Yes. In my previous company, we were responsible for maintaining all our proofing equipment. I know the consequences of not properly maintaining equipment.*

The Mac operator is usually responsible for the maintenance of the proofing equipment. It's important to show the interviewer not only that you understand

Career Changers: Few people choose prepress work as a second career. Even professionals in the industry, such as experienced press people, tend to stay in their particular areas throughout their careers. If you do want to switch careers, you'll need to take a few classes at a vocational school to learn the technical aspects of the field. In addition to classes in traditional printing, you should also take classes in electronic prepress equipment. In your interview discuss why you've decided to make this change, and what attracted you to the position.

it's your responsibility, but that you know the correct way to keep the proofer up and running. If the machines aren't kept clean, jams can occur, slowing down production. If proofs can't go out you'll start missing deadlines for press time and other related finishing functions.

Q: What size presses have you prepped for?

A: *I've stripped for many different sizes, from multi-lith to forty-inch four- and six-color presses. However, I did most of my work on larger presses.*

In bigger printing shops, workers tend to specialize in and work with only a certain size press. If you're applying for a position in a midsized or small shop, you'll be expected to work with several different sizes. Show the interviewer that you have experience with everything from the smallest to the biggest presses. If you have experience with only one kind of machine, emphasize your eagerness to learn; the company may be willing to train you.

Q: Do you have experience trapping multi-color files?

A: *Yes. I have more than ten years' experience trapping six-color and four-color files with critical traps.*

Experience in this area is essential. Show the interviewer that you understand how to use chokes and spreads—which are basically ways to adjust color—in order to make two colors trap properly. If this procedure is done incorrectly, there will be issues on press and you'll have a lot of down time.

Q: What problems would you encounter trapping solid cyan to solid magenta?

A: *These particular colors require a very tight, almost nonexistent trap. If you put too much trap, you'd create a black line where the colors overlap.*

Though a black line can also appear when trapping other color combinations, if you can answer this question correctly, the interviewer will know you're an experienced operator. Cyan and magenta are an unusual combination, and a correct answer will show that you have an in-depth understanding of color. A very fine trap is required, because if a black line appears, you need to start the entire stripping and trapping process over again.

> **Experienced Professionals:** Be sure to bring some samples of your work to the interview. The sophistication of the projects you bring in will give the interviewer a better idea of your level of experience, and if you specialized in any particular areas, such as color correction or platemaking. Discuss any experience you have with electronic prepress work, and if you have little, discuss what steps you're taking to stay current with the new technology.

Q: **Are you experienced with book work, including making dummies and doing page imposition?**

A: *I've done some work with making dummies and page imposition. I'm familiar with the processes and understand what can go wrong if they aren't done correctly, but I wouldn't call myself an expert on the subject.*

You should expect this question if you're applying to a printer that does book work. Interviewers will expect you to have some experience and understanding of this area. If either of these processes are done incorrectly, the entire book will have to be redone, which will waste money as well as hours of hard work.

Q: **Do you know the difference between a saddle-wire and a perfect-bound book?**

A: *Yes, these are two different types of binding. The signatures of a saddle-wire book are collated one inside the other. After the cover is put on, the signatures are stitched together on the edge. Perfect binding is used for books with more than seventy or eighty pages. In this case, the book's signatures are stacked one on top of the other, then glued together on the side when the cover is put on.*

Show the interviewer that you understand which type of binding is appropriate to use on a particular book. Even if you don't have specific experience in this area, the interviewer will want to see that you have some knowledge of the binding process. This is particularly true if you're applying to a small or midsized printing shop, where all workers are expected to have an understanding of all areas.

Q: **What's most important when imposing a book for perfecting?**

A: *The pages need to be imposed so they're positioned in the exact center of the sheet. When the sheet is tumbled, the pages must back each other up perfectly.*

Demonstrate an understanding of the perfecting process. Perfecting is an essential part of the prepress process. If the pages don't line up against each other exactly, they'll need to be redone.

Q: **If the ink rotation changes on a job that has metallic inks, and the files have already been trapped, how would you identify any potential problems?**

A: *It's very important to know your ink rotation when trapping metallic colors. Where the metallic ink falls in the rotation will determine what colors will make the shape. I would go back and examine the ripped files to see if there are any issues. In most cases, the files would need to be retrapped, but I would only fix and replace the problem pages so that I'm not wasting time on redoing pages that are already correct.*

Your answer here will give the interviewer an indication of your problem-solving experience. Generally, only the most experienced operators will understand how to fix this problem. If you can answer this question correctly, the interviewer will know that you've "been around"—that is, that you're a highly skilled operator.

Q: **What's the best way to print a solid black known as Rich Black?**

A: *Rich Black requires printing a 40 to 60 percent screen tint under the solid black. I've found that cyan is the best color to use. Other colors will tint the black that particular color, which may produce an unfavorable result on the final product.*

Again, this question tests the candidate's knowledge of color. This problem is often encountered in printing situations. The press cannot lay down enough ink in one run to make the dense color of "Rich Black." Any experienced prepress worker should understand how to produce this color.

Q: **What's the most important precaution to take when making plates?**

A: *Handling the chemistry and cleaning the processor. It's important to take all the necessary precautions when handling plate chemicals. Gloves, goggles, and smocks should always be used during maintence to prevent injuries from the extremely corrosive developer. If the processor is not kept clean, debris can get on the rollers and cause problems.*

Throughout the prepress process, the cleanliness of the equipment is of the utmost importance. It's essential to show the interviewer that you recognize the implications of having debris on the plate. If the mistake isn't caught early, it won't be noticed until the actual printing process, and the entire process may have to be redone.

Candidates Re-entering the Workforce: Discuss the type of work you've done in the past. Be sure to bring samples of your work for the interviewer to get a better idea of your skills. Although technology doesn't change rapidly in terms of conventional prepress equipment, the field is becoming more automated and computerized. Discuss any computer experience you have, or show the interviewer that you're taking steps to familiarize yourself with the new automated processes. For example, some vocational institutes offer job retraining with which you can learn the new technology.

Technical Writer
(Computers)

Q: How would you describe the role of a technical writer?

A: *The writer's job is to present complex, technical material to an audience in a manner that meets the needs of that audience. It can be compared to translating a foreign language to English. Before you begin a project, you must find out what the audience wants and the best way to deliver it.*

"Know your audience" is the credo of every good technical writer. It helps to be an expert on the topic about which you're writing, but knowing how to get the information the audience needs, and then how to deliver it clearly, is the most important trait a technical writer can have. For example, if you're writing a reference manual for a computer software program, you need to determine if it should be task oriented (explaining how to do the job) or process heavy (explaining how the system works). If you're writing for advanced users, you can keep the manual at a higher level, but if the audience isn't expert, you should provide more overview. If you have a mixed audience, then you have to organize the material in such a way that each user can quickly get to what he or she needs and then get back to work.

Q: What writing experience have you had?

A: *I worked as a technical writer for three years, and I have a certificate in technical writing.*

Writing experience is great, but the best writing often comes from journalists, because newspaper environments encourage clear, factual, concise writing. Journalism positions also offer great experience at getting information from many different sources, which is crucial to the technical writer's job. Your job is essentially to get information from a specification, a product, or a person and present it in the best way to meet the user's needs. Be sure to mention any relevant training or education you may have, including degrees in journalism or technical writing.

Q: How do you work under pressure?

A: *I try to plan effectively enough not to have to work under pressure, but I'll put in long hours if the situation calls for it.*

There will often be tight deadlines and stressful projects for a technical writer. However, a good writer anticipates this and can prioritize well. The recruiter needs to know that the candidate will try to use a project plan up front. Employers are less concerned with bad estimates than with last-minute surprises.

Q: Are you familiar with a development process?

A: *Yes. The place I worked last had a product cycle with a beta period.*

There is no right or wrong answer to this question, but since technical writers are usually a part of a development process, it's beneficial for you to understand a typical product cycle. This may include a requirements phase, specifications, alpha, beta, and a general release. Candidates with development experience, or experience on a development team, are desirable.

Q: Have you ever used FrameMaker? How do you feel about learning or using desktop-publishing software?

A: *Yes, I use FrameMaker all the time. I enjoy learning new software programs and make a point to stay up to date on the latest applications.*

If the employer has some time to get you up to speed, you may not need to know the specific program used by that company. If you aren't familiar with the employer's software, communicate a willingness to learn and mention any other similar desktop-publishing programs you've used (such as PageMaker or Microsoft Word).

Q: Can you explain "kerning" to me?

First-time Job Seekers: You should join the STC (the Society of Technical Communication), which can help you find jobs, learn skills, and keep up with changes in the industry. If you have trouble breaking into a company, apply for an internship. Many companies hire interns, who sometimes end up as full-time employees. Failing that, try working for a magazine or a newspaper. The skills you learn in this field (including clear, concise writing, knowledge of typography, and page layout) will transfer well to technical writing.

Some useful nonwriting skills to acquire include HTML (a hypertext markup language that lets you publish on the World Wide Web); and a proficiency with Adobe Acrobat, Adobe Exchange, FrameMaker, and Microsoft Word. Familiarize yourself with a style guide, learn editing marks, and read about editing skills. Popular guides, including *The Chicago Manual of Style* and the *AP Style Guide*, can be found at your local bookstore or library.

A: *Kerning is closing the spacing between letters in order to create visually-consistent letter spacing. The larger the letters, the more critical it is to adjust their spacing.*

You may be asked this or some other comparable quiz question. If you know any typography, you'll be able to answer the question readily.

Q: Have you ever studied Information Mapping?

A: *No, but I've heard of it. It's all about separating information types and writing in a modular fashion.*

Information Mapping is a very popular writing methodology that many universities and companies teach or use. It's a great approach for technical or business writing, and a super background for writers of any kind of online documentation.

Q: Have you ever worked with standards before? Do you understand why they're important?

A: *Yes. My previous company used standards to make sure that our documentation maintained a consistent look. We had editors who enforced the standards and kept us up to date on them.*

Professional writers understand the power of standards. There are several well-known style guides that many institutions use. *The Chicago Manual of Style*, and the *AP Style Guide* are two. Often a company needs to create a short style guide of its own, which is a set of guidelines rather than rigid rules. If you don't have any experience working with standards, you can say something like, "We didn't work with standards at my last company, but we should have. I was constantly trying to figure out what spelling or what look my company wanted to use. Without a standard we'd end up with inconsistencies within our documents and from book to book."

Q: Are you familiar with the STC?

A: *Yes. In fact, I'm a member of the STC. I find it helps me keep up with changes in the industry.*

Career Changers: Depending on what your former career was, you may have excellent skills that can be easily transferred to a career in technical writing. In fact, the best technical writers often come from newspaper environments, which encourage clear, factual, concise writing. Join the STC (the Society of Technical Communication), which can help you find jobs, learn skills, and keep up with changes in the industry.

Ideally, you should know about this international group called the Society of Technical Communication. It's an invaluable resource for industry trends, experts, and research. The STC has a web site, a mailing list, a trade magazine, newsletters, and seminars.

Q: Have you ever attended industry seminars? Which ones?

A: *Yes, I've recently attended seminars on usability testing and online help authoring.*

This question is designed to encourage the candidate to talk about any areas of technical writing that he or she might be interested in. The interviewer will also want to know how you keep up with changes in the field. Attending seminars and finding other ways of honing your skills are especially important if you don't have a certificate or degree.

Q: If you could join an SIG (special interest group) tomorrow, which would you pick?

A: *I'd choose online help, the Internet, graphics, printing, and production.*

The recruiter wants to know which areas of technical communication interest you. You should name a few that show how current you are on developments in the field.

Q: Have you published with HTML? Adobe Acrobat?

A: *Yes, I've worked with both.*

Much of the world is using the Internet to communicate. HTML and Adobe Acrobat are different developing arenas that require some background and training. Although the mastery of them may not be required by all employers, you should at least be familiar with them. HTML, or Hypertext Markup Language, is the language for writing on the World Wide Web. Usually, a technical communicator will write the articles that are published through the Web. Since the language is so simple, you may be expected to learn it and to write in this format. Otherwise, a programmer would have to get involved. Adobe Acrobat is a platform-independent book-publishing tool. It lets companies distribute books electronically. It also allows customers to print the

Experienced Professionals: Emphasize the breadth of your experience and your flexibility in a variety of mediums, such as textbooks, online documentation, and so on. Tell the interviewer how you can apply your varied experience to that particular company. Portray yourself as someone who's a good writer and communicator, good with people, diplomatic, energetic, willing and able to troubleshoot and learn new things, inquisitive, and knowledgeable about the importance of keeping the audience in mind at all times.

books from this file on an as-needed basis. Because it's becoming a standard delivery mechanism for technical writers, you should familiarize yourself with at least the basics.

Q: **What's your feeling about the trend for reference manuals to go online? What do you think are important considerations?**

A: *Some things are good online and some things don't work as well. If you did have to put a manual online, you should be sure to give your users plenty of navigational tools. For example, if there's a sophisticated search engine for an online manual, that may help the user to find a topic. Otherwise, the user must scroll through electronic pages. It's also harder for a user to read online. You need to use smaller pages and larger fonts. If you've access to hypertext, it couldn't hurt to use that too.*

Your answer should address how the user's needs are different for online and paper, how you need to present and write differently for these environments, how it's easier to test and review writing when it's built into the product. You should also be sure to distinguish between an online manual and online help.

Q: **How would you expect to be edited? How do you generally respond to edits from editors and reviewers?**

A: *Editing is essential. I'm careful when I work but fully expect and desire to be edited. No one catches everything, and I'd rather fix the mistakes before the product goes out. It's also good to see how other people write, since I often get ideas that way.*

Editing, including peer editing, is an important part of the writing process. A good writer welcomes feedback. Remember the old saying, "God is perfect, everyone else gets edited."

Q: **What would you do if a technical expert told you to change your work in a way that you knew would confuse the reader? How would you handle that?**

Candidates Re-entering the Workforce: Technical communicators need to keep up with trends and changes. You'll need to convince the recruiter, for example, that you're proficient in the latest desktop-publishing programs and HTML (a hypertext markup language that lets you publish on the World Wide Web). Basic knowledge of the latest programming software and familiarity with Information Mapping will go a long way toward making your candidacy attractive to employers.

A: *I'd give reasons why I believed the suggestions were missing the mark. I'd suggest alternate methods instead of just telling the expert he or she was wrong. Many people are willing to trust you when you can back up your decisions.*

It's important to hire a candidate with diplomacy skills. The interviewer wants to see that the candidate has the confidence to let technical reviewers know he or she can handle the writing end of the project, while welcoming any feedback they may have. Just as you wouldn't question the way in which something was coded or built, a reviewer should trust you with the mechanics of writing. When there's a complete disagreement that you can't resolve, you may try to have a user look at both samples. This is called usability testing. Remember, your goal is not to argue over design, grammar, or presentation with your team; it's to get an idea across to a user.

Q: Could I see a sample? References?

A: *Yes, I've brought several recent samples of my writing and three references to give to you.*

Remember to bring samples and references with you to each interview. Make copies of each so that you can leave them with the employer. The interviewer will scrutinize your samples for clear procedures, good writing and flow, use of active voice, and concise, clear writing.

Q: How organized are you? Do you use any project-planning strategies?

A: *I tend to be very organized and very neat. Project planning is essential to the writer's life. Often enhancements are made and deadlines changed. The better organized I am up front, the better prepared I am to handle change when it comes.*

Because you'll often be juggling several projects at once, it's important to be able to break down a writing project into many small chunks. This enables you to plan projects, and to be ready to switch parts of a project around at any time.

Q: What programming skills do you have?

A: *I'm proficient in both Pascal and C++.*

The bonus of knowing or having exposure to programming is that if the writer can read the code, he or she can work more independently. This is a nice plus for some positions, though it's usually not considered essential. For example, an engineering firm that doesn't code wouldn't expect you to be able to.

INDEX
(Parts I–III, pages 000–000)

J

INDEX OF JOB INTERVIEWS

E

F

G

H

I

L

M